ALL · IN · ONE

CompTIA
Cloud+™
Certification

EXAM GUIDE

(Exam CV0-003)

Prior edition published as part of the Study Guide series under the title
CompTIA Cloud+ Certification Study Guide, Second Edition (Exam CV0-002).

Eric Vanderburg

New York   Chicago   San Francisco
Athens   London   Madrid   Mexico City
Milan   New Delhi   Singapore   Sydney   Toronto

Sponsoring Editor
Lisa McClain

Editorial Supervisor
Patty Mon

Project Manager
Neelu Sahu,
    KnowledgeWorks Global Ltd.

Acquisitions Coordinator
Emily Walters

Technical Editor
Daniel Lachance

Copy Editor
Lisa McCoy

Proofreader
Tricia Lawrence

Indexer
Ted Laux

Production Supervisor
Thomas Somers

Composition
KnowledgeWorks Global Ltd.

Illustration
KnowledgeWorks Global Ltd.

Art Director, Cover
Jeff Weeks

To my children, Faith and Jacob Vanderburg. May your curiosity know no bounds as you continually grow and learn. This book is for you with all my love.

ABOUT THE AUTHOR

Eric Vanderburg is a Christian cybersecurity leader, consultant, author, and thought leader. He is best known for his insight on cybersecurity, privacy, cloud, and storage. He is passionate about sharing cybersecurity and technology information on strategies, techniques, current events, and best practices. He regularly presents at conferences, seminars, and other events, and has been honored to be the commencement speaker at Remington College and Vatterott College. His blog and social media channels are often cited as must-read sources for those interested in technology and security.

Eric is a continual learner and has earned over 40 technology certifications from Microsoft, Cisco, CompTIA, (ISC)², Rapid7, EMC, CWNP, and Hitachi Data Systems. He holds an MBA with a concentration in Information Systems from Kent State University, a BS in Technology, and an AS in Computer Information Systems. He also studied Japanese technology management practices at Kansai Giada University.

He leads the cybersecurity consulting division at TCDI. TCDI's cybersecurity division, which provides companies with peace of mind in our digital world by protecting the confidentiality, integrity, and availability of data and critical systems. TCDI security practitioners, analysts, engineers, and forensic investigators apply their unique skills to create confidence in information systems and policies.

In addition to being the Vice President of Cybersecurity at TCDI, Eric is the affiliate faculty at the Cleveland State University Cleveland-Marshall College of Law, and Technology Director at Grace Baptist Church in Westlake, Ohio. He serves on the editorial board for the HITSF Journal and on advisory boards for a number of colleges. He has published books on storage networking and cloud computing, and has served as a technical editor for several other publications. Additionally, he frequently writes articles for magazines, journals, and other publications.

Vanderburg lives in Cleveland, Ohio, with his wife Aimee. He has two children, Faith and Jacob. In his spare time, he can often be found building arcade and pinball machines or reading novels.

Twitter: @evanderburg
LinkedIn: https://www.linkedin.com/in/evanderburg
Facebook: https://www.facebook.com/VanderburgE

About the Technical Editor

Daniel Lachance, CompTIA Security+™, CompTIA A+*, CompTIA Network+*, CompTIA Server+™, CompTIA Cloud Essentials, Cloud+, as well as various Microsoft Azure and Amazon Web Services certifications, is the owner of Lachance IT Consulting, Inc., based in Halifax, Nova Scotia, Canada. He is the author of *CompTIA Cloud Essentials Certification Study Guide* and co-author of *CompTIA Security+ Certification Practice Exams*.

Since the early 1990s, Dan has worked in various capacities as a computer programmer, network and server technician, and security analyst. He is also an experienced trainer, having delivered IT training online, in Canada, and in the Caribbean since the 1990s on topics ranging from the enterprise use of Microsoft Active Directory, Microsoft Hyper-V, Microsoft System Center Configuration Manager, Microsoft Azure, and Amazon Web Services, as well as Unix, Linux, Security, and Networking.

Dan has recorded numerous tech support videos for products such as Microsoft Azure, Amazon Web Services, Microsoft System Center Configuration Manager, various cybersecurity and mobility topics, and Linux.

He enjoys spending time with his spouse, Tammy; their children, Roman, Trinity, Abby, and Jacob; families and friends; and the family dogs, Dori and Louis. He also enjoys jogging, reading nonfiction, and listening to and playing various styles of music.

CONTENTS AT A GLANCE

CONTENTS

ACKNOWLEDGMENTS

I would like to thank my wife, Aimee Vanderburg, for having patience with me while I finished this project. Without her love, encouragement, and support, this project would not have been possible. The support by my family throughout this project is the primary reason for its success.

In addition to my wife, I want to thank my children, Faith and Jacob, for their understanding when Daddy had to work instead of conquering dragons, constructing LEGO skyscrapers, or playing games with them. I am thankful for my parents and the example they set of working hard to accomplish great things, modeling excellence and integrity, and giving me the freedom to fail enough to succeed.

No matter the size, each book is a team effort. It has been an absolute pleasure to work with the professional editors at McGraw Hill, especially Lisa McClain and Emily Walters. Thank you for your patience, flexibility, and honest feedback. Dan Lachance deserves special mention for his outstanding contributions as technical editor. His comments, clarifying notes, and perspective brought polish and refinement to this work. It has been a blessing to work with such a skilled editorial team. Lastly, I want to acknowledge the excellent work of McGraw Hill's production team.

Thank you all so much! May this book be a testimony to your efforts, assistance, and guidance.

INTRODUCTION

Cloud technologies form the backbone for most of the services companies and individuals use on a daily basis. It is the reason we can utilize immense computing power from a small cell phone app or carry over similar user experiences and sessions from one device to another. Cloud technologies host our applications, synchronize our data, back up our systems, connect our software with common APIs, and give us a place to develop new applications swiftly.

The ubiquity of the cloud means that its definition is very broad. Also, since the cloud involves so many facets, it is ever-changing and continually adapting to different use cases to solve new business problems. This also means that the skill sets required to support cloud computing environments are in high demand. Most companies have implemented cloud solutions to some degree while considering additional ways to further employ it to reduce costs and increase capabilities.

Cloud computing provides something that the IT industry has always needed: a way to increase capacity and add resources as necessary without having to invest in infrastructure. It enables an organization to expand its business on demand as it grows.

As more and more organizations adopt a cloud model, the need for cloud administrators increases. Whether the organization is implementing a private cloud, public cloud, or hybrid cloud, it is going to need someone to administer and maintain that cloud environment. Having the skills necessary to support a cloud environment will set you apart.

About the Exam

CompTIA Cloud+ is a global certification that validates the skills needed to deploy and automate secure cloud environments supporting the high availability of business systems and data. While not requirements, CompTIA recommends candidates have five years of IT experience, including two to three years of experience in systems administration or networking, CompTIA Network+ and Server+ accreditation or equivalent knowledge, and familiarity with any major hypervisor technology for server virtualization and cloud service models.

To validate the skills needed to implement modern cloud solutions, CompTIA indicates the relative importance of each domain with the following weighting on the exam:

Domain	% of Exam
1.0 Cloud Architecture and Design	13%
2.0 Security	20%
3.0 Deployment	23%
4.0 Operations Support	22%
5.0 Troubleshooting	22%

The Cloud+ exam is administered at authorized testing centers or via remote online. It consists of a maximum of 90 multiple-choice and performance-based questions, which must be answered in no more than 90 minutes. To pass, you must score 750 points out of a maximum possible 900 points.

About the Book

This book is valuable for anyone wishing to learn more about cloud technologies, but it is specifically geared toward those taking the CompTIA Cloud+ Exam CV0-003. While many individuals taking the exam have been in the IT industry for many years, the terminology used in a cloud computing environment and on the exam may be new to them. Understanding this terminology is a key step to passing the CompTIA Cloud+ exam and becoming a cloud administrator. Throughout the book, you will learn the different components that make up a cloud environment along with the best practices for implementing those components in the cloud. If you are an experienced IT professional, some of these components will be familiar to you, but this book helps you understand how those components work together to provide cloud solutions.

This book is divided into the following chapters based on meeting the objectives of the CompTIA Cloud+ exam:

Chapter 1: Cloud Computing Concepts, Models, and Terminology Chapter 1 is foundational in understanding cloud concepts and delivery models. In this chapter, you will learn about the various cloud service models, along with cloud deployment models, object storage, and key terms as they relate to cloud computing. The chapter wraps up with a discussion on how the cloud supports technologies such as machine learning, artificial intelligence, and the Internet of Things.

Chapter 2: Disk Storage Systems This chapter discusses how disk configurations and redundancy are implemented in the cloud. You will learn the different file types that are part of a cloud environment, along with how to use data tiering to maximize the organization's storage.

Chapter 3: Storage Networking After becoming familiar with the disk storage systems involved in a cloud environment, the next thing to understand is how to implement and provision those disk storage systems. In this chapter, you will learn about the various storage technologies, how to implement them in the most efficient manner, and how to protect storage through high availability and replication.

Chapter 4: Network Infrastructure Network configuration is a primary component of cloud computing. In this chapter, you will learn the different types of network configurations and how to optimize those networks. You will also be introduced to the different network ports and protocols that are part of cloud computing.

Chapter 5: Virtualization Components Virtualization is the key component of cloud computing. This chapter explains the basic concepts of virtualization, including the virtualization host, hypervisor, and virtual machines. You will also learn about virtualized infrastructure service elements, including DNS, DHCP, certificate services, and load balancing.

Chapter 6: Virtualization and the Cloud   Chapter 6 expands on the virtualization components introduced in Chapter 5 to demonstrate how virtualization is utilized in a cloud environment. The chapter begins by discussing cloud virtualization benefits, including how virtualization scales in the cloud, resource sharing, and infrastructure consolidation. Next, you will learn how to migrate an organization's current environment to a virtual environment using the various tools that are available, including P2V and V2V. The chapter wraps up by introducing software-defined networking, storage, and data centers.

Chapter 7: Cloud Adoption   Cloud adoption is the process of employing new cloud technologies. This is a process you will frequently engage in as you move systems, purchase new cloud systems, or develop applications in the cloud. This chapter describes the planning, deployment, and post-deployment validation stages of cloud adoption and then moves into implementation steps for specific service models and solutions.

Chapter 8: DevOps   DevOps teams are a combination of software development and IT operations that more effectively support applications throughout their life cycle. This chapter covers some primary areas of responsibility for DevOps, including secure coding methods, version control, build processes, and application retirement or replacement. The chapter presents life cycle management, an overarching concept in DevOps for how applications are specified, developed, tested, deployed, and maintained. Lastly, cloud transformation through DevOps continuous integration/continuous delivery, Infrastructure as Code, and business changes is introduced.

Chapter 9: Performance Tuning   Optimizing performance and allocating resources need careful consideration and planning. You will learn how to configure virtualization host resources and guest resources and how to optimize those configurations.

Chapter 10: Systems Management   This chapter explores the nontechnical aspects of implementing a cloud environment. You will learn how to implement the proper policies and procedures as they pertain to a cloud environment, along with best practices for systems management, such as how to perform system maintenance, important metrics, dashboards, and standards.

Chapter 11: Security in the Cloud   This chapter explains a variety of security concepts as they pertain to a cloud environment. You will learn how to secure the network and the data that is part of the cloud environment.

Chapter 12: Security Best Practices   This chapter expands on the security concepts introduced in Chapter 11 through cloud security best practices. It includes security governance strategies, vulnerability management, system hardening, and layered security. The chapter concludes with incident response processes, planning, training, and procedures.

Chapter 13: Business Continuity and Disaster Recovery   Disaster recovery and business continuity are still primary concerns for an organization when implementing a cloud environment. This chapter describes the different options an organization has when building both business continuity and disaster recovery plans and implementing high availability. It ends with a discussion on backup and recovery methods.

Chapter 14: Testing, Automation, and Changes Service and maintenance availability must be considered when choosing a cloud provider. This chapter explains the testing techniques that can be used to ensure adequate performance, proper functionality, and availability. The chapter then introduces methods to automate and orchestrate activities and then discusses how to manage changes and configurations.

Chapter 15: Troubleshooting Knowing how to solve issues effectively will set you apart from other professionals. This chapter teaches you troubleshooting tools, documentation, and analysis. The chapter then introduces CompTIA's troubleshooting methodology and explains how to troubleshoot deployment, capacity, automation, connectivity, and security issues using the CompTIA troubleshooting methodology.

Using the Exam Objectives Map

The exam objectives map in Appendix A has been constructed to help you cross-reference the official exam objectives from CompTIA with the relevant coverage in the book. A reference has been provided for each exam objective exactly as CompTIA has presented it, the chapter, and the section that covers that objective.

Online Practice Exams

This book includes access to practice exams that feature the TotalTester Online exam test engine, which enables you to generate a complete practice exam or to generate quizzes by chapter module or by exam domain. Online resources also include a glossary. See Appendix B for more information and instructions on how to access the exam tool.

Cloud Computing Concepts, Models, and Terminology

In this chapter, you will learn about
- Cloud service models
- Cloud deployment models and services
- Cloud characteristics and terms
- Advanced cloud services

Moving some or all of an organization's infrastructure to the cloud provides a number of benefits to that organization, including power savings, on-demand storage, ease of administration, ability to pay for only the resources it uses, and a metered environment that can offer almost 100 percent uptime if included in the service level agreement (SLA)—a costly undertaking when provided by the organization itself. An SLA is a contract between a cloud service provider (CSP) and a cloud consumer that formally defines the cloud service and who is responsible for it.

This chapter covers the basic concepts, models, and terminology that are the building blocks of cloud computing. It lays a foundation for the rest of the book by building scenarios for cloud deployments that the subsequent chapters can be compared to and modeled against for a better understanding of what cloud computing is, how it can be deployed, and the value it provides both to information technology (IT) organizations and the customers that they support.

Cloud Service Models

A cloud service model is a set of IT-related services offered by a CSP. The CSP is responsible for supplying cloud-based IT resources to a cloud consumer under a predefined and mutually agreed upon SLA. The CSP is responsible for administrative maintenance and management of the cloud infrastructure, which allows the cloud consumer to focus its administrative effort on other aspects of the business. In essence, the cloud consumer is buying or leasing its IT infrastructure from the CSP.

The entity that legally owns the cloud service is known as the cloud service owner. Either the CSP or the cloud consumer can be the cloud service owner, depending on the terms of the SLA.

It is critical to understand who is responsible for the services hosted in the cloud. Before an organization migrates any piece of its business to the cloud, it needs to understand who is "in control" of those resources. A variety of cloud service models offer the cloud consumer a number of different options. To implement a successful cloud deployment, you need to understand each of the cloud service models and the service that each provides. In this section, you will learn about each of the different cloud service models and when to implement each.

Infrastructure as a Service

Infrastructure as a Service (IaaS) is the model by which the cloud consumer outsources responsibility for its computer hardware, network, and operating systems to an external CSP. The CSP not only owns the equipment that provides the infrastructure resources but is also responsible for the ongoing operation and maintenance of those resources. In this model, the cloud consumer is charged on a "pay-as-you-use" or "pay-as-you-grow" basis. IaaS can include the server storage, infrastructure, and connectivity domains. For example, the cloud consumer could deploy and run its own applications and operating systems, while the IaaS provider would handle the following:

- Storage resources, including replication, backup, and archiving
- Compute resources, which are the resources traditionally provided by servers or server farms, including processor, memory, disk, and networking
- Connectivity domains, including infrastructure management and security, such as network load balancing and firewalls

When an organization utilizes IaaS, it no longer has to buy, maintain, or upgrade server hardware, which can help it save resources, time, and money. Since IaaS allows an organization to pay only for the resources it uses, the organization no longer needs to outlay expenditures for hardware resources it either is not using or is not using to maximum capacity. IaaS allows an organization to spin up additional resources quickly and efficiently without having to purchase physical hardware. For example, the IT department might need a development environment to test a new application; with IaaS, this development environment could be spun up quickly and then removed when the new application has been fully tested. IaaS allows an organization to meet hardware capacity spikes without having to add resources to its data center. Figure 1-1 shows you a graphical representation of the services that are offered by an IaaS provider.

Figure 1-1
Infrastructure as
a Service (IaaS)
provider services

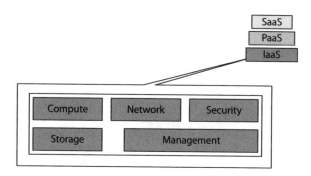

Platform as a Service

Platform as a Service (PaaS) enables customers to have applications deployed without the time, cost, and human resources required to buy and manage their own back-end hardware and software. PaaS applications are either consumer created or acquired web applications or services that are entirely accessible from the Internet. The tools and programming languages used to create PaaS applications are usually supplied by the CSP.

PaaS web applications enable cloud consumers to control the deployed applications via an application programming interface (API) without having to manage the complexity of all the underpinning servers, operating systems, or storage. In some circumstances, the cloud consumer is also allowed to control the application hosting environment. PaaS offers cloud consumers a speedy time to market and an integrated way to provision services over the Web. PaaS facilitates the immediate delivery of business requirements such as application design, development, and testing at a fraction of the cost.

PaaS providers offer a variety of services and service combinations spanning the entire application deployment life cycle. Some of the service features are source code, application usage tracking, versioning, and testing tools. Figure 1-2 shows a graphical representation of the services offered by PaaS providers.

Figure 1-2
Platform as a
Service (PaaS)
provider services

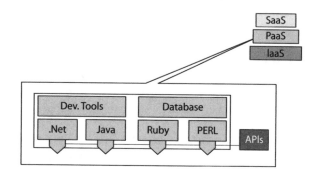

Figure 1-3
Software as a
Service (SaaS)
provider services

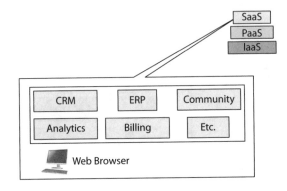

Software as a Service

Software as a Service (SaaS) is a cloud service model that enables a cloud consumer to use on-demand software applications delivered by the CSP via a thin client device, typically a web browser over the Internet. The web-based application features of SaaS have been around for quite some time before cloud became a term. Such applications were referred to as application service provider (ASP) software. SaaS customers delegate both the management and control of the infrastructure, such as storage, servers, network, or operating systems, to their CSP.

SaaS is a quick and efficient service model for key business applications such as customer relationship management (CRM), enterprise resource planning (ERP), human resources (HR), and payroll. Figure 1-3 shows you a graphical representation of the services offered by SaaS providers.

 EXAM TIP It is important to understand the difference between IaaS, PaaS, and SaaS. These are the three primary service models that all others are based on, and you will need to know who the users of each model are for the exam; IaaS is primarily for IT service providers, PaaS is primarily used by developers, and SaaS is used by end users.

Database as a Service

Database as a Service (DBaaS) is essentially a form of software specializing in the delivery of database operations. This service enables CSPs to offer database functionality to multiple discrete cloud consumers. DBaaS infrastructures support the following competencies:

- Self-service database instance provisioning for the customer
- Monitoring of attributes and quality-of-service levels to ensure compliance with provider-defined service agreements

- Carefully measured usage of database services, enabling chargeback functionality for each individual cloud consumer

A DBaaS infrastructure may also support service elasticity, secure multitenancy, access using a wide range of devices, automated resource management, and capacity planning. These concepts will be discussed later in this chapter.

Communications as a Service

Communications as a Service (CaaS) enables customers to utilize enterprise-level voice over IP (VoIP), virtual private networks (VPNs), private branch exchange (PBX), and unified communications without the costly investment of purchasing, hosting, and managing their own infrastructure. With the CSP being responsible for the management and operation of this infrastructure, the customer also has the advantage of not having to source and staff its own trained personnel, bringing significant relief to both operational and capital costs.

Business Process as a Service

Business Process as a Service (BPaaS) mixes business process management (BPM) with one or more aspects of a cloud service model (SaaS, IaaS, or PaaS). BPM is an approach that aims to make a company's workflow more effective, efficient, and agile, allowing it to respond quickly to changes driven by business requirements. This kind of workflow enables businesses to be more flexible and to decrease their spending.

Traditional business process management systems (BPMSs) integrate business processes and keep track of running their corresponding instances. A BPMS coordinates the execution of a business process step by step. Each process instance is monitored by the BPMS and provides users with feedback on progress to validate successful completion or to alert on failures. In case of a failure, the BPMS shows where the process failure occurred. By monitoring, analyzing, and identifying where business processes fail, companies can act proactively and optimize the deployment of their business service. This ultimately leads to lower costs and improved customer satisfaction.

A BPaaS is any business process that is delivered as a service by utilizing a cloud solution. With BPaaS, one or more business processes are uploaded to a cloud service that performs each process step and monitors them while they execute. As with any other cloud environment, BPaaS enables customers to use cloud software in a pay-per-use model instead of having to invest in hardware and maintenance.

Essentially, BPaaS is a cloud service that frees up not just internal computing resources but also human resources who may have been dedicated to performing that process. For example, a cloud-based payroll system can perform the functions of a payroll or HR employee by issuing paychecks and tax statements and processing deductions and benefits. Similarly, a cloud CRM can offload some tasks associated with qualifying leads, communicating with prospects, and sales project management.

Anything as a Service

Anything as a Service (XaaS) is the delivery of IT as a service through a combination of cloud service models; it works with one or a combination of SaaS, IaaS, PaaS, CaaS, DBaaS, or BPaaS. The *X* in XaaS is a variable that can be changed to represent a variety of different cloud services.

Accountability and the Shared Responsibility Model

Now that you understand all the different cloud service models, you need to become familiar with who is responsible for those services. Accountability in the cloud can be split between multiple parties, including cloud consumers, infrastructure providers, and CSPs. Accountability in cloud computing is about creating a holistic approach to achieve security in the cloud and to address the lack of consumer trust. The very nature of cloud computing brings a new level of complexity to the issue of determining who is responsible for a service outage, and CSPs are faced with the difficult task of achieving compliance across geographic boundaries. A service outage can be the result of a variety of issues, such as software vulnerabilities, power outages, hardware failure, network disruption, application error, or user error.

The three primary service models in cloud computing have differing security approaches for businesses. With SaaS, the CSP is responsible for maintaining the agreed-upon service levels between the CSP and the cloud consumer and for security, compliance, and liability expectations. When it comes to PaaS and IaaS, the cloud consumer is responsible for managing the same expectations, while the CSP takes some of the responsibility for securing the underlying infrastructure. Service outages can also be attributed to the end-user device having misconfiguration or hardware failures. Table 1-1 provides a quick reference for the party responsible for maintaining the service levels of each cloud service model.

Responsibility	SaaS	PaaS	IaaS
Data	Consumer	Consumer	Consumer
End-User Systems	Consumer	Consumer	Consumer
User and Service Account Management	Consumer	Consumer	Consumer
Directory/Identify Infrastructure	Both	Both	Consumer
Applications	Provider	Both	Consumer
Databases	Provider	Both	Consumer
Operating Systems	Provider	Both	Consumer
Hypervisors	Provider	Provider	Provider
Physical Network	Provider	Provider	Provider
Data Center	Provider	Provider	Provider

Table 1-1 Service Level Responsibility

Figure 1-4
Cloud service models and their consumers

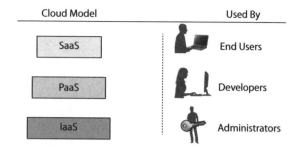

When discussing accountability and responsibility in the cloud, it is important to classify risk according to the service model being utilized and the location of the data. For example, if a business is using a hybrid cloud, both the consumer and the CSP can be responsible for the same risks, since part of the data is in the cloud and part is in the internal data center. It is important that the SLAs and any other agreements signed between the cloud consumer and CSP clearly state who is responsible for preventing and remedying outages and how those outages are classified, identified, and measured. Figure 1-4 shows who the typical cloud consumer is for each cloud model.

Another consideration is the division of responsibility for maintenance tasks in a cloud environment. Patching and maintenance contribute greatly to the overall security and performance in a cloud solution. Responsibility is broken out in such a way that the CSP is responsible for the patching and maintenance "of" the cloud, and the cloud consumer is responsible for patching "in" the cloud. We will explore this concept further in Chapter 10 when diving into systems management.

Cloud Deployment Models and Services

You have just learned about the different service models available for implementing a cloud computing solution. To realize the value from these service models and for the customers to have access to them, a deployment model must be chosen. Implementing a cloud deployment model can vastly affect an organization. Implementation requires careful consideration and planning to be successful. If your role is the IT administrator, it is your responsibility to educate the organization on the benefits and challenges of implementing a cloud deployment model. You need to evaluate the business needs and determine what benefits a cloud deployment model would bring to your organization. Whichever cloud deployment model you choose, whether it be private, public, or hybrid (all described next), it needs to map well to the business processes you are trying to achieve.

Private Cloud

In a private cloud deployment model, the cloud is owned by a single organization and enables central access to IT resources for departments and staff distributed among a variety of locations. A private cloud solution is implemented behind the corporate firewall and is maintained by the same organization that is using it. A private cloud utilizes internal resources and is designed to offer the same benefits of a public cloud without relinquishing control, security, and recurring costs to a CSP. In a private cloud model, the same organization is both the cloud consumer and the CSP.

The decision to implement a private cloud is usually driven by the need to maintain control of the environment because of regulatory or business reasons. For example, a bank might have data security issues that prevent it from using a public cloud service, so the bank might implement a private cloud to achieve the benefits of a cloud computing model.

A private cloud is a combination of virtualization, data center automation, chargeback metering, and identity-based security. Virtualization allows for easy scalability, flexible resource management, and maximum hardware utilization. A private cloud solution also involves having the ability to auto-provision physical host computers through orchestration software, which is discussed later in this chapter. Some organizations use private clouds to share storage between internal systems or departments. This is referred to as a private cloud space (PCS).

One of the downsides to a private cloud is that an organization does not get the return on investment it does with other cloud models. This is because the organization is still responsible for running and managing the resources instead of passing that responsibility to a CSP.

 EXAM TIP A private cloud allows you to take advantage of a cloud environment without losing flexibility and control of the systems and data.

Public Cloud

Unlike a private cloud that is owned by the organization, a public cloud is a pool of computing services delivered over the Internet via a CSP. A CSP makes resources such as applications and storage available to organizations over the Internet. Public clouds use a pay-as-you-go model, which gives organizations the benefit of paying only for the resources that they consume. Public clouds allow for easy and inexpensive setup because the hardware, application, and bandwidth costs are covered and maintained by the CSP and charged as part of the service agreement.

You may recognize SaaS offerings such as cloud storage and online office applications (e.g., Microsoft Office 365) as public cloud offerings. What you may not know is that IaaS and PaaS offerings, including cloud-based web hosting and development environments, can be part of a public cloud as well.

Public clouds are used when an organization is less likely to need full customization or the level of flexibility and control offered by private clouds. Organizations requiring data security can still utilize public clouds to make their operations significantly more efficient with the storage of nonsensitive content, online document collaboration, and webmail.

A public cloud offers ultimate scalability because cloud resources are available on demand from the CSP's vast pool of resources. Organizations do not need to purchase and implement hardware to scale the environment; they just need to obtain more resources from the CSP. The availability of the public cloud via an Internet connection allows the services to be used wherever the client is located, making a public cloud location-independent. Some examples of public CSPs are Microsoft Azure, Google Cloud, SAP Cloud Platform, Oracle Cloud, IBM Cloud Foundry, VMware vCloud, and Amazon Web Services.

Hybrid Cloud

A hybrid cloud is a cloud service that utilizes both private and public clouds to perform distinct functions within the same organization. An organization might have a need for both a local server running specific applications for security reasons and a public cloud hosting additional applications, files, and databases. These two environments would be configured for scalability and interoperability.

In a hybrid cloud model, an organization continues to provide and manage some resources internally, while other resources are provided externally by a CSP. A hybrid cloud allows an organization to take advantage of the scalability and cost-effectiveness of a public cloud without exposing mission-critical data to a public CSP.

A cloud model is defined as a hybrid cloud if an organization is using a public development platform that sends data to a private cloud. Another example of a hybrid cloud model is when an organization uses multiple SaaS applications and moves that application data between a private cloud or an internal data center.

A cloud is not considered a hybrid if an organization uses SaaS applications and does not move the data to a private cloud or internal data center. A cloud environment is labeled a hybrid cloud only if there is a combination of private and public clouds or if data is moved between the internal data center and the public cloud. You can see an example of a hybrid cloud environment in Figure 1-5.

 EXAM TIP Make sure you understand the different use cases for each type of cloud: private, public, and hybrid. A hybrid cloud is a combination of both a private cloud and a public cloud.

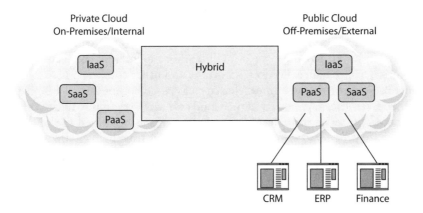

Figure 1-5 Components of a hybrid cloud environment

Community Cloud

A community cloud is a cloud offering where the infrastructure is shared between several organizations from a specific group with common computing needs or objectives. Community clouds are built and operated specifically for a targeted group of entities that have common cloud requirements and whose ultimate goal is to work together to achieve a specific business objective.

Community clouds are usually implemented for organizations working on joint projects that require a central cloud for managing and executing those projects. A finance community cloud, for example, could be set up to provide specific security requirements or optimized to provide low latency to perform financial transactions. A community cloud can be either on-premises or off-premises and can be managed by a CSP or by the organizations themselves.

 EXAM TIP A community cloud provides a segregated approach to cloud computing for increased security. The key to a community cloud is that it can be scoped to a specific group.

Cloud Within a Cloud

Cloud within a cloud offers the flexibility of a private cloud without the investment and operational cost of the infrastructure. Essentially, public cloud resources are used to create a private cloud for the consumer. The consumer would use the public cloud resources to provision the virtual infrastructure and systems for their services and manage access to those systems.

On-Premises vs. Off-Premises Hosting

On-premises hosting is the solution that IT professionals are likely most familiar with. On-premises hosting is the traditional way of managing a data center. In an on-premises environment, the virtualized servers are hosted on-site at the organization's internal data center, and the organization owns and maintains that server hardware. The benefit of on-premises hosting is that the organization has complete control over the daily management and maintenance of its servers. The downside to on-premises hosting is that the organization has to pay the costs of maintaining the internal data center, including power, security, maintenance, licenses, hardware, and other costs.

Off-premises hosting is sometimes referred to as cloud computing. With off-premises hosting, the IT resources are hosted in the cloud and accessed online. Off-premises hosting can be used for server virtualization or applications to be hosted in the cloud. One of the benefits of off-premises hosting is that the cost is usually lower than on-premises hosting because the resources are hosted online instead of in the organization's data center. This allows the organization to convert IT costs to the pay-as-you-grow model, keeping IT costs down. Off-premises hosting is sometimes perceived as less secure or as having a higher security risk, since the organization loses control of its data because it is hosted in the cloud.

Orchestration Platforms

Automation of day-to-day administrative tasks is becoming more and more of a requirement for IT departments. Orchestration platforms provide an automated way to manage the cloud or computing environment. They make it possible to achieve a dynamic data center by aligning business requests with applications, data, and infrastructure. A typical business model defines policies and service levels that an IT department must meet. Orchestration platforms help an IT department meet these requirements through automated workflows, provisions, and change management features. This allows for a dynamic and scalable infrastructure that is constantly changing based on the needs of the business. For example, with an orchestration platform, a developer could request the creation of a virtual machine via a service portal, and the orchestration software would automatically create that virtual machine based on a predefined template. Orchestration software can also be used for centralized management of a resource pool, including billing, software metering, and chargeback or showback for resource utilization.

Orchestration platforms provide companies with automated tools to perform tasks that would typically take a team of administrators to complete. These platforms offer an automated approach to creating hardware and software, allowing them to work together to deliver a predefined service or application. Orchestration platforms make it possible for the cloud environment to easily scale and provision new applications and services on demand through workflows.

Some examples of orchestration platforms include Cloudify, Terraform, Ansible, IBM Cloud Orchestrator, Flexiant Cloud Orchestrator, and Microsoft System Center Orchestrator. All of the orchestration platforms allow for the creation of workflows to automate day-to-day administrative tasks.

Multicloud

Most organizations today utilize a large number of cloud systems. Multicloud is the use of two or more cloud systems to comprise a system. Multicloud allows a company to take the best components from multiple vendors and combine them together into a solution that meets their needs. Some cloud solutions may be too rigid for a company's needs, so they take the pieces they need from multiple providers. In other cases, a single CSP presents too much risk to the organization, so they spread an application across two or more providers for redundancy. If one CSP goes down, services are rebalanced across the other providers.

Cloud Characteristics and Terms

When implementing a cloud computing model, an organization needs to understand the terminology of cloud computing and the characteristics of remote provisioning of a scalable and measured IT resource. The IT administrator, as a cloud consumer, needs to work with the CSP to assess these characteristics and measure the value offering of the chosen cloud platform.

Elasticity

Elasticity can be thought of as unlimited space that allows the organization to dynamically provision and deprovision processing, memory, and storage resources to meet the demands of its network. Elasticity allows an organization to shift and pool resources across dissimilar infrastructure, allowing data to be more synchronized and avoiding overprovisioning of hardware. It is one of the many benefits of cloud computing because it allows an IT department to be scalable without having to purchase and stand up hardware in its internal data center. The primary difference between elasticity and scalability is that scalability is the ability of a system to increase its workload on the current hardware resources, whereas elasticity is the ability of a system to increase its workload by adding hardware resources or shrink resources for decreasing workloads.

Demand-Driven Service

In an on-demand self-service environment, users have access to cloud services through an online portal. This gives them the ability to provision cloud resources on demand wherever and whenever they need to. On-demand, or "just-in-time," self-service allows cloud consumers to acquire computing resources automatically and on demand without human interaction from the CSP.

Pay-as-You-Grow

One of the advantages of the public cloud is the pay-as-you-grow philosophy. The pay-as-you-grow charging model allows an organization to pay for services by the hour or based on the compute resources it uses. Therefore, pay-as-you-grow does not require a large up-front investment by the organization for infrastructure resources. It is important for an organization to design and plan its cloud costs before deploying its first application in the cloud. Most CSPs have a calculator to help organizations figure the costs they would incur by moving to the cloud. This gives organizations a better understanding of the pay-as-you-grow model when it comes to cloud pricing and using the public cloud infrastructure.

Chargeback

IT chargeback is an accounting strategy that attempts to decentralize the costs of IT services and apply them directly to the teams or divisions that utilize those services. This system enables organizations to make better decisions about how their IT dollars are spent, as it can help determine the true cost of a particular service. Without a chargeback system, all IT costs are consolidated under the IT department umbrella, and the ability to determine the true profitability of the individual business services the IT department supports is limited or impossible. Most private clouds and internal IT departments use the term "showback" instead of chargeback to describe the amount of resources being consumed by a department.

Ubiquitous Access

With ubiquitous access, a CSP's capabilities are available over the network and can be accessed through standard mechanisms by many different types of clients, and without the requirement for application deployment or a specific operating system configuration. This does not necessarily mean Internet access. Ubiquitous access does, however, allow a cloud service to be widely accessible via a web browser from anywhere. A cloud consumer can get the same level of access, whether at home, at work, or in a coffee shop.

Metering

Metering is the ability of a cloud platform to track the use of its IT resources and is geared primarily toward measuring usage by cloud consumers. A metering function allows the CSP to charge a cloud consumer only for the IT resources actually being used. Metering is closely tied to on-demand or demand-driven cloud usage.

Metering is not only used for billing purposes; it can also be used for general monitoring of IT resources and usage reporting for both the consumer and the provider. This makes metering a benefit for not only public clouds but private cloud models as well.

Multitenancy

Multitenancy is an architecture that provides a single instance of an application to serve multiple clients or tenants. Tenants are allowed to have their own view of the application and make customizations while remaining unaware of other tenants who are using the same application.

Multitenant applications ensure that tenants do not have access to change the data and configuration of the application on their own. However, tenants are allowed to change the user interface to give the application a personalized look and feel.

Implementing a multitenant application is, of course, more complicated than working with a single-tenant application. Multitenant applications must support the sharing of multiple resources by multiple users (e.g., databases, middleware, portals) while maintaining the security of the environment.

Cloud computing has broadened the definition of multitenancy because of the new service models that can take advantage of virtualization and remote access. A SaaS service provider can run an instance of its application on a cloud database and provide web access to multiple customers. Each tenant's data is isolated and remains invisible to other tenants.

Cloud Bursting

Cloud bursting is the concept of running an application on the organization's internal computing resources or private cloud and "bursting" that application into a public cloud on demand when the organization runs out of resources on its internal private cloud. Cloud bursting is normally recommended for high-performance, noncritical applications that have nonsensitive data. It allows a company to deploy an application in an internal data center and "burst" to a public cloud to meet peak needs.

When an organization is looking to take advantage of cloud bursting, it needs to consider security and regulatory compliance requirements. An example of when cloud

Figure 1-6
Operating within the organization's internal computing resources (no public cloud needed)

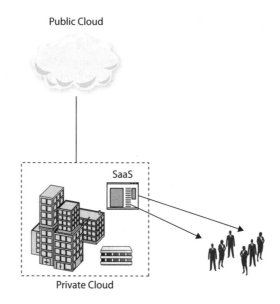

bursting is a good option is in the retail world, where a company might experience a substantial increase in demand during the holiday season. The downside to this is that the retailers could be putting sensitive data into the public cloud and exposing their customers to risk. Figures 1-6 and 1-7 show an example of an application experiencing heavy use and subsequently "bursting" into the public cloud.

Figure 1-7
Operating after cloud bursting (using the public cloud)

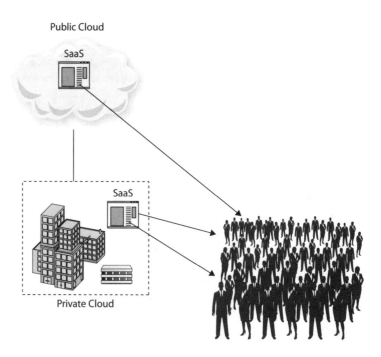

EXAM TIP   Cloud bursting is a short-term way to increase your available cloud resources on demand.

Auto-Scaling Technology

Auto-scaling is the logical next step after cloud bursting for the demand-driven cloud. Cloud consumers can capitalize on the elasticity and orchestration of a CSP by bursting resources to the cloud automatically when necessary. This feature takes the enablement of cloud resources to the next level by provisioning not just more compute resources as necessary for the subscribed set of virtual machines or instances but also provisioning more virtual machines and instances themselves to deliver the performance and availability that the consumer is looking to achieve. Auto-scaling technology can help consumers offset unknown or unexpected spikes in demand without adversely affecting their deliverables.

Baselines

Baselines are the starting point for all measurements to be compared against. A baseline is a recorded state or configuration against which planned changes and performance comparisons can be made. Establishing a baseline is the first step in controlling any environment.

Organizations typically take a baseline of an existing system when migrating it to the cloud. They take another baseline when the system is deployed and under normal load to compare performance metrics between the two baselines and ensure that performance meets the needs of the business and application. Baselines should be taken at different milestones in the cloud life cycle. For example, when a cloud is deployed and is being used by the workforce, conduct a baseline to understand normal activity. However, the system's usage may grow or shrink over time, and new behavior will be considered normal, thus requiring a new baseline. Similar applications on the same platform should also be baselined and compared against each other to ensure that the organization takes advantage of optimizations that may be in place in one application but not another.

The importance of baselines cannot be overemphasized in cloud operations. Appropriate tools and procedures should be put in place to perform the following functions:

- Evaluate performance
- Ensure user satisfaction
- Fulfill service level agreement requirements
- Demonstrate proof of compliance

The inability to prove compliance may put a company at risk financially, as many contracts specify penalties if the company is unable to demonstrate their fulfillment of the stated requirements.

The following methodology can be used to demonstrate proof of compliance:

1. *Establish baselines.* Create a baseline measurement of the environment for each area that has defined service levels.

2. *Monitor baselines.* Establish procedures to regularly and consistently monitor and measure the baseline and to understand the pattern of varying measurements over the course of time, in a process known as trending. The cloud service administrator (CSA) also needs to be alerted to significant deviations from the baseline so that they can restore service to the previously defined baseline state.

3. *Make baselines available.* Share baselines with customers to provide evidence of SLA compliance.

4. *Maintain baseline states.* Once the baselines have been established, documented, and contractually agreed upon, it is then the goal of service operations to ensure that they consistently beat baseline performance metrics.

Source and Target Hosts

When moving workloads in a cloud environment, the compute resources that run the workload in the current position are owned by the "source" host. The host that owns the compute resources that an administrator intends to move to is referred to as the "target" host.

Existing Systems

Cloud environments are not usually developed as an entirely new solution running by itself. Workloads are often shared by existing systems and cloud systems to provide continuity. Migration plans are established, and existing systems are slated for removal over time as functionality is slowly migrated to the cloud.

Cloud Elements

The cloud is not made up only of virtual machines and virtualization hosts. Services have been developed that allow consumers to leverage cloud objects such as storage, databases, and applications from disparate CSPs. A wide variety of computing resources are available to cloud consumers through cloud services. These resources can become pieces of a larger system or solution. When utilizing cloud services, application components are called from APIs and are referred to as "target objects."

This enables a diverse approach to cloud computing and gives consumers more choice on how they can develop the solutions they want to build. As a foundation for understanding cloud computing, it is important to understand how the terms cloud element and target object are used. Cloud elements are the pieces that make up a cloud solution. Some of those pieces could be accessed by cloud consumers and programs, while others are used in support of those resources. When cloud consumers reference cloud elements, those elements are referred to as target objects. For example, when a backup program is pointed to cloud storage to archive it onto another storage medium, the cloud storage is the target object. Table 1-2 shows a number of cloud elements and how they can be a target object. It provides an example of how it would be a target object and chapter references for where you can learn more. Since these are foundational terms, you will learn much more about them as they are used in conveying other important cloud concepts.

Cloud Element	Example	Chapter and Section Reference
Hypervisor	A patch management system would reference hypervisors to apply patches to them.	Ch. 5, "Hypervisor" Ch. 10, "Patch Management"
Virtual resources (vCPU/memory)	Virtual resources would be a target object for a management tool that collects resource utilization metrics, benchmarks, and thresholds.	Ch.10, "Baselines and Thresholds"
Virtual machine	A virtual machine would be a target object for a cloud backup solution.	Ch. 5, "Virtual Machine" Ch. 13, "Backup Targets"
Virtual appliance	A virtual appliance such as a cloud firewall or a CASB would be a target object for cloud dashboards.	Ch. 5, "Firewall" Ch. 10, "Virtual Appliances" Ch. 11, "Firewall" and "Cloud Access Security Broker"
Applications	Application components would be target objects for systems that call their APIs.	Ch. 11, "APIs"
Storage	Clients synchronize with cloud storage in solutions like Dropbox. The cloud storage, in this case, would be the target object for the synchronization.	Ch. 3, "Storage Types and Technologies"
Logs	When a security information and event management (SIEM) system pulls logs from cloud servers, these logs would be target objects.	Ch. 11, "SIEM"
Workflow	A workflow would be the target object of orchestration.	Ch. 14, "Automation and Orchestration"
Cluster	Code updates may be deployed to cluster nodes independently by a deployment tool or orchestration tool. This tool would trigger failovers and code updates on the target objects.	Ch. 10, "Clusters" and "Code Updates"

Table 1-2 Cloud Elements and Target Objects

Advanced Cloud Services

The cloud is the platform supporting some of the latest technologies, including Internet of Things (IoT), machine learning, and artificial intelligence. This section introduces both of those concepts, as well as the ability to deploy applications with a serverless architecture.

Machine Learning and Artificial Intelligence

Many companies want to develop services that utilize a level of machine learning (ML) or artificial intelligence (AI). ML is a computer program that can make increasingly better decisions or predictions based on data as it observes more patterns and relationships between the data. For example, the prediction ML in Netflix suggests programs you might be interested in based on programs you have watched before and programs viewed by others who viewed the same or similar programming. Likewise, Amazon uses an ML model to suggest other products that you might like based on previous purchase decisions. ML algorithms go through a process of training where they are given data to learn from. They develop a model from this training that then is applied to larger data sets.

Another method ML uses is reinforcement learning. Reinforcement learning is where a program is given metrics for success and then it uses the tools available to perform millions of iterations, where it attempts to achieve the most optimal solutions.

Similar to ML, AI learns from its interactions with data to make better decisions. However, AI is a broader concept of which ML is a part. AI is concerned with developing computer programs that exhibit learning and problem-solving abilities similar to that of human cognition.

There are huge barriers to creating new ML or AI models and algorithms from scratch. Fortunately, CSPs like Google and Amazon have been pioneers in this space and offer consumers the ability to utilize pretrained and tuned models for their applications. For example, if you want to develop an application that needs to receive speech-based instructions, you can utilize a predeveloped speech AI platform to do that portion of the application. Figure 1-8 shows Google's AI Hub, where you can select predeveloped AI services.

Some predeveloped ML/AI solutions include

- Image recognition
- Video analysis
- Personalized recommendations
- Natural language processing (NLP)
- Speech recognition
- Code review
- Forecasting
- Enterprise search
- Anomaly detection
- Language translation
- Transcription

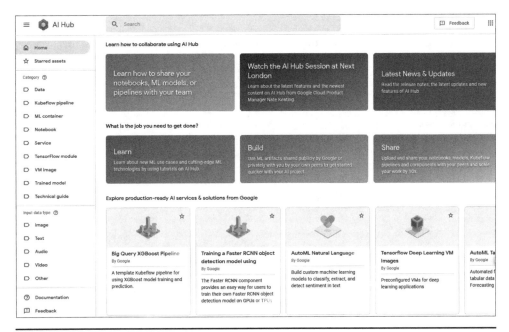

Figure 1-8   Predeveloped AI services in Google's AI Hub

Serverless

Serverless computing uses cloud resources to host an application, and the CSP manages the provision of the system and management of its resources transparently to the cloud consumer. This makes it very fast and easy to develop and deploy applications. The consumer is charged only for the resources they use, and there is no set minimum. Let's try an exercise.

Exercise 1-1: Creating a Basic Serverless Application on AWS Lambda

In this exercise, we will create a serverless application using AWS Lambda. You will need an AWS account to perform these steps. The application is a simple Hello World application that will run on an AWS server instance, but we will not need to configure the server to run our code. We will also be using some built-in templates to make it simpler.

1. Log in to your AWS account. You will be presented with the management console, which will show the available services you can choose from.

2. Click on Lambda under the All Services/Compute section, and the AWS Lambda functions screen will load.

3. Click Create Function.

4. AWS Lambda gives you some precreated functions that you can use under Blueprints. Click Use A Blueprint and a list of blueprints will appear.

5. Type **hello-world** in the search box and then press ENTER.

6. Select the hello-world blueprint.

7. The basic information screen will load. Enter a function name and leave the default options selected, as shown next, and then click Create Function.

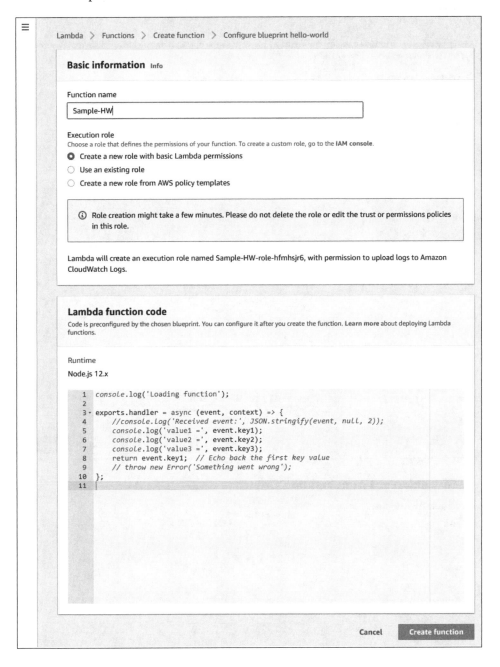

8. Click the test button in the upper right to display the Configure Test Event screen.

9. Give the event a name and click Create.

10. Click Test again.

11. Expand the execution result details, and it will show the resulting output shown here.

Note that the log output shows the memory that you were billed for to perform the operation. In this case, we were billed for 128MB of memory for 100 milliseconds. Amazon allocated the resources needed for the work and then removed them when we were done. We are only billed for what was actually used.

```
START RequestId: cd3d9d26-9ccd-450e-b2f9-fb4d1af2af2c Version: $LATEST
2020-10-10T15:49:45.515Z        cd3d9d26-9ccd-450e-b2f9-fb4d1af2af2c        INFO    value1 = value1
2020-10-10T15:49:45.515Z        cd3d9d26-9ccd-450e-b2f9-fb4d1af2af2c        INFO    value2 = value2
2020-10-10T15:49:45.515Z        cd3d9d26-9ccd-450e-b2f9-fb4d1af2af2c        INFO    value3 = value3
END RequestId: cd3d9d26-9ccd-450e-b2f9-fb4d1af2af2c
REPORT RequestId: cd3d9d26-9ccd-450e-b2f9-fb4d1af2af2c        Duration: 1.89 ms        Billed
Duration: 100 ms   Memory Size: 128 MB    Max Memory Used: 64 MB  Init Duration: 126.18 ms
```

Internet of Things

The cloud is an ideal way of managing the IoT. IoT refers to devices that are connected to the Internet. The primary purpose of IoT is not computing, but some other task. Some IoT devices include IP cameras, sensors, lights, thermostats, and many other devices. The primary purpose of the IoT camera is to record footage, but it also is connected to the Internet to allow for remote management, footage archiving, and live streaming. Manufacturing uses IoT to embed sensors into equipment so as to better track utilization and determine when maintenance is required. Companies may have digital signage that displays content from the cloud, tracking systems for assets, or sensors to measure heat, humidity, or other things. IoT has also entered the home with smart water heaters, sprinkler systems, light bulbs, thermostats, security systems, and entertainment devices.

IoT can be provisioned quickly when it is cloud-enabled. Out of the box, a device can connect back to a cloud service to report in and then be attached to the customer's cloud account for ongoing management and operations. This is especially important for sensors or equipment that is distributed around the globe, outside organizational boundaries, or mobile. As long as the IoT has Internet access, it can connect to the CSP to allow for data exchange or management. For example, a water company could deploy IoT sensors at homes so that data can be collected automatically. This saves them the trouble of sending someone out to record the data from each sensor, and they receive the data in real time so they can make better decisions.

Cloud IoT allows for effective global asset management. For example, a car rental company could place sensors on its fleet to track location, speed, or other data. An IoT cloud platform would allow the devices to be managed wherever the customer drives them. Furthermore, because cloud resources are distributed across the globe, a company can manage systems centrally but communicate with IoT devices close to the device to reduce latency for high-speed or real-time processing of data that would not be possible if distributed systems were tied directly to a central hub.

Lastly, IoT cloud platforms make it easy for consumers to take the data from IoT devices and analyze that data with other cloud services. It can be hard to collect and analyze data from devices when they are managed on-premises, but cloud systems can be easily scaled or the data can be ported from one system to another with standard APIs for ease of management and analysis. Suppose the company wants to integrate the data with another service. In that case, it is as simple as connecting the new service to the existing platform API.

Chapter Review

The cloud offers multiple ways for consumers to deploy and manage applications with varying levels of complexity. It also allows consumers to reduce their security and compliance burden by sharing it with the CSP. Understanding the similarities and differences between the cloud models is key to understanding which one meets the business needs of the application or service you want to provide. It is equally important to grasp how the cloud can benefit an organization. Cloud computing also makes it easy for customers to integrate IoT systems into their cloud infrastructure or deploy ML or AI solutions. Cloud computing is a growing industry, and IT professionals are going to be required to grow with it.

Questions

The following questions will help you gauge your understanding of the material in this chapter. Read all the answers carefully because there might be more than one correct answer. Choose the best response(s) for each question.

1. Which of the following would be considered an example of IaaS?

   A. Providing productivity software for use over the Internet

   B. A multiuser program that is hosted by a third party

   C. Providing hardware resources over the Internet

   D. A database that is hosted in the cloud

2. Which term is used to define the increasing number of services delivered over the Internet?

   A. XaaS

   B. CaaS

   C. MaaS

   D. C-MaaS

3. Voice over IP (VoIP) is an example of what type of cloud service?

   A. IaaS

   B. PaaS

   C. MaaS

   D. CaaS

4. Which of the following cloud solutions provides only hardware and network resources to make up a cloud environment?

   A. SaaS

   B. CaaS

   C. PaaS

   D. IaaS

5. Which of the following would give developers a place to build applications and services over the Internet?

   A. IaaS

   B. SaaS

   C. PaaS

   D. Virtual machines

6. What type of computing solution would be defined as a platform that is implemented within the corporate firewall and is under the control of the IT department?

   A. Private cloud

   B. Public cloud

   C. VLAN

   D. VPN

7. A cloud deployment has been created explicitly for the finance department. What type of cloud deployment would this be defined as?

   A. Public cloud

   B. Hybrid cloud

   C. Community cloud

   D. Private cloud

8. Which of the following statements would be used to explain a private cloud but not a public cloud?

   A. Used as a service via the Internet

   B. Dedicated to a single organization

   C. Requires users to pay a monthly fee to access services

   D. Provides incremental scalability

9. Which of the following statements is a benefit of a hybrid cloud?

   A. Data security management

   B. Requirement of a major financial investment

   C. Dependency of internal IT department

   D. Complex networking

10. Which of the following would be considered an advantage of cloud computing?

    A. Increased security

    B. Ability to scale to meet growing usage demands

    C. Ease of integrating equipment hosted in other data centers

    D. Increased privacy for corporate data

11. Which statement defines chargeback?

    A. The recovery of costs from consumers of cloud services

    B. The process of identifying costs and assigning them to specific cost categories

    C. A method of ensuring that cloud computing becomes a profit instead of a cost

    D. A system for confirming that billing occurs for the cloud services being used

12. When you run out of compute resources in your internal data center and expand to an external cloud on demand, this is an example of what?

    A. SaaS

    B. Hybrid cloud

    C. Cloud bursting

    D. Elasticity

13. A company wants to deploy a private cloud but does not want to invest in the infrastructure associated with a private cloud. Which solution should they consider?

    A. Hybrid cloud

    B. Cloud within a cloud

    C. Community cloud

    D. On-premises hosting

14. Given the shared responsibility model, under which of the following services models would the CSP only be responsible for the directory infrastructure?

   A. SaaS

   B. PaaS

   C. IaaS

   D. All of the above

Answers

  1. C. Providing hardware resources over the Internet is an example of IaaS. Infrastructure as a Service (IaaS) is a cloud service model that offers server storage, infrastructure, and connectivity domains to a cloud consumer.

  2. A. XaaS is a collective term that means "Anything as a Service" (or "Everything as a Service").

  3. D. Voice over IP is an example of Communications as a Service (CaaS) because it is a cloud-based phone system, which is a form of communications.

  4. D. In a cloud service model, IaaS providers offer computers and other hardware resources. Organizations would outsource the equipment needed to support their business.

  5. C. PaaS provides a platform that an organization can use to build their applications and services on. These systems can then be accessed over the Internet. PaaS is hosted in the cloud and accessed with a web browser.

  6. A. A private cloud is a cloud computing solution that is implemented behind a corporate firewall and is under the control of the internal IT department.

  7. C. A community cloud is a cloud solution that provides services to a specific or limited number of individuals who share a common computing need.

  8. B. A private cloud is dedicated to a single organization and is contained with the corporate firewall.

  9. A. A hybrid cloud offers the ability to keep the organization's mission-critical data behind a firewall and outside of the public cloud.

 10. B. One of the benefits of cloud computing is the ability to easily scale and add resources to meet the growth of the organization.

 11. A. The purpose of a chargeback system is to measure the costs of IT services, hardware, or software and recover them from the business unit or cloud consumer that used them.

12. **C.** Cloud bursting allows you to add resources from an external cloud on an on-demand basis. The internal resource is the private cloud, and the external resource is the public cloud.

13. **B.** Cloud within a cloud offers the flexibility of a private cloud without the investment and operational cost of the infrastructure.

14. **C.** Under IaaS, the CSP is responsible for everything except data, end-user systems, and user and service account management.

Disk Storage Systems

In this chapter, you will learn about
- Disk types and configurations
- Tiering
- File system types

Storage devices are the foundation of a storage network and are the building blocks of storage in a disk subsystem, stand-alone server, or cloud data center. Disk system performance is a key factor in the overall health of the cloud environment, and you need to understand the different types of disks that are available and the benefits of each. Once an organization chooses the type of disk to use in its cloud environment, it needs to protect the data that is stored on the disk. Along with describing the different types of disks and how to connect those disks to the system, this chapter illustrates how data can be tiered to provide better utilization of disk resources and better application performance. Those who have passed the Network+, Server+, or Storage+ exam might possibly skip this chapter.

Disk Types and Configurations

Disk drive technology has advanced at an astonishing rate over the past few years, making terabytes of storage available at a relatively low cost to consumers. Evaluating what types of disks to buy requires careful planning and evaluation of the purpose of the disk.

Two main factors are used in determining the appropriate disk type for a use case. These are speed and capacity. Speed is typically measured in input/output operations per second (IOPS). You want to use a disk type that can offer the IOPS needed by the application or system. For example, if you were looking for a type of drive to support a database environment, this requires high IOPS to support queries across large data sets and many random reads and writes. In this case, you would be interested in a disk type with high IOPS, such as flash. However, if you were selecting a drive to support a file share on a test network, a disk type with medium IOPS would be acceptable, whereas archival storage such as backup might be able to use a drive type with low IOPS.

The second factor is capacity. You want to choose a drive type that will provide enough storage for the application or system data, not just for now, but also factoring in future growth.

Companies have limited resources, so they must balance speed and capacity when choosing the drive type. Storage with high IOPS such as flash costs significantly more than storage with low IOPS, like spinning disk. In the following sections, we examine each of the different disk types and clarify these distinctions.

Rotational Media

Disk storage is a generic term used to describe storage mechanisms where data is digitally recorded by various electronic, magnetic, optical, or mechanical methods on a rotating disk or media. A disk drive is a device that uses this storage mechanism with fixed or removable media. Removable media refers to an optical disc, memory card, flash media, or USB drive, and fixed or nonremovable media refers to a hard disk drive.

A hard disk drive (HDD) uses rapidly rotating disks called platters coated with a magnetic material known as ferrous oxide to store and retrieve digital information. An HDD retains the data on the drive even when the drive is powered off. The data on an HDD is read in a random-access manner. What this means is that an individual block of data can be stored or retrieved in any order rather than only being accessible sequentially, as in the case of data that might exist on tape.

An HDD contains one or more platters with read/write heads arranged on a moving arm that floats above the ferrous oxide surface to read and write data to the drive. HDDs have been the primary storage device for computers since the 1960s. Today the most common sizes for HDDs are the 3.5 inch, which is used primarily in desktop computers, and the 2.5 inch, which is mainly used in laptop computers. The primary competitors of the HDD are the solid-state drive (SSD) and flash memory cards. HDDs should remain the dominating medium for secondary storage, but SSDs have replaced rotating hard drives for primary storage.

 EXAM TIP Hard disk drives are used when speed is less important than total storage space.

Solid State Drive

An SSD is a high-performance storage device that contains no moving parts. It includes either dynamic random-access memory (DRAM) or flash memory boards, a memory bus board, a central processing unit (CPU), and sometimes a battery or separate power source. The majority of SSDs use "not and" (NAND)–based flash memory, which is a nonvolatile memory type, meaning the drive can retain data without power. SSDs produce the highest possible I/O rates because they contain their own CPUs to manage data storage. SSDs are less susceptible to shock or being dropped, are much quieter, and have a faster access time and lower latency than HDDs. SSDs and traditional hard disks have the same I/O interface, allowing SSDs to easily replace a traditional HDD without changing the computer hardware.

While SSDs can be used in all types of scenarios, they are especially valuable in a system where I/O response time is critical, such as a database server, a server hosting a file share, or any application that has a disk I/O bottleneck. Another example of where an

SSD is a good candidate is in a laptop. SSDs are shock-resistant; they also use less power and provide a faster startup time than HDDs. Since an SSD has no moving parts, both sleep response time and system response time are improved. SSDs are currently more expensive than traditional HDDs but are less of a risk for failure and data loss. Table 2-1 shows you some of the differences between SSDs and traditional HDDs.

 TIP   SSDs have faster response times than HDDs and are used in high-performance servers where speed is more important than total storage space.

Drive Characteristic	Solid-State Drive	Hard Disk Drive
Startup time	Almost instantaneous. There are no moving parts to start on an SSD.	Disk spin-up can take a few seconds. If a system has multiple hard disks, it might stagger spin-up to limit power usage.
Fragmentation	Very small. Defragmenting an SSD could actually cause wear by making additional writes to the memory.	Files that are frequently written become fragmented over time. Defragmentation is required to ensure optimum performance.
Noise	Virtually none, since an SSD has no moving parts.	Noise levels vary between different models and manufacturers.
Temperature control	Able to tolerate higher temperatures than an HDD. Special cooling is usually not required.	Ambient temperatures above 95°F can shorten life. Additional cooling could be required.
Susceptibility to failure	Extremely resistant to shock and vibrations because it has no moving parts.	Susceptible to shock and vibrations due to moving heads above rapidly rotating platters.
Reliability and expected lifetime	Not as likely to have a mechanical failure, since it has no moving parts. Reliability varies across manufacturers.	Potential for mechanical failure from normal use due to moving parts.
Power consumption	Flash-based, on average, requires half the power of an HDD. High-performance DRAM requires as much power as an HDD.	Anywhere from 0.35 watts to 20 watts, depending on size and performance.
Cost	More expensive per GB compared to HDD.	Less expensive per GB than SSD.
Installation	Not sensitive to location or orientation. No exposed circuitry.	Circuits can be exposed and should not come in contact with other metal parts. Needs to be mounted to protect against vibrations.
Data transfer rate	Delivers consistent read/write speed. Sleep recovery is greatly improved compared to an HDD due to no moving parts.	Slower response time because of constantly seeking to read files from various locations on the disk.

Table 2-1   SSD vs. HDD

SSDs are made up of flash memory cells that can hold one or more bits. A bit is a binary 0 or 1, and it is the foundation of information storage. The cells are organized into rows and columns. Current is sent to the cell to give it a charge. The voltage is stored in the cell and can be read by evaluating the voltage level. Writing new data requires setting a new voltage level in the cell. Cells have a limited lifespan. While you can read from the cell as many times as you wish, each time data is written to the cell, charge deteriorates the layer of the cell that conducts the voltage to it. Eventually, the conductive layer will break down and no longer allow for the cell to be charged.

SSDs come in four different types based on how many bits can be stored in each cell. The types are named accordingly, as follows:

- Single-level cell (SLC)
- Multi-level cell (MLC)
- Triple-level cell (TLC)
- Quad-level cell (QLC)

SLC flash stores only one bit in each cell. A binary one is represented by a charge, and a binary zero by no charge. MLC flash can store two bits per cell. This equates to four binary possibilities: 00, 01, 10, and 11. It does this by setting four different voltage levels in a cell. A charge of 25 percent equates to a binary value of 11, 50 percent is 01, 75 percent is 00, and a full charge is 10. Similarly, TLC flash stores three bits, which equates to eight binary possibilities, and QLC flash stores four bits, with sixteen binary possibilities. Each of these possible binary values in the cell must have a corresponding voltage level that can be set in the cell and read by the flash media. This requires more precise charging and voltage evaluation methods.

Adding more bits to the memory cell increases capacity, but it reduces the access speed and longevity of the cell because a change to any of the bits in that cell requires changing the voltage level of the cell. This equates to more frequent cell writes as compared to cells containing fewer bits.

Each of the SSD types has an average number of Program Erase (PE) cycles that can be performed per cell. Enterprise variants of some types will allow for more PE cycles. These drives also cost more but are better suited to commercial purposes where drives are utilized more intensely than consumer drives. SSDs will perform an action called write leveling to balance writes across the cells to avoid premature deterioration of some cells over others.

Following the release of TLC flash, a change occurred in the industry. The organization of cells based on rows and columns was augmented to include a third axis by stacking the cells on top of one another. This version of flash is referred to as 3D NAND, and the former is known as 2D NAND. 3D NAND cells are larger, which improves reliability through higher PE cycles per cell. Some TLC flash uses the 2D NAND, and some 3D NAND. QLC only comes in a 3D NAND version. QLC is the slowest of the flash types and it has the lowest PE cycle rating. However, it is also the cheapest. Table 2-2 compares the different SSD types.

	SLC Flash	MLC Flash	TLC Flash	QLC Flash
Bits per cell	1	2	3	4
Possible voltage levels	2	4	8	16
PE cycles	50,000–100,000	20,000–30,000 (Enterprise) 5,000–10,000 (Consumer)	2,000–4,000 (2D NAND) 3,000–10,000 (3D NAND)	1,000
Speed	Highest	Medium	Low	Lowest
Cost	Highest	Medium	Low	Lowest

Table 2-2   SSD Types

NOTE   There is a Penta-Level Cell (PLC) currently in development that is planned to house five bits per cell.

USB Drive

A universal serial bus (USB) drive is an external plug-and-play storage device that can be plugged into a computer's USB port and is recognized by the computer as a removable drive and assigned a drive letter by the computer. Unlike an HDD or SSD, a USB drive does not require a special connection cable and power cable to connect to the system because it is powered via the USB port of the computer. Since a USB drive is portable and retains the data stored on it as it is moved between computer systems, it is a great device for transferring files quickly between computers or servers. Many external storage devices use USB, such as hard drives, flash drives, and DVD drives.

Tape

A tape drive is a storage device that reads and writes data to magnetic tape. Using tape as a form of storage has been around for a long time. The role of tape has changed tremendously over the years and is still changing. Tape is now finding a niche in the market for longer-term storage and archiving of data, and it is the medium of choice for storage at an off-site location.

Tape drives provide sequential access to the data, whereas an HDD provides random access to the data. A tape drive has to physically wind the tape between reels to read any one particular piece of data. As a result, it has a slow seek time, having to wait for the tape to be in the correct position to access the data. Tape drives have a wide range of capacity and allow for data to be compressed to a size smaller than that of the files stored on the disk.

TIP   Tape storage is predominantly used for off-site storage and archiving of data.

Interface Types

HDDs interface with a computer in a variety of ways, including via ATA, SATA, Fibre Channel, SCSI, SAS, and IDE. Here we look at each of these interface technologies in greater detail. HDDs connect to a host bus interface adapter with a single data cable. Each HDD has its own power cable that is connected to the computer's power supply.

- *Advanced Technology Attachment (ATA)* is an interface standard for connecting storage devices within computers. ATA is often referred to as Parallel ATA (or PATA).

- *Integrated Drive Electronics (IDE)* is the integration of the controller and the hard drive itself, which allows the drive to connect directly to the motherboard or controller. IDE is also known as ATA.

- *Serial ATA (SATA)* is used to connect host bus adapters to mass storage devices. Designed to replace PATA, it offers several advantages over its predecessor, including reduced cable size, lower cost, native hot swapping, faster throughput, and more efficient data transfer.

- *Small Computer System Interface (SCSI)* is a set of standard electronic interfaces accredited by the American National Standards Institute (ANSI) for connecting and transferring data between computers and storage devices. SCSI is faster and more flexible than earlier transfer interfaces. It uses a bus interface type, and every device in the chain requires a unique ID.

- *Serial Attached SCSI (SAS)* is a data transfer technology that was designed to replace SCSI and to transfer data to and from storage devices. SAS is backward compatible with SATA drives.

- *Fibre Channel (FC)* is a high-speed network technology used in storage networking. Fibre Channel is well suited to connect servers to a shared storage device such as a storage area network (SAN) due to its high-speed transfer rate of up to 16 gigabits per second. Fibre Channel is often referred to as FC in the industry and on the Cloud+ exam.

Table 2-3 explains the different connection types and some of the advantages and disadvantages of each interface.

 EXAM TIP Understanding the differences in the interface types is key for the test. You need to know when to use each connector and the benefits of that connector.

Access Speed

Just knowing the types of hard disks and the interface is not enough to calculate which drive type is best for a particular application. Understanding the speed at which a drive can access the data that is stored on that drive is critical to the performance of the application.

Connector	Advantages	Disadvantages
Integrated Drive Electronics (IDE)	• Lower cost • Large capacity	• Only one device can read/write at a time if used in the typical master/slave configuration
Serial ATA (SATA)	• Lower cost • Large capacity • Faster transfer rates than ATA • Easy configuration	• Slower transfer rates than SCSI • No native support in older operating systems
Small Computer System Interface (SCSI)	• Faster speeds • Greater scalability • Compatible with older SCSI devices • Reliability • Appropriate for large amounts of data	• Higher cost • Large variety of interfaces • Higher RPM, causing more noise and heat • More difficult configuration
Serial Attached SCSI (SAS)	• Compatibility with SATA • Higher transfer speeds • Serial communication vs. parallel • Increased availability	• Higher cost • Use of SCSI command set

Table 2-3   HDD Interface Types

A hard drive's speed is measured by the amount of time it takes to access the data that is stored on the drive. Access time is the response time of the drive and is a direct correlation between seek time and latency. The actuator arm and read/write head of the drive must move for data to be located. First, the actuator arm must move the head to the correct location on the platter. The time it takes for the arm to move to the correct location is known as seek time. At the same time, the platter must rotate to the desired sector. The time it takes for the platter to spin to the desired location is known as rotational latency or just latency for short.

The access time of an HDD can be improved by either increasing the rotational speed of the drive or reducing the time the drive has to spend seeking the data. Seek time generally falls in the range of 3 to 15 milliseconds (ms). The faster the disk can spin, the faster it can find the data and the lower the latency for that drive will be. Table 2-4 lists the average latency based on some common hard disk speeds.

Redundant Array of Independent Disks (RAID)

So far in this chapter, you have learned about the different disk types and how those disk types connect to a computer system. The next thing you need to understand is how to make the data that is stored on those disk drives as redundant as possible while

Table 2-4	Rotational Speed (RPM)	Average Latency (ms)
Hard Disk Speed and Latency	3600	8.3
	4200	7.1
	5400	5.6
	7200	4.2
	10,000	3.0
	15,000	2.0

maintaining a high-performance system. RAID is a storage technology that combines multiple hard disk drives into a single logical unit so that the data can be distributed across the hard disk drives for both improved performance and increased security according to their various RAID levels.

There are four primary RAID levels in use and several additional RAID levels, called nested RAID levels, that are built on top of the four primary types. RAID 0 takes two disks and stripes the data across them. It has the highest speed, but a failure of any disk results in data loss for the entire RAID set. RAID 1, also known as a mirror, stores identical copies of data on two drives for reliability. However, speeds are limited to the capabilities of a single drive, and twice as much storage is required for data. RAID 5 stripes data across disks in the set and uses parity to reconstruct a drive if it fails in the set. RAID 5 requires at least three drives. It has good read performance, but the computation of parity can reduce write speeds in what is known as the write penalty. RAID 6 is like RAID 5, except it stores double parity and can recover from a loss of two drives. It has a higher write penalty.

Nested RAID consists of RAID 10 (RAID 1+0), which takes a number of mirror sets and stripes data over them. It has high read and write performance but requires double the drives for storage. RAID 50 is another type of nested RAID where two RAID 5 sets are striped together. It can offer higher performance than the RAID 5 arrays could individually while still retaining the parity on the underlying RAID 5.

Table 2-5 compares the different RAID configurations to give you a better understanding of the advantages and requirements of each RAID level.

Two different options are available when implementing RAID: software RAID and hardware RAID using a RAID controller. Software RAID is implemented on a server by using software that groups multiple logical disks into a single virtual disk. Most modern operating systems have built-in software that allows for the configuration of a software-based RAID array. Hardware RAID controllers are physical cards that are added to a server to offload the overhead of RAID and do not require any CPU resources; they allow an administrator to boot straight to the RAID controller to configure the RAID levels. Hardware RAID is the most common form of RAID due to its tighter integration with the device and better error handling.

Level	Description	Minimum Number of Disks	Fault Tolerance	Storage Efficiency
RAID 0	Blocks are striped. No mirror or parity.	2	None	100%
RAID 1	Blocks are mirrored. No striping or parity.	2	1 drive	50% or $n/2$
RAID 5	Blocks are striped. Distributed parity.	3	1 drive	Number of drives: 1
RAID 6	Blocks are striped with double distributed parity.	4	2 drives	Number of drives: 2
RAID 10	Blocks are mirrored and striped.	4	1 drive per span up to a maximum of 2	50%
RAID 50	Blocks are striped across two or more RAID 5 sets.	6	1 drive per RAID 5 set	Number of drives: number of RAID 5 sets

Table 2-5 RAID Level Benefits and Requirements

 EXAM TIP You need to understand the difference between each RAID level and when each particular level is appropriate to use.

Write Once, Read Many (WORM)

WORM is storage that cannot be overwritten. WORM typically refers to optical storage such as CD-R or DVD-R devices that allow you to write data once to them and then never again. The data can be read from the CD or DVD as many times as you want, but you cannot overwrite the data with new data as you can with a hard drive. Writing data to a CD-R or DVD-R is called burning. WORM can also refer to storage that has write protection enabled. Floppy disks used to have a tab that could be moved to determine whether the data could be overwritten. Software disks would often lack this tab so that consumers could not switch them to writable mode. Similarly, some SD cards have firmware that prevents modifying or deleting data stored on them. This can be used for delivering content that you do not want the end user to change.

Another important reason for WORM is to protect the data on the storage from malicious alteration. Configuration data can be stored on WORM so that a malicious program cannot modify it. The disadvantage is that new storage must be created with the new configuration parameters, and then that storage is placed in the device. For example, a computer could be used as a firewall with a live version of Linux running off a DVD. The firewall configuration would be burned to the DVD and cannot be changed.

To change this configuration, a new DVD would need to be burned with the updated configuration, and then the firewall would be shut down, the DVDs swapped, and the firewall started again to take on the new configuration.

 CAUTION CD-R and DVD-R are both WORM, but CD-RW and DVD-RW are not. The RW in CD-RW and DVD-RW stands for rewritable, meaning that data can be changed after the initial burn.

Tiering

In the previous section, we discussed the different types of disks and the benefits of each. Now that you understand the benefits of each disk, you know that storing data on the appropriate disk type can increase performance and decrease the cost of storing that data. Having flexibility in how and where to store an application's data is key to the success of cloud computing.

Tiered storage permits an organization to adjust where its data is being stored based on the performance, availability, cost, and recovery requirements of an application. For example, data that is stored for restoration in the event of loss or corruption would be stored on the local drive so that it can be recovered quickly, whereas data that is stored for regulatory purposes would be archived to a lower-cost disk, like tape storage.

Tiered storage can refer to an infrastructure that has a simple two-tier architecture, consisting of SCSI disks and a tape drive, or to a more complex scenario of three or four tiers. Tiered storage helps organizations plan their information life cycle management, reduce costs, and increase efficiency. Tiered storage requirements can also be determined by functional differences, for example, the need for replication and high-speed restoration.

With tiered storage, data can be moved from fast, expensive disks to slower, less expensive disks. Hierarchical storage management (HSM), which is discussed in the next section, allows for automatically moving data between four different tiers of storage. For example, data that is frequently used and stored on highly available, expensive disks can be automatically migrated to less expensive tape storage when it is no longer required on a day-to-day basis. One of the advantages of HSM is that the total amount of data that is stored can be higher than the capacity of the disk storage system currently in place.

Performance Levels of Each Tier

HSM operates transparently to users of a system. It organizes data into tiers based on the performance capabilities of the devices, with tier 1 containing the devices with the highest performance and each tier after that containing storage with lower performance than the tier before it. HSM tiers can include a wide variety of local and remote media such as solid state, spinning disk, tape, and cloud storage.

HSM places data on tiers based on the level of access required and the performance and reliability needed for that particular data or based on file size and available capacity. Organizations can save time and money by implementing a tiered storage infrastructure. Each tier has its own set of benefits and usage scenarios based on a variety of factors. HSM can automatically move data between tiers based on factors such as how often data is used, but organizations can also specify policies to further control where HSM stores data and what priority it gives to migration operations between tiers.

The first step in customizing HSM policies is to understand the data that will reside on HSM storage. Organizations and IT departments need to define each type of data and determine how to classify it so that it can configure HSM policies appropriately. Ask yourself some of the following questions:

- Is the data critical to the day-to-day operation of the organization?
- Is there an archiving requirement for the data after so many months or years?
- Is there a legal or regulatory requirement to store the data for a period of time?

Once the data has been classified, the organization can create HSM policies so that data is moved to the appropriate tier and given the correct priority.

Tier 1

Tier 1 data is defined as mission-critical, recently accessed, or secure files and should be stored on expensive and highly available enterprise flash drives such as RAID with parity. Typically tier 1 drives would be SLC or MLC flash drives for the best speed. Tier 1 storage systems have better performance, capacity, reliability, and manageability.

Tier 2

Tier 2 data is data that runs major business applications, for example, e-mail and Enterprise Resource Planning (ERP) software. Tier 2 is a balance between cost and performance. Tier 2 data does not require subsecond response time but still needs to be reasonably fast. This typically consists of lower-speed flash drives, such as MLC or TLC flash, or a hybrid of flash media and spinning disks, such as spinning disks with flash as cache.

Tier 3

Tier 3 data includes financial data that needs to be kept for tax purposes but is not accessed on a daily basis and so does not need to be stored on the expensive tier 1 or tier 2 storage systems. Tier 3 storage typically uses QLC flash or spinning disks.

Tier 4

Tier 4 data is data that is used for compliance requirements for keeping e-mails or data for long periods of time. Tier 4 data can be a large amount of data but does not need to be instantly accessible. Tier 4 storage is long-term storage such as offline drives, tape, or other media.

Policies

A multitiered storage system provides an automated way to move data between more expensive and less expensive storage systems. Using a multitiered storage system, an organization can implement policies that define what data fits each tier and then manage how data migrates between the tiers. For example, when financial data is more than a year old, the policy could be to move that data to a tier 4 storage solution, much like the HSM defined earlier.

Tiered storage provides IT departments with the best solution for managing the organization's data while also saving time and money. Tiered storage helps IT departments meet their service level agreements at the lowest possible cost and the highest possible efficiency.

 TIP Tiered storage allows companies to achieve greater return on investment (ROI) on disk investments by utilizing a combination of storage types and capitalizing on their strengths.

File System Types

After choosing a disk type and configuration, an organization needs to be able to store data on those disks. The file system is responsible for storing, retrieving, and updating a set of files on a disk. It is the software that accepts the commands from the operating system to read and write data to the disk. It is responsible for how the files are named and stored on the disk.

The file system is also responsible for managing access to the file's metadata ("the data about the data") and the data itself and for overseeing the relationships to other files and file attributes. It also manages how much available space the disk has. The file system is responsible for the reliability of the data on the disk and for organizing that data in an efficient manner. It organizes the files and directories and tracks which areas of the drive belong to a particular file and which areas are not currently being utilized.

This section explains the different file system types. Each file system has its own set of benefits and scenarios under which its use is appropriate.

Unix File System

The Unix file system (UFS) is the primary file system for Unix and Unix-based operating systems. UFS uses a hierarchical file system structure where the highest level of the directory is called the root and all other directories span from that root.

 NOTE The Unix root directory is depicted with the / character. This character is pronounced "slash."

Figure 2-1
Unix file system
(UFS) structure

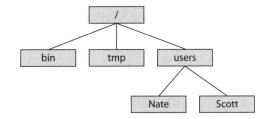

Under the root directory, files are organized into subdirectories and can have any name the user wishes to assign. All files on a Unix system are related to one another in a parent/child relationship, and they all share a common parental link to the top of the hierarchy.

Figure 2-1 shows an example of the UFS structure. The root directory has three subdirectories called bin, tmp, and users. The users directory has two subdirectories of its own called Nate and Scott.

Extended File System

The extended file system (EXT) is the first file system created specifically for Linux. The metadata and file structure are based on the Unix file system. EXT is the default file system for most Linux distributions. EXT is currently on version 4, or EXT4, which was introduced in 2008 and supports a larger file and file system size. EXT4 is backward compatible with EXT3 and EXT2, which allows for mounting an EXT3 and EXT2 partition as an EXT4 partition.

File Allocation Table File System

The file allocation table (FAT) file system is a legacy file system that provides good performance but does not deliver the same reliability and scalability as some of the newer file systems. The FAT file system is still supported by most operating systems for backward-compatibility reasons. Still, it has mostly been replaced by NTFS (more on this in a moment) as the preferred file system for the Microsoft operating system. If a user has a drive running a FAT32 file system partition, however, they can connect it to a computer running Windows 7 and retrieve the data from that drive because all modern versions of Windows, including 7, 8, and 10, still support the FAT32 file system.

FAT originally came in two flavors, FAT16 and FAT32, the difference being that FAT16 supported fewer files in the root directory, smaller maximum file sizes, and smaller maximum partition size. Modern iterations of FAT use exFAT, which further increases the maximum file and partition sizes.

The FAT file system is used by a variety of removable media, including solid-state memory cards, flash memory cards, and portable devices. The FAT file system does not support the advanced features of NTFS like encryption, VSS, and compression.

New Technology File System

The New Technology File System (NTFS) is a proprietary file system developed by Microsoft to support the Windows operating systems. It first became available with Windows NT 3.1 and has been used on all of Microsoft's operating systems since then. NTFS was Microsoft's replacement for the FAT file system. NTFS has many advantages over FAT, including improved performance and reliability, larger partition sizes, and enhanced security. NTFS uses the NT LAN Manager (NTLM) protocol for authentication.

Starting with version 1.2, NTFS added support for file compression, which is ideal for files that are written on an infrequent basis. However, compression can lead to slower performance when accessing the compressed files; therefore, it is not recommended for .exe or .dll files or for network shares that contain roaming profiles due to the extra processing required to load roaming profiles.

NTFS version 3.0 added support for volume shadow copy service (VSS), which keeps a historical version of files and folders on an NTFS volume. Shadow copies allow you to restore a file to a previous state without the need for backup software. The VSS creates a copy of the old file as it is writing the new file, so the user has access to the previous version of that file. It is best practice to create a shadow copy volume on a separate disk to store the files.

Exercise 2-1: Formatting a Disk with the NTFS Partition in Windows

In this exercise, we will create an NTFS partition on a USB drive. Please note that this operation removes all data from the drive, so please move any data you want to save off the drive before creating the partition.

1. Insert the USB drive into your Windows computer.
2. The contents of the drive will appear. Please note the drive letter of the device if it already has a partition. If you have never used the drive before, it will likely prompt you to format the drive to begin working with it.
3. Right-click on the Start button and select Disk Management.
4. Scroll down to the disk that you want to create the partition on.

5. For this example, I inserted a 4GB flash drive that has a FAT32 volume on it called ELEMENTARY.

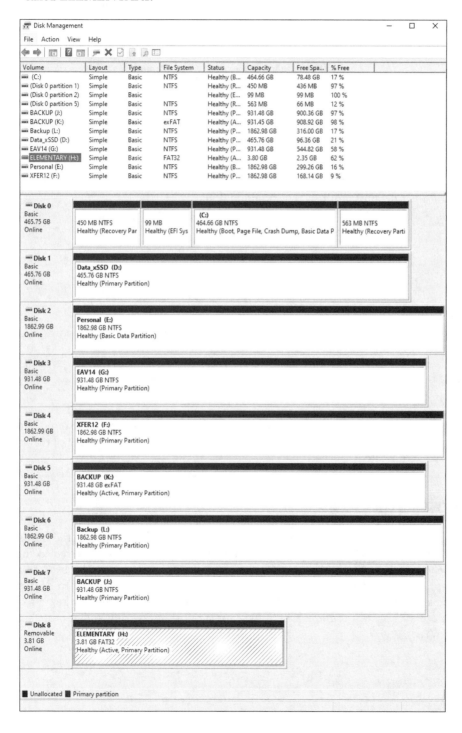

6. Right-click on the partition you want to remove and then select Format.

7. You will be warned that all data will be lost. Select Yes.

8. A format box will appear. Give the partition a name and then select the NTFS file system from the second drop-down box. We will leave the rest of the fields at their defaults. Your screen should look like this:

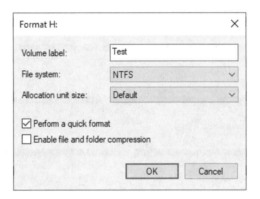

9. Click OK. The disk will now be formatted using the NTFS file system. The quick format option usually only takes a few seconds, and then the operation will complete.

Encrypting File System

The Encrypting File System (EFS) provides an encryption method for any file or folder on an NTFS partition and is transparent to the user. EFS encrypts a file by using a file encryption key (FEK), which is associated with a public key that is tied to the user who encrypted the file. The encrypted data is stored in an alternative location from the encrypted file. To decrypt the file, EFS uses the private key of the user to decrypt the public key that is stored in the file header. If the user loses access to their key, a recovery agent can still access the files. NTFS does not support encrypting and compressing the same file.

Disk quotas allow an administrator to set disk space thresholds for users. This gives an administrator the ability to track the amount of disk space each user is consuming and limit how much disk space each user has access to. The administrator can set a warning threshold and a deny threshold and deny access to the user once they reach the deny threshold.

Resilient File System

The Resilient File System (ReFS) is a proprietary file system developed by Microsoft to support the Windows operating systems. It first became available with Windows Server 2012 and is supported on Windows Server 2012 and later server operating systems, as well as Windows 8.1 and later versions.

Rather than fully replacing NTFS, ReFS offers support for some new features by sacrificing some other features. ReFS's new features include the following:

- **Integrity checking and data scrubbing**   These features are a form of file integrity monitoring (FIM) that checks data for errors and automatically replaces corrupt data with known good data. It also computes checksums for file data and metadata.

- **Storage virtualization**   Remote mounts such as SAN storage can be formatted as local storage. Additionally, mirroring can be applied to disks in a logical volume to provide redundancy and striping to provide better performance.

- **Tiering**   Multiple storage types with different capacity and performance ratings can be combined together to form tiered storage.

- **Disk pooling**   A single ReFS logical volume can consist of multiple storage types. Unlike RAID, the drives do not need to be the same size and type to be in a pool.

- **Support for longer file paths than NTFS**   NTFS was limited to 256-character filenames and file paths, but ReFS can support filenames and file paths up to 32,768 characters in length each. This allows for more descriptive names and deeper folder hierarchies.

- **Block cloning**   A feature that decreases the time required for virtual machine copies and snapshots.

- **Sparse valid data length (VDL)**   A feature that reduces the time required for the creation of thick-provisioned virtual hard disks.

These new features, however, come at a cost. Microsoft has sacrificed some NTFS features that system administrators have become quite comfortable with, including support for EFS, compression, data deduplication, and disk quotas.

 EXAM TIP   Take careful note of which features are needed when selecting the correct file system. The newest file system may not necessarily be the right answer. For example, if encryption was required, NTFS would be a better choice than ReFS.

Virtual Machine File System

The Virtual Machine File System (VMFS) is VMware's cluster file system. It is used with VMware ESXi server and vSphere and was created to store virtual machine disk images, including virtual machine snapshots. It allows for multiple servers to read and write to the file system simultaneously while keeping individual virtual machine files locked. VMFS volumes can be logically increased by spanning multiple VMFS volumes together.

Z File System

The Z File System (ZFS) is a combined file system and logical volume manager designed by Sun Microsystems. The ZFS file system protects against data corruption and support for high storage capacities. ZFS also provides volume management, snapshots, and continuous integrity checking with automatic repair.

ZFS was created with data integrity as its primary focus. It is designed to protect the user's data against corruption. ZFS is currently the only 128-bit file system. It uses a pooled storage method, which allows space to be used only as it is needed for data storage.

Table 2-6 compares a few of the different file system types, lists their maximum file and volume sizes, and describes some of the benefits of each system.

 NOTE Some of the data sizes shown here or referenced elsewhere in this text use rather large numbers. For reference, 1000 bytes (B) = 1 kilobyte (KB), 1000KB = 1 megabyte (MB), 1000MB = 1 gigabyte (GB), 1000GB = 1 terabyte (TB), 1000TB = 1 petabyte (PB), 1000PB = 1 exabyte (EB), 1000EB = 1 zettabyte (ZB), 1000ZB = 1 yottabyte (YB).

 EXAM TIP You should know the maximum volume size of each file system type for the exam. For example, if the requirement is a 3TB partition for a virtual machine drive, you would not be able to use the FAT file system; you would need to use NTFS.

File System	Maximum File Size	Maximum Volume Size	Encryption	Resizable Volumes
Unix File System (UFS)	32PB	1YB	No	Offline but cannot be shrunk
New Technology File System (NTFS)	16TB	256TB	Yes	Online
File Allocation Table (FAT32)	4GB	2TB	No	Offline
Virtual Machine File System (VMFS)*	2TB	64TB	No	Offline but cannot be shrunk*
Z File System (ZFS)	18EB	295ZB	Yes	Online but cannot be shrunk

*The newest version of VMFS allows dynamic resizing but must be supported by the OS for it to be utilized without a reboot or additional sizing tools.

Table 2-6 File System Characteristics

Chapter Review

Understanding how different storage technologies affect the cloud is a key part of the CompTIA Cloud+ exam. This chapter discussed the various physical types of disk drives and how those drives are connected to systems and each other. It also covered the concept of tiered storage with HSM. We closed the chapter by giving an overview of the different file system types and the role proper selection of these systems plays in achieving scalability and reliability. It is critical to have a thorough understanding of all these issues as you prepare for the exam.

Questions

The following questions will help you gauge your understanding of the material in this chapter. Read all the answers carefully because there might be more than one correct answer. Choose the best response(s) for each question.

1. Which type of storage device has no moving parts?

   A. HDD

   B. SSD

   C. Tape

   D. SCSI

2. Which type of storage device would be used primarily for off-site storage and archiving?

   A. HDD

   B. SSD

   C. Tape

   D. SCSI

3. You have been given a drive space requirement of 2TB for a production file server. Which type of disk would you recommend for this project if cost is a primary concern?

   A. SSD

   B. Tape

   C. HDD

   D. VLAN

4. Which of the following storage device interface types is the most difficult to configure?

   A. IDE

   B. SAS

   C. SATA

   D. SCSI

5. If price is not a factor, which type of storage device interface would you recommend for connecting to a corporate SAN?

   A. IDE

   B. SCSI

   C. SATA

   D. FC

6. You need to archive some log files, and you want to make sure that they can never be changed once they have been copied to the storage. Which type of storage would be best for the task?

   A. SSD

   B. Rotational media

   C. WORM

   D. USB drive

7. What RAID level would be used for a database file that requires minimum write requests to the database, a large amount of read requests to the database, and fault tolerance for the database?

   A. RAID 10

   B. RAID 1

   C. RAID 5

   D. RAID 0

8. Which of the following statements can be considered a benefit of using RAID for storage solutions?

   A. It is more expensive than other storage solutions that do not include RAID.

   B. It provides degraded performance, scalability, and reliability.

   C. It provides superior performance, improved resiliency, and lower costs.

   D. It is complex to set up and maintain.

9. Which data tier would you recommend for a mission-critical database that needs to be highly available all the time?

   A. Tier 1

   B. Tier 2

   C. Tier 3

   D. Tier 4

10. Which term describes the ability of an organization to store data based on performance, cost, and availability?

    A. RAID

    B. Tiered storage

    C. SSD

    D. Tape drive

11. Which data tier would you recommend for data that is financial in nature, is not accessed on a daily basis, and is archived for tax purposes?

    A. Tier 1

    B. Tier 2

    C. Tier 3

    D. Tier 4

12. Which of the following file systems is used primarily for Unix-based operating systems?

    A. NTFS

    B. FAT

    C. VMFS

    D. UFS

13. Which of the following file systems was designed to protect against data corruption and is a 128-bit file system?

    A. NTFS

    B. UFS

    C. ZFS

    D. FAT

14. Which file system was designed to replace the FAT file system?

    A. NTFS

    B. ZFS

    C. EXT

    D. UFS

15. Which of the following file systems was the first to be designed specifically for Linux?

    A. FAT

    B. NTFS

    C. UFS

    D. EXT

Answers

1. **B.** A solid-state drive is a drive that has no moving parts.

2. **C.** Tape storage is good for off-site storage and archiving because it is less expensive than other storage types.

3. **C.** You should recommend using an HDD because of the large size requirement. An HDD would be considerably cheaper than an SSD. Also, since it is a file share, the faster boot time provided by an SSD is not a factor.

4. **D.** SCSI is relatively difficult to configure, as the drives must be configured with a device ID and the bus has to be terminated.

5. **D.** Fibre Channel delivers the fastest connectivity method, with speeds of up to 128 Gbps, but it is more expensive than the other interface types. If price is not a factor, FC should be the recommendation for connecting to a SAN.

6. **C.** WORM is the correct answer because it cannot be overwritten once the data has been stored on it.

7. **C.** RAID 5 is best suited for a database or system drive that has a lot of read requests and very few write requests.

8. **C.** Using RAID can provide all these benefits over conventional hard disk storage devices.

9. **A.** Tier 1 data is defined as data that is mission-critical, highly available, and secure data.

10. **B.** Tiered storage refers to the process of moving data between storage devices based on performance, cost, and availability.

11. **C.** Tier 3 storage would be for financial data that you want to keep for tax purposes and is not needed on a day-to-day basis.

12. **D.** UFS is the primary file system in a Unix-based computer.

13. **C.** ZFS was developed by Sun Microsystems and is focused on protecting the user's data against corruption. It is currently the only 128-bit file system.

14. **A.** NTFS was designed by Microsoft as a replacement for FAT.

15. **D.** EXT was the first file system designed specifically for Linux.

Storage Networking

In this chapter, you will learn about
- Storage types and technologies
- Storage access protocols
- Storage provisioning
- Storage protection

Storage is the foundation of a successful infrastructure. The traditional method of storing data is changing with the emergence of cloud storage. Storage is the instrument that is used to record and play back the bits and bytes that the compute resources process to provide their functions for delivering cloud services and applications.

Cloud storage is being leveraged for a wide range of enterprise functions, from end-user computing to enterprise storage and backup. Furthermore, cloud storage is a platform for explosive growth in organizational data because it is highly available and almost infinitely scalable. Understanding the advantages and disadvantages of storage types and technologies is a key concept for IT and cloud professionals because it will be your responsibility to help the organization understand the risks and the benefits of moving to cloud storage.

Storage Types and Technologies

Just as there are many different environments in which computers are used, there are many types of storage to accommodate each of those environment's needs. Some storage types are designed to meet primary organizational storage concerns such as cost, performance, reliability, and data security. Figure 3-1 displays a graphical comparison of the three storage types—DAS, SAN, and NAS—which we explore in more detail directly. A fourth type is object storage.

In addition to the four storage types, this section covers two storage technologies. These technologies—deduplication and compression—improve storage efficiencies by removing unnecessarily redundant data.

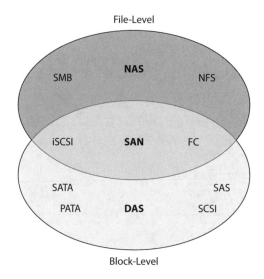

Figure 3-1
Three major
storage types:
DAS, SAN,
and NAS

File-Level

SMB   **NAS**   NFS

iSCSI   **SAN**   FC

SATA   SAS

PATA   **DAS**   SCSI

Block-Level

Direct Attached Storage

Direct attached storage (DAS) is one or more drives connected to a machine as additional block-level storage. Some storage protocols used to access these storage devices are eSATA, USB, FC, SCSI, and SAS. USB and eSATA are most frequently utilized by desktops and laptops to connect to DAS, while companies typically connect DAS to servers using FC, SCSI, or SAS.

DAS is typically the least expensive storage option available for online storage (as opposed to offline storage such as a tape). As its name suggests, this type of storage is directly attached to the host computer that utilizes it and does not have to traverse a network to be accessed by that host. Direct attached storage is made available only to that local computer and cannot be used as shared storage. Shared storage in this context refers to storage that is made available to multiple machines at the block level. A machine can share out storage that was provided to it by DAS.

EXAM TIP   Direct attached storage (DAS) cannot provide shared storage to multiple hosts.

Storage Area Network

A storage area network (SAN) is a high-performance option employed by many data centers as a high-end storage solution with data security capabilities and a very high price tag to go along with it. A SAN is a storage device that resides on its own network and provides block-level access to computers that are attached to it.

The disks that are part of a SAN are combined into RAID groups for redundancy and higher performance. These RAID groups are then carved into subdivisions called logical unit numbers (LUNs) that provide block-level access to specified computers. LUNs can be interacted with just like a logical drive.

SANs are capable of highly complex configurations, allowing administrators to divide storage resources and access permissions granularly and with very high-performance capabilities. However, SAN maintenance and operations can be complicated, often requiring specialized skill sets and knowledge of proprietary technology (because each SAN solution is vendor-specific). The role of SANs is mission-critical, so there is little, if any, margin for error. Many storage administrators go to specialized training for their specific SAN solution, and they spend much of their time in the workplace, giving SANs constant monitoring and attention. These administrative burdens add to the cost of deploying a SAN solution.

SANs can also provide shared storage or access to the same data at the same time by multiple computers. This is critical for enabling high availability (HA) in data center environments that employ virtualization solutions that require access to the same virtual machine files from multiple hosts. Shared storage allows hosts to perform migrations of virtual machines without any downtime, as discussed in more detail in Chapter 5.

Computers require a special adapter to communicate with a SAN, much like they need a network interface card (NIC) to access their data networks. The network that a SAN utilizes is referred to as a fabric and can be composed of fiber-optic cables, Ethernet adapters, or specialized SCSI cables.

A host bus adapter (HBA) is the most common device used to connect a machine to a SAN. An HBA is usually a PCI add-on card that can be inserted into a free slot in a host and then connected either to the SAN disk array directly or, as is more often the case, to a SAN switch. Virtual machines can use a virtual HBA, which emulates a physical HBA and allocates portions of the physical HBA's bandwidth to virtual machines. Storage data is transferred from the disk array over the SAN to the host via the HBA, which prepares it for processing by the host's compute resources.

Two other adapters may be used to connect to a storage network. A converged network adapter (CNA) can be used in lieu of an HBA. CNAs are computer expansion cards that can be used as an HBA or a NIC. NetApp has a proprietary adapter called universal target adapter (UTA). UTA has ports for one or more Ethernet or Fibre Channel transceivers and can support Ethernet transceivers up to 10 Gbps and Fibre Channel transceivers at native Fibre Channel speeds.

In addition to SANs, organizations can use a virtual SAN (VSAN), which can consolidate separate physical SAN fabrics into a single larger fabric, allowing for easier management while maintaining security. A VSAN allows identical Fibre Channel IDs to be used at the same time within different VSANs. VSANs allow for user-specified IDs that are used to identify the VSAN. VSANs can also span data centers using VXLANs, discussed more in Chapter 4, or with encapsulation over routable network protocols.

HBAs usually can significantly increase performance by offloading the processing required for the host to consume the storage data without utilizing its processor cycles. This means that an HBA enables greater efficiency for its host by allowing its processor to focus on running the functions of its operating system (OS) and applications instead of on storage I/O.

Network Attached Storage

Network attached storage (NAS) offers an alternative to storage area networks for providing network-based shared storage options. NAS devices utilize TCP/IP networks for sending and receiving storage traffic in addition to data traffic. NAS provides file-level data storage that can be connected to and accessed from a TCP/IP network. Because NAS utilizes TCP/IP networks instead of a separate SAN fabric, many IT organizations can utilize existing infrastructure components to support both their data and storage networks. This use of common infrastructure can greatly cut costs while providing similar shared storage capabilities. Expenses are reduced for a couple of reasons:

- Data networking infrastructure costs significantly less than storage networking infrastructure.
- Shared configurations between data and storage networking infrastructure enable administrators to support both without additional training or specialized skill sets.

One way to differentiate NAS from a SAN is that NAS appears to the client operating system as a file server, whereas a SAN appears to the client operating system as a disk (typically a LUN) that is visible in disk management utilities. This allows NAS to use Universal Naming Convention addressable storage. Network attached storage leverages protocols such as file-sharing protocols like SMB/CIFS and NFS.

NAS also differs from SAN in that NAS natively allows for concurrent access to shares. However, there are some functions that can only be performed on block storage such as booting from SAN storage or loading applications from SAN storage. SAN connections usually offer much higher throughput to storage for high-performance needs.

 EXAM TIP A storage area network (SAN) provides much better performance than network attached storage (NAS).

NAS uses file-sharing protocols to make shares available to users across a network. NAS systems typically support both the Common Internet File System (CIFS)/Server Message Block (SMB) for Windows and the Network File System (NFS) for Linux. Many NAS devices also support uploading and downloading files to it via FTP or SSL/TLS-enabled FTP, such as FTPS and SFTP.

Network File System

NFS is a protocol used for network file sharing. It is mainly used on Unix and Linux systems and suffers from very little overhead because of its use of the stateless User Datagram Protocol (UDP) transport protocol. Many NAS operating systems run some version of Linux because there are no licensing costs with it, and NAS vendors can customize the software for their needs. This allows those NAS systems to support NFS out of the box.

Since NFS is a stateless protocol, it does not retain some information on the communication session that CIFS would, such as the current working directory or open files. Each set of requests and responses in NFS is independent. This requires that each response contain all the necessary information to process the request rather than relying on the server to track current network operations. The advantage of such a stateless protocol is that the

NAS does not need to retain this information, nor does it need to clean up such information when transactions complete.

Common Internet File System

CIFS is an open network file-sharing protocol compatible with Microsoft's SMB protocol. The initial version of SMB/CIFS suffered from lower network performance due to increased broadcast traffic and weak authentication. However, these issues have been resolved in modern versions of CIFS, which use TCP instead of NetBIOS as the transport protocol and better methods of securing the authentication process.

CIFS is a stateful protocol. The advantage of this is that CIFS can restore connections to shares and files after an interruption, and it can enforce locks on files to prevent users from making changes to files that are currently being modified by another client. However, it has slower network performance than NFS.

Object Storage

Traditional file systems tend to become more complicated as they scale. Take, for example, a system that organizes pictures. Thousands of users may be requesting pictures from the site simultaneously, and those pictures must be retrieved quickly. The system must track each picture's location and, to retrieve them quickly, maintain multiple file systems and possibly multiple NAS devices for that data. As the user base grows further from the data center, latency issues can come up, so the data must be replicated to multiple sites and users directed to the location that has the lowest latency. The application now tracks the NAS where each picture resides, the location on that NAS, and which country the user is directed to. It must keep the data synchronized between each site by tracking changes to the pictures. This application complexity makes applications harder to maintain and results in more processing to perform normal application functions. The solution is object storage.

Object-based storage is a concept that was developed to help provide a solution to the ever-growing data storage needs that have accompanied the IT explosion since the late twentieth century. It acts as a counterpart to block-based storage, allowing large sets of files to be grouped and to move the processing power for those files away from server and workstation CPUs and closer to the storage itself. This processing power is utilized to assist in the implementation of such features as fine-grained security policies, space management, and data abstraction.

Object storage is a storage system that abstracts the location and replication of data, allowing the application to become more simplified and efficient. Traditional file systems store data in blocks that are assembled into files, but the system does not know what each file actually contains. That is the responsibility of the application. However, object storage knows where the data is located and what the data is by utilizing metadata as a file organization method. For example, an application residing on top of object storage can ask the storage for the picture of John Doe at Middleton Beach on August 4, 2020, and the object storage will retrieve it for the application. In an object storage system, data is stored within buckets that have a unique identifier within the namespace that is used to access the data.

With object storage, capacity planning is done at the infrastructure level rather than the application level. This means that the application owners and the application itself do not need to monitor its capacity utilization, and it allows the system to be much more scalable.

Object storage is scalable because it uses a scale-out method that creates new object stores to handle additional data. These stores can exist at multiple sites, and redundancy can be defined per data type or per node so that the object store replicates data accordingly, both to ensure that it is available if a single copy is lost and to avoid latency issues with satisfying application requests.

However, you should be aware that object storage requires changes to the application. You can move between different storage and database models, usually by changing a few parameters in the application, but moving to object storage requires the application to interface with the storage differently, so developers will need to modify their code accordingly. The change from traditional storage to object storage, therefore, is a dev change rather than an ops change.

 EXAM TIP　Object storage provides better scalability than hierarchical file systems.

Object ID

Since object-based storage is not addressed in blocks, like most of the storage used in standard workstation and server environments, the object storage device (OSD) interface requires some way to find out how to address the data it contains. Objects are the individual pieces of data that are stored in a cloud storage system. Objects are composed of parts: an object data component, which is usually a file designated to be stored in the cloud storage system, and an object metadata component, which is a collection of values that describe object qualities. The OSD interface uses object IDs as a unique identifier for the combination of data and metadata that comprises each of the objects.

Metadata

Object storage is heavily reliant upon metadata. Along with all the files that each object contains is an associated set of metadata that can describe the data component of a specific object to classify it or define relationships with other objects. This metadata is an extensible set of attributes that are either implemented by the OSD directly for some of the more common attributes or interpreted by higher-level storage systems that the OSD uses for its persistent storage.

Data and metadata are stored separately, and metadata can be expanded as needed in order to track additional details about the data. Object storage indexes metadata so that the data can be located using multiple criteria. Object stores are also application-agnostic, supporting multiple applications for the same data set. In this way, the same data can be utilized for multiple applications, avoiding redundancy in storage and complexity in managing the data.

Policy Tags

Policy tags are similar to metadata in that they are attributes associated with the object. The difference is that policy tags contain information that is associated with a particular security mechanism. Policy tags are often used with data classification labels such as public, sensitive, financial, personal, or health and can be interpreted by data loss prevention (DLP) systems to restrict their use to acceptable actions only. See more on DLP in Chapter 11 and data classification in Chapter 12.

Tenant

Tenants are accounts that allow access to object storage. Tenant accounts are usually created for a specific type of object storage. For example, you would have one tenant account for Google Cloud storage buckets and another for OpenStack Swift containers. Tenants are given their own unique namespace, so their bucket names are associated with their tenant ID.

Bucket

Buckets are storage locations for data in an object storage system. Bucket names must be unique within their namespace. Buckets can store any type of data. Object storage has lower storage overhead because of the way data is organized. Applications requesting data from a bucket do not need to know where the data is stored. They simply need to reference the bucket ID. Object storage further avoids overhead by using a flat organization method rather than a hierarchical storage system. Hierarchical storage systems can only expand so far until suffering from latency in traversing directory trees, but object storage does not utilize such directory trees.

 EXAM TIP Buckets are a basic storage mechanism in the cloud and foundational for other cloud processes.

Exercise 3-1: Creating Object Storage

In this exercise, we will create a bucket on Amazon S3 to store data.

1. Log in to your AWS account. You will be presented with the management console, which will show the available services you can choose from.

2. Go to the storage section and select S3.

3. You will be presented with a screen showing your existing buckets, as shown here.

4. Click Create Bucket, and then you will be presented with the following screen.

Amazon S3 > Create bucket

Create bucket

Buckets are containers for data stored in S3. Learn more ⧉

General configuration

Bucket name

cloud-example

Bucket name must be unique and must not contain spaces or uppercase letters. **See rules for bucket naming** ⧉

Region

US East (Ohio) us-east-2 ▼

Copy settings from existing bucket - *optional*
Only the bucket settings in the following configuration are copied.

Choose bucket

Bucket settings for Block Public Access

Public access is granted to buckets and objects through access control lists (ACLs), bucket policies, access point policies, or all. In order to ensure that public access to this bucket and its objects is blocked, turn on Block all public access. These settings apply only to this bucket and its access points. AWS recommends that you turn on Block all public access, but before applying any of these settings, ensure that your applications will work correctly without public access. If you require some level of public access to this bucket or objects within, you can customize the individual settings below to suit your specific storage use cases. **Learn more** ⧉

☑ **Block *all* public access**
Turning this setting on is the same as turning on all four settings below. Each of the following settings are independent of one another.

☑ Block public access to buckets and objects granted through *new* access control lists (ACLs)
S3 will block public access permissions applied to newly added buckets or objects, and prevent the creation of new public access ACLs for existing buckets and objects. This setting doesn't change any existing permissions that allow public access to S3 resources using ACLs.

☑ Block public access to buckets and objects granted through *any* access control lists (ACLs)
S3 will ignore all ACLs that grant public access to buckets and objects.

☑ Block public access to buckets and objects granted through *new* public bucket or access point policies
S3 will block new bucket and access point policies that grant public access to buckets and objects. This setting doesn't change any existing policies that allow public access to S3 resources.

☑ Block public and cross-account access to buckets and objects through *any* public bucket or access point policies
S3 will ignore public and cross-account access for buckets or access points with policies that grant public access to buckets and objects.

Bucket Versioning

Versioning is a means of keeping multiple variants of an object in the same bucket. You can use versioning to preserve, retrieve, and restore every version of every object stored in your Amazon S3 bucket. With versioning, you can easily recover from both unintended user actions and application failures. Learn more ⧉

Bucket Versioning
◉ Disable
○ Enable

5. Give the bucket a name. In this example, I called it cloud-example. This bucket will just be for us, so keep the Block All Public Access checkbox checked.

6. The next option is related to versioning. In some cases, you may enable versioning if you think you will need to retrieve previous versions of bucket contents. For example, if you were storing temporary screenshots in the bucket but one was overwritten before the desired process performed an action on it, you could go back and retrieve that version if this function were enabled. For this example, we will leave it disabled.

7. The next option is tags, as shown next. Tags are metadata associated with the bucket. Let's add a few tags for this example. Click Add Tag and then give it a key and a value. For this example, I created the first tag with a key of 1 and a value of sample and then repeated the process to create a tag with a key of 2 and a value of cloud+.

8. The last option is for encrypting the contents of the bucket. Do not enable encryption for this bucket. It is disabled by default, so you will not need to change anything.

9. Lastly, click Create Bucket. Your new bucket will appear in the buckets screen.

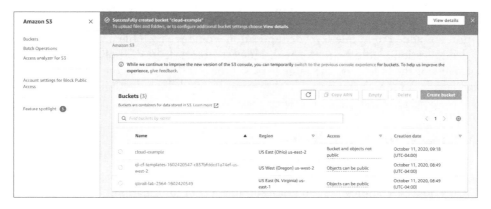

Congratulations! You have just created an Amazon S3 bucket that can be used to store data.

Replicas

Many systems use object storage for replicas. Replicas are essentially copies of one large set of data. They are used to both increase availability and reduce the amount of risk associated with keeping a large amount of data in one location. Replicas are good candidates for object-based storage for several reasons:

- They are large data sets that require a copying mechanism that can run efficiently without requiring expensive error correction or filtering.

- They do not affect user performance SLAs if they are faced with I/O latency, which is often associated with object-based storage and can introduce a performance bottleneck.

Object storage from more than one cloud service provider (CSP) can be used to house replicas of the data so that it will still be available if one CSP is unavailable.

Deduplication Technologies

Deduplication technologies remove redundant data from a storage system to free up space. There are two forms of deduplication technologies: file-level deduplication and block-level deduplication.

File-level deduplication hashes each file on a file system and stores those hashes in a table. Suppose it encounters a file with a hash that is already in its table. In that case, it places a pointer to the existing file on the file system rather than storing the data twice. Imagine a document that is e-mailed to 100 people at an office. Because each person who stores that file would be storing a duplicate on the system, file-level deduplication would save only one copy of that data, with pointers for all the remaining ones. File-level deduplication can remove many duplicates, but it is not nearly as efficient as block-level deduplication.

Block-level deduplication hashes each block that makes up a file. This allows deduplication to occur on the pieces of a file, so deduplication does not require that a file be 100 percent identical to perform deduplication. For example, a user may store nine versions of a spreadsheet. Each version is slightly different from the others as new information was added to it. File-level deduplication would see each file hash as different, so no deduplication would be performed. However, block-level deduplication would see that many of the blocks are the same between these different versions and would store only one block for each duplicate. In this example, block-level deduplication could save up to 90 percent of the space otherwise used.

Compression Technologies

Compression is another method used to reduce space. Some forms of compression result in a loss of information. These forms are known as lossy compression. Other types, known as lossless compression, do not result in a loss of information.

In most cases, you will want to employ lossless compression. Still, there are cases, such as in the transmission of audio or video data, where lossy compression may be utilized to transmit data at a lower quality level when sufficient bandwidth for higher quality is not available or when it would interrupt more time-sensitive data streams. Lossy compression might also be used on a website to increase the speed at which site objects load.

Lossless compression uses mathematical formulas to identify areas of files that can be represented in a more efficient format. For example, an image might have a large section that is all one color. Rather than storing the same color value repeatedly for that section, the lossless compression algorithm would note the range of pixels that contain that color and the color code.

Data BLOB

A binary large object, or BLOB, is a collected set of binary data that is stored as a single, discrete entity in a database management system. By gathering this binary data into larger collections, database administrators are able to better copy large amounts of data between databases with significantly reduced risk of error correction or data filtering.

Storage Access Protocols

Now that you have learned about the various storage technologies that are available, we can turn our attention to the access protocols and applications that utilize these technologies to transmit, shape, and prioritize storage information between hosts and their storage devices.

Fibre Channel

Fibre Channel is a technology for transmitting data between computers at data rates of up to 128 Gbps. IT organizations have made Fibre Channel the technology of choice for interconnecting storage controllers and drives when building high-performance infrastructure requirements. The Fibre Channel architecture is composed of many interconnected individual units, which are called nodes. Each of these nodes has multiple ports. These ports connect the nodes in a storage unit architecture using one of three different interconnection topologies: point-to-point, arbitrated loop, and switched fabric. Fibre Channel also can transmit over long distances. When deployed using optical fiber, it can transmit between devices up to about six miles apart. While Fibre Channel is the transmission medium, it still utilizes SCSI riding on top of it for its commands.

 CAUTION   Each component in the storage system, from the SAN or NAS, to switches and connected devices such as servers, must support the storage access protocol.

Fibre Channel Protocol

The SCSI commands that ride atop the Fibre Channel transport are sent via the Fibre Channel Protocol (FCP). This protocol takes advantage of hardware that can utilize protocol offload engines (POEs) to increase performance. This assists the host by offloading processing cycles from the CPU, thereby improving system performance.

FCP uses addresses to reference nodes, ports, and other entities on the SAN. Each HBA has a unique worldwide name (WWN), which is an 8-byte identifier similar to an Ethernet MAC address on a network card. There are two types of WWNs on an HBA: a worldwide node name (WWNN), which can be shared by either some or all of the ports of a device, and a worldwide port name (WWPN), which is unique to each port. Fibre switches also have WWPNs for each switch port. Other devices can be issued a worldwide unique identifier (WWUI) so that they can communicate on the SAN.

The frames in Fibre Channel Protocol consist of three components: an encapsulating header called the start-of-frame (SOF) marker, the data frame itself, and the end-of-frame (EOF) marker. This encapsulated structure enables the Fibre Channel frames to be transported across other protocols, such as TCP, if desired.

Fibre Channel over Ethernet

Fibre Channel over Ethernet (FCoE) enables the transport of Fibre Channel traffic over Ethernet networks by encapsulating Fibre Channel frames. Fibre Channel over Ethernet can utilize Ethernet technologies up to 10 Gigabit Ethernet (10GigE) networks and higher speeds as they are developed while still preserving the Fibre Channel protocol.

Ethernet

Ethernet is an established standard for connecting computers to a local area network (LAN). Ethernet is a relatively inexpensive and reasonably fast LAN technology, with speeds ranging from 10 Mbps to 10 Gbps. Because it enables high-speed data transmission and is relatively inexpensive, Ethernet has become ubiquitous in IT organizations and the Internet. Ethernet technology operates at the OSI model's physical and data link layers (layers 1 and 2). Although it is capable of high speeds, it is limited by both the length and the type of cables over which it travels. The Ethernet standard divides its data traffic into groupings called frames. These frames are utilized by storage protocols to deliver their data from one point to another, such as from a NAS device to a server.

TCP/IP

Internet Protocol (IP) is a protocol that operates at the network layer of the OSI model (layer 3) and provides unique IP addresses and traffic-routing capabilities. Computers utilizing the IPv4 protocol are addressed using dotted decimal notation with four octets divided by dots. As the name suggests, IP is the protocol that enables the Internet. Like Ethernet networks, it is ubiquitous in IT departments. TCP/IP provides a proven, relatively inexpensive, and well-understood technology on which to build storage networks.

Transmission Control Protocol (TCP) is a protocol that provides reliable transport of network data through error checking. TCP uses ports that are associated with certain services and other ports that can be dynamically allocated to running processes and services. TCP is most often combined with IP, and it operates at the transport layer of the OSI model (layer 4).

Internet Fibre Channel Protocol

Internet Fibre Channel Protocol (iFCP) enables the transport of Fibre Channel traffic over IP networks by translating Fibre Channel addresses to IP addresses and Fibre Channel frames to IP packets. iFCP reduces overhead compared with other protocols that transport Fibre Channel over IP because it does not use tunneling to connect Fibre Channel devices.

Internet Small Computer System Interface

Internet Small Computer System Interface (iSCSI) is a protocol that utilizes serialized IP packets to transmit SCSI commands across IP networks and enables servers to access remote disks as if they were locally attached. iSCSI "initiator" software running on the requesting entity converts disk block-level I/O into SCSI commands that are then serialized into IP packets that traverse any IP network to their targets. At the destination storage device, the iSCSI packets are interpreted by the storage device array into the appropriate commands for the disks it contains. Figure 3-2 shows an example of how multiple servers can leverage iSCSI to connect to shared storage over an IP network.

iSCSI is limited by the transmission speeds of the Ethernet network it travels over; when administrators design iSCSI networks, they should pay close attention to the design to isolate the storage network traffic from the data network traffic. Although its performance is not as high as that of a Fibre Channel SAN, iSCSI can be an inexpensive entry into shared storage for IT departments or a training ground using repurposed equipment for administrators who want to get hands-on experience with storage networking. iSCSI can be implemented on a NAS device or on a general-purpose machine. iSCSI's flexibility and ease of implementation make it a popular and versatile storage protocol.

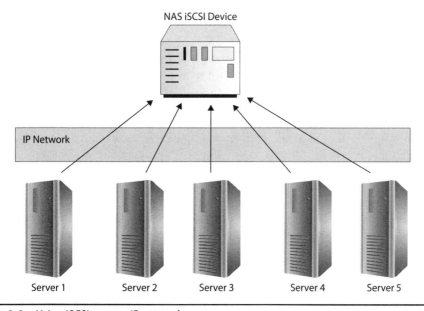

Figure 3-2   Using iSCSI over an IP network

The iSCSI address given to an initiator is known as an iSCSI qualified name (IQN). Initiators reside on clients in an iSCSI network, and initiators connect to targets such as storage resources over the iSCSI network. An IQN uses the following naming convention: iqn.yyyy-mm.naming-authority:unique name.

Nonvolatile Memory Express Over Fabrics

Nonvolatile Memory Express Over Fabrics (NVMe-oF) is a storage network protocol that can run over high-speed storage protocols such as InfiniBand or FC and Ethernet. It is specially designed to work well with flash SSD storage over the network. NVMe-oF is based on the NVMe storage protocol used for high-speed SSD storage over the PCI-e bus. NVMe-oF can directly share data in memory and without using CPU cycles, so the CPU is not overburdened. This sharing occurs using the Remote Direct Memory Access (RDMA) protocol.

 EXAM TIP　NVMe-oF is an ideal storage networking protocol to use when working primarily with flash-based storage.

Storage Provisioning

Now that you understand the technologies, protocols, and applications for moving storage data around networks, we will explore how that data is presented to computers. Data can be made available to computers in many ways, with varying degrees of availability and security.

Performance

Everyone has an expectation of performance for a system, and these expectations tend to increase as computing power increases. Storage systems also cannot stay the same. They must keep up with the application and end-user demand. To do this, storage systems need a way to measure performance in a meaningful way. The most common method is input/output operations per second (IOPS). Storage must be provisioned to provide the required IOPS to the systems that utilize that storage. This requires having an understanding of the read and write throughput that different RAID sets and drive types can produce, as well as the performance enhancements that can be gained from storage tiering.

IOPS

IOPS is a measurement of how much data is provided over a period of time. It is usually expressed in bits per second (bps), bytes per second (Bps), megabytes per second (MBps), or gigabytes per second (GBps). Drives are typically rated regarding the IOPS they can support. Hard disk drives may provide values for average latency and average seek time, or those values can be computed from their spindle speed. The formula for IOPS is as follows:

IOPS = 1 / (average latency + average seek time)

For example, if a SATA drive running has an average latency of 3.2 ms and an average seek time of 4.7 ms, we would take 1 / (.0032 + .0047), which gives us 126.58, or 127 IOPS rounded to the nearest integer.

When drives are combined together into a RAID array, the RAID technology will utilize a combination of these IOPS. For example, a RAID 5 array of six drives, each with 127 IOPS, would provide 635 IOPS. The array would have five drives for striping and one for parity, so that is 5 times 127 to produce the 635 read IOPS. There is a difference between read and write IOPS, as will be explained next.

Read/Write Throughput

The RAID types chosen, as well as the caching settings, can determine how many IOPS will be produced by a logical volume. Read and write throughput are also expressed as either sequential reads or writes or random reads or writes. Sequential reads are when data is read from contiguous portions of the disk, while random reads are when data is read from various locations on the disk. It is more efficient to pull data from adjacent parts of the disk because then drives do not need to spend as much time seeking the data.

Caching can also have an impact on read and write IOPS. Caching settings can be optimized for reading or writing or a little of both. A cache can hold files that were recently requested in case they are asked for again, improving read speeds when those files are fetched from cache instead of disk. Similarly, files can be placed in cache and then written to the disk when it is most efficient to store the data so that the application does not need to wait for the data to actually be written to the disk if it exists in the write cache. The four read/write throughput values are thus as follows:

- **Random read IOPS**   The average number of read I/O operations that can be performed per second when the data is scattered around the disk

- **Random write IOPS**   The average number of write I/O operations that can be performed per second when the data must be written to scattered portions of the disk

- **Sequential read IOPS**   The average number of read I/O operations that can be performed per second when the data is located in contiguous sections of the disk

- **Sequential write IOPS**   The average number of write I/O operations that can be performed per second when the data must be written to contiguous sections of the disk

Storage Tiers

Storage tiering is an essential part of storage optimization. Not all data will be requested all the time, so it does not have to be treated the same way. Tiering combines multiple classes of storage into a single storage pool to intelligently satisfy storage demands. Higher-speed storage is used for the most often needed data or that the system predicts will be required. In contrast, data that is requested less often is moved down to lower tiers.

For example, the highest-speed storage tier could be made up of 5TB of high-speed SLC SSD storage, while the second tier would be 10TB of lower-speed MLC SSD storage, the third tier 20TB of TLC SSD storage, and the fourth tier 50TB of 15k SAS storage drives that spin at 15,000 rotations per minute. This is shown in Figure 3-3.

Figure 3-3
Tiered storage
pool

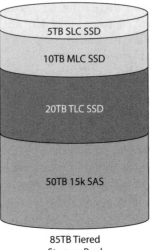

5TB SLC SSD

10TB MLC SSD

20TB TLC SSD

50TB 15k SAS

85TB Tiered
Storage Pool

The application would see an 85TB pool of storage available to it that is made up of these different types of storage. The storage system intelligently moves the data around on the different tiers so that data is most often served from the highest speed storage.

TIP Solid-state storage was discussed in Chapter 2. There are three common types of SSDs in use today. Single-level cell (SLC) is the fastest but can store only one binary value in a cell, making it the SSD storage type with the smallest capacity. Looking at it another way, SLC has the highest cost per gigabyte. Multilevel cell (MLC) can store two binary values in each cell but is slower than SLC. Triple-level cell (TLC) is the slowest of the three but has the highest capacity because it can store three binary values per cell. This makes TLC the lowest cost per gigabyte in SSDs.

Logical Unit Numbers

LUNs, introduced earlier, have been around for a long time and were originally used to identify SCSI devices as part of a DAS solution for higher-end servers. Devices along the SCSI bus were assigned a number from 0 to 7, and SCSI 2 utilized 0 to 15, which designated the unique address for the computer to find that device. In storage networking, LUNs operate as unique identifiers, but now they are much more likely to represent a virtual hard disk from a block of allocated storage within a NAS device or a SAN. Devices that request I/O process are called initiators, and the devices that perform the operations requested by the initiators are called targets. Each target can hold up to eight other devices, and each of those devices is assigned a LUN.

Network Shares

Network shares are storage resources available across the network that appear as if they are resources on the local machine. Traditionally, network shares are implemented using the SMB protocol when using Microsoft products and the NFS protocol in Linux. It is also possible to share the same folder over NFS and SMB so that both Linux and Windows clients can access it. Access to these shares happens within an addressable file system as opposed to using block storage.

Zoning and LUN Masking

SANs are designed with high availability and performance in mind. In order to provide the flexibility that system administrators demand for designing solutions that utilize those capabilities, servers need to be able to mount and access any drive on the SAN. This flexible access can create several problems, including disk resource contention and data corruption. To mitigate these problems, storage devices can be isolated and protected on a SAN by utilizing zoning and LUN masking, which allow for dedicating storage on the SAN to individual servers.

Zoning controls access from one node to another. It enables the isolation of a single server to a group of storage devices or a single storage device or associates a set of multiple servers with one or more storage devices. Zoning is implemented at the hardware level on Fibre Channel switches and is configured with what is referred to as "hard zoning" on a port basis or "soft zoning" using a WWN. In Figure 3-4, the Fibre Channel switch is controlling access to the red server and the blue server to connect to storage controllers 0–3. It grants access to the blue server to the LUNs on controllers 0 and 3, while the red server is granted access to all LUNs on all storage controllers.

LUN masking is executed at the storage controller level instead of at the switch level. By providing LUN-level access control at the storage controller, the controller itself enforces access policies to the devices. LUN masking provides more detailed security

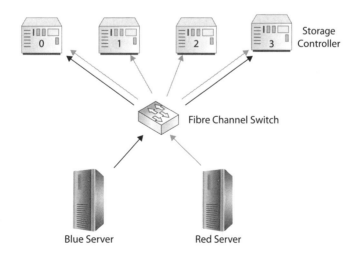

Figure 3-4
Zoning using a
Fibre Channel
switch

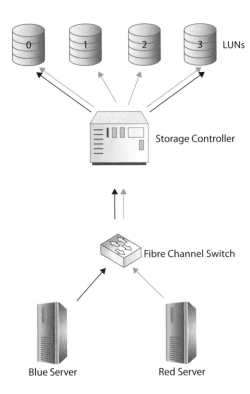

Figure 3-5
LUN masking using the storage controller

0 1 2 3 LUNs

Storage Controller

Fibre Channel Switch

Blue Server   Red Server

than zoning because LUNs allow for sharing storage at the port level. In Figure 3-5, LUN masking is demonstrated as the blue server is granted access from the storage controller to LUNs 0 and 3. In contrast, the red server is granted access to all LUNs.

Multipathing

Whereas zoning and LUN masking are configuration options that limit access to storage resources, multipathing is a way of making data more available or fault-tolerant to the computers that need to access it. Multipathing does exactly what its name suggests, in that it creates multiple paths for the machine to reach the storage resources it is attempting to contact.

The redundant paths in multipathing are created by a combination of hardware and software resources. The hardware resources are multiple NICs, CNAs, or HBAs deployed to a single computer. These multiple adapters provide options for the software to run in multipath mode, which allows it to use either of the adapters to send traffic over in case one of them were to fail.

Setting up multipathing on the computer, however, is not enough to ensure high availability of the applications designed to run on it. The entire network infrastructure that the data traffic travels upon should be redundant so that a failure of any one component will not interrupt the storage data traffic. This means that to implement an effective multipath solution, redundant cabling, switches, routers, and ports on the storage devices must be considered. Enabling this kind of availability may be necessary to meet the business requirements of the applications being hosted, but such a configuration can be very expensive.

Provisioning Model

Cloud storage administrators will need to determine how to best provision storage depending on how the storage will be utilized and the available storage at hand. Some storage needs increase slowly, while others increase quickly. There are two options for provisioning storage. One is known as thick provisioning and the other as thin provisioning. Each has its own set of benefits and drawbacks.

Virtual hard disks on hypervisors can be provisioned as a thick disk or a thin disk. The size of a thick disk (termed a fixed disk in Microsoft Hyper-V) is specified and allocated during the virtual disk creation. A thin disk (termed a dynamically expanding disk in Microsoft Hyper-V) starts out small. It adds space as required by the virtual machine.

While the different virtualization manufacturers use different terms to define their virtual disks, the concepts are similar. Whether you are using Hyper-V, VMware ESXi, or XenServer, you still need to decide which type of disk to use for which application. If you are concerned about disk space, then using a thin disk or dynamically expanding disk would be the best option. If size is not a concern, then you could use a fixed-size or thick disk.

Now that you understand the basics, let's look at thin and thick provisioning in more detail.

Thick Provisioning

Thick provisioning allocates the entire size of the logical drive upon creation. This means that the virtual disk is guaranteed and consumes whatever amount of disk space is specified during the creation of that virtual disk. Thin provisioning ensures that space will not be claimed by some other application and keeps the provisioned storage in contiguous space on the disk. Thick provisioning provides better performance because the drive size is not being built as the application requires more drive space. Thick provisioning is best suited for volumes that are expected to multiply in size or for those that require dedicated performance.

For example, a thick-provisioned volume of 400GB will consume 400GB of space on the storage system. This storage will be allocated entirely upon creation and made available to the system.

Thin Provisioning

Thin provisioning allocates only the space that is actually consumed by the volume. For example, a 400GB thin-provisioned volume will start off consuming zero bytes of storage. As data is written to the volume, the storage system will continue to allocate more storage out of a storage pool until the volume reaches its max of 400GB. This results in storage space allocated from wherever there is free space on the drive at the time it is needed, so not all space assigned to the thin-provisioned volume will be in contiguous space.

Thin provisioning does not have the same performance level as a thick disk and needs to be monitored closely to prevent running out of available disk space, since storage space is, by definition, overcommitted.

Here are a few things to keep in mind when comparing thin and thick provisioning to determine which one works best in the organization's environment. First, determine the system's performance requirements, including the amount of data reads and writes you expect the system to perform. Each time new data is added to a thin-provisioned disk, space from the pool on which the thin-provisioned disk resides is allocated to the disk. This can lead to extensive fragmentation of the thin-provisioned volume if it grows frequently and rapidly. For example, an application that writes a lot of data to the drive, such as a database application, would not perform as well on a thin-provisioned disk. On the other hand, if space is a concern and a web server is not writing to the virtual disk that often, a thin-provisioned disk would be more appropriate.

Second, determine how often the data will grow. Excessive growth of thin-provisioned disks can fill up the storage pool on which the disks reside if overprovisioning, discussed next, is not properly controlled.

 EXAM TIP The application workload is often the determining factor in choosing the type of virtual disk.

Storage Overprovisioning

Storage overprovisioning, also known as overcommitting or oversubscribing, is the process of creating multiple volumes using thin provisioning with a total maximum size that exceeds available storage. Overprovisioning is often done because some volumes will never utilize the maximum available, yet applications perform better when there is some space available for temporary data. However, storage administrators must monitor overprovisioned storage closely to ensure that it does not fill up and cause downtime to the systems that are provisioned from it.

Each of the major virtualization manufacturers has different terms when describing virtual disk configurations. For example, if you are using Microsoft Hyper-V, you would have the option of making a dynamically expanding virtual disk, a fixed virtual disk, or a differencing virtual disk. If you are creating a fixed-size disk, you would specify the size of the disk when it is created. If you are creating a dynamically expanding virtual disk, the disk starts at a small size and adds storage as needed.

Encryption Requirements

Disk encryption is quickly becoming a minimum requirement for regulated industries and for protecting the data of cloud consumers. Some customers require their volumes to be encrypted so that other tenants or the CSP cannot read their data.

Disk encryption takes an entire drive and converts it to a form that is unreadable unless the decryption key is provided. Disk encryption can be performed on local drives or removable media. The process is mostly transparent to the user. Users provide their decryption key when they log onto the computer. From that point on, files are encrypted when stored and decrypted when opened without additional interaction. Disk encryption is also referred to as full disk encryption (FDE). Some software-based disk encryption methods encrypt all contents but not the Master Boot Record (MBR), the section of the disk that describes the logical partitions and contains the boot loader information that the computer uses to start up the operating system when the computer is powered up.

In contrast, hardware disk encryption methods are able to encrypt the contents and the MBR. Hardware disk encryption does not store the decryption key in memory. Drives encrypted with hardware disk encryption are also known as self-encrypting drives (SEDs). Many disk encryption systems support trusted platform module (TPM), a processor on the system mainboard that can authenticate the encrypted hard drive to the system to prevent an encrypted drive from being used on another system.

Some disk encryption limitations include the fact that once a user is logged in, the entire disk is available to them. Malicious code or a lost password could allow access to the entire drive even if it is encrypted. Additionally, some disk encryption systems have been circumvented, including those with TPM, by stealing the keys stored in memory shortly after a cold shutdown (not a controlled shutdown) before memory data fully degrades. Still, disk encryption is an effective way to prevent unauthorized access to data stored on local drives and removable disks.

Tokenization

Tokenization can separate sensitive data from storage media that does not have a high enough security classification. Tokens are identifiers that can be mapped to sensitive data. The token is just an identifier and cannot create the data without interfacing with the tokenization system.

A system storing data on a cloud might store public data and then store a token in place of each sensitive data element, such as personally identifiable information (PII) or protected health information (PHI). The PII or PHI would be stored in the tokenization system, and the public cloud storage would retain the token for that information. When retrieving the data, the system would retrieve public data directly from the cloud storage but would need to query the tokenization system to pull out the sensitive data, a process known as detokenization.

Storage Protection

Storage protection guards against data loss, corruption, or unavailability. Users expect their data to be present when they request it, and data loss is almost always considered unacceptable to cloud consumers. Storage protection must guard against equipment failures, site failures, user error, data corruption, malware, and other threats that could damage data integrity or availability.

High Availability

HA refers to systems that are available almost 100 percent of the time. These systems are usually measured in terms of how many "nines" of availability they offer. For example, a system that offers 99.999 percent availability is offering 5 nines of availability. This equates to 5.39 minutes of downtime in a year.

HA systems achieve such availability through redundancy of components and sites. HA systems might also replicate data to multiple sites, colocations (COLOs), or cloud services to protect against site failure or unavailability. Storage replication is discussed after failover zones.

Failover Zones

HA systems utilize clusters to divide operations across several systems. Some systems are active-active, where all systems can service application requests. In contrast, others are active-passive, where one or more systems service requests while one or more remain in a standby state until needed. Active-active systems must retain enough available resources to handle the remaining load if a system in the cluster becomes unavailable. This is known as N + 1 redundancy because they can suffer the loss of one system.

HA systems require regular maintenance, and yet in the 5 nines example, 5.39 minutes of downtime per year is hardly enough time to perform regular maintenance. HA systems accomplish this by performing upgrades to redundant equipment independently. In a cluster, the services on one cluster node are failed over to other cluster nodes. That node is upgraded and then services are failed back to it. Maintenance or upgrades continue on the other nodes in the same fashion until all are upgraded. Throughout the process, the user does not experience any downtime. Clustering typically requires some level of shared storage where each node can access the same storage. When shared storage is not available, systems will use some form of replication to keep each system consistent with other systems. For example, when failover is performed across sites, replication is usually required to keep both sites consistent.

Storage Replication

Storage replication transfers data between two systems so that any changes to the data are made on each node in the replica set. A replica set consists of the systems that will all retain the same data. Multiple sites are used to protect data when a single site is unavailable and to ensure low-latency availability by serving data from sources that are close to the end user or application.

Regional Replication

Regional replication uses replication to store data at a primary site and a secondary site. In regional replication, the secondary site is located in a different region from the primary site so that conditions affecting the primary site are less likely to affect the secondary site. Site unavailability is usually the result of a natural disaster such as a flood, fire, tornado, or hurricane. Many data centers are placed in regions where natural disasters are less common. For example, you will not find many data centers on the Florida coast. Not only is this land very expensive but it is also prone to floods and hurricanes, which could render the site unavailable. Redundant sites are usually chosen in different regions that are far enough apart from one another that a single disaster will not affect both sites.

When implementing sites in different regions, also consider the power distribution method. Choose regions that are serviced by different power suppliers so that a disruption in the power network will not affect both sites.

Data will need to be replicated to these regions. This requires a connection between the data centers. This can be a leased line such as an MPLS network or dark fibre (fiber-optic cable that is not owned and operated by a telco), or it could be a VPN tunnel over a high-speed Internet link. Ensure that the link between the sites will support the amount of replication data plus some overhead and room for spikes. Some Internet service providers will allow for a consistent data rate with bursting for the occasional large transfer. Bursting allows the connection to exceed the normal data transmission limits, but it comes at a charge from the ISP.

Multiregional Replication

Multiregional replication replicates data between many different sites in multiple regions. Replication schemes should be planned so that the entire replica set can be consistent with a minimum of effort and yet still provide redundancy in case of site link failures.

 CAUTION Regulations may require that data remain within specific countries or regions. Be sure to check to see if data can be replicated outside the country before enabling such features. Cloud systems can be restricted to a specific country or region, if necessary.

Each site typically has one or more replication partners, but they will not replicate with all sites. This saves on bandwidth costs and latency, since longer-distance links will incur additional latency and cost more to operate. A hub-and-spoke model is often utilized, with redundant links added in to protect against site link failure. This is depicted in Figure 3-6.

Synchronous and Asynchronous Replication

Two forms of replication can be used to keep replica sets consistent: synchronous and asynchronous. Synchronous replication writes data to the local store and then immediately replicates it to the replica set or sets. The application is not informed that the data has been written until all replica sets have acknowledged receipt and storage of the data. Asynchronous replication stores the data locally and then reports to the application that the data has been stored. It then sends the data to replication partners at its next opportunity.

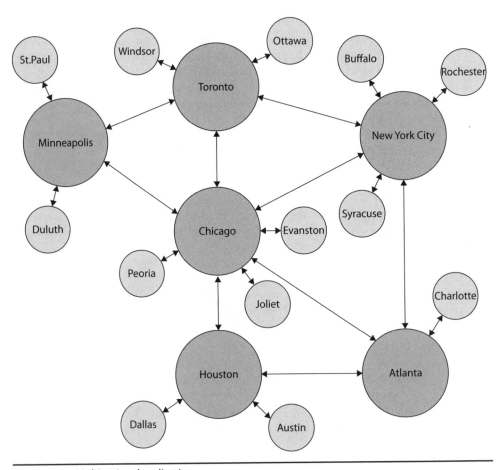

Figure 3-6 Multiregional replication

Synchronous replication requires high-speed, low-latency links between sites in order to ensure adequate application performance. Synchronous replication ensures greater consistency between replication partners than asynchronous replication.

Asynchronous replication can tolerate fluctuations that are more significant in latency and bandwidth, but not all members of the replica set may be fully consistent in a timely manner if latency is high or bandwidth is low. This can lead to issues with multiple concurrent access from different sites that are dependent upon transactions being current. Figure 3-7 shows the multiregional replication scheme with a combination of asynchronous and synchronous replication. The sites that are farther away are using asynchronous replication, while the closer sites with lower latency are using synchronous replication.

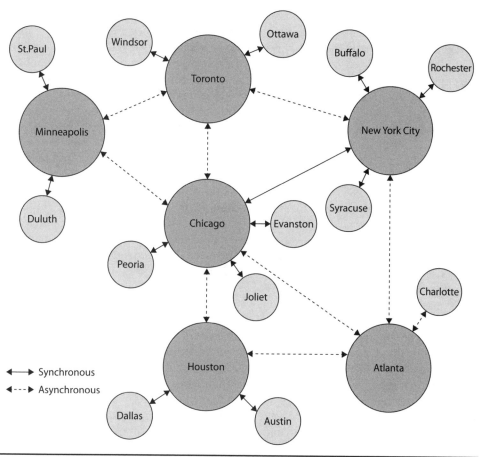

Figure 3-7 Synchronous and asynchronous multiregional replication

Chapter Review

Storage networking is an essential component of the CompTIA Cloud+ exam, and it is the foundation of a successful cloud infrastructure. This chapter discussed storage types and technologies, how to connect storage to devices, how to provision storage and make it available to devices, and how to protect storage availability through replication and redundancy.

The chapter began with a discussion on storage types and technologies. Understanding when to use the different storage types is important for optimizing a cloud deployment. These include direct attached storage (DAS), consisting of one or more drives that are connected to a single machine to provide block-level storage; SAN storage that is made available to one or more machines at the block level; NAS shares that make data available to multiple machines at the file level; and object storage, a system that stores and retrieves data based on its metadata, not on its location within a hierarchy.

In addition to the four storage types, this section covered two storage technologies. These technologies are deduplication and compression, and they are designed to improve storage efficiency. Deduplication improves storage efficiency by removing unnecessarily redundant data, while compression improves efficiency by decreasing the amount of storage required to store the data. Lossy compression results in some reduction in data quality, while lossless does not change the data when it is decompressed.

Storage needs to be connected to devices for it to be useful. The second section of this chapter provided details on storage connectivity. Connecting to storage can be simple, as in the case of DAS, since it is connected to only one machine. Still, NAS and a SAN can involve complex networking to ensure adequate storage performance and reliability needed in today's cloud environments. This includes how devices are connected to storage networks or how NAS is connected to traditional networks, as well as the benefits of each connection type. Connection types include Fibre Channel, FCP, FCoE, Ethernet, IP, iFCP, and iSCSI.

The next section covered how storage is provisioned. The first step is to create storage that meets the application's performance requirements. SAN storage may be created from many disks, and the portions that are carved out from those disks are called LUNs. Next, storage is made available only to the devices that need it through the use of zoning and LUN masking. There are some options when provisioning storage on how much space is allocated when new storage is created. Thin and thick provisioning offer two different methods to provision storage. Thick provisioning consumes all the allocated storage immediately, while thin provisioning allocates only what is actually used. Thin provisioning can help companies maximize capacity and utilization, but it can affect performance. Thick provisioning results in underutilized resources in order to offer more reliable performance.

The chapter closed with a discussion on some methods used to protect storage against data loss, corruption, or unavailability. The concept of high availability (HA) was presented first. HA systems are available almost 100 percent of the time. Next, storage replication was discussed. Storage replication transfers data between two systems so that any changes to the data are made on each node in the replica set. A replica set consists of the systems that will all retain the same data. Multiple sites are used to protect data when a single site is unavailable and to ensure low-latency availability by serving data from sources that are close to the end user or application.

Questions

The following questions will help you gauge your understanding of the material in this chapter. Read all the answers carefully because there might be more than one correct answer. Choose the best response(s) for each question.

1. Which type of storage system is directly attached to a computer and does not use a storage network between the computer and the storage system?

   A. NAS

   B. SAN

   C. DAS

   D. Network share

2. Which of the following characteristics describe a network attached storage (NAS) deployment?

   A. Requires expensive equipment to support

   B. Requires specialized skill sets for administrators to support

   C. Delivers the best performance of any networked storage technologies

   D. Provides great value by utilizing an existing network infrastructure

3. Which statement would identify the primary difference between NAS and DAS?

   A. NAS cannot be shared and accessed by multiple computers.

   B. DAS provides fault tolerance.

   C. DAS does not connect to networked storage devices.

   D. NAS uses an HBA and DAS does not.

4. Which storage type can take advantage of Universal Naming Convention addressable storage?

   A. SAN

   B. NAS

   C. DAS

   D. SATA

5. Which storage type provides block-level storage?

   A. SAN

   B. NAS

   C. DAS

   D. SATA

6. Which of the following connects a server and a SAN and improves performance?

   A. Network interface card

   B. Host bus adapter

   C. Ethernet

   D. SCSI

7. Which of the following protocols allows Fibre Channel to be transmitted over Ethernet?

   A. HBA

   B. FCoE

   C. iSCSI

   D. SAN

8. Which of the following is considered a SAN protocol?

   A. FCP

   B. IDE

   C. SSD

   D. DTE

9. Which of the following allows you to connect a server to storage devices with speeds of 128 Gbps?

   A. Ethernet

   B. iSCSI

   C. Fibre Channel

   D. SAS

10. Which of the following uses IP networks that enable servers to access remote disks as if they were locally attached?

   A. SAS

   B. SATA

   C. iSCSI

   D. Fibre Channel

11. Warren is a systems administrator working in a corporate data center, and he has been tasked with hiding storage resources from a server that does not need access to the storage device hosting the storage resources. What can Warren configure on the storage controller to accomplish this task?

   A. Zoning

   B. LUN masking

   C. Port masking

   D. VLANs

12. Which of the following would increase availability from a virtualization host to a storage device?

   A. Trunking

   B. Multipathing

   C. Link aggregation

   D. VLANs

13. A website administrator is storing a large amount of multimedia objects in binary format for the corporate website. What type of storage object is this considered to be?

   A. BLOB

   B. Replica

    C. Metadata

    D. Object ID

14. Which of the following allows you to provide security to the data contained in a storage array?

    A. Trunking

    B. LUN masking

    C. LUN provisioning

    D. Multipathing

15. Which provisioning model would you use if data is added quickly and often? The solution must ensure consistent performance.

    A. Thin provisioning

    B. Thick provisioning

    C. Overprovisioning

    D. Encryption

16. Which HA solution involves multiple servers that each service requests concurrently but can assume the load of one member if that member fails?

    A. Active-passive

    B. Active-active

    C. Passive-passive

    D. Passive-active

17. Which of the following are requirements for adequate application performance when using synchronous replication? (Choose two.)

    A. Object storage

    B. Low latency

    C. Multipathing

    D. High-speed links

Answers

    1. C. DAS is a storage system that directly attaches to a server or workstation without a storage network in between the devices.

    2. D. Network attached storage can utilize existing Ethernet infrastructures to deliver a low-cost solution with good performance.

    3. C. DAS is a storage system that directly attaches to a server or workstation without a storage network in between the devices.

    4. B. NAS appears to the client operating system as a file server, which allows it to use Universal Naming Convention addressable storage.

5. **A.** A SAN is a storage device that resides on its own network and provides block-level access to computers that are attached to it.

6. **B.** An HBA card connects a server to a storage device and improves performance by offloading the processing required for the host to consume the storage data without having to utilize its own processor cycles.

7. **B.** Fibre Channel over Ethernet (FCoE) enables the transport of Fibre Channel traffic over Ethernet networks by encapsulating Fibre Channel frames over Ethernet networks.

8. **A.** The Fibre Channel Protocol is a transport protocol that transports SCSI commands over a Fibre Channel network. These networks are used exclusively to transport data in FC frames between storage area networks and the HBAs attached to servers.

9. **C.** You can use Fibre Channel to connect servers to shared storage devices with speeds of up to 128 Gbps. Fibre Channel also comes in 64, 32, 16, 8, 4, and 2 Gbps versions.

10. **C.** iSCSI utilizes serialized IP packets to transmit SCSI commands across IP networks and enables servers to access remote disks as if they were locally attached.

11. **B.** LUN masking is executed at the storage controller level instead of at the switch level. By providing LUN-level access control at the storage controller, the controller itself enforces access policies to the devices, making it more secure. This is the reason that physical access to the same device storing the LUNs remains "untouchable" by the entity using it.

12. **B.** Multipathing creates multiple paths for the computer to reach the storage resources it is attempting to contact, improving fault tolerance and possibly speed.

13. **A.** A BLOB is a collection of binary data that is stored as a single entity. BLOBs are primarily used to store images, videos, and sound.

14. **B.** LUN masking enforces access policies to storage resources, and these storage policies make sure that the data on those devices is protected from unauthorized access.

15. **B.** Thick provisioning would consume all the allocated space upon creation of the LUN, but performance would be consistent for a LUN that expects data to be added quickly and often because storage would not need to be continually allocated to the LUN and the storage would not be fragmented.

16. **B.** Active-active solutions allow for all systems to service application requests.

17. **B, C.** Synchronous replication requires high-speed, low-latency links in between sites in order to ensure adequate application performance.

Network Infrastructure

In this chapter, you will learn about
- Network types
- Network optimization
- Routing and switching
- Network ports and protocols

Network configuration is an integral piece of cloud computing and is key to cloud computing performance. One of the factors an organization must consider is the impact of networking on cloud computing performance and the differences that exist between their current network infrastructure and what would be utilized in a cloud computing infrastructure.

This chapter introduces you to networking components that are used in cloud computing. After reading this chapter, you should understand the different types of networks and how to optimize an organization's network for cloud computing. You will also learn how network traffic is routed between the various cloud models and how to secure that traffic. And you will find out about the different network protocols used in cloud computing and when to use those protocols. It is important for you to have a thorough understanding of these topics for the exam.

Network Types

A network is defined as a group of interconnected computers and peripherals that are capable of sharing resources, including software, hardware, and files. The purpose of a network is to provide users with access to information that multiple people might need to perform their day-to-day job functions.

There are numerous advantages for an organization to construct a network. It allows users to share files so that multiple users can access them from a single location. An organization can share resources such as printers, fax machines, storage devices, and even scanners, thus reducing the total number of resources they have to purchase and maintain. A network also allows for applications to be shared by multiple users as long as the application is designed for this and the appropriate software licensing is in place.

There are three types of networks: intranet, Internet, and extranet. They all rely on the same Internet protocols but have different levels of access for users inside and outside the organization. This section describes each of these network types and when to use them.

Intranet

An intranet is a private network based on the Internet Protocol (IP) that is configured and controlled by a single organization and is only accessible to users that are internal to that particular organization. An intranet can host multiple private websites and is usually the focal point for internal communication and collaboration.

An intranet allows an organization to share information and websites within the organization and is protected from external access by a firewall or a network gateway. For example, an organization may want to share announcements, the employee handbook, confidential financial information, or organizational procedures with its employees but not with people outside the organization.

An intranet is similar to the Internet, except that an intranet is restricted to specific users. For example, a web page that is designed for the intranet may have a similar look and feel like any other website that is on the Internet, with the only difference being who is authorized to access the web page. Public web pages that are accessible over the Internet are typically available to everyone. In contrast, an intranet is owned and controlled by the organization and that organization decides who can access that web page. Figure 4-1 shows an example of an intranet configuration.

Internet

The Internet is a global system of interconnected computer networks that use the same Internet protocols (TCP/IP) as an intranet network uses. Unlike an intranet, which is controlled by and serves only one organization, the Internet is not controlled by a single organization and serves billions of users around the world. The Internet is a network of multiple networks relying on network devices and common protocols to transfer data from one intermediate destination (sometimes called a hop) to another until it reaches its final destination.

Figure 4-1
An intranet
network
configuration,
where access
is private

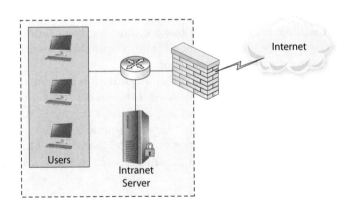

Figure 4-2
An extranet network configuration, where outside access is limited

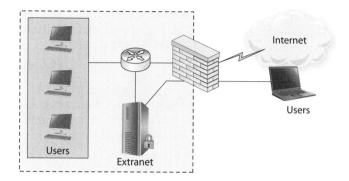

Aside from a few countries that impose restrictions on what people in their country can view, the Internet is largely unregulated, and anyone can post or read whatever they want on the Internet. The Internet Corporation for Assigned Names and Numbers (ICANN) is a nonprofit organization that was created to coordinate the Internet's system of unique identifiers, including domain names and IP addresses.

Extranet

An extranet is an extension of an Intranet, with the primary difference being that an extranet allows controlled access from outside the organization. An extranet permits access to vendors, partners, suppliers, or other limited third parties. Access is restricted using firewalls, access profiles, and privacy protocols. It allows an organization to share resources with other businesses securely. For example, an organization could use an extranet to sell its products and services online or to share information with business partners.

Both intranets and extranets are owned and supported by a single organization. The way to differentiate between an intranet and an extranet is by who has access to the private network and the geographical reach of that network. Figure 4-2 shows an example configuration of an extranet network.

EXAM TIP   The difference between an intranet and an extranet is that an intranet is limited to employees, while an extranet is available to a larger group of people, such as vendors, partners, or suppliers.

Network Optimization

Now that you know about the different types of networks, you need to understand the components of those networks and how they can be optimized. In this section, you will learn about the components that make up intranet and extranet networks and how to configure them so that they perform most efficiently.

Network optimization is the process of keeping a network operating at peak efficiency. To keep the network running at peak performance, an administrator must perform a variety of tasks, including updating the firmware and operating system on routers and switches, identifying and resolving data flow bottlenecks, and monitoring network utilization. By keeping the network optimized, a network administrator as well as CSPs can more accurately meet the terms of the organization's SLA.

Network Scope

The scope of a network defines its boundaries. The largest network on Earth was described earlier. It is the Internet, but millions of other networks span organizational or regional boundaries. The terms LAN, MAN, and WAN are used to differentiate these networks.

LAN

A local area network (LAN) is a network topology that spans a relatively small area like an office building. A LAN is a great way for people to share files, devices, pictures, and applications and is primarily Ethernet-based.

There are three different data rates of modern Ethernet networks:

- **Fast Ethernet**   Transfers data at a rate of 100 Mbps (megabits per second)
- **Gigabit Ethernet**   Transfers data at 1000 Mbps
- **10 Gigabit Ethernet**   Transfers data at 10,000 Mbps

MAN

A metropolitan area network (MAN) is similar to a LAN except that a MAN spans a city or a large campus. A MAN usually connects multiple LANs and is used to build networks with high data connection speeds for cities or college campuses. MANs are efficient and fast because they use high-speed data carriers such as fiber optics.

WAN

A wide area network (WAN) is a network that covers a large geographic area and can contain multiple LANs or MANs. WANs are not restricted by geographic areas. The Internet is an example of the largest WAN. Some corporations use leased lines to create a corporate WAN that spans a large geographic area containing locations in multiple states or even countries. Leased lines are private network circuits that are established through a contract with an ISP. These connect one or more sites together through the ISP's network.

Network Topologies

How the different nodes or devices in a network are connected and how they communicate is determined by the network's topology. The network topology is the blueprint of the connections of a computer network and can be either physical or logical. Physical topology refers to the design of the network's physical components: computers, switches, cable installation, etc. Logical topology can be thought of as a picture of how the data flows within a network.

Figure 4-3
Network
configuration
using a bus
topology

Backbone

The primary physical topologies to be considered are bus, star, ring, mesh, and tree. There are various pros and cons of the different network topologies. After evaluating the needs of the organization, you can then choose the most efficient topology for the intended purpose of the network.

Bus

In a bus topology, every node is connected to a central cable, referred to as the bus or backbone. In a bus topology, only one device is allowed to transmit at any given time. Since a bus topology uses a single cable, it is easy to set up and cost-effective.

The bus topology is not recommended for large networks because of the limitations to the number of nodes that can be configured on a single cable. Troubleshooting a bus topology is much more difficult than troubleshooting a star topology because in a bus topology, you have to determine where the cable was broken or removed. In a star topology, the central device offers a simple place to conduct troubleshooting. Figure 4-3 shows an example of a network configured to use a bus topology.

Star

In a star topology, each node is connected to a central hub or switch. The nodes communicate by sending data through the central hub. New nodes can easily be added or removed without affecting the rest of the nodes on the network.

The star topology offers improved performance over a bus topology. It is also more resilient because the failure of one node does not affect the rest of the network. Problematic nodes can be easily isolated by unplugging that particular node. If the problem disappears, it can be concluded that it is related to that node, making troubleshooting much more straightforward in a star topology.

The main drawback to the star topology is that if the central hub or switch fails, all the nodes connected to it are disconnected and unable to communicate with the other nodes. This is known as a single point of failure. Figure 4-4 shows an example of a network configured to use a star topology.

Ring

In a ring topology, each node is connected to another, forming a circle or a ring. Each packet is sent around the ring until it reaches its target destination. The ring topology is hardly used in today's enterprise environment because all network connectivity is lost if one of the links in the network path is broken. Figure 4-5 shows an example of a network configured to use a ring topology.

Figure 4-4
Network
configuration
using a star
topology

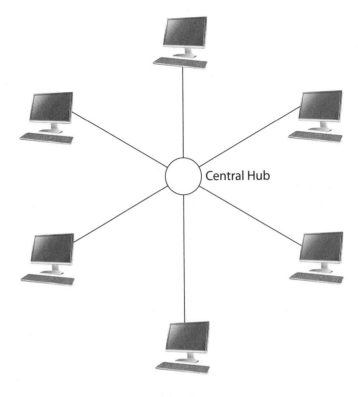

Figure 4-5
Network
configuration
using a ring
topology

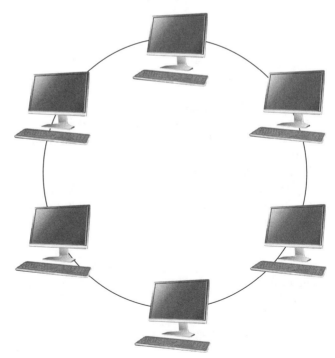

Figure 4-6
Network
configuration
using a mesh
topology

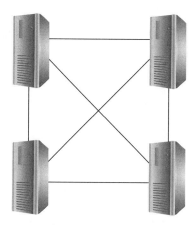

Mesh

In a true mesh topology, every node is interconnected to every other node in the network, allowing transmissions to be distributed even if one of the connections goes down. A mesh topology, however, is difficult to configure and expensive to implement and is not commonly used. It is the most fault-tolerant of the physical topologies, but it requires the most amount of cable. Since cabling is expensive, the cost must be weighed against the fault tolerance achieved. Figure 4-6 shows an example of a network configured to use a mesh topology.

Most real-world implementations of a mesh network are actually a partial mesh, where additional redundancy is added to the topology without incurring the expense of connecting everything to everything.

Tree

In a tree topology, multiple star networks are connected through a linear bus backbone. As you can see in Figure 4-7, if the backbone cable between the two star networks fails, those two networks would no longer be able to communicate; however, the computers on the same star network would still maintain communication with each other. The tree topology is the most commonly used configuration in today's enterprise environment.

Bandwidth and Latency

Now that you understand the different network topologies that you can configure, you need to know what other factors affect network performance. When moving to the cloud, network performance is crucial to the success of your deployment because the data is stored off-site. Two of the necessities for determining network performance are bandwidth and network latency. Bandwidth is the speed of the network. Network latency is the time delay encountered while data is being sent from one point to another on the network.

There are two types of latency: low latency and high latency. A low-latency network connection is a connection that experiences very small delays while sending and receiving traffic. A high-latency network has long delays while sending and receiving traffic. When it is excessive, network latency can create bottlenecks that prevent data

Figure 4-7
Network
configuration
using a tree
topology

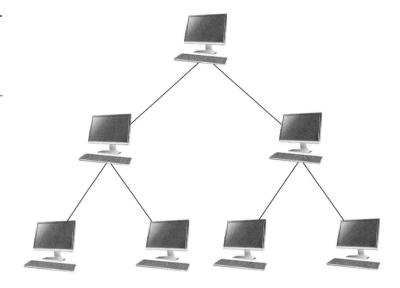

from using the maximum capacity of the network bandwidth, thereby decreasing the effective bandwidth.

Compression

Compression is defined as the reduction in the size of data traveling across the network, which is achieved by converting that data into a format that requires fewer bits for the same transmission. Compression is typically used to minimize the required storage space or to reduce the amount of data transmitted over the network. When using compression to reduce the size of data that is being transferred, a network engineer sees a decrease in transmission times, since there is more bandwidth available for other data to use as it traverses the network. Compression can result in higher processor utilization because a packet must be compressed and decompressed as it traverses the network.

Network compression can automatically compress data before it is sent over the network to improve performance, especially where bandwidth is limited. Maximizing the compression ratio is vital to enhancing application performance on networks with limited bandwidth. Compression can play a key role in cloud computing. As an organization migrates to the cloud network, compression is vital in controlling network latency and maximizing network bandwidth.

 EXAM TIP Compression requires compute power to perform. The higher the compression, the higher the compute cost.

Caching

Caching is the process of storing frequently accessed data in a location closer to the device that is requesting the data. For example, a web cache could store web pages and web content either on the physical machine that is accessing the website or on a storage device like a proxy server. This would increase the response time of the web page and reduce the amount of network traffic required to access the website, thus improving network speed and reducing network latency.

 EXAM TIP The most common type of caching occurs with proxy servers.

There are multiple benefits to caching, including the cost savings that come with reducing the bandwidth needed to access information via the Internet and the improved productivity of the end users (because cached information loads significantly faster than noncached information). With your data now being stored in the cloud, it is crucial to understand how caching works and how to maximize caching to improve performance and maximize your network bandwidth.

Load Balancing

Throughout this section, we have discussed the importance of optimizing network traffic and infrastructure. Data must be routed as efficiently as possible to optimize network traffic. For example, if an organization's network has five routers and three of them are running at 5 percent and the other two are running at 90 percent, the network utilization is not as efficient as it could be. If the load were balanced such that each of the routers was running at 20 percent utilization, it would improve network performance and limit network latency.

Similarly, websites and cloud servers can only handle so much traffic on their own. E-commerce sites may receive thousands or millions of hits every minute. These systems service such a huge number of requests through load-balanced systems by splitting the traffic between multiple web servers that are part of a single web farm, referenced by a single URL. This increases performance and removes the single point of failure connected with having only one server respond to the requests.

Load balancing is the process of distributing incoming HTTP or application requests evenly across multiple devices or web servers so that no single device is overwhelmed. Load balancing allows for achieving optimal resource utilization and maximizing throughput without overloading a single machine. Load balancing increases reliability by creating redundancy for your application or website by using dedicated hardware or software. Figure 4-8 shows an example of how load balancing works for web servers.

Network Service Tiers

Network service tiers determine the level of network performance and resiliency provided to the cloud environment. CSPs may have multiple tiers to choose from, each of them offering different options. Some of the options include network performance, reliability, and geographic distribution.

 NOTE There is no standard network service tier package that every vendor uses. You will need to evaluate what each tier offers to choose the one that best meets your needs.

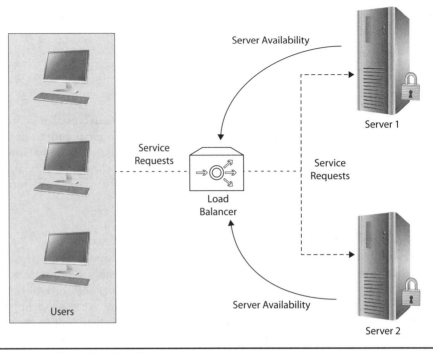

Figure 4-8 An illustration of load balancing

Network Performance

The first way network services tiers differentiate themselves is through network performance. Premium tiers will offer the lowest network latency, higher bandwidth, and more concurrent connections. In contrast, lower tiers will have higher latency, bandwidth caps or throttling, and fewer concurrent connections.

 CAUTION Don't assume that the premium or highest tier is necessarily the best solution. Tiers give customers the option to only pay for what they need. Business needs should drive the decision on which tier to select.

Reliability

The second way network service tiers are differentiated is through higher availability. Higher tiers will have less downtime in their SLA, and they may offer more advanced routing and DNS capabilities so that fewer packets are lost when systems fail over or when network links go down or routes are updated. Conversely, lower tiers will have more downtime in their SLAs and may lose more packets when such events occur. This does not mean that they will lose data, only that the data will need to be retransmitted, which can mean slower speeds or potential timeouts for customers in such events.

Geographic Distribution

The third way network service tiers differentiate themselves is through geographic distribution. A cloud service can be load-balanced across multiple nodes in different regions or even different countries. A low tier might host the systems on a single instance, while a middle tier may load-balance across multiple servers in a local region, called regional load balancing. A premium tier might load-balance across multiple servers in multiple regions across the globe, called global load balancing.

Exercise 4-1: Configuring Network Service Tiers in Google Cloud

In this exercise, you will learn how to change the network service tier for a Google Cloud project. The process is rather simple, which just shows how powerful the cloud is. If you were to upgrade the service tier of a locally hosted application, you would need to purchase additional bandwidth, upgrade networking hardware, configure replication to multiple sites, and establish partnerships or hosting contracts with each of those sites. With the cloud, a system can be upgraded to a higher service tier with a few clicks.

1. Log in to your Google Cloud dashboard.
2. Click the three lines in the upper right and scroll down until you find the networking category and then you will see network service tiers, as shown next. Please note that Google shortens the name to "network service…" in its list.

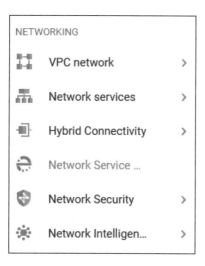

3. Select the project you wish to modify.
4. Click the Change Tier button.
5. If you have never changed the tier before, it will be set to the default network tier you have specified. Select the tier you wish to change it to.
6. Click Change.

Figure 4-9
Proxy server

Web Server   Proxy Server   User

User unknown
to web server

Proxy Servers

Proxy servers are used to route traffic through an intermediary. The proxy server can receive requests for data, such as a website request, and then make the request for the user. The web server would interact with the proxy, sending back the response, and then the proxy would forward it on to the end user. Proxy servers hide the client from the server because the server communicates with the proxy instead of the client or user, as shown in Figure 4-9.

This first example approached the proxy server from the client perspective. Proxy servers can also be used in reverse. This is known as a reverse proxy. A reverse proxy accepts requests for resources and then forwards the request on to another server. A reverse proxy hides the server from the client because the client or user connects only to the reverse proxy server, believing that the resources reside on the reverse proxy when they actually reside somewhere else, as shown in Figure 4-10.

Figure 4-10
Reverse Proxy
server

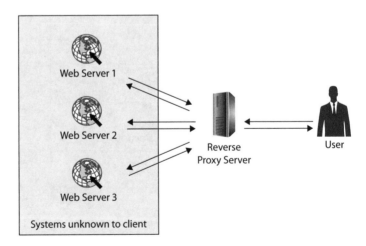

Web Server 1

Web Server 2

Reverse
Proxy Server

User

Web Server 3

Systems unknown to client

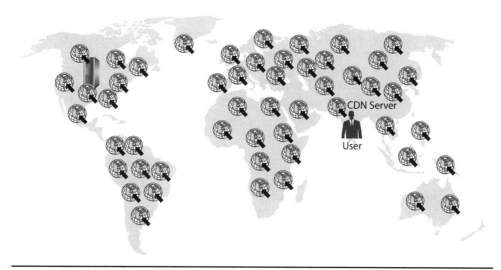

Figure 4-11 CDN Delivering Web Content to a User in India

Content Delivery Network

A content delivery network (CDN) is a collection of servers that are geographically distributed around the world to provide content to users via local servers. CDNs allow companies to deploy content to one place but have it locally available around the world. Local connections have lower latency than remote ones. For example, if you did not have a CDN and a user in India wanted to access your website that is hosted in the United States, they may have to traverse many network links, otherwise known as hops, in between their computer and the data center hosting your website. However, if you are using a CDN, they will only have a few hops between their computer and the closest CDN server in India, so the website will be much more responsive for them, as shown in Figure 4-11.

Routing and Switching

We have discussed the different options and configurations that are available for setting up a network. Now let's explore how to route traffic to and from networks. Knowing how a network operates is the most important piece to understanding routing and switching. In the previous section, you learned that a network operates by connecting computers and devices in a variety of different physical configurations. Routers and switches are the networking devices that enable other devices on the network to connect and communicate with each other and with other networks. They are placed on the same physical network as the other devices.

While routers and switches may give the impression they are somewhat similar, these devices are responsible for very different operations on a network. A switch is used to connect multiple devices to the same network or LAN. For example, a switch connects computers, printers, servers, and a variety of other devices. It allows those devices to share network resources with each other. This makes it possible for users to share resources, saving valuable time and money for the organization.

A router, on the other hand, is used to connect multiple networks together and allows a network to communicate with the outside world. An organization would use a router to connect its network to the Internet, thus allowing its users to share a single Internet connection. A router can analyze the data that is being sent over the network and change how it is packaged so that it can be routed to another network or even over a different type of network.

A router makes routing decisions based on the routing protocol configured on it. Each routing protocol uses a specific method to determine the best path a packet can take to its destination. Some routing protocols include Border Gateway Protocol (BGP), Interior Gateway Routing Protocol (IGRP), Open Shortest Path First (OSPF), and Routing Information Protocol (RIP). BGP uses rule sets; IGRP uses delay, load, and bandwidth; OSPF uses link-state; and RIP uses hop count to make routing decisions.

 EXAM TIP A router connects outside networks to your local network, whereas a switch connects devices on your internal network.

Network Address Translation

Now that you know a router can allow users to share a single IP address when browsing the Internet, you need to understand how that process works. Network address translation, or NAT, allows a router to modify packets so that multiple devices can share a single public IP address. Most organizations require Internet access for their employees but do not have enough valid public IP addresses to allow each individual to have his or her own public address to locate resources outside of the organization's network. The primary purpose of NAT is to limit the number of public IP addresses an organization needs.

NAT allows outbound Internet access, including for cloud-based virtual machines, but prevents inbound connections initiated from the Internet directly to inside machines or cloud-based virtual machines, which route through the NAT devices as their default gateway.

For example, most organizations use a private IP address range, which allows the devices on the network to communicate with all the other devices on the network and makes it possible for users to share files, printers, and the like. But if those users need to access anything outside the network, they require a public IP address. If Internet queries originate from various internal devices, the organization would need to have a valid public IP address for each device. NAT consolidates the addresses needed for each internal device to a single valid public IP address, allowing all of the organization's employees to access the Internet with the use of a single public IP address.

To fully understand this concept, you first need to know what makes an IP address private and what makes an IP address public. Any IP address that falls into one of the IP address ranges reserved for private use by the Internet Engineering Task Force (IETF) is considered a private IP address. Table 4-1 lists the different private IP address ranges.

Table 4-1
Private
IP Addresses

Address Range	Usable IPs	Network Class
10.0.0.0–10.255.255.255	16,777,216	Class A network
172.16.0.0–172.31.255.255	1,048,576	Class B network
192.168.0.0–192.168.255.255	65,536	Class C network
169.254.0.0–169.254.255.255	65,534	Class B network

A private network that adheres to the IETF published standard RFC 1918 is a network address space that is not used or allowed on the public Internet. These addresses are commonly used in a home or corporate network or LAN when a public IP address or globally routed address is not required on each device. Because these address ranges are not made available as public IP addresses and consequently are never explicitly assigned for use to any organization, they receive the designation of "private" IP addresses. IP packets that are addressed by private IP addresses cannot be transmitted onto the public Internet over the backbone.

There are two reasons for the recent surge in using RFC 1918 addresses: one is that Internet Protocol version 4 (IPv4) address space is rapidly diminishing, and the other is that a significant security enhancement is achieved by providing address translation, whether it is NAT or PAT (described shortly) or a combination of the two. A perpetrator on the Internet cannot directly access a private IP address without the administrator taking significant steps to relax the security. A NAT router is sometimes referred to as a poor man's firewall. In reality, it is not a firewall at all, but it shields the internal network (individuals using private addresses) from attacks and from what is sometimes referred to as Internet background radiation (IBR).

An organization must have at least one "routable" or public IP address to access resources that are external to its network. This is where NAT comes into play. NAT allows a router to change the private IP address into a public IP address to access resources that are external to it. The NAT router then tracks those IP address changes. When the external information being requested comes back to the router, the router changes the IP address from a public IP address to a private IP address to forward the traffic back to the requesting device. Essentially, NAT allows a single device like a router to act as an agent or a go-between for a private network and the Internet. NAT provides the benefits of saving public IP addresses, higher security, and ease of administration.

In addition to public and private IP addresses, there is automatic private IP addressing (APIPA, sometimes called Autoconfig), which enables a Dynamic Host Configuration Protocol (DHCP) client to receive an IP address even if it cannot communicate with a DHCP server. APIPA addresses are "nonroutable" over the Internet and allocate an IP address in the private range of 169.254.0.1 to 169.254.255.254. APIPA uses Address Resolution Protocol (ARP) to verify that the IP address is unique in the network.

EXAM TIP   You need to quickly identify a private IP address, so it is advantageous to memorize the first octet of the IP ranges (i.e., 10, 172, and 192).

Port Address Translation

Like NAT, port address translation (PAT) allows for mapping of private IP addresses to public IP addresses and mapping multiple devices on a network to a single public IP address. Its goal is the same as that of NAT: to conserve public IP addresses. PAT enables the sharing of a single public IP address between multiple clients trying to access the Internet.

An excellent example of PAT is a home network where multiple devices are trying to access the Internet simultaneously. In this instance, your ISP would assign your home network's router a single public IP address. On this network, you could have multiple computers or devices trying to access the Internet at the same time using the same router. When device Y logs on to the Internet, it is assigned a port number appended to the private IP address. This gives device Y a unique IP address. If device Z were to log on to the Internet simultaneously, the router would assign the same public IP address to device Z but with a different port number. The two devices are sharing the same public IP address to browse the Internet, but the router distributes the requested content to the appropriate device based on the port number the router has assigned to that particular device.

 EXAM TIP Basic NAT provides a one-to-one mapping of IP addresses, whereas PAT provides a many-to-one mapping of IP addresses.

Subnetting and Supernetting

Subnetting is the practice of creating subnetworks, or subnets. A subnet is a logical subdivision of an IP network. Using subnets may be useful in large organizations where it is necessary to allocate address space efficiently. They may also be utilized to increase routing efficiency and offer improved controls for network management when different networks require the separation of administrator control for different entities in a large or multitenant environment. Inter-subnet traffic is exchanged by routers, just as it would be exchanged between physical networks.

All computers that belong to a particular subnet are addressed with the use of two separate bit groups in their IP address, with one group designating the subnet and the other group designating the specific host on that subnet. The routing prefix of the address can be expressed in either classful notation or classless inter-domain routing (CIDR) notation. CIDR has become the most popular routing notation method in recent years. This notation is written as the first address of a network, followed by a slash (/), then finishing with the prefix's bit length. To use a typical example, 192.168.1.0/24 is the network prefix starting at the given address, having 24 bits allocated for the network prefix, and the remaining 8 bits reserved for host addressing. An allocation of 24 bits is equal to the subnet mask for that network, which you may recognize as the familiar 255.255.255.0.

Whereas subnetting is the practice of dividing one network into multiple networks, supernetting does the exact opposite, combining multiple networks into one larger network. Supernetting is most often utilized to combine multiple class C networks. It was created to solve the problem of routing tables growing too large for administrators to manage by aggregating networks under one routing table entry. It also provided a solution to the problem of class B network address space running out.

In much the same fashion as subnetting, supernetting takes the IP address and breaks it down into a network bit group and a host identifier bit group. It also uses CIDR notation. The way to identify supernetted networks is that the network prefix is always lower than 23, which allows for a greater number of hosts (on the larger network) to be specified in the host bit group.

Routing Tables

A routing table is a set of procedures stored on a router that the router uses to determine the destination of network packets that it is responsible for routing. The routing table contains information about the network topology that is located adjacent to the router, as well as information gathered from neighboring routers. This information is used by routers to determine which path to send packets down to efficiently deliver information to its destination.

Routers may know of multiple paths to a destination. The routing table will rank each of these paths in order of efficiency. The method of ordering the paths depends on the routing protocol used. If the most efficient path is unavailable, the router will select the next best path as defined by its routing table.

 EXAM TIP   Routers can maintain multiple routing tables simultaneously, allowing for identical IP addresses to coexist without conflict through a technology called virtual routing and forwarding (VRF).

Network Segmentation and Micro-segmentation

Network segmentation and micro-segmentation are techniques to divide the network into smaller pieces to isolate or better control traffic and to apply more granular policies to those network segments. Both segmentation and micro-segmentation can be used to reduce the spread of malicious code or make attacks harder, as attackers will need to figure out how to move between network segments before they can attack nodes in another segment.

Segmentation and micro-segmentation methods include traditional VLANs, as well as newer technologies such as VXLAN, NVGRE, STT, and GENEVE. Each of these protocols operates on top of other network protocols such as TCP and IP. Therefore, they are often referred to collectively as network overlays. These protocols aim to make the network more scalable and flexible, a requirement when networks span multiple clouds and when clouds host thousands or millions of customers.

Virtual Local Area Network

A virtual local area network, or VLAN, is the concept of partitioning a physical network to create separate, independent broadcast domains that are part of the same physical network. VLANs are similar to physical LANs but add the ability to break up physical networks into logical groupings of networks, all within the same physical network.

VLANs were conceived out of the desire to create logical separation without the need for additional physical hardware (i.e., network cards, wiring, and routers). VLANs can even traverse physical networks, forming a logical network or VLAN even if the devices exist on separate physical networks. With a virtual private network (VPN), which extends a private network over a public network such as the Internet, a VLAN can even traverse the entire Internet. For example, you could implement a VLAN to place only certain end users inside the VLAN to help control broadcast traffic.

VLAN tagging is the process of inserting a 4-byte header directly after the destination address and the Ethernet frame header's source address. There are two types of VLAN tagging mechanisms: Inter-Switch Link (ISL), which is proprietary to Cisco equipment, and IEEE 802.1Q, which is supported by everyone, including Cisco, and is usually the VLAN option of choice. Approximately 4095 different VLAN IDs can be achieved on the same physical network segment (depending on what is supported by the switch and router devices) utilizing the IEEE 802.1Q protocol.

A VLAN is usually associated with an IP subnet, so all the devices in that IP subnet belong to the same VLAN. To configure a VLAN, you must first create a VLAN and then bind the interface and IP address. VLANs must be routed, and there are various methods for assigning VLAN membership to switch ports. Switch ports can be assigned membership to a particular VLAN on a port-by-port basis manually. Switch ports can also be dynamically configured from a VLAN membership policy server that tracks MAC addresses and their associated VLANs, or they can be classified based on their IP address if the packets are untagged or priority tagged.

Broadcasts, by their very nature, are processed and received by each member of the broadcast domain. VLANs can improve network performance by segmenting the network into groups that share broadcast traffic. For example, each floor of a building might have its own subnet. It might make sense to create a VLAN for that subnet to control broadcasts to other floors of the building, thus reducing the need to send broadcasts to unnecessary destinations (in this case, another floor of the building). The general rule for VLANs is to keep the resources that are needed for the VLAN and that are consumed by members of the VLAN on that same VLAN. Latency issues will occur whenever a packet must cross a VLAN, as it must be routed. This situation should be avoided if possible.

The type of port that supports a VLAN is called an access link. When a device connects using an access link, it is unaware of any VLAN membership. It behaves as if it were a component of a broadcast domain. All VLAN information is removed by switches from the frame before it gets to the device connected to the access link. No communication or interaction can occur between the access link devices and the devices outside of their designated VLAN. This communication is only made possible when the packet is routed through a router.

A trunk link, also known just as a trunk, is a port that transports packets for any VLAN. These trunk ports are usually found in connections between switches and require the ability to carry packets from all available VLANs because those VLANs span multiple switches. Trunk ports are typically VLAN 0 or VLAN 1, but there is nothing magical about those numbers. It is up to the manufacturer to determine which ID is designated as the trunk port. Specifications are spelled out in the 802.1Q protocol. Like any other blueprint, some manufacturers will make their own interpretation of how trunk ports should be implemented.

For cloud VLANs, it is important to understand another type of VLAN known as a private VLAN or PVLAN. PVLANs contain switch ports that cannot communicate with each other but can access another network. PVLANs restrict traffic through the use of private ports so that they communicate only with a specific uplink trunk port. A good example of the utilization of a PVLAN is in a hotel setting. Each room of the hotel has a port that can access the Internet, but it is not advantageous for the rooms to communicate with each other.

Virtual Extensible LAN

The virtual extensible LAN (VXLAN) is a network overlay protocol used to subdivide a network into many smaller segments. VXLAN tunnels or encapsulates frames across UDP port 4789. The data addressed to another member of a VXLAN is placed inside the UDP packet and routed to its destination, at which point it is de-encapsulated so that the receiving port, known as a VXLAN tunnel endpoint (VTEP), can receive it as if it were sent over a local network. The primary vendors behind VXLAN are Cisco, VMware, Brocade, Citrix, Red Hat, Broadcom, and Arista. VXLAN has a moderate overhead of 50 bytes.

VXLAN is primarily used in cloud environments to segment different tenants. VXLANs were created because VLAN uses a 12-bit VLAN ID that can have a maximum of 4096 network IDs assigned at one time. This is not enough addresses for many large cloud environments. VXLAN uses a 24-bit segment ID that allows for 16 million segments, which provides enough segments for many more customers. Similar to VLANs, switch ports can be members of a VXLAN. VXLAN members can be either virtual or physical switch ports.

Network Virtualization Using Generic Routing Encapsulation

Network Virtualization Using Generic Routing Encapsulation (NVGRE) is another network overlay protocol used to subdivide a network into many smaller segments. As the name implies, NVGRE uses the GRE protocol for tunneling. The primary vendors behind the NVGRE protocol are Microsoft for use with their Hyper-V hypervisors on Azure, Huawei, and HP. NVGRE has a moderate overhead of 42 bytes.

Like VXLAN, NVGRE is also used to segment a much larger network set than the traditional VLAN. Also, just like VXLAN, NVGRE uses a 24-bit Virtual Subnet Identifier (VSID) that uniquely identifies the network segment. This allows for 16 million segments. However, unlike VXLAN, NVGRE headers include an extra 8-bit field called the flow ID, which devices can use to better prioritize traffic. Also, NVGRE frame sizes are larger than VXLAN and STT, so intermediary nodes will need to support this larger 1546-byte frame.

Stateless Transport Tunneling

Stateless Transport Tunneling (STT) is another network overlay protocol used to subdivide a network into many smaller segments. STT can be implemented entirely in software so that it can operate on top of existing network technologies. STT runs over TCP/IP and supports the largest number of networks with its 64-bit network ID.

	VXLAN	NVGRE	STT
Network ID Size	24-bit	24-bit	64-bit
Supported Networks	16 million	16 million	18 quintillion
Encapsulation	UDP	GRE	TCP/IP
Overhead	50 bytes	42 bytes	76 bytes
Offload Supported	No	No	Yes
Primary Vendors Supporting the Technology	Cisco, VMware, Brocade, Citrix, Red Hat, Broadcom, and Arista	Microsoft, Huawei, and HP	VMware and Broadcom

Table 4-2 Network Overlay Protocols Compared

This allows for 18 quintillion networks. This larger ID also increases its overhead. It has the most overhead of each of the network overlay protocols, at 76 bytes. However, STT does support offloading of processing to the NIC to reduce its burden on the systems encapsulating and de-encapsulating its content.

The primary vendors behind STT are VMware and Broadcom. VXLAN, NVGRE, and STT are compared in Table 4-2.

Generic Network Virtualization Encapsulation

Generic Network Virtualization Encapsulation (GENEVE) is the answer to VXLAN, NVGRE, and STT. Each of these protocols has different vendors behind them, but we live in a world that requires increasing interconnectivity and interoperability. GENEVE was created as a multivendor effort to allow for this interoperability. GENEVE is an overlay protocol, but it only specifies the data format. It does not specify a control format like VXLAN, NVGRE, and STT. The goal of the protocol was to allow it to evolve over time and offer maximum flexibility. It operates over TCP/IP. To support each of the aforementioned protocols, GENEVE includes a 64-bit metadata field for network virtualization. This increases the overhead much like STT. GENEVE utilizes Type-Length-Value (TLV) encoding for the metadata so that hardware can skip over parts it does not support without resulting in an error. GENEVE has the support of many vendors and software systems.

Network Ports and Protocols

Now that you understand how to select the physical network configuration and segment and route network traffic, you need to learn about the different ports and protocols that are used in cloud computing. A network port is an application-specific endpoint to a logical connection. It is how a client program finds a specific service on a device. A network protocol, on the other hand, is an understood set of rules agreed upon by two or more parties that determine how network devices exchange information over a network. In this section, we discuss the different protocols used to securely connect a network to the Internet so that it can communicate with the cloud environment.

Hypertext Transfer Protocol and Hypertext Transfer Protocol Secure

Hypertext Transfer Protocol (HTTP) is an application protocol built on TCP to distribute Hypertext Markup Language (HTML) files, text, images, sound, videos, multimedia, and other types of information over the Internet. HTTP typically allows for communication between a web client or web browser and a web server hosting a website. HTTP defines how messages between a web browser and a web server are formatted and transmitted and which actions the web server and browser should take when issued specific commands. HTTP uses port 80 to communicate by default.

Hypertext Transfer Protocol Secure (HTTPS) is an extension of HTTP that provides secure communication over the Internet. HTTPS is not a separate protocol from HTTP; it layers the security capabilities of Secure Sockets Layer (SSL) or Transport Layer Security (TLS) on top of HTTP to provide security to standard HTTP, since HTTP communicates in plaintext. HTTPS uses port 443 by default.

When a web client first accesses a website using HTTPS, the server sends a certificate with its embedded public key to the web client. The client then verifies that the certificate is in its trusted root store during the standard authentication process, thus trusting the certificate was signed by a trusted certificate authority. The client generates a session key (sometimes called a symmetric key) and encrypts the session key with the server's public key. The server has the private key, which is the other half of the public-private key pair and can decrypt the session key, which allows for an efficient, covert, and confidential exchange of the session key. No entity other than the server has access to the private key.

Once both the web client and the web server know the session key, the SSL/TLS handshake is complete and the session is encrypted. As part of the protocol, either the client or the server can ask that the key be "rolled" at any time. Rolling the key is merely asking the browser to generate a new 40-, 128-, or 256-bit key or above, forcing a would-be attacker to shoot at a moving target.

 EXAM TIP   Some organizations may use a proxy for connecting to the Internet. Proxy automatic configuration (PAC) is a system that automatically configures devices to use a proxy server if one is required for a web connection. PAC is also known as proxy auto-config.

File Transfer Protocol and FTP over SSL

Unlike HTTP, which is used to view web pages over the Internet, the File Transfer Protocol (FTP) is used to download and transfer files over the Internet. FTP is a standard network protocol that allows for access to and transfer of files over the Internet using either the FTP client or command-line interface. An organization hosts files on an FTP server so that people from outside the organization can download those files to their local computers. Figure 4-12 shows an example of a graphical-based FTP client.

FTP is built on a client-server architecture and provides a data connection between the FTP client and the FTP server. The FTP server is the computer that stores the files and authenticates the FTP client. The FTP server listens on the network for incoming

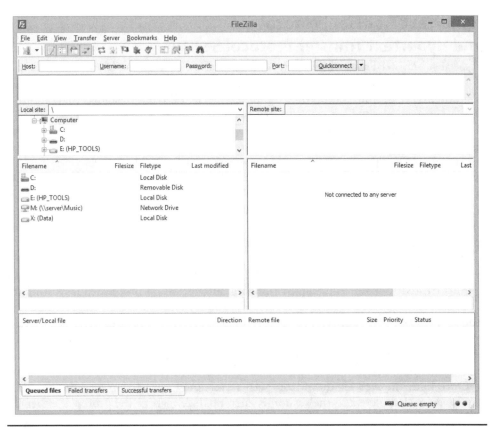

Figure 4-12 Screenshot of a graphical-based FTP client

FTP connection requests from FTP clients. The clients, on the other hand, use either the command-line interface or FTP client software to connect to the FTP server.

After the FTP server has authenticated the client, the client can download files, rename files, upload files, and delete files on the FTP server based on the client's permissions. The FTP client software has an interface that allows you to explore the directory of the FTP server, just like you would use Windows Explorer to explore the content of your local hard drive on a Microsoft Windows–based computer.

Similar to how HTTPS is an extension of HTTP, FTPS is an extension of FTP that allows clients to request that their FTP session be encrypted. FTPS allows for the encrypted and secure transfer of files over FTP using SSL or TLS. There are two different methods for securing client access to the FTP server: implicit and explicit. The implicit mode gives an FTPS-aware client the ability to require a secure connection with an FTPS-aware server without affecting the FTP functionality of non-FTPS-aware clients. With explicit mode, a client must explicitly request a secure connection from the FTPS server. The security and encryption method must then be agreed upon between the FTPS server and the FTPS client. If the client does not request a secure connection, the FTPS server can either allow or refuse the client's connection to the FTPS server.

Secure Shell File Transfer Protocol

Secure Shell File Transfer Protocol (SFTP) is a network protocol designed to provide secure access to files, file transfers, file editing, and file management over the Internet using a Secure Shell (SSH) session. Unlike FTP, SFTP encrypts both the data and the FTP commands, preventing the information from being transmitted in cleartext over the Internet. SFTP differs from FTPS in that SFTP uses SSH to secure the file transfer and FTPS uses SSL or TLS to secure the file transfer.

SFTP clients are functionally similar to FTP clients, except SFTP clients use SSH to access and transfer files over the Internet. An organization cannot use standard FTP client software to access an SFTP server, nor can it use SFTP client software to access FTP servers.

There are a few things to consider when deciding which method should be used to secure FTP servers. SFTP is generally more secure and superior to FTPS. Suppose the organization is going to connect to a Linux or Unix FTP server. In that case, SFTP is the better choice because it is supported by default on these operating systems. If one of the requirements for the FTP server is that it needs to be accessible from personal devices, such as tablets and smartphones, then FTPS would be the better option, since most of these devices natively support FTPS but may not support SFTP.

 EXAM TIP It is important to understand that FTPS and SFTP are not the same. FTPS uses SSL or TLS and certificates to secure FTP communication, and SFTP uses SSH keys to secure FTP communication.

Domain Name System

The Domain Name System (DNS) distributes the responsibility for both the assignment of domain names and the mapping of those names to IP addresses to the authoritative name servers within each domain. An authoritative name server is responsible for maintaining its specific domain name. It can also be authoritative for subdomains of that primary domain. For example, if you want to go to a particular web page like https://www.cwe.com, all you do is type the web page's name into your browser, and it displays the web page. For your web browser to show that web page by name, it needs to locate it by IP address. This is where DNS comes into play.

DNS translates Internet domain or hostnames into IP addresses. DNS would automatically convert the name https://www.cwe.com into an IP address for the web server hosting that web page. To store the full name and address information for all the public hosts on the Internet, DNS uses a distributed hierarchical database. DNS databases reside in a hierarchy of database servers where no one DNS server contains all the information. Figure 4-13 shows an example of how a client performs a DNS search.

DNS consists of a tree of domain names. Each branch of the tree has a domain name and contains resource records for that domain. Resource records describe specific information about a particular object. The DNS zone at the top of the tree is called the root zone. Each zone under the root zone has a unique domain name or multiple domain names. The owner of that domain name is considered authoritative for that DNS zone. Figure 4-14 shows the DNS hierarchy and how a URL is resolved to an IP address.

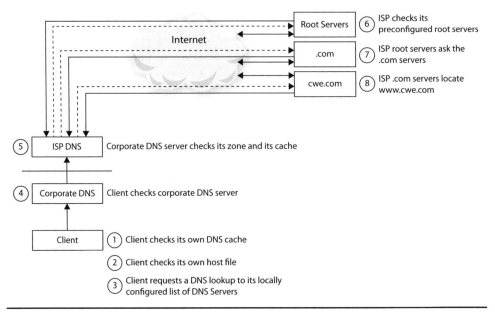

Figure 4-13 The steps in a DNS search

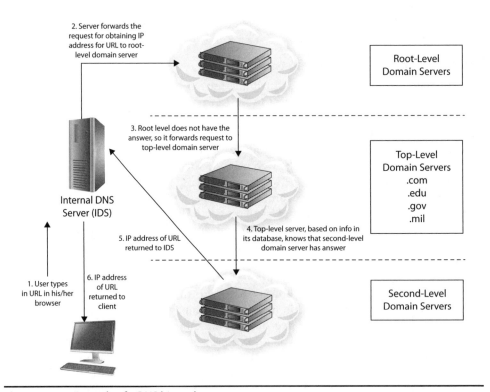

Figure 4-14 Example of a DNS hierarchy

DNS servers manage DNS zones. Servers store records for resources within one or more domains that they are configured and authorized to manage. A host record, or "A" record, is used to store information on a domain or subdomain along with its IP address. A canonical name (CNAME) record is an alias for a host record. For example, a CNAME record testing for the comptia.org domain pointing to www would allow for users to enter the URL www.comptia.org or testing.comptia.org to go to the same site. A mail exchanger (MX) record stores information on the mail server for the domain, if one exists.

DNS is one of the protocols the Internet and cloud services are based on because, without it, users cannot resolve the names for the services they wish to reach. Because of this importance, DNS has also been the target for attacks to disrupt its availability. In addition, DNS has privacy implications, since the resolving servers can view the queries made to it and where those queries came from. Several protocols have been developed to help mitigate these concerns. These include DNS Security (DNSSEC), DNS over HTTPS (DoH), and DNS over TLS (DoT).

DNS Security

DNSSEC was developed to address data integrity issues with DNS. Namely, when a client issues a request for DNS resolution, they have no way of validating that the response they receive is correct because attackers can spoof the DNS IP address and then reply back with incorrect IP addresses for common URLs that send users to websites that may look and feel like real websites but are designed to steal their information. For example, a DNS server may provide the wrong IP address for ebay.com, which sends the user to an attacker's page, where attackers harvest user credentials or credit card information and then pass them back to the real ebay.com.

DNSSEC signs DNS records with digital signatures so that user systems can independently validate the authenticity of the data they receive. Each DNS zone has a public and private key. The private key is used to sign the DNS data in the zone so that users can use the public key to verify its authenticity. The keys used by DNSSEC can be trusted because they are signed with the parent zone's private key, so machines validate the private keys used to sign the DNS data by validating the chain all the way up to the root-level domain, which each of the systems trusts implicitly.

DNS over HTTPS and DNS over TLS

DoH and DoT were developed to address the data confidentiality and privacy issues with DNS. Just like HTTPS encapsulates HTTP in SSL, DoH encapsulates DNS requests in SSL. Some significant vulnerabilities have been discovered in SSL, so it has been superseded by TLS. DoT operates with the same goal as DoH. It takes DNS and encapsulates it in TLS. Both of these protocols encrypt the traffic so that other parties cannot view it as it traverses the Internet. DoH transmits traffic over port 443, while DoT uses port 853.

Dynamic Host Configuration Protocol

DHCP is a network protocol that allows a server to automatically assign IP addresses from a predefined range of numbers, called a scope, to computers on a network. DHCP is responsible for assigning IP addresses to computers, and DNS is responsible for resolving those IP addresses to names. A DHCP server can register and update resource records on a DNS server on behalf of a DHCP client. A DHCP server is used any time an organization does not wish to use static IP addresses (IP addresses that are manually assigned).

DHCP servers maintain a database of available IP addresses and configuration options. The DHCP server leases an IP address to a client based on the network to which that client is connected. The DHCP client is then responsible for renewing its lease or IP addresses before the lease expires. DHCP supports both IPv4 and IPv6. It can also create a static IP address mapping by creating a reservation that assigns a particular IP address to a computer based on that computer's media access control (MAC) address.

If an organization's network has only one IP subnet, clients can communicate directly with the DHCP server. If the network has multiple subnets, the company can still use a DHCP server to allocate IP addresses to the network clients. To allow a DHCP client on a subnet that is not directly connected to the DHCP server to communicate with the DHCP server, the organization can configure a DHCP relay agent in the DHCP client's subnet. A DHCP relay agent is an agent that relays DHCP communication between DHCP clients and DHCP servers on different IP subnets. DNS and DHCP work together to help clients on an organization's network communicate as efficiently as possible and allow the clients to discover and share resources located on the network.

IP Address Management

IP Address Management (IPAM) is a centralized way to manage DHCP and DNS information for an enterprise. An enterprise may have DHCP systems in various locations and clouds that each operates independently. This can be difficult to manage. IPAM includes tools to discover DHCP and DNS servers and then centrally manage each of the scopes in use and the IP addresses assigned to systems. IPAM stores the information it collects in a database. This makes it easier to administer the network, identify redundancies, and monitor which systems have which IP addresses across the enterprise.

Simple Mail Transfer Protocol

Documents and videos are not the only pieces of information you might want to share and communicate over the Internet. While HTTP and FTP allow you to share files, videos, and pictures over the Internet, Simple Mail Transfer Protocol (SMTP) is the protocol that enables you to send an e-mail over the Internet. SMTP uses port 25 and provides a standard set of codes that help to simplify the delivery of e-mail messages between e-mail servers. Almost all e-mail servers that send an e-mail over the Internet use SMTP to send messages from one server to another. After the e-mail server has received the message, the user can view that e-mail using an e-mail client, such as Microsoft Outlook. The e-mail client also uses SMTP to send messages from the client to the e-mail server.

Network Time Protocol

Have you ever tried to schedule a meeting with someone who you didn't know was in another time zone? You schedule the appointment for 2:30, and then they e-mail you shortly after 1:30, wondering why you aren't on the call. Similarly, computers need to have reliable time to reliably communicate.

Network protocols rely on accurate time to protect against attacks where authentication data is replayed back to the server. This is why Microsoft's Active Directory will reject connections if the machine's system time is over five minutes off from the domain controller. Similarly, TLS and DNSSEC each rely upon accurate time to operate.

Network Time Protocol (NTP) is a protocol operating on UDP port 123 that is used to dynamically set the system clock on a machine by querying an NTP server. In a domain, computers are typically configured to all set their system clocks to authoritative time servers to ensure that they are all correct. Similarly, network devices such as routers or firewalls often use NTP to ensure their time is right. Windows machines use the Windows Time service (W32Time), and some Linux distributions use chrony to set the system time from an NTP server.

Public NTP servers can be queried by anyone. An organization can also set up their own internal private NTP server. Some companies implement a private NTP server that connects to a public NTP server so that each individual NTP request does not need to go out to the Internet to be resolved. Public NTP servers usually reside within a pool where a group of servers actually respond to the NTP request. Some of these pools have servers in various geographic locations to reduce latency for queries.

Despite NTP's usefulness, it is vulnerable to man-in-the-middle (MITM) attacks and has been used in distributed denial of service (DDoS) reflection attacks. MITM attacks involve an attacker who intercepts traffic intended for the NTP server and replies back with false time information, while DDoS reflection attacks submit NTP queries to a server from a spoofed IP so that the NTP servers flood the real IP address with NTP responses. A solution to some of the security concerns was developed in the Network Time Security (NTS) protocol.

Network Time Security

NTS expands on NTP to include a key exchange to properly authenticate client and server. This helps defend against MITM attacks because the client can validate that they are talking to the correct NTP server. NTS uses the TLS protocol for secure key exchange. There is an optional client authentication component as well.

Well-Known Ports

Ports are used in a TCP or UDP network to specify the endpoint of a logical connection and how the client can access a specific application on a server over the network. Port binding is used to determine where and how a message is transmitted. Link aggregation can also be implemented to combine multiple network connections to increase throughput. The Internet Assigned Numbers Authority (IANA) assigns the well-known ports that range from 0 to 1023. The IANA is responsible for maintaining the official assignments of port numbers for a specific purpose. You do not need to know all of the well-known ports for the CompTIA Cloud+ exam, so we will focus only on the ports that are relevant to the exam. Table 4-3 specifies server processes and their communication ports.

 EXAM TIP Make sure you know the ports listed in Table 4-3 and which service uses which port.

Service	Port(s)	Transport Protocol	Description
FTP	20, 21	TCP	File Transfer Protocol, used to transfer data.
SFTP	22	TCP	Secure Shell File Transfer Protocol, used for secure logins, file transfers, and port forwarding.
Telnet	23	TCP	Telnet, used to send unencrypted text messages.
SMTP	25	TCP	Simple Mail Transfer Protocol, used to route e-mails between mail servers.
DNS and DNSSEC	53	TCP/UDP	Domain Name System and Domain Name System Security
DHCP	67, 68	UDP	Dynamic Host Configuration Protocol, used to assign IP addresses to computers.
HTTP	80	TCP	World Wide Web Hypertext Transfer Protocol.
POP	110	TCP	Post Office Protocol, used for retrieving mail from a mail server.
NTP	123	UDP	Network Time Protocol, synchronizes the system clock with a time server.
IMAP	143	TCP	Internet Message Access Protocol, another protocol used to send and receive mail. It is considered more advanced than POP, with push methods and other features.
SNMP	161	TCP/UDP	Simple Network Management Protocol, used to send network management information.
LDAP	389	TCP/UDP	Lightweight Directory Access Protocol, used for exchanging directory information.
HTTPS	443	TCP	HTTP over Secure Sockets Layer (SSL).
DoH	443	TCP	DNS over HTTPS.
DoT	853	TCP	DNS over TLS.
FTPS	990	TCP	One of two secure versions of FTP. FTPS runs over SSL/TLS.

Table 4-3   Well-Known Server Processes and Communication Ports

Chapter Review

A network's physical topology is a key factor in its overall performance. This chapter explained the various physical topologies and when to use each of them. It also discussed how traffic is routed across the network, which is key to understanding how to implement cloud computing. Since most information is accessed over an Internet connection, it is crucial to know how to properly configure a network and how it is routed.

There are various ways to reduce network latency and improve network response time and performance, including caching, compression, load balancing, and maintaining the physical hardware. These issues are critical for ensuring that an organization meets the terms of its SLA.

Questions

The following questions will help you gauge your understanding of the material in this chapter. Read all the answers carefully because there might be more than one correct answer. Choose the best response(s) for each question.

1. Which network type is not accessible from outside the organization by default?

   A. Internet

   B. Extranet

   C. Intranet

   D. LAN

2. Which of the following statements describes the difference between an extranet and an intranet network configuration?

   A. An intranet does not require a firewall.

   B. An extranet requires less administration than an intranet.

   C. An intranet is owned and operated by a single organization.

   D. An extranet allows controlled access from outside the organization.

3. Which of the following is a network of multiple networks relying on network devices and common protocols to transfer data from one destination to another until it reaches its final destination and is accessible from anywhere?

   A. Intranet

   B. Extranet

   C. Internet

   D. LAN

4. Which of the following terms defines the amount of data that can be sent across a network at a given time?

   A. Network latency

   B. Bandwidth

   C. Compression

   D. Network load balancing

5. Which of the following causes network performance to deteriorate and delays network response time?

   A. Network latency

   B. Caching

   C. Network bandwidth

   D. High CPU and memory usage

6. After taking a new job at the state university, you are asked to recommend a network topology that best fits the large college campus. The network needs to span the entire campus. Which network topology would you recommend?

   A. LAN

   B. WAN

   C. MAN

   D. SAN

7. You administer a website that receives thousands of hits per second. You notice the web server hosting the website is operating at close to capacity. What solution would you recommend to improve the performance of the website?

   A. Caching

   B. Network load balancing

   C. Compression

   D. Network bandwidth

8. Which process allows a router to modify packets so that multiple devices can share a single public IP address?

   A. NAT

   B. DNS

   C. VLAN

   D. Subnetting

9. Which of the following IP addresses is in a private IP range?

   A. 12.152.36.9

   B. 10.10.10.10

   C. 72.64.53.89

   D. 173.194.96.3

10. Which of the following technologies allows you to logically segment a LAN into different broadcast domains?

    A. MAN

    B. WAN

    C. VLAN

    D. SAN

11. Which of the following protocols and ports is used to secure communication over the Internet?

    A. HTTP over port 80

    B. SMTP over port 25

    C. FTP over port 21

    D. HTTPS over port 443

12. SFTP uses _____ to secure FTP communication.

    A. Certificates

    B. FTPS

    C. SSH

    D. SMTP

13. In a network environment _____ is responsible for assigning IP addresses to computers and _____ is responsible for resolving those IP addresses to names.

    A. DNS, DHCP

    B. DHCP, DNS

    C. HTTP, DNS

    D. DHCP, SMTP

14. Which of these ports is the well-known port for the Telnet service?

    A. 25

    B. 22

    C. 23

    D. 443

15. Which protocol is responsible for transferring e-mail messages from one mail server to another over the Internet?

    A. DNS

    B. HTTPS

    C. FTP

    D. SMTP

Answers

    1. C. An intranet is a private network that is configured and controlled by a single organization and is only accessible by users that are internal to that organization.

    2. D. An extranet is an extension of an intranet, with the primary difference being that an extranet allows controlled access from outside the organization.

    3. C. The Internet is not controlled by a single entity and serves billions of users around the world.

    4. B. Bandwidth is the amount of data that can traverse a network interface over a specific amount of time.

5. **A.** Network latency is a time delay that is encountered while data is being sent from one point to another on the network and affects network bandwidth and performance.

6. **C.** A metropolitan area network (MAN) can connect multiple LANs and is used to build networks with high data connection speeds for cities or college campuses.

7. **B.** Network load balancing is used to increase performance and provide redundancy for websites and applications.

8. **A.** NAT allows your router to change your private IP address into a public IP address so that you can access resources that are external to your organization; then the router tracks those IP address changes.

9. **B.** 10.0.0.0 to 10.255.255.255 is a private class A address range.

10. **C.** A VLAN allows you to configure separate broadcast domains even if the devices are plugged into the same physical switch.

11. **D.** HTTPS is an extension of HTTP that provides secure communication over the Internet and uses port 443 by default.

12. **C.** SFTP uses SSH to secure FTP communication.

13. **B.** DHCP is responsible for assigning IP addresses to computers, and DNS is responsible for resolving those IP addresses to names.

14. **C.** Telnet uses port 23 by default for its communication.

15. **D.** SMTP is used to transfer e-mail messages from one e-mail server to another over the Internet.

Virtualization Components

In this chapter, you will learn about

- Hypervisor
- Virtualization host
- Virtual machine
- Virtualized infrastructure service elements

Virtualization technologies have grown substantially over the years. Before that, many major software vendors would not support their applications if they were being run in a virtualized environment. Now virtualization is the standard when it comes to creating an efficient data center, and almost all application vendors support their applications running in a virtualized environment. Virtualization allows a cloud provider to deliver resources on demand to a cloud consumer as needed rather than wasting time or losing opportunities because IT could not keep up with demand. Resource flexibility and scalability are key elements of cloud computing and some of the primary reasons for its rapid adoption.

The IT world has shifted from a one-to-one application-to-hardware model to a many-to-one model. Virtualization uses one physical computer to run multiple virtual servers, each with its own independent operating system and applications. Virtualization has made the IT industry more efficient. Virtualization results in better utilization of existing computing assets and technology cost savings.

Virtualization plays a key role in cloud computing by empowering cloud providers to deliver lower-cost hosting environments to cloud consumers. With virtualization, an organization can do more with less physical hardware and can deliver applications to its users faster than ever.

Virtualization makes the most of the physical hardware by running multiple virtual servers on one physical server. This consolidates infrastructure and reduces the total cost of ownership (TCO) by cutting data center space, power consumption, and cooling costs.

One key piece of software that has allowed the shift to virtualization is the hypervisor. Know this term for the exam. This chapter begins by looking at the various types of hypervisors and how they operate.

Hypervisor

A hypervisor is software that creates and manages the virtual infrastructure, including virtual switches (vSwitch), virtual CPUs (vCPU), virtual memory, virtual disks, and virtual machines.

The hypervisor is the entity that allows multiple operating systems to run on a single physical machine. The computer running the hypervisor is defined as the "host" computer. The virtual machines that are running on the host are called "guest" machines. The hypervisor is responsible for managing the guest operating system resources, including memory, CPU, and other resources that the guest operating system might need.

There are currently two distinct types of hypervisors: type 1 and type 2. Understanding the two types of hypervisors is critical to creating a successful virtualization environment and integrating that environment with the cloud computing models discussed in Chapter 1.

Type 1

A type 1 hypervisor is one that is created and deployed on a bare-metal installation. The first thing installed on a type 1 hypervisor is the hypervisor itself; it acts as the operating system for the bare-metal machine.

Type 1 hypervisor software communicates directly with the physical server hardware and boots before the operating system (OS). Almost all of the major virtualization distributors, including VMware, Microsoft, Citrix, Oracle, and Red Hat, currently use type 1 hypervisors. Figure 5-1 shows an example of what a type 1 hypervisor looks like. The image is meant to give you a graphical representation of the layered design, with the hypervisor layer building on top of the hardware layer.

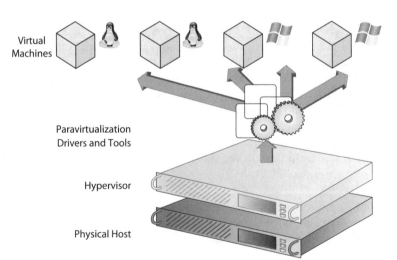

Figure 5-1 The layered design of a type 1 hypervisor

Virtual Machines

Paravirtualization Drivers and Tools

Hypervisor

Physical Host

Type 2

Unlike a type 1 hypervisor that is loaded on a bare-metal server, a type 2 hypervisor is loaded on top of an already existing operating system installation. For example, a system running Microsoft Windows 10 might have a VMware workstation installed on top of that operating system.

Type 2 hypervisors create a layer they must traverse as they are distributed to the guest virtual machines. A type 2 hypervisor relies on the operating system and cannot boot until the operating system is loaded and operational. Since type 2 relies heavily on the underlying operating system, if the system crashes or doesn't boot, all of the guest virtual machines are affected. This makes type 2 hypervisors much less efficient than type 1 hypervisors.

Type 1 hypervisors are the best choice for high performance, scalability, and reliability, since they operate directly on top of the host hardware and expose hardware resources to virtual machines. This results in less overhead and less complexity.

Type 2 hypervisors sit on top of the operating system, making the virtualized environment less scalable and more complex to manage. Figure 5-2 gives a graphical representation of a type 2 hypervisor. Notice the difference in layering as compared to the type 1 hypervisor.

 EXAM TIP   The primary difference between a type 1 hypervisor and a type 2 hypervisor is that type 1 is installed natively on the server and boots before the operating system, while type 2 is installed on top of or after the operating system.

Figure 5-2
Image of a type 2 hypervisor

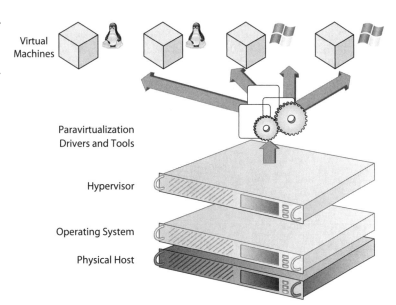

Proprietary

When a company is choosing which type of hypervisor to use, it needs to understand the difference between proprietary and open-source hypervisors. A proprietary hypervisor is developed and licensed under an exclusive legal right of the copyright holder. Proprietary hypervisors are created and distributed under a license agreement to the customer. Hyper-V, vSphere, OVM, and FusionSphere are examples of proprietary hypervisors.

Open Source

Some say that the open-source market is growing and advancing faster than the proprietary product market. It can also be argued that the open-source hypervisors are more secure than the proprietary hypervisors because of the underlying operating system running the hypervisor.

An open-source hypervisor is provided at no cost, yet it delivers the same basic functionality as a proprietary hypervisor to run multiple guest virtual machines on a single host. Some examples of open-source hypervisors are Citrix Xen, kernel-based virtual machine (KVM), and OpenVZ. However, many differences arise when evaluating advanced feature sets, migration capabilities, performance, scalability, and integration with other virtualization environments.

Choosing between proprietary and open-source hypervisors can be a difficult decision. Some of the factors that need to be considered are security, the reliability of the vendor, and the operating systems that are supported by the hypervisor. Some organizations also choose not to use an open-source hypervisor because their IT staff is not familiar with the interface. For example, an organization may choose to use Microsoft Hyper-V over Citrix Xen because its IT staff is already familiar with the Microsoft product line. This will reduce the learning curve to become proficient in managing the system compared to if the organization were to choose an open-source hypervisor.

Table 5-1 shows some of the most popular hypervisors, the companies or groups behind them, and whether they are proprietary or open source. The list is arranged alphabetically.

Hypervisor	Organization	Proprietary/Open Source
FusionSphere	Huawei	Proprietary
Hyper-V	Microsoft	Proprietary
KVM	KVM Project	Open Source
OpenVZ	Virtuozzo	Open Source
OVM	Oracle	Proprietary
Red Hat Virtualization	Red Hat	Open Source
vSphere / ESXi	VMware	Proprietary
Xen XenServer	Citrix	Open Source Proprietary

Table 5-1 Popular Hypervisors

Consumer vs. Enterprise

Hypervisors are available in many flavors to meet the varied needs of everyone from end users, to developers, to enterprise data centers. Many of the current desktop operating systems come with a virtualization option already built in. These operating systems offer a consumer hypervisor that allows users to create virtual machines on a standard PC. For example, Microsoft Windows 8 and later versions come packaged with Hyper-V, allowing desktop-level hardware to run a virtual environment. Similarly, KVM can be added to Linux by pulling down a few packages.

However, not all hypervisors are the same. Consumer and enterprise use cases differ significantly. Thus, when selecting a hypervisor, it is essential to consider the user's or group's specific virtualization goals.

The enterprise virtualization goal is to host the required virtual servers and their associated data and applications on the least amount of hardware to provide acceptable performance and redundancy. Enterprises want to run many virtual machines on each physical machine. Those virtual machines, running independent operating systems, must support many concurrent users and a variety of applications and workloads. This is the job for a type 1 hypervisor because it is built to effectively handle this type of use case and workload.

In comparison, the average consumer's goal is to configure a virtual environment on a desktop or laptop machine that was not designed primarily for the purpose of virtualization. The device may serve other purposes such as gaming, word processing, or Internet browsing in addition to functioning as a hypervisor. Consumers are typically not looking to support a large number of users.

Desktop virtualization is popular with developers and IT professionals. Developers often test out applications locally in virtual machines without the complexity of managing a dedicated hypervisor. IT professionals may want to test new operating systems or applications in an isolated environment separate from the operating system running on their desktop. Similarly, Linux or Mac users may use virtualization such as KVM or Parallels to run another operating system so that they can run OS-specific applications or games.

The type 2 hypervisor is more likely to fit consumers' needs because type 2 hypervisors allow the desktop to continue to run the original operating system and its applications side by side with virtualized operating systems and applications.

Virtualization Host

Now that you understand what a hypervisor is and how it interacts with a computer, you need to understand the virtualization host that runs the hypervisor software. The virtualization host is the system that is installed first and then hosts or contains the guest virtual machines. The host server provides all of the underlying hardware and compute resources for the guest virtual machines, including memory, CPU, hard disk, and network I/O. Since the host machine provides the resources for the guest, it must contain at least enough hardware resources to meet the minimum requirements for its guest virtual machines.

Figure 5-3
A graphical
representation of
a virtualization
host

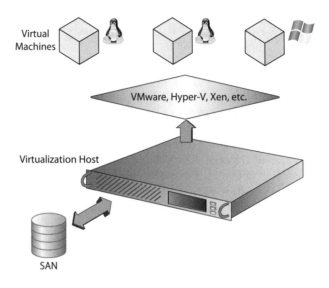

A virtualization host computer allows different operating systems to coexist on the same host computer. For example, you could have a virtual machine running Microsoft Windows Server 2016 and another virtual machine running your favorite Linux distro. The first step in configuring a virtualization host is to confirm that your system meets the virtualization host's requirements. Hardware requirements include BIOS configuration, sufficient memory, CPU, and at least one NIC. Figure 5-3 shows an example of a virtualization host computer.

Hardware-Assisted Virtualization

Hardware-assisted virtualization enables efficient full virtualization, which is used to simulate a complete hardware environment or a virtual machine. It is basically software that allows the hardware to provide architectural support for the host computer to support running guest virtual machines. Hardware-assisted virtualization helps make virtualization more efficient by utilizing the hardware capabilities built into the host computer's processor. Both AMD and Intel support hardware-assisted virtualization.

If an organization wants to find out whether its hardware supports hardware-assisted virtualization, an excellent place to start is with the AMD and Intel websites. Both websites have a list of all the processors that support hardware-assisted virtualization. It should also be noted that all processors manufactured after 2003 have hardware-assisted virtualization built in.

 EXAM TIP   Hardware-assisted virtualization enables efficient full virtualization using the hardware capabilities of the host computer.

If an organization has already purchased the hardware or wants to repurpose older hardware as a virtualization host, it can download and run free software tools to check to see if its hardware supports hardware-assisted virtualization. For example, suppose a company is trying to use an older server as a virtualization host to run Microsoft Hyper-V. In that case, Microsoft has a free software tool that can determine if that server supports hardware-assisted virtualization and Microsoft Hyper-V.

Single Root Input/Output Virtualization

Single root input/output virtualization (SR-IOV) allows the PCI Express bus to be shared by multiple virtual machines. Devices plugged into the PCI Express bus, such as a graphics card or network card, have physical functions (PFs) shared with the virtualization host. Virtual machines map to virtual functions (VFs) that share the PFs of the device.

SR-IOV provides a PCI Express Requester ID for each PF and VF. This allows different access requests to be identified so that access can be managed for the resource. SR-IOV provides for the sharing of PCI Express resources without having to go through the virtualization stack. This dramatically improves performance and reduces overhead.

BIOS

The Basic Input/Output System (BIOS) is software residing on a ROM chip or a flash memory chip installed from the manufacturer. The system mainboard or motherboard has a system BIOS, and some advanced components such as RAID controllers and HBAs have their own BIOSs as well.

The system BIOS determines which features a computer supports without having to access any additional software that is loaded on the computer. For example, the system BIOS can contain the software needed to control the keyboard, the display settings, disk drives, USB settings, power options, and multiple other options. The system BIOS allows a computer to boot itself and is available even if the hard disks in the computer fail or are corrupted, because it is self-contained on the chip.

So what does the BIOS have to do with virtualization? The system BIOS plays a key role when enabling virtualization on a host computer. In order for a modern computer to act as a host and have the ability to host guest virtual machines, modern operating systems rely on the system BIOS to support hardware-assisted virtualization. Some older computers do not have this feature available in the system BIOS. Other computers might need a firmware update for the system BIOS before the feature can be enabled. However, most of the newer servers from mainstream manufacturers, including the latest desktop computers, support this feature.

With the advancement in virtualization and desktop computers, it is no longer a requirement to have a host machine running server-class hardware. Much of the desktop hardware now natively supports hardware-assisted virtualization.

A BIOS has several limitations that necessitated its eventual replacement with UEFI, discussed next. A BIOS is limited to 16-bit processing and 1MB of addressable memory. The BIOS can only boot to drives that are 2.1TB or less due to limitations in the master boot record (MBR).

UEFI

The Unified Extensible Firmware Interface (UEFI) is a replacement for BIOS that was introduced in 2007. UEFI is supported on Windows Vista SP1 and newer Windows operating systems, as well as most Linux versions, including Ubuntu, Fedora, Red Hat Enterprise, CentOS, and OpenSUSE.

UEFI addresses the limitations in BIOS by allowing both 32-bit and 64-bit processing, which can significantly improve system boot times. It also allows for more than 1MB of addressable memory during the boot process when the process is in real mode. UEFI supports hard drives larger than 2.1TB and the GUID Partition Table (GPT) instead of the MBR. UEFI also supports secure boot, a technology that performs OS integrity checking. This helps prevent rootkits from starting up a modified version of the OS.

 EXAM TIP UEFI can emulate BIOS for boot disks and other media if necessary.

Firmware Configurations

Firmware is a set of instructions that are programmed for a specific hardware device. The firmware tells the hardware device how to communicate with the computer system. Firmware upgrades can be performed on many devices, including motherboards, network cards, and hard drives. Firmware upgrades are generally carried out so that the hardware can support new features and functionality. For example, you might do a firmware upgrade on a network card so that the card is supported in a new operating system.

In some cases, it might be necessary to do a firmware upgrade to a computer's BIOS for it to support hardware-assisted virtualization. This would generally be done on older hardware, as most new hardware purchased today already supports hardware-assisted virtualization. Motherboard manufacturers place firmware updates and the software needed to update the BIOS firmware on their websites for customers to download.

Hyperconverged Systems and Infrastructure

Hyperconverged infrastructure (HCI) is a virtualization effort to reduce complexity, improve flexibility, and improve the manageability of systems. HCI operates by combining the compute, storage, graphics, and networking hardware into a single system compared with virtualization that uses dedicated hardware for compute, networking, or storage functions, otherwise known as converged infrastructure. HCI reduces complexity because converged infrastructure can be challenging to configure. Converged infrastructure components are sometimes only compatible with equipment from a select few vendors. Upgrading such equipment often involves upgrading several other connected systems as well. All too often, a single system can hold back an entire upgrade because newer technologies on the compute or storage side do not support technologies of other parts of the infrastructure.

HCI can reduce the need for multiple teams to support the virtualization solution, reducing the number of people necessary to manage the system, and improving communication because team members are working from the same frame of reference. Converged infrastructure may require the efforts of a storage team to manage the SAN, a network infrastructure team to manage network connectivity, a server team to manage the server hardware, and a virtualization team to handle the host and VMs. Conversely, HCI can be managed by a more generalist team, rather than multiple teams of specialists.

HCI can operate off more generic hardware because complex hardware configurations are instead performed within software. This software also allows for resources to be shared more easily across the HCI. Virtualization software in HCI combines the underlying hardware resources such as storage, compute, networking, or graphics hardware into easy-to-manage pools that can be easily allocated to virtual machines.

VM Sizing Considerations

Now that you understand the prerequisites to creating a host machine, you need to know how to properly size a host machine. Host machines may be physical servers located in an organization's data center, or they could be cloud hypervisors that the organization rents from a cloud vendor. Ensuring that the host machine can support at least the minimum number of guest virtual machines that the organization is trying to run is a critical step in creating a successful virtualization environment.

One of the many benefits of virtualization is the ability to provision virtual machines on the fly as the organization's demands grow, making the purchase of additional hardware unnecessary. Suppose the host computer is not sized correctly. In that case, however, it is not possible to add virtual machines without adding compute resources to the host computer or purchasing additional resources from a cloud vendor.

In this section, we will look at some of the primary resources assigned to virtual machines. Storage was already covered in earlier chapters, but this section covers the CPU, GPU, memory, and NIC.

CPU

The central processing unit (CPU) is the device in a computer system that performs the mathematical operations specified in computer code. When you break down computer operations to their most basic form, it is just math. The CPU, sometimes just referred to as the processor, is designed to perform such math quickly and efficiently. The first step to sizing the CPU on a host machine is purchasing the correct type and number of CPUs. Both AMD (AMD-V) and Intel (Intel VT) support virtualization, so the manufacturer is not as critical as the number of CPU cores and the CPUs' speed. A multicore processor is a single physical CPU with two or more independent CPUs called cores.

Once the organization has defined the host computer processor, it needs to evaluate how to assign those CPU resources to the guest virtual machines. Not surprisingly, virtual machines use virtual CPUs (vCPUs), which can be added to a virtual machine when it is created. The number of vCPUs that the company should add is dependent on a number of factors, but it is possible to assign multiple vCPUs to a single virtual machine.

EXAM TIP Some products are licensed based on the number of CPUs, cores, or vCPUs. It is important to know how many CPUs you are licensed for when assigning resources so that you do not violate your license or cause a program to fail activation checks.

Simultaneous Multithreading

Simultaneous multithreading (SMT) is a technology that allows for a processor core to work on multiple independent threads at the same time. These threads do not have to be related to one another. Processors with SMT are capable of fetching instructions from multiple threads in a single CPU cycle. The CPU accomplishes SMT by creating multiple logical cores from its physical cores.

SMT allows for a CPU to better use its resources and reduce overall power consumption compared with those that do not support SMT. SMT was introduced with the Pentium 4 in 2002, and today, nearly all modern processors are equipped with SMT.

SMT increases the system's ability to run parallel processes, but whether performance increases using hyperthreading depends upon the application's ability to execute multiple steps on processors in parallel. SMT is not the same as having multiple cores in a CPU because SMT shares the CPU's pipeline, cache, and system bus interface instead of dedicating cache and interfaces to distinct cores.

SMT is beneficial in virtualization, allowing for higher oversubscription ratios of vCPUs to physical CPUs, discussed later in this chapter. Hypervisors with only a few processor cores will see the most significant advantage from SMT because they are likely running out of available processors to allocate to virtual machines.

Hyperthreading

Hyperthreading is a proprietary SMT technology for Intel CPUs. Hyperthreading creates two logical CPU cores for each physical CPU core that supports hyperthreading. It was introduced in 2002 with the Xeon server and Pentium 4 desktop processors. Hyperthreading requires operating system support for symmetric multiprocessing (SMP), a feature that all current operating systems support.

Clock Speed

Clock speed, also known as clock rate, is the measurement of how many cycles per second the CPU operates at. Clock speed is measured in hertz (Hz), with modern processors running in the billions of cycles per second, measured in gigahertz (GHz). The computer motherboard has a front-side bus (FSB) speed that is also measured in Hz. The processor, memory, and other components on the motherboard will run at some multiplier of this. The CPU clock speed will be a multiple of the FSB speed. In Figure 5-4, you can see the results of the CPU-Z tool for an AMD Ryzen 7 3800X. The FSB bus speed is just labeled as bus speed in CPU-Z. It is operating at 99.19 MHz. The CPU is running at 41 times the FSB speed, so its clock speed is 4066.76 MHz, or 4.06 GHz.

Figure 5-4
Processor
specifications as
shown in CPU-Z

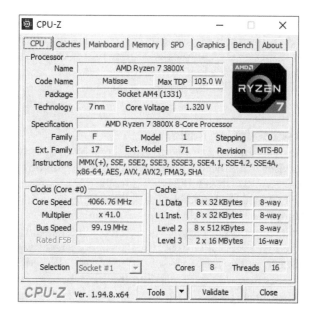

Clock speed is important because it determines how much work the processor can perform in a given amount of time. The CPU performs one or more instructions in each clock cycle. Some operations will be more efficient than others, depending on how capable the processor is at breaking the operations down into steps and performing them with its available resources. Processors use instruction pipelines to streamline this process by defining common processor workflows.

Clock Speed vs. Cores

As a general virtualization rule, more cores are usually better than higher processor clock speeds. It is typically better to invest in more cores with more cache than faster CPU speed because this will allow computing resources to be distributed more effectively.

For example, imagine that you are setting up a new virtualization host and trying to choose the best processor for the workload between two alternatives. The first option is to put two 6-core processors running at 2.6 GHz into the host. The second option is to equip it with two 4-core processors running at 3.2 GHz. Between these two choices, the system with two 6-core processors is the better choice. This is because, with virtualization, the company can spread the virtual machine load across more CPU cores, which translates into faster and more consistent virtual machine performance. Also, if you do the math, two 6-core processors equal 12 cores running at 2.6 GHz, equaling 31.2 GHz of total processing power. In comparison, two 4-core processors equal 8 cores running at 3.2 GHz, equaling 25.6 GHz. However, even if the math favored the higher speed over cores, the best choice is still additional cores.

VT-x

VT-x is a set of instructions performing virtualization functions that are built into the CPU. VT-x decreases the complexity of hypervisors that run on top of supported VT-x hardware. In fact, VT-x is a requirement of most modern hypervisors. VT-x also improves the speed of hypervisor functions because they can be performed in hardware rather than software.

CPU Oversubscription Ratio

It is possible to assign more vCPUs to virtual machines than available physical CPU cores in the hypervisor in a process known as oversubscription or overcommitment. However, assigning more vCPUs than CPU cores must be done with care. Before undertaking such a move, the technicians should evaluate all the virtual machines' workload on the server and whether or not that workload is processor intensive.

Virtual machines often require more CPU when starting up or when loading processes for the first time. CPU usage usually then decreases significantly, with occasional increases due to utilization. Oversubscription can allow the hypervisor to host more virtual machines than otherwise possible and make better use of the available processors. The hypervisor manages CPU requests, providing each virtual machine with the CPU the resources it needs up to its max.

However, oversubscription can result in contention for CPU resources when multiple machines attempt to utilize all their vCPUs at the same time. This results in reduced performance for the virtual machines and the applications that run on them. For this reason, it is important to understand what a reasonable oversubscription ratio is.

 TIP Hypervisors can be configured to start virtual machines with a delay so that they do not all start at the same time or resume from a saved state at the same time.

It is generally safe to maintain an oversubscription ratio of 5:1, with five vCPUs for each physical CPU, so a server with four physical CPU cores could assign up to 20 vCPUs. You may be able to increase this, especially for hosts with a large number of rarely used virtual machines. Monitor resources closely when using an oversubscription ratio of 6:1 to 7:1 because it is easy to produce a situation where virtual machines are waiting for available CPU cycles.

Most of the time, it is unsafe to assign more than seven vCPUs for every CPU core on the server. However, this number may vary based on virtual machine vCPU utilization, so evaluating the environment and the goal of that environment is key.

Another important consideration is that you should not allocate more vCPUs to an individual virtual machine than you have physical cores in the hypervisor. This is because the virtual machine may try to use all assigned vCPUs. If the VM tries to use more cores than are available at once, some processes that were meant to be in parallel will be serialized because there will never be enough CPUs available to satisfy the demand. This will result in less-than-ideal performance. For example, if a hypervisor has four CPUs with 4 cores each, it has 16 cores. Assign no more than 16 cores to an individual virtual machine on the host, even if your oversubscription ratio is below the recommended 5:1 ratio.

It is best to allocate one vCPU to a machine and then monitor performance, adding additional vCPUs as needed. When a virtual machine attempts to use a vCPU, the hypervisor must wait for the physical CPU associated with that vCPU to become available. The virtual machine believes that vCPU to be idle and will attempt to spread the load around if the application is configured for multiprocessing, but this can have an adverse impact on virtual machine performance if the physical CPU has a large number of processes in the queue. Furthermore, even idle processors place some load on the hypervisor from host management processes, so it is best to not provision more than will be necessary.

Monitor hypervisor metrics to determine if oversubscription bottlenecks are occurring. The most important metric to watch is the CPU-ready metric. CPU ready measures the amount of time a virtual machine has to wait for physical CPU cycles to become available. It is also important to monitor CPU utilization within each virtual machine and on the host. High CPU utilization might indicate the need for additional vCPUs to spread the load. High host CPU utilization could indicate that virtual machines are not properly balanced across hosts. If one host has high CPU utilization and others have available resources, it may be best to move one or more virtual machines to another host to relieve the burden on the overtaxed host. Host resources could also be expanded for physical hosts or requested for those provisioned in the cloud.

For example, a heavily used Microsoft SQL server will be a very processor-intensive virtual machine. In that scenario, an organization would want a one-to-one CPU-to-vCPU assignment. VMware, Hyper-V, and Citrix all have calculators available to help determine exactly how to distribute vCPUs based on best practices for that particular virtualization product. Table 5-2 displays the maximum number of logical CPUs and virtual CPUs for some of the virtualization products currently available.

GPU

The graphics processing unit (GPU) is the device in a computer system that performs the mathematical operations associated with displaying content on the screen. GPUs process the pixels that fill your screen, but they also do many other computations to determine

Component	VMware ESXi 6.5	Hyper-V (Server 2016) Gen 2	XenServer 7.0
Logical CPUs per host	576	512	288
Virtual CPUs per host	4096	2048	2048
RAM per host	12TB	24TB	5TB
Virtual machines per host	1024	1024	1000
Network cards per host	128	No limits imposed by Hyper-V	512

Table 5-2   Virtualization Host Maximum Resources

what should be displayed on the screen. These computations include determining texture mappings, rendering shapes, and determining the physics for games and other applications. The GPU may be bundled with a motherboard, or it can exist on a dedicated graphics card. Multiple graphics cards may be linked together so that the combined power of multiple GPUs can be applied to workloads.

GPUs started out as something only needed to play video games, but they have evolved to become a far more essential part of the modern computing platform. In the beginning, GPUs were just CPUs that were put onto a video card to improve video performance. However, the specific requirements for graphics processing led to a divergence in GPU architecture. GPUs need to break down problems, not into a couple or a dozen parallel tasks, but rather into thousands or millions of tasks. For this reason, GPUs are designed with hundreds or thousands of cores and have pipelines optimized for such processing. This makes them much more efficient at completing such tasks.

The GPU role was greatly expanded with the development of the Compute Unified Device Architecture (CUDA), which allows developers to create applications that take advantage of the GPU architecture to perform specialized tasks that would be overly burdensome for a CPU. Some workloads that utilize CUDA include blockchain, cryptocurrency mining, deep learning, cryptography, genomics research, artificial intelligence, climate modeling, data analytics, scientific visualization, physics, neuroscience, seismic prediction, augmented reality, and virtual reality. Therefore, GPU selection for the host should be based on the type of workloads that will be performed on the VMs it will house. It is also essential to know which operating systems the VMs on the host will be running. Some GPUs may support Linux VMs, but not Windows, and vice versa.

Once the technician has defined the GPUs for the host computer, he or she needs to evaluate how to assign those GPU resources to the guest virtual machines. There are three options for allocating GPU resources, as follows:

- Sharing the GPU among multiple VMs
- Dedicating the GPU to a single VM
- Dedicating multiple GPUs to a single VM

Virtual/Shared

The GPU can be virtualized so that it can be shared among multiple virtual machines on the host. The physical GPU is divided into multiple logical GPUs, called virtual GPUs (vGPUs), which can be added to a virtual machine. vCPUs are commonly used when provisioning virtual desktops. Standard enterprise desktops do not need a lot of processing power. Still, it is more efficient to allocate a portion of the GPU to the virtual desktop than to have graphics tasks processed by the vCPU.

When a VM using a vGPU starts up, the host starts a corresponding process for it on the host system. This process communicates with the graphics driver running within the VM and then sends the commands to the host's coordinating service to be delivered to the GPU. The coordinating service may juggle requests from multiple VMs concurrently, so some requests may have to wait for available GPU cycles. Assigning more vGPUs than the number of GPUs in a machine is called GPU oversubscription.

GPU Oversubscription Ratio

Virtualization allows for more vGPUs to be assigned to virtual machines than available physical GPU cores in the hypervisor in a process known as oversubscription. Oversubscription can enable the hypervisor to host more virtual machines than otherwise possible and make better use of the available graphics processors. The hypervisor manages GPU requests, providing each virtual machine with the GPU resources it needs up to its max.

Assigning more vGPUs than GPU cores must be done with care. Too much oversubscription can result in contention for GPU resources. This results in reduced performance for the virtual machines and the applications that run on them. For this reason, it is crucial to understand what a reasonable oversubscription ratio is.

There is no standard oversubscription ratio for GPU. The ratio depends on the GPU model, so you will need to determine the maximum vGPUs supported for the GPUs you are considering. For example, the Nvidia Tesla M60 can support 8 vGPUs; however, the Nvidia GRID K100 supports 32 vGPUs.

Pass-through

GPU pass-through is used when one or more GPUs are dedicated to a single VM. Pass-through allows the VM to address the GPU directly without having to go through the hypervisor stack. This significantly improves performance for the application. Pass-through is used for very GPU-intensive workloads such as deep learning, artificial intelligence, and data analytics.

Memory

After a company has determined how many and what type of CPUs and GPUs they will purchase for the virtualization host, the next step is to plan the amount of random-access memory (RAM) that the host machine will need. Planning the amount of memory required on a host machine is quite different from planning the number of CPUs. Planning for memory is critical. The more RAM and the faster the RAM speed, the better for a virtualization host.

Hypervisors have a virtual allocation table (VAT) that uses methods such as nested page tables or shadow page to map virtual memory to that of the host. Some virtualization platforms allow for adjusting virtual machine memory on the fly, essentially allowing one virtual machine to borrow memory from another virtual machine without shutting down the system. Each of the virtualization products supports virtual machine memory allocation differently, but the one consistent thing is that more memory on the host machine is always better. The IT administrator's job is to maximize the cost savings of virtualization and the value it brings to the organization.

Careful planning is required to provide enough memory on the host machine to dynamically provision virtual machines as the organization's needs grow and, at the same time, to make the most cost-efficient choices. Table 5-2, shown earlier, includes the maximum amount of memory allowed on a host machine for some of the virtualization products currently available.

Memory Ballooning

Virtual machines often require more memory when starting up or when loading processes for the first time. Memory usage often then decreases significantly, with occasional increases due to utilization. However, when oversubscription ratios are high, there might not be enough memory to start new machines.

Memory ballooning comes into play when there are not enough resources available to handle new memory requests from virtual machines. Ballooning requests memory resources from other virtual machines. These virtual machines decide which processes they can swap out to free up space, and then they loan those memory pages to the hypervisor. The hypervisor places all the memory pages lent to it into a balloon that is temporarily allocated to a machine that urgently needs it.

The beauty of ballooning is that the hypervisor does not need to seize the memory, and the virtual machine can make an intelligent decision about which memory to swap out to have the least impact on the virtual machine. The ballooning process runs as a standard Windows process in the VM guest. As it requests memory, Windows allocates pages to it as it would any other process. The hypervisor then takes those pages and makes them available to others. The virtual machine believes the memory is in use by the ballooning process until the ballooning process releases it back to the virtual machine.

Memory Bursting

Virtual machines can be configured with a minimum and a maximum memory size in a technique known as dynamic memory. The machine can request up to the max amount of memory, and the hypervisor will allocate pages to the virtual machine. The burst memory is the maximum amount of memory that the virtual machine can utilize. When configuring burst values, consider how much the machine will use at peak levels and then add a buffer to that value for the burst/max memory.

 EXAM TIP Once a virtual machine bursts, it may keep the additional memory for some time even after actual utilization has dropped back to normal levels. It does not release the memory back immediately.

Transparent Page Sharing

Transparent page sharing is a technology that deduplicates hypervisor memory allocated to virtual machines. Several virtual machines may load the same data into memory, especially when running the same application. In a virtual desktop infrastructure (VDI), this is even more prevalent, with users commonly running office productivity, web browsing, and other apps on their virtual desktops. Operating systems also load many processes into memory that may be deduplicated.

Transparent page sharing maps duplicate pages to a single page or fixed block of memory. When transparent page sharing finds a duplicate, the memory references for the pages assigned to virtual machines are mapped to a single page on the hypervisor so that only one copy is retained.

Memory Compression

When memory is entirely consumed, operating systems are configured to dump data from memory into a page file. The page file is located on disk and is much slower to access than memory. Hypervisors can be configured to compress memory when available memory is low rather than page that memory. This consumes CPU resources to perform the compression and decompression, but it reduces memory read and write I/O, since the data does not have to be read from disk.

Memory Oversubscription Ratio

Virtual machines can be configured with a minimum and a maximum memory size. The machine can request up to the max amount of memory, and the hypervisor will allocate pages to the virtual machine. When the memory is not needed anymore, the hypervisor reclaims it for use on other virtual machines. In this way, the total maximum amount of memory configured for virtual machines can exceed the available physical memory, known as memory oversubscription. This works as long as the actual consumption remains lower than physical memory. Other technologies, such as memory compression and transparent page sharing, can further reduce memory consumption, allowing for more oversubscription.

Oversubscription can allow the hypervisor to host more virtual machines than otherwise possible and make better use of the available memory. However, oversubscription ratios are much lower for memory than they are for CPU.

It is generally safe to maintain an oversubscription ratio of 1.25:1, with 125 percent of physical memory allocated to virtual machines. Thus, a server with 256GB of memory could assign up to 320GB of memory to virtual machines. You may be able to increase this comfortably to 1.5:1, in particular for hosts that have a significant number of similar virtual machines, as transparent page sharing will reduce actual memory consumption. A 1.5:1 oversubscription ratio would allow for 384GB of memory to be allocated to virtual machines in a host that has 256GB of physical memory. Monitor resources closely when using an oversubscription ratio higher than 1.25:1. In such cases, it can be easy to produce a situation where virtual machines consume all available physical memory and the host is forced to page memory to disk.

Most of the time, it is unsafe to operate at an oversubscription ratio above 1.5:1. Be extremely careful if you operate at this level and ensure that memory metrics are configured with alerts so that administrators are aware when memory thresholds are reached. Set alerting thresholds below the level where paging will occur to avoid performance issues, and adjust virtual machine memory settings accordingly.

CAUTION Be sure to have some reserve memory when oversubscribing memory because virtual machines or applications may crash if they run out of memory.

NIC

In addition to choosing CPU, GPU, and memory, choosing the type of network interface card (NIC) to use is just as important when planning the hardware for a virtualization host. Choosing the correct network configuration and type of card is critical to a virtual environment's success because, without reliable network connectivity, VMs will not be accessible or might be less available. Network latency can diminish the speed of a virtual environment, so the organization needs to carefully plan for which features its network cards on the host computer need to support.

The first step when planning the NICs for the host computer is to understand the physical aspects of the network. This includes how the host will be connected to other resources and how users will connect to it. Next, one should consider which features will provide the required network performance for the desired workloads.

Performance Considerations

Server-class NICs provide the best possible network performance for virtualization. It is also necessary to verify that the source and destination NIC infrastructure does not introduce a bottleneck. For example, if the organization is using a 10 Gbps NIC to connect to a 10 Gbps port on a switch, it must make sure that all the patch cables support 10 Gbps speeds and that the switch is configured to use 10 Gbps and is not hardcoded to use 1 Gbps speeds. The network can only be as fast as the slowest link, so having a misconfigured switch or a bad cable can cause a bottleneck and slower performance.

There are some other key features to consider when purchasing NICs for the virtualization host computer. Table 5-3 lists those features and gives a brief description of each.

Feature	Description
Checksum Offload	Offloads the process of TCP packets to the network controller from the CPU
TCP Segmentation Offload (TSO)	Converts large chunks of data into smaller packets to be transmitted through the network
64-Bit Direct Memory Access (DMA) Addresses	Permits high-throughput and low-latency networking
Jumbo Frames (JF)	Extends Ethernet to 9000 bytes, allowing for less packet overhead on the server and fewer server interrupts
Large Receive Off-Load (LRO)	Increases inbound throughput by reducing CPU overhead, aggregating multiple incoming packets from a single stream into a larger buffer

Table 5-3 NIC Hardware Features

NIC Oversubscription Ratio

Multiple virtual machines can share the same NIC in a similar fashion to the sharing of other resources, such as GPU, CPU, or memory. Assigning more virtual network resources than physical network resources available is NIC oversubscription.

As with other resources, it is important to understand the workload of the systems that you will be attaching to each physical NIC. Some types of systems utilize more network traffic than others. For example, a file server or e-mail server might consume a significant portion of a NIC's bandwidth. In contrast, a certificate server might use only a small percentage.

Network oversubscription ratios are usually relatively high. Systems typically have lower utilization of network resources than they do for CPU, GPU, or memory. It is generally safe to maintain an oversubscription ratio of 10:1, but as with other resources, pay attention to network utilization metrics and tweak this if utilization stays consistently high so that you can avoid contention.

Exercise 5-1: Creating a Virtual Switch in Hyper-V

In this exercise, we will create a virtual switch from a physical NIC to be used for Hyper-V on Windows 10 Enterprise, Pro, or Education edition. To follow these steps, you must have the Hyper-V installed. You can install it by opening PowerShell as administrator and then running the following command:

```
Enable-WindowsOptionalFeature -Online -FeatureName Microsoft-Hyper-V -All
```

Follow along with these steps to create a new virtual switch in Hyper-V.

1. Open the Hyper-V Manager tool.

2. Click Virtual Switch Manager in the Actions pane on the right side of the Hyper-V Manager.

3. Select External under Create Virtual Switch on the right pane of the window and then click Create Virtual Switch. This will create a virtual switch that is mapped to a physical adapter on the host, allowing the host to communicate with the network outside of the host. This is shown in the following illustration. The internal or private virtual switches can be used for traffic that will not leave the host, such as traffic between VMs on the host. The internal switch allows VMs on the host to communicate, and the host can communicate with them. The private switch is the same as the internal switch, except that the host cannot communicate with the VMs on the private switch.

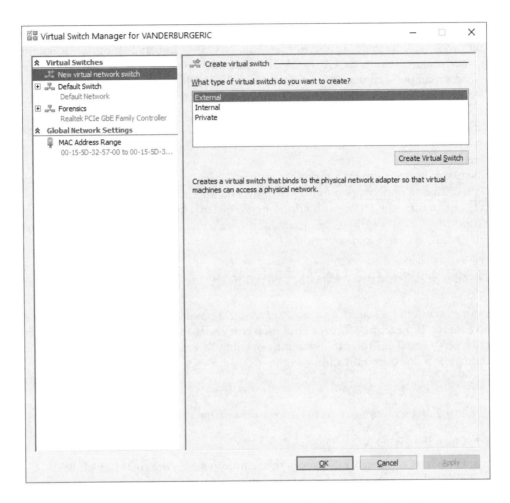

4. Give the switch a name. In this example, we will call it Cloud Switch.

5. Next, map this virtual switch to a physical NIC in the host. In this example, a Realtek PCIe GbE Family Controller NIC was selected.

6. If this is the only NIC in your machine, leave "Allow management operating system to share this network adapter" checked. However, uncheck this if you will dedicate this NIC to virtual machines. The following illustration shows the cloud switch on a dedicated NIC, so the option is unchecked. Click OK when you have finished setting these options, and the virtual switch will be created.

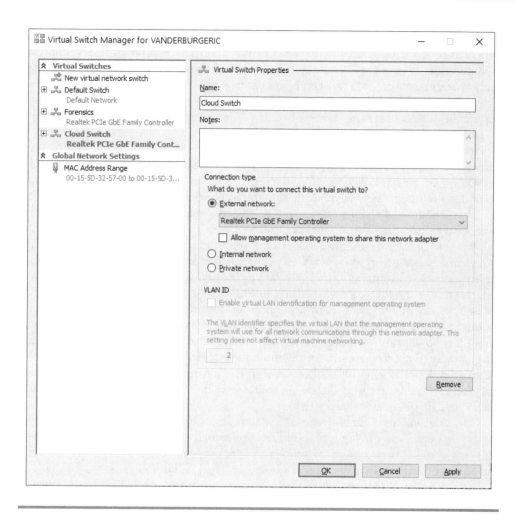

Virtual Machine

After the virtualization host computer has been carefully planned and designed, it is ready to support guest virtual machines. However, there is just as much planning, if not more, that needs to go into configuring the virtual machines. With virtualization comes the ability to maximize the physical server and no longer have "unused" resources. While this is a considerable advantage and cost savings to an organization, it also requires more planning than the one-to-one way of thinking before virtualization.

Before virtualization, IT administrators were confined to the physical resources available on the server running a particular application. With virtualization, an IT administrator can now add compute resources to a virtual machine without purchasing additional hardware, as long as the virtualization host computer has been designed with this in mind.

The concept of a virtual machine is sometimes tricky to grasp for those new to the term. Think of a virtual machine in the same way you think of a physical server hosting an application. A virtual machine emulates a physical computer, with the only difference being that its resources are managed by a hypervisor that translates resource requests to the underlying physical hardware. You can think of a virtual machine as a portable file that can be moved, copied, and reassigned to a different virtualization host with minimal administration.

Virtualization separates the physical hardware from the virtual hardware running on a virtual machine, so virtual machines can be moved to another hardware platform easily. Physical servers are typically on a refresh cycle of several years. Every few years, the IT team would have to build a new server, configure the applications, and migrate software. With virtualization, the underlying hardware can be upgraded while the virtual machines stay the same. This reduces the IT maintenance burden.

With full virtualization, guest operating systems are unaware that they are running in a virtual environment as opposed to paravirtualization, a virtualization method that presents a more customized virtual interface to host system hardware. Applications and software can be installed on a virtual machine as if it were a physical server. Isolation of applications is just one of the many advantages of running a virtual environment. Applications can be installed on separate virtual machines, which provides complete isolation from other applications running on the host computer or another virtual machine. This is a great way to test new applications without interfering with existing applications or to create a development environment that is segmented from the production environment. Isolation can also be performed through containers rather than allocating an entire VM. Containers are discussed in Chapter 7.

Virtualization is used for both servers and desktops. Organizations will virtualize desktops so that end users can log into their desktop remotely. Desktops are maintained centrally in a cloud or data center environment, where they can be more effectively managed and secured. Desktop virtualization is known as virtual desktop infrastructure (VDI).

The remainder of this section explains the compute resources that make up a virtual machine and how to manage and plan for those resources in a virtual environment.

Virtual Disks

Just like a physical server, a virtual machine needs to have a place to install an operating system and applications and to store files and folders. Simply put, a virtual disk is a file that represents a physical disk drive to the virtual machine. VMware virtual machine disks (VMDKs) have an extension of .vmdk, while Hyper-V virtual hard disks (VHDs) have an extension of .vhdx.

A virtual disk file resides on the host computer and is accessed by the guest virtual machine. It contains the same properties and features of a physical drive, including disk partitions, a file system, and files and folders.

When creating a virtual disk, you need to make a few decisions, including the type of disk, the name and location of the disk, and the disk's size. Each of the significant virtualization manufacturers uses different terminology to describe virtual disk configurations. For example, if you are using Microsoft Hyper-V, you would have the option of making a dynamically expanding virtual disk, a fixed virtual disk, or a differencing virtual disk. If you are creating a fixed-size disk, you will specify the disk's size when it is created. If you create a dynamically expanding virtual disk, the disk starts at the minimum size required to hold the data and adds storage as needed.

Differencing virtual disks are used in parent-child virtual disks, where a parent virtual disk holds files inherited by its children. For example, five Windows 10 machines could all share a parent virtual disk for the operating system, while user profile directories and applications would reside on the child disks. This results in lower disk consumption and easier updating.

On the other hand, if you are creating a virtual disk in VMware ESXi, you have the option of creating a thick disk or a thin disk. A thick disk is similar to a fixed disk in Microsoft Hyper-V in that the size is specified and allocated during the creation of the virtual disk. A thin disk is similar to a dynamically expanding disk in Microsoft Hyper-V in that the disk starts out small and adds space as required by the virtual machine.

While the different virtualization vendors use different terms to define their virtual disks, the concepts are similar. Whether you are using Hyper-V, ESXi, or XenServer, you still need to decide which type of disk to use for which application. If you are concerned about disk space, then using a thin disk or dynamically expanding disk would be the best option. If disk size is not a concern, then you could use a fixed-size or thick disk.

Virtual disks also use instruction sets and queueing techniques just like physical disks, and virtual disks must be created using a specific virtual disk interface such as IDE or SCSI. Some virtual machine types can only boot from a virtual IDE drive, while others, such as those requiring secure boot, require a SCSI boot drive. Table 5-4 shows the maximum number of virtual IDE and SCSI disks available for various types of virtual machines. Please note that XenServer does not emulate SCSI or IDE and uses a unique disk format with a maximum of 16 disks.

vNIC

Configuring and planning the virtual network interface cards are just as important as planning the virtual disk configuration. The network interface card in a computer is a device that allows a physical computer to interact with other virtual machines and devices on the network. Likewise, a virtual NIC (vNIC) is associated with a physical NIC

Components (per virtual machine)	VMware ESXi	Microsoft Hyper-V	Citrix Hypervisor
Memory	6TB	12TB	1.5TB
Virtual CPUs	768	512	32
Virtual IDE hard disks	4	4	255
Virtual SCSI disks	256	256	255
Virtual NICs	10	12	7
Virtual GPUs	16	12	8

Table 5-4 Virtual Machine Limits

and allows a virtual machine to communicate on the network. Proper configuration of the vNIC and network settings is a crucial component to minimizing bottlenecks in the virtual environment.

A vNIC does not have any physical components; it is a software component made up of software drivers that mimic a physical NIC. A vNIC allows an organization to change some of the properties of the vNIC, including MAC address settings, network connections, and VLAN ID. This allows for greater control over the vNIC from within the hypervisor software. Once the settings are configured and the vNIC is installed on the virtual machine, it functions like a physical NIC installed on a physical server.

After attaching a vNIC to a virtual machine, you can add the vNIC to a virtual network. A virtual network is a group of network devices configured to access local or external network resources and consists of virtual network links. In effect, a virtual network is a network where traffic between the virtual servers is routed using virtual switches (vSwitches) and virtual routers.

A virtual router is a software-based router that allows a virtualization host to act as a hardware router over the network. This is required if you wish to enable inter-VLAN communication without a hardware router. A virtual network allows the virtual machine to interact with the rest of the LAN.

In addition to configuring a vSwitch, you may configure bridged networking, which allows the virtual machine to communicate with the outside world using the physical NIC so it can appear as a normal host to the rest of the network.

You need to consider some options when configuring a virtual machine to communicate with the rest of the LAN. Sometimes an organization may want to prevent a virtual machine from communicating with devices on the LAN, in which case you can isolate the virtual machine on a private network so that it can communicate only with other virtual machines on the same host. Virtual machine isolation with a private network is common when setting up a test lab from cloned virtual machines. The cloned machines would conflict with existing production machines if they could talk on the network, so they are isolated to only talk among themselves on a private network. Also, clustered virtual machines use private networks for heartbeat connections.

In a different scenario, an organization might want to bridge the connection between its virtual machine and the LAN used by the host computer so that the virtual machine can communicate with devices that are external to the host computer. Determining how the vNIC and virtual machine use virtual networks is an essential piece of virtualization. Remember, one of the many benefits of virtualization is the ability to isolate applications for testing and deployment, but that is only possible if the virtual network and vNIC are correctly configured.

After the virtual machine's operating system recognizes and installs the vNIC, it can be configured just like a physical NIC. It is possible to set the IP address, DNS servers, default gateway, subnet mask, and link speed. The actual network configuration of the vNIC is identical to that of a physical network adapter. So the virtual machine connects to the network in the same manner that a physical device would that has the same IP address and subnet mask configuration. A virtual machine can be configured to use one or more virtual Ethernet adapters, allowing each adapter to have its own MAC and IP address. Table 5-4, shown earlier, includes the maximum number of vNICs available on various types of virtual machines.

Virtual Switches

Once the organization has created and added a vNIC to its virtual machine, the next step in the process is to assign a vSwitch to the machine so that it can communicate with other network devices. Similar to a physical switch, a vSwitch makes it possible to connect other network devices together.

A vSwitch controls how the network traffic flows between the virtual machines and the host computer, as well as how network traffic flows between the virtual machine and other network devices in the organization. Virtual switches also allow the organization to isolate network traffic to its virtual machines. A vSwitch can provide some of the same security features that a physical switch provides, including policy enforcement, isolation, traffic shaping, and simplified troubleshooting.

A vSwitch can support VLANs and is compatible with standard VLAN implementations. However, a vSwitch cannot be attached to another vSwitch; instead, more ports can be added to the existing switch.

An organization can create different types of vSwitches to control network connectivity to a virtual machine. An external vSwitch allows the virtual machine to communicate with other virtual machines on the same host and with other network devices located outside the host computer. An internal vSwitch allows the virtual machines and the host to communicate with each other, but the virtual machine is unable to communicate with network devices located outside the host computer.

 EXAM TIP   You need to understand how to configure a vSwitch so that a virtual machine can communicate with the correct network devices.

Planning the vSwitch configuration is extremely important to an organization's virtualization design. It is equally important for the organization to make sure the vSwitch that the virtual machine uses to communicate is configured correctly. Proper design of the vSwitch environment is critical to the virtual machine being able to communicate to the correct part of the network.

Memory

Managing memory on a virtual machine is different than managing memory on a physical server. When dealing with a physical server, an organization has to decide at the time of purchase how much memory a server needs to have. When building or deploying a virtual machine, the organization can change the memory on the fly as needed. Also, a virtual machine only consumes memory if that virtual machine is running, so memory can be freed up by shutting down less important virtual machines if necessary.

Managing virtual machine memory is easier and allows the organization to maximize its resources for that virtual machine. It can set the initial size of the virtual machine's memory and change that setting after the virtual machine has been created and is operational. For example, the organization may have a virtual machine running file and print services and may be uncertain what the memory requirements ultimately will be. In this instance, it can configure a low amount of memory to start and then monitor the virtual machine to determine its memory utilization. If the virtual machine reaches 90 to 100 percent utilization, the organization can easily increase the amount of memory without having to purchase additional hardware.

Keep in mind, however, that increasing virtual machine memory is only possible if there is additional memory available on the virtualization host computer. The host computer must also have enough physical memory available to start the virtual machine; if there is not enough available physical memory, the virtual machine will not be allowed to start. Earlier in this chapter, you learned how to plan memory allocation on the virtualization host; now you can see why planning the host computer resources is so important.

There are three things that you should consider when provisioning a virtual machine and assigning memory to it:

- **Operating system requirements**   Ensure that the amount of memory meets the minimum recommendations for the operating system that the virtual machine will be running.

- **Application requirements**   Consider the applications the virtual machine will be running. Applications that require a lot of memory on a physical server may also need a similar setup on a virtual machine.

- **Virtual machine neighbors**   Consider what other virtual machines are running on the host computer that will be competing with this virtual machine for memory resources and whether other applications are going to be running on the host computer that might need resources as well.

Resource contention is not typically a significant factor in a type 1 hypervisor, since best practice is not to run any additional software on the host computer. However, if additional applications are running on the host computer besides the hypervisor, you should consider their impact on resource contention with virtual machines when planning memory size. On a type 2 hypervisor, other applications would be running on the host computer. These applications require memory, so the memory necessary for those applications will need to be factored in when determining memory size for the virtual machine.

Memory can be assigned to a virtual machine in a couple of ways. One option is to configure a static amount of memory assigned to the virtual machine at all times. Static memory is a predefined amount of memory that is allocated to the virtual machine. If an organization uses this setting for all the virtual machines on a host computer, then the host computer must have at least enough physical memory to support those virtual machines.

A second option is to use dynamic memory, which allows a company to assign a minimum and maximum amount of memory to a virtual machine. With dynamic memory, a virtual machine consumes memory based on its current workload. Dynamic memory also allows for overcommitting the host computer's physical memory so that more virtual machines can be run on that host computer.

Dynamic memory can be enabled on a per-virtual-machine basis, targeting only those virtual machines that can benefit from it. One way for a company to determine if it should use static or dynamic memory is by considering the application the virtual machine will be running. For example, if the company has a virtual machine running an application that uses a fixed amount of memory, the better option is to use static memory and allocate precisely the amount of memory that the virtual machine needs. Managing virtual machine memory is a crucial component of the performance of the virtualization environment and thus needs to be carefully planned and executed. Table 5-4, shown earlier, lists the maximum amount of memory available for various types of virtual machines.

Storage Virtualization

Planning where to store the virtual disks and configuration files for the virtual machine is something that needs careful consideration. Storage virtualization groups multiple network storage devices into a single storage unit that can be managed from a central console and used by a virtual machine or host computer.

Storage virtualization usually occurs in a storage area network (SAN), where a high-speed collection of shared storage devices can be used. Managing storage devices can be a complex and tedious task for an administrator. Storage virtualization simplifies the administration of common storage tasks, such as archiving, recovery, backups, and storage configuration.

A virtualized storage environment has some distinct advantages over nonvirtualized storage. In a nonvirtualized storage environment, the host computers connect directly to the internal storage to the host or to an external array. In this scenario, the server takes complete ownership of the physical storage, with an entire disk tied to a single server.

Virtualized storage enables the use of shared storage devices. Virtualized storage addresses the challenge of a single server owning storage by allowing multiple host servers and virtual machines to simultaneously access storage. Shared storage can present storage to a host computer, and the host computer, in turn, can present the storage to the virtual machine. Multiple host computers can access the shared storage simultaneously, which allows the virtual machines to migrate between host computers. Virtualization software supports all the common storage interconnects for block-based storage, including Fibre Channel, iSCSI, Fibre Channel over Ethernet (FCoE), and direct-attached storage. The virtualization software provides an interface to simplify how the virtual machine accesses the storage. It also presents SCSI and IDE controllers to the virtual machines so that the operating system can recognize the storage. The virtual machine sees only a simple physical disk attached via the IDE or SCSI controller provided by the virtualization software.

Virtual storage offers the following advantages to a virtual machine:

- Ease of management
- Improved efficiency
- Support for a range of storage types that the native operating system might not support
- Flexible placement and migration

Suppose an organization uses Fibre Channel to connect to shared storage. In that case, it is taking advantage of N_Port ID Virtualization (NPIV), a technology that allows multiple host computers to share a single physical Fibre Channel port identification, or N_Port. This allows a single host bus adapter to register multiple worldwide names (WWNs) and N_Port identification numbers. Using NPIV, each host server can present a different WWN to the shared storage device, allowing each host computer to see its own storage.

In addition to storage virtualization, an organization might use clustered storage to provide increased performance, capacity, and reliability for the storage environment that the virtual machines access. Clustered storage combines multiple storage devices together to distribute the workload between storage devices and provide access to the virtual machine files, regardless of the physical location of the files.

Guest Tools

Guest tools are software additions added to a virtual machine after the operating system has been installed. They enhance a virtual machine's performance and improve the interaction between the virtual machine and the host computer. Guest tools also make it easier to manage a virtual machine by providing enhanced features, such as faster graphics performance, time synchronization between host and guest, increased network performance, and the ability to copy files between the virtual machine and the host computer. The guest tools are also responsible for integrating the drivers into the guest virtual machine operating system.

A guest virtual machine operating system can run without installing guest tools, but it loses important functionality and ease of administration without them. Installing the guest tools is easy and straightforward on all mainstream virtualization applications and is sometimes even built into the operating system. For example, a Windows Server 2019 virtual machine created using Microsoft Hyper-V has the virtual machine integration services already loaded. Most operating systems, including Microsoft Windows, Linux, Oracle Solaris, FreeBSD, and macOS, support the installation of guest tools.

 EXAM TIP Guest tools help the virtual machine interact with the host machine, such as by keeping clocks in sync. Some virtual machine features may not work without the guest tools being installed on that virtual machine.

Exercise 5-2: Creating a Virtual Machine in Hyper-V

In this exercise, you will create a new virtual machine using Hyper-V.
Follow along with these steps to create a new virtual machine in Hyper-V.

1. Open the Hyper-V Manager tool.

2. Click New | Virtual Machine under the actions pane on the right or right-click on your computer name on the left and select New | Virtual Machine.

3. Click Next.

4. Give the virtual machine a name. In this example, the machine is named Cloud-Test.

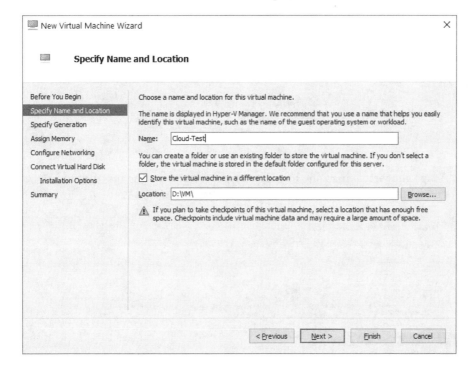

5. Check the box labeled "Store the virtual machine in a different location," and then select a folder on your disk that has enough space. In this example, the location is on the D drive in a folder called VM so that it does not contend with the programs running on the C system drive. Click Next when you are finished.

6. On the screen shown next, choose Generation 2, and click Next. The only reason to select Generation 1 will be if you are installing a 32-bit operating system. Generation 1 machines are much more limited. They use IDE-based virtual hard disks and do not allow for some of the more advanced virtualization features.

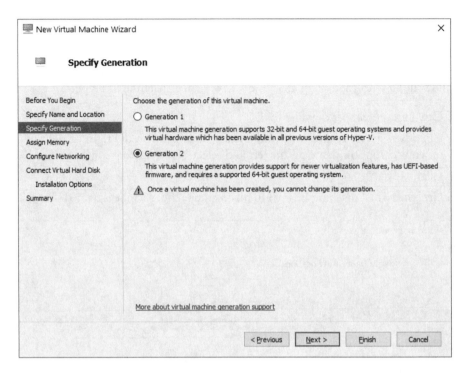

7. Assign the virtual machine memory. Hyper-V specifies the memory in MB, so if you want 16GB of memory, you will allocate 16,384MB.

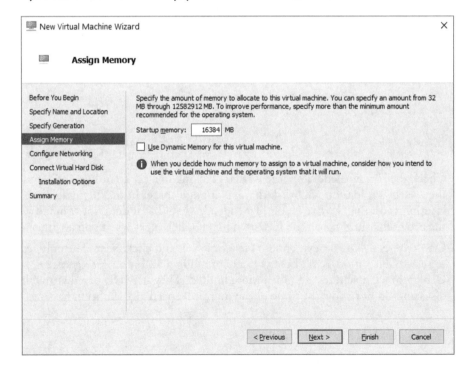

Depending on your machine's available memory, you may need to assign less memory to this machine. If you are unsure about how much available memory you have, right-click on your taskbar and then select Task Manager. Click the Performance tab, and then you will see how much memory you have available. The system shown next is using 104GB out of 128GB of memory. This leaves 24GB. Do not assign all available memory to the virtual machine because you will want to leave some buffer for increased use on the host. Uncheck the box to use dynamic memory. Dynamic memory allows Hyper-V to grow and shrink the amount of memory assigned to the machine according to demand. Click Next when you are done.

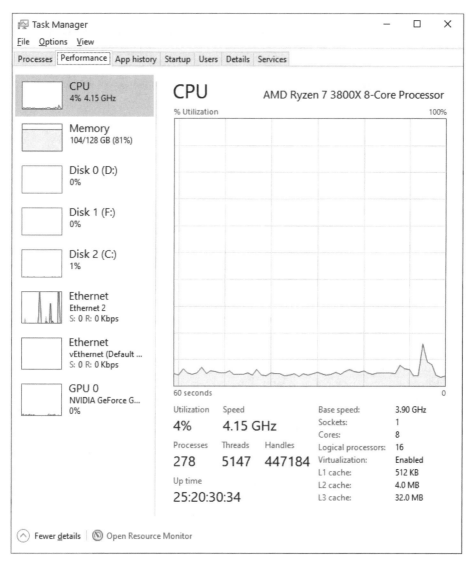

8. Choose a virtual switch to attach this machine to. If this were a physical server, the system would have a NIC, and an Ethernet cable would connect it to a switch for network access. As a VM, the machine is given a vNIC associated with a virtual switch mapped to a physical NIC in the host. In this example, the switch "Cloud Switch" created in this chapter's earlier exercise was chosen, shown next. After you have set these options, click Next.

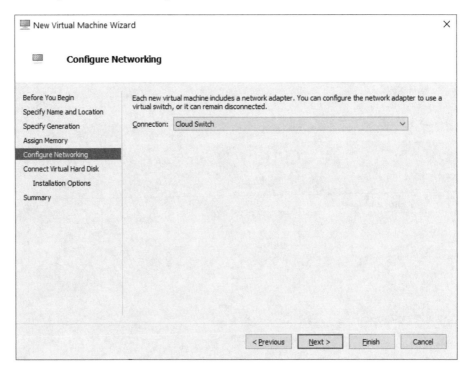

9. The next step is to give the virtual machine a virtual hard disk. You will need to select a name, location, and maximum size for the virtual disk. Alternatively, if you already have a virtual disk, you can use that instead. You might choose this option if you were creating a machine from a virtual hard disk template. The last option is to attach a disk later. However, if you choose this option, your VM will not have a hard disk. You might choose this if you were going to run a live VM from an ISO such as a live Kali Linux VM. In this exercise, we will give the virtual hard disk the name Cloud-Test_System.vhdx, as shown next. Hyper-V defaults the name of the hard disk to the name of the virtual machine. However, it is a good practice to add a bit more information to the virtual hard disk name. Often VMs will have more than one hard disk, so in this example, we appended the "_System" at the end of the name to indicate that this is the system drive. The system drive is the one where the operating system and default applications are installed. Give the hard disk a maximum size of 160GB. The disk will only consume the actual space used by the VM, but it will be able to grow to this size. Last, click Next.

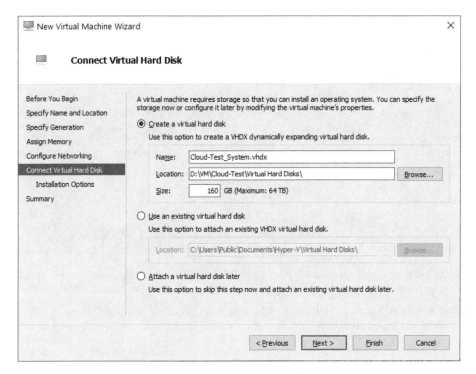

10. The next screen allows you to mount an ISO to install an operating system. You can also point the system to a server to install an OS or choose to install an operating system later. For this example, we will create an Ubuntu VM. Download the Ubuntu install ISO from https://ubuntu.com/download/desktop and then choose "Install an operating system from a bootable image file" and click the Browse button. Next, navigate to the location where you downloaded the Ubuntu ISO, select the ISO, and then click Open. You will be returned to

the installation options screen, which should look like the following illustration, except that your ISO file's location will be wherever you placed it on your system. Click Next when you are done.

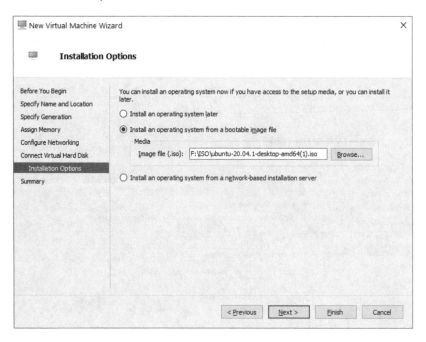

11. You are now shown a summary of the settings you selected. Click Finish to complete the process.

12. The virtual machine will now appear in your Hyper-V manager. It will have a state of Off, as shown here.

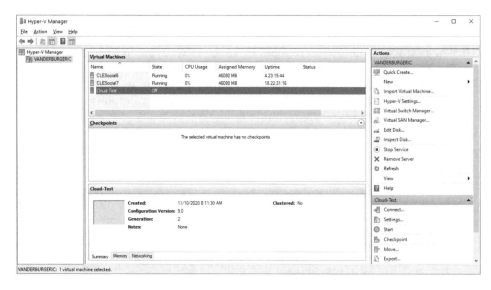

13. You might have noticed that we did not choose how many vCPUs to assign to the VM. Hyper-V does not include this in the wizard. Instead, it assigns just one vCPU, but this can be changed once the machine is created. Please note that the machine must be in an Off state to modify the vCPU settings. Right-click on the Cloud-Test VM and select Settings.

14. Select Processor on the left. On the right side of the window, you can adjust how many vCPUs are assigned to the VM by typing a number in the box labeled Number Of Virtual Processors or clicking on the up arrow next to the box, as shown next. In this example, four vCPUs were assigned to the VM. Once you set this value to your preferred number of vCPUs, click OK to save the settings.

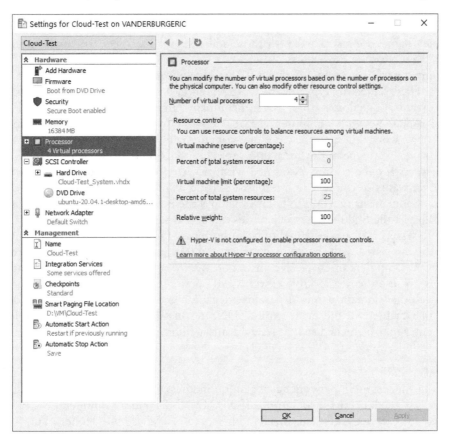

Virtualized Infrastructure Service Elements

Experts used to debate about which workloads were suitable for virtualization and which were not. However, today, most workloads are safe to run in a virtual machine. Virtualization is not just used for testing or development environments. Rather, enterprise-grade production systems run in highly virtualized environments. Of course, the purpose of virtual machines is to run services or applications, and this section presents some of the types of services you should be familiar with as you build out a virtualized infrastructure into a given cloud solution.

DNS

Domain Name System (DNS) is the backbone of network communication, for it provides name resolution for devices on the local network, the domain, or the Internet. DNS servers respond to queries for name resolution for hosts that reside within their particular space. This space is called a zone. Name resolution is the process whereby a name such as cloudplus.comptia.com is translated into its associated IP address. Each machine requires a unique IP address to communicate on a network. On the Internet, those addresses are assigned and distributed to companies. DNS servers maintain records of which names are associated with those addresses so that users and applications can access the services on those hosts.

Computers that are configured with IP are usually configured with one or more DNS servers. These servers are typically the DNS servers closest to the computer, such as those of an organization's domain or a user's or company's Internet service provider (ISP). On a local domain network, computers can be referenced by just their name. For example, a user using a workstation on the cloudplus.com domain who wants to connect to a server called server1 can type in the hostname, server1, and their computer will query the local DNS server for the address associated with server1.cloudplus.com. However, when a computer wants to connect to a resource outside its own network, it must use a fully qualified domain name (FQDN). This includes the name of the host and the domain. For example, the FQDN of server1 in this example is server1.cloudplus.com.

DNS servers can be configured to be authoritative for a zone. Those that are authoritative are associated with the domain owner, and they provide the most accurate results. However, computers often receive answers to DNS queries that are nonauthoritative. That is because their local DNS server issues queries on their behalf when it does not know of other domain names. It retains a local cache of queries and can respond back from that cache until the cache expires. DNS servers inform other servers how long a DNS entry may be cached so that stale records are not provided back to users.

DHCP

Each machine on an IP network needs a unique address to communicate. These addresses can be assigned manually or automatically. Dynamic Host Configuration Protocol (DHCP) is a service that hands out IP addresses to machines upon request. This is most often used for end-user workstations or for devices that connect to an ISP. DHCP servers are configured with one or more scopes. Each scope can hand out IP addresses from a specific range. Within that range, some addresses can be reserved for a particular machine by assigning an IP address to the MAC address of the desired node in the DHCP configuration. A MAC address is a unique identifier that is placed on a network interface port from the manufacturer.

DHCP servers usually hand out other information in addition to the IP address. This information includes the DNS server, default gateway, local time server, and other options, such as where server boot images can be found. (DNS servers were discussed in the previous section.) The default gateway is the device that computers will send traffic to if its destination does not reside on the local network, VLAN, or VXLAN.

Certificate Services

Certificates are cryptographic entities that can encrypt data in a public key infrastructure (PKI) or verify the authenticity of devices, program code, or websites. Certificates are cryptographic in that they are a function of an encryption algorithm where a public and private key pair can be used to sign data from one another (e.g., that requires the use of a public and private key pair to sign and validate data sent between the certificate holders). Data encrypted with a public key can only be decrypted by the associated private key. Similarly, data encrypted by the private key can only be decrypted by the associated public key. Data that is signed with the private key can prove authenticity because the signature can be decrypted with the public key, proving that the signer has the private key. This is called a digital signature. Signing data with a private key is not used to encrypt the data (protecting confidentiality). It is only used for validating authenticity.

As you can surmise from the names, the private key is not shared, and the public key is made available to anyone who wants it. Private keys are stored in a secure file or cryptographic store. To validate itself as authentic, a website, program code, or device can sign data with its digital signature (private key). If the digital signature can be read with the public key, the certificate is validated because the private key is not shared.

PKI is required to manage the exchange of keys and validation of certificates. Computers obtain public keys and certificate serial numbers from a certificate server to validate the certificates issued by it. However, computers do not simply trust any certificate server. Computers are configured by default to trust several root certificate authorities. These authorities can issue certificates to other certificate servers, granting them the right to issue certificates for a specific domain. The certificate authority must go through a process to prove its identity before the root provides it with a subordinate certificate used to issue certificates. Externally validated certificates from trusted third parties are not free. Organizations must pay for these certificates. Most certificates are purchased for a specific use from a trusted third-party certificate authority.

Companies can issue their own certificates without being part of the trusted certificate chain leading back to a trusted certificate authority. This is often performed for authentication or encryption on a domain. Computers in the domain can be configured to trust the domain certificate authority. The certificate authority then issues certificates to the machines on the domain so that they can authenticate each other. However, if a company tries to use certificates generated on its own domain for use over the Internet, those outside the organization will not trust the certificates assigned to the sites, and they will receive warnings or errors in displaying the page.

Local Agents

A variety of services utilize agent software to perform functions on a virtual machine. This includes backup software, licensing modules, performance monitoring, and security software, to name a few. A centralized tool coordinates tasks that run on local agents installed on individual virtual machines. The local agent can talk to the centralized tool to report back metrics, perform backup tasks, or obtain licensing information, and then this information can be reviewed within the central tool. Local agents make it possible for enterprise software to manage individual devices to a greater degree than would be allowed through remote management configuration.

Cloud services offer virtual machine extensions that offer the same or similar functionality to local agents. For example, a company using Azure, Amazon Web Services, or Rackspace might purchase extensions for backup recovery, antivirus, software installation, or other features as defined by the cloud service. This makes it easy to manage cloud systems from the same centralized consoles that control other organizational machines.

Antivirus

Antivirus software is a necessity for virtual machines. Antivirus software scans files resident on a device and processes in memory and analyzes them for signatures or anomalous behavioral patterns. Signatures describe what a malicious process or file looks like so that antivirus software can recognize it. Behavioral patterns analyze the way a system operates to identify conditions that are outside the norm or indicative of malicious behavior, in response to which the antivirus software takes action to restrict, block, or log activity based on the software's configuration.

Some hypervisor-aware antivirus software can perform a function called hypervisor introspection where the antivirus software resides on the host rather than on individual machines. Since the host has access to the virtual memory for each virtual machine and the virtual hard disks, the hypervisor-aware antivirus software can monitor all memory for viruses and block any it recognizes as malicious without requiring a separate agent on each machine.

Load Balancing

Some services can be configured to run on multiple machines so that the work of processing requests and servicing end users can be divided among multiple servers. This process is known as load balancing.

With load balancing, a standard virtual machine can be configured to support a set number of users. When demand reaches a specific threshold, another virtual machine can be created from the standard template and joined into the cluster to balance the load.

Load balancing is also valuable when performing system maintenance, as systems can be added or removed from the load-balancing cluster at will. However, load balancing is different from failover clustering in that machines cannot be failed over immediately without a loss of connection with end users. Instead, load-balanced machines are drain stopped. This tells the coordinating process not to send new connections to the node.

The node finishes servicing all the user requests and then can be taken offline without affecting the overall availability of the system.

Multifactor Authentication

Usernames and passwords are not always sufficient for authenticating to sensitive servers and services. Multifactor authentication is a method whereby several authenticating values are used instead of just one. The possible combinations include something you know, something you are, something you have, something you do, and somewhere you are.

The username/password is something you know. Something you are is a biometric value such as a fingerprint, iris scan, or facial scan. Something you have can be a token authenticator, a small device that generates a unique numeric value at regular intervals. A companion device on the server also keeps track of the same numbers. Users provide the token value along with their username and password to authenticate. Other forms of multifactor authentication include the use of proximity cards, which activate when brought close to an authenticator, account cards such as an ATM card that is used in conjunction with a PIN, or software that runs on a mobile phone or a secondary device. Such software is configured to receive a PIN or code that can be entered on another device. Users must have the device with the software on it in order to authenticate it.

Evaluate the servers in your environment based on the security risk they represent and determine which ones should require multifactor authentication to access. Virtualization hosts are commonly selected for multifactor authentication by companies because access to the host can provide the ability to disrupt operations for the virtual machines on the host or possibly to access the data on the virtual machines.

Firewall

Firewalls are software or hardware designed to screen traffic traversing a network link. Some firewalls sit between the Internet and a location or between more and less secure network segments. Virtual machines and physical computers can also run firewall software that blocks access to the computer when that access does not meet specific criteria. These firewalls are called host-based firewalls.

IDS/IPS

An intrusion detection system (IDS) or an intrusion prevention system (IPS) is a system designed to evaluate data on a device or network link for signs of malicious behavior. The IDS or IPS operates like antivirus software for network data by using signatures of known attack patterns and heuristics to detect behavior that appears malicious. Both IDSs and IPSs notify administrators if they detect attacks, but IPSs can also block the traffic or perform other actions as configured to prevent intrusion.

An IDS or IPS that exists on a network device is called a network-based IDS (NIDS) or network-based IPS (NIPS), while an IDS or IPS that exists on a virtual machine, workstation, or other node is called a host-based IDS (HIDS) or host-based IPS (HIPS).

Chapter Review

Knowing how to plan a virtualization environment is of great importance to any organization wishing to adopt a cloud computing infrastructure. A virtualization host computer uses software called a hypervisor that allows a single physical computer to host multiple guests called virtual machines, which can run different operating systems and have different amounts of compute resources assigned to each guest. Understanding how a host computer and a guest virtual machine interact and share resources is a key concept not only to the CompTIA Cloud+ exam but also to a successful cloud computing implementation.

Questions

The following questions will help you gauge your understanding of the material in this chapter. Read all the answers carefully because there might be more than one correct answer. Choose the best response(s) for each question.

1. Which of the following hypervisors would provide the best performance for a host machine?

   A. Type 1

   B. Type 2

   C. Open source

   D. Proprietary

2. You are evaluating which technology is best suited for virtualizing a server operating system for personal use on a desktop computer. Which of the following technologies would you recommend?

   A. Type 1

   B. Type 2

   C. SAN

   D. RAID 6

3. Which of the following hypervisors runs on a bare-metal system?

   A. Open source

   B. Proprietary

   C. Type 1

   D. Type 2

4. What type of hypervisor is provided to an enterprise to use without cost?

   A. Proprietary

   B. Open source

   C. Type 1

   D. Type 2

5. An administrator is testing a variety of operating systems while performing other functions like surfing the Internet and word processing. What type of hypervisor is the admin most likely using?

   A. Type 1

   B. Enterprise hypervisor

   C. Type 2

   D. Open source

6. You are deploying two virtual servers. One of the virtual servers is a heavily used database server, and the other is a lightly used print server. What virtual CPU configuration would you recommend?

   A. One virtual CPU for the database server and two virtual CPUs for the print server

   B. Two virtual CPUs for the database server and two virtual CPUs for the print server

   C. Two virtual CPUs for the database server and one virtual CPU for the print server

   D. Three virtual CPUs for the print server and two virtual CPUs for the database server

7. An administrator is trying to enable hardware-assisted virtualization in the BIOS of a computer and notices it is not an option. He checks the specification on the manufacturer's website and finds that the system should support hardware-assisted virtualization. What is most likely the reason why he can't enable it?

   A. The BIOS needs a firmware update.

   B. The BIOS is corrupt.

   C. Hardware-assisted virtualization is enabled in the operating system, not the BIOS.

   D. The firmware is corrupt.

8. You have been tasked with planning the purchase of a new virtualization host computer. When it comes time to recommend the processor type, which processor capability is more important?

   A. CPUs are more important than CPU cores and cache.

   B. CPU cores and cache are more important than CPUs.

   C. CPU speed is more important than CPU cores and cache.

   D. CPU cores and cache are more important than CPU speed.

9. Which of the following would be a requirement when planning the compute resources for a host computer?

   A. The host computer does not need to have enough compute resources to support the virtual machine workload.

   B. The host computer must have enough compute resources to support the virtual machine workload.

   C. The host computer must be running a support operating system.

   D. The number of virtual machines running Microsoft Windows must be known.

10. In a virtual machine, which component appears as an Ethernet adapter?

    A. Virtual HBA

    B. Virtual NIC

    C. Virtual switch

    D. Virtual router

11. An administrator deploys a new virtual machine. After logging on to the virtual machine, she notices that it has a different time setting than the host. What is most likely the cause of this issue?

    A. The virtual machine cannot communicate with the network.

    B. The guest tools are not installed.

    C. The vNIC is not configured correctly.

    D. The VLAN tag is incorrect.

12. Which of the following virtualization technologies groups multiple network storage devices into a single storage unit that can be managed from a central console and used by a virtual machine or host computer?

    A. Virtual switch

    B. Virtual HBA

    C. Virtual NIC

    D. Storage virtualization

13. Which type of memory allows a virtual machine to start with a smaller amount of memory and increase it based on the workload of the virtual machine?

    A. Startup RAM

    B. Static memory

    C. Virtual memory

    D. Dynamic memory

14. Which component controls how the network traffic flows between the virtual machines and the host computer and how network traffic flows between the virtual machine and other network devices in the organization?

A. Virtual NIC

B. Virtual storage

C. Virtual HBA

D. Virtual switch

15. Which piece of information is required to create a DHCP reservation?

A. MAC address

B. Default gateway

C. Server name

D. Host record

16. Which of the following could not be used as one part of a multifactor authentication solution?

A. Fingerprint

B. Token

C. Reference

D. Proximity card

Answers

1. A. A type 1 hypervisor is one that is created and deployed on a bare-metal installation. The hypervisor communicates directly with the physical server hardware and boots before the operating system. Due to the way the hypervisor interacts with the host computer, a type 1 hypervisor will provide improved performance versus the other choices.

2. B. A type 2 hypervisor is more suited for personal use because it can be installed directly on top of an existing operating system. Most desktop manufacturers support hardware virtualization on their desktops, which would allow you to run a type 2 hypervisor on your existing operating system.

3. C. A type 1 hypervisor is one that is created and deployed on a bare-metal installation.

4. B. An open-source hypervisor is provided at no cost and delivers the same ability as a proprietary hypervisor to run multiple guest virtual machines on a single host.

5. C. A type 2 hypervisor allows an administrator to run virtual machines on top of an existing operating system while surfing the Internet and running word processing on the host computer.

6. C. When assigning virtual CPUs, you want to assign as many as possible to the heavily used application. If an application is not going to be heavily utilized, you should assign the minimum amount of virtual CPUs. In this case, the database server is heavily utilized, so it should get more CPUs than the lightly used print server.

7. A. If the manufacturer states that the hardware should support hardware-assisted virtualization and the option is unavailable in the BIOS, the most likely cause is that the BIOS needs a firmware update to add the feature.

8. D. You are better off spending money on more cores with more cache rather than on faster CPU speed. When it comes to virtualization, you want as many CPU cores as possible to assign to the virtual machine.

9. B. When you are planning for and determining the compute resources for a host computer, you need to make sure there are enough resources to handle the virtual machine workload that the host computer is expected to support.

10. B. A virtual network interface card does not have any physical components; it is a software component made up of software drivers that mimics a physical NIC and appears as an Ethernet adapter on a virtual machine.

11. B. Guest tools are software additions that are added to a virtual machine after the operating system has been installed. Among other things, the guest tools allow a virtual machine to synchronize its time with a host computer.

12. D. Storage virtualization consolidates multiple storage devices into a single unit and simplifies the administration of common storage tasks.

13. D. Dynamic memory allows you to assign a minimum and maximum amount of memory to a virtual machine. This allows a virtual machine to consume memory dynamically based on its current workload.

14. D. The vSwitch is responsible for how the network traffic flows between virtual machines and the host and between virtual machines and other network devices.

15. A. DHCP reservations use the system's MAC address to set aside an IP address for that machine.

16. C. References are used in the real world to validate a person. However, computers do not accept references as a method of authentication. The other items are all forms of multifactor authentication.

Virtualization and the Cloud

In this chapter, you will learn about

- Benefits of virtualization in a cloud environment
- Virtual resource migrations
- Migration considerations
- Software defined

Virtualization is the key building block to cloud computing, and it is used by cloud providers to offer services to cloud consumers. Virtualization is the component that makes it possible for cloud services to provide a scalable, elastic, and on-demand environment. For example, cloud services may have thousands of hypervisors. When a cloud consumer requests a new server, the cloud provider provisions a new VM from a hypervisor. No new physical hardware needs to be put in place to service the request.

Virtualization allows an organization to efficiently scale its computing environment both up and down to meet its needs. When combined with cloud computing, virtualization takes advantage of the unlimited computing resources provided externally by a cloud provider to provide flexible and scalable virtualization solutions.

Virtualization will continue to play a significant role in cloud computing, as it is the technology that allows a cloud provider to deliver low-cost hosting environments to organizations no matter the size of the enterprise.

Benefits of Virtualization in a Cloud Environment

Cloud computing and virtualization go hand in hand. Virtualization makes cloud computing more efficient and easier to manage. Virtualization consolidates many physical servers into VMs running on fewer physical servers functioning as hosts. Through virtualization, a single host can run many guest operating systems and multiple applications instead of a single application on each server. Virtualization reduces the number of servers needed to host IT services, in turn, lessening rack space, power consumption, and administration.

Virtualization transforms compute resources into a centralized, sharable pool of resources that an organization can allocate to its business units on demand while still maintaining control of resources and applications.

Shared Resources

Cloud computing can provide compute resources as a centralized resource through shared resources. Shared resources are distributed on an as-needed basis to the cloud consumer. Thus, sharing resources improves efficiency and reduces costs for an organization.

Virtualization helps to simplify the process of sharing compute resources. As we discussed in Chapter 5, virtualization also increases the efficiency of hardware utilization. The cloud, on the other hand, adds a layer of management that allows a VM to be created quickly and scaled to meet the demands of the organization.

Figure 6-1 shows an example of how shared resources are configured.

Elasticity

Elastic computing allows compute resources to vary dynamically to meet a variable workload. A primary reason organizations implement a cloud computing model is the ability to dynamically increase or decrease the compute resources of their virtual environment.

A cloud provider can support elasticity by using resource pooling. Resource pooling allows compute resources to be pooled to serve multiple consumers by using a multitenant model. Resource pooling can provide a unique set of resources to cloud consumers

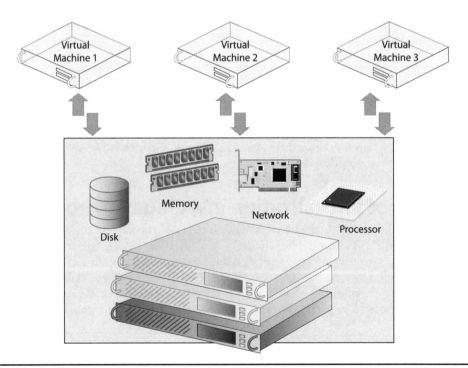

Figure 6-1   An illustration of shared resources in a cloud environment

so that physical and virtual resources can be dynamically assigned and reassigned based on cloud consumer demands.

With cloud computing and elasticity, the time to add or remove cloud resources and the time it takes to implement an application can both be drastically reduced. When an organization implements cloud computing and virtualization, it can quickly provision a new server to host an application and then provision that application, which in turn reduces the time it takes to implement new applications and services.

Elasticity allows an organization to scale resources up and down as an application or service requires. In this scenario, the organization becomes a cloud consumer, and the resources in the cloud appear to the consumer to be infinite, allowing the organization to consume as many or as few resources as it requires. With this new scalable and elastic computing model, an organization can respond to compute resource demands in a quick and efficient manner, saving it time and money. Not only can a cloud consumer dynamically scale the resources it needs, but it can also migrate its applications and data between cloud providers, making the applications portable. With the cloud, an organization can deploy applications to any cloud provider, making its applications portable and scalable.

While virtualization alone could provide many of these same benefits of elasticity and scalability, it would rely on compute resources purchased and owned by the organization rather than leased from a seemingly infinite resource like a cloud provider.

Another benefit of combining cloud computing and virtualization is the ability to self-provision virtual systems. An IT department in a cloud computing model can grant permissions that give users in other departments the ability to self-provision VMs. The IT department still controls how the VM is created and what resources are provided to that VM without actually having to create it. The IT department even can charge or keep track of the users who are creating the VM, making the users accountable for whether they actually need the machine and the resources it requires.

 EXAM TIP   Elasticity allows an organization to quickly and easily scale the virtual environment both up and down as needed.

Network and Application Isolation

As discussed previously, cloud computing and virtualization can enhance network security, increase application agility, and improve the scalability and availability of the environment. Cloud computing can also help to create network and application isolation.

Without network isolation, it might be possible for a cloud consumer to intentionally or unintentionally consume a significant share of the network fabric or see another tenant's data in a multitenant environment. Proper configuration of the network to include resource control and security using network isolation helps to ensure these issues are mitigated.

There are also circumstances where specific network traffic needs to be isolated to its own network to provide an initial layer of security, to afford higher bandwidth for particular applications, to enforce chargeback policies, or for use in tiered networks.

Virtualization and cloud computing now provide a means to isolate an application without having to deploy a single application to a single physical server. By combining virtualization and network isolation, it is possible to isolate an application just by correctly configuring a virtual network. Multiple applications can be installed on one physical server, and then a given application can be isolated so that it can communicate only with network devices on the same isolated segment.

For example, you can install an application on a VM that is the same version or a newer version of an existing application, yet have that install be completely isolated to its own network for testing. The ability of an organization to isolate an application without having to purchase additional hardware is a crucial factor in the decision to move to virtualization and cloud computing.

 EXAM TIP Virtualization makes it possible for an application to be installed on a VM and be isolated from other network devices. This feature is typically utilized in the entry-level stages of testing applications because the identical environment running in the IT department can be easily replicated.

Infrastructure Consolidation

Virtualization allows an organization to consolidate its servers and infrastructure by allowing multiple VMs to run on a single host computer and even providing a way to isolate a given application from other applications that are installed on other VMs on the same host computer. Cloud computing can take it a step further by allowing an organization not only to benefit from virtualization but also to purchase compute resources from a cloud provider. If an organization purchases its compute resources from a cloud provider, it requires fewer hardware resources internally.

Cost Considerations

Consolidating an organization's infrastructure using virtualization and cloud compute resources results in lower costs to the organization, since it no longer needs to provide the same power, cooling, administration, and hardware that would be required without virtualization and cloud computing. The organization can realize additional cost savings in reduced time spent on maintaining the network environment, since the consolidated infrastructure is often easier to manage and maintain.

Energy Savings

Consolidating an organization's infrastructure using virtualization and cloud compute resources results in lower energy consumption to the organization, since it no longer needs to provide the same power to equipment that was virtualized or replaced by cloud compute resources. Less hardware also results in reduced cooling needs and less square footage used in an office space.

Dedicated vs. Shared Compute Environment

A dedicated compute environment offers consistent performance because the organization does not need to contend with other tenants for compute resources. However, a dedicated compute environment is more expensive to lease than a shared compute environment because the cloud provider cannot distribute the costs for the compute resources over as many tenants.

Dedicated resources may be a requirement for some regulated industries or for companies with specific data handling or contractual isolation requirements.

Virtual Data Center Creation

Another option an organization has regarding infrastructure consolidation is a virtual data center. A virtual data center offers data center infrastructure as a service and is the same concept as a physical data center with the advantages of cloud computing mixed in.

A virtual data center offers compute resources, network infrastructure, external storage, backups, and security, just like a physical data center. A virtual data center also offers virtualization, pay-as-you-grow billing, elasticity, and scalability. An administrator can control the virtual resources by using quotas and security profiles.

A cloud user of a virtual data center can create virtual servers and host applications on those virtual servers based on the security permissions assigned to their user account. It is also possible to create multiple virtual data centers based on either geographic or application isolation requirements.

Virtual Resource Migrations

Now that you understand how cloud computing benefits from virtualization, you need to know how to migrate an organization's current resources into either a virtual environment or a cloud environment.

Migrating servers to a virtual or cloud environment is one of the first steps in adopting a cloud computing model. Organizations do not want to start from scratch when building a virtual or cloud environment; they want the ability to migrate what is in their current data center to a cloud environment.

With the advancements in virtualization and consolidated infrastructures, organizations now see IT resources as a pool of resources that can be managed centrally, not as a single resource. IT administrators can now quickly move resources across the network from server to server; from data center to data center; or into a private, public, or hybrid cloud, giving them the ability to balance resource and compute loads more efficiently across multiple, even global, environments.

This section explains the different options for migrating an organization's current infrastructure to a virtual or cloud environment.

Virtual Machine Templates

When an organization is migrating its environment to the cloud, it needs to have a standardized installation policy or profile for its virtual servers. The virtual machines (VMs) need to have a similar base installation of the operating system so that all the machines have the same security patches, service packs, and base applications installed.

VM templates provide a streamlined approach to deploying a fully configured base server image or even a fully configured application server. VM templates help decrease the installation and configuration costs when deploying VMs and lower ongoing maintenance costs, allowing for faster deploy times and lower operational costs.

 EXAM TIP VM templates create a standardized set of VM configuration settings that allow for quick deployment of one or multiple VMs.

A VM template can be exported from one virtualization host and then imported on another virtualization host and be used as a master VM template for all virtualization hosts.

VM templates provide a standardized group of hardware and software settings that can repeatedly be reused to create new VMs that are configured with those specified settings. For example, a VM template can be defined to create a VM with 8192MB of memory, four vCPUs, two vGPUs, and three virtual hard disks. Alternatively, a VM template can be set up based on an existing, fully configured VM.

In essence, a VM template acts as a master image that an organization can use to quickly and efficiently deploy similar VM instances in its environment. The organization can then maintain the VM templates by applying operating system updates and application patches so that any new VM instances that are created with the template are up to date and ready to use instantly. Figure 6-2 displays a graphical representation of how VM templates work.

Figure 6-2
Representation
of a VM template

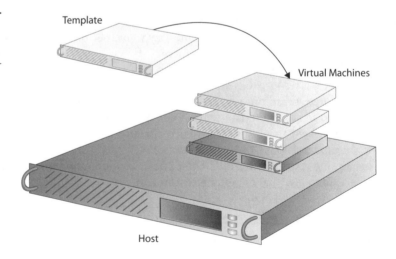

Physical to Virtual

Along with creating new VMs and provisioning those VMs quickly and efficiently using VM templates, there will be occasions when an organization needs to convert a physical server to a virtual server. The process of creating a VM from a physical server is called physical to virtual (P2V). Figure 6-3 illustrates how a P2V migration works.

P2V enables the migration of a physical server's operating system, applications, and data to a newly created guest VM on a host computer. There are three different ways to convert a physical server to a virtual server:

- **Manual**   You can manually create a new VM on a host computer and copy all the files from the OS, applications, and data from the source physical server. The manual process is time-consuming and not very effective.

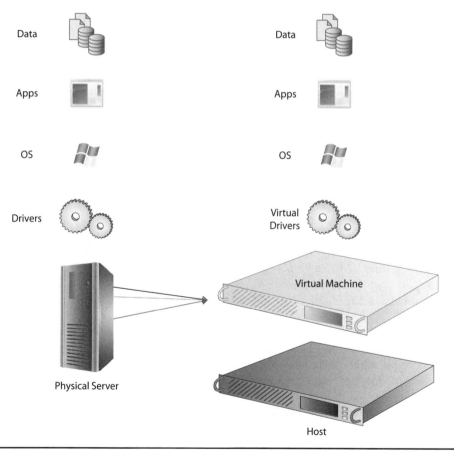

Figure 6-3   A graphical representation of physical-to-virtual (P2V) migration

- **Semiautomated** A semiautomated P2V approach uses a software tool to assist in the migration from a physical server to a virtual server. This simplifies the process and gives the administrator some guidance when migrating the physical server. There are also free software tools that help migrate a physical server from a virtual server.

- **Fully automated** The fully automated version uses a software utility that can migrate a physical server over the network without any assistance from an administrator.

Migrating a VM from a physical server can be done either online or offline. With an online migration, the physical computer or source computer remains running and operational during the migration. One of the advantages of the online option is that the source computer is still available during the migration process. This may not be a big advantage, however, depending on the application that is running on the source computer.

When doing an offline P2V conversion, the source computer is taken offline during the migration process. An offline migration provides for a more reliable transition, since the source computer is not being utilized. For example, if you are doing a migration of a database server or a domain controller, it would be better to do the migration offline, since the system is constantly being utilized.

Before migrating a physical machine to a VM, it is always advisable to check with the application vendor to make sure it supports the hardware and application in a virtual environment.

Virtual to Virtual

Similar to P2V, virtual to virtual (V2V) is the process of migrating an operating system, applications, and data, but instead of migrating them from a physical server, they are migrated from a virtual server.

Just like for P2V, software tools are available to fully automate a V2V migration. V2V can be used to copy or restore files and programs from one VM to another. It can also convert a VMware VM to a Hyper-V–supported VM or vice versa.

If the conversion is from VMware to Hyper-V, the process creates a .vhdx file and copies the contents of the .vmdk file to the new .vhdx file so that the VM can be supported in Hyper-V.

The Open Virtualization Format (OVF) is a platform-independent, extensible, open packaging and distribution format for VMs. OVF allows for efficient and flexible allocation of applications, making VMs mobile between vendors because the application is vendor and platform-neutral. An OVF VM can be deployed on any virtualization platform. Similarly, an Open Virtual Appliance (OVA) is an open standard for a virtual appliance that can be used in a variety of hypervisors from different vendors.

Client Tool Changes when Migrating or Upgrading

You may need to upgrade the client tools on a VM to a newer version if you move the VM to a host with a newer hypervisor version or upgrade the hypervisor software. Virtual machine client tools provide many features to the virtual machine. In addition to heartbeat connections, client tools offer the ability to take snapshots, synchronize the virtual machine clock with the host, direct data transfers from host to virtual machine, and send a remote shutdown or restart command to the virtual machine from the hypervisor without connecting to the virtual machine directly. Client tools need to be installed on the virtual machine in order for these features to work, and their version must match up with the hypervisor software version to support full functionality.

Virtual to Physical

The virtual-to-physical (V2P) migration process is not as simple as a P2V. A variety of tools are needed to convert a VM back to a physical machine. Here is a three-step process for doing a V2P conversion:

1. *Generalize the VM security identifiers.* Install and run Microsoft Sysprep on the VM to prepare the image for transfer and allow for hardware configuration changes.

2. *Gather drivers.* Prepare all the drivers for the target physical server before doing the migration.

3. *Convert using a third-party tool.* Use a software tool such as Symantec Ghost or Acronis Universal Restore to facilitate the virtual-to-physical conversion and load the necessary hardware drivers onto the physical machine.

While a V2P conversion is not something that is often done, sometimes it is required, for a couple of different reasons. One of the reasons is to test how the application performs on physical hardware. Some applications may perform better on physical hardware than on virtual hardware. This is not a common circumstance, however, and it is fairly easy to increase the compute resources for a VM to improve the performance of an application that is hosted there.

The more common reason to perform a V2P is that some application vendors do not support their product running a virtual environment. Today almost all vendors do support their application in a virtual environment, but there are still a few who do not. This fact and the complexities of V2P over P2V make V2P a less common scenario. Unlike the P2V process, which requires only the software tool to do the migration, the V2P process involves more planning and utilities and is much more complex.

Physical to Physical

The physical-to-physical (P2P) migration process is used to convert one physical system to another. This is a common practice when upgrading the server hardware. IT administrators would do the P2P conversion to the new hardware and then retire the original machine. The process for P2P conversions is mostly the same as the V2P conversion:

1. *Generalize the source system security identifiers.* Install and run Microsoft Sysprep on the source system to prepare the image for transfer and allow for hardware configuration changes.

2. *Gather drivers.* Prepare all the drivers for the target physical server before doing the migration.

3. *Image the source system using a third-party tool.* Use a software tool such as Symantec Ghost or Acronis to image the source.

4. *Restore the image to new hardware.* Boot the new system to the imaging software, point it to the image, and run the restore operation. The imaging tool should include a function to load the necessary hardware drivers onto the physical machine. For example, this is called Universal Restore in Acronis.

Virtual Machine Cloning

Whether an organization creates a VM from scratch or uses one of the migration methods we just discussed, at some point, it might want to make a copy of that VM, called a clone.

Installing a guest operating system and all applications is a time-consuming process, so VM cloning makes it possible to create one or multiple copies of a VM or a VM template. Clones can also be used to create VM templates from existing machines.

When a company creates a VM clone, it is creating an exact copy of an existing VM. The existing VM then becomes the parent VM of the VM clone. After the clone is created, it is a separate VM that can share virtual disks with the parent VM or create its own separate virtual disks.

Once the VM clone is created, any changes made to the clone do not affect the parent VM and vice versa. A VM clone's MAC address and universally unique identifier (UUID) are different from those of the parent VM.

VM cloning allows for deploying multiple identical VMs to a group. This is useful in a variety of situations. For example, the IT department might create a clone of a VM for each employee, and that clone would contain a group of preconfigured applications. Or the IT department might want to use VM cloning to create a development environment. A VM could be configured with a complete development environment and cloned multiple times to create a baseline configuration for testing new software and applications.

 EXAM TIP VM clones provide an efficient way to create a copy of a VM to quickly deploy a development environment.

Virtual Machine Snapshots

A VM snapshot captures the state of a VM at the specific time that the snapshot is taken. A VM snapshot can be used to preserve the state and data of a VM at a specific point in time. Reverting to a snapshot is extremely quick compared to restoring from a backup.

It is common for snapshots to be taken before a major software installation or other maintenance. If the work fails or causes issues, the VM can be restored to the state it was in when the snapshot was taken in a very short amount of time.

A snapshot includes the state the VM is in when the snapshot is created. So if a VM is powered off when the snapshot is created, the snapshot will be of a powered-off VM. However, if the VM is powered on, the snapshot will contain the RAM and current state, so that restoring the snapshot will result in a running VM at the point in time of the snapshot. The snapshot includes all the data and files that make up the VM, including hard disks, memory, and virtual network interface cards.

Multiple snapshots can be taken of a VM. A series of snapshots are organized into a snapshot chain. A snapshot keeps a delta file of all the changes after the snapshot was taken. The delta file records the differences between the current state of the virtual disk and the state the VM was in when the snapshot was taken.

Clones vs. Snapshots

Clones and snapshots have different uses, and it is important not to confuse their use cases. VM cloning is used when you want to make a separate copy of a VM for either testing, separate use, or archival purposes.

However, if you are looking to save the current state of a VM so that you can revert to that state in case of a software installation failure or an administrative mistake, you should create a VM snapshot, not a VM clone.

Storage Migration

Storage migration is the process of transferring data between storage devices. Storage migration can be automated or done manually. Storage migration makes it possible to migrate a virtual machine's storage or disks to a new location and across storage arrays while maintaining continuous availability and service to the VM. It also allows for migrating a VM to a different storage array without any downtime to the VM. Figure 6-4 displays how storage is migrated between storage devices.

Figure 6-4
Using storage
migration
in a virtual
environment

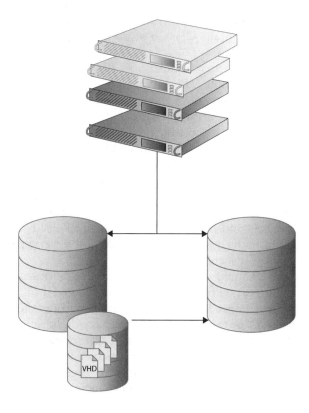

Storage migration eliminates service disruptions to a VM and provides a live and automated way to migrate the virtual machine's disk files from the existing storage location to a new storage destination. Migrating VM storage to different storage classes is a cost-effective way to manage VM disks based on usage, priority, and need. It also provides a way to take advantage of tiered storage, which we discussed in Chapter 2.

Storage migration allows a VM to be moved from SAN-based storage to NAS, DAS, or cloud-based storage according to the VM's current needs. Storage migration helps an organization prioritize its storage and the VMs that access and utilize that storage.

Block, File, and Object Migration

Storage migration can differ based on the type of data being moved. Block storage is migrated using tools on the source storage system or cloud storage to map it to the destination cloud. File migration can be configured at the storage layer (using storage or cloud software), similar to the block storage migration, or it can be performed within the system that is mapped to the storage. This involves using a tool within the operating system to copy the files from source to destination. Object storage can be moved using a RESTful API to interface with the object storage.

Host Clustering and HA/DR

High availability (HA) and disaster recovery (DR) functions of a hypervisor enable automatic failover with load balancing. A cluster consisting of multiple hypervisors, typically utilizing shared storage, must be configured to use HA. Some systems require management tools such as VMware's vSphere or Microsoft System Center VM Manager to take advantage of some of the more advanced HA capabilities, profiles, and customization.

A high-availability cluster auto-balances VMs across the available hypervisors. It can also fail a VM over to another host if the host experiences issues or suffers from resource constraints. Each host in the cluster must maintain a reserve of resources to support additional VM migrations in the case of a host failure. HA clusters also periodically rebalance VMs across the cluster hosts to ensure that a comfortable resource ceiling is maintained.

Depending on the cluster size, some or all hosts in the cluster will be configured to monitor the status of other hosts and VMs. This is accomplished through heartbeat connections that tell other nodes that the hypervisor or VM is still active and functioning. Suppose a heartbeat is not received from a host for a predetermined amount of time (15 seconds for VMware). In that case, the VMs on that host will be failed over to other hosts in the cluster, and the host will be marked as inactive until a heartbeat signal is received again from the host. On-premises physical servers or VMs can be configured to fail over to cloud VMs, and vice versa.

Administrators should configure a dedicated network segment or VLAN for heartbeat traffic. Heartbeat traffic does not need to be routed if all hosts are on the same LAN. However, if hosts are spread across sites such as in multisite failover scenarios, the heartbeat network will need to be routed to the other site as well. In cloud environments, a VXLAN, NVGRE, STT, or GENEVE segment is a perfect solution for the heartbeat connection. VXLAN, NVGRE, STT, and GENEVE segmentation was covered in Chapter 4.

A dedicated virtual NIC does not need to be assigned to VMs on a cluster. The hypervisor client tools will send the heartbeat information to the hypervisor. Hypervisors can be configured to take specific actions if a heartbeat signal is not received from a VM, such as restarting the VM, notifying an administrator, reverting to a saved state, or failing the VM over to another host.

CPU Effect on HA/DR

The hypervisor only has so much information when it chooses the placement of a VM. Some VMs might not have many processors configured, but they are still processor intensive. If you find that your HA cluster frequently rebalances the machines in a suboptimal way, there are some actions you can take to remedy the situation.

HA resource determinations are based on a number of factors, including the following:

- Defined quotas and limits
- Which resource is requested by which VM
- The business logic that may be applied by a management system for either a VM or a pool of VMs
- The resources that are available at the time of the request

It is possible for the processing power required to make these decisions to outweigh the benefit of the resource allocations, and in those situations, administrators can configure their systems to allocate specific resources or blocks of resources to particular hosts to shortcut that logic and designate which resources to use for a specific VM or pool on all requests.

CPU affinity is one such application in which processes or threads from a specific VM are tied to a specific processor or core, and all subsequent requests from those processes or threads are executed by that same processor or core. Organizations can utilize reservations for VMs to guarantee an amount of compute resources for that VM.

Cloud Provider Migrations

It may become necessary to migrate VMs, data, or entire services from one cloud provider to another. There is a high level of standardization with most cloud platforms, but the migration process still requires a high level of integration between cloud providers for seamless migration.

It is important, when evaluating cloud providers, to ensure that they offer integration and migration options. One cloud provider may not meet your scalability or security requirements, necessitating a move to another cloud provider. Additionally, you may wish to diversify cloud resources across several providers to protect against data loss or service downtime from a single provider's downtime.

In worst-case scenarios, you may need to export the VMs into a compatible format and then manually import them or import them with a script into the new cloud provider's environment.

Extending Cloud Scope

A major advantage of cloud systems is that cloud consumers can extend existing workloads into the cloud or extend existing cloud systems, making the cloud a powerful and flexible system for companies to rely upon for changing business needs. This can be advantageous even in temporary situations, such as in cloud bursting, where traffic is routed to cloud resources when the load exceeds available local resources.

Vendor Lock-in

Vendor lock-in is a situation where a cloud consumer is unable to easily move to another cloud provider. Lock-in can occur when the vendor does not support common standards or data export and migration functions. If the cloud provider does not support common standards such as data export in a common format that the industry supports, cloud consumers will not be able to import their data into another provider and would be forced to re-create the data manually. Similarly, the cloud provider may not support data or VM export or migration, so the consumer would have no method of taking their business elsewhere. Lock-in occurs whenever the cost to switch to another provider is substantial.

PaaS or SaaS Migrations

It is important to determine which type of migration you want to conduct when migrating to the cloud or from cloud to cloud. A SaaS migration is often the easiest because the cloud vendor takes on most of the migration burden. However, there are cases where a PaaS migration may make more sense, such as lower ongoing subscription costs or a higher level of control. Let's consider an example. Consider a company that has a locally hosted Exchange e-mail server that they want to migrate to the cloud. If they choose the PaaS solution, they would export their local Exchange server and import it into the cloud provider's virtualization platform. If the Exchange server is not a stand-alone server, they may also need to reconfigure authentication for the system or move other supporting resources to the cloud so that it will function. In this scenario, the company would pay for the server hosting, and they would be responsible for maintaining the server.

Now, if the company chooses the SaaS approach, it would export the mailboxes from their local exchange into the cloud e-mail system, such as Office 365. In this SaaS solution, the company would pay a monthly subscription for each e-mail account, but they would no longer be responsible for server maintenance.

Similarly, a company could have resources in the cloud and choose to migrate those to another cloud provider. They can make the same choices here. The PaaS-to-SaaS migration would be similar to the local-to-SaaS migration. However, the SaaS-to-PaaS migration would require the company to set up the e-mail system within the new provider's platform before exporting and importing the accounts into their new system.

Migration Firewall Configuration

When moving resources to a new cloud, you will need to ensure that you also move any firewall rules associated with those resources. Otherwise, the migrated resources will be unable to connect to other services properly, or end users will be unable to communicate with them. Follow these steps to migrate the firewall configuration:

1. Verify feature support.

2. Review current firewall rules.

3. Review network connections between migrated and nonmigrated resources.

4. Create the rules on the new firewall.

5. Test communication.

6. Migrate resources.

7. Perform final validation.

The first step is to verify that the new cloud provider's firewall supports the essential features you need. All firewalls have the primary support for access control lists (ACLs) and some level of logging, but other features such as bandwidth control, IDS or IPS functionality, malware scanning, VPN, data loss prevention (DLP), deep packet inspection, or sandboxing may or may not be included. This is the first step because it is a deal-breaker. If the provider does not support the required features, you will need to select a different provider.

The second step is to review the current firewall rules to identify those that apply to the migrated resources. If we use the e-mail server example from before, there would be firewall rules for web-based e-mail, IMAP, POP3, and SMTP. Document each of these rules so that they can be created on the new firewall.

Third, review network connections between migrated and nonmigrated resources. These communications take place between systems in the cloud or the local environment, and new firewall rules will need to be created to support this communication once the resources have been moved to the new provider. In the e-mail example, there may be communication to the backup server for continuous backups, domain controller for authentication, the DNS server for DNS lookups, and an NTP server for time synchronization. Document these communication requirements so that rules can be created for them.

In the fourth step, new firewall rules are created based on the documentation drafted in steps two and three. For the e-mail server example, rules would be created for web-based e-mail, IMAP, POP3, SMTP, backup, DNS, authentication, and NTP.

The fifth step is to verify connectivity for all the required resources. It is essential to do this step before migrating to ensure that the rules are configured correctly. Skipping this step could result in unexpected downtime to the system following its migration. Make sure you verify connectivity to each port and service that you configured. If you have a test copy of the system, you can restore it there but not modify external DNS pointers to it so that clients do not establish connections with it. Next, verify that the services can connect to it and then manually test a sample client connection. If everything works, you can move on to the next step.

The sixth step is to perform the migration of the resources, and this is followed by the final phase of validating that those resources can still connect to the required systems and that clients can connect to the migrated resources.

Migration ACLs   You may need to configure some ACLs to perform the migration. For example, you may create an ACL that allows communication to and from the VMware server over port 8000 to support vMotion if moving VMs between two VMware systems.

It is crucial to remove migration ACLs once you have completed the migration, as these ACLs increase the attack surface, making the systems potentially more vulnerable to attacks. They should be promptly removed, since they are no longer needed. In the example earlier, if vMotion is no longer required following the migration, you would remove the ACL that allows connections over port 8000 once the migration was complete.

Exercise 6-1: Creating a Cloud Firewall on Azure

In this exercise, we will create a cloud firewall on Azure and add firewall ACLs to allow SMTP, POP3, and web-based e-mail traffic to an internal system with the IP address 10.0.0.1.

 NOTE   You will need to have an Azure subscription to perform this task. You can sign up for a free 12-month subscription if you do not have one.

1. Sign in to the Azure portal (https://portal.azure.com), as shown here.

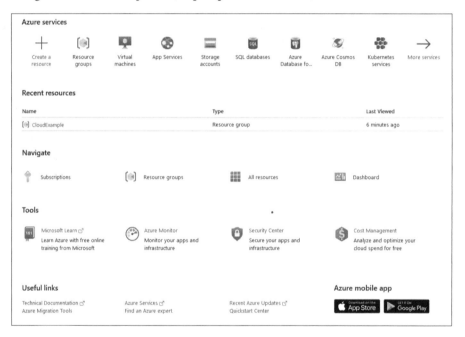

2. Select Create A Resource, and a new window will load.
3. Type **firewall** in the search bar (see the illustration on the following page), then press ENTER.
4. Various options from the marketplace will be displayed. Choose the firewall from Microsoft. This should be the first one displayed.

Firewall

Microsoft

Azure Firewall is a managed cloud-based network security service that protects your Azure Virtual

Create ∨   ♡

5. Click Create.

6. Select your Azure subscription in the subscription drop-down box. Then select a resource group. The resource group chosen for this example is one that I created previously called CloudExample. Give the instance a name. In this example, we called it CloudExample_FW1. Select a region and an availability zone from the drop-down boxes. In this example, we selected East US for the region and Zone 1 for the availability zone. Choose to create a new virtual network and give it a name. This example calls it CloudExample_Net1.

Give it an address space of 10.0.0.0/16. Next, assign the subnet address space 10.0.0.0/24.

7. The last option is for the public IP address. Click the Add New button and give it a name. This example calls it FW-IP. In the end, your screen should look like the following illustration, except that your resource group may be different. Click the blue Review + Create button at the bottom. This will display a screen that shows the values you just entered. Click the blue Create button at the bottom.

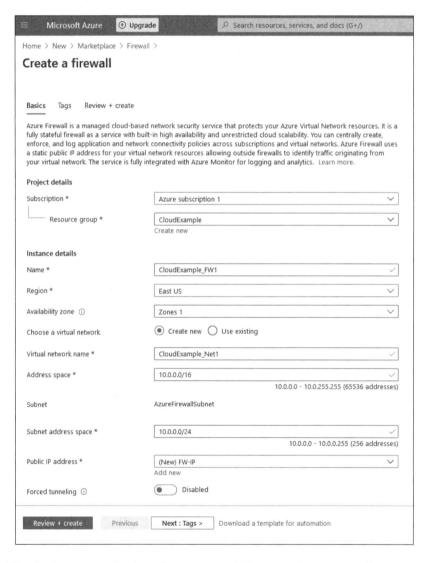

8. The deployment will take a few minutes. When it is done, you will see a screen like the following illustration, stating that the deployment is complete. Click the Go To Resource button.

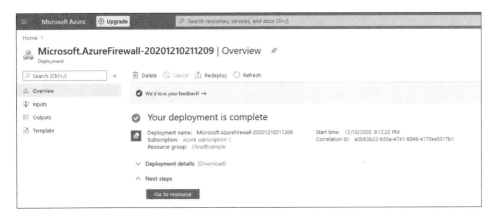

9. Under settings, on the left side, select Rules.

10. Click the Network Rule Collection tab and then click Add Network Rule Collection to create a new network rule.

11. The Add Network Rule Collection screen will appear. Enter a name for the network rule. This example named it CloudExample-E-mail. Set the priority to **100** and the action to **allow**.

12. Under the IP addresses section, create three rules. The first will be SMTP with the TCP protocol, * for the source address, a destination address of 192.168.10.1, and port 587. The second will be POP3 with the TCP protocol, * for the source address, a destination address of 192.168.10.1, and ports 110 and 993. You can specify two ports by putting a comma between them (e.g., 110,993). The third will be Mail-Web with the TCP protocol, * for the source address, a destination address of 192.168.10.1, and port 443. Your screen should look like this:

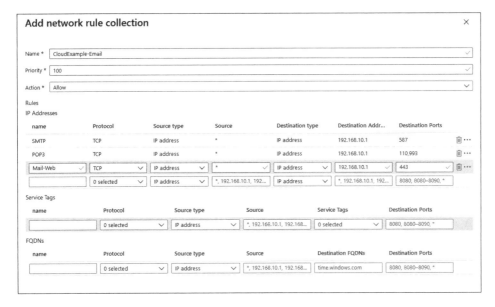

13. Click the Add button. It will take a moment for the rule to be created. Wait for the screen to display the new rule.

Migration Considerations

Before an organization can migrate a VM using one of the migration methods discussed in the previous section, it needs to consider a few things. Among the most important of those considerations are the compute resources: the CPU, memory, disk I/O, and storage requirements. Migrating a physical server to a VM takes careful planning for it to be successful. Planning the migration of physical servers to the virtual environment is the job of IT administrators, and they must perform their due diligence and discover all the necessary information about both the server and the application that the server is hosting.

Requirements Gathering

It is essential to gather as much information as possible when preparing to migrate physical servers to a virtual environment. This information will help determine which servers are good candidates for migration and which of those servers to migrate first.

When evaluating a physical server to determine if it is the right candidate for a virtual server, it is important to monitor that server over a period of time. The monitoring period helps to produce an accurate profile of the physical server and its workload.

A monitoring tool such as Windows Performance Monitor or a comparable tool in the Linux environment can be used to accurately assess the resource usage for that particular server. The longer the physical server trends are monitored, the more accurate the evaluation of resource usage will be.

The time spent monitoring the system also varies depending on the applications the physical server is hosting. For example, it would make sense to monitor a database server for a more extended period than a print server. In the end, the organization needs to have an accurate picture of memory and CPU usage under various conditions so that it can use that information to plan the resources the physical server might need after it is converted to a VM.

Another consideration to make when determining if a physical server is the right candidate for virtualization is the file system's status. When converting a physical server to a virtual server, all the physical server data is copied to the virtual server as part of the P2V process. Files and data that are not required are sometimes kept on a server, and those files do not need to be migrated as part of the P2V process, nor should they be. It is important to examine the hard drive of the physical server before performing a migration and remove all files and data that are not required for the server to function and provide the application it is hosting. Examples of these files might be drivers or hardware applications such as Wi-Fi tools, firmware update utilities, or other files meant to be used only by a physical machine.

 EXAM TIP During a P2V migration, the host computer must have a sufficient amount of free memory because much of the data will be loaded into memory during the transfer process.

Migration Scheduling

After gathering the proper information to perform a successful physical-to-virtual migration, you need to plan when the project should be completed. Migrations will not result in downtime for systems that meet your specific P2V migration tool's online migration requirements, such as the VMware vCenter converter or the Microsoft VM converter. However, systems under migration will likely experience slower performance while the migration is underway. It may be advisable to schedule migrations during downtime or a period where the activity is typically at its lowest, such as in the late evening or overnight.

Expect some downtime as part of the migration of a physical server to a virtual server if it does not meet the requirements of your P2V conversion tool. At a minimum, the downtime will consist of the time to start the new VM and shut down the old physical server. DNS changes may also need to be made and replicated to support the new virtual instance of the physical server.

Maintenance schedules should also be implemented or taken into consideration when planning a physical server's migration to a virtual server. Most organizations have some maintenance schedule set up for routine maintenance on their server infrastructure, and these existing scheduled blocks of time might be suitable for P2V conversions.

Provide the business case for some downtime of the systems to the change management team before embarking on the P2V migration process. Part of that downtime goes back to the resource provisioning discussion earlier in this chapter. It is a balance between underprovisioning the new virtual servers from the beginning or overprovisioning resources. Underprovisioning causes additional and unnecessary downtime of the virtual server and the application the virtual server is hosting. On the other hand, overprovisioning reserves too many resources to the VM and consumes precious host resources where they are not required. This can sometimes even have a detrimental effect on performance.

Upgrading

In addition to P2V, V2P, and V2V, an organization may upgrade an existing VM to the latest virtual hardware or the newest host operating system. VM hardware corresponds to the physical hardware available on the host computer where the VM is created.

It may be necessary to upgrade the VM hardware or guest tools on a VM to take advantage of some of the host's features. The host file system or hypervisor may also need to be updated to support these improvements. VM hardware features might include BIOS enhancements, virtual PCI slots, and dynamically configuring the number of vCPUs or memory allocation.

Another scenario that might require upgrading a VM is when a new version of the host operating system is released (e.g., when Microsoft releases a new version of Hyper-V or VMware releases a new version of ESXi). In this instance, an organization would need to upgrade or migrate its VMs to the new host server.

Upgrading to a new host operating system and migrating the VMs to that new host requires the same planning that would be needed to perform a P2V migration. Make sure you understand the benefits of the new host operating system and how those benefits will affect the VMs and, specifically, their compute resources. Once again, careful planning is critical before the upgrading process starts.

Workload Source and Destination Formats

The most straightforward migrations are performed when the source and destination formats are the same, but life is not always straightforward, and there will be times when an upgrade includes transitioning from one format to another.

Migrations or upgrades may include transitioning P2V, V2P, or V2V and from one platform such as Microsoft Hyper-V to VMware or Citrix Hypervisor. Migrations may also involve more advanced features such as virtual disk encryption or multifactor authentication that must be supported and configured on the destination server.

Virtualization Format   P2V migrations can be performed manually by setting up a new operating system and then installing applications, migrating settings, and copying data. However, this is time-consuming and often error-prone. It is more efficient to use software tools to fully or partially automate the P2V conversion process. Tools are specific to the destination virtualization platform. Such tools gather the required information from the physical machine and then create a VM on the destination virtualization platform such as Hyper-V or VMware.

V2P migrations can be performed by running Microsoft Sysprep on the VM to prepare the image for transfer and allow for hardware configuration changes. Next, all the drivers for the target physical server would need to be prepared before doing the migration, and then a software tool would be used to facilitate the virtual-to-physical migration and load the necessary hardware drivers onto the physical machine. Alternatively,

V2P migrations can be performed manually by setting up a new operating system and then installing applications, migrating settings, and copying data.

V2V migration can be performed by exporting the VMs from the previous version and importing them into the new version of the host operating system software. Additionally, some software such as VMware VMotion or Microsoft SCVMM can perform migrations from one hypervisor version to another. However, this is often a one-way move because moving from a newer version to an older version is not usually supported.

Application and Data Portability   Migrations also may move from an encrypted format to a nonencrypted format or vice versa. Migrating encrypted VMs does require the encryption keys, so you must ensure that these are available prior to migration and ensure that the destination system supports the same encryption standards. Certificates or other prerequisites may need to be in place first to support this or other features of the VM.

Standard Operating Procedures for Workload Migrations

You will likely perform migrations many times. The first time you complete a migration, create a standard process for future migrations. You may find along the way that you can improve the process here or there. Feel free to add more details to the standard procedure as you discover enhancements.

A standard process ensures that others who perform the same task will do so with the same level of professionalism that you do. Standard operating procedures also ensure consistent implementation, including the amount of time it takes to perform the task and the resources required.

Standard operating procedures can also be used to automate processes. Once a process has been performed several times and is sufficiently well documented, there may be methods of automating the process so that it is even more streamlined. The documentation will ensure that you do not miss a critical step in the automation, and it can help in troubleshooting automation later on.

Environmental Constraints

Upgrades are also dependent upon various environmental constraints such as bandwidth, working hour restrictions, downtime impact, peak timeframes, and legal restrictions. We also operate in a global economy, so it is essential to understand where all users are working and the time zone restrictions for performing upgrades.

Bandwidth   Migrations can take a lot of bandwidth depending on the size of the VM hard drives. When migrating over a 1 Gbps or 10 Gbps Ethernet network, this is not as much of a concern, but bandwidth can be a considerable constraint when transferring machines over a low-speed WAN link, such as a 5 Mbps MPLS connection.

Evaluate machines that are to be migrated and their data sizes and then estimate how much time it will take to migrate the machines over the bandwidth available. Be sure to factor in other traffic as well. You do not want the migration to affect normal business operations in the process. Also, be sure that others are not migrating machines at the same time.

Working Hour Restrictions   Working hours can be a restriction on when upgrades or migrations are performed. Working hour restrictions may require that some work be performed outside of regular business hours, such as before 9:00 A.M. or after 5:00 P.M. Working hours may differ in your company. For example, they may be 7:00 A.M. to 7:00 P.M. in places where 12-hour shifts are common.

Working hour restrictions also affect how work is assigned to people who work in shifts. For example, suppose an upgrade is to take three hours by one person. In that case, it must be scheduled at least three hours prior to the end of that person's shift, or the task will need to be transitioned to another team member while still incomplete. It generally takes more time to transition a task from one team member to another, so it is best to try to keep this to a minimum. Sometimes more than one person works on a task, but those people leave, and a new group takes over at some point so that a single person or group does not get burned out trying to complete a major task.

It is also important to factor in some buffer time for issues that could crop up. In the example, if the task is expected to take three hours and you schedule it precisely three hours before the employee's shift ends, that provides no time for troubleshooting or error. If problems do arise, the task would be transitioned to another team member, who would need to do troubleshooting that might require input from the first team member to avoid rework, since the second employee may not know everything that was done in the first place. For this reason, it is crucial to keep a detailed log of what changes were made and which troubleshooting steps were performed, even if you do not anticipate transitioning the task to another person. This can also be helpful when working with technical support.

Downtime Impact   Not all migrations and upgrades require downtime, but it is very important to understand which ones do. Upgrades or migrations that require the system to be unavailable must be performed during a downtime. Stakeholders, including end users, application owners, and other administrative teams, need to be consulted prior to scheduling a downtime so that business operations are not affected. The stakeholders need to be informed of how long the downtime is anticipated to take, what value the change brings to them, and the precautions that the IT team is taking to protect against risks.

For systems that are cloud-consumer facing, if the cloud provider can't avoid downtime to conduct a migration or upgrade, it needs to schedule the downtime well in advance and give cloud consumers plenty of notice so that the company does not lose cloud-consumer confidence by taking a site, application, or service down unexpectedly.

Peak Timeframes   Upgrades that do not require downtime could still affect the VM's performance and the applications that run on top of it. For this reason, it is best to plan upgrades or migrations for times when the load on the system is minimal.

For example, it would be a bad idea to perform a migration on a DHCP server at the beginning of the day when users log into systems because that is when the DHCP server has the most significant load. Users would likely see service interruptions if a migration or an upgrade occurs during such a peak time.

Legal Restrictions   Migrating a VM from one location to another can present data sovereignty issues. Different countries have different laws, especially when it comes to privacy, and you will need to understand the type of data that resides on VMs and any limitations to where those VMs can reside.

Upgrades can also run into legal constraints when new features violate laws in the host country. For example, an upgrade may increase the encryption capabilities of software to the degree that it violates local laws requiring no more than a specific encryption bit length or set of algorithms.

Legal constraints can come up when upgrades violate laws for users of the system even if the application resides in a different country from the users. For example, the European Union's General Data Protection Regulation (GDPR) affects companies that do business with Europeans, even if those businesses are not located in Europe. Consult with legal and compliance teams to ensure that you adhere with local laws and regulations.

Time Zone Constraints   Virtualized and cloud systems may have users spread across the globe. Additionally, it may be necessary to coordinate resources with cloud vendors or support personnel in different global regions. In such cases, time zones can be a considerable constraint for performing upgrades. It can be challenging to coordinate a time that works for distributed user bases and maintenance teams.

For this reason, consider specifying in vendor contracts and SLAs an upgrade schedule so that you do not get gridlocked by too many time zone constraints and are unable to perform an upgrade.

Follow the Sun   Follow the sun (FTS) is a method where multiple shifts work on a system according to their time zone to provide 24/7 service. FTS is commonly used in software development and customer support. For example, customer support calls might be answered in India during India's regular working hours, after which calls are transitioned to the Philippines, and so on so that each group works its normal business hours. Similarly, a cloud upgrade could be staged so that teams in the United States perform a portion of the upgrade, and then as soon as they finish, a team in the UK starts on the next batch. When the UK team completes their work, a group in China begins, and then back to the United States the following morning.

Testing

The process of P2V, or V2V for that matter, generally leaves the system in complete working and functional order, and the entire system is migrated and left intact. With that said, any system that is being migrated should be tested both before and after the migration process. The IT administrator needs to define a series of checks that should be performed after the migration and before the virtual server takes over for the physical server. Some of the tests that should be completed on the virtual server after migration are as follows:

- Remove all unnecessary hardware from the VM. (If you are migrating from a physical server to a virtual server, you might have some hardware devices that were migrated as part of the P2V process.)

- When first booting the VM, disconnect it from the network. This allows the boot to occur without having to worry about duplicate IP addresses or DNS names on the network.

- Reboot the VM several times to clear the logs and verify that it is functioning as expected during the startup phase.

- Verify network configurations on the virtual server while it is disconnected from the network. Make sure the IP address configuration is correct so that the VM does not have any issues connecting to the network once network connectivity is restored.

Performing these post-migration tests will help to ensure a successful migration process and to minimize any errors that might arise after the migration is complete. As with anything, there could still be issues once the VM is booted on the network, but performing these post-conversion tests will lessen the likelihood of problems.

Databases

A database is a storage method for data, such as financial transactions, products, orders, website content, and inventory, to name a few. A database organizes data for fast data creation, retrieval, and searching. The two main methods of organizing information, relational and nonrelational, are discussed later in this section. The software that databases reside in is known as a database management system (DBMS).

Databases in the cloud can be deployed on top of virtualized servers that the company operates, or they can be utilized as a part of a Database as a Service (DBaaS) solution. The DBaaS solution requires the least amount of work for the cloud consumer. The cloud provider takes care of the database software and maintenance, and the consumer creates their database objects, such as tables, views, and stored procedures, then populates it with data.

Relational

A relational database organizes data into tables where each record has a primary key, a unique value that can be used to reference the record. Data is stored to minimize duplication of data within the database. Relationships between data in multiple tables are established by referencing the primary key from another table known as a foreign key.

For example, we may have a customer table that has a customer ID as the primary key. We might also have an orders table that stores each and every order placed. Its primary key is the order ID. However, we can determine which customer placed the order by including the customer ID in the orders table as a foreign key. Similarly, we can obtain the orders a customer made by querying the order table for each record that contains the customer ID. The most common application for relational databases is Online Transaction Processing (OLTP).

Relational databases are stored within software known as a relational database management system (RDBMS). Some RDBMSs include Microsoft SQL Server, MySQL, Oracle Database, and IBM DB2.

Nonrelational

Nonrelational databases store data in a less structured format. This allows them to be more flexible. Data sets do not have to contain the same pieces of data. For example, one name field might have several pieces of data associated with it. For one customer, it might include first name and last name; for another, first name, last name, middle initial, and title; and another first name, last name, and maiden name.

Nonrelational databases are sometimes called NoSQL databases because SQL is not used to query the data set. This does not mean that SQL cannot be used, but SQL will need to be translated into the query method for the nonrelational database.

Some advantages of a nonrelational database include simple design, support for multiple data types, flexible data organization and growth, and the ability to derive new insights from data without needing to first establish a formal relationship. However, there are some drawbacks. Nonrelational databases suffer from data duplication, which can result in more extensive data storage requirements. It is also more challenging to enforce transactional business rules at the database level because the underlying relationships have not been established. This has to be performed at the application level. Lastly, the semistructured approach to nonrelational databases and the agility it offers can give some the wrong impression, resulting in systems that are developed with too little structure. It is still crucial for developers to consider their data model when they develop an application that uses a nonrelational database.

Nonrelational databases are ideal when collecting data from multiple data sources, such as in data warehousing and Big Data situations. It is also useful in artificial intelligence, where the meaning of the data is unknown until the program acts on it. Some popular nonrelational databases include Cassandra, Coachbase, DocumentDB, HBase, MongoDB, and Redis.

Database Migrations

It is quite common to move databases between providers because much of the software and systems developed in the cloud utilize databases for the storage of the data required for their operation. Thus, when moving services to a cloud provider or between cloud providers, you will also need to move the associated databases. Cloud providers offer tools that can perform the migrations for you. For example, the Amazon database migration service and the Azure database migration service can both be used to perform a database migration. When using the Amazon service, the only cost is the compute resources required to do the migration. Azure offers its offline tool for free. This will result in some downtime while the migration is in progress. Their online tool can move the database without downtime, and it is available for premium tiers.

- **Amazon Database Migration Service** https://aws.amazon.com/dms/
- **Azure Database Migration Service** https://azure.microsoft.com/en-us/ services/database-migration/

Cross-Service Migrations

You may need to convert from one database service to another. For example, you may want to move from Oracle to SQL Server or PostgreSQL to MySQL. The good news is that cloud migration tools allow you to move the data into a different database service with minimal effort. Both the Amazon and Azure services mentioned earlier offer schema conversion functions that will take the source elements and convert them into the format required for the destination database type.

The process typically involves analyzing the source database with the tool to generate a report on what can be converted and which areas will need to be modified before the conversion can be performed. Cross-service migrations require conversion of the following database elements:

- **Constraints**   Constraints are used to apply rules to the data that can be put into a table or a column. Some of the most common constraints include requiring that all values in a column be unique, excluding null values (places where no data was provided), default values when none are provided, indexed values, or relational concepts like primary key or foreign key constraints.

- **Data types**   Data types specify the kind of data contained in a database column, such as an integer, decimal, date, or binary data.

- **Functions**   Functions are computed values such as an average, sum, or count.

- **Indexes**   An index is used to perform fast searches on data. Indexes require additional data to be stored for each searchable item, which increases the time for data writes, but they vastly improve search query time because the query does not need to go through every row sequentially until it finds the desired data.

- **Procedures**   Procedures perform a task using one or more Structured Query Language (SQL) statements.

- **Schema**   The schema is an outline of how the database is structured.

- **Sequences**   Sequences are used to automatically insert an incrementing numeric value into a database column each time new data is added.

- **Synonyms**   Synonyms are alternative names given to database objects to make it easier to reference them in queries or procedures.

- **Tables**   Tables are the basic building blocks of a database. Tables store the data in a database. They are organized into columns for each piece of data that comprises a record and rows for each discrete record. For example, a table might contain customers, so the columns might be customer ID, first name, last name, address, city, state, ZIP code, loyalty number, and join date. There would be a row for each customer.

- **Views**   Views are alternative ways of accessing the data in one or more tables. They are formed from a SQL query and can include indexes for fast searching of specific data across the database or to provide restricted access to only a portion of the data contained in tables. Views do not hold the data itself. The data still resides in the underlying tables.

Software Defined

Rapidly changing business needs and customer expectations are driving companies to seek ever more agility from their technology. This has spawned a set of technologies, termed "software defined," that perform physical functions within software. These software defined technologies include software defined network (SDN), software defined storage (STS), and software defined data center (SDDC). Each of these technologies is leveraged to provide today's flexible and scalable cloud solutions.

Software Defined Network

The goal of SDN is to make networks that are easier to manage and more flexible in terms of handling changing application requirements. SDN does this by decoupling the data forwarding role of the network from the control role. SDN uses a controller that has visibility across the enterprise network infrastructure, including both physical and virtual devices from heterogeneous vendors and platforms. This visibility is used to provide faster detection and remediation of equipment faults or security incidents.

The controller is the hub for the information flow. Commands from the controller and information from the network devices are exchanged through APIs, called Southbound APIs. Similarly, information exchanged between the controller and policy engines or applications is done through Northbound APIs.

SDN offers greater flexibility because network resources can be dynamically assigned, expanded, or removed, depending on application needs. SDN improves security because security applications can reconfigure the network to mitigate attacks based on network intelligence.

Software Defined Storage

Like SDN, SDS's goal is to improve the manageability and more flexibility of storage so that it can handle dynamically changing application requirements. SDS allows companies to utilize storage from multiple sources and vendors and automatically provision, deprovision, or scale the storage to meet application demands.

Centralized control and management of enterprise storage allow for storage types to be virtualized and addressed in a single place. Policies can be applied to the storage so that it can be configured in one place, rather than relying on multiple vendor-specific interfaces. Application data can span across multiple storage platforms for improved data redundancy and to combine best-of-breed solutions into a solution. All-flash arrays can be combined with spinning disks or VTL, which is then mirrored to replica sets in other locations. This occurs over multiple storage fabrics and platforms, without the software needing to understand the underlying pieces.

Software Defined Data Center

The SDDC is a combination of virtualization, SDN, and SDS to provide a single method of controlling the infrastructure to support operations, monitor security, and automate management functions. SDDC can be used to manage resources at multiple physical data centers or clouds to best allocate resources. SDDC makes it easier for companies to shift workloads among technologies or to replace underlying technologies without affecting the applications that run on top of them.

Chapter Review

There are many benefits to adopting a virtualized environment, including shared resources, elasticity, and network isolation for testing applications. Migrating to a virtual environment takes careful planning and consideration to define proper compute resources for the newly created VM. Understanding how to correctly perform a P2V migration is a key concept for the test and the real world, as you will be required to migrate physical servers to a virtual environment if you are working with virtualization or the cloud.

Questions

The following questions will help you gauge your understanding of the material in this chapter. Read all the answers carefully because there might be more than one correct answer. Choose the best response(s) for each question.

1. Which of the following allows you to scale resources up and down dynamically as required for a given application?

   A. Subnetting

   B. Resource pooling

   C. Elasticity

   D. VLAN

2. Which of the following data centers offers the same concepts as a physical data center with the benefits of cloud computing?

   A. Private data center

   B. Public data center

   C. Hybrid data center

   D. Virtual data center

3. How does virtualization help to consolidate an organization's infrastructure?

   A. It allows a single application to be run on a single computer.

   B. It allows multiple applications to run on a single computer.

   C. It requires more operating system licenses.

   D. It does not allow for infrastructure consolidation and actually requires more compute resources.

4. Which of the following gives a cloud provider the ability to distribute resources on an as-needed basis to the cloud consumer and in turn helps to improve efficiency and reduce costs?

   A. Elasticity

   B. Shared resources

   C. Infrastructure consolidation

   D. Network isolation

5. Your organization is planning on migrating its data center, and you as the administrator have been tasked with reducing the footprint of the new data center by virtualizing as many servers as possible. A physical server running a legacy application has been identified as a candidate for virtualization. Which of the following methods would you use to migrate the server to the new data center?

  A. V2V

  B. V2P

  C. P2P

  D. P2V

6. You have been tasked with migrating a VM to a new host computer. Which migration process would be required?

  A. V2V

  B. V2P

  C. P2P

  D. P2V

7. An application was installed on a VM and is now having issues. The application provider has asked you to install the application on a physical server. Which migration process would you use to test the application on a physical server?

  A. V2V

  B. V2P

  C. P2P

  D. P2V

8. You have been tasked with deploying a group of VMs quickly and efficiently with the same standard configurations. What process would you use?

  A. V2P

  B. P2V

  C. VM templates

  D. VM cloning

9. Which of the following allows you to move a virtual machine's data to a different device while the VM remains operational?

  A. Network isolation

  B. P2V

  C. V2V

  D. Storage migration

10. You need to create an exact copy of a VM to deploy in a development environment. Which of the following processes is the best option?

    A. Storage migration

    B. VM templates

    C. VM cloning

    D. P2V

11. You are migrating a physical server to a virtual server. The server needs to remain available during the migration process. What type of migration would you use?

    A. Offline

    B. Online

    C. Hybrid

    D. V2P

12. You notice that one of your VMs will not successfully complete an online migration to a hypervisor host. Which of the following is most likely preventing the migration process from completing?

    A. The VM needs more memory than the host has available.

    B. The VM has exceeded the allowed CPU count.

    C. The VM does not have the proper network configuration.

    D. The VM license has expired.

13. After a successful P2V migration, which of the following tests, if any, should be completed on the new VM?

    A. Testing is not required.

    B. Remove all unnecessary software.

    C. Verify the IP address, DNS, and other network configurations.

    D. Run a monitoring program to verify compute resources.

14. You are planning your migration to a virtual environment. Which of the following physical servers should be migrated first? (Choose two.)

    A. A development server

    B. A server that is running a non–mission-critical application and is not heavily utilized day to day

    C. A highly utilized database server

    D. A server running a mission-critical application

Answers

1. **C.** Elasticity allows an organization to scale resources up and down as an application or service requires.

2. **D.** A virtual data center offers compute resources, network infrastructure, external storage, backups, and security, just like a physical data center. A virtual data center also offers virtualization, pay-as-you-grow billing, elasticity, and scalability.

3. **B.** Virtualization allows an organization to consolidate its servers and infrastructure by allowing multiple VMs to run on a single host computer.

4. **B.** Shared resources give a cloud provider the ability to distribute resources on an as-needed basis to the cloud consumer, which helps to improve efficiency and reduce costs for an organization. Virtualization helps to simplify the process of sharing compute resources.

5. **D.** P2V would allow you to migrate the physical server running the legacy application to a new VM in the new virtualized data center.

6. **A.** V2V would allow you to migrate the VM to a new VM on the new host computer.

7. **B.** One of the primary reasons for using the V2P process is to migrate a VM to a physical machine to test an application on a physical server if requested by the application manufacturer.

8. **C.** VM templates would allow you to deploy multiple VMs, and those VMs would have identical configurations, which streamlines the process.

9. **D.** Storage migration is the process of transferring data between storage devices and can be automated or done manually and allows the storage to be migrated while the VM continues to be accessible.

10. **C.** When you create a VM clone, you are creating an exact copy of an existing VM.

11. **B.** With an online migration, the physical computer or source computer remains running and operational during the migration.

12. **A.** During a P2V migration, the host computer must support the source computer's memory. More than likely the host does not have enough available memory to support the import of the VM in a migration scenario.

13. **C.** After a successful migration, the network settings should be checked and verified before bringing the VM online.

14. **A, B.** When planning a migration from a physical data center to a virtual data center, the first servers that should be migrated are noncritical servers that are not heavily utilized. A development server would be a good candidate, since it is most likely not a mission-critical server.

Cloud Adoption

In this chapter, you will learn about
- Planning
- Implementation
- Post-deployment validation
- Remote access tools

Cloud adoption is the process of employing new cloud technologies. This is a process you will frequently engage in as you move systems, purchase new cloud systems, or develop applications in the cloud. The cloud adoption process consists of planning, deployment, and then post-deployment validation.

Once the cloud adoption is complete, the organization will move into the operational phase, where the cloud system is used for normal business operations. Regular maintenance and monitoring tasks are performed at this point. Specific operational tasks will be discussed in later chapters, but we will introduce remote access tools here. Since cloud systems are inherently remote to cloud consumers, remote access tools are valuable for performing operational tasks. They are also used by employees when connecting to their virtual desktop systems.

Planning

Careful planning is required to select the right cloud solution. Generally, the more time spent planning, the less time is spent deploying and troubleshooting solutions later. Obviously, there will be a point of diminishing returns, but this section will outline the planning phases and what activities should be performed in each. The five phases are shown in Figure 7-1.

The first phase in the planning process is to identify the requirements for the system. Next, you design a solution based on the requirements. This then leads to selecting a solution that meets the requirements. This is followed by creating a deployment plan that outlines the steps necessary to deploy the solution, who will perform those steps, when the actions will occur, and how stakeholders will be kept up to date during the process. Lastly, the deployment plan must be approved by appropriate organizational decision-makers.

Figure 7-1
Planning phases

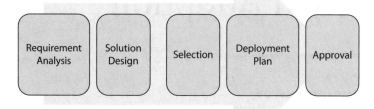

Requirement Analysis

The first phase of the planning process is called requirement analysis. The first phase in the planning process is to answer the question, "What do I need this cloud solution to do?" From this, you will then establish the other requirements for the solution to satisfy your user, business, compliance, security, and budgetary needs.

User and Business Requirements

The first part of requirement analysis is to determine the user and business requirements. User requirements define what the users will do with the system. For example, users may wish to track tasks in a task management system and have it automatically enter time for them in a time tracking system so that they do not have to track things twice. Another example might be users wishing to search an in-house knowledge management system for issues and problems that have been resolved to make troubleshooting future issues easier.

User requirements are often captured in a document called a user requirements document (URD). This document describes what the user is seeking from the system and formally documents that user's needs.

Business requirements establish the anticipated benefits for the company, such as reduced expense entry time, support for a more interactive website experience, or better insight into customer purchase decisions. Similar to the URD, business requirements are often documented in a business requirements document (BRD).

Compliance Requirements

Depending on the type of data collected and the industry the business resides in, there may be some compliance requirements that the company will need to be aware of. For example, suppose the company is in the healthcare industry. In that case, HIPAA will require them to apply certain protections to healthcare data and patient records. If they are doing business in California or the EU, regulations like the California Consumer Privacy Act (CCPA) or the General Data Protection Regulation (GDPR) will require the system to notify users of the information being collected on them and govern how that data may be used and how users can request copies or removal of that data.

These requirements will need to be built into the application. The good news about developing in the cloud is that many cloud vendors have already implemented these features. Document the functions you require and then select a cloud vendor that has implemented these features. You will then need to ensure that those features are turned on and integrated correctly into your solution.

Some requirements that may come out of compliance include

- **Data retention**   How long data will be stored. This may be defined for different data types. For example, customer data may be stored for 5 years, financial data for 10 years, and employee data for 20 years.

- **Encryption requirements**   Encrypting data in transit or when stored to prevent those without the decryption keys from viewing it.

- **Vulnerability management requirements**   Testing the system for weaknesses using vulnerability scanning tools or through penetration testing.

- **Auditing requirements**   How security controls will be evaluated, tested, and validated.

- **Privacy notices**   When and where users will be notified of their privacy rights and the privacy practices of the organization in regard to the system and the data collected.

Security Requirements

Security requirements will define how the data you store or process in the application is protected from loss or disclosure to unauthorized parties. Security requirements are derived from the risk level the organization is comfortable with and the potential threats to the data in the system. Some security requirements might include

- **Authentication mechanisms**   How users log into the system. This includes password requirements and possibly the use of multifactor authentication.

- **Log management**   How logs will be audited, archived, stored, and monitored.

- **Patch management**   How often patches will be applied and in what manner.

- **Privileges**   Access levels to data and system functions.

- **Access**   How the system may be accessed, such as over the Web, via mobile devices, through remote administration consoles, and so forth.

- **Hardening requirements**   How the system will be configured to reduce its attack surface.

Budgetary Requirements

The last part of requirement analysis is to determine the budgetary requirements. The business goals established earlier should provide the company with a measurable benefit. Based on that, the company will set a budget that will result in the desired return on investment (ROI).

ROI is a percentage and is calculated by taking the value of the system's benefit, then subtracting the cost of the system. This is then divided by the cost times 100. The formula is shown here:

ROI = (Return – Cost) / Cost times 100

The budget is the amount that can be spent on the project. Project managers will need to ensure that their expenses do not exceed this number. Budgets may or may not include sunk costs such as employee time, so you will need to be aware of this when doing calculations.

Designing a Solution

The second phase is to design the solution based on these requirements. The solution needs to achieve the business and user goals within the established budget. The solution design includes how the system will be secured, how it will integrate with other systems or clouds, the technical design, and the amount of downtime required.

Security Design

In the security design phase, the team will evaluate the security requirements and determine how to implement them. For example, if multifactor authentication is required, the team will decide which type of multifactor authentication would best fit the solution and how that will be implemented.

A big part of the security design will be identifying the data flows in the system and how the data will be secured at different places. A data flow diagram is often created at this point. The data flow diagram shows the type of data and how it moves between system components, which networks it traverses, where it is stored, and whether it is encrypted or not at each point.

Another part of the security design is how the system will be segmented. You will need to determine whether certain functions need to be on their own networks and how access will be governed between those networks. A typical web application framework is to have web, database, and storage tiers. Web servers would sit in the web tier, database servers on the database tier, and the storage systems on the storage tier. In between each tier is a firewall with access control lists that define how traffic can traverse the networks. For example, users would be allowed to access the web servers over the Internet. Only the web servers would be able to connect to the database tier. Only the databases would be able to connect to the storage tier. This is a bit simplistic, as there might be some other services required to connect to these networks, such as backup or authentication services, but it serves to demonstrate how this part of the security design phase is performed.

Technical Design

The technical design outlines the computing resources and services that will be used to put the solution together. This includes software, hardware, networking, routing, and subnets.

Software The software portion of the technical design will include the applications that comprise the solution. This will consist of the software required for the user and business goals, as well as compliance and security goals. The user and business software are needed to meet those functional requirements, while the software necessary to implement security or privacy controls is specified for those elements.

For the functional portion, you will need to specify which operating systems the servers will run, the applications that will run on them, and the major service components. For example, a solution might require ten Fedora Linux installations. Five of those will be web servers, running Apache with PHP. Another five machines will run the MySQL database service.

The security and compliance portion will specify which software will provide the necessary controls. This may include intrusion detection or prevention systems, identify and access management systems, software firewalls or web application firewalls (WAFs), DNS, and authentication systems, among other software.

Some software will require licenses, so this is the time to calculate the license costs to determine the best way to satisfy the solution. Keep in mind your budget. You may need to adjust the software design if it exceeds the software allocation in the budget. You will also want to track when those licenses need to be renewed. In some cases, existing software licenses can be transferred to be used in the cloud solution. Transferring licenses in this way is known as bring your own license (BYOL).

An application architecture diagram is often created at this step. This will show the software that is in use and how it is integrated with other software. A software inventory spreadsheet is also commonly created at this stage.

Hardware   The next part of the design will outline the hardware that is required to implement the solution. In an on-premises solution, this will include specifying the server type and size, then the processor, memory, storage, and networking included in each server. However, for some cloud resources, the hardware specified will be the vCPU, vNIC, and memory required for each server. If your solution is a SaaS solution, you will just specify the service that will be utilized, since the actual hardware required is not part of your consideration.

Network   The next step is to design the network portion of the solution. Each system on the network will need an address to communicate. Most systems will require one or more IP addresses. Some systems, like storage devices, may require another type of address. Determine how you will assign those addresses. Some systems may have static addresses assigned, while others will receive theirs through an addressing system like DHCP. The network design will need to include these IP address scopes and the static addresses that will be assigned.

Another part of the network design is the segments and their purposes. Earlier in the security section, we defined different network segments. These segments often correspond to network virtualization technologies, such as VXLAN, NVGRE, STT, or GENEVE networks, which were covered in Chapter 4. Specify which systems will reside on which segments, the IDs, and names.

The network design will also need to include how network redundancies will be put in place, such as how many network connections systems will have and how those systems will be connected together to provide the appropriate level of resiliency. Enterprise configurations usually have at least two network connections to each server. Each of these connections will be cabled to a different switch to protect against cable failure, NIC failure, or switch failure. You will also want to consider how your switches will be connected to each other to avoid a single point of failure in the network.

Lastly, consider what other network services will be part of the solution. This could include network load balancers to distribute the load, caching systems, proxies or reverse proxies, and other network optimization systems.

Network Sizing   As part of the network design, you will need to determine how much bandwidth and reliability are required for systems. This is especially important in cloud systems where network service levels may be assigned per resource. Review the application documentation to determine how much network bandwidth it will require based on the expected utilization. If you have a similar existing environment, collect network statistics to obtain a baseline for the application.

Routing   Routing is required to allow network segments to communicate with one another. Even if you only have one network segment, you will still need to configure routing so that those devices can connect to the Internet. Routing is the network process that directs traffic from source to destination on different networks. Devices such as routers, firewalls, and layer 3 switches can perform routing. They do this by understanding the networks that they are directly connected to to send packets to the next leg of their journey, known as a hop. Routers may know of multiple paths to a destination, and they rank these by hop count (how many links the packet must traverse to get there). Lower hop counts are prioritized above higher hop count links so that packets are delivered as quickly as possible.

You will need to determine which routing protocols you will use on your network and whether you will have any static routes in place. Routing was discussed in Chapter 4, so please see that section for more detail on routing specifics.

Subnetting   A single address space is usually not the right fit for an organization. Each segment will need to have a subnet within the overall address space for the systems on that network. The links between networks will also need their own subnets. The first step is to determine overall how many subnets you need, and then you can select which type of overall network you need. Table 7-1 shows classes A, B, and C of addresses and subnet masks. It also shows how many networks and addresses per network can be in each one before any subnetting occurs.

Subnetting allows a single address space to be divided into multiple networks. This makes it easier to manage and can improve both performance and security on a network.

Class	Range	Default Subnet Mask	Total Addresses	Networks	Addresses per Network
Class A	0.0.0.0–127.255.255.255	255.0.0.0	2,147,483,648	128	16,777,216
Class B	128.0.0.0–191.255.255.255	255.255.0.0	1,073,741,824	16,384	65,536
Class C	192.0.0.0–223.255.255.255	255.255.255.0	536,870,912	2,097,152	256

Table 7-1   Class A, B, and C Subnet Capabilities

The subnet mask is used to determine which network a system belongs to. Without subnetting, each octet in the subnet mask will be either a 255 or a 0.

Small sites may require only a few of the available addresses from even a class C address. Point-to-point WAN links only require two addresses but must reside on their own network. Without subnetting, a separate address range would have to be purchased for each site or WAN link, resulting in a large number of wasted addresses and inefficient use of resources.

Plan out how many networks you will need and how many hosts you will need on the networks. It is important to note that each network will have a network address and a broadcast address that you cannot use for your systems. Also, many virtual network subnets in the cloud reserve a few IP addresses for internal use.

Various subnetting tools are available for those setting up a network. One such tool is available on https://www.subnet-calculator.com. However, it is distracting to switch between a program and the calculator when doing regular tasks. Also, once you learn a few quick methods, you will be able to subnet so quickly that the task of entering subnet information into a calculator will seem laborious.

Computers use the subnet mask for an IP address to find which network the address resides in. The mask and IP address are combined in a process known as binary ANDing. The process works like this. Computer A wants to send data to computer B. Computer A will find the network address for computer B by ANDing B's IP address and subnet mask and comparing it with its own, which is also obtained by the same process. At this point, most people resort to converting everything to binary, and everyone gets confused. That's why I put together this different technique.

Let's avoid that confusion by using this simple method. There are three subnetting tasks that you will want to be able to do. The first is to determine what subnet mask will satisfy your required subnets and hosts per subnet. The second is to determine which network an IP address resides on, and the third is to find out how many hosts and networks can be created from a subnet mask.

Determining the Subnet Mask

When setting up an IP addressing scheme, you will want to know how many networks you can create and how many hosts will be in each network. A standard class C subnet mask without subnetting looks like this: 255.255.255.0. The standard subnet mask allows 256 addresses in a single network. However, only 254 of those addresses can be used for hosts because each network requires a network address and a broadcast address. These two addresses consume two of the subnet's available ones.

An IP address is made up of four numbers, each separated by a period. When represented in binary form, these numbers, consisting of eight binary numbers, are referred to as an octet. Each digit can be a one or a zero. Ones represent network bits and zeroes host bits. Subnetting takes some host bits and turns them into network bits, dividing that one network into many networks with fewer hosts on each. Table 7-2 shows each of the possible class C subnet addresses and their binary form. Please note that the table does not offer options for one or zero host bits because one host bit would only allow a network and broadcast address, and zero host bits would not allow for even that, so both of those options would allow for zero hosts.

Subnet in Decimal Form	Subnet in Binary Form	Host Bits	Network Bits
255.255.255.0	11111111.11111111.11111111.00000000	8	0
255.255.255.128	11111111.11111111.11111111.10000000	7	1
255.255.255.192	11111111.11111111.11111111.11000000	6	2
255.255.255.224	11111111.11111111.11111111.11100000	5	3
255.255.255.240	11111111.11111111.11111111.11110000	4	4
255.255.255.248	11111111.11111111.11111111.11111000	3	5
255.255.255.252	11111111.11111111.11111111.11111100	2	6

Table 7-2 Subnet Decimal and Binary Forms

The number of networks and hosts we can create depends on what class of address we are using. IP addresses can be class A, B, or C. In class C addresses, the first three octets are always used for network identification. An octet with all network bits has a value of 255. With three octets for networks, one is left for hosts. We can only steal host bits. Notice that we steal bits, but I have only mentioned octets. There are eight bits in each octet. Class B addresses allocate two octets, or 16 bits, to hosts, and class A allocates three octets, with 24 bits, for hosts.

Let's find the subnet mask we would need if we want five networks given a class C address space. Borrowing one bit from the eight available host bits would provide two networks. This is because that one bit represents a binary number that can be either a zero or a one, so there are two options. As you increase the bits allocated, that value increases by a power of two. For example, with two bits, there are four possible combinations, and with three bits, there are eight possible combinations. Each time we borrow another bit, the number of networks double, and the usable networks is simply the number of networks.

It helps to know the powers of two when working with computers. For reference, Table 7-3 lists the powers of two up to ten. These "magic numbers" should look familiar to you because they crop up all the time when working with computers. For example, the number of colors supported with 16-bit color is 65,536 or 216. RAM modules come in sizes such as 128MB, 256MB, or 512MB. Take a little time to practice these steps, and you will soon be quick at subnetting.

2^1	2^2	2^3	2^4	2^5	2^6	2^7	2^8	2^9	2^{10}
2	4	8	16	32	64	128	256	512	1024

Table 7-3 Powers of Two

128	64	32	16	8	4	2	1

Table 7-4   Binary Conversion Chart

We must borrow three bits to obtain five networks. We will actually have eight usable networks ($2^3 = 8$), of which we will use five. If we borrow three bits for subnets, there will be five bits left over for hosts because there are eight bits in the octet. The binary for this eight-bit octet would look like this:

Before subnetting: 11111111.11111111.11111111.00000000
After subnetting: 11111111.11111111.11111111.11100000

With five bits, we have two to the fifth, or 32, possible addresses, but we must subtract 2 for the network and broadcast address, so each network will support up to 30 hosts.

Borrowing three bits changes three zeroes in the last octet of our subnet mask to ones. Each binary bit has a value. Table 7-4 shows a chart that you can use to determine the decimal number for a binary octet. There are eight blanks where you can fill in the network and host bits as zeroes or ones.

Add the values in each place where you see a one to get the value for the octet in the subnet mask that is composed of a mix of binary ones and zeroes. Table 7-5 shows the binary octet when we borrowed three bits. Those bits are represented as the first three ones.

128 + 64 + 32 = 224, so this is the value of that octet in the subnet mask. Combine this together with the first three octets to get 255.255.255.224. Remember that the first three octets are used for network identification, so they are entirely composed of network bits or ones. An entire octet of eight binary ones (2^8) adds up to 255 if we count zero as the first number. For reference, Table 7-6 shows the subnet mask and how many subnets and hosts could be obtained from each class C mask.

128	64	32	16	8	4	2	1
1	1	1	0	0	0	0	0

Table 7-5   Binary Conversion Chart

Table 7-6 Class C Subnet and Host Addresses	Subnet Mask	CIDR	Network Bits	Subnets	Hosts
	255.255.255.192	/26	2	2	62
	255.255.255.224	/27	3	6	30
	255.255.255.240	/28	4	14	14
	255.255.255.248	/29	5	30	6
	255.255.255.252	/30	6	62	2

Also included in the table is the Classless Inter-Domain Routing (CIDR) notation. The CIDR notation shows how many total bits are used for networks. In the class A addresses, you can see that the smallest one has a CIDR notation of /10. This represents the eight bits that make up the first 255 in the subnet mask and then the two bits borrowed for subnets.

Let's try another example with a class B network. Our default class B subnet mask looks like this: 255.255.0.0 or 11111111.11111111.00000000.00000000 in binary, so there are 16 hosts bits. Suppose we want to find the subnet mask we would need if we want 100 networks with 500 hosts on each.

If we look back at Table 7-3, we see that borrowing seven host bits as network bits will give us 128 networks ($2^7 = 128$). We cannot go any smaller because six bits only gives us 64 networks. Borrowing seven bits leaves nine for hosts. The binary for this would be 11111111.11111111.11111110.00000000. With nine bits, we have two to the ninth, or 512, possible addresses, but we must subtract 2 for the network and broadcast address, so each network will support up to 510 hosts.

Finally, add the values in each place where you see a one to get the value for the octet in the subnet mask composed of a mix of binary ones and zeroes. In this case, it is the third octet, so we can use Table 7-4 again and plug the ones in to get 128 + 64 + 32 + 16 + 8 + 4 + 2, which equals 254, so the subnet mask is 255.255.254.0. For reference, Table 7-7 shows the subnet mask and how many subnets and hosts could be obtained from each class B mask.

Just to round things out, we will do one more example with a class A network. The default class A subnet mask looks like this: 255.0.0.0 or 11111111.00000000.000000 00.00000000 in binary, so there are 24 hosts bits. Suppose we want to find the subnet

Subnet Mask	CIDR	Network Bits	Subnets	Hosts
255.255.192.0	/18	2	2	16,382
255.255.224.0	/19	3	6	8190
255.255.240.0	/20	4	14	4094
255.255.248.0	/21	5	30	2046
255.255.252.0	/22	6	62	1022
255.255.254.0	/23	7	126	510
255.255.255.0	/24	8	254	254
255.255.255.128	/25	9	510	126
255.255.255.192	/26	10	1022	62
255.255.255.224	/27	11	2046	30
255.255.255.240	/28	12	4094	14
255.255.255.248	/29	13	8190	6
255.255.255.252	/30	14	16,382	2

Table 7-7 Class B Subnet and Host Addresses

mask we would need if we want 1000 networks and the maximum number of hosts on each network.

If we look back at Table 7-3, we see that borrowing ten host bits as network bits will give us 1024 networks ($2^{10} = 1024$). Borrowing 10 bits leaves 14 for hosts. The binary for this would be 11111111.11111111.11000000.00000000. With 14 bits, we have two to the fourteenth, or 16,384, possible addresses and 16,382 usable addresses once we subtract 2 for the network and broadcast address.

Finally, add the values for the ones in the significant octet. We need to find the significant octet because that is where we will focus our attention. The significant octet is the number that is neither 255 nor 0, or in binary, a mix of ones and zeroes. In this case, it is the third octet, so we can use Table 7-4 again and plug the ones in to get 128 + 64, which equals 192, so the subnet mask is 255.255.192.0. For reference, Table 7-8 shows the subnet mask and how many subnets and hosts could be obtained from each class A mask.

Subnet Mask	CIDR	Network Bits	Subnets	Hosts
255.192.0.0	/10	2	2	4,194,302
255.224.0.0	/11	3	6	2,097,150
255.240.0.0	/12	4	14	1,048,574
255.248.0.0	/13	5	30	524,286
255.252.0.0	/14	6	62	262,142
255.254.0.0	/15	7	126	131,070
255.255.0.0	/16	8	254	65,534
255.255.128.0	/17	9	510	32,766
255.255.192.0	/18	10	1022	16,382
255.255.224.0	/19	11	2046	8190
255.255.240.0	/20	12	4094	4094
255.255.248.0	/21	13	8190	2046
255.255.252.0	/22	14	16,382	1022
255.255.254.0	/23	15	32,766	510
255.255.255.0	/24	16	65,534	254
255.255.255.128	/25	17	131,070	126
255.255.255.192	/26	18	262,142	62
255.255.255.224	/27	19	524,286	30
255.255.255.240	/28	20	1,048,574	14
255.255.255.248	/29	21	2,097,150	6
255.255.255.252	/30	22	4,194,302	2

Table 7-8 Class A Subnet and Host Addresses

Finding the Network Number   Now that we know how to determine what subnet mask will satisfy your required subnets and hosts per subnet, the next thing to learn is how to determine on which network an IP address resides. The network address is how we uniquely identify a network.

The first step is to look at the subnet mask. We need to find the significant octet because that is where we will focus our attention. If you remember, the significant octet is the number that is neither 255 nor 0, or in binary, a mix of ones and zeroes. There are 256 possible numbers in each octet, numbering from 0 to 255. Take 256 and subtract the number in the significant octet from it.

Next, look at the significant octet for the IP address. This is the same octet you evaluate for the subnet mask. Use the number you obtained in the first step, and ask yourself how many times that number goes into the number in the IP address's significant octet, and then multiply that number by the number you obtained earlier to get the network address.

Let's consider an example. Two machines, computer A and computer B, want to communicate, so we want to determine if a router will be needed to establish communication between them. If they are on the same network, no router will be necessary. However, if they are on different networks, a router will properly relay the packets to their destination.

Computer A has the IP address of 192.168.5.11 and a subnet mask of 255.255.255.240. Computer B has an IP address of 192.168.5.19 and the same subnet mask. These two machines may have the same subnet mask, but that does not mean that they are on the same network. As you know from the exercise earlier, this subnet mask gives us 16 subnets so that these machines could be on any one of those.

Let's look at the subnet mask and find the significant octet. In this case, it is the fourth octet where you see the number 240. Take 256 and subtract the number in the significant octet from it to get 16. Now that we have the number 16, we are ready to move to the next step.

Next, look at the significant octet for computer A's IP address. Remember that the fourth octet was significant, so the number we look at is 11. Ask yourself how many times 16 goes into 11. Sixteen goes into eleven zero times. Take 16 times 0, and you get 0. Now combine this with the rest of the address, and we have our network address: 192.169.5.0. Let's take a look at computer B. Computer B has the same subnet mask, so we can skip step 1. Step 2 asks how many times 16 goes into 19. The answer is 1, so we take 1 times 16 and get 16. The network address for computer B is 192.169.5.16, so these two addresses are not on the same network, so their communication will require a router to communicate.

Finding Subnets and Hosts   We can work backward to find the number of hosts and subnets from a subnet mask that has already been created. In our network example, we used the address 192.169.5.11 with a subnet mask of 255.255.255.240. From the table earlier, we see this is a class C address. We can find how many bits were stolen by converting the decimal number 240 from the subnet mask to binary. We only need to look at the last octet because the first three are used for network identification and thus are unusable.

128	64	32	16	8	4	2	1
1	1	1	1	0	0	0	0

Table 7-9 240 in Binary

We can obtain the binary of the decimal number 240 if we use the binary conversion chart introduced earlier. To begin, start filling in the chart by adding the numbers together from left to right until you get to 240, as shown in Table 7-9. Place a 1 in each slot where you added a number.

For example, 128 + 64 + 32 + 16 = 240, so the first four bits are ones. The rest become zeroes. Counting the host and subnet bits in this octet gives us four subnet bits and four host bits.

We use two formulas to find the available subnets and hosts using the number of bits for each. The number of subnets equals two raised to the power of the number of subnet bits. Two to the fourth is 16, so we have 16 available subnetwork addresses. Almost the same formula is used for the host bits, of which we also have four. Take two and raise it to the power of the number of host bits and subtract two, so the answer is 14. Our subnet mask 255.255.255.240 will support 16 subnets, each with 14 hosts.

Integration

The different components of the solution do not operate in isolation. You will need to design how they will work together. One portion of this is the data flow. How will data be exchanged between systems? Which data standards will be required to support this exchange?

Another integration element to consider is authentication. Will all the systems be part of the same authentication domain, or will they be broken up into separate units? You may choose to make them all part of the same domain for ease of management, or you might split them to isolate control over portions of the environment.

Downtime

If the cloud solution is replacing a current solution, the team will need to determine whether the implementation will cause downtime. Downtime is a period where the system is unavailable to end users. It is important to know the duration of the downtime and whether it can fit into existing maintenance windows or whether a new downtime will need to be scheduled and communicated to stakeholders.

Selection

The planning team will then select a solution that meets their requirements in the third phase. This includes evaluating the different offerings and weighing the pros and cons of each. Some key considerations include ensuring that the data and privacy provisions in contractual agreements meet security and compliance requirements and that SLAs are aligned with availability requirements.

Evaluate Cloud Offerings

Consider the different cloud offerings that can satisfy portions of your solution and weigh the pros and cons of these. This will involve evaluating their features, how others rate their service, and how their price fits into your budget.

Contractual Fit

The next step is to review the contractual provisions to ensure that they meet your business and compliance requirements. Two main areas to look at are the data privacy and security provisions and the service level agreement (SLA).

Data Privacy and Security Provisions
Data privacy and security provisions specify how the CSP will protect the systems that you are using. You will want to ensure that the contract specifies how quickly the CSP will notify you in the case of a data breach or other security incident affecting you and your customers. Shorter notification times will give you more time to perform your portion of the investigation to determine whether notification is required, who needs to be notified, and its impact on your company and its customers.

You will also need to make sure the contract has sufficient privacy protections to meet your compliance requirements. Make sure that the contract specifies how long the CSP will retain data if it is responsible for that portion of the service. You will also want to ensure that they provide methods to export the data in standard formats to avoid vendor lock-in and that they ensure the same compliance in their providers that they rely upon to provide the service to you.

Service Level Agreement
Another necessary contractual provision is the SLA. The SLA will specify the promised maximum amount of downtime and service credits or other payments provided to the consumer if it exceeds that maximum. They may also define the workflow for handling technical issues. Ensure that the SLA meets your application requirements and the SLA that you are providing to your own customers. You cannot give your own customers an SLA that exceeds the SLAs of the cloud services your solution relies upon.

Deployment Plan

The fourth phase of the planning process is to put together a deployment plan that outlines the steps necessary to deploy the solution, who will perform those steps, when the actions will occur, and how stakeholders will be kept up to date during the process.

Tasks

With the cloud service selected and the solution designed, the team can now break the deployment down into discrete tasks. Next, determine how much time will be required for each task and then determine dependencies. Sometimes, groups of tasks will together form a milestone.

Some tasks are dependent upon others. These are known as sequential tasks because they must be performed in a particular order. Other tasks may be performed simultaneously. These are known as parallel tasks. The tasks should be documented in a task tree.

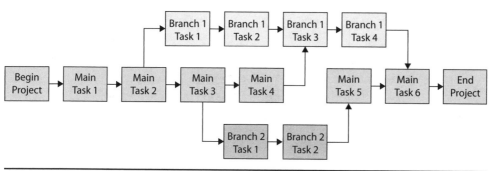

Figure 7-2 Task tree

Sequential tasks are placed in a row, with each task leading to the next. When tasks can be performed in parallel, they form a branch off the task tree. A sample task tree is shown in Figure 7-2.

The diagram shows the main tasks that then branch off into two different branches. Later steps in the main path are dependent upon the completion of the branches, and task three in branch one is dependent upon both the task before it and main task four. There is a period where the main task path must wait for branch three to complete before main task five can be started. This is a potential area where the planner might be able to put more resources in later to speed up the completion of the overall project.

Assign Responsibilities

Tasks will need to be performed by one or more people. You will need to assign these responsibilities to appropriate personnel or teams. Your task tree may need to be adjusted if parallel tasks require the same personnel, since a person cannot be in two places at once. This is a chance to identify alternative resources that may be able to perform the task. The result of this process will be a work breakdown structure. The work breakdown structure can take many forms, but a sample is shown in Figure 7-3.

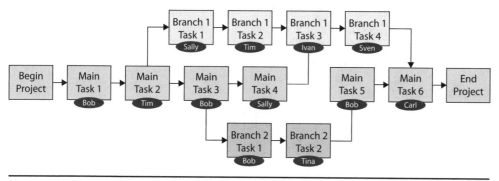

Figure 7-3 Work breakdown structure

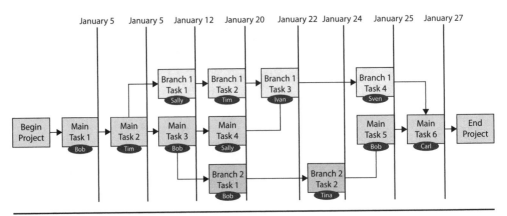

Figure 7-4   Timeline

Timeline

The next step is to take the tasks that were identified earlier and plot them out on a timeline. First, choose a reasonable starting date. Next, plot out the steps from the work breakdown structure. Give each one a date based on the estimated duration for the task and its dependencies. Some tasks may have the same due date because they are being performed in parallel.

You will also need to consider other dependencies, such as the availability of resources when assigning dates. For example, a step in the process requires a report that is received from a vendor every 30 days, and the task must be completed within 7 days of receipt of the report. You would need to ensure that the schedule meets this requirement.

The timeline process is not something that is done arbitrarily, but in coordination with those who will be performing the tasks. Discuss each step to ensure that the timeline represents realistic, achievable goals. A sample timeline is shown in Figure 7-4.

Communication

It is important to keep stakeholders informed of the expected duration of the project and significant project milestones. You might also need to notify customers or employees of downtimes that will occur. Document these communications as substeps in the plan and document whether deliverables will need to be shared with those people. Deliverables could be reports of data moved or users migrated or an update to a project plan.

Overall Project Plan

A project plan is a final step in the planning process. This document should include all the information put together in the previous steps, such as the step, deliverable, dependency, assigned person, estimated duration, and due dates. Many plans include reference numbers for each task so that you can refer to the task by the number rather than the task description. A sample project plan is shown in Figure 7-5.

Ref No.		Step	Deliverable	Dependent Upon	Assigned Person	Est. Hours	Hrs %	Due
1		Milestone 1						
1.1		Main Task 1			Bob	2		January 5
1.2		Main Task 2		Main Task 1	Tim	6		January 7
1.3		Branch 1 Task 1		Main Task 1	Sally	4		January 12
1.4		Main Task 3		Main Task 2	Sven	5		January 12
1.5		Branch 1 Task 2		Branch 1 Task 1	Tim	8		January 20
1.6		Main Task 4	Deliverable 1	Main Task 3	Sally			January 20
	a	Subtask 1			Ivan	2		January 18
	b	Subtask 2			Tina	6		January 20
1.7		Branch 2 Task 1		Main Task 3	Bob	3		January 20
1.8		Branch 1 Task 3		Main Task 4, Branch 1 Task 2	Ivan	9		January 22
1.9		Branch 2 Task 2		Branch 2 Task 1	Tina	3		January 24
1.10		Main Task 5		Main Task 4	Bob	5		January 25
1.11		Branch 1 Task 4		Branch 1 Task 3	Sven	4		January 25
1.12		Main Task 6	Deliverable 2	Main Task 5, Branch 1 Task 4	Carl	1		January 27
					Subtotal	58	55%	
2		Milestone 2						
2.1		Main Task 1			Ivan	2		February 7
2.2		Main Task 2		Main Task 1	Sally	2		February 11
2.3		Branch 1 Task 1	Deliverable 3	Main Task 2	Bob	8		February 11
2.4		Main Task 3		Main Task 2	Tim			February 14
	a	Subtask 1			Paul	1		February 12
	b	Subtask 2			Carl	2		February 13
	c	Subtask 3			Carl	7		February 14
2.5		Branch 1 Task 3		Branch 1 Task 1	Tina	4		February 16
2.6		Main Task 4		Main Task 3, Branch 1 Task 3	Bob	1		February 18
					Subtotal	27	25%	
3		Milestone 3						
3.1		Main Task 1			Paul			February 24
	a	Subtask 1			Sally	2		February 20
	b	Subtask 2	Deliverable 4		Tim	8		February 24
3.2		Main Task 2		Main Task 1	Bob			February 28
	a	Subtask 1			Ivan	5		February 25
	b	Subtask 2			Tina	1		February 28
3.3		Main Task 3		Main Task 2	Sally	2		March 5
3.4		Main Task 4		Main Task 3	Tim			March 9
	a	Subtask 1			Paul	1		March 7
	d	Subtask 2	Deliverable 5		Sven	2		March 9
					Subtotal	21	20%	
TOTAL NORMAL HOURS						106		

Figure 7-5   Project plan

Approval

The last step is to get the deployment plan approved by the appropriate organizational decision-makers. Typically, the project plan and budgetary items are distributed to the stakeholders. The project manager will explain how the project will meet the business and user goals and how it will stay within the prescribed budget. They will walk the stakeholders through the timeline for completion and then seek approval to move forward. Some projects require approval from multiple groups before the project can begin. Ensure that you have sign-off from those who are authorized to approve the project before you start the project activities.

Implementation

Hooray! The planning process is finally complete, and you are approved to begin implementing the solution. The implementation phase involves contracting with cloud providers for their solutions; developing the software that will be deployed; and then deploying the virtual systems, networks, and containers that comprise the solution.

Service Model Solutions

Implementation strategies for deploying solutions in the cloud differ based on the service model. As you remember from Chapter 1, some of the cloud services models include IaaS, PaaS, SaaS, and CaaS.

IaaS

IaaS solution deployments involve the cloud consumer implementing systems on top of a CSP's storage, networking, and other supporting infrastructure. IaaS cloud deployments involve the following high-level steps:

1. Create virtual machines
2. Install operating systems
3. Install software or roles
4. Configure firewall rules

The first step is to create virtual machines in the cloud. You will create or migrate a virtual machine for each server that is part of your solution. For example, you may have several web servers, two database servers, a domain controller, and a file server.

The next step is to install operating systems on each of these servers. Once this is complete, install applications or enable server roles on the virtual machines so that they can perform their assigned role. For example, you may need to install SQL Server on a database server or enable the Active Directory or DNS roles.

 NOTE If you are migrating from a different environment, steps 2 and 3 would be replaced with a P2V or V2V conversion of the existing systems into the cloud.

Lastly, configure firewall rules to allow appropriate traffic to your systems. For example, a web server would need an access rule to allow data over port 443 to and from it.

PaaS

PaaS solution deployments involve the cloud consumer implementing systems on top of an operating system provided by the CSP. The CSP supports the operating system, along with the underlying storage, networking, and other supporting infrastructure, so the deployment focuses on the application components.

In a PaaS solution, you would provision the systems using the cloud self-service tools and then select the necessary software to be included on them. The CSP then deploys the systems for you. One example of this is serverless computing, mentioned in Chapter 1, where the CSP provisions the system and manages its resources transparently to the cloud consumer. You would then need to configure access rules to the systems.

SaaS

SaaS deployments involve provisioning users and configuring options within an on-demand software application delivered by the CSP over the Internet. Deploying to a SaaS solution would involve provisioning accounts or licenses for your users and possibly migrating data from one solution into the SaaS solution.

CaaS

CaaS deployments involve provisioning users and configuring options within an on-demand voice over IP (VoIP), e-mail, or messaging application delivered by the CSP over the Internet.

VoIP To deploy a cloud VoIP solution, first provide the cloud vendor with the telephone numbers you will be migrating. The next step is to purchase phones. This is an optional step because you can use a cloud software-based VoIP solution without any physical phones. The cloud vendor may support multiple phone models, or they might require you to purchase the phones from them.

There are two types of VoIP phones: softphones and hard phones. Softphones are those that are implemented entirely via software. An application on a computer or a cell phone app can be used to send and receive calls. Softphones are very useful because they are often integrated into other messaging suites so that you can easily schedule conference calls on your calendar or initiate calls from a chat window. You can also easily move around with a softphone rather than being tied to your workplace. Since the software can be installed on multiple devices, you could have the software installed on your work machine and a home machine or a cell phone. This allows you to take calls in each of these locations. However, it can be slightly annoying to hear a computer, cell phone, and a hard phone all ring at once when a new call comes in. Softphones can also be used in conjunction with hard phones. Hard phones are physical phones that connect to the cloud VoIP system to make calls.

When the phones arrive, you will connect each one to the network to ensure that they have Internet access and then follow the steps from the cloud provider to link each phone with a user. A user may be associated with a hard phone and multiple softphones.

The last step is to cut over from your existing phone system. Much like moving to a new cell phone, on the cutover date, the existing phone numbers are moved from the current phone system to the new one. At this point, the old phone system can be retired.

E-mail Cloud e-mail systems are prevalent today. There are many solutions out there, but two of the most popular are Microsoft Office365 and Google's Gmail. If you are a new company setting up cloud-based e-mail, the process is as simple as purchasing and assigning a domain name for the e-mail, then purchasing licenses for each user. The users will then log into their e-mail, set their password, and can begin sending and receiving mail immediately.

For established companies, e-mail is a fundamental technological need, so these companies most likely already have some solution. This could be an in-house system such as Microsoft Exchange, Sendmail, HCL Notes, and many others, or it could be an existing cloud e-mail system.

You will need to follow the instructions from the cloud vendor to migrate an in-house system to the cloud. This often involves establishing a federation between the local system and the cloud system. The cloud system is then configured as a front end for the local system so that mail flows through it and then back to the local system. You then use migration tools to begin moving accounts from one system to another. This allows for e-mail to route to the appropriate mailbox during the migration.

When migrating from one cloud provider to another, first ensure that the cloud provider supports migration from your existing solution. If they do, you can use their migration tools to perform the migration.

Messaging The last type of CaaS is a messaging system. These systems allow teams to easily communicate with one another via chat. Employees can easily see others on their team or look up employees to communicate with them. Messaging systems are much easier for long-running conversations. It is much easier to track a conversation using these programs rather than going through a long chain of e-mails. Files and pictures can easily be embedded into the chat so that teams can coordinate work in one place.

Deploying a messaging system is as easy as licensing the users through the cloud portal, installing the messaging software on systems, and then having users log into the application with their cloud credentials. Some solutions do not even require the installation of software. For example, chatting on the Google Workspace requires only a browser. There are often phone apps that can be used too, so that using the messaging solution is as easy as sending a text message.

Solutions

A variety of cloud solutions can be deployed. We already mentioned some of the communication solutions. Some other popular solutions include

- Web services
- Collaboration tools
- Financial solutions
- CRM
- Identity management
- Directory services

Web Services

Web services are one of the most well-known cloud services. Cloud consumers can easily create websites by signing up for one of these services. The cloud provider hosts the website and often maintains the back-end content management system (CMS), such as WordPress, Drupal, Joomla, or Magento. This allows the cloud consumer to focus on developing the content for the website. This could be anything from an informative company site to an e-commerce platform or a blog.

Collaboration Tools

Collaboration tools are designed to make it easier for teams to work together and manage projects or tasks.

- **Document collaboration**   Document collaboration tools, such as Google Docs, Microsoft SharePoint, HyperOffice, and Box.com, allow multiple people to access, edit, and comment on documents as they are developed. These solutions provide a portal where the documents reside. The portal can be organized with a hierarchy consisting of folders, and access can be assigned at file or folder levels. Document collaboration tools track the changes made to files using a version history so that previous versions of documents or individual changes with the documents can be viewed. Changes are marked with the user who made the change.

- **Project management**   Solutions like Trello, Asana, and Monday allow users to create projects and then track and assign tasks within projects. They offer visual tools so tasks can be moved around between different buckets to show status. Comments can be placed within tasks to keep team members and project managers informed of the status.

Financial Solutions

Financial solutions allow companies to perform accounting or other financial functions online through a single portal. These include accounting tools like QuickBooks and benefit and payroll tools like ADP.

CRM

Customer relationship management (CRM) software offers an easy way for salespeople and managers to identify leads, contact those leads, track engagement through the sales pipeline, and track sales productivity metrics.

Identity Management

Identity management solutions help track and manage users' access to enterprise resources. Identity management systems can be linked to a variety of cloud services or in-house systems that an organization wishes to manage. Credentials are then provisioned for users, and access can be granted to those systems. A user does not need to have access to all systems, and their access to a particular system can be granularly managed. Individual application roles can be mapped to roles with the identity management solution so that it is easy to establish access to multiple resources for a single employee, contractor, or customer role.

Directory Services

Directory services are used to organize computer and user entities within one or more domains. Each entity has a unique identifier within the domain. Users can be assigned permissions and roles that govern their access to resources. Directory services can also be connected to one another to provide access to resources for users in other domains or federations.

Deploying Virtual Systems

You will likely find yourself needing to deploy virtual systems to the cloud. This section discusses how to deploy virtual machines, virtual appliances, and virtual desktops to cloud systems.

Virtual Machines

If you are using an IaaS solution, you will be deploying the systems to the CSP's infrastructure. However, in PaaS solutions, you will use the CSP's self-service portal or other tools to create new virtual machines. In both solutions, the deployment of virtual systems is quite streamlined.

The first step will be to determine the performance needs of the virtual machine. Cloud VM deployment can be performed through a guided deployment from the cloud portal, templates, custom images, or CLI scripting languages.

Guided Deployment   The wizard-based guided deployment is often the easiest for a small number of VMs because the system walks you through all the options. You will choose to create a new machine and then be able to select from various performance profiles. Each profile comes with an associated monthly cost. For example, at the time of writing this text, a low-end Azure VM in their Bs-Series costs $2.74 per month and is a fairly bare-bones setup with few resources. Toward the other end of the scale is the H-Series with 60 vCPU cores, 4GB of RAM per core, four logical drives, and 260 GB/sec of memory bandwidth at the cost of $581.08 per month. It is easy to vertically scale the VM later on to a profile with more resources. The idea is to right-size the VM so that it achieves your required performance and capacity at the lowest cost.

These VMs come in Windows or Linux. The wizard will walk you through configuring the remaining settings, such as networking, security groups, and remote access. The primary disadvantage to the guided deployment is that it is very repetitive for large-scale deployments, and it lacks some configuration options.

Templates   VM templates are virtual machines that are already partially configured. VM templates are typically generalized so that unique system identifiers are generated when the template is used to create a new machine. These templates allow for new virtual machines to be rapidly created. Cloud vendors often use templates to spool up new machines quickly when requested, and you can use them too. Templates can be divided into two types: OS templates and solution templates.

- **OS templates**   OS templates are VMs that are preconfigured with the operating system but no other software. These are best used when you are creating a new virtual machine that will have a unique role but run a standard operating system.

- **Solution templates**   Solution templates are VMs that are preconfigured with the operating system, patches, applications, and software dependencies, such as frameworks or necessary supplemental tools. Cloud vendors have a marketplace of solution templates that you can choose from to meet your needs for specific applications.

Custom Images   Custom images can also be created. Custom images are highly configured templates that can be used to quickly deploy an almost entirely functional machine. Custom images are often made when you know you will create many VMs of the same type, such as web servers or virtual desktops, because they take more time to configure and reduce deployment time.

Appliances

Virtual appliances are self-contained software solutions that perform a specific role. These are often provided by a vendor. For example, you may wish to deploy a spam firewall as a virtual appliance in your cloud. You can purchase the system and obtain a VM from the vendor that you load into your cloud instead of plugging in actual hardware. There are also open-source appliances that you can download for free.

Virtual Desktop Infrastructure

Virtual desktop infrastructure (VDI) is a method of providing a desktop PC experience to end users over the network or cloud. VDI solutions use virtualization to host multiple desktop operating systems. Users connect to their desktops over the Internet from a variety of devices, such as thin clients, laptops, or tablets. The desktop software runs within the cloud or data center, isolating the processing, storage, and networking from the system that accesses the VDI.

VDI hosts many virtual desktops on the same host. VDI can be configured as persistent and nonpersistent. Persistent VDI allocates a virtual desktop per user, and user changes to that specific machine are retained. If the user downloads a file to the desktop or changes configuration settings, those settings will remain. Users will be connected to the same machine when they return. The advantage of persistent VDI is that users can personalize their desktop and customize it for their work or continue work from day to day.

In nonpersistent VDI, users are connected to whichever desktop is available, rather than a specific one. Changes are not retained on the desktop, and each desktop system is identical. The advantage of nonpersistent VDI is that it is simpler to deploy and manage because IT does not need to support custom configurations. If a desktop system is not working correctly, it can be removed and replaced with an identical one without changing the user experience.

Scripted Deployment

You can develop scripts to perform a wide variety of virtual deployment tasks with minimal effort. For example, you could automatically spin up new VMs from templates or custom images, deploy appliances, or move VMs between performance tiers. Scripts can be kicked off manually or be scripted to execute based on certain conditions, such as expanding a VDI with more virtual desktops when a new employee is hired. Rather than walk through a process many times, a script could create many machines in one operation. Scripts can also be optimized to perform many tasks in parallel to accelerate the deployment process.

Networking

Cloud systems require many different networking components to function correctly. Some of these components may be configured by the CSP, but others you will need to configure. This section covers virtual networks, cloud firewalls, virtual routing, VPNs, and VPCs.

Virtual Networks

You may need to establish virtual networks to connect your VMs or segment VMs into different networks. Companies typically segment different types of machines so that they can strictly govern the type of traffic allowed between zones. For example, you may have a virtual network for web servers and allow connections from the Internet to this zone. You can then specify another network for virtual desktops and only allow connections to this network over a VPN.

Exercise 7-1: Creating a Virtual Network in Azure

In this exercise, we will create a virtual network in Azure. Note: You will need to have an Azure subscription to perform this task. You can sign up for a free 12-month subscription if you do not have one.

   1. Sign in to the Azure portal (https://portal.azure.com).

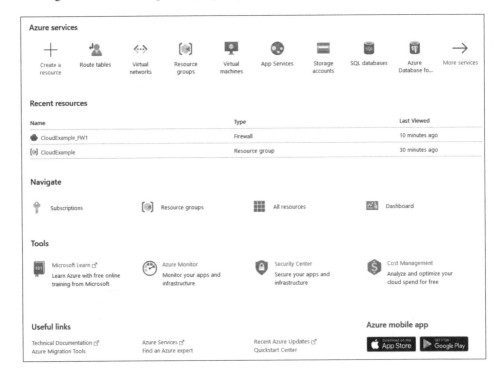

2. Select Virtual Networks. When the screen changes, select the Add button.

3. In the Create Virtual Network screen, enter the following options. Select your Azure subscription in the subscription drop-down box. Then select a resource group. The resource group chosen for this example is one that I created previously called CloudExample. Name the instance **CloudExample_Net1** and choose a region. In this example, we chose the East US region. When you are done, your screen will look like this:

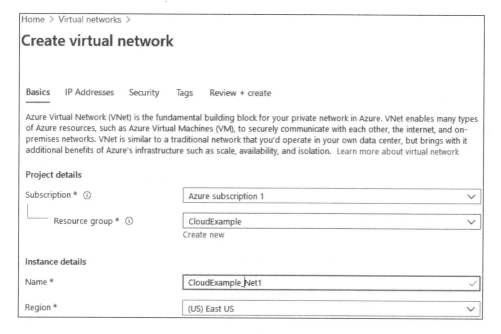

4. Click the blue Review + Create button at the bottom. This will display a screen that shows you the values you just entered. Click the blue Create button at the bottom.

5. The deployment will take a few minutes. When it is done, you will see a screen like the following illustration, stating that the deployment is complete. Click the Go To Resource button.

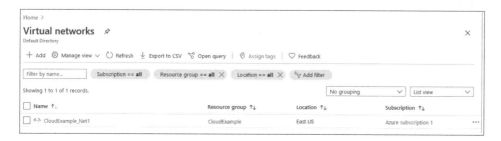

Cloud Firewalls

Firewalls are devices that sit between networks to govern the traffic flow. They use access control lists (ACLs) to determine which traffic is allowed and which should be denied. There are a variety of other, more advanced features. Cloud firewalls are discussed in more detail in Chapter 11. This section explores how to deploy them. Cloud vendors will often have firewall functionality that you can configure within the cloud portal.

Common features that are available to consumers include defining the traffic types allowed and which machines can receive that traffic. You may also be able to specify inspection rules from a set of prebuilt templates. You can also deploy firewalls as virtual appliances. Many of the same companies that make hardware firewalls also make virtual appliances with the same functionality. These firewalls can offer features that built-in firewalls do not have, or they can allow for a company to implement a consistent firewall strategy within each cloud and on-premises location by using a mix of cloud and hardware firewalls along with centralized management tools.

Virtual Routing

Virtual routing is necessary in order to make various virtual networks talk to one another. A virtual router makes decisions on how to send and receive data between networks based on the routing protocol configured on it. Each routing protocol uses a specific method to determine the best path a packet can take to its destination. Some routing protocols include Border Gateway Protocol (BGP), Interior Gateway Routing Protocol (IGRP),Open Shortest Path First (OSPF), and Routing Information Protocol (RIP). BGP uses rule sets; IGRP uses delay, load, and bandwidth; OSPF uses link-state; and RIP uses hop count to make routing decisions.

Cloud vendors will often have routing functionality that you can configure within the cloud portal to specify static routes or enable routing protocols.

Static and Dynamic Routes   Static routes are manually configured instructions that tell a router always to send traffic over a specific link. These differ from dynamic routes that are built using routing protocols that obtain routing information by querying neighboring routers. Dynamic routes can change with network conditions such as a failed link, but static routes will not change.

Static routes are often used for routing where there is only one option, such as the default route that establishes a single connection to the outside world. They do not require updating, so they use fewer system resources on the router. Dynamic routes are best when there are multiple possible ways to get from source to destination. Dynamic routes can determine the most optimal path to take and can automatically adjust based on link availability. However, they do need to be maintained, and this consumes processing on the router and network resources when exchanging routing information with other routers.

Exercise 7-2: Creating a Default Route on Azure

In this exercise, we will create a static default route in Azure.

   1. Sign in to the Azure portal (https://portal.azure.com).

2. Type **route tables** in the search bar at the top and select Route Tables once it appears. You will be presented with the following screen:

3. We will need a route table before we can create routes. Click Create Route Table.

4. Select your Azure subscription in the subscription drop-down box. Then select a resource group. The resource group selected for this example is one that I created previously called CloudExample. Select a region from the drop-down box. In this example, we selected East US. Give the instance a name. In this example, we called it CloudExample-FWDefaultRoute, as shown next. Click the blue Review + Create button at the bottom. This will display a screen that shows you the values you just entered. Click the blue Create button at the bottom.

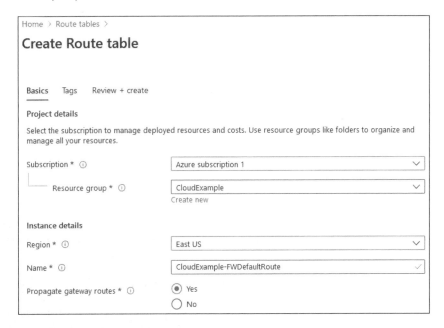

5. The deployment will take a few minutes. When it is done, you will see a screen like the following illustration, stating that the deployment is complete. Click the Go To Resource button.

6. Now that we have a route table, we can create routes inside it. Under settings, on the left side, select Routes.

7. When the route screen appears, click the Add button.

8. The Add Route screen will appear. Enter a route name. In this example, we named it FWDefaultRoute. Set the address prefix to 0.0.0.0/0 so that it will be used for target addresses that are not covered by other explicit routes. Set the next hop type to the virtual network gateway, as shown next. Click the OK button at the bottom.

9. It will take a moment for the rule to be created. Wait for the screen to display the new rule, as shown here:

Virtual Private Network

A virtual private network (VPN) connects systems over a public network, such as the Internet, so that they can operate as if they were on the same LAN segment. A VPN can connect multiple office locations together into a single network, or it can be used to connect remote employees into the company's cloud. It is quite common to create a VPN to cloud resources so that users can access those resources like they would for local office servers. VPNs are also used by administrators to perform maintenance and other tasks.

Virtual Private Cloud

A virtual private cloud (VPC) is used to isolate resources within a public cloud for an organization. A subnet is created for the VPC, and then the resources are segmented off from other cloud resources with one or more VXLAN, NVGRE, STT, or GENEVE segments and associated routing and access control lists to govern traffic flow. Traffic that exits the VPC is encrypted.

 NOTE Microsoft refers to their VPC as a VNet, not a VPC, with no difference in functionality from other cloud providers' VPCs.

Hub and Spoke   The hub and spoke VPC model funnels connections back to the VPC in the cloud. The VPC acts as the central place for communication. As you can see in Figure 7-6, each of these offices is connected together and to the cloud resources through the VPC.

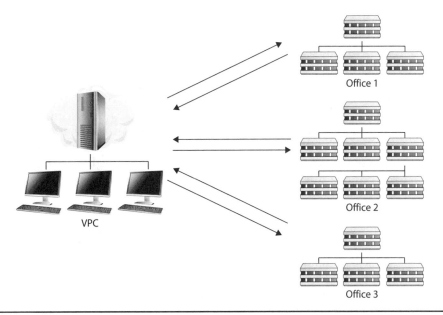

Figure 7-6   Hub and spoke VPC

Peering   VPC peering is a way to link multiple VPCs together over the SCP backbone. You may do this if you have several cloud accounts from the same CSP that you want to connect together into a shared network space. Mergers and acquisitions often go through this, but it is also very common when multiple departments set up cloud resources and then later determine that they should be shared with other parts of the organization.

Still, VPC peering can be a planned event from the beginning when combining the best from multiple cloud providers into a single solution or solution set. The advantage of VPC peering over other connection methods is that the traffic does not traverse the public Internet. Rather, the traffic flows through the network links owned and operated by the CSP using private IP addresses instead of public, Internet-facing ones.

To set up VPC peering, the owner of one VPC sends a peering request to the owner of the other VPC. Once the request is accepted, static routes will need to be created in each VPC to point to the other. Next, configure security rules to allow traffic between the VPCs to the resources you want to share. Lastly, enable and configure hostname resolution for the VPC connections so that systems will be able to connect to resources by name.

 CAUTION   Make sure that you are using distinct IP address spaces before you set up VPC peering. Otherwise, you will have IP conflicts.

Containers

Containers are isolated silos that house applications. Containers should not be confused with virtual machines. Containers are much smaller than a virtual machine because they only need to retain their application components, not the underlying operating system. This means that they consume less storage space and less memory than deploying applications over virtual machines. Containers can be created or destroyed at will so that they only consume resources when they are needed. Running containers typically use nonpersistent or volatile storage, such as memory, to operate. Some primary features of containers include their isolation, portability, and ease of deployment.

Containers isolate applications because they are self-contained. An application within a container is packaged with all the code, runtime libraries, files, dependencies, and frameworks necessary for its operation. Because of this, containers do not interfere with other applications or containers that run on the machine. Containers allow you to have multiple versions of the same application or multiple applications that rely on their own framework versions that can run on the same platform without conflict. This is a great way to test new applications or various application builds in parallel without interfering with existing applications. It also gives you the freedom to deploy applications without worrying about their impact on the host system other than their resource consumption.

 EXAM TIP   Container isolation is considered lightweight isolation as compared to the isolation provided through virtual machines. Dedicated virtual machines for applications offer more security boundaries between applications that run on different VMs.

Containers allow for easy portability because they are platform agnostic. Containers operate within a container runtime that is installed on the platform to serve as an interface between the container and the platform, much like the virtualization layer between a hypervisor and guest virtual machines. Container vendors, including Docker, Google, and CoreOS, created the Open Container Initiative (OCI) to create open container format and runtime standards. OCI has released a runtime specification and an image specification to aid in developing standard runtime support on different platforms. The same application can easily run on multiple different platforms that each have the container runtime.

Containers are easy to deploy because DevOps teams do not need to troubleshoot compatibility issues or perform machine-specific configurations in order for the applications to run in the environment. More extensive applications can be broken down into many smaller pieces that are each containerized. These containers can then be combined into a larger unit called a cluster that is then managed with a container orchestrator, such as Kubernetes.

Configure Environment Variables

Environment variables are used by containers to store values that can be used to customize the application. Environment variables are often used to enable or disable features or customize them for a customer or setting. Here are some examples for setting environment variables for different container runtimes.

The following code will assign two variables, FirstFeature and SecondFeature, the value of 1. If this were a feature that you wished to enable, you could do it by setting these values to 1 and disable them by setting their values to 0.

```
web:
    environment:
        - FirstFeature=1
        - SecondFeature=1
```

This is the same code that will run on Amazon:

```
"environment": [
    {
        "name": "FirstFeature",
        "value": "1"
    }
    {
        "name": "SecondFeature",
        "value": "1"
    }
]
```

This code sets the environment variable in the Azure CLI when creating a container called cloudtest:

```
az container create \
--name cloudtest \
--environment-variables 'FirstFeature' ='1' 'SecondFeature' ='1'
```

Configure Secrets

Secrets are items that must be protected from unauthorized access. They include data such as passwords, private keys, SSL certificates, or other sensitive data. Secrets are stored and transmitted in an encrypted form. Only authorized containers can access the data in the secrets.

The following code creates a Docker secret named AppCertificateFingerprintSHA-1 and assigns it the value 9F:FB:59:0D:2F:62:0E:DF:58:30:EE:02:17:97:2D:4F:CE:09: EB:6C.

```
docker secret create AppCertificateFingerprintSHA-1 9F:FB:59:0D:2F:62:0E:DF:5
8:30:EE:02:17:97:2D:4F:CE:09:EB:6C
```

 CAUTION   Do not pass sensitive information to your containers using environment variables because environment variables are not encrypted. This could expose those passwords to others and compromise the security of your container. Use secrets instead.

Configure Storage

Containerized apps utilize storage that resides outside the container for data. This is ideal because the container is typically running in nonpersistent storage, and many containers may need access to the data. Containers access storage by mounting the volumes or bind points within the container.

Mounting a volume allocates the entire logical disk to the container, while bind points allocate a directory tree consisting of folders, files, and subfolders to the container. Volumes usually provide better performance, but bind mounts are better used for shared configuration files. The following code mounts a volume called mydisk to a folder called data in the container called cloudtest:

```
docker run -d \
  --name cloudtest \
  --mount source=mydisk,target=/data \
```

Post-Deployment Validation

The last step in the deployment process is to validate that the application accomplishes the user and business requirements set forth at the beginning of the project. Establish specific test cases to evaluate this and then go through a checklist to ensure that each objective is met. Do not rely on just a single person to do this validation. Ensure you have a good sampling of testers, including stakeholders who sponsored and suggested the need for the solution in the first place.

Remote Access Tools

The cloud computing environment is inherently in a different location from the working environment because of the environment needs servers have and the economies of scale that can be achieved by housing thousands of servers in the same place. The cloud consumer might not even know where the cloud provider's servers are being hosted. This is why remote access is required to manage, service, and maintain systems.

Remotely accessing a server does not always have to mean accessing the server from an offsite location. There are times when simply connecting to a host computer or virtual machine from a workstation is more convenient than physically walking over to the server and logging in. When a quick fix or change needs to be made to a virtual machine or host computer, accessing that server from a local workstation saves time. Remote access prevents the need to walk or drive to the data center and physically sit at the machine that requires the change.

Being able to remotely access and troubleshoot a virtualization host or virtual machine requires less time and makes fixing and maintaining the environment easier to accomplish. Some remote access tools include remote hypervisor access and Remote Desktop Protocol (RDP).

Remote Hypervisor Access

There are a variety of ways to remotely connect to a hypervisor. Most vendors allow a console to be installed on a workstation or server that is not the hypervisor. This allows a user to manage the hypervisor from their workstation. The machine with remote management tools is often referred to as a jump or step machine. Multiple hypervisors can be managed from a single console on a workstation, giving a single-pane-of-glass approach to hypervisor management.

Remote hypervisor tools enable administrators to perform most host management tasks as if they were connecting directly to the actual hypervisor. The client console gives them the ability to create or modify virtual machines or virtual hard disks, configure virtual machine settings, and so on. This allows them to do all the administrative tasks that are required on a day-to-day basis from a single workstation.

Users of remote hypervisor tools need to have the correct administrative permissions on the hypervisor to modify the host computer's settings or the virtual machines. Using a console from a workstation is an excellent way to connect to a hypervisor host because it looks and acts just as it would if the user were locally logged into the hypervisor host.

RDP

RDP differs from installing the hypervisor console on a workstation. It allows for remotely connecting and logging into the Windows-based hypervisor host's desktop. RDP provides remote display and input capabilities over the network. RDP connections are made through software that supports RDP over TCP port 3389. RDP is built into Windows machines and can be executed by typing **mstsc** from the command prompt or run command. Figure 7-7 shows an example of RDP client software that is used to connect to a hypervisor host remotely. RDP is a multichannel protocol that provides separate virtual channels for transmitting device communication and presentation data from the server.

Figure 7-7
Remote desktop
connection:
An example of
RDP software

Employing a Console to Connect to a Remote Hypervisor Host

I remember a time when I was working with an organization that had deployed multiple hypervisor hosts in its environment. The organization had a total of 20 hypervisor hosts and 250 virtual machines. The data center that the hypervisor hosts were installed on was in an adjacent building, and the time it took administrators to walk to the data center was time that they could have spent doing other tasks. The organization needed a way to centrally manage the hosts from the administrators' workstation computers without logging in to each one individually.

The solution was to install the console on each of the administrators' workstations and add the hypervisor hosts into the single console. This allowed each administrator to see all 20 of the hypervisor host computers and manage those hosts. It was a great solution that satisfied the organization's needs by saving the administrators' time and effort and managing all 20 hypervisor hosts from a single console. The console installed on each workstation looks and responds just like the console installed on the hypervisor host computer.

The advantage of using RDP to connect to a hypervisor is that the user has direct access to the hypervisor server without having to be physically sitting at the hypervisor host. RDP allows users to interact with the server just as if they were sitting in front of it. So instead of just having access to the hypervisor console, RDP enables access to the entire server. The user can launch other applications on the server, as well as change system settings on the hypervisor host computer itself. RDP allows for complete control of the server operating system, not just the hypervisor settings, without physically attending the hypervisor host computer.

One of the disadvantages of using RDP for managing a virtualization environment is that an administrator cannot manage multiple hypervisor hosts in a single RDP session like a remote hypervisor client console. The option to use RDP is currently only available for the Microsoft hypervisor. Connections made to other modern hypervisors such as VMware, Citrix, and Oracle require the use of a software client installed on a jump machine.

Console Port

A console port allows an administrator to use a cable to connect directly to a hypervisor host computer or a virtual machine. The administrator can use a parallel or serial port to connect peripherals to a virtual machine, add serial ports, and change the logical COM port configuration. The virtual serial port can connect to a physical serial port or a file on the host computer. Using a console port allows for managing a virtualization host computer directly from another computer connected to the host computer with a console cable.

SSH

The Secure Shell (SSH) protocol provides a secure way to manage network devices, including hypervisor hosts, remotely. SSH is capable of using public-key cryptography to exchange a symmetric key covertly between the SSH client and the SSH server, creating a fast and secure channel, and then using that channel to authenticate a remote computer and user if required. It can also use a traditional username and password for authentication. The default port for SSH is port 22.

SSH can use a manually generated public-private key pair to perform authentication. The symmetric key is used to encrypt the connection. SSH can be used to log into a remote computer and execute certain command strings against a hypervisor host machine.

SSH provides strong authentication if using the latest version and secure communication over an insecure channel. It was designed to replace remote shell (RSH) and Telnet because RSH and Telnet send unencrypted traffic over the network, making them insecure communication methods.

When designing a virtualization environment, it is not recommended to directly expose the hypervisor host to the Internet. Normally, the hypervisor host is installed behind a firewall or some other form of protection, which makes it difficult to access the hypervisor host off-site. SSH allows for the creation of a secure management tunnel to the hypervisor host computer or virtual machine and provides a secure way to manage those devices, since all the traffic is sent through an encrypted tunnel.

 EXAM TIP SSH provides a way to access a hypervisor host or virtual machine securely from an off-site location.

HTTP

Another option for remotely accessing a hypervisor host machine is through a web console using HTTP or HTTPS. Hypertext Transfer Protocol (HTTP) is an application protocol built on TCP to distribute Hypertext Markup Language (HTML) files, text, images, sound, videos, multimedia, and other types of information over the Internet. HTTP operates by default over port 80, and HTTPS operates by default over port 443.

HTTP typically allows for communication between a web client or web browser and a web server hosting a website. Most hypervisor vendors have a web console that allows an administrator to access a hypervisor host from virtually anywhere as long as the hypervisor's DNS name can be resolved and HTTPS access is permitted through perimeter devices.

Administrators may have to install an additional component when doing the initial hypervisor host installation to provide web access to a host computer. The hypervisor host web service should be configured to use HTTPS to ensure a secure way to connect. Some hypervisors (like Microsoft IIS) may require additional software on the host computer as well. Connecting to a hypervisor host computer using a web console is a quick and easy way to perform simple configuration on a virtual machine.

Chapter Review

The importance of planning before deploying cloud solutions cannot be overstated. This chapter provided you with the tools and techniques to conduct the requirement analysis for a new solution, design that solution, select a cloud offering, and then build a deployment plan. This is then presented to management to seek approval for deployment. We then walked through the implementation of various cloud solutions and virtual systems, networking, and containers. Finally, remote access tools were described so that you can manage the systems you deploy in the cloud.

Questions

The following questions will help you gauge your understanding of the material in this chapter. Read all the answers carefully because there might be more than one correct answer. Choose the best response(s) for each question.

1. Which of the following are steps in the requirement analysis process? (Choose all that apply.)

   A. Technical requirements

   B. Compliance requirements

   C. User and business requirements

   D. Data requirements

2. You are planning the network for a new VDI cloud deployment. You need seven networks, and the largest subnet will have 25 hosts on it. Which subnet mask would you choose for a class C network?

   A. Console port

   B. SSH

   C. Hypervisor console

   D. 255.255.255.224

3. You are reviewing a cloud service contract to determine if it is the right fit. Which section would you review to determine the maximum amount of downtime allotted in the contract?

   A. Data privacy and security provisions

   B. Indemnification

   C. SLA

   D. Force majeure

4. You are reviewing a cloud service contract to determine if it is the right fit. You receive an alert that a virtual machine is down. The server does not respond to a ping. What tool should you use to troubleshoot the server if you are off-site?

   A. Console port

   B. SSH

   C. Hypervisor console

   D. SMTP

5. Which of the following would you use to remotely access a virtualization host in a secure fashion?

   A. Telnet

   B. Ping

   C. HTTPS

   D. Console port

6. The primary stakeholder for your project has asked for a document showing the responsibilities of each task. Which document should you send them?

   A. Task tree

   B. Work breakdown structure

   C. Timeline

   D. User responsibilities design

7. You would like to deploy a new task management system to your cloud. The vendor offers a virtual machine that has its software already installed and configured on it. What should you look for in the cloud portal to deploy this?

A. Solution template

B. Custom image

C. VDI image

D. Software download link

8. You are deploying a container to a QA platform so that multiple testers can begin evaluating the application. What would you use to enable certain functions within the application for each test group?

A. Configuration settings

B. Secrets

C. Deployment scripts

D. Environment variables

9. Which of the following would be used to directly connect to a hypervisor host remotely to modify operating system settings on the hypervisor host?

A. RDP

B. Console port

C. SMTP

D. HTTPS

10. Which of the following is a benefit of remote hypervisor administration?

A. Only being able to modify one hypervisor host at a time

B. Being able to remotely manage multiple hypervisor hosts from a single console

C. Not having access to a hypervisor host

D. Remotely accessing a hypervisor host has no benefit

Answers

1. B, C. Requirement analysis consists of (1) user and business requirements, (2) compliance requirements, (3) security requirements, and (4) budgetary requirements.

2. D. 255.255.255.224 has three subnet bits, allowing for eight subnets and five host bits, allowing for 30 hosts per subnet.

3. C. The SLA specifies the promised maximum amount of downtime and damages provided to the consumer if it exceeds that maximum.

4. B. Secure Shell (SSH) provides a secure way to remotely manage network devices, including hypervisor hosts.

5. C. HTTPS gives you a way to access a virtualization host remotely in a secure fashion.

6. B. The work breakdown structure shows each of the tasks and whom they are assigned to.

7. A. A solution template will provide you with the software in the marketplace, and the software will already be packaged within the VM for deployment.

8. D. Environment variables will allow you to enable or disable certain features from the containerized application.

9. A. The Remote Desktop Protocol (RDP) lets you establish a remote connection directly to a hypervisor host. It allows you to change system settings on the hypervisor host computer itself.

10. B. The ability to remotely manage multiple hypervisor hosts from a single console from your workstation allows for a quick and easy way to make changes to multiple hosts and is an important benefit of remote hypervisor administration.

CHAPTER 8

DevOps

In this chapter, you will learn about

- Application life cycle
- Ending applications
- Secure coding
- DevOps cloud transformation

Many companies have combined the distinct functions of development (programming) and IT (operations) into a single group called DevOps. Instead of one team writing software and another deploying and supporting it, a single team is responsible for the entire life cycle. This has led to improved agility and better responsiveness of DevOps teams to the issues faced by end users because the team works directly with them rather than one department removed. This chapter covers some DevOps functions, including resource monitoring, remote access, and life cycle management.

Organizations need to be able to manage the applications that they put in place, and they need to ensure those applications are developed securely. Life cycle management includes everything from the requirements stage to retirement. Each stage has inputs and outputs that connect the stages to one another. The application life cycle enables an organization to manage each of its service offerings as efficiently and effectively as possible and ensure that each of those services continues to provide value throughout its life cycle.

Application Life Cycle

Just as creatures are born and eventually die, applications are created and eventually retired. This process is called the application life cycle, also known as the software development life cycle (SDLC). The application life cycle consists of five phases: specifications, development, testing, deployment, and maintenance. Figure 8-1 shows the application life cycle.

EXAM TIP No official version of the SDLC exists. There are several versions, some of which have six, seven, or even ten phases. However, each version still covers the same things, just more or less granularly. It is important to understand the things that are taking place in the process no matter how many phases are described.

Figure 8-1
Application
life cycle

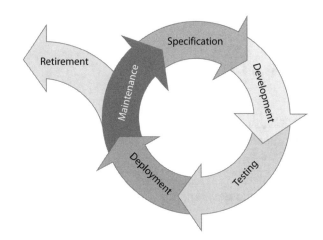

Phase 1: Specifications

The first phase of the application life cycle is the specifications phase. In this phase, the application's reason for being is documented. Users and stakeholders explain what they would like the application to do and what problem it will solve for them. For applications that have already been developed, this phase is about identifying improvements or bug fixes.

Roadmap

A software development roadmap is a strategic plan for a development project. It describes the goals and objectives of the application. The roadmap should be aligned with the overall business strategy to show how the application will provide business value.

Next, the roadmap lays out the activities that will be performed throughout the application life cycle. Some of the benefits of a roadmap include:

- Better communication of goals and objectives
- Team members understand their responsibilities
- Communicates the value of the project to stakeholders

Phase 2: Development

In the development phase, project managers turn specifications identified in the first phase into a model for a working program. They map out the requirements for different discrete tasks with the idea of creating the smallest discrete functional set of code that can be tested and validated. In this way, when bugs or flaws are identified, it is easy to pinpoint where they came from. Those tasks are assigned to developers who write that segment. Application developers or programmers then write source code for the current project that has been designed.

Source code is written in a selected programming language. There are a wide variety of programming languages. Some popular languages include C, Java, Python, Perl, and Ruby. Some languages are only supported on certain platforms, such as Windows systems, web platforms, or mobile platforms. Programming languages also differ in how structured they are. Some have very rigid rules, while others give developers a great degree of freedom. They may also differ in how much error checking they perform.

Source code is made up of modules that contain functions and procedures. Within these functions and procedures, the elements of code are written. These include variables that store a value; classes that define program concepts containing properties and attributes; Boolean operations such as AND, OR, and NOR; looping functions that repeat sections of code; and sorting and searching functions.

Developers write source code in an integrated development environment (IDE) that can check the code's syntax, similar to how spell checking works in a word processing application. Source code is written in a selected language, and each of the developers will use the same language when writing a program together. Cloud development tools allow development teams to easily collaborate on code together. AWS has a whole suite of development tools such as their CodeCommit repository, CodeDeploy deployment suite, or CodePipeline CI/CD system. Similarly, Microsoft has its long-standing Visual Studio IDE that can be tied to many of their cloud tools, such as Azure DevOps Server, a version control, project management, and CI/CD system.

Builds

The source code developed to accomplish the specifications is known as a build. This includes the set of bug fixes or features identified in the first phase. Only small parts of the code are written at a time to keep everything as simple to manage as possible—the more complex the code, the greater the chance that bugs will pop up. Builds go through a process of compilation and linking to allow the source code to run on a computer.

- **Compilation** A process that transforms the source code, programming statements written in a programming language into instructions that a computer can understand. These instructions are known as object code. The compilation process is typically platform-specific, meaning that the source code would be transformed differently for different operating systems or versions. The compilation process will also perform some basic error checking.

- **Linking** A process that combines the object code with related libraries into a program that can be executed on a computer.

Figure 8-2 shows the build process for an application written in the ASP.NET Core app in Microsoft Azure. The build process checks for basic errors and identified an issue with the namespace name.

The development phase continues until all the elements required in the specifications have been created in the program. However, it is iterative in that small portions of the feature set may be sent to the testing phase and then return to the development phase until the feature set is completed. Developers do some initial testing on the functions

```
↻  |  Azure Cloud Shell

                                                          Program.cs                                                    ...
FILES                        ↻     4    using Microsoft.Extensions.Configuration;
▶ bin                              5
▲ Controllers                      6    namespace KeyVaultDemoApp
    SecretTestController.cs        7    {
    WeatherForecastController.cs   8        public class Program
▶ obj                              9        {
▶ Properties                      10            public static void Main(string[] args)
    appsettings.Development.json  11            {
    appsettings.json             12                CreateWebHostBuilder(args).Build().Run();
    KeyVaultDemoApp.csproj       13            }
    Program.cs                   14
    Startup.cs                   15            public static IHostBuilder CreateHostBuilder(string[] args) =>
    WeatherForecast.cs           16                Host.CreateDefaultBuilder(args)
                                 17                    .ConfigureWebHostDefaults(webBuilder =>
                                 18                    {
                                 19                        webBuilder.UseStartup<Startup>();
                                 20                    })
                                 21                    .ConfigureAppConfiguration((context, config) =>
                                 22                    {
                                 23                        // Build the current set of configuration to load values from
                                 24                        // JSON files and environment variables, including VaultName.
                                 25                        var builtConfig = config.Build();
                                 26
                                 27                        // Use VaultName from the configuration to create the full vault URL.
                                 28                        var vaultName = builtConfig["CloudTest"];
                                 29                        Uri vaultUri = new Uri($"https://CloudTest.vault.azure.net/");
                                 30
                                 31                        // Load all secrets from the vault into configuration. This will autom
                                 32                        // authenticate to the vault using a managed identity. If a managed id
                                 33                        // is not available, it will check if Visual Studio and/or the Azure C
```

```
Microsoft (R) Build Engine version 16.7.0+7fb82e5b2 for .NET
Copyright (C) Microsoft Corporation. All rights reserved.

  Determining projects to restore...
  All projects are up-to-date for restore.
Program.cs(15,23): error CS0246: The type or namespace name 'IHostBuilder' could not be found (are you missing a using di
rective or an assembly reference?) [/home/isconsultants/KeyVaultDemoApp/KeyVaultDemoApp.csproj]

Build FAILED.

Program.cs(15,23): error CS0246: The type or namespace name 'IHostBuilder' could not be found (are you missing a using di
rective or an assembly reference?) [/home/isconsultants/KeyVaultDemoApp/KeyVaultDemoApp.csproj]
    0 Warning(s)
    1 Error(s)

Time Elapsed 00:00:05.56
```

Figure 8-2   Building an Azure application

they create to ensure that they perform as they were designed to do. Once enough programming elements are gathered together to create a build, they are passed on to the testing phase.

Builds are organized as either trunks or branches. A trunk is the current stable build, while branches contain new features that have yet to be subjected to a full range of testing or integration with other components. Branches are created from a copy of the trunk code. They are rolled back into the trunk when they have been sufficiently tested.

Version Control

In the past, developers kept multiple copies of application code as they worked on a project and might roll back to versions if issues were encountered in testing later on. They might have taken copious notes within the source code to help inform them of its purpose. Still others just relied upon their memory to maintain their code. This may have worked for small development projects with a single developer, but it does not scale to the type of projects worked on today. Furthermore, it made it much harder for developers to maintain software developed by others.

Development teams today often involve many people working in tandem to write pieces of the application. These people may be geographically distributed and need to be able to track and manage source code changes. Software version control (SVC) systems are used to manage code throughout the application life cycle. SVC systems perform the following core tasks:

- Store software trunks and branches in their various revision states
- Receive code from multiple developers
- Track changes made to source code, the developer making the change, and when the change occurred
- Store related documentation on software versions

 NOTE SVC systems are also known as revision control systems, source code management systems, or code repositories.

Developers are provisioned with accounts on the SVC and then a project for the program source code is created within the SVC. The developers are granted access to that project so that they can publish, or commit, source code to it. There are usually multiple different roles. Some users may be able to post code but not merge branches into trunks, while others may be able to create projects. Each time a change is made to the code, the developers publish the new code to the SVC. Some SVC systems can be used to establish workflow so that newly published code is made available for testing automatically.

Cloud SVC systems may be centralized where the project files and source code remain on a central system or set of systems that each person must access. One example would be the Apache Subversion SVC. In a centralized SVC, source code is published directly to the central repository. On the other hand, distributed SVC systems still have a central repository, but they also keep a local repository on developer machines that developers can use to work on their current branch. This can speed up commit time, and it can allow developers to continue working on tasks even if they do not have a connection to the SVC. However, this can pose a security risk for sensitive development projects, since the code is mirrored to multiple machines that may have different sets of security controls and be subject to potential physical loss or theft.

A company may have multiple versions of the same application that will each need to be updated. There may be versions specific to certain industry segments or user groups that differ from other versions but share much of the core functionality. It is important to be able to track the differences in the source code for these application versions so that new changes can be applied to each of the versions that are affected or would benefit from the change.

Phase 3: Testing

In this phase, the build developed in the development phase is subjected to testing to ensure that it performs according to specifications, without errors, bugs, or security issues. Development code should never be ported directly to the production environment because developers may not be aware of bugs or other problems with the build that the testing phase can reveal. Testers may be other developers, or their full job may be in testing builds. Either way, they are members of the DevOps team and an overall part of delivering the program.

Builds are typically deployed to a development environment, where the build is subjected to automated testing and individual testing by users and groups. This occurs for each distinct element that is coded so that errors can be identified and isolated. Most IDEs have built-in syntax checking, variable validation, and autocomplete to help keep the majority of typos from causing problems.

Some development environments exist locally on the developer's machine. This streamlines the process for deploying source code changes. Local development environments allow for the code to be executed in the development environment with breakpoints and other objects to find errors and monitor the details of program execution.

Once a build is stable in the development environment, it is moved to a staging or quality assurance (QA) environment. This is when quality assurance kicks in: testers go to staging servers and verify that the code works as intended.

The staging environment needs to be provisioned, or the existing environment needs to be made current. This includes making the patch level consistent with the production environment and installing add-ons or configuration changes that have been made in production since the last release. Testers use information from the change management database on recent production changes to obtain a list of changes to be made in the QA environment.

The testing phase should include people involved in the specifications phase to ensure that the specifications were correctly translated into an application. When bugs or issues are identified with the application, developers fix those issues until the application is ready to be deployed into production.

Lastly, procedures should be documented for how the system will be deployed and used. Deployment documentation will be used in phase 4, and user documentation will be used to train users on how to use the program and its new features appropriately. Documentation should also include a brief list of updates that can be distributed to users for reference.

Phase 4: Deployment

In the deployment phase, the application developed and tested in previous phases is installed and configured in production for stakeholders to use. The first step is to ensure that the resources required for the application deployment are available, including compute, memory, storage resources, and personnel. Teams may need to provision or deprovision cloud resources. Only then can the remainder of the deployment be scheduled.

It can be tempting to automate this process. However, deployment needs to be performed by a human and at a time when others are available to troubleshoot if necessary. Automatic deployments can lead to issues, particularly if someone accidentally triggers an automatic deployment to production.

Developers should do a final check of their code in this phase to remove testing elements such as debugger breakpoints and performance hogs such as verbose logging.

Then, project managers work with stakeholders and customers to identify an ideal time to do the deployment. They need to select a time that is convenient for the DevOps team and one that does not fall in peak times when customers have urgent need of the application. DevOps teams may be deploying application releases every other week, so they may need to have a regularly scheduled downtime for this. Other options include blue-green deployments where the site is deployed and tested and then a switch is quickly made to make that site live with minimal disruption to the user base. See Chapter 9 for more information on deployment methodologies.

It is critical to take a backup or snapshots of the application servers before rolling out the new version. Despite all the testing in the previous phase, problems still can arise, and you will want to have a good clean version to go back to if a problem arises. Sometimes issues are encountered when deploying to production, despite the testing that occurred in previous phases of the application life cycle. In such cases, DevOps teams may need to roll back to the snapshot if they cannot fix the deployment issues in a timely manner.

Once the application is deployed, users need to be trained on the new features or changes of the release. This could be as simple as sending out release notes or including links to video tutorials and bundling tooltips into the application, or it could be more involved such as requiring one-on-one training.

Software Release Management Systems

Software release management systems (SRMS) are software used to manage the deployment process and streamline the workflow surrounding moving releases through deployment to different environments such as QA, beta, or production. The SRMS serves as the orchestration hub for deployments and can efficiently deploy systems using deployment scripts. Deployments can be easily customized so that an update to code affecting multiple sites with differing configurations can be deployed with a few clicks. Some SRMS tools include CloudBees, Jenkins for Google Cloud, and the open-source tool Electric Cloud.

You may also choose to fully or partially automate deployment steps using an SRMS. Deployment can occur based on triggering events in a process known as software delivery automation (SDA). Detailed workflows for managing development life cycle tasks can greatly reduce the time it takes to get new releases out the door. SRMS are sometimes combined with SVC systems so that builds and releases can be tracked and managed in one central tool.

SRMS can deploy releases to a variety of different test or production systems. Some standard categories of software releases have arisen based on the level of testing the release has undergone. These categories include canary, beta, stable, and long-term support (LTS).

Canary

Canary builds get their name from the canaries coal miners used to take down with them into mines. Canaries are more susceptible to harmful gases than people are. Coal miners would observe the canary and listen for its singing. If the canary stopped singing or showed signs of illness, the coal miners would see that as a warning that dangerous gases might be present. This often saved the lives of coal miners. In a similar way, developers release a canary build to customers to see what issues they find with the software so that they can fix it for the next release. The customers of the canary build are used as an extension of the company's own testing team. There is usually very little gap between development and release of the canary build.

Canary builds usually have quite a few bugs in them, and they are not recommended for production use. Canary builds are quickly replaced with new versions, sometimes daily. Cloud customers do not need to reinstall canary builds because the developers do all the work for them. They just connect to the site and use the application. One example of an SRMS tool that can be used for canary releases is LaunchDarkly. It aids DevOps teams with deploying canary releases and obtaining bug information so that issues can be quickly identified and corrected with updated releases for the testers for the canary release.

Customers will often adopt a canary release to try out new features or generate interest in the latest version. Developers will build in functions to send back error information to the DevOps team so that they can identify, categorize, and prioritize bug files for later releases.

Beta

Beta builds, similar to canary builds, are still likely to have some bugs in them, but they are much more stable than the canary release. Beta builds are the last release before the stable build is released. Beta builds are often desired by consumers who want the latest feature and are willing to tolerate a few bugs in the process.

Stable

Stable builds are those that have gone through the canary and beta testing process and emerged with their bugs fixed. The company labels it stable because it has a reasonable level of confidence in the build's stability or ability to operate without encountering bugs. However, the true test of stability is time, and that is why there is another type of build called long-term support. The support offered for stable releases is often limited. It is usually less than one year, so companies will need to keep updating to newer stable versions if they want to continue receiving support.

Long-Term Support

LTS builds are those that have been exposed to normal usage as part of a stable build for some time. For this reason, enterprises can have a much higher degree of confidence in the build's stability, and the software manufacturer offers much longer support agreements for LTS software. These agreements can range from three to five years. Companies that favor stability over features will opt for the LTS software build.

Phase 5: Maintenance

Along the way, after deployment, various patches will be required to keep the application, or the resources it relies upon, functioning correctly. This phase is called the maintenance phase. Here the DevOps team will fix small user-reported bugs or configuration issues, field tickets from users, and measure and tweak performance to keep the application running smoothly.

There is an element of maintenance that involves a micro version of the entire application life cycle because small issues will result in specifications, which will lead to development and testing, and ultimately deployment into the production environment. Some of the tasks listed previously fall into this category. Suffice to say, this element is somewhat recursive.

Before adding new code, changing code, or performing other maintenance tasks that might affect application availability, the DevOps team works with stakeholders and customers to identify an ideal time to perform the activity. Some deployments may be urgent, such as fixes to address a critical vulnerability that was just discovered or a serious issue that users or customers are experiencing. In these cases, these limitations may be waived due to the criticality of the update.

It is important to note the difference between patches and releases here. Releases offer new features, while patches fix bugs or security problems.

Life Cycle Management

Life cycle management is the process or processes put in place by an organization to assist in the management, coordination, control, delivery, and support of its configuration items from the requirements stage to retirement. ITIL has established a framework for implementing life cycle management, and Microsoft has a framework that is based on ITIL.

ITIL

Information Technology Infrastructure Library (ITIL) provides a framework for implementing life cycle management. ITIL's model is a continuum consisting of the following five phases:

1. Service strategy

2. Service design

3. Service transition

4. Service operation

5. Continual service improvement

Each phase has inputs and outputs that connect the stages to one another, and continual improvement is recognized via multiple trips through the life cycle. Each time through, improvements are documented and then implemented based on feedback from each of the life cycle phases. These improvements enable the organization to execute each of its service offerings as efficiently and effectively as possible and ensure that each of those services provides as much value to its users as possible. Figure 8-3 shows the ITIL model. The three inner processes are cyclical, while the strategy and continuous improvement processes encapsulate them.

Figure 8-3
ITIL life cycle
management
continuum

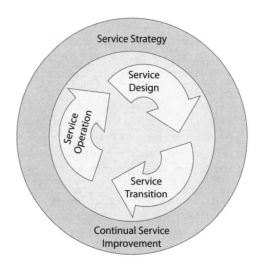

Microsoft Operations Framework

Microsoft Operations Framework (MOF) is based on ITIL. MOF has shortened the life cycle to four phases:

1. Plan
2. Deliver
3. Operate
4. Manage

These phases are usually depicted graphically in a continuum, as we see in Figure 8-4. This continuum represents the cyclical nature of process improvement, with a structured system of inputs and outputs that leads to continual improvement.

Figure 8-4
A representation
of the MOF life
cycle continuum

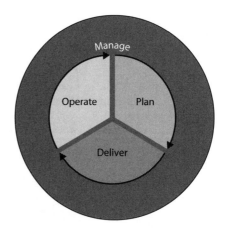

Ending Applications

Applications do not last forever. In addition to the software development frameworks, DevOps professionals should understand the functions involved in application replacement, retirement, migration, and changes in feature use.

Application Replacement

Eventually, the application reaches a point where significant changes are required to make it useful. This could be due to shifts in the environment, other business processes, or the underlying technology that the application was built upon. At this point, specifications are drafted for a replacement application or a newer version of the application, and the cycle begins anew.

Old/Current/New Versions

During the application life cycle, you may have multiple versions of an application running simultaneously. These versions include old systems that are no longer used for day-to-day activities, current systems that are in active use, and new versions on which the company is migrating toward.

It is not always possible, nor advisable, to simply cut over from one system to another. Users need to be trained on the new system, standard operating procedures may need to be documented, or dependencies may need to be resolved on the client side before the new system can fully take the place of its replacement.

Companies often run the current and new versions side by side when replacing the application. Keeping data consistent between these versions can be challenging. In some of the worst cases, users are forced to enter data into two systems during this process. As you can imagine, this is burdensome for users and should be avoided by automating the process of keeping the data consistent between the current and new versions.

The easiest and oftentimes most effective method to keep data consistent would be to utilize an application from the application vendor. However, vendors do not always have such a program, so companies are forced to seek a solution elsewhere. This requires configuring scripts or other tools to keep the data synchronized.

Most application data will be contained in a database. However, if your data consists of only files, not transactional database data, you can use file-based or block-based storage replication tools. For more information on these methods, see the sections on storage replication in Chapter 3.

There are various database-specific synchronization tools, but they may or may not be feasible, depending on how the database architecture has changed between the current and new versions. Some of these include transactional replication using a publisher-subscriber model, snapshot replication, log shipping, or merge replication. Another option might be to configure triggers on database fields that will initiate updates on their corresponding fields in the other system. However, this method is dependent upon the database architecture, such as how you are creating primary keys.

CAUTION Be careful not to create circular triggers when synchronizing database updates. This can occur if you have triggers configured on both sides that automatically initiate upon updates to the table. An update on one side would trigger an update on the other side, which would then trigger another update. This would continue indefinitely, creating a large amount of junk data.

A third option might be to configure a daily job that queries tables from both databases to identify new unique records and then creates an update script for each database to bring it up to date with the changes made to the corresponding database. As you can see, there are quite a variety of ways to keep the data synchronized and many more besides the ones mentioned here. The method you select depends largely on how the current and new systems are designed.

You will also encounter scenarios where old and current systems are running side by side. Companies may keep an old system around when they have not migrated data from that system to a new system. They may choose not to perform this migration due to the costs to migrate or because their need for regular or recurring access to that data is very low. For example, a company may move to a new order tracking system but only move the last 12 months of data from their old solution to the new one due to the cloud provider's costs for maintaining that data. They may determine that they only need to generate data from the old system if there is a specific request for it or for financial auditing purposes, so the old system is kept around just to run reports against it, and the new system is used for day-to-day activities. The primary challenge with this situation is that maintenance must still be performed on the old system so that it is available when needed and kept secure from new security threats.

Application Retirement

All applications eventually reach a point where they no longer provide value to the organization. At this point, the application should be retired. Program procedures and processes are documented, and the resources the application uses are released for some other purpose.

Deprecation

Application components are often retired due to deprecation. Deprecation is a process where functions or APIs are declared unsupported or no longer safe for use. These components are then no longer included in new versions of the software.

Deprecation typically occurs when significant security vulnerabilities are discovered and the company behind the software determines it is better to replace the component with a re-engineered one rather than trying to fix the vulnerabilities. Another reason for deprecation is when new methods of operation are discovered or largely adopted, making the old methods obsolete.

New software versions will replace components that have been deprecated unless those functions are part of some dependency. You will often need to update source code or scripts that reference deprecated functions for your code to work once the new software has been deployed.

NOTE Be sure to read the release notes for new software versions to identify if components have been deprecated. Many administrators have learned the hard way when they did not read the release notes and then found parts of their systems did not work following the upgrade. It is far better to identify these issues ahead of time and then rewrite the code that relies upon the deprecated functions before installing the new software.

End of Life

All software eventually reaches a point where it is no longer supported or supported in only a limited fashion, often at a much higher cost to consumers. This is known as end of life (EOL). Software that is EOL will no longer have updates and patches released for it, so consumers using that software may be at risk of exploitation of new vulnerabilities identified for that EOL software. For this reason, it is not advisable to continue using such software.

Software manufacturers will issue many notices when an application is nearing the end of life to ensure that customers understand and to give them the opportunity to purchase newer versions of the software.

Many companies have a formal process for classifying their software as EOL. They communicate this policy to their customers so that EOL announcements do not come as a surprise. For example, Microsoft has some products that are under their fixed life cycle policy. For these products, Microsoft offers mainstream support for five years and then extended support for the next five years. Such products are declared EOL after ten years.

Application Migration

Applications may need to be migrated to different hardware as their usage increases or decreases. The application may need to be migrated as the underlying technology environment changes. For example, the organization may move to more powerful hardware or from one cloud provider to another or from one virtualization platform to a competing platform.

Application Feature Use (Increase/Decrease)

The use of an application will change over time. Application use will be relatively limited as it is introduced because it takes a while for users to adopt a new solution. However, as the value of the program is demonstrated and more people tell others about it, the use will gradually increase. Eventually, application use will plateau and stay at a relatively consistent level for some time before it finally diminishes when other applications or newer processes supplant the application or as business conditions change. A major thing touted in new releases is what new features the release adds.

Secure Coding

Whether you are developing a new application or maintaining an existing one, secure coding is one of the most important things to know. Companies spend vast sums of money each year to resolve vulnerabilities discovered in applications. Some of these vulnerabilities could have been avoided if secure coding techniques had been utilized earlier in the project life cycle.

Security is important throughout the SDLC. It should be built in during the specifications and development phase and then tested. Vulnerabilities will be identified in the operational phase, and this should feed back into the development phase to correct these issues.

A good place to start in secure coding is to review the OWASP top ten application security risks. You can find them here: https://owasp.org/www-project-top-ten/. Some of the most common security mistakes take place around authentication and authorization. Authentication is the process of identifying the identify of user or system, while authorization is the process of giving accounts access to the resources they have a right to access. This section will introduce some of the coding basics of secure authentication and authorization, including

- Avoid hardcoded passwords
- Service account best practices
- Utilizing password vaults
- Key-based authentication

Avoid Hardcoded Passwords

Hardcoded passwords are those that are embedded into the application code. For example, a developer might code a database connection string into the application so that the software can issue queries to the database without having to set up the connection and account during installation or deployment of the application. This simplifies the deployment but comes with a serious security risk.

The issue with this is that the password cannot be customized for a specific deployment or customer installation. Attackers who discover the password in the application through methods such as disassembling the application could then use that password on any other installation, since it is built into the software. The only way to change this password would be for the developers to release a patch.

Sometimes hardcoded passwords are placed into source code by developers for testing, with the intention to later remove it. This is still a bad practice because developers may forget to remove these features, leaving the application vulnerable until someone discovers the issue and informs them of it.

Service Account Best Practices

Service accounts are used by application components to access system or network resources such as files on the local machine or network, databases, or cloud systems. Each function should have clearly defined access requirements, and the service account should be configured with the rights to perform those functions only and nothing else. This is known as least privilege. This makes it more difficult for a compromised service account to be used to perform malicious actions.

As an example, suppose a service account is used to allow access to a server data drive so that files can be uploaded or downloaded through the application. Permissions on this account should only grant access to the specific folder where these files exist. This prevents an exploit from within the application from changing the directory to somewhere else on the system to send attackers potentially sensitive information.

Specific access rights for each service account should be well documented. It also makes it easier for security operations to monitor for inappropriate access because they have clearly defined access expectations. It is possible in some cases for attackers to escalate privileges for an account to perform other actions, and that is why it is best to both limit the privileges and monitor for noncompliance.

The best practice for service accounts is to establish an individual service account for discrete access functions rather than creating one service account per application. To demonstrate this practice, Microsoft's database application, SQL Server, has up to 13 service accounts that must be created, based on the database components the company elects to install on the server. Some of these include the account for running the database service, an account to run the agent service for monitoring jobs and sending alerts, a service for full-text searching, a service to provide database connection name resolution, and a service for backup operations. Consider the functions your application will need to perform and then allow for the specification of service accounts for those functions. If you are deploying the application, create these service accounts following the vendor's guidelines.

Password Vaults

As you can see, a single application can potentially have many accounts associated with it. These passwords are created when the service accounts are established, and they are needed when the application is configured on the server. Therefore, they must be documented, but the documentation should be secure.

It is far too commonplace for companies to store passwords in an Excel file, Word document, or another nonencrypted file. The best practice is to store passwords in a password vault. A password vault is an encrypted repository where usernames and passwords can be entered. Multiple administrators may need access to the password vault, and they will use a very complex master password to access it and retrieve credentials.

Many password vaults have features to keep copied passwords in the clipboard for a short period so that they are not accidentally pasted into a form or document later or scraped by another application or remote session.

Password vaults can also be used for services to obtain their credentials. Password vaults associated with a cloud service can store keys in their vault and allow applications to invoke the keys by referencing their Uniform Resource Identifier (URI), a unique character string used to represent the key. Homogenous key vaults ensure that keys do not leave their cloud, so it reduces the threat of key interception over the Internet. Key vaults can generate new keys, or users can import their own existing keys into them.

Let's look at an example of Azure Key Vault. We can create a secret that will be used by an app within Key Vault with these steps. After logging into the Azure Cloud Shell CLI, we create a secret with the following code. Please note that this requires a key vault

```
  ↻  | Azure Cloud Shell
}
isconsultants@Azure:~$ az keyvault secret set \
>       --name CloudTestSecret \
>       --value Testing4FunKeys \
>       --vault-name CloudTest
{
  "attributes": {
    "created": "2021-02-22T18:34:37+00:00",
    "enabled": true,
    "expires": null,
    "notBefore": null,
    "recoveryLevel": "Recoverable+Purgeable",
    "updated": "2021-02-22T18:34:37+00:00"
  },
  "contentType": null,
  "id": "https://cloudtest.vault.azure.net/secrets/CloudTestSecret/1ad098c0077f412abda7cac0f8
c19024",
  "kid": null,
  "managed": null,
  "name": "CloudTestSecret",
  "tags": {
    "file-encoding": "utf-8"
  },
  "value": "Testing4FunKeys"
}
```

Figure 8-5   Creating a secret in the Azure Key Vault

to have been created. In this example, our key vault is named CloudTest. We will create a secret to be used by an app, and the name will be CloudTestSecret with a value of Testing4FunKeys. The output from this command is shown in Figure 8-5.

```
az keyvault secret set \
    --name CloudTestSecret \
    --value Testing4FunKeys \
    --vault-name CloudTest
```

Cloud key vaults can automatically rotate secrets stored there for associated identities. This reduces the maintenance required for maintaining secure rotating secrets.

Key-Based Authentication

Key-based authentication can be used as an alternative to authenticating using a username and password. This form of authentication uses public key cryptography, where the account has a private key that is used to authenticate it to the system. The private key is paired to a public key that can decrypt data encrypted with the private key and vice versa. Common authentication systems will encrypt a number or a string with the public key and then have the account decrypt the value to confirm its identity. Only the user or service with the private key would be able to accomplish this, so it is an effective way of establishing authentication.

Exercise 8-1: Setting Up SSH Keys for Key-Based Authentication

In this exercise, we will create an SSH key pair for authentication to an Ubuntu Linux server. You will be able to use this to remotely connect to the server.

1. Start by creating a key pair on your machine. Open the Terminal application and type the following command to create a 2048-bit RSA key:

   ssh-keygen

2. You will receive the output shown next. Press ENTER to save the SSH key in the default directory, the .ssh subdirectory in your home directory.

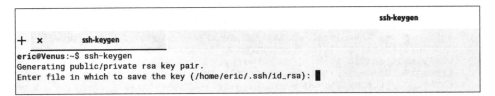

3. Now enter a passphrase. The passphrase will be used to encrypt the key on the local machine. Choose something secure. Type the passphrase and then press ENTER. You will then need to enter the passphrase again and press ENTER a second time to confirm the passphrase. You will then be shown a screen showing you the fingerprint of the key and its randomart image, as shown here:

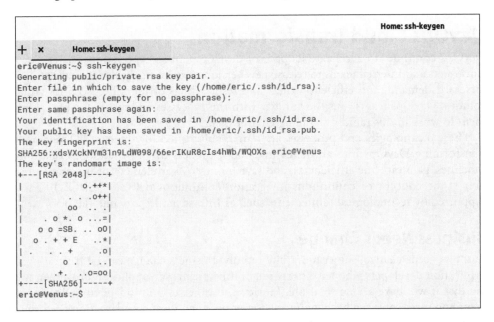

4. Now that you have the key, you will need to copy it to the server so that it can be used. Type the following command to display the public key, as shown in the illustration:

```
cat ~/.ssh/id_rsa.pub
```

5. Establish a shell connection with the remote computer.

6. Place the public key in the authorized_keys file with the following command, substituting the key shown here with the one you obtained from step 4:

```
echo ssh-rsa AAAAB3NzaC1yc2EAAAADAQABAAAABAQC8R7wUL+h2rNljTbpSRKw/Zkf4
CF8qVdY6IS3mqn2hkK4PT5hkdtuEjDMYQxS2rvKJVvUw+Ny2HnojoRA4KDqkYk7dj8XC/
WI9Iyix50fjdBMCit71SjXV+QYhuqtRUsihAxuxwnSqGdRFdHh8hikO55M4ibzTvRankAqS
t1SBvgtEq6Gcc4gO55lY1tXEJ4nKTYcBECfm3X+NZ9PRX6Ox4YbctJ3EwOMK2CosdjSTwB
oX7296hG/sj+LfDBgiB0aMgQRsCsY0Jva4D+Iev9ewTbcA+yyNX+JT4+cqxnXSn6AsOczrqx
7OAfrNdmMtVOMKQbG1mnas4pZ2E8JNmn4V>> ~/.ssh/authorized_keys
```

7. Lastly, assign ownership to the file for the user account that will authenticate with it. In this example, the user is eric, but you will need to substitute your username for it.

```
chown -R eric:eric ~/.ssh
```

DevOps Cloud Transformation

DevOps continues to accelerate its pace of development as expectations increase from consumers and internal teams to release new versions more quickly, dynamically scale for increased demand, and efficiently track and resolve bugs or identified security vulnerabilities. DevOps teams must be familiar with the processes and technologies to enable them to work in this rapidly changing environment.

These technologies and processes are remarkably suited for the cloud. The cloud is transforming DevOps into an increasingly agile process that can reduce development timelines, gain pipeline efficiencies, and save money. A key element of this transformation is the concept of continuous integration/continuous delivery (CI/CD). This is supported by technological refinements such as Infrastructure as Code (IaC).

Business Needs Change

Business needs change, sometimes quite rapidly. Business change can be frustrating for application developers who have spent much time putting an application together, hoping that it will have a long shelf life. However, businesses must adapt to their environment and meet continually changing customer needs and wants. Adaptation necessitates changes to applications, tools, systems, and personnel to adjust the technology environment to these new requirements.

Cloud technologies make such changes much easier. Cloud services can be expanded, contracted, or terminated simply by contacting the cloud vendor and requesting the change. Some services may have a contract period, with a penalty for breaking the contract, but many services are flexible.

It is also important to note that personnel changes are not as dramatic when using cloud services. If a company decides to stop using one cloud service and adopt two others, this might result in no changes to personnel. By contrast, if these were on-premises applications, one person might need to go through training to be familiar with the new application, and another person may need to be hired to support the new one.

Some business changes that affect cloud professionals include

- Mergers, acquisitions, and divestitures
- Cloud service requirement changes
- Regulatory and legal changes

Mergers, Acquisitions, and Divestitures

When two companies decide to combine their businesses, this is known as a merger. One company can also choose to purchase another in an acquisition. Some companies decide to change direction and sell off a portion of their business through divestiture.

Every company has a unique technology infrastructure that supports its business, and any company that goes through a merger, acquisition, or divestiture has to adapt its infrastructure to meet the requirements of the new corporate form. Physical hardware must be moved from one site to another; possibly rebranded; and adapted to meet the policies, standards, and compliance requirements of the new company.

Cloud services streamline this operation. Cloud accounts can be moved from one company to another and still reside with the same provider. Cloud integrations can be migrated from one system to another if necessary. Cloud migrations are easiest if cloud service integrations are performed using standard APIs.

Cloud Service Requirement Changes

Cloud service providers are continually upgrading their systems to take advantage of new technologies and improvements in processes. Unlike on-premises solutions where new software versions must be deployed by IT staff, cloud updates are deployed by the cloud provider on the organization's behalf. It is important to stay on top of what changes are made by the cloud provider in case changes are needed on the organizational side as well.

Companies may also request changes to their cloud services. In some cases, a cloud provider might offer a buffet of services, and customers can add or remove these services at will. Other solutions may be highly customized for the customer, in which case negotiation with the provider and adequate lead time are necessary for changes to be made to the environment to meet the customer requirements.

Regulatory and Legal Changes

The regulatory and legal environment is also an area that sees frequent change. When a country promulgates a new regulation or law (or changes an existing one) that affects business practices, companies that do business in that country must adhere to the new or changed law or regulation. Global organizations often have entire teams of people who monitor changes in the global regulatory environment and then work with organizational departments to implement appropriate changes.

Corporate legal teams often work with vendor management or IT to coordinate with cloud providers to ensure that legal and regulatory requirements are met. One way to validate that a cloud provider supports new regulatory requirements is through a vendor risk assessment. This involves sending a document listing each of the requirements to the cloud provider and asking the cloud provider to verify that it has the appropriate controls and measures in place to meet the compliance requirements.

Vendor risk assessments take time to administer and time to complete. It is important to give vendors plenty of time to work through the details. Some vendors will need to implement additional procedures or controls to meet the requirements, and others may decide that they do not want to make changes, forcing your organization to move its business from one cloud provider to another to remain compliant.

Continuous Integration/Continuous Delivery

CI/CD are DevOps processes that aim to improve efficiencies and reduce costs through greater automation of the SDLC. The CI portion is concerned with planning, regularly building, testing, and merging new branches of code into the trunk. The CD portion is concerned with deploying the application to stakeholders or customers, managing the application, and monitoring for issues. When issues are identified, those are fed back into the planning step of the CI process. Figure 8-6 shows the CI/CD processes. The CI tasks begin with planning, then building, testing, and merging. This leads into the CD processes of deployment, maintaining, and monitoring.

Cloud tools such as AWS CodePipeline or Azure Pipeline can automate development tasks such as building, testing, and releasing code. Workflow for the entire set of CI/CD processes are reflected in such tools. Planning is aided with visualization and modeling tools. These tools allow DevOps teams to outline the workflow that will be accomplished at each point in the pipeline. The cloud development platform then guides developers through the workflow and tracks progress so that team leads can manage the project tasks effectively.

Figure 8-6
Continuous integration/ continuous delivery processes

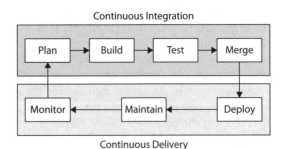

Standardization is key to ensuring that each build is tested using the right criteria. Establish your testing workflow, and cloud tools can execute that workflow for each build automatically when new changes are committed to the repository. This may involve human tasks as well, but the tools notify testers or approvers to perform their role as soon as their step in the workflow is reached. This helps reduce delays in the process. Errors and other issues are quickly identified and sent back to developers so that they can fix them while the code is still top of mind.

Infrastructure as Code

Virtualization and the cloud have gone a long way toward abstracting the underlying hardware components of a solution, paving the way for new innovations in software-defined networks, storage, and data centers. These concepts were introduced in Chapter 6, and DevOps utilizes these software-defined processes to take the task of provisioning networking, storage, server, and application resources and automate it through software. IaC automates the provisioning of the resources required for an application using definition files that outline how the systems will be provisioned and configured. IaC is an essential part of continuous deployment.

IaC automation aids in configuring test and production environments similarly to ensure that testing accurately reflects the situations encountered in the production environment. It also aids in deploying many systems quickly or simultaneously. Consider a situation where your team has developed a patch for your application and you need to deploy it for 3,500 customer sites. IaC automation could update each site with minimal effort.

IaC configurations can be stored beside the code. Changes to the configuration are tracked within the code repository right along with the associated code for the build.

Microsoft Azure implements IaC with Azure Resource Manager (ARM) templates, and Amazon has AWS CloudFormation. Both systems use JavaScript Object Notation (JSON) statements that are written to describe the configuration logic behind what you want to set up. Configurations can be broken out into modular parts that are shared among similar projects. This makes updating elements simpler because you only need to update it in one place. Templates are provided for commonly configured items so that you do not need to start from scratch.

Infrastructure Components and Their Integration

Prior to IaC, infrastructure components ended up with very different custom configurations. The industry calls these snowflakes because each snowflake is unique. Snowflakes are hard to support because each configuration might require different steps or additional coding to address future issues. IaC aids in establishing a standard and using that each time new systems are deployed. Some of the infrastructure components you should configure with IaC include system storage, virtual machines, virtual networks, security segments and ACLs, and application configuration settings. These components work together to provide the solution. If one of these is misconfigured, the solution will not likely work.

Chapter Review

DevOps teams, the combination of software development and IT operations, are responsible for developing, deploying, and maintaining applications. As such, DevOps is responsible for the entire application life cycle. This includes creating the program specifications, development, testing, deployment, and maintenance.

There is a point where the application no longer serves a purpose and will be retired or replaced. At this point, DevOps will remove those applications or create new replacement applications and potentially migrate data to them.

DevOps teams need to be cognizant of security throughout the SDLC so that it is built into the applications they develop, evaluated in testing phases, and monitored in operational phases. Many applications suffer from insecure authentication or authorization functions. Authentication is the process of identifying the identity of a user or system, while authorization is the process of giving accounts access to the resources they have a right to access. The best practice is to never use hardcoded passwords, define service accounts for specific application functions, limit service account permissions to the minimum necessary, document permissions, store passwords in password vaults, and implement key-based authentication when possible.

The cloud has transformed DevOps to make it much more agile. This aids DevOps teams in adjusting to changes quickly. CI/CD processes improve DevOps efficiency through automation of the SDLC, while IaC automates the deployment of applications and application updates. IaC is powerful and can significantly enhance DevOps agility and avoid snowflakes (unique system configurations), but it must be implemented correctly. There are many components to an application that will need to be correctly configured. Some of these components include storage, virtual machines, virtual networks, security segments and ACLs, and application configuration settings.

Questions

The following questions will help you gauge your understanding of the material in this chapter. Read all the answers carefully because there might be more than one correct answer. Choose the best response(s) for each question.

1. You have just finished development on a new version of your company's primary application, and you would like to have a small group test the features to identify potential bugs. Which type of release would this be?

   A. Stable

   B. Canary

   C. LTS

   D. Beta

2. Choose the answer that lists the SDLC phases in the correct order.

   A. Specifications, Testing, Development, Maintenance, Deployment

   B. Development, Specifications, Deployment, Testing Maintenance

   C. Specifications, Development, Testing, Deployment, Maintenance

   D. Specifications, Development, Deployment, Maintenance, Testing

3. What is the desired end result of ITIL?

   A. CAB

   B. Continual service improvement

   C. Service strategy

   D. Service operation

4. Which of the following terms best describes life cycle management?

   A. Baseline

   B. Finite

   C. Linear

   D. Continuum

5. You are planning to migrate to a new ERP system. You will be running the old and new systems simultaneously for six to nine months and want to ensure that the data is kept consistent between the versions. Which method would not work to accomplish this?

   A. Have users enter the data into both systems

   B. Use a tool from the software vendor to keep the data synchronized

   C. Configure database synchronization jobs

   D. Point both old and new applications to the same database

6. Which scenario would be the best case in which to hardcode the password into the application?

   A. The username and password will not change

   B. Customers should not know the password

   C. You want to decrease deployment time

   D. None of the above

7. Which of the following is not a service account best practice?

   A. Configure a service account for each key application.

   B. Restrict services by creating only local accounts on the systems instead of domain accounts.

   C. Limit access rights to only those absolutely necessary for the service's role.

   D. Monitor service account access based on documented privileges.

8. Which one of these tasks is not a continuous integration task?

   A. Plan

   B. Build

   C. Merge

   D. Deploy

9. Which one of these tasks is not a continuous delivery task?

   A. Monitor

   B. Test

   C. Maintain

   D. Deploy

10. Which technology aids in provisioning the systems and resources required for deploying an application?

    A. Software version control

    B. Infrastructure as code

    C. Compiler

    D. Continuous integration

Answers

1. **B.** The canary build is used when testing features immediately after it has been developed.

2. **C.** The order is Specifications, Development, Testing, Deployment, Maintenance.

3. **B.** The end result of each cycle within ITIL is to identify opportunities for improvement that can be incorporated into the service to make it more efficient, effective, and profitable.

4. **D.** Life cycle management is a continuum with feedback loops going back into itself to enable better management and continual improvement.

5. **D.** You cannot keep the data in sync by pointing both the new and old applications to the same database.

6. **D.** You should never hardcode credentials into an application.

7. **B.** Creating local accounts instead of domain accounts is not a best practice. This may seem like it is limiting the scope of the account, but local accounts cannot be managed centrally and are more susceptible to tampering.

8. **D.** Deploy is a continuous delivery task, not a continuous integration task.

9. **B.** Test is a continuous integration task, not a continuous delivery task.

10. **B.** Infrastructure as code automates the provisioning of the resources required for an application using definition files that outline how the systems will be provisioned and configured.

Performance Tuning

In this chapter, you will learn about

- Host resource allocation
- Guest resource allocation
- Optimizing performance
- Common performance issues

Appropriately distributing compute resources is one of the most important aspects of a virtualized cloud environment. Planning for future growth and the ability to adjust compute resources on demand is one of the many benefits of a virtualized environment. This chapter explains how to configure compute resources on a host computer and a guest VM and how to optimize the performance of a virtualized environment.

Host Resource Allocation

Building a virtualization host requires careful consideration and planning. First, you must identify which resources the host requires and plan how to distribute those resources to a VM. Next, you must plan the configuration of the guest VM that the host computer will serve.

You must attend to the configuration of resources and the licensing of the host in the process of moving to a virtualized environment or virtual cloud environment. This consists of the following:

- Compute resources
- Quotas and limits
- Licensing
- Reservations
- Resource pools

Compute Resources

Adequate compute resources are key to the successful operation of a virtualization host. Proper planning of the compute resources for the host computer ensures that the host can deliver the performance needed to support the virtualization environment.

Figure 9-1
Host compute
resources:
processor,
disk, memory,
and network

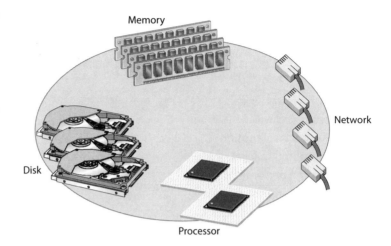

Compute resources can best be defined as the resources that are required for the delivery of VMs. They are the disk, processor, memory, and networking resources that are shared across pools of VMs and underpin their ability to deliver the value of the cloud models, as covered in Chapter 1.

As a host is a physical entity, the compute resources that the host utilizes are naturally physical, too. However, cloud providers may allocate a subset of their available physical resources to cloud consumers to allocate to their own VMs. Compute resources are displayed in Figure 9-1.

For disk resources, physical rotational disks and solid state hard drives are utilized, as well as their controller cards, disk arrays, host bus adapters, and networked storage transmission media. For network resources, network interface cards (NICs) and physical transmission media such as Ethernet cables are employed. Central processing units (CPUs) are employed for the processor, and physical banks of RAM are used to supply memory.

Quotas and Limits

Because compute resources are limited, cloud providers must protect them and make certain that their customers only have access to the amount that the cloud providers are contracted to provide. Two methods used to deliver no more than the contracted amount of resources are quotas and limits.

Limits are a defined floor or ceiling on the amount of resources that can be used, and quotas are limits that are defined for a system on the total amount of resources that can be utilized. When defining limits on host resources, cloud providers have the option of setting a soft or hard limit. A soft limit will allow the user to save a file even if the drive reaches 100GB, but will still log an alert and notify the user. A hard limit, on the other hand, is the maximum amount of resources that can be utilized. For example, a hard limit of 100GB for a storage partition will not allow anything to be added to that partition once it reaches 100GB, and the system will log an event to note the occurrence and notify the user.

The quotas that are typically defined for host systems have to do with the allocation of the host compute resources to the host's guest machines. These quotas are established according to service level agreements (SLAs) that are created between the cloud provider and cloud consumers to indicate a specific level of capacity.

Capacity management is essentially the practice of allocating the correct amount of resources in order to deliver a business service. The resources that these quotas enforce limits upon may be physical disks, disk arrays, host bus adapters, RAM chips, physical processors, and network adapters. They are allocated from the total pool of resources available to individual guests based on their SLA.

Quotas and limits on hosts can be compared to speed limits on the highway; very often, there are both minimum and maximum speeds defined for all traffic on the roads. A quota can be defined as the top speed, and a limit can be defined as the slowest speed for all vehicles using that road's resources.

Licensing

After designing the host computer's resources and storage limits, an organization or cloud provider needs to identify which vendor it will use for its virtualization software. Each virtualization software vendor has its own way of licensing products. Some of them have a free version of their product and only require a license for advanced feature sets that enable functionality, like high availability, performance optimization, and systems management. Others offer an utterly free virtualization platform but might not offer some of the more advanced features with their product.

Choosing the virtualization platform is a critical step, and licensing is a factor in that decision. Before deploying a virtualization host and choosing a virtualization vendor, the organization must be sure to read the license agreements and determine exactly which features it needs and how those features are licensed. In addition to licensing the virtualization host, the guest requires a software license.

Reservations

Reservations work similarly to quotas. Whereas quotas are designed to ensure the correct capacity gets delivered to customers by defining an upper limit for resource usage, reservations are designed to operate at the other end of the capacity spectrum by ensuring that a lower limit is enforced for the amount of resources guaranteed to a cloud consumer for their guest VM or machines.

A reservation for host resources is important to understand because it ensures certain VMs always have a defined baseline level of resources available to them regardless of the demands placed on them by other VMs. The reason these guest reservations are so important is that they enable cloud service providers to deliver against their SLAs.

 CAUTION Reserving resources makes them unavailable to other machines and may result in less efficient utilization of resources.

Resource Pools

Resource pools are slices or portions of overall compute resources on the host or those allocated from the cloud provider to consumers. These pools include CPU, memory, and storage, and they can be provided from a single host or a cluster of hosts. Resources can be partitioned off in resource pools to provide different levels of resources to specific groups or organizations, and they can be nested within a hierarchy for organizational alignment.

Resource pools provide a flexible mechanism with which to organize the sum total of the compute resources in a virtual environment and link them back to their underlying physical resources.

Guest Resource Allocation

Before creating a guest VM, an organization needs to consider several factors. A guest VM should be configured based on the intended application or task that the guest will support. For example, a guest running a database server may require special performance considerations, such as more CPUs or memory based on the VM's designated role and the overall system load. In addition to CPUs and memory, a guest may require higher-priority access to certain storage or disk types.

An organization must consider not only the role of the VM, the load of the machine, and the number of clients it is intended to support but also the performance of ongoing monitoring and assessment based on these factors. The amount of disk space the guest is using should be monitored and considered when deploying and maintaining storage.

The allocation of resources to VMs must be attended to in the process of moving to a virtualized environment or virtual cloud environment because the organization will either be allocating these resources from its available host resources or paying for them from a cloud provider. Organizations should evaluate each of the following resources:

- Compute resources
- Quotas and limits
- Licensing
- Physical resource redirection
- Resource pools
- Dynamic resource allocation

Compute Resources

The compute resources for VMs enable service delivery in the same way that compute resources for hosts do. However, the resources themselves are different in that they are virtualized components instead of physical components that can be held in your hand or plugged into a motherboard.

Guest compute resources are still made up of disk, network, processor, and memory components, but these components are made available to VMs not as physical resources but as abstractions of physical components presented by a hypervisor that emulates those physical resources for the VM.

Physical hosts have a Basic Input/Output System (BIOS) that presents physical compute resources to a host so they can be utilized to provide computing services, such as running an operating system and its component software applications. With VMs, the BIOS is emulated by the hypervisor to provide the same functions. When the BIOS is emulated and these physical resources are abstracted, administrators have the ability to divide the virtual compute resources from their physical providers and distribute those subdivided resources across multiple VMs. This ability to subdivide physical resources is one of the key elements that make cloud computing and virtualization so powerful.

When splitting resources among multiple VMs, vendor-specific algorithms can help the hypervisor make decisions about which resources are available for each request from its specific VM. There are requirements of the host resources for performing these activities, including small amounts of processor, memory, and disk. These resources are utilized by the hypervisor for carrying out the algorithmic calculations to determine which resources will be granted to which VMs.

Quotas and Limits

As with host resources, VMs utilize quotas and limits to constrain the ability of users to consume compute resources and thereby prevent users from either monopolizing or completely depleting those resources. Quotas can be defined either as hard or soft. Hard quotas set limits that users and applications are barred from exceeding. If an attempt to use resources beyond the set limit is registered, the request is rejected, and an alert is logged that can be acted upon by a user, administrator, or management system. The difference with a soft quota is that the request is granted instead of rejected, and the resources are made available to service the request. However, the same alert is still logged so that action can be taken to either address the issue with the requester for noncompliance with the quota or charge the appropriate party for the extra usage of the materials.

Licensing

Managing hardware resources can be less of a challenge than managing license agreements. Successfully tracking and managing software license agreements in a virtual environment is a tricky proposition. The software application must support licensing a virtual instance of the application.

Some software vendors still require the use of a dongle or a hardware key when licensing their software. Others have adopted their licensing agreements to coexist with a virtual environment. A guest requires a license to operate just as a physical server does. Some vendors have moved to a per-CPU-core type of license agreement to adapt to virtualization. No matter if the application is installed on a physical server or a virtual server, it still requires a license.

Organizations have invested heavily in software licenses. Moving to the cloud does not always mean that those licenses are lost. Bring Your Own License (BYOL), for example, is a feature for Azure migrations that allows existing supported licenses to be migrated to Azure so that companies do not need to pay for the licenses twice. Software assurance with license mobility allows for licenses to be brought into other cloud platforms such as Amazon Web Services (AWS) or VMware vCloud.

Physical Resource Redirection

There are so many things that VMs can do that sometimes we forget that they even exist on physical hardware. However, there are occasions when you need a guest to interface with physical hardware components. Some physical hardware components that are often mapped to VMs include USB drives, parallel ports, serial ports, and USB ports.

In some cases, you may want to utilize USB storage exclusively for a VM. You can add a USB drive to a VM by first adding a USB controller. When a USB drive is attached to a host computer, the host will typically mount that drive automatically. However, only one device can access the drive simultaneously without corrupting the data, so the host must release access to the drive before it can be mapped to a VM. Unmount the drive from the host, and then you will be ready to assign the drive to the VM.

Parallel and serial ports are interfaces that allow for the connection of peripherals to computers. There are times when it is useful to have a VM connect its virtual serial port to a physical serial port on the host computer. For example, a user might want to install an external modem or another form of a handheld device on the VM, and this would require the guest to use a physical serial port on the host computer. It might also be useful to connect a virtual serial port to a file on a host computer and then have the guest VM send output to a file on the host computer. An example of this would be to send data that was captured from a program running on the guest via the virtual serial port and transfer the information from the guest to the host computer.

In addition to using a virtual serial port, it is helpful in certain instances to connect to a virtual parallel port. Parallel ports are used for a variety of devices, including printers, scanners, and dongles. Much like the virtual serial port, a virtual parallel port allows for connecting the guest to a physical parallel port on the host computer.

Besides supporting serial and parallel port emulation for VMs, some virtualization vendors support USB device pass-through from a host computer to a VM. USB pass-through allows a USB device plugged directly into a host computer to be passed through to a VM. USB pass-through allows for multiple USB devices such as security tokens, software dongles, temperature sensors, or webcams that are physically attached to a host computer to be added to a VM.

The process of adding a USB device to the VM usually consists of adding a USB controller to the VM, removing the device from the host configuration, and then assigning the USB device to the VM. When a USB device is attached to a host computer, that device is available only to the VMs that are running on that host computer and only to one VM at a time.

Resource Pools

A resource pool is a hierarchical abstraction of compute resources that can give relative importance, or weight, to a defined set of virtualized resources. Pools at the higher level in the hierarchy are called parent pools; these parents can contain either child pools or individual VMs. Each pool can have a defined weight assigned to it based on either the business rules of the organization or the SLAs of a customer.

Resource pools also allow administrators to define a flexible hierarchy that can be adapted at each pool level as required by the business. This hierarchical structure comes with several advantages, as follows:

- Efficiently maintain access control and delegation of the administration of each pool and its resources.

- Establish isolation between pools.

- Enable resource sharing within the pools.

- Separates the compute resources from discrete host hardware.

The hardware abstraction offered through resource pools frees administrators from the typical constraints of managing the available resources from the host they originated from. Instead, resources are bubbled up to a higher level for management and administration when utilizing pools.

 EXAM TIP   Understanding the advantages and usage of resource pools is key for the test. You need to know when to use a resource pool and why it provides value.

Dynamic Resource Allocation

Just because administrators can manage their compute resources at a higher level with resource pools, it does not mean they want to spend their precious time doing it. Enter dynamic resource allocation. Instead of relying on administrators to evaluate resource utilization and apply changes to the environment that result in the best performance, availability, and capacity arrangements, a computer can do it for them based on business logic that has been predefined by either the management software's default values or the administrator's modification to those values.

Management platforms can manage compute resources for performance, availability, and capacity reasons and realize more cost-effective implementation of those resources in a data center, employing only the hosts required at the given time and shutting down any resources that are not needed. By employing dynamic resource allocation, providers can reduce power costs and go greener by shrinking their power footprint and waste.

Optimizing Performance

Utilization of the allocation mechanisms we have talked about thus far in this chapter allows administrators to achieve the configuration states that they seek within their environment. The next step is to begin optimizing that performance. Optimization includes the following:

- Configuration best practices
- Common issues
- Scalability
- Performance concepts
- Performance automation

Configuration Best Practices

There are some best practices for the configuration of each of the compute resources within a cloud environment. The best practices for these configurations are the focus for the remainder of this section. These best practices center on those allocation mechanisms that allow for the maximum value to be realized by service providers. To best understand their use cases and potential impact, we investigate common configuration options for memory, processor, and disk.

Memory

Memory may be the most critical of all computer resources, as it is usually the limiting factor on the number of guests that can run on a given host, and performance issues appear when too many guests are fighting for enough memory to perform their functions. Two configuration options available for addressing shared memory concerns are memory ballooning and swap disk space.

Memory Ballooning   Hypervisors have device drivers that they build into the host virtualization layer from within the guest operating system. Part of this installed toolset is a balloon driver, which can be observed inside the guest. The balloon driver communicates to the hypervisor to reclaim memory inside the guest when it is no longer valuable to the operating system. If the hypervisor host begins to run low on memory due to memory demands from other VM guests, it will invoke (inflate) the balloon driver in VMs requiring less memory. Hypervisors such VMware use a balloon driver installed in the guest VM; Microsoft Hyper-V calls this setting "Dynamic memory." This reduces the chance that the physical host will start to utilize virtualized memory from a defined paging file on its available disk resource, which causes performance degradation. An illustration of the way this ballooning works can be found in Figure 9-2.

Swap Disk Space   Swap space is disk space allocated to service memory requests when the physical memory capacity limit has been reached. When virtualizing and overcommitting memory resources to VMs, administrators must make sure to reserve enough

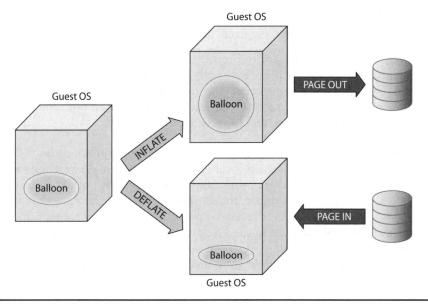

Figure 9-2 How memory ballooning works

swap space for the host to balloon memory in addition to reserving disk space within the guest operating system for it to perform its swap operations.

VMs and the applications that run on them will take a significant performance hit when memory is swapped out to disk. However, you do not need that large of a disk for swap space, so it is a good practice to keep a solid state drive in the host that can be used for swap space if necessary. This will ensure that those pages moved to swap space are transferred to high-speed storage, reducing the impact of memory paging operations.

Processor

CPU time is the amount of time a process or thread spends executing on a processor core. For multiple threads, the CPU time of the threads is additive. The application CPU time is the sum of the CPU time of all the threads that run the application. Wait time is the amount of time that a given thread waits to be processed; it could be processed but must wait on other factors such as synchronization waits and I/O waits.

High CPU wait times signal that there are too many requests for a given queue on a core to handle, and performance degradation will occur. While high CPU wait time can be alleviated in some situations by adding processors, these additions sometimes hurt performance.

CAUTION   Be careful when adding processors, as there is a potential for causing even further performance degradation if the applications using them are not designed to be run on multiple CPUs.

Another solution for alleviating CPU wait times is to scale out instead of scaling up, two concepts that we explore in more detail later in this chapter.

CPU Affinity   It is also important to properly configure CPU affinity, also known as processor affinity. CPU affinity is where threads from a specific VM are tied to a specific processor or core, and all subsequent requests from that process or thread are executed by that same processor or core. CPU affinity overrides the built-in processor scheduling mechanisms so that threads are bound to specific processor cores.

- **Benefits**   The primary benefit of CPU affinity is to optimize cache performance. Processor cache is local to that processor, so if operations are executed on another processor, they cannot take advantage of the cache on the first processor. Furthermore, the same data cannot be kept in more than one processor cache. When the second processor caches new content, it must first invalidate the cache from the first processor. This can happen when a performance-heavy thread moves from one processor to another. This process of invalidating the cache can be prevented by assigning the VM thread to a processor so that its cache never moves. CPU affinity can also ensure that the cache that has been created for that processor is utilized more often for that VM thread.

  Another benefit is preventing two CPU-intensive VMs from operating on the same vCPU. Since many vCPUs are oversubscribed or are mapped to hyperthreaded CPU cores, these cores end up being mapped back to the same physical core. This is fine when the load is minimal because the oversubscription and hyperthreading allow for the hypervisor to make better use of CPU resources. However, when two processor-intensive VMs are operating on the same vCPU, they can easily cause contention.

- **Caveats**   Assigning CPU affinity can cause many problems and should be used sparingly. In many cases, the best configuration will be not to configure CPU affinity and to let the hypervisor choose the best processor for the task at hand. This is primarily because CPU affinity does not prevent other VMs from using the processor core, but it restricts the configured VM from using other cores; thus, the preferred CPU could be overburdened with other work. Also, where the host would generally assign the virtual machine's thread to another available CPU, CPU affinity would require the VM to wait until the CPU became available before its thread would be processed.

Test CPU affinity before implementing it in production. You may need to create CPU affinity rules for all other VMs to ensure that they do not contend for CPU cores. Document affinity settings so that other administrators will be aware of them when migrating VMs or performing other changes to the environment.

CPU Anti-Affinity   CPU anti-affinity ensures that threads from a specific VM will not execute on a particular processor or core, and all subsequent requests from that process or thread are executed by processors other than the excluded one. Similar to CPU affinity, CPU anti-affinity overrides the built-in processor scheduling mechanisms.

CPU anti-affinity is often used in conjunction with CPU affinity, such as when trying to isolate the processes of CPU-intensive VMs. When one machine has affinity for the CPU, the other one can be given anti-affinity for it. Similarly, suppose you have a VM that needs very predictable performance. In that case, you may dedicate a vCPU to it with CPU affinity and then use CPU anti-affinity rules to ensure that other machines are not allocated time on that vCPU when the dedicated VM is not using it.

Exercise 9-1: Setting CPU Affinity and Anti-Affinity Rules in VMWare Cloud

In this exercise, we will set CPU affinity and nonaffinity rules within VMWare Cloud.

1. Log into VMWare Cloud Service Manager and then click on Clouds to select your cloud, as shown here:

2. Click on the Inventory tab, and you will see a breakdown of the machines, services, and groups that you have in your cloud.

3. Select the VM button on the left side, as shown next.

4. You will see your VMs presented. Select the one you wish to change the CPU affinity on and then select Edit Settings.

5. Select CPU under Virtual Hardware.

6. There is a section called Scheduling Affinity. Under this, select Physical Processor Affinity.

7. You can now enter which processors you want this VM to use. The VM will be given affinity for the processors you enter here and will be given anti-affinity for any that you do not enter here. Each processor you wish to add should be added by a number separated by a comma. You can also reference them by range. For example, if you want the processor to run only on processors 17 through 32, you would enter "17-32" in the field. For this example, let's have the VM run on processors 25 through 32, so we will enter **25-32** and then select Save Settings.

Disk

Poor disk performance, or poorly designed disk solutions, can have performance ramifications in traditional infrastructures, slowing users down as they wait to read or write data for the server they are accessing. In a cloud model, however, disk performance issues can limit access to all organization resources because multiple virtualized servers in a networked storage environment might be competing for the same storage resources, thereby crippling their entire deployment of virtualized servers or desktops. The following sections describe some typical configurations and measurements that assist in designing a high-performance storage solution. These consist of the following:

- Disk performance
- Disk tuning
- Disk latency
- I/O throttling
- I/O tuning

Disk Performance   Disk performance can be configured with several different configuration options. The media type can affect performance, and administrators can choose between the most standard types of traditional rotational media or chip-based solid state drives. Solid state drives, while becoming more economical in the last few years, are still much more expensive than rotational media and are not utilized except where only the highest performance standards are required.

The next consideration for disk performance is the speed of the rotational media, should that be the media of choice. Server-class disks start at 7200 RPM and go up to 15,000 RPM, with seek times for the physical arm reading the platters being considerably lower on the high-end drives. In enterprise configurations, the price point per gigabyte is primarily driven by the rotation speed and only marginally by storage space per gigabyte. When considering enterprise storage, the adage is that you pay for performance, not space.

Once the media type and speed have been determined, the next consideration is the type of RAID array that the disks are placed in to meet the service needs. Different levels of RAID can be employed based on the deployment purpose. These RAID levels should be evaluated and configured based on the type of I/O and on the need to read, write, or a combination of both.

Disk Tuning   Disk tuning is the activity of analyzing what type of I/O traffic is taking place across the defined disk resources and moving it to the most appropriate set of resources. Virtualization management platforms enable the movement of storage, without interrupting current operations, to other disk resources within their control.

Virtualization management platforms allow either administrators or dynamic resource allocation programs to move applications, storage, databases, and even entire VMs among disk arrays with no downtime to ensure that those virtualized entities get the performance they require based on either business rules or SLAs.

Disk Latency   Disk latency is a counter that provides administrators with the best indicator of when a resource is experiencing degradation due to a disk bottleneck and needs to have action taken against it. If high-latency counters are experienced, a move to either another disk array with quicker response times or a different configuration, such as higher rotational speeds or a different array configuration, is warranted. Another option is to configure I/O throttling.

I/O Throttling   I/O throttling does not eliminate disk I/O as a bottleneck for performance, but it can alleviate performance problems for specific VMs based on a priority assigned by the administrator. I/O throttling defines limits that can be utilized specifically for disk resources allocated to VMs to ensure that they are not performance or availability constrained when working in an environment that has more demand than the availability of disk resources.

I/O throttling may be a valuable option when an environment contains both development and production resources. The production I/O can be given a higher priority than the development resources, allowing the production environment to perform better for end users.

Prioritization does not eliminate the bottleneck. Rather, prioritizing production machines just passes the bottleneck on to the development environment, which becomes even further degraded in performance while it waits for all production I/O requests when the disk is already overallocated. Administrators can then assign a priority or pecking order for the essential components that need higher priority.

I/O Tuning   When designing systems, administrators need to analyze I/O needs from the top-down, determining which resources are necessary to achieve the required performance levels. In order to perform this top-down evaluation, administrators first need to evaluate the application I/O requirements to understand how many reads and writes are required by each transaction and how many transactions take place each second.

Once administrators understand the application requirements, they can build the disk configuration. Configurations elements that will need to be considered to support the application requirements include some of the following:

- Type of media
- Array configuration
- RAID type
- The number of disks in a RAID set
- Access methods

Scalability

Most applications will see increases in workloads in their life cycles. For this reason, the systems supporting those applications must be able to scale to meet increased demand. Scalability is the ability of a system or network to manage a growing workload in a proficient manner or its ability to be expanded to accommodate the workload growth. All cloud environments need to be scalable, as one of the chief tenets of cloud computing is elasticity, or the ability to quickly adapt to growing workloads.

Scalability can be handled either vertically or horizontally, more commonly referred to as "scaling up" or "scaling out," respectively.

Vertical Scaling (Scaling Up)

To scale vertically means to add resources to a single node, thereby making that node capable of handling more of a load within itself. This type of scaling is most often seen in virtualization environments where individual hosts add more processors or more memory with the objective of adding more VMs to each host.

Horizontal Scaling (Scaling Out)

More nodes are added to a configuration to scale horizontally instead of increasing the resources for any particular node. Horizontal scaling is often used in application farms. In such cases, more web servers are added to a farm to handle distributed application delivery better. The third type of scaling, diagonal scaling, is a combination of both, increasing resources for individual nodes and adding more of those nodes to the system. Diagonal scaling allows for the best configuration to be achieved for a quickly growing, elastic solution.

 EXAM TIP   Know the difference between scaling up and scaling out.

Performance Concepts

There are some performance concepts that underlie each of the failure types and the allocation mechanisms discussed in this chapter. As we did with the failure mechanisms, let's look at each of these according to their associated compute resources.

Disk

The configuration of disk resources is an integral part of a well-designed cloud system. Based on the user and application requirements and usage patterns, numerous design choices need to be made to implement a storage system that cost-effectively meets an organization's needs. Some of the considerations for disk performance include

- IOPS
- Read and write operations
- File system performance
- Metadata performance
- Caching

IOPS   IOPS, or input/output operations per second, are the standard measurement for disk performance. They are usually gathered as read IOPS, write IOPS, and total IOPS to distinguish between the types of requests that are being received.

Read and Write Operations   As just mentioned, two types of operations can take place: reading and writing. As their names suggest, reads occur when a resource requests data from a disk resource, and writes occur when a resource requests new data be recorded on a disk resource. Different configuration options exist both for troubleshooting and performance tuning based on which type of operation occurs.

File System Performance   File system performance is debated as a selling point among different technology providers. File systems can be formatted and cataloged differently based on the proprietary technologies of their associated vendors. There is little to do in the configuration of file system performance outside of evaluating the properties of each planned operation in the environment.

Metadata Performance   Metadata performance refers to how quickly files and directories can be created, removed, or checked. Applications exist now that produce millions of files in a single directory and create very deep and wide directory structures, and this rapid growth of items within a file system can have a significant impact on performance. The ability to create, remove, and check their status efficiently grows in direct proportion to the number of items in use on any file system.

Caching   To improve performance, hard drives are architected with a disk cache mechanism that reduces both read and write times. On a physical hard drive, the disk cache is usually a RAM chip that is built in and holds data that is likely to be accessed again soon. On virtual hard drives, the same caching mechanism can be employed by using a specified portion of a memory resource.

Network

Similar to disk resources, the configuration of network resources is critical. Based on the user and application requirements and usage patterns, numerous design choices need to be made to implement a network that cost-effectively meets an organization's needs. Some of the considerations for network performance include

- Bandwidth
- Throughput
- Jumbo frames
- Network latency
- Hop counts
- Quality of service (QoS)
- Multipathing
- Load balancing

Bandwidth   Bandwidth is the measurement of available or consumed data communication resources on a network. The performance of all networks is dependent on having available bandwidth.

Throughput   Throughput is the amount of data that can be realized between two network resources. Throughput can be substantially increased through bonding or teaming of network adapters, which allows resources to see multiple interfaces as one single interface with aggregated resources.

Jumbo Frames   Jumbo frames are Ethernet frames with more than 1500 bytes of payload. These frames can carry up to 9000 bytes of payload, but depending on the vendor and the environment they are deployed in, there may be some deviation. Jumbo frames are utilized because they are much less processor-intensive to consume than a large number of smaller frames, thereby freeing up expensive processor cycles for more business-related functions.

Network Latency   Network latency refers to any performance delays experienced during the processing of any network data. A low-latency network connection is one that experiences short delay times, such as a dedicated T-1, while a high-latency connection frequently suffers from long delays, like DSL or a cable modem.

Hop Counts   A hop count represents the total number of devices a packet passes through to reach its intended network target. The more hops data must pass through to reach its destination, the greater the delay is for the transmission. Network utilities like ping can be used to determine the hop count to an intended destination.

Ping generates packets that include a field reserved for the hop count, typically referred to as the Time to Live (TTL). Each time a capable device, usually a router, along the path to the target receives one of these packets, that device modifies the packet, decrementing the TTL by one. Each packet is sent out with a particular TTL value, ranging from 1 to 254. The TTL count is decremented for every router (hop) that the packet traverses on its way to the destination.

The hop count is also decremented by one each second that the packet resides in the memory of a routing device at a hop along the path to its destination. The receiving device compares the hop count against a predetermined limit. It discards the packet if its hop count is too high. If the TTL is decremented to zero at any point during its transmission, an "ICMP port unreachable" message is generated, with the IP of the source router or device included, and sent back to the originator. The finite TTL is used as it counts down to zero to prevent packets from endlessly bouncing around the network due to routing errors.

Quality of Service   QoS is a set of technologies that can identify the type of data in data packets and divide those packets into specific traffic classes that can be prioritized according to defined service levels. QoS technologies enable administrators to meet their service requirements for a workload or an application by measuring network bandwidth, detecting changing network conditions, and prioritizing the network traffic accordingly. QoS can be targeted at a network interface, toward a given server's or router's performance, or regarding specific applications. A network monitoring system is typically deployed as part of a QoS solution to ensure that networks perform at the desired level.

Multipathing   Multipathing is the practice of defining and controlling redundant physical paths to I/O devices. When an active path to a device becomes unavailable, the multipathing configuration can automatically switch to an alternative path to maintain service availability. The capability of performing this operation without intervention from an administrator is known as automatic failover.

 EXAM TIP   Remember that multipathing is almost always an architectural component of redundant solutions.

A prerequisite for taking advantage of multipathing capabilities is to design and configure the multipathed resource with redundant hardware, such as redundant network interfaces or host bus adapters.

Load Balancing   A load balancer is a networking solution that distributes incoming traffic among multiple servers hosting the same application content. Load balancers improve overall application availability and performance by preventing any application server from becoming a single point of failure.

If deployed alone, however, the load balancer becomes a single point of failure by itself. Therefore, it is always recommended to deploy multiple load balancers in parallel. In addition to improving availability and performance, load balancers add to the security profile of a configuration by the typical usage of network address translation, which obfuscates the back-end application server's IP address.

Performance Automation

Various tasks can be performed to improve performance on machines. It is typical for these tasks to be performed at regular intervals to maintain consistent performance levels. However, it can be quite a job to maintain a large number of systems, and organizational

IT departments are supporting more devices per person than ever before. They accomplish this through automation. Automation uses scripting, scheduled tasks, and automation tools to do the routine tasks so that IT staff can spend more time solving the real problems and proactively looking for ways to make things better and even more efficient.

PowerShell commands are provided in many examples because these commands can be used with the AWS Command Line Interface (CLI) or the Microsoft Azure Cloud Shell. PowerShell was chosen for its versatility. However, other scripting languages can also be used, depending on the platform. Scripts can be combined into tasks using AWS Systems Manager or Microsoft Azure runbooks.

This section discusses different performance-enhancing activities that can be automated to save time and standardize. They include the following:

- Archiving logs
- Clearing logs
- Compressing drives
- Scavenging stale DNS entries
- Purging orphaned resources
- Reclaiming resources

Archiving Logs

Logs can take up a lot of space on servers, but you will want to keep logs around for a long time in case they are needed to investigate a problem or a security issue. For this reason, you might want to archive logs to a logging server and then clear the log from the server.

A wide variety of cloud logging and archiving services are available that can be leveraged instead of setting up a dedicated logging server. Some services include Logentries, OpenStack, Sumo Logic, Syslog, Amazon S3, Amazon CloudWatch, and Papertrail. Cloud backup services can also be used to archive logs. Services such as AWS Glacier can be configured to pull log directories and store them safely on another system, so they are not lost. These systems can consolidate logs, then correlate and deduplicate them to save space and gain network intelligence.

Clearing Logs

There is very little reason to clear logs unless you have first archived them to another service or server. The previous section outlined how to archive logs to a local logging server or to cloud services. Ensure that these are configured and that they have been fully tested before clearing logs that could contain valuable data. Logs are there for a reason. They show the activity that took place on a device, and they can be very valuable in retracing the steps of an attacker or in troubleshooting errors. You do not want to be the person who is asked, "How long has this been going on?" and you have to answer, "I don't know because we cleared the logs last night." Attackers will often clear log files to cover their tracks after committing some malicious deed, such as compromising a server or stealing data.

Here is a PowerShell function to clear the logs from computers 1 through 4 called ClearComputer1-4Logs. You first provide the function with a list of computers. It then puts together a list of all logs, goes through each, and clears the log.

```
function ClearComputer1-4Logs ($ComputerName="Computer1", "Computer2",
"Computer3", "Computer4")
{
    $Logs = Get-EventLog -ComputerName $ComputerName -List | ForEach {$_.Log}
    $Logs | ForEach {Clear-EventLog -ComputerName $ComputerName -Log $_ }
    Get-EventLog -ComputerName $ComputerName -List
}
```

Compressing Drives

Compressing drives can reduce the amount of space consumed. However, accessing files on the drives will require a bit more CPU power to decompress before the file can be opened. Here is the command you can use to compress an entire drive. You can place this in a Windows group policy to encrypt the data drives (D:\) of various machines, depending on how you apply the group policy. The following command specifies that the D:\ directory and everything below it should be compressed. The –recurse command is what causes the compression to take place on all subfolders.

```
Enable-NtfsCompression -Path D:\ -Recurse
```

Scavenging Stale DNS Entries

As mentioned in Chapter 4, DNS distributes the responsibility for both the assignment of domain names and the mapping of those names to IP addresses to the authoritative name servers within each domain. DNS servers register IP address assignments as host records in their database. Sometimes a record is created and then that host is removed or it is assigned a new address. The DNS server would retain a bogus record in the former case and redundant addresses in the latter case.

Scavenging is the process of removing DNS entries for hosts that no longer respond on that address. You can configure automatic scavenging on DNS servers. All you have to do is enable the scavenging feature and set the age for when DNS records will be removed. If a host cannot be reached for the specified number of days, its host record in DNS will automatically be deleted.

Purging Orphaned Resources

Applications, hypervisors included, do not always clean up after themselves. Sometimes child objects or resources from deleted or moved objects still remain on systems. These are known as orphaned resources.

In Microsoft System Center Virtual Machine Manager (SCVMM), you can view orphaned resources by opening the Library workspace and clicking Orphaned Resources. You can right-click the object to delete it, but we want to automate the task. A script to remove all orphaned resources from SCVMM would take many pages of this book, so we will point you to a resource where you can obtain an up-to-date script for free: https://www.altaro.com/hyper-v/free-script-find-orphaned-hyper-v-vm-files/

Orphaned resources show up in the VMware vSphere web client with "(Orphaned)" after their name. You can remove them with this script after logging into the command line on the host:

```
$VMSet=Get-VM
foreach ($vm in $VMSet)
{
 if ($vm.ExtensionData.Runtime.ConnectionState -eq "orphaned") {$vm | Remove-VM}
}
```

Reclaiming Resources

Many companies have inactive VMs that continue to consume valuable resources while providing no business value. Metrics can identify machines that might not be used. At this point, a standard message can be sent to the VM owner, notifying them that their system has been flagged for reclamation unless they confirm that the VM is still providing business value. Alternatively, you can give the owner the option of keeping or reclaiming the resources themselves rather than automatically doing it. However, if the owner of the VM does not respond in a timely manner, the organization may decide to have the machine reclaimed automatically.

If reclamation is chosen, the machine can be archived and removed from the system, and the resources can be freed up for other machines. The automation can be initiated whenever metrics indicate an inactive machine. VMware vRealize has this capability built-in for vCenter, and similar automation can be created for other tools. In Microsoft Azure, the Resource Manager can be configured to reclaim resources.

 NOTE Do not enable reclamation functions until you have a good idea of how they will operate. Double-check settings to avoid reclaiming too much.

Common Performance Issues

Some failures can occur within a cloud environment, and the system must be configured to be tolerant of those failures and provide availability in accordance with the organization's SLA or other contractual agreements.

Mechanical components in an environment will experience failure at some point. It is just a matter of time. Higher-quality equipment may last longer than cheaper equipment, but it will still break down someday. This is something you should be prepared for.

Failures occur mainly on each of the four primary compute resources: disk, memory, network, and processor. This section examines each of these resources in turn.

Common Disk Issues

Disk-related issues can happen for a variety of reasons, but disks fail more frequently than the other compute resources because they are the only compute resource that has a mechanical component. Due to the moving parts, failure rates are typically quite high. Some common disk failures include

- Physical hard disk failures
- Controller card failures
- Disk corruption
- HBA failures
- Fabric and network failures

Physical Hard Disk Failures

Physical hard disks frequently fail because they are mechanical, moving devices. In enterprise configurations, they are deployed as components of drive arrays, and single failures do not affect array availability.

Controller Card Failures

Controller cards are the elements that control arrays and their configurations. Like all components, they fail from time to time. Redundant controllers are costly to run in parallel, as they require double the amount of drives to become operational, and that capacity is lost because it is never in use until failure. Therefore, an organization should do a return-on-investment analysis to determine the feasibility of making such devices redundant.

Disk Corruption

Disk corruption occurs when the structured data on the disk is no longer accessible. This can happen due to malicious acts or programs, skewing of the mechanics of the drive, or even a lack of proper maintenance. Disk corruption is hard to repair, as the full contents of the disks often need to be reindexed or restored from backups. Backups can also be unreliable for these failures if the corruption began before its identification, as the available backup sets may also be corrupted.

Host Bus Adapter Failures

While not as common as physical disk failures, host bus adapter (HBA) failures need to be expected, and storage solutions need to be designed with them in mind. HBAs have the option of being multipathed, which prevents a loss of storage accessibility in the event of a failure.

Fabric and Network Failures

Similar to controller card failure, fabric or network failures can be relatively expensive to design around, as they happen when a storage networking switch or switch port fails. The design principles to protect against such a failure are similar to those for HBAs, as multipathing needs to be in place to make sure all hosts that depend on the fabric or network have access to their disk resources through another channel.

Common Memory Issues

Memory-related issues, while not as common as disk failures, can be just as disruptive. Good system design in cloud environments will take RAM failure into account as a risk and ensure that there is always some RAM available to run mission-critical systems in case of memory failure on one of their hosts. The following are some types of memory failures:

- Memory chip failures
- Motherboard failures
- Swap files that run out of space

Memory Chip Failures

Memory chip failures happen less frequently than physical device failures, since memory chips have no moving parts and mechanical wear does not play a role. They will, however, break from time to time and need to be replaced.

Motherboard Failures

Similar to memory chips, motherboards have no moving parts, and because of this, they fail less frequently than mechanical devices. When they do fail, however, VMs are unable to operate, as they have no processor, memory, or networking resources that they can access. In this situation, they must be moved immediately to another host or go offline.

Swap Files Out of Space

Swap space failures often occur in conjunction with a disk failure, when disks run out of available space to allocate to swap files for memory overallocation. They do, however, result in out-of-memory errors for VMs and hosts alike.

Network Issues

Similar to memory components, network components are relatively reliable because they do not have moving parts. Unlike memory, network resources are highly configurable and prone to errors based on human mistakes during implementation. Network redundancy, such as redundant links to a CSP, can help mitigate the risk of some network issues. This is important because network communication is the foundation for using cloud services. Some common types of network failures include

- Physical NIC failures
- Speed or duplex mismatches
- Switch failures
- Physical transmission media failures

Physical NIC Failures

Network interface cards can fail in a similar fashion to other printed circuit board components like motherboards, controller cards, and memory chips. Because they fail from time to time, redundancy needs to be built into the host through multiple physical NICs and into the virtualization through designing multiple network paths using virtual NICs for the VMs.

Speed or Duplex Mismatches

Mismatch failures happen only on physical NICs and switches, as virtual networks negotiate these automatically. Speed and duplex mismatches result in dropped packets between the two connected devices and can be identified through getting a significant number of cyclical redundancy check (CRC) errors on the devices.

Switch Failures

Similar to fabric and network failures, network switch failures are expensive to plan for, as they require duplicate hardware and cabling. Switches fail only a small percentage of the time, but more frequently have individual ports fail. When these individual ports do fail, the resources that are connected to them need to have another path available, or their service will be interrupted.

Physical Transmission Media Failures

Cables break from time to time when their wires inside are crimped or cut. This can happen either when they are moved, when they are stretched too far, or when they become old, and the connector breaks loose from its associated wires. As with other types of network failures, multiple paths to the resource using that cable is the way to prevent a failure from interrupting operations.

Physical Processor Issues

Processors fail for one of three main reasons: they get broken while getting installed, they are damaged by voltage spikes, or they are damaged due to overheating from failed or ineffective fans. Damaged processors either take hosts completely offline or degrade performance based on the damage and the availability of a standby or alternative processor in some models.

Chapter Review

When building a virtualization host, special consideration needs to be given to adequately planning the resources to ensure that the host can support the virtualized environment. Creating a VM requires thorough planning regarding the role the VM will play in the environment and the VM's resources to accomplish that role. Planning carefully for the VM and the primary resources of memory, processor, disk, and network can help prevent common failures.

Questions

The following questions will help you gauge your understanding of the material in this chapter. Read all the answers carefully because there might be more than one correct answer. Choose the best response(s) for each question.

1. Which of the following would be considered a host compute resource?

   A. Cores

   B. Power supply

   C. Processor

   D. Bandwidth

2. Quotas are a mechanism for enforcing what?

   A. Limits

   B. Rules

   C. Access restrictions

   D. Virtualization

3. How are quotas defined?

   A. By management systems

   B. According to service level agreements that are defined between providers and their customers

   C. Through trend analysis and its results

   D. With spreadsheets and reports

4. When would a reservation be used?

   A. When a maximum amount of resources needs to be allocated to a specific resource

   B. When a minimum amount of capacity needs to be available at all times to a specific resource

   C. When capacity needs to be measured and controlled

   D. When planning a dinner date

5. How does the hypervisor enable access for VMs to the physical hardware resources on a host?

   A. Over Ethernet cables

   B. By using USB 3.0

   C. Through the system bus

   D. By emulating a BIOS that abstracts the hardware

6. What mechanism allows one core to handle all requests from a specific thread on a specific processor core?

   A. V2V

   B. CPU affinity

   C. V2P

   D. P2V

7. In a scenario where an entity exceeds its defined quota but is granted access to the resources anyway, what must be in place?

   A. Penalty

   B. Hard quota

   C. Soft quota

   D. Alerts

8. Which of the following must be licensed when running a virtualized infrastructure?

   A. Hosts

   B. VMs

   C. Both

   D. Neither

9. What do you need to employ if you have a serial device that needs to be utilized by a VM?

   A. Network isolation

   B. Physical resource redirection

   C. V2V

   D. Storage migration

10. You need to divide your virtualized environment into groups that can be managed by separate groups of administrators. Which of these tools can you use?

    A. Quotas

    B. CPU affinity

    C. Resource pools

    D. Licensing

11. Which tool allows guest operating systems to share noncritical memory pages with the host?

    A. CPU affinity

    B. Memory ballooning

    C. Swap file configuration

    D. Network attached storage

12. Which of these options is not a valid mechanism for improving disk performance?

   A. Replacing rotational media with solid state media

   B. Replacing rotational media with higher-speed rotational media

   C. Decreasing disk quotas

   D. Employing a different configuration for the RAID array

Answers

1. **C.** The four compute resources used in virtualization are disk, memory, processor, and network. On a host, these are available as the physical entities of hard disks, memory chips, processors, and network interface cards (NICs).

2. **A.** Quotas are limits on the resources that can be utilized for a specific entity on a system. For example, a user could be limited to storing up to 10GB of data on a server or a VM limited to 500GB of bandwidth each month.

3. **B.** Quotas are defined according to service level agreements that are negotiated between a provider and its customers.

4. **B.** A reservation should be used when there is a minimum amount of resources that need to have guaranteed capacity.

5. **D.** The host computer BIOS is emulated by the hypervisor to provide compute resources for a VM.

6. **B.** CPU affinity allows all requests from a specific thread or process to be handled by the same processor core.

7. **C.** Soft quotas enforce limits on resources, but do not restrict access to the requested resources when the quota has been exceeded.

8. **C.** Both hosts and guests must be licensed in a virtual environment.

9. **B.** Physical resource redirection enables VMs to utilize physical hardware as if they were physical hosts that could connect to the hardware directly.

10. **C.** Resource pools allow the creation of a hierarchy of guest VM groups that can have different administrative privileges assigned to them.

11. **B.** Memory ballooning allows guest operating systems to share noncritical memory pages with the host.

12. **C.** Decreasing disk quotas helps with capacity issues, but not with performance.

CHAPTER 10

Systems Management

In this chapter, you will learn about
- Policies and procedures
- Systems management best practices
- Systems maintenance
- Monitoring techniques

Up until this point, this book has primarily focused on the technologies required to deliver cloud services. This chapter explores the nontechnical aspects of cloud service delivery in policies, procedures, and best practices. These components are critical to the efficient and effective execution of cloud solutions.

The chapter begins with the documents that define the rule sets by which users and administrators must abide, called policies, and the prescribed documented actions that will carry out the expectations of the policies, known as procedures. After this, maintenance activities are introduced. These maintenance activities must be performed to keep cloud systems operating at expected performance levels and to avoid unexpected downtime.

The chapter then introduces monitoring techniques. Monitoring the cloud environment is a fundamental component of successful cloud computing environment management. Proper monitoring helps uncover problems early on, and it aids in detecting network outages quickly and efficiently, which leads to increased availability of servers, services, and applications. Valuable data obtained in monitoring metrics can be used to plan for future resource utilization and to become more proactive instead of reactive.

An organization needs to be able to monitor and manage the cloud environment quickly and efficiently. Remotely administering cloud virtualization is a flexible way to administer the environment and respond to issues or alerts that might arise. There are various options for managing and monitoring the cloud environment securely and remotely, which are covered in this chapter.

Policies and Procedures

Policies and procedures are the backbone of any IT organization. While the hardware, software, and their associated configurations are the products that enable the functionality businesses desire from their IT services, it is a cloud service provider's or cloud consumer's policies and procedures that allow IT service implementation, maintenance, and ongoing support.

Policies define the rule sets by which users and cloud service administrators (CSAs) must abide, and procedures are the prescribed methodologies by which activities are carried out in the IT environment according to those defined policies.

While most IT professionals focus on the technical aspects of IT, a growing percentage of all IT organizations are emphasizing policy and procedure development to ensure that they get the most out of their technology investment. Policies can be used to enforce IT best practices to significantly affect not only the operational efficiency and effectiveness of the businesses they serve but to also protect the organization from risk by defining compliance expectations and ensuring adherence to industry regulation.

This section provides information on some key business processes that aid in managing the technology environment, making it more efficient, and planning for the future. These processes include

- Creating standard operating procedures
- Workflow
- Capacity management

Standard Operating Procedures

Standard operating procedures (SOPs) are a form of knowledge management. The experience gained from one individual can be documented so that others do not need to go through the same experience, possibly involving failure, to learn from it.

SOPs help ensure that tasks are performed consistently, without significant deviation from expectations. It is likely that you will perform routine tasks many times. The first time you perform such a job, it is best to create an SOP for future migrations. You may find along the way that you can improve the SOP here or there. Feel free to add more details to the SOP as you discover enhancements.

An SOP will ensure that others who perform the same task do so with the same level of professionalism that you do. SOPs also ensure consistent implementation, including the amount of time it takes to perform the task and the resources required.

Workflow

Workflows are business processes organized in sets of discrete tasks from the beginning to the end of the operations. Workflow task details include the dependencies and requirements such as the personnel, technology, tools, and environment required to complete the task.

Workflow modeling can help visualize a workflow by placing each task on a timeline, with dependencies shown as prerequisite tasks and parallel tasks shown about one another. Relationships are depicted using paths. Each path is a set of functions that can be performed independently of other tasks. Some paths may diverge and then join back together to express group dependencies and then there is a period where tasks can be carried out at the same time. Some paths may take longer to complete than others. A project management technique known as *critical path analysis* identifies paths where there is no extra time available. When resources are scarce, tasks on the critical path should be given a higher priority.

Workflow can be helpful in managing standard processes, but it can be even more effective when those processes are automated. The SOPs an organization creates in the course of doing business can now be used in establishing workflow automation. Once a process has been performed several times and sufficiently well documented, there may be methods of automating the process so that it is even more streamlined. The documentation will ensure that you do not miss a critical step in the workflow, and it can help in troubleshooting workflows later on. Workflow automation with runbooks is discussed in more detail in Chapter 14.

Capacity Management

Capacity management is the process of ensuring that both the current and future capacity and performance demands of an IT organization's customers regarding service provision are delivered according to justifiable costs. Capacity management has overall responsibility for ensuring adequate IT capacity (as the name suggests) to meet required service levels, that the appropriate stakeholders are correctly advised on how to match capacity and demand, and that existing capacity is optimized.

Successful capacity management requires considerable attention to be paid to the design of the system. The design phase must ensure that all service levels are understood and that the capacity to fulfill them is incorporated into the design's configuration. Once the configuration has been adequately designed and documented, operations can establish a baseline. This baseline is a measuring stick against which capacity can be monitored to understand both the current demand and trend for future needs.

The capacity management process includes producing and maintaining an appropriate capacity plan that reflects the current and future requirements of its customers. The plan is designed to accomplish the following objectives:

- Provide advice and guidance to all other areas of the business and IT on all capacity- and performance-related issues.

- Ensure that service performance achievements meet or exceed all their agreed-upon performance targets by managing the performance and capacity of both services and resources.

- Ensure the current and future capacity and performance demands of the customer regarding IT service provision are delivered within justifiable costs.

- Assist with the diagnosis and resolution of both performance- and capacity-related incidents and problems.

- Assess the impact of any changes to the capacity plan and the performance and capacity of all IT services and resources.

- Ensure that proactive measures to improve the performance of services are implemented.

When building this capacity plan, its architects must factor in all IT resources, including both human and technical resources. Keep in mind that people are resources as well.

Records Management

Records management is a governance process surrounding organizational information. Much of a company's ability to operate and its organizational value may reside within its data, so it is important to effectively manage that information so that it can be easily obtained by those who need it, revised when necessary, protected from accidental or malicious modification or deletion, and removed when it no longer provides value. Records management includes both physical and digital information. Such information includes work products created by employees or others on behalf of the company or information obtained by the company.

Records have a life cycle, beginning with their creation and ending with their destruction. The life cycle is shown in Figure 10-1. The first stage is the creation of the document. The record then may go through various modifications. The third phase is the movement of the document. This may include moving to other storage mediums or platforms. The last stage is destruction.

Records management seeks to control organizational information through the following activities:

- Identifying newly created data.
- Tracking relevant metadata.
- Storing the data.
- Documenting access to data.
- Tracking revisions to the data. This may also include preserving previous versions.
- Destroying documents.

Identifying New Data

The first priority of a records management system is to track when new data is created. In some cases, the company requires that new data be stored within the records management system and leaves it to employees to comply with the requirement. However, some data can potentially fall through the cracks with this approach, so some records management systems will have agents that run on systems to identify when new data is created and then automatically archive the data within the records management system.

Tracking Metadata

The next step is to track relevant metadata on the data. Some important metadata includes creator, creation date, data classification, data owner, and revisions. Figure 10-2 shows the metadata of a sample Microsoft Word document. This is information that the application and the operating system collect automatically.

Figure 10-1
Records life cycle

Creation ⟩ Modification ⟩ Movement ⟩ Destruction

Figure 10-2
Record metadata

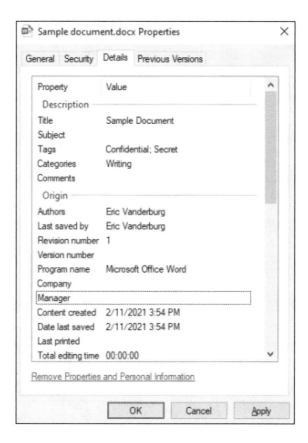

The actual metadata fields may differ based on the document type. For example, Figure 10-3 shows the metadata for a picture. As you can see, the camera recorded additional metadata specific to a photo, including the camera make, model, exposure time, ISO speed, and more.

Storing the Data

The next step is to store the data. We covered storage mechanisms back in Chapters 2 and 3, so we will not rehash all the options available for storage, except to say that some records management systems will store the data in the application as part of the database, others will store the files on a file system and include pointers to their location within their database, and still others will leave the files where they are at and simply record their current location.

Access

The records management system should also document who has access to the file. This will typically not list each and every user that can access the data. Rather, the system may include which groups can access it. The actual access permissions may be governed by the permissions of the underlying file system or permissions within the database, depending on how the data is accessed.

Figure 10-3
Photo metadata

Versioning

The next step in the records management process is tracking changes made to organizational data and storing previous copies so that older versions can be retrieved if needed. One component of versioning is to lock out earlier copies so that they can no longer be modified. In some cases, previous versions are stored on WORM media so that they cannot be changed. If you recall from Chapter 3, write once, read many (WORM) media is storage that cannot be modified once it has been written. It does this through write protection or by physically blocking write capabilities.

Retention

The records management system should track when information is set to expire. Typically, organizations will establish data retention rates for certain types of data. These retention rates may be set according to the organization's determination on how long data typically has value to the company weighed against the cost to continue managing and securing the data. Additionally, compliance requirements, such as Securities and Exchange Commission (SEC) regulations or Gramm-Leach-Bliley Act (GLBA) for financial documents or Health Insurance Portability and Accountability Act (HIPAA)

Record Type	Retention Period
Accounting ledgers and schedules	7 years
Bank statements	7 years
Credit card records	2 years
Legal documents	Close of matter + 7 years
Employee benefit information	4 years after termination
Payroll deductions	Termination + 7 years
Employee tax documents (e.g., W-2)	Termination + 7 years
Employment records	Hire date + 3 years
Correspondence, property deeds, assessments, licenses, rights of way	Indefinite
Original purchase/sale/lease agreement	Indefinite

Table 10-1 Sample Record Retention Periods

for health information, may specify certain retention rates. Table 10-1 shows an example of some record retention periods and how specific they might be.

Destruction

The last step in records management is removing data that is no longer needed. This is typically performed by implementing policies to purge data that has expired organizational retention rates or is otherwise no longer useful to the company.

Systems Management Best Practices

The processes and procedures that IT organizations implement to achieve results more effectively and efficiently are the results of careful design, standardized environments, and thorough documentation.

With a view to building sustainable technology solutions that consistently deliver their intended value, system maintenance must be performed at every step of the application life cycle. Documentation of the business requirements for any proposed IT service additions or changes should be the first phase of the life cycle, followed by documentation for the proposed technical design, continuing into implementation planning documents and support documentation, and coming full circle in the life cycle through documented service improvement plans.

Documentation

Documentation is an important part of systems management. The Information Technology Infrastructure Library (ITIL) is a collection of best practices for IT service management. It was put together initially by the British government but was spun off under a private best practices body called AXELOS in 2013. ITIL is one of the most widely used IT service management best practices globally, and it is very helpful in understanding best practices in IT documentation. ITIL is divided into five publications, called volumes, that cover the following categories:

- Service strategy
- Service design
- Service transition
- Service operation
- Continual service improvement

ITIL provides a framework for documentation for each of the five sections, and this section will discuss documentation in that context.

During the ITIL service strategy phase, business requirements are documented as the entry point for all IT services. The key piece of documentation in this stage is the service portfolio. The service portfolio is a comprehensive list of quantified services that will enable the business to achieve a positive return on its investment in the service.

During the service design phase, technical solutions, support processes, and service level agreements (SLAs) are documented in the service design package (SDP). The SDP includes the technical solutions, such as routers, switches, servers, and storage; support processes for maintaining the service; and SLAs with the customer regarding the mutually agreed-upon levels of capacity, availability, and performance.

The service transition phase focuses on delivering the SDP and all of its detail into a living, breathing operational environment. This documentation stage consists of change and configuration documentation. See Chapter 14 for further information on change and configuration management.

Lastly, a service improvement register documents opportunities for improving IT services as follows:

- Opportunities are categorized as short-term, medium-term, or long-term options.
- Opportunities are assessed as part of the service strategy phase once the life cycle restarts.
- Opportunities are assigned a business value that can be weighed against implementation cost.
- Opportunity time frames, value, and costs are evaluated to determine which services to add or modify to provide the highest value to customers.

Documentation is one vehicle that drives effective systems administration. Documentation allows CSAs to expand their ability to comprehend complex environments without keeping all the information in their heads. Another very effective way to accomplish this goal is through standardization.

 EXAM TIP All service levels must be documented and agreed upon by both the service provider and the customer.

Standardization

Standardization reduces system administration complexities because CSAs only need to learn the standard way of doing things, since that method and configuration are applicable across many systems.

Standardization focuses on two areas: procedures and configurations. Standard procedures were discussed earlier in the "Standard Operating Procedures" section. Now we will focus on standardizing configuration. Some of the advantages of standardization include

- Systems management is performed consistently.
- System access is better controlled.
- System communication protocols are the same across applications and services.
- Uniform system logging and auditing settings are employed.
- Systems are deployed in the same manner each time.

Standardization allows for systems to be managed consistently in the same way. Organizations can specify which management protocols to use and whether centralized management utilities will be put in place. When new systems are evaluated, the selection group then ensures that new software or cloud services meet the standard requirements so that they can be managed in the same way. Consistent management reduces the amount of time spent managing devices and makes employees more efficient as they get more comfortable with the process. Consistent management means that administrators need to be familiar with fewer tools, so training administrators is easier and the company spends less on licensing because fewer tools need to be licensed.

Standardization mandates which entities have access by default. Some devices come with default configurations that may not be secure or in the company's best interests. Standards define which users have administrative access and which users should have functional access to newly deployed systems. This ensures that end users do not have access to systems until the systems have been fully provisioned and tested for use.

Standardization is used to enforce how systems communicate with one another. Using standard communication models allows the organization to specify fewer traffic rules on intermediary devices. This decreases the complexity of management and decreases the attack surface of systems and networks, since only a small set of authorized communication protocols is allowed through. Communication standardization also makes it easier to detect unauthorized communication attempts if such attempts utilize a nonstandard communication method.

Standardization ensures consistent system logging and auditing settings are applied to servers, computers, and network devices to retain accurate data. Some logging settings such as file access logging or the logging of both successes and failures may not be configured everywhere, but having such information can be very useful when there are questions about what happened on a device. Standard logging methods ensure that each device will have the information the organization needs to make decisions or remediate an incident. Furthermore, the organization will have a more complete picture because each device will be recording the same types of information.

Lastly, standardization can help confirm that systems are deployed the same way each time. This is especially important as continuous improvement, and continuous delivery models produce more frequent software deployments. Each deployment should go through the same standard steps so that it is deployed correctly and efficiently.

Organizations often specify their own standards for how systems must be configured, but these standards may be based on industry standards such as the following:

- International Organization for Standardization/International Electrotechnical Commission (ISO/IEC) 27000 series
- The National Institute of Standards and Technology (NIST) standards
- The Information Systems Audit and Control Association's (ISACA) Control Objectives for Information and Related Technologies (COBIT)
- The Cloud Security Alliance (CSA) Cloud Controls Matrix (CCM)
- The Organization for the Advancement of Structured Information Standards (OASIS) Cloud Application Management for Platforms (CAMP) standard

Metrics

Metrics are an excellent way to track company performance. Metrics can be defined for all sorts of indicators. Another name for metrics is key performance indicators (KPIs). Metrics should be defined for items that are essential for organizational success. Some companies establish parameters because another company or trusted source uses them, but unless the metric contributes to the company's goals and mission, it is more likely a waste of time.

Metrics fall under the role of operations, and cloud operations (or "ops") teams often identify and track cloud-based metrics. As you can tell from the name, ops teams are part of DevOps, introduced in Chapter 8.

Cloud environments can be quite complex, with many different cloud solutions integrated into a hybrid multicloud. Metrics can help the cloud operations team and management track how systems are performing and the efficiency of processes.

Metrics are essential in evaluating whether service level agreements are being met and demonstrating to customers how the provider is achieving service level agreements. Metrics also help in identifying problems.

Reporting Based on Company Policies

Company policies specify the expectations the company has for employee behavior and how systems should operate. These items are of obvious importance to the organization because leaders took the time to write these expectations out in policy and made employees aware of the policy requirements. For this reason, policy elements can be a good guide for identifying metrics to track. For example, if the company policy says that high vulnerabilities must be remediated within seven days, it would make sense to establish a vulnerability remediation metric to track how long it takes to remediate vulnerabilities, including high vulnerabilities.

Reporting Based on SLAs

An SLA is a contract that specifies the level of uptime that will be supported by the service provider. SLAs include provisions for how the service provider will compensate customers if SLAs are not met, so it is in the organization's best interest to ensure that SLAs are met.

Metrics can be defined to measure SLA performance. For example, if the SLA states that an application must be available 99.999 percent of the time, an important metric to track would be site availability.

 EXAM TIP   Similar to SLAs are operational level agreements (OLAs), which are documents that describe the expectations of internal units so that SLAs can be met.

Dashboards

Gathering metrics is useful, but metrics truly become valuable when made available for decision-making and performance monitoring. Dashboards and reporting are two methods commonly used to make metrics available to those who need them. Dashboard panels, often consisting of a web portal or a linked spreadsheet, contain a series of metrics on specific areas. Web portals can be viewed anywhere, so they are available when needed. Spreadsheets are similarly shared, if not quite as easy to use as a web dashboard. One downside with spreadsheets is that they will not update if the resources from which they obtain their data are inaccessible, making the spreadsheet data stale. Stale spreadsheets can happen if the spreadsheet is created by someone who is authorized to collect the data and then later shared with another who is not. For this reason, web portals are far superior to spreadsheets for tracking metrics.

Metrics can also be tracked with reports that are set out at periodic intervals. This is typically an automated procedure, but upper-management reports are often consolidated from other reports and prepared by hand to give them added polish. Applications can be configured to e-mail reports with selected metrics on performance at certain intervals. Of course, this requires that data regarding these metrics be available to the application.

System Availability

System availability metrics are a core metric of any service provider, including cloud service providers (CSPs). Customers are purchasing an IT service, and they need to know when and how often that service is unavailable through such metrics as system uptime, bandwidth, or error rate. Some services can ping websites and send out notifications if a site becomes unavailable. These sites also track availability percentages and provide dashboards for viewing all checks.

It is also possible to collect availability metrics on the underlying components that make up a system, such as web services, database services, file systems, critical service dependencies, and so forth. Notifications can be similarly configured for such systems, with dashboards for viewing the status of all essential functions in one place.

- **Uptime**   Uptime can be a differentiating factor for service providers if uptime numbers are particularly high. Uptime is often measured as a percentage and described in terms of how many consecutive "nines" are in the percent. For example, a system that provides 99.999 percent availability is offering five 9s of availability, while a system that offers 99.999999 percent availability is offering eight 9s. A service provider can conduct a competitive analysis to reveal what competing service providers are offering for uptime availability metrics so that it can be sure to meet or exceed those numbers.

- **Downtime**   Periods of unavailability are called downtime, and most cloud service providers want to minimize this because disruptions for customers mean that they are finding less value in the service offering. The number of nines was used to demonstrate uptime, but downtime is represented either as the inverse percentage or as a specific amount of time the systems were unavailable. For example, the downtime number for five 9s would be 0.001 percent, and the number for eight 9s would be 0.000001 percent. If we were to measure these in the actual amount of time the systems were unavailable, five 9s would equate to 5.39 minutes of downtime in a year, while eight 9s would be less than 1 second of downtime.

Connectivity

Connectivity metrics measure things like bandwidth consumption, congestion, and packet loss. Connectivity metrics are essential for ensuring responsive services and applications and avoiding performance or availability problems.

Track connectivity metrics to ensure that communication mediums do not get congested. By tracking connectivity metrics, a service provider can expand bandwidth or implement throttling to control available resources. Cloud dashboards can quickly show if, for example, a select group of virtual desktop users is utilizing more bandwidth than others. The cloud administrator may decide to implement throttling on those users if the cloud account as a whole is approaching a bandwidth limit, or they may choose to upgrade to a plan that includes more bandwidth if the bandwidth-consuming activity is for legitimate business purposes. Connectivity metrics are also applicable to conducting trending on connectivity metrics to determine when upgrades will be necessary.

Connectivity dashboards can show connectivity parameters for links within the network and across sites. Some system tools for collecting network connectivity data include PRTG Network Monitor and SolarWinds NetFlow Traffic Analyzer. You can use SNMP and RMON to collect device statistics. Some companies perform protocol analysis as well to gain additional insight into connectivity.

Latency

Latency metrics measure site, service, or link response time. Latency metrics are essential for ensuring responsive services and applications and avoiding performance or availability problems.

Track latency metrics to ensure that services meet established SLAs and that end users are receiving data from devices with the lowest latency. Implement changes or add local services when regions are not well served. Often performance issues can be avoided by monitoring latency metrics in replication. Synchronous replication is particularly sensitive to latency.

Capacity

Capacity metrics measure how much storage is allocated, used, and free. Capacity metrics are helpful in ensuring that enough storage is available to users and applications. Track capacity metrics to ensure that volumes do not get full. Expand volumes or add storage as needed when capacity reaches established thresholds. You should also consider conducting trending on capacity metrics to determine when upgrades will be necessary.

Storage vendors produce dashboards and tools for viewing capacity metrics. These can sometimes be integrated into other reporting suites with Web-Based Enterprise Management (WBEM) or through custom vendor integration tools or application programming interfaces (APIs).

Overall Utilization

Detailed metrics are great for solving problems and for reporting, but it helps to have an overall picture of usage across the board. Overall utilization metrics can be obtained by consolidating individual metrics to give decision-makers and operations teams valuable insight on current usage and trends and can enable forecasting of future needs and opportunities.

Cost

Cost is a fundamental metric in any scenario. IT costs can be a significant portion of a company's budget, so it is crucial for those managing IT to know where the money is being spent and how those costs contribute to business operations. In a cloud-based environment, billing is often based on consumption, so IT needs to be able to show with metrics how that consumption is contributing to IT costs.

Cost metrics will also need to be calculated for chargebacks and showbacks to show which clients or departments should be billed for IT services as part of a chargeback initiative or just to track consumption for showbacks.

Chargebacks　　IT is often seen as purely an organizational cost to be reduced. IT frequently has to defend its actions and budget. IT can push the costs of technology services onto the company departments that use those services through chargebacks.

Chargebacks track usage of systems by departments or individuals and then bill the department for their utilization of the service. Chargebacks are popular in consulting organizations, law firms, accounting firms, and others that bill services to clients, because costs such as printing, faxing, and cloud service usage can be charged back to their clients as a cost of providing the service.

Showbacks   Showbacks track usage of IT services so that management can see the value of IT services in relation to their costs. This makes budgeting much more manageable. Also, when cutbacks are needed, management will have the data necessary to reduce services that have the least organizational impact.

Incidents

Incidents can and will happen in your organization. It is important to have an incident response plan and to specify metrics on how long certain tasks will take. Notification periods for investigations are strict, and there will be a lot of pressure during the incident to meet those deadlines. Be familiar with these metrics before the incident. Some metrics include investigation time, detection time, number of records affected, number of users affected, remediation cost, remediation hours, and investigation hours.

Health

Health metrics are valuable to gauge when equipment replacement is likely. Some CSAs may choose to replace equipment proactively in particularly critical environments. Health metrics also provide information useful for determining which spare equipment should be purchased for expected substitutes. Some important hardware health metrics include

- Mean time between failures (MTBF)
- Mean time to repair (MTTR)
- Self-monitoring, analysis, and reporting technology (SMART)

MTBF is the average time a device will function before it fails. MTBF can be used to determine approximately how long a hard drive will last in a server.

MTTR, on the other hand, is the average time that it takes to repair a failed hardware component. MTTR is often part of the maintenance contract for virtualization hosts. An MTTR of 24 hours or less would be appropriate for a higher-priority server. In contrast, a lower-priority server might have an MTTR of seven days.

Lastly, SMART is a set of hard disk metrics used to predict failures by monitoring over 100 metrics such as read error rate, spin-up time, start and stop count, reallocated sectors count, and seek error rate. SMART has predefined thresholds for each metric, and those thresholds are used to determine if a drive is in an OK, warning, or error status.

Elasticity

Elasticity is a measurement of how sensitive one variable is to changes in another. Elasticity is important in tracking metrics because some metrics may depend upon one another or may affect one another. Elasticity can track how changes in one metric affect other metrics.

Elasticity cause and effect, in turn, can be used to focus better efforts to improve performance. For example, a company may find that several key performance metrics improve when training time is increased. From a more technical perspective, backup time metrics may improve if bandwidth utilization is reduced.

Planning

Once the baseline states are documented, agreed upon in writing, and put in place, what happens when maintenance needs to occur or system upgrades occur? Such events almost certainly disrupt a baseline. These events must be planned for under controlled circumstances by the systems administrator. They cannot happen at random times without the consent of the customer. Maintenance windows need to be established as part of any IT environment for all of its configuration items. These windows should be scheduled at periods of least potential disruption to the customer, and the customer should be involved in the maintenance scheduling process. After all, the customer knows their patterns of business activity better than the systems administrators ever could.

All technology upgrades and patches should utilize these maintenance windows whenever possible. Furthermore, the timing of patch or upgrade implementation should be consistently reviewed as part of the standard change management process by the change advisory board (CAB). Change management is discussed in Chapter 14.

Systems Maintenance

IT systems require regular maintenance to help them remain free from errors and bugs and keep up with the latest technologies and processes. Maintenance and development updates can consume a great deal of IT personnel time, and yet their functions are core to the business. Additionally, some functions overlap, and others benefit from increased integration. A blended group of software developers and IT operations has evolved called DevOps to handle both objectives. DevOps was introduced back in Chapter 8, and system maintenance is also a function of the DevOps team. This section covers the following core systems maintenance activities:

- Code updates
- Patch management
- Maintenance automation

Code Updates

There is usually a queue of code updates, including requests, bugs, and features, that DevOps teams try to tackle. Teams may be working on different branches of code. Each branch is a portion of the program that is duplicated so that teams can work in parallel.

Two concepts that are often discussed within DevOps are continuous integration (CI) and continuous delivery (CD). Continuous integration involves automating the elements of the coding and testing processes. CI automates testing routines so that each time a new piece of code is committed, it is subjected to testing to ensure that it meets quality standards. Additional testing still needs to be performed, but this function helps catch the most routine issues early on in the development cycle with less effort.

Continuous delivery is a process that creates a pipeline of tasks leading toward the deployment of regular software releases. In CD, DevOps teams make frequent iterative changes to the code rather than working on a large portion of the program for an extended period. This decreases the time from the introduction of new code to the deployment of that code in production. CD also allows for software users to have more current versions and for stable releases to be produced in a short time frame. CD is also known as continuous development.

Some DevOps teams operate on short-term release schedules called *sprints* to accomplish some shared objective. Sprints allow developers to work as a team and celebrate the small successes rather than working on a huge project and only seeing the reward at the end.

Code Repository

Keeping track of changes in the code is essential. As the complexity of code increases, changes may cause unintended behavior that may not be caught until testing. For this reason, DevOps teams will keep a code repository. Code repositories can organize code branches to keep code consistent even when multiple teams work on the same areas in parallel.

Developers publish code changes or commits to the repository, where a record is kept of the code that has been updated since the previous submission. Developers tag commits with a short statement on what the change accomplished. Developers can synchronize their local development environments with the code repository to receive new updates to the code or select or create branches of the code to work from. Furthermore, developers can easily revert to previous versions of code that they or others worked on through the code repository.

Version Updates

Updating versions on end-user machines can be a big job. Three methods are used to complete version updates:

- **Manual version updates**   Manual version updates require the most time from the DevOps team. Companies that use this method send teams out to update end-user machines.

  Distributed environments may not be connected enough for end-user updating or package managers, so updates are sent to local staff at branch or regional offices, who update applications for the users in their location. Some companies use this method to customize the application for particular regions or languages. For example, an accounting firm may deploy different versions of its application to offices in different states or countries so that those users receive an interface that is most compatible with their tax codes and processes.

- **End-user updating** In the end-user updating method, new versions are pushed to an update server. The team then notifies end users that a new update is available. Notifications can be sent through e-mail or by posting to a company message board or intranet. Users are expected to keep their applications updated to the latest version. In some cases, the program may not work if it is not running the newest version.

- **Package manager** The third option is to use a package manager to deploy updates. The package manager resides on each end-user machine. New versions are released to a server, and the package manager checks for an update on the server when the user loads the program. If a new version exists, the package manager automatically pulls down any new code to upgrade the application to the current version.

  Package managers can also check for the local language settings on the operating system and region to load the appropriate software modules into their application.

Rollback

Developers used to save copies of an entire program or specific modules, functions, or subroutines each time a milestone was reached. If the next set of changes broke the program and the solution was not apparent, it was easiest to replace the existing code with the last backup rather than find all the changes and remove them.

Code repositories make rollback much simpler. In fact, they are now standard practice. If developers detect an error in testing and cannot find the cause, the code can be rolled back to a previous version by selecting the commit from the repository and deploying it back to the development environment. The code repository only stores the changes, so it takes much less space to store and less time to roll back.

Deployment Landscapes

Deployments are typically rolled out in four landscapes: development, quality assurance (QA), staging, and production. The landscapes can be available to diverse teams that are responsible for specialized areas of development. As code is more refined, it moves to a different landscape and undergoes additional testing.

Landscapes are efficient because the most straightforward and automated testing can be performed to small code segments first. Since this testing is frequent or a regularly scheduled activity, it can be automated. Furthermore, those tests' findings can be quickly resolved because the developer is familiar with the code he or she just wrote. Later efforts can then focus on more complex testing. Second, landscapes provide higher levels of assurance as the testing environment moves closer to that of production. Landscapes also offer some isolation and separation of duties so that the people testing the product are not influenced by those writing the code. Releases go through development, QA, staging, and production landscapes as they make their way from code sections to a functional release.

Development

The first landscape is a development environment where developers can test small changes to ensure that their code changes provide the correct results for any new features. This provides an environment where new features and modifications can be previewed without committing. Testing at this phase is mostly automated.

Quality Assurance

Once a group of small changes reaches the point where it can be packaged together into a functioning element of the specifications, it is ready to move to the QA landscape. The QA landscape is where software testers evaluate both the added code and the impact those changes could have on other parts of the application.

The application is tested as a whole in the QA landscape to ensure potential unintended actions, memory leaks, or security vulnerabilities do not occur. QA testing evaluates the edge cases to ensure that the application will not process data that is not within the program's bounds. Testers will work from multiple defined use cases of the program and seek to break it by performing actions the developers might not have anticipated.

In addition to regular QA testers, the QA landscape sometimes includes select individuals from the specifications phase (the first phase of the application life cycle) to ensure that the specifications were correctly translated into an application. The product must be thoroughly tested in the QA landscape before heading to the next landscape. The lead QA tester will usually sign off on the code in QA before it is moved.

Staging

In the staging landscape, code is placed into an environment that mirrors the production environment as closely as possible. The DevOps team will provision virtual machines (VMs) with the exact same specifications and configurations so that they can perform tests to better ensure that additional issues will not come up when the application or code is introduced to the production landscape. The team will test the deployment of the application, configuration, and access to the system, as well as any new features or application changes. The staging landscape, sometimes called pre-production, is the last landscape the code enters before going to production. Testing in the staging landscape may include canary and beta testers.

Production

In the production landscape, code is placed into production, where it is available for end users. Companies will usually implement segregation of duties in this landscape so that the same person who can deploy to the QA landscape cannot deploy to the production landscape and vice versa. These are usually separate individuals from those doing the testing as well.

The production landscape is where the maintenance and support start. Any updates have to go through the other two landscapes first to make sure that the best quality product is delivered. If there are any changes to the production environment in the future, then the end users must be contacted and notified of any potential downtime that may occur.

Deployment Methodologies

Recall from the discussion of the application life cycle in Chapter 8 that deployment is the fourth phase of the application life cycle. For review, the phases are specifications, development, testing, deployment, and maintenance. In the deployment phase, the application is installed and configured for use and procedures are documented for how the system should be employed. Users are then trained on how to use the system, and the application starts performing the job it was designed for.

DevOps will need to provision the resources required for the application, such as compute, memory, and storage resources. Deployments do not happen in a day, but methodologies such as those mentioned in the following sections aim to keep deployments moving along on a regular schedule of releases. Some deployment methods include the following:

- **Rolling updates** A methodology that can be used to keep an application at a stable release, with another always in the queue to be deployed shortly after that.

- **Blue-green deployment** These deployments always have an active system and one that is used for testing. When testing is complete, the testing system becomes active, and the former production system is available for testing. One system is labeled "blue" and the other "green."

- **Rapid deployment** Virtualization and containerization technologies are used to create new application environments faster than ever before.

- **Failover clusters** Deployment can be performed to more than one server that work together to provide the service. Failover cluster deployments may use some of the same techniques as other deployments, but they are given their own section because the implementation of that deployment methodology may differ for a clustered environment.

Rolling Updates

Traditionally, software development is done in individual release versions. However, implementing CI and CD is quickly becoming the norm as DevOps teams work through queues of requests, bugs, and features.

Legacy release schedules have too much overhead associated with them to meet such expectations without increasing costs exponentially. Instead of having release versions that take a long time to deploy and test, developers work off increasingly smaller code segments so that issues are identified sooner and testing is simpler.

DevOps teams do not write code from different versions. Instead, they work with a single code base, using branching to differentiate project elements and development work products from one another. Updates to the software are rolled out as releases, which usually are very small and happen frequently. A single code base ensures that only one version of the software needs to be supported at a time.

With rolling updates, the program is never really finished. The application is always at a stable release, but DevOps teams have another one in the queue with regular deployment dates.

Blue-Green Deployment

Blue-green deployment is an excellent method for DevOps teams to test changes to systems when releases are made rapidly or as part of a continuous delivery model. However, blue-green deployment is not limited to such either. Blue-green deployment uses two environments, one called blue and the other called green. One of the environments faces the customer, while the other is used for testing.

When QA teams complete testing for a new release, the two environments are swapped. For example, the blue environment is operating for production and the green for test. A new release is deployed to green and tested. When testing is complete, the DevOps team makes green the production environment, and blue becomes the new test environment.

Blue-green deployment is faster than deploying from test to production, since the testing environment becomes the production environment. Swapping rather than redeploying eliminates one step in the deployment process. Additionally, blue-green environments allow for a rapid rollback if necessary.

Blue-green switches are performed to make one environment online and open to customers and the other available to test. Blue-green switches can be implemented on cloud virtualization in a number of ways. Two ways outlined here involve virtual network swapping and resource group swapping.

For example, a CSP may host several virtual machines. These virtual machines are part of either the blue or green network, depending on which virtual network they are assigned to. One set of systems may have its virtual network interface cards (NICs) on the blue virtual switch, while the other set has its virtual NIC configured for the green virtual switch, where blue is production and green is test. CSAs swap the virtual switch to physical switch mapping on the hypervisor when they want to switch from blue to green or vice versa. Depending on the cloud platform, the actual switch may need to be performed by the CSP based on a request from the cloud consumer.

Another option is to use resource group swapping. In Microsoft Azure, resources can be deployed into groups, one for the green environment and one for the blue environment. The cloud servers in the resource group are all given private IP addresses, and an application gateway is configured with the outside IP address. The application gateway is then used to direct traffic to whichever environment is the current production environment. The CSP can redirect the application gateway to the other environment when it's time to swap. For example, in Microsoft Azure, you could create a deployment slot for blue and green deployments. Azure lets you choose which deployment slot to send new code to. You can quickly change which one is the production deployment slot so that you can switch between your blue and green deployments.

Rapid Deployment

Rapid deployment is a way for DevOps teams to provision and release solutions with minimal management effort or service provider interaction. Rapid deployment is enabled by enhanced virtualization and container technologies such as virtual machine clones, parent-child relationships, application containerization, virtual machine templates, self-service portals, and orchestration tools that allow IT organizations to roll out systems faster than ever before.

Failover Clusters

A failover cluster is multiple systems configured to operate together to offer a set of services. If one system in the cluster fails, the others are configured to pick up the failed server's load without a loss of availability to the application.

To deploy a failover cluster, first provision several machines. You will need at least two to form a cluster. Next, provision shared storage to all servers. Shared storage is storage from a storage array over a storage area network (SAN) such as iSCSI, Fibre Channel, or InfiniBand. Configure storage adapters in the machines such as host bus adapters (HBAs), converged network adapters (CNAs), or NICs.

NOTE If using NICs for iSCSI, it is best to use ones with TCP offload to reduce the processing burden on the CPU for storage traffic.

Put the worldwide names (WWNs) for each of the cluster members (or IP addresses of the iSCSI adapters if using iSCSI) into a host group on the storage array and then enable the storage group for concurrent access. Lastly, assign storage resources, referenced by their logical unit number (LUN), to the storage group. The storage should now be visible on each device. However, do not configure the storage yet.

Install the clustering features on each node in the cluster. The installation will set up some basic cluster resources off the bat, such as a quorum, the service that monitors if enough devices are connected to the cluster to offer services. Configure each of the LUNs as a resource in the cluster and give the storage resources a name that makes sense. For example, database components like to have dedicated storage resources for different types of I/O. Typically, databases will have drives for the following types of data: tables, log files, indexes, full-text catalogs, temporary data, and backups. The storage requirements for each of these are different based on the reads and writes expected of the storage resource.

Next, install application services on the nodes and add services to the cluster. Set dependencies on the services so that the cluster will know in what order to start the services. Assign credentials to run the services and test the credentials on each node.

Lastly, start the application and ensure that it runs. Then test failing over elements from one node to another. Ensure that each one can be successfully failed over to each node in the cluster.

Patch Management

Software vendors regularly release patches for their software. Patches are software packages that modify existing software. Patches are created to fix software bugs or discovered vulnerabilities or to add new features.

Patches must be deployed to organizational systems to protect against new vulnerabilities in the software that could be exploited by attackers or to fix bugs in the software that could cause problems for users. The strategy employed to deploy patches is known as patch management.

Some software vendors release patches on a set schedule. This helps companies stay on top of patches because they can check for patches or schedule deployment and associated downtimes regularly. For example, Microsoft releases patches on the second and fourth Tuesdays of every month. Apple, Adobe, Oracle, and many others have similar practices. Still, some vendors release patches on an as-needed basis.

Hotfixes

Hotfixes, or quick fix engineering (QFE) updates, are small patches that address a specific issue. Many vendors use hotfixes to address urgent problems such as a critical vulnerability or a bug that the company cannot wait to address in its regular patching schedule.

Some hotfixes are released to address an issue that only some customers may face. Companies issues hotfix release information (Microsoft documents them in Knowledge Base articles) to describe the issue and the patch that fixes it. Customers can then request the hotfix if they encounter the problem. Other customers need not apply the hotfix. This approach is usually taken when the hotfix has the potential of disrupting other systems, so it is only applied when the need to resolve the issue outweighs the potential drawbacks. Be aware of the drawbacks by reading the Knowledge Base article associated with the hotfix carefully before applying the hotfix.

Rollups

Companies issue patch rollups to address the issue of updating an out-of-date software application that has been around for a while. Rollups combine multiple patches in the same category, such as security, or a specific product component, into a single package that can be deployed more easily. Without rollups, customers would need to deploy a long list of updates in sequence.

Service Packs

Service packs are another type of rollup that combines even more together into a single deployment package. Companies package all patches from the last main software release or patches from the last service pack into a single update package called a service pack. This makes it much easier to bring a system up to date from its initial installation package. Simply install the service packs in order and then apply any remaining patches.

Server Upgrades and Patches

Server upgrades and patches provide enhancements to the software running on servers that can either provide fixes for known errors or add functionality. Patches are developed and released in much the same way as patches for desktop operating systems. However, server upgrades and patches differ typically in their deployment. Desktop patches are often rolled out automatically or delegated to users to deploy. However, servers are more complicated to patch because patches often require a restart, which affects the availability of services that run on the server.

Clustering, discussed later in this chapter, is often used to allow for patching and other maintenance to be performed to servers without downtime to the overall system. Clusters enable the components to be failed over to other nodes in the cluster while one machine is restarted.

Patch Management Tools

Deploying patches can be time-consuming if performed manually. Fortunately, a variety of tools are available to automate the patch management process. These tools identify the installed software version number and then query the vendor's patch list to identify which patches need to be installed and in which order. Some tools are specific to a vendor, some are built in, and some are available from third parties. For example, Microsoft has packaged an update system into Microsoft Windows. The user can set their system to download and install updates automatically on a set schedule or as soon as they are released. Other third-party solutions can query the system to identify all applications and then identify the patches available for those systems. There are also central patch management tools that can deploy and track the patch status of groups of machines. Figure 10-4 shows the Microsoft Windows Update Services console used to centrally manage Windows updates.

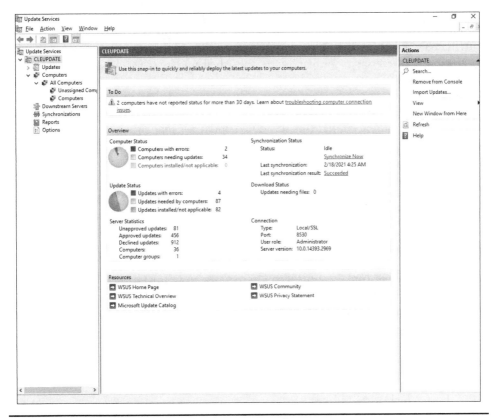

Figure 10-4   Microsoft Windows Update Services console

Patch management systems can be configured to install available updates automatically or to install only approved updates. In approval mode, an administrator reviews updates, potentially applying them to a series of test systems, and if the patches appear stable, the administrator approves the patches for deployment across the enterprise.

If systems are configured to download patches automatically, those patches might trigger a restart of the system. Ensure that patch installation occurs during a period where the workstation or server can be taken offline.

Patch Testing

Application vendors test their patches before releasing them, but they may not test all configurations or compatibility with applications you may have in your environment. For this reason, many companies test patches before deploying them to production systems.

Scheduled Updates

It is prudent to schedule updates to be applied on a regular basis so that systems are kept up-to-date without excessive management effort. Major software companies have made this process simpler and predictable. For example, Microsoft releases patches on the second Tuesday of each month. They may release additional patches on the fourth Tuesday of the month if necessary. Companies can time their update schedules so that they apply updates shortly after their release by the software vendor.

Scheduled updates can be configured to download and then install automatically, or they can be configured just to download and then prompt for installation. The important thing to note when configuring scheduled updates is that automatic installation may result in a restart of the machine so ensure that you have scheduled downtime for the systems you are patching if you are using automatic installation.

Exercise 10-1: Configuring Group Policy for Automatic Updates

In this exercise, we will create and configure the Windows group policy for a domain so that computers automatically download updates.

1. Log in to your domain controller. Go to Start | Administrative Tools and select Group Policy Management.

2. Expand the forest and domain, as shown next. Please note that the domain name has been blurred out. Next, right-click Default Domain Policy and select Edit.

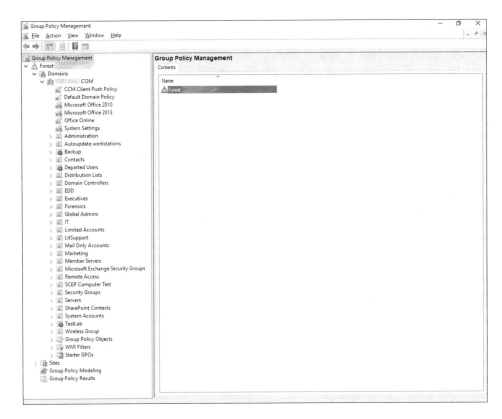

3. A new window will open, allowing you to modify the default domain policy:

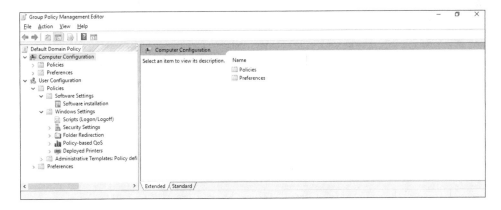

4. Navigate as follows: Computer Configuration | Policies | Administrative Templates Policy Definitions | Windows Components | Windows Update. This will display the Windows update settings, as shown in the following illustration. Please note that some of your settings may be configured differently depending on how your domain is set up.

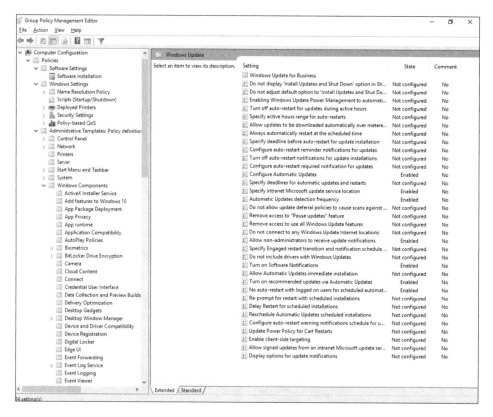

5. Double-click the Configure Automatic Updates setting and select the Enabled option in the upper left. Set the automatic updating setting to 4 – Auto Download And Schedule The Install and then check the Every Week checkbox, as shown on the following page.

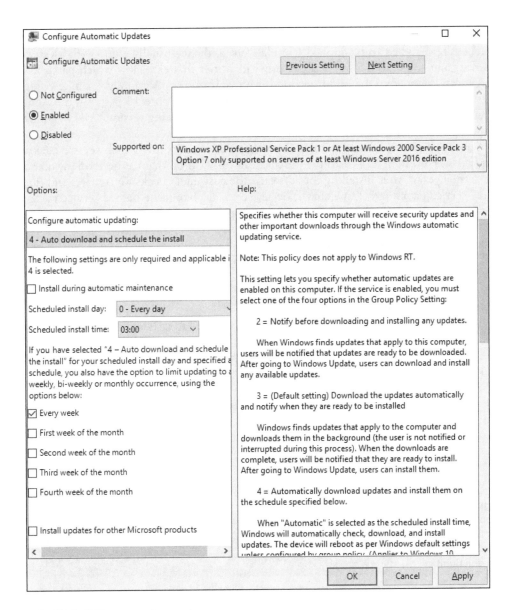

6. Click OK to save the setting.

7. You can now close the Group Policy Management Editor and Group Policy Management applications and log off the domain controller. Please note that the group policy will not immediately be applied to all machines. It can take time for it to propagate to each system. If you need to apply the policy to a machine immediately, run `gpupdate /force` on the local machine or script this command to run on multiple machines. This will make the machine check for and apply a new policy from the domain.

Patching Order of Operations

Patches are designed to be applied cumulatively, and they usually come with a version number and sometimes a build ID or other identifier that can show which patch level you are at. If you go to the About section in your software application, you can see which version you are running to identify if you need patches. Figure 10-5 shows the About screen from LibreOffice 5. As you can see, this system is running version 5.3.4.2, and the build ID is provided for querying for updates.

Service packs are usually numbered so that customers know which service pack to apply first. For example, a customer purchases an application that has been on the market for several years. After installing the software, the customer checks for updates and finds three service packs and 22 patches. The service packs would be named service pack 1, service pack 2, and service pack 3, and the customer would install them in that order.

Newly released patches are designed to be deployed to applications running the latest service pack, so a customer would need to install service packs first and then the most recent patches. In the example, the customer would install service packs 1, 2, and 3 and then install the 22 patches in sequence.

Prioritization of Patch Application

You may have to apply many patches to a system to bring it up to date in some cases. You will need to test these patches before deploying them for any mission-critical systems to avoid unnecessary downtime or application issues. Thus, it is helpful to know in what order the patches should be applied to best protect the systems.

Patches are deployed for one of three reasons. They either fix software bugs or discovered vulnerabilities or add new features. Your first priority should be to apply security patches to address existing known vulnerabilities. After you have installed the security patches, consider some of the patches addressing bugs. You should ask yourself whether system users are experiencing issues related to any of the bugs addressed in these patches.

Figure 10-5
About screen for LibreOffice 5 showing the version number

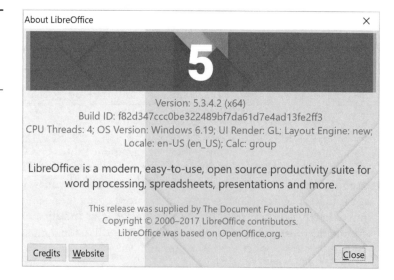

About LibreOffice   ✕

5

Version: 5.3.4.2 (x64)
Build ID: f82d347ccc0be322489bf7da61d7e4ad13fe2ff3
CPU Threads: 4; OS Version: Windows 6.19; UI Render: GL; Layout Engine: new;
Locale: en-US (en_US); Calc: group

LibreOffice is a modern, easy-to-use, open source productivity suite for word processing, spreadsheets, presentations and more.

This release was supplied by The Document Foundation.
Copyright © 2000–2017 LibreOffice contributors.
LibreOffice was based on OpenOffice.org.

Credits   Website   Close

If so, identify the patches related to those issues and add them to your priority list. Once this is complete, apply the rest of the bug fixes and then move on to the feature updates.

Dependency Considerations

Patches have dependencies. Cumulative updates, of course, are dependent upon previous patches. Other patch dependencies include specific software modules or features that may or may not have been installed when the program was deployed to the machine. Attempting to deploy a patch to a system where the dependencies are not present will result in an error. If you receive an error, double-check to ensure that you have the required dependencies. You may find that you do not need to install the patch because you do not have the component addressed in the update.

Operating System Upgrades

Operating system upgrades take an operating system from one major version to another. For example, an upgrade would take Windows 7 and bring it to Windows 10 or macOS 10.15 (Catalina) to macOS 11 (Big Sur).

Carefully consider how the upgrade will affect your applications before pursuing it. You will want to test key applications in the new operating system and test the upgrade procedure before performing it on production systems. Some applications may not be compatible with the new operating system, or they may require an update to make them compatible.

OS vendors sometimes have compatibility-checking applications that can review the applications and configurations of a system to let administrators know which items will need to be removed or updated before an OS upgrade can be performed. Document the changes required to system configurations or applications so that those can be performed on the system once the upgrade has been tested.

Once you have completed the testing, you can begin by updating the applications or modifying configurations on the production system to prepare it for the upgrade. In some cases, applications may need to be uninstalled and then reinstalled after the upgrade is complete. You will then perform the upgrade to bring the OS to the latest version. This should be immediately followed by applying the available patches to the system to protect from known vulnerabilities or bugs. Lastly, install any applications that were uninstalled before the upgrade. You should then go through a final checklist to ensure that applications and key services operate as expected, and then you can make the system available to users.

Rollbacks

You may encounter situations where patches cause some issue with the system, necessitating a rollback. Rollbacks remove a patch to bring the system back to its state before the patch was applied.

Rollbacks are also performed if the patch fails to apply for some reason. Some of the most common reasons why a patch might fail are lost Internet connectivity, lack of hard drive space, or failed dependency checks. If Internet connectivity is lost while the patch is being downloaded and applied, the system will wait for connectivity to be restored, but it may eventually time out, and the system will need to roll back to the previous state to revert any changes made by the patch. Many systems perform the download first and then check the integrity of the download before even starting the installation process to avoid this issue. The second issue you might see is the lack of hard drive space. The patch may fail if there is not enough hard drive space to apply it. Patches require the room for the download and the additional data copied to the system as part of the patch process. Patches may also need some space to decompress container files such as .zip, .msi, or .tar files. It is always good to have at least 20 percent free space for the regular operation of a system so that the system has room to expand files and add new data. Ensure that you have enough hard drive space before applying patches so that you will not need to roll back. The last reason a patch might fail is if it fails a dependency check. The patch might require a previous patch to be applied first, or it might require a system component to be at a specific level to function. Patches typically check for these dependencies as part of the installation process so that they can alert you to the condition before applying the patch, but you may encounter a situation where the patch fails because a dependency is missing, and then it will need to be rolled back.

Patches can also fail for other reasons. You could run into disk errors, or the system could crash while the patch is being applied. For whatever reason, rollbacks serve the purpose of reverting the system so that you can get it back to an operational state following a failed patch deployment.

N-1

You may not always want to run the latest version of a software application or service. Frequently bugs are identified in newly released versions, and those bugs are corrected with patches. To avoid such risks, some companies upgrade systems to the n-1 release. N stands for the current release, so n-1 means the last release before the current one.

Firmware

Firmware is software that is installed on computing hardware, such as a firewall, switch, or camera or hardware components within a machine, such as a network card, RAID controller, or system BIOS. Firmware requires updates just like other software, so it is important to check for new versions of the hardware's firmware. The process of updating the firmware is known as flashing. Figure 10-6 shows the firmware update screen for a QNAP NAS device.

Flashing computer hardware firmware often requires a utility from the hardware vendor. For devices such as firewalls, a web interface allows the firmware to be downloaded and installed. You can download the firmware elsewhere and then use the interface to upload the firmware to the system for installation. Other systems may require you to send the firmware to the device over a protocol such as Trivial File Transfer Protocol (TFTP). Some systems allow for many devices to be updated at the same time. For example, Cisco has software that can be used to deploy firmware updates to many devices simultaneously. You may also want to deploy software that can monitor systems for new firmware updates. Figure 10-7 shows the QFinder application that continually monitors three NAS devices for new firmware updates. The figure shows that the one named WORMHOLE has a new firmware version available.

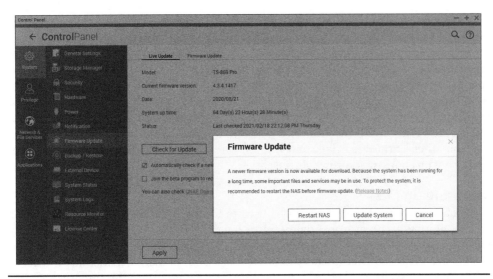

Figure 10-6 QNAP firmware update

Figure 10-7 QFinder app monitoring for new firmware

It is important to only install official firmware obtained from the manufacturer. Some unofficial firmware may advertise advanced features or ways to get around the manufacturer's programming, but these come at a cost. Some users have applied custom firmware to their cable modems in the hopes of obtaining faster Internet speeds but later discovered back doors hidden in this firmware that allowed attackers onto their systems. Unofficial firmware for mobile phones offers to allow users to obtain software from unofficial repositories at no cost. Installing such firmware is known as jailbreaking or rooting the phone. However, these firmware versions are not updated with the same security patches that the official firmware offers, and the software available on their repositories sometimes contains bugs or security vulnerabilities.

Signature Updates

A signature is a data sample that can be used to identify other data as data of the same type. Security software such as antivirus, intrusion prevention, antispam, or Internet filtering software uses signatures to identify the content they wish to block. Antivirus signatures help antivirus software identify malware. Each piece of malware, once identified, has a signature created for it. These signatures must then be applied to the antivirus software to understand what the malware looks like and take appropriate action. Figure 10-8 shows the Trend Micro antivirus client and the state of its signatures. Trend Micro calls its signatures agent patterns.

Similarly, intrusion detection systems (IDSs) use signatures to identify malicious traffic. An IDS would have a signature for TCP session hijacking, UDP port scan, or a Loki attack. Antispam systems use signatures to identify certain types of spam, while Internet filtering software can use signature lists to identify malicious web content and block it from being delivered to users.

Similar to patches and firmware, software must be kept up-to-date with the latest signatures, or it will not be able to identify new malware, attacks, spam, or malicious

Figure 10-8
Trend signature (agent pattern) status

web content. Most security products can be configured to automatically download and apply new signatures. This relieves the burden of maintaining signatures. Put processes and software in place to monitor systems to ensure that they have the latest signatures. It is common for enterprises to have central software that antivirus systems check into and report back on their status, including their signature level, whether they have identified malware, their last scan date, and so forth.

Component Updates

There are some differences in updating different system components such as virtual machines, virtual appliances, hypervisors, networking equipment, storage, and clusters. A well-rounded IT professional needs to understand how to update each of these components.

Cloud services allow for some or many of the components to be managed by the CSP. This can reduce the time organizations spend on routine maintenance. For example, Amazon Web Services Relational Database Service (AWS RDS) hosts a database for use with applications or websites. The cloud consumer does not need to maintain the underlying server, operating system, database software, and networking. Instead, they can focus their efforts on the database housed within AWS RDS.

In another example, hosted options running software such as cPanel allow cloud consumers to deploy databases to a MySQL instance and then access them from cloud servers or websites. Some basic maintenance tasks, such as resetting the database administrator password or changing backup schedules and restores, can be performed by the cloud consumer, but the remaining maintenance is performed by the CSP.

Virtual Machines

Virtual machines can be updated independently using the same tools as a physical machine, but you also have some additional options. Some hypervisors can deploy updates to virtual machines. For example, vSphere Update Manager can deploy updates to virtual machines that reside on hypervisors managed by vSphere.

Here is the high-level procedure for automating the update process for the virtual machines:

1. Configure repositories for where Update Manager can find updates. Repositories are indexed sources for updates.

2. Create a baseline consisting of patches, service packs, upgrades, and hotfixes.

3. Schedule synchronization with repositories so that Update Manager is aware of new patches, hotfixes, upgrades, and service packs.

4. Assign virtual machines to a baseline.

5. Scan virtual machines against the baseline to determine which patches need to be applied.

6. Stage the patches by having Update Manager download the updates to vSphere for deployment.

7. Deploy patches to the virtual machines.

Virtual Appliances

Appliances are fully built and functional virtual machines that are purchased or downloaded from a vendor to perform a specific task. Before the age of virtualization, appliances would be rebranded servers or small rack-mounted equipment that would be purchased from a vendor to perform a task. Some vendors still offer physical equipment, but this is largely a thing of the past.

The advantage of using an appliance versus installing and configuring the software on a server is that the appliance is set up and mostly configured by the vendor. The company is provided with a ready-to-deploy virtual machine, which saves the organization valuable deployment time.

Some virtual appliances are available for free from open-source groups. Vendors may offer stripped-down appliances at no cost, or they may provide a fully functional unit to educational or nonprofit groups. If you purchase a virtual appliance or get it for free, you can download it from the vendor site as a virtual hard drive. Simply copy the virtual hard drive to your hypervisor, assign it resources, and start it up.

Virtual appliances will walk you through a configuration wizard to get the product up and running. When it comes time to update the virtual appliance, the vendor will package underlying updates together with its own software updates so that you can receive all updates in one vendor package. You can configure the appliance to download updates from the vendor and deploy them on a scheduled basis. Updates from the vendor have already been tested on the virtual machine, so there is a high likelihood that they will be deployed without issue.

Public CSPs, and in some cases private clouds, often have a marketplace where virtual machine templates and appliances can be selected to deploy new virtual machines in the cloud rapidly. These systems have already been confirmed to be compatible with the underlying cloud infrastructure, and they can be offered cost-effectively because of the CSP's economies of scale. Research options for your CSP, because some offer many different solutions while others, usually small providers, may only offer one or two solutions. The options available to you may not be the ones ideal for your workload.

Firewall, IDS, and intrusion prevention system (IPS) virtual appliances are covered in the "Network Security" section of Chapter 12.

Hypervisors

Patching hypervisors will likely result in downtime to the virtual machines that reside on them unless the hypervisor is part of a cluster. You update a hypervisor in much the same way as you would a normal computer, but any updates that require a restart or updates to hypervisor services will make the virtual machines go into a saved state or shut down.

Networking Components

Devices such as firewalls, routers, switches, and Internet of Things (IoT) equipment have updates called firmware that can be downloaded from the manufacturer. Firmware updates are usually installed manually, but some vendors, such as Cisco, release tools that can update a multitude of systems simultaneously or in sequence. Check with the vendor of your equipment to find out which deployment options you have. It also helps to subscribe to the vendor's mailing list for firmware updates so that you can be notified as soon as they are released.

Applications

It can be difficult to keep track of all the application updates to keep your application protected. Many applications will include an agent that keeps track of your software version and then notifies you when a new software version is available. Some agents will download the new software and then prompt for installation. Unfortunately, for the average computer running many applications, this can result in applications requesting to update all the time.

The solution is to turn off the agents and use a single third-party tool to manage the updates. Third-party solutions can scan the entire server or workstation to identify the software on it. The third-party vendor keeps track of the latest versions of all software and pushes the updates down to the computer through its tool.

Storage Components

Storage systems are one of the more complex items to update. An update to a storage system, also called storage array firmware or microcode, could affect other items in the data path, such as SAN switches or HBAs. Before applying a storage system update, ensure that devices on the data path (everything from the SAN to the initiator) support the upgrade. Devices on the data path often include the switch and HBA versions but could consist of other devices as well.

If all firmware versions for the devices in the data path meet the acceptable level for the storage upgrade, go ahead and install it. However, if a device is not supported at its current firmware level, you will need to upgrade it to a supported level first. Ensure that when you upgrade it, the updated version is supported on the current SAN version.

Clusters

Updates for cluster nodes can be done typically with no downtime to the end user. This is great for the end user, but the upgrade process is a bit more complicated for IT administrators. You will need to fail over services to free up a node so that it is not actively hosting any of the cluster resources and then update that node. You can then fail back services to that node and fail over the services on another node. Complete this process on all nodes until each node is running the same software versions.

Maintenance Automation

It can be quite a job to maintain many systems, and organizational IT departments are supporting more devices per person than ever before. They accomplish this through automation. Automation uses scripting, scheduled tasks, and automation tools to do the routine tasks so that IT staff can spend more time solving the real problems and proactively looking for ways to make things better and even more efficient.

PowerShell commands are provided in many examples because these commands can be used with the AWS CLI or the Microsoft Azure Cloud Shell. Scripts can be combined into tasks using AWS Systems Manager or Microsoft Azure runbooks.

This section discusses different activities that can be automated to save time and standardize. They include the following:

- Patch management
- Shutdown and restart
- Entering maintenance mode
- Enabling or disabling monitoring checks

Patch Deployment

Patch deployments can be scripted or controlled using patch management tools to streamline or automate the process of patch deployment. For example, with the following PowerShell command, an administrator can deploy all patches to a machine and reboot, if necessary. This command could be part of a script that iterates through a list of machines to then deploy patches on them with a few modifications. Also, please note that the PSWindowsUpdate module must be installed to make this update command available.

```
Get-WindowsUpdate -Install -AcceptAll -AutoReboot
```

Restarting

Systems run better when they are restarted regularly. However, regular restarts are not an option for all environments, but for those that can, a scheduled restart can help keep systems fresh and functional. Scheduled restarts are useful in other scenarios, such as performing maintenance on a host or some other system that requires many machines to be restarted.

Here is a PowerShell command that restarts four computers named computer1, computer2, computer3, and computer4. You can schedule this script to run as a scheduled task from a management machine with rights on each of the other servers.

```
Restart-Computer -ComputerName "Computer1", "Computer2", "Computer3", "Computer4"
```

Shutting Down

Scheduled shutdown events are applicable in maintenance or triage scenarios, such as when you are turning off all nonessential systems to save on resources.

Here is a PowerShell command that shuts down four computers named computer1, computer2, computer3, and computer4. You can schedule this script to run as a scheduled task from a management machine with rights on each of the other servers.

```
Stop-Computer -ComputerName "Computer1", "Computer2", "Computer3", "Computer4"
```

Entering Maintenance Mode

Whenever you do work on a host, it is important to put that host in maintenance mode. In fact, many maintenance tasks cannot be performed unless the host is first in maintenance mode. Some maintenance activities include restarting the host, applying firmware updates, or applying patches to the host.

Maintenance mode will migrate all the virtual machines to another host in a cluster and prepare the host for maintenance. Exiting maintenance mode will allow for virtual machines to be rebalanced across hosts in the cluster.

Many maintenance tasks can be scripted, and the transition to maintenance mode can also be placed in the maintenance script to automate the entire process. The following command can be scripted to enter into maintenance mode. Here we will assume our username is ESXAdmin and our password is 77}N50&a9fr-Q=i.

```
esxcli –username ESXAdmin --password 77}N50&a9fr-Q=i system maintenanceMode
set --enable true
```

You can then script the transition out of maintenance mode in the script when the maintenance is complete. The following command can be placed at the end of the script to exit maintenance mode (assuming the same username and password):

```
esxcli –username ESXAdmin --password 77}N50&a9fr-Q=i system maintenanceMode
set --enable false
```

Enabling or Disabling Monitoring Alerts

It can be very annoying to receive hundreds or thousands of e-mail notifications because someone forgot to disable monitoring alerts when doing server maintenance. Everyone who has gone through this knows what this means, because it simply destroys a mailbox. The good news is that if you forget, your coworkers are likely to remind you and not let you forget again.

Disabling alerts greatly depends on which tool is being used to send out the alerts, but there is usually a master pause function that can be enabled for the downtime. If you have regularly occurring downtimes such as patch downtimes, you can likely script this action.

Monitoring Techniques

Effective monitoring techniques provide an efficient means of monitoring all aspects of cloud infrastructure without placing a significant performance burden on the systems and network. Monitoring techniques track the performance of enterprise systems and provide detailed information on the current usage of the cloud environment that can be consolidated and displayed on dashboards or reports.

Cloud computing provides an efficient way of load balancing, task scheduling, and allocating compute resources. Monitoring compute resources is an important part of maintaining a cloud environment and ensuring that systems have adequate resources to perform their tasks. Some key benefits of resource monitoring include providing input for chargebacks and showbacks, more intelligent resource provisioning and proactive resource expansion or contraction, more effective capacity planning, and improved technology agility in response to an ever-changing environment.

One of the goals of monitoring the environment is to ensure the overall health of key systems and applications. System health information can be published to a corporate intranet site, allowing the entire organization or select decision-makers access to the health data. For example, an administrator might publish a dashboard on the company intranet site that shows the current SLAs of the organization and whether or not the IT department has met those SLAs.

Another place to use monitoring is in a chargeback situation. An IT department can monitor the environment and get a report on who consumed which compute resources and for how long, allowing the organization to charge departments for their use of compute resources.

The first part of understanding resource monitoring is understanding the protocols and methods used for resource monitoring, as discussed next. Then, this section discusses configuring baselines and thresholds and forecasting resource capacity. Finally, automation can be used to send alerts for specific events and thresholds, so this section concludes with a discussion on how that can be accomplished.

Collector Protocols and Methods

When defining a monitoring solution, it is crucial to understand the different collector protocols available for monitoring and the alerting options to problems that might arise in the cloud environment. Monitoring is enabled through a series of protocols and alerting methods that, in conjunction, can provide a robust system of threshold monitoring and alerting.

The following protocols and methods are presented in this section:

- Simple Network Management Protocol (SNMP)
- Windows Management Instrumentation (WMI) and WBEM
- Out-of-band management and Intelligent Platform Management Interface (IPMI)
- Syslog

SNMP

One of the common protocols used to manage and monitor an environment is SNMP. SNMP is commonly supported on devices such as routers, switches, printers, and servers and is used to monitor these devices for issues or conditions that might arise on the devices that would require administrative attention.

A monitoring solution that uses SNMP has an administrative computer, commonly referred to as a manager, that monitors or manages a group of network devices. Each managed device runs an agent, which reports information, using SNMP, back to the manager. For example, an SNMP agent on a router can provide information about the router's network configuration and operations (such as network interface configurations and routing tables) and transmit that information back to the manager.

A variety of vendors use SNMP to monitor devices on the network; they use the information from SNMP to give an administrator a means of monitoring and managing network performance or reporting on and troubleshooting network issues. This knowledge enables administrators to better understand and prepare for network growth.

In addition to monitoring and managing an environment, SNMP allows for alerts to be generated. An administrator can use SNMP to modify and apply new configurations to network devices and be alerted when certain conditions are present on monitored network devices. SNMP uses notifications, known as SNMP traps, to alert on important information. SNMP traps are network packets that contain data relating to a particular component of the network device running the SNMP agent; they can notify the management stations by way of an unsolicited SNMP message that a particular event has occurred. SNMP traps are triggered when particular preprogrammed conditions are present on the monitored device.

WMI

Another option for monitoring an environment is WMI, Microsoft's version of WBEM. WBEM is an industry initiative to develop a standardized way of accessing management information in an enterprise environment.

WMI allows you to write scripts to automate certain administrative tasks and run those scripts against remote computers. WMI can query and set information on a workstation, server, application, or supported network device.

WMI provides a way to gather hardware information from multiple physical servers or virtual servers. WMI information can be placed into a centralized database, allowing for the collection and reporting on a variety of information, including CPU, memory, operating system, and hard drive space.

WMI information can assist in determining if a system is close to maximizing compute resources, which may necessitate an upgrade to meet demands. For example, Microsoft System Center Configuration Manager (SCCM) uses WMI to gather hardware information from its clients and allows an administrator to manage and report on those systems based on the information gathered from the WMI queries.

 EXAM TIP WMI can gather information about the installed software and the operating system version on a computer, along with hardware information.

Out-of-Band Management and IPMI

Out-of-band management allows an administrator to remotely manage and monitor a device using a separate network segment from normal production traffic. Out-of-band monitoring can be implemented with the IPMI protocol, which can monitor a device that is not powered on. IPMI operates independently of the operating system, which allows BIOS settings to be remotely monitored or configured.

 EXAM TIP Out-of-band management allows for remotely monitoring BIOS settings.

Syslog

One of the most common ways to gather event messages is with the use of Syslog. Syslog is a logging standard that provides a mechanism for a network device to send event messages to a logging server or Syslog server over UDP port 514 or TCP port 514.

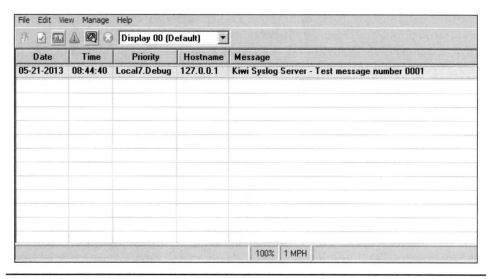

Figure 10-9   A sample Syslog entry

One of the benefits of a Syslog server is that the Syslog protocol is supported by a wide range of devices and can log different types of events. Syslog cannot poll devices to gather information as SNMP does; it merely gathers messages sent by various devices to a central Syslog server when a specific event has triggered. Each device is configured with the location of the Syslog collector and sends its logs to that server for collection. Syslog can be used to consolidate logs from multiple devices into a single location for review, analysis, or archival purposes. Figure 10-9 shows an example of a standard Syslog server entry.

Tagging

Tagging is a method of adding metadata or classification to log entries. Tags can be used to enable faster searching of data or more enhanced log processing. Tagging can be performed automatically as part of a processing task.

Let us consider several examples. An application may add tags to the log to give context to the events. A spam filter, for example, might tag specific messages as junk, spam, or bulk. Tags can also be applied manually by the engineers, who review the logs to more easily work with the data. For example, an engineer may identify a potential indicator of compromise (IOC) and could tag the event for further follow-up and research.

Log Analysis

Servers, network devices, and cloud services all produce logs. These logs show activity to varying degrees of specificity, depending on the logging settings, and they can be analyzed to re-create a situation or identify a threat.

Log Types

Log types and formats vary based on the device type and the services running on it, but there are some logs that are common to most machines. Windows systems have the following log files on them at a minimum:

- **Application log**   The application log contains information related to drivers and software installed on the machine.

- **Security log**   The security log contains successful and failed authentication to the system. It also records when an account escalates its privileges and audited events.

- **Setup log**   The setup log contains information on patches that have been applied.

- **System log**   The system log records information on operating system messages and the launching or termination of services.

The Windows logs can be viewed through the Event Viewer program. You can access this by going to Start | Run and then typing **eventvwr.msc**. The Event Viewer is shown in Figure 10-10.

Linux systems keep a wide variety of logs. Some of the most crucial logs to monitor include the boot log, which records information on boot-up processes and issues; the security log, which logs failed and successful authentication; and the Yum log, which records installations that use the yum command.

Servers running Active Directory store a record of all domain authentication requests in their security log. This is an important log to review to determine when a user logged on and to what resource.

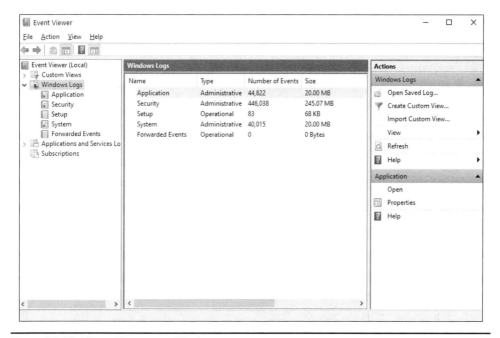

Figure 10-10   Event Viewer on a Windows computer

Table 10-2	**Linux Log File**	**Location**
Linux Log File Locations	Boot log	/var/log/boot.log
	Security log	/var/log/auth.log or /var/log/secure
	Yum log	/var/log/yum.log
	HTTP log	/var/log/httpd/

Web server logs are important for identifying connections to the server. This can be used to investigate attacks or troubleshoot transactions. Apache web servers store their data in the HTTP log, and Windows IIS servers store their logs in the webserver log. Table 10-2 shows some of the Linux log files and their locations on the system.

Event Correlation

Logs can be reviewed for each device individually, but this is hardly efficient. Furthermore, each log represents a microcosm of the whole. A firewall log will give you part of the picture, but when combined with the authentication records from a domain controller or the file access logs of a file server, they reveal the whole picture. Logs are immensely more valuable when correlated with logs from other systems and network devices. Cloud machines do not operate in a vacuum, so log review should also take into consideration other devices when investigating issues or detecting threats. This is where event correlation steps in.

Event correlation can combine authentication requests from domain controllers, incoming packets from perimeter devices, and data requests from application servers to gain a more complete picture of what is going on. Software exists to automate much of the process.

SIEM

A security information and event management (SIEM) system archives logs and reviews logs in real time against correlation rules to identify possible threats or problems. Additionally, a SIEM system monitors baselines and heuristics to identify issues that crop up before they balloon into more significant issues. The information is presented so that log analysts can easily filter, sort, and report on the data or investigate threats. A dashboard with metrics from the SIEM LogRhythm is shown in Figure 10-11.

For example, when analyzed together, several informational events may present a more severe issue that can be resolved before it creates problems for end users. Without such a system, administrators would likely not notice the events until errors or warnings appeared in the log, which would probably be the same time users of the system also experienced issues. Figure 10-12 shows how log entries are displayed in a SIEM.

It is much easier to fix issues before end users discover them and begin complaining. IT administrators tend to think more clearly and logically when not under pressure. SIEM can change how IT administrators investigate issues, eventually causing them to focus more on proactive indicators of a problem rather than fighting fires.

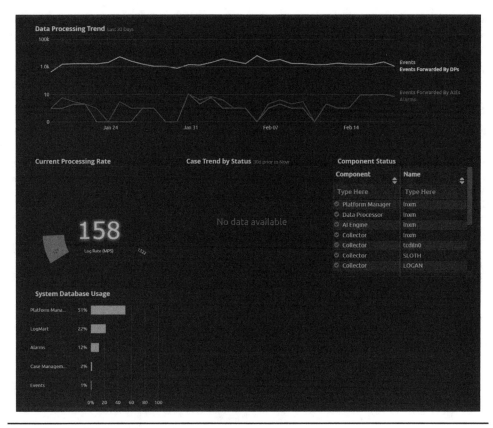

Figure 10-11 SIEM metrics

Event Collection and Event Collection Policies

A server can consume a lot of space with event logs. All too often, companies configure small log sizes with rollover so that recent events automatically replace old ones. However, these same companies often find out too late that the events they need to see have already been overwritten.

Establish policies to ensure that events are retained for a sufficiently long period of time. Your data retention policy is an excellent place to start. A good retention rate for

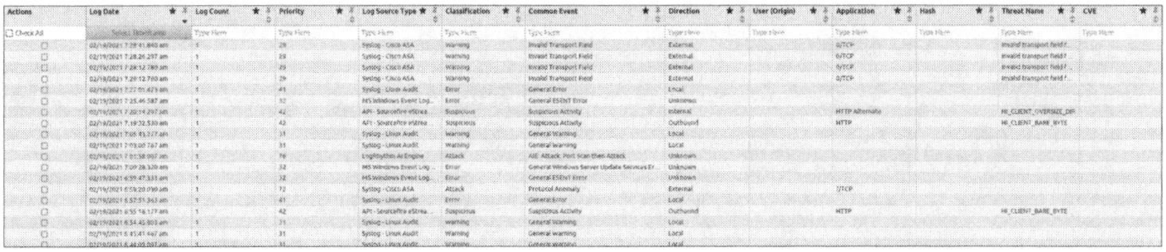

Figure 10-12 SIEM log entries

logs is 18 months. This can consume a lot of space on the local machine, so it is a best practice to archive logs off to lower-cost secondary storage or to a log review platform. A log review platform can also centralize log review, log analysis, and alerting functions, simplifying the entire event management process. After an organization chooses and configures its event collection policy, its next step is to develop a baseline.

Severity Categorization

Each item in a log is referred to as an event. These events can be categorized based on their severity level. The Windows event severity levels include critical, warning, error, and information. You can filter the event log based on items of a specific severity level, and log collection systems will use this value when evaluating events. The filter settings for the Windows event log are shown in Figure 10-13.

CAUTION   Just because an event is labeled as information does not mean that it is not essential in an investigation. SIEM systems may identify a threat from information events on multiple machines.

Figure 10-13
Filter logs by severity level

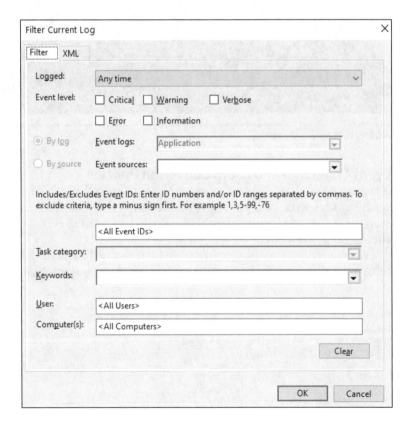

Baselines

The purpose of establishing a baseline is to create a sample of resources consumed by the cloud services, servers, or virtual machines over a set period and provide the organization with a point-in-time performance chart of its environment. Establish a baseline by selecting a sampling interval and the objects to monitor and then collecting performance data during that interval.

A good baseline must include an accurate sampling of everyday activities. If the activity is roughly the same from week to week, then one week's baseline might be sufficient. However, if activity fluctuates from week to week, the baseline needs to be longer. If a baseline were created for only a week and activity differed the next week, those differences would appear as outliers and be flagged as potential problems when they are actually just regular activity that was not captured in the baseline. However, do not go overboard on baseline collection, because a lengthy sampling interval can consume a significant amount of disk space and bandwidth.

Performance metrics collected when users report sluggish performance or slow response times can be easily compared to the baseline to see if performance is within normal tolerance. Continue to collect metrics at regular intervals to get a chart of how systems are consuming resources.

For example, suppose a user says that a database server is responding exceptionally slowly. In that case, the IT department can use a baseline to compare the performance of the server when it was performing well to when the user reported the slow performance.

Some software products such as VMware vCenter Operations Manager (VCOP) and Microsoft System Center Virtual Machine Manager (SCVMM) build an internal baseline over time. The baseline can be used to reveal patterns and outliers. For example, a cloud administrator may notice over 12 months that the average memory usage has increased 10 percent, which helps plan for additional resources for the server in the near future.

Target Object Baselines

Baselines should be collected not only for entire systems but also for objects within the system, such as CPU utilization, memory pages per second, CPU queue depth, memory utilization, data reads per second, data writes per second, and so forth. These values can be instrumental in determining how to improve performance over time, optimize resources for utilization, and upgrade components so that they provide maximum value to the organization.

Target Anomalies

Baselines can be used to detect anomalies. Anomalies are events that are outside the norm. The baseline shows the norm, and the anomaly can indicate a short-term increase in utilization or a problem in the works. A pattern can be inferred from baseline data, and this pattern can be used to identify anomalous data collected thereafter.

Thresholds

In addition to establishing a baseline, an organization needs to configure thresholds. When it comes to monitoring a cloud environment, thresholds are a key piece of the process. Thresholds can be set so that if a virtualization host consumes more than 95 percent of its CPU for more than 10 minutes, it sends an alert via either SMTP or SMS to the appropriate party (as described later in the chapter).

Setting a threshold allows for a more robust alerting system. Thresholds can also be used to automatically and dynamically create and orchestrate resources in the cloud computing environment. ("Orchestration" refers to automated tasks that could be scripted to happen based on particular conditions and triggers.)

Cloud computing allows a cloud consumer to define a threshold policy to check and manage resources when workload demands require. This allows the cloud provider to create instances of resources depending on how much the workload exceeds the threshold level. For example, a defined threshold could state that if CPU utilization for a particular virtual machine reaches 95 percent for 5 minutes, utilizing orchestration APIs, an additional processor should be added dynamically. The next step after determining thresholds is to perform trending.

Trending

Baselining and thresholds are useful in comparing current data to historical data and identifying some alert conditions. The same information can also be used for trending. Trending looks at baseline values over time to predict likely future utilization.

Trending can be used to forecast resource capacity to ensure that you have the resources you need and the associated budget for them when those resources are required. It can also easily show how resource consumption will increase or decrease.

Forecasting Resource Capacity

Trending can be used to identify future resource needs. It is often helpful to compare year-to-date numbers and compare corresponding months across years. Start tracking this data now, and you will see how useful it will be later. Some trends are based on the annual cycle, so it is sensible to look at trends over a 12-month period.

 CAUTION Far too many companies wait to start collecting resource metrics until they urgently need answers. If you are not collecting data now, you will not have it available for analysis later when you need it, so put such systems in place right away.

Upsize/Increase

Trends may show an increase or upsize over time. For example, suppose storage consumption was 100GB in January, 105GB in February, 109GB in March, 117GB in April, and 121GB in June. In that case, we can conclude that storage will need to increase a minimum of 5GB per month and that some months will increase more than that.

Downsize/Decrease

Conversely, trends may show a decrease over time. This could be due to efficiencies in the system or decreasing use of the application or system. For example, if memory consumption was 28GB in January, 24GB in February, 26GB in March, 22GB in April, and 23GB in June, we can conclude that storage will decrease about 2GB per month with a standard deviation of 4GB per month.

Automated Event Responses

While monitoring and alerting are great ways to minimize problems in the cloud environment, some issues arise with using these features. When an organization is monitoring and alerting on all its devices, the number of alerts that might arise could be staggering. If an administrator gets too many alerts, he or she may not have enough time to respond to those alerts. This may result in some issues going unnoticed or not given the attention they deserve.

This is where automated event responses can help. For example, let's say an administrator gets an alert that a hard drive is at 99 percent capacity. Instead of manually logging into the server and deleting files or running a disk cleanup program, the entire process can be scripted and executed by a trigger on the threshold. Once the threshold is hit, that triggers the script to run that performs the task. Automating minor tasks can save administrators considerable time and allow them to focus on more pressing issues. It also ensures that the tasks are carried out correctly and promptly.

As an example, one time, I was asked to help an organization manage its monitoring environment. I recommended the organization buy monitoring software that allows for automated responses. I configured thresholds and alerts based on the organization's needs. I then configured the most common alerts with an automated response that would run a script to fix the issue and resolve the alert in the monitoring software.

Common Alert Methods/Messaging

An organization needs a way to be alerted when certain events occur. For example, if the organization is monitoring a server and that server loses network connectivity, IT administrators need to be notified of that occurrence so they can fix the issue that is causing the problem.

Many vendors offer network monitoring and alerting solutions both for on-premises and cloud-based deployments. Most vendors provide a website or some form of web service to monitor an organization's cloud environment centrally, whether the cloud is private or public. The web service provides a dashboard that gives the administrator a quick and easy view of the entire cloud environment.

SMTP   One of the most common alerting methods used is the Simple Mail Transfer Protocol (SMTP), discussed in Chapter 4. When configured on a device, SMTP sends an e-mail when a monitored event occurs. The alert can be configured to send an e-mail to a single user or to a group of users so that more than one person receives the alert. SMTP is a quick and easy way of sending alerts from the monitoring software when certain events occur on the network.

SMS Another option for receiving alerts is the Short Message Service (SMS), a text messaging service that allows an alert to be sent to a mobile device. SMS is a great way to notify an on-call technician when an alert has been generated after hours. Monitoring an environment is normally a 24-hour job because the network needs to be available 24 hours a day.

Enabling and Disabling Alerts

There is a balancing act when enabling and disabling alerts. It might seem like a good idea to enable everything so that you are aware of what is going on, but no one has time to review every alert, and IT administrators quickly become numb to the alerts and no longer review them if you configure alerting in this way. It is important, therefore, to select only the alerts that matter to your organization.

Cloud portals usually have a section for alerts where you can configure how alerts will be processed. Some may be e-mailed to a recipient or group, while others will be retained in the dashboard for review when someone logs on or when investigating an issue. Figure 10-14 shows the Office 365 Security & Compliance alerting section.

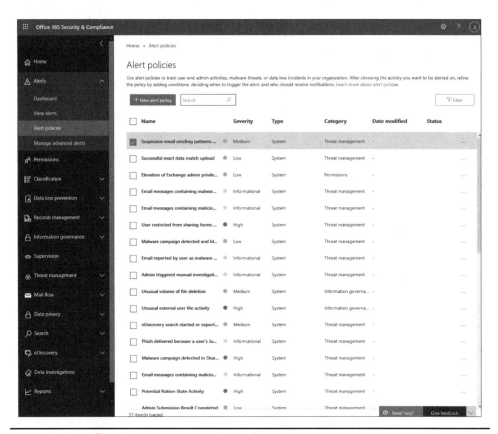

Figure 10-14 Office 365 Security & Compliance alerting section

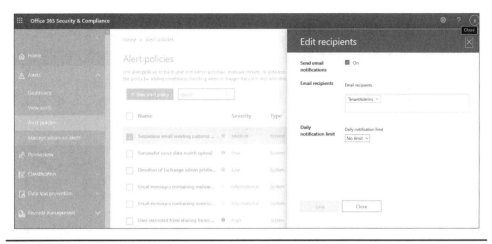

Figure 10-15   Configuring e-mail alerts for Office 365 alert policies

For example, the suspicious e-mail sending patterns alert could be configured to e-mail a group by selecting the alert policy and then clicking Edit Policy. The Edit Policy screen allows for e-mail recipients to be set, as shown in Figure 10-15.

Maintenance Mode   Servicing a virtualization host can cause problems for the machines running on the host if it is not done properly. Setting a host to maintenance mode will migrate the VMs that are currently running on that machine to other hosts so that you can perform work on it. The host will not allow VMs to be deployed or migrated to it while it is in maintenance mode.

You can put a VMWare host into maintenance mode with the following procedure:

1. Log into your virtualization environment. This step will depend on where it is hosted.

2. Browse to the host you want to service and right-click it.

3. Select Maintenance Mode | Enter Maintenance Mode

4. Wait while the machines are migrated off it. The host will show a status of "Under Maintenance" when the process has been completed.

5. Perform your maintenance.

6. Return the host to service by selecting Maintenance Mode | Exit Maintenance Mode.

Alerting Based on Deviation from Baseline

Make sure to save your baseline data. You can use simple spreadsheets, but a database is the best way to protect such data because it allows you to write queries to analyze the data in different ways. As you gather the data, configure alerts to let administrators know of significant deviations from the baseline. Resources may need to be adjusted to handle short-term spikes in demand, or this could indicate the start of a new trend. Either way, it is valuable to be aware of these changes as soon as possible.

Alerts can be configured such that when metrics are a certain percentage above the baseline, an alert is sent to a specific individual or a distribution group. For example, you may want to send out an alert if CPU utilization is 40 percent more than average for a sustained duration of at least ten minutes. You can also configure alerts to go out when certain static thresholds are met. For example, you may plan to expand a LUN when it reaches 100GB, so you set an alert that notifies you when the LUN reaches that point.

Policies to Communicate Events Properly

Metrics are not the only thing that should prompt alerting. Some events require immediate attention. These events cannot wait until an administrator reviews the logs. For such cases, policies should be created defining which events need notification and how administrators should respond to such alerts. For example, the policy may state that a critical event requires immediate notification to the on-call administrators and that administrators must respond to the event within five minutes and resolve the event within one hour.

Once the policy is defined, technical controls can be implemented to carry out the policy. Triggers can be created to alert on such events to a person or group right away, and systems can be put in place to track resolution time and who is on call.

Appropriate Responses

The appropriate responses to events should be thought out ahead of time. For example, if you are e-mailing an alert to an IT team, what do you expect them to do with that alert? The appropriate response should include investigating the alert and possibly taking some action on it. If it was important enough to e-mail out, it should be important enough to act on.

The specific actions will depend on the type of alert. For example, a message about a detected virus may prompt a full scan of the machine, while an event for multiple failed login attempts might prompt reaching out to the user to see if they are having trouble logging in. Define these expectations so that your teams will effectively respond.

Log Scrubbing

You may share log information with others as part of your normal course of business. Some log entries may contain sensitive information that you do not want to be divulged to other parties. For example, you may share logs with consumers so that they can investigate issues with their own service, but you will want to exclude entries from other clients. You could share logs with others in your supply chain to help remediate issues that affect multiple entities, but you might hide the internal IP addresses or names of specific machines.

The process of removing sensitive information from logs is called log scrubbing, and it is typically implemented by applying scrubbing policies to the process of exporting or exposing the logs to another application. If you are making your logs available via an API call, this would be performed as part of the API response process.

Verification of Continuous Monitoring Activities

Systems can be configured to continuously monitor applications or cloud services, but how do you know if those services are continuing to function properly? Regular checks of routine activities such as continuous monitoring are essential to ensure that such services continue to perform their function. The last thing you want is to find out that a key service was not functioning when its need is mission-critical. In the case of monitoring, you want to know it is running so that a security threat does not fly under your radar.

Establish processes to routinely check such services, or have checks built into other services to cross-check each other and notify you if a service becomes unavailable or if monitoring functions change.

Management Tools

There are a wide range of tools to manage cloud systems. They can be divided into three different types: CLI, Web GUI, and Cloud Portal. Each offers its own features and advantages depending on your purpose. Management tools can have different interfaces, and there are pros and cons to the interface depending on how the application is going to be used.

CLI

The command-line interface (CLI) is an interface that is text-based. The user must type instructions to the program using predefined syntax in order to interact with the program. For example, Microsoft Azure and Amazon Web Services each have their own CLI. Figure 10-16 shows the Azure Cloud Shell CLI.

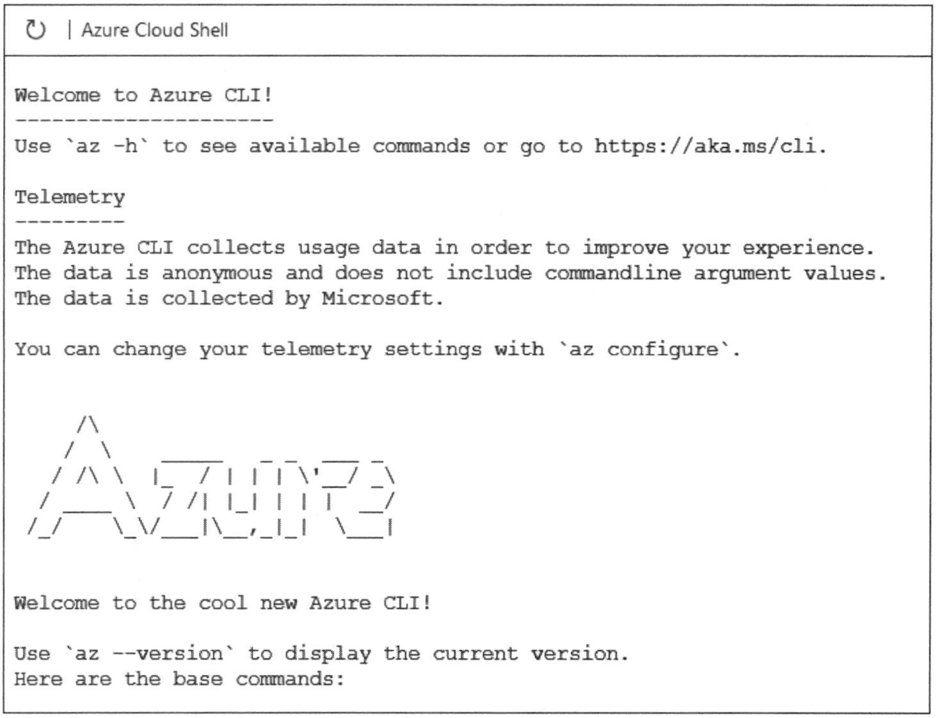

```
 ↻  | Azure Cloud Shell

Welcome to Azure CLI!
---------------------
Use `az -h` to see available commands or go to https://aka.ms/cli.

Telemetry
---------
The Azure CLI collects usage data in order to improve your experience.
The data is anonymous and does not include commandline argument values.
The data is collected by Microsoft.

You can change your telemetry settings with `az configure`.


      /\
     /  \    _____   __ _____  ___
    / /\ \  |___  / | | | '__/ _ \
   /  ___ \  / /| |_| | | |  __/
  /_/    \_\/___|\__,_|_|  \___|


Welcome to the cool new Azure CLI!

Use `az --version` to display the current version.
Here are the base commands:
```

Figure 10-16 Azure Cloud Shell CLI

CLI tools can seem cumbersome to those most familiar with graphical user interfaces (GUIs), but their power comes with the ability to script them. A task that could take 30 minutes of clicking in a GUI to accomplish could be achieved in a few minutes with a script because all the functions are preprogrammed with a series of commands. CLI tools are usually more lightweight, so they are easier to deploy and have less of a burden on systems.

Web GUI

Graphical user interfaces are easy to work with. Simply point and click on something to take an action. Users can get to work on an application very quickly if it has a GUI. Web GUIs offer that functionality from a web browser. The advantage of a web GUI is that tools can be administered from any machine that can connect to the web server and has the authorization to administer the tool.

Cloud Portal

A cloud portal is an interface that is accessed over the Internet to manage cloud tools or integrate with other tools. The portal displays useful dashboards and information for decision-making and ease of administration.

Cloud portals are like web GUIs, but they can be accessed from almost anywhere. Cloud portals are great for administering cloud tools and for integrating with a variety of legacy tools that would have required logging into many different web GUIs, launching traditional applications, or sending SSH commands to a CLI.

Chapter Review

Successful delivery of a cloud solution is driven not just by the technical components that make up that solution but by clear policies and standard operating procedures. The successful design, documentation, and methodical implementation and support of those technical resources result in an effective solution that is profitable for the IT provider and valuable to its customers.

Processes and procedures allow for control of the environment through life cycle metrics, dashboards and reporting, standardization, and planning. These control mechanisms make certain that the environments are designed to meet business requirements and are deployed and supported according to that design.

IT systems require regular maintenance to keep them free from vulnerabilities and bugs and to keep up with the latest technologies and processes. Maintenance and development updates can consume a great deal of IT personnel time. Maintenance and development are core to the business. This includes making code updates, documenting those updates in code repositories, ensuring that patches are applied to systems in a timely manner, and automating common maintenance tasks to do more with limited IT resources.

Monitoring the network is a key component of DevOps and cloud computing. Monitoring allows an organization to plan for future resource utilization and respond to issues that arise in the cloud environment. Combining monitoring and alerting gives an administrator a way to be proactive instead of reactive when it comes to the cloud environment.

Questions

The following questions will help you gauge your understanding of the material in this chapter. Read all the answers carefully because there might be more than one correct answer. Choose the best response(s) for each question.

1. Which of the following defines the rule sets by which users and administrators must abide?

   A. Procedures

   B. Change management

   C. Policies

   D. Trending

2. Capacity management has responsibility for ensuring that the capacity of the IT service is optimally matched to what?

   A. Demand

   B. Future trends

   C. Procedures

   D. Availability

3. Carlos works in the IT department at Sample Bank. He uses a cloud-based e-mail system and has been asked by his manager to establish metrics on mailbox usage per department so that department budgets can be billed for the expense of hosting department e-mail. What is this practice known as?

   A. Chargeback

   B. Billback

   C. Pass-through charge

   D. Showback

4. When should maintenance windows be scheduled?

   A. In the morning

   B. In the evening

   C. On weekends

   D. When they will least affect customers

5. Which of the following is not a benefit of standardization?

   A. Consistent management

   B. Better control of system access

   C. Uniform logging across systems

   D. Flexible deployment scenarios

6. Donna has been developing software for her company. She makes a copy of the directory where her code is stored each time she makes a significant change. However, the project she started years ago is now much larger, and two other developers also work on the program with her. She would like a way to better manage the code so that she can revert to previous states if necessary and track changes made by each person. Which technology would you suggest?

A. Continuous integration application

B. Code repository

C. Workflow automation

D. Chargebacks for each developer

7. Which of the following is not a method for deploying application updates?

A. Manual version updating

B. End-user updating

C. Using DevOps ticketing

D. Using a package manager

8. Which landscape is used for testing small changes made to code immediately after development?

A. Development

B. Quality assurance

C. Testing

D. Production

9. Which of the following can be used to identify which operating system version is installed on a virtual machine?

A. WMI

B. SMTP

C. SMS

D. IMAP

10. Which of these can be used by both a cloud consumer and a cloud provider to give a visual picture of performance metrics?

A. API

B. SNMP

C. Dashboard

D. SMTP

11. Which of the following utilizes UDP port 514 when collecting events?

    A. SNMP

    B. Syslog

    C. WMI

    D. Web services

12. Which of the following can be used to create scripts that can be run against target computers to perform simple administrative tasks?

    A. WMI

    B. SMTP

    C. SMS

    D. IMAP

13. Which of the following constantly executes a software component called an agent, which reports information using the protocol back to a manager?

    A. WMI

    B. SMTP

    C. SMS

    D. SNMP

14. Which of the following alerting methods allows a technician to receive an alert on a mobile device such as a cell phone?

    A. SMTP

    B. SMS

    C. SNMP

    D. Syslog

15. Which of the following alerting methods can be configured to send an e-mail when a certain alert is triggered?

    A. SMTP

    B. SMS

    C. SNMP

    D. Syslog

16. Which of the following allows for out-of-band management of a computer?

    A. WMI

    B. SMS

    C. SNMP

    D. IPMI

17. You have been tasked with gathering a list of software installed on all the computers in your environment. You want to gather this information remotely. Which of the following would you use to gather this information?

   A. WMI

   B. SNMP

   C. HTTP

   D. Syslog

Answers

1. **C.** Policies are defined as rule sets by which users and administrators must abide.

2. **A.** Capacity management's primary objective is to ensure that the capacity of an IT service is optimally matched with its demand. Capacity should be planned to meet agreed-upon levels, no higher and no lower. Because controlling costs is a component of capacity management, designs that incorporate too much capacity are just as bad as designs that incorporate too little capacity.

3. **A.** Chargebacks can be used to establish metrics on mailbox usage per department so that department budgets can be billed for the expense of hosting department e-mail.

4. **D.** A maintenance window is an agreed-upon, predefined time period during which service interruptions are least impactful to the customer. This could fall at any time and depends on the patterns of business activity for that particular customer.

5. **D.** Flexible deployment scenarios is not a benefit of standardization because standardization establishes consistent deployment scenarios and does not allow for each one to be deployed however the user or administrator wishes.

6. **B.** A code repository organizes code branches to keep code consistent even when multiple teams are working on the same areas in parallel. Developers can publish code changes to the repository, can synchronize their local copy of the code with the repository, or can revert to previously published versions.

7. **C.** DevOps ticketing is not a method for deploying application updates. The methods are manual version updating, end-user updating, and using a package manager.

8. **A.** Small changes made to code are tested immediately in the development landscape before being passed to other landscapes.

9. **A.** Windows Management Instrumentation (WMI) provides an administrator a way to gather hardware information from multiple physical servers or virtual servers and put that information into a centralized database.

10. **C.** A dashboard is a great way for both the cloud consumer and cloud provider to access key metrics when it comes to monitoring cloud resources. A dashboard can give a summary of the current usage of the cloud resources in an easy-to-view format of charts and graphs.

11. B. Syslog provides a mechanism for a network device to send event messages to a logging server or Syslog server using UDP port 514 or TCP port 514.

12. A. Windows Management Instrumentation (WMI) allows you to write scripts to automate certain administrative tasks and run those scripts against remote computers.

13. D. A monitoring solution that uses SNMP has an administrative computer, commonly referred to as a manager, that monitors or manages a group of network devices. Each managed device constantly executes a software component, called an agent, that reports back to the manager.

14. B. Short Message Service (SMS) is a text messaging service that allows an alert to be sent to a mobile device.

15. A. Simple Mail Transfer Protocol (SMTP) can be configured to send an e-mail alert when a certain monitored event occurs.

16. D. The Intelligent Platform Management Interface (IPMI) operates independently of the operating system. It provides out-of-band management and monitoring of a system before the operating system is loaded, which allows BIOS settings to be remotely monitored or configured.

17. A. With Windows Management Instrumentation (WMI), it is possible to query workstations remotely and gather a list of all the software installed on those workstations.

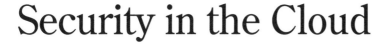

CHAPTER 11

Security in the Cloud

In this chapter, you will learn about
- Data security
- Network security
- Endpoint protection
- Access control

This chapter covers the concepts of security in the cloud as they apply to data both in motion across networks and at rest in storage, as well as the controlled access to information in both states. Our security coverage begins with some high-level best practices and then delves into the details of the mechanisms and technologies required to deliver against those practices. Some of these technologies include encryption (data confidentiality) and digital signatures (data integrity) and their supporting systems.

Access control is the process of determining who should be able to view, modify, or delete information. Controlling access to network resources such as files, folders, databases, and web applications requires effective access control techniques.

Data Security

Data security encompasses data as it traverses a network, as well as stored data or data at rest. Data security is concerned with data confidentiality (encryption), ensuring that only authorized parties can access data, and data integrity (digital signatures), ensuring that data is tamper-free and comes from a trusted party. These can be implemented alongside a public key infrastructure (PKI). Encryption is also used to create secure connections between locations in a technique called tunneling. These control mechanisms can be used separately or together for the utmost security, and this section will explore them in detail in the following sections:

- Encryption
- Public key infrastructure
- Encryption protocols
- Tunneling protocols

- Ciphers
- Storage security
- Protected backups

Encryption

Encryption is the process of making data unreadable to anyone except those who have the correct decryption key. Encryption is performed by changing the bits that make up the data by running them through an encryption algorithm. The algorithm uses a mathematical formula and a unique key or a key pair to take readable data and turn it into encrypted data that is unreadable. To help you better understand encryption, this section will first explain a few encryption terms. These include obfuscation, plaintext, and ciphertext. We will then talk through how encryption is employed for data in two different states: data at rest and data in transit.

Obfuscation

Obfuscation is the practice of using some defined pattern to mask sensitive data. This pattern can be a substitution pattern, a shuffling of characters, or a patterned removal of selected characters. Obfuscation is more secure than plaintext but can be reverse-engineered if a malicious entity were willing to spend the time to decode it.

Plaintext

Before data is encrypted, it is called plaintext. When an unencrypted e-mail message (i.e., an e-mail in plaintext form) is transmitted across a network, a third party can intercept and read that message in its entirety.

Ciphertext

Ciphers are mathematical algorithms used to encrypt data. Applying an encryption algorithm (cipher) and a value to make the encryption unique (key) against plaintext results in ciphertext; it is the encrypted version of the originating plaintext.

Encryption at Rest

Encrypting data when stored on a media such as a hard drive, USB drive, or DVD is known as encryption at rest. Don't forget that whenever data is stored in the cloud, it is stored on some media in the CSP's data center, so this is considered data at rest. Some of the options for encrypting data at rest include encrypting the storage, file system, operating system, database, or files and folders.

- **Storage**   Storage encryption is implemented at the hardware level through self-encrypting drives.
- **File system**   File system encryption is performed by software and managed by the storage controller.

- **Operating system**   Operating system encryption is similar to file system encryption in that it is performed by software, but it is managed with built-in tools in the operating system. Some examples include BitLocker from Microsoft or FileVault from Apple.

- **Database**   Database encryption encrypts data within rows or columns within a database. For example, you could encrypt the Social Security number field, or you could have certain records encrypted instead, such as encrypting only records marked top secret.

- **Files and folders**   File and folder encryption is implemented by software. It can be selectively performed on a single file, a group of files, or one or more folders. Some file and folder encryption methods are built into operating systems, but the majority of options are available as software that is installed on the machine. If you move encrypted files or folders to another machine, you will need to install the software first and then provide the decryption key before the data can be accessed.

Encryption in Transit

Data does not always remain on storage. It must also be protected when it travels from one machine to another. Data that is being transferred is referred to as data in transit. Several methods are used to encrypt data in transit, including LAN encryption, browser encryption, and API endpoint encryption.

- **LAN encryption**   Data can be encrypted over the local network via protocols such as IPSec. This helps protect data traversing the network from being observed by others on the network.

- **Browser encryption**   Browser encryption encrypts a browser session between the client and server using protocols such as SSL or TLS. Encrypted browser connections use a certificate, and their URLs are prefaced with https://.

- **API endpoint encryption**   API endpoint encryption protects data traveling between clients and the API endpoint. The encryption is performed using SSL or TLS.

Public Key Infrastructure

A PKI is a hierarchy of trusted security certificates. These security certificates (also called X.509 certificates or PKI certificates) are issued to users, applications, or computing devices. PKI certificates are primarily used in two ways. The first is to encrypt and decrypt data. The second is as a digital identity, to sign and verify an entity's integrity such as a computer, user, website, application, or code.

Each certificate contains a unique, mathematically related public and private key pair. When the certificate is issued, it has an expiration date; certificates must be renewed before the expiration date. Otherwise, they are not usable.

To help you better understand encryption and PKI, this section is divided into the following topics:

- Certificate management
- Cryptographic key
- Key management
- Symmetric encryption
- Asymmetric encryption
- Digital signatures
- Secret management

Certificate Management

Certificate management is the set of processes to issue, renew, store, authenticate, and revoke digital certificates. It is an integral part of a PKI. It consists of several elements, including a root certificate authority (CA), subordinate CAs, and the systems that receive certificates.

The root CA exists at the top of the PKI hierarchy. The root CA can issue, revoke, and renew all security certificates. Under it reside either user, application, and device certificates or subordinate certificate authorities. Computers are configured by default to trust several root certificate authorities. These authorities can issue certificates to other certificate servers, known as subordinate CAs. You can also set up an internal CA hierarchy for issuing internal certificates.

When a CA grants a certificate to a subordinate CA, it gives them the right to issue certificates for a specific domain. Subordinate CAs can issue, revoke, and renew certificates for the scope of operations provided in their mandate from the CA above them in the hierarchy.

A large enterprise, for example, Acme, might have a CA named Acme-CA. For each of its three U.S. regions, Acme might create subordinate CAs called West, East, and Central. These regions could be further divided into sections by creating subordinate CAs from each of those, one for production and one for development. Such a subordinate CA configuration would allow the cloud operations and development personnel in each of the three regions to control their own user and device PKI certificates without controlling resources from other areas or departments. This hierarchy is shown in Figure 11-1.

Certificates have a defined expiration date, but some need to be deactivated before their expiration. In such cases, administrators can revoke the certificate. Revoking a certificate places the certificate on the certificate revocation list (CRL). Computers check the CRL to verify that a certificate is not on the list when they validate a certificate.

Companies can issue their own certificates without being part of the trusted certificate chain leading back to a trusted certificate authority. This is often performed for authentication or encryption on a domain. Computers in the domain can be configured to trust the domain certificate authority. The certificate authority then issues certificates to the machines on the domain to authenticate each other. However, suppose a company tries to use certificates generated on its own domain for use over the Internet. In that case,

Figure 11-1
Illustration of
a public key
infrastructure
hierarchy

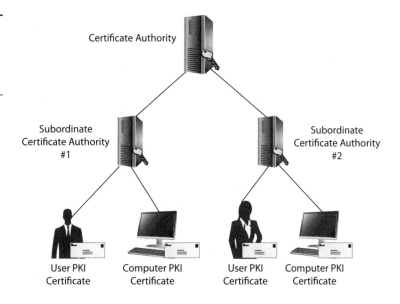

those outside the organization will not trust the certificates assigned to the sites. They will receive warnings or errors in displaying the page.

Cryptographic Key

Many people can own the same lock model, while each has its own unique key that opens that specific lock. The same is valid for cryptography. Multiple people can each use the same cryptographic algorithm, but they will each use a unique cryptographic key, or key for short, so that one person cannot decrypt the data of another.

Let's continue with the lock example. Some locks have more tumblers than others, and this makes them harder to pick. Similarly, some keys are longer than others. Longer keys result in more unique ciphertext, and this makes the resulting ciphertext harder to break. Keys are used for data at rest (stored data) and data in motion (transmission data).

Key Exchange Keys are generated and distributed as part of the encryption process, or they are configured before encryption begins. Keys that are generated as part of the encryption process are said to be created in-band. The key generation and exchange process occurs during the negotiation phase of communication. Similarly, systems that encrypt stored data will need to generate a key when encrypting the data if one has not been provided before encryption.

The other approach is to provide keys before engaging in encrypted communication or encryption. For transmission partners, keys are generated out-of-band, meaning that they are created separately and distributed to transmission partners before communication starts. Such a key is known as a pre-shared key (PSK).

Software or tools that encrypt stored data may be provided with a key upon installation or configuration, and then this key will be used in the encryption process. Some systems use a PSK to encrypt unique keys generated for each file, backup job, or volume.

This allows a different key to be used for discrete portions of data, but these keys do not all have to be provided beforehand. Without such a process, new jobs or drives would require more administrative involvement before being encrypted.

Distributed Key Generation   Multiple devices can work together to create a key in a process known as distributed key generation. Distributed key generation makes it harder for the system to be corrupted because there is no single device responsible for the key. An attacker would need to compromise several systems. This is the method blockchain uses to create keys for Bitcoin and the many other services that depend on the blockchain.

Elliptic Curve Cryptography   Elliptic curve cryptography (ECC) is a cryptographic function that allows for smaller keys to be used through the use of a finite-field algebraic structure of elliptic curves. The math behind it is a bit complex, but the simple description is that ECC uses a curve rather than large prime number factors to provide the same security as those with larger keys. Also, a key using ECC of the same length as one using prime number factors would be considered a stronger key.

Key Management

However they are provided, each key must be documented and protected so that data can be decrypted when needed. This is performed through a key management system (KMS).

Key Management System   Organizations can deploy a KMS to manage the process of issuing, validating, distributing, and revoking cryptographic keys so that keys are stored and managed in a single place. Cloud KMSs include such systems as AWS KMS, Microsoft Azure Key Vault, Google Cloud KMS, and Oracle Key Manager.

Symmetric Encryption

Encrypting data requires a passphrase or key. Symmetric encryption, also called private key encryption, uses a single key that encrypts and decrypts data. Think of it as locking and unlocking a door using the same key. The key must be kept safe, since anybody with it in their possession can unlock the door. Symmetric encryption is used to encrypt files, secure some VPN solutions, and encrypt Wi-Fi networks, just to name a few examples.

To see symmetric encryption in action, let's consider a situation where a user, Stacey, encrypts a file on a hard disk:

1. Stacey flags the file to be encrypted.
2. The file encryption software uses a configured symmetric key (or passphrase) to encrypt the file contents. The key might be stored in a file or on a smartcard, or the user might be prompted for the passphrase at the time.
3. This same symmetric key (or passphrase) is used when the file is decrypted.

Encrypting files on a single computer is easy with symmetric encryption, but when other parties that need the symmetric key are involved (e.g., when connecting to a VPN using symmetric encryption), it becomes problematic: How do we securely get the symmetric key to all parties? We could transmit the key to the other parties via e-mail or text message, but we would already need to have a way to encrypt this transmission in the first place. For this reason, symmetric encryption does not scale well.

Asymmetric Encryption

Asymmetric encryption uses two different keys to secure data: a public key and a private key. This key pair is stored with a PKI certificate (which itself can be stored as a file), in a user account database, or on a smartcard. Using two mathematically related keys is what PKI is all about: a hierarchy of trusted certificates, each with its own unique public and private key pairs.

The public key can be freely shared, but the private key must be accessible only by the certificate owner. Both the public and private keys can be exported to a certificate file or just the public key by itself. Keys are exported to exchange with others for secure communications or to use as a backup. If the private key is stored in a file, the file should be password protected.

The recipient's public key is required to encrypt transmissions to them. Bear in mind that the recipient could be a user, an application, or a computer. The recipient then uses their mathematically related private key to decrypt the message.

Consider an example, shown in Figure 11-2, where user Roman sends user Trinity an encrypted e-mail message using a PKI, or asymmetric encryption:

1. Roman flags an e-mail message for encryption. His e-mail software needs Trinity's public key. PKI encryption uses the recipient's public key to encrypt. If Roman cannot get Trinity's public key, he cannot encrypt a message to her.

2. Roman's e-mail software encrypts and sends the message. Anybody intercepting the e-mail message will be unable to decipher the message content.

3. Trinity opens the e-mail message using her e-mail program. Because the message is encrypted with her public key, only her mathematically related private key can decrypt the message.

Unlike symmetric encryption, PKI scales well. There is no need to find a safe way to distribute secret keys because only the public keys need to be accessible by others, and public keys do not have to be kept secret.

Figure 11-2
Sending an
encrypted
e-mail message

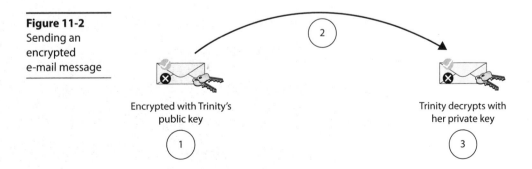

Encrypted with Trinity's
public key

Trinity decrypts with
her private key

Cloud providers use asymmetric encryption for communication between VMs. For example, AWS generates key pairs for authentication to Windows cloud-based VMs. AWS stores the public key, and you must download and safeguard the private key.

Digital Signatures

A PKI allows us to trust the integrity of data by way of digital signatures. When data is digitally signed, a mathematical hashing function is applied to the message's data, which results in what is called a message digest or hash. The PKI private key of the signer is then used to encrypt the hash: this is the digital signature.

Notice that the message content has not been secured; for that, encryption is required. Other parties needing to trust the digitally signed data use the mathematically related public key of the signer to validate the hash. Remember that public keys can be freely distributed to anyone without compromising security.

As an example of the digital signature at work, consider user Ana, who is sending user Zoey a high-priority e-mail message that Zoey must trust really did come from Ana:

1. Ana creates the e-mail message and flags it to be digitally signed.

2. Ana's e-mail program uses her PKI private key to encrypt the generated message hash.

3. The e-mail message is sent to Zoey, but it is not encrypted in this example, only signed.

4. Zoey's e-mail program verifies Ana's digital signature using Ana's mathematically related public key; if Zoey does not have Ana's public key, she cannot verify Ana's digital signature.

Using a public key to verify a digital signature is valid because only the related private key could have created that unique signature. Hence, the message had to have come from that party. This is referred to as nonrepudiation. If the message is tampered with along the way, the signature is invalidated. Again, unlike symmetric encryption, there is no need to safely transmit secret keys; public keys are designed to be publicly available.

For the utmost security, data can be encrypted and digitally signed, whether it is transmitted data or data at rest (stored).

 EXAM TIP Data confidentiality is achieved with encryption. Data authentication and integrity are achieved with digital signatures.

Secret Management

Secrets in the cloud must also be managed. Secrets include things like API keys, passwords, and other sensitive data that your applications need to securely access. Secret management includes provisioning secrets, providing access to authorized entities, rotating secrets, and auditing. The major cloud vendors each have their tools for secret management. For example, you can manage secrets in Google's cloud using Google's Secret Manager.

Encryption Protocols

Many methods can be used to secure and verify the authenticity of data. These methods are called encryption protocols, and each is designed for specific purposes, such as encryption for confidentiality and digital signatures for data authenticity and verification (also known as nonrepudiation).

IPSec

Internet Protocol Security (IPSec) secures IP traffic using encryption and digital signatures. PKI certificates, symmetric keys, and other methods can be used to implement this type of security. IPSec is flexible because it is not application-specific. If IPSec secures the communication between hosts, it can encrypt and sign network traffic regardless of the application generating the traffic. IPSec can be used as both an encryption protocol and a tunneling protocol, discussed in the next section.

SSL/TLS

Unlike IPSec, Secure Sockets Layer (SSL) or Transport Layer Security (TLS) is used to secure the communication of specially configured applications. Like IPSec, encryption and authentication (signatures) are used to accomplish this level of security. TLS is SSL's successor.

Most computer people associate SSL/TLS with secure web servers. However, SSL/TLS can be applied to any network software that supports it, such as Simple Mail Transfer Protocol (SMTP) e-mail servers and Lightweight Directory Access Protocol (LDAP) directory servers. SSL and TLS rely on PKI certificates to obtain the keys required for encryption, decryption, and authentication. Take note that some secured communication, such as connecting to a secured website using Hypertext Transfer Protocol Secure (HTTPS), uses public and private key pairs (asymmetric) to encrypt a session-specific key (symmetric). Most public cloud services are accessed over HTTPS.

Tunneling Protocols

Tunneling is the use of encapsulation and encryption to create a secure connection between devices so that intermediary devices cannot read the traffic and so that devices communicating over the tunnel are connected as if on a local network. Tunneling creates a secure way for devices to protect the confidentiality of communications over less secure networks such as the Internet. This is a great way to extend an on-premises network into the public cloud.

Encapsulation is the packaging of data within another piece of data. Encapsulation is a normal function of network devices as data moves through the TCP/IP layers. For example, layer 3 IP packets are encapsulated inside layer 2 Ethernet frames. Tunneling encapsulates one IP packet destined for the recipient into another IP packet, treating the encapsulated packet simply as data to be transmitted. The reverse encapsulation process is de-encapsulation, where the original IP packet is reassembled from the data received by a tunnel endpoint.

The nodes that form encapsulation, de-encapsulation, encryption, and decryption of data in the tunnel are called tunnel endpoints. Tunnel endpoints transmit the first packets of encapsulated data that will traverse the intermediary network.

Not all tunneling protocols encrypt the data that is transmitted through them, but all do encapsulate. Suppose connectivity that seems local is all you are looking for. In that case, a protocol that does not encrypt could work because it will operate faster without having to perform encryption on the data. However, for most tunneling uses, encryption is a necessity because traffic is routed over an unsecured network. Without encryption, any node along the route could reassemble the data contained in the packets.

Tunneling consumes more network bandwidth and can result in lower speeds for connections over the tunnel because rather than transmitting the packets themselves, network devices must take the entire packet, including header information, and package that into multiple packets that traverse from node to node until they reach their destination and are reassembled into the original packets that were sent.

Tunneling protocols are network protocols that enable tunneling between devices or sites. They consist of GRE, IPSec, PPTP, and L2TP. Table 11-1 compares each of these tunneling protocols.

GRE

Generic Routing Encapsulation (GRE) is a lightweight, flexible tunneling protocol. GRE works with multiple protocols over IP versions 4 and 6. It is not considered a secure tunneling protocol because it does not use encryption. GRE has an optional key field that can be used for authentication using checksum authentication or keyword authentication.

IPSec

IPSec is a tunneling and encryption protocol. Its encryption features were mentioned previously in this chapter. IPSec tunneling secures IP traffic using Encapsulating Security Protocol (ESP) to encrypt the data tunneled over it using PKI certificates or asymmetric

Protocol Name	Considered Secure as of 2021	Authentication	Encryption
Generic Routing Encapsulation (GRE)	No	Yes, checksum or keyword	No
Internet Protocol Security (IPSec)	Yes	Yes, AH	Yes, ESP
Point-to-Point Tunneling Protocol (PPTP)	No	Yes, PAP, CHAP, MS-CHAP version 1 or version 2, EAP-TLS, PEAP	Yes, MPPE
Layer 2 Tunneling Protocol (L2TP)	Yes (only in L2TP/IPSec mode)	Yes, AH (only in L2TP/IPSec mode)	Yes, ESP (only in L2TP/IPSec mode)

Table 11-1 Tunneling Protocols Compared

keys. Keys are exchanged using the Internet Security Agreement Key Management Protocol (ISAKMP) and Oakley protocol and a security association (SA) so that endpoints can negotiate security settings and exchange encryption keys.

IPSec also offers authentication through the Authentication Header (AH) protocol. The main disadvantage of IPSec is that it encrypts the data of the original IP packet but replicates the original packet's IP header information, so intermediary devices know the final destination within the tunnel instead of just knowing the tunnel endpoint. IPSec functions in this way because it offers end-to-end encryption, meaning that the data is encrypted not from the endpoint to endpoint, but from the original source to the final destination.

PPTP

Point-to-Point Tunneling Protocol (PPTP) is a tunneling protocol that uses GRE and Point-to-Point Protocol (PPP) to transport data. PPTP has a very flexible configuration for authentication and encryption, so various implementations can utilize a variety of authentication and encryption protocols. PPP or GRE frames can be encrypted, compressed, or both. The primary benefit of PPTP is its speed and its native support in Microsoft Windows.

The most widely used variation of PPTP is used in Microsoft VPN connections. These connections use PAP, CHAP, MS-CHAP version 1, or MS-CHAP version 2 for authentication. At the time of this publication, weaknesses have been found in most of these protocols. The only secure implementation currently available for PPTP is Extensible Authentication Protocol Transport Layer Security (EAP-TLS) or Protected Extensible Authentication Protocol (PEAP).

PPTP data is encrypted using the Microsoft Point-to-Point Encryption (MPPE) protocol. MPPE uses RC4 key lengths of 128 bits, 56 bits, and 40 bits. Negotiation of keys is performed using the Compression Control Protocol (CCP). At the time of this publication, weaknesses in the RC4 protocol make PPTP implementations insecure because data can be decrypted using current toolsets.

L2TP

Layer 2 Tunneling Protocol (L2TP) offers improvements over PPTP. L2TP does not offer built-in encryption but can be combined with IPSec to provide encryption and authentication using ESP and AH. However, L2TP is CPU intensive when encryption is used because data must be encapsulated twice, once with L2TP and another time with IPSec.

L2TP is a flexible tunneling protocol, allowing a variety of protocols to be encrypted through it. L2TP has been used to encrypt and tunnel IP, Asynchronous Transfer Mode (ATM), and Frame Relay data.

Ciphers

Recall that plaintext fed to an encryption algorithm results in ciphertext. "Cipher" is synonymous with "encryption algorithm," whether the algorithm is symmetric (same key) or asymmetric (different paired keys). There are two categories of ciphers: block ciphers and stream ciphers. Table 11-2 lists some of the more common ciphers.

Cipher Name	Creation Date	Encryption Type	Cipher Type	Cipher Strength	Usage
Advanced Encryption Standard (AES)	1998	Symmetric	Block	256 bits	Replaced DES in 2001 as the U.S. federal standard
Digital Encryption Standard (DES)	1975	Symmetric	Block	56 bits	U.S. federal standard until 2001
3DES or "triple-DES"	1998	Symmetric	Block	168 bits	An improvement on DES that performed DES operations three times
Digital Signature Algorithm (DSA)	1991	Asymmetric	Block	2048 bits	U.S. federal standard for digital signatures
Rivest Cipher (RC4)	1987	Symmetric	Stream	128 bits	Byte-oriented stream operation
Rivest Cipher (RC5)	1994	Symmetric	Block	2048 bits	A simple and fast algorithm
Rivest, Shamir, Adleman (RSA)	1977	Asymmetric	Stream	4096 bits	Some hardware and software may not support up to 4096 bits

Table 11-2   Common Block and Stream Ciphers

Block Ciphers

Designed to encrypt chunks or blocks of data, block ciphers convert plaintext to ciphertext in bulk as opposed to one data bit at a time, either using a fixed secret key or by generating keys from each encrypted block. A 128-bit block cipher produces a 128-bit block of ciphertext. This type of cipher is best applied to fixed-length segments of data, such as fixed-length network packets or files stored on a disk.

Some block ciphers include DES, AES, RC5, DSA, and 3DES. Each of these ciphers is shown in Table 11-2.

DES   Data Encryption Standard (DES) is a symmetric block cipher that uses block sizes of 64 bits and 16 rounds of encryption. 3DES, or "triple-DES," encrypts data with DES three times using three keys. It is marginally better than DES and managed to extend the life of DES for a short time. DES and 3DES are now outdated protocols. They were succeeded by AES in 2001 as the new standard for government encryption.

AES   Advanced Encryption Standard (AES) is a symmetric block cipher that uses a 128-bit block and variable key sizes of 128, 192, and 256 bits. It performs 10 to 14 rounds of encryption depending on the key size used. AES replaces DES as the new standard for government encryption.

RC5   Rivest Cipher 5 (RC5) is a symmetric block cipher used to encrypt and decrypt data. It is named for its creator, Ron Rivest. RC5 is a block cipher that uses symmetric keys for encryption. RC5 replaces RC4 and supports a cipher strength of up to 2048 bits. RC5 uses 1 to 255 rounds of encryption.

DSA   The digital signature algorithm (DSA) is an asymmetric block cipher used for message or data signing and verification. DSA creates keys of variable lengths and can create per-user keys. DSA is accepted as a federal information processing standard in FIPS 186. DSA has a maximum cipher strength of 2048 bits and was created in 1991.

Stream Ciphers

Unlike block ciphers that work on a chunk of data at a time, stream ciphers convert plaintext into ciphertext one binary bit at a time. Stream ciphers are considerably faster than block ciphers. Stream ciphers are best suited when an unknown or variable amount of data needs to be encrypted, such as variable-length network transmissions. Some stream ciphers include RC4 and RSA, shown in Table 11-2.

RC4   Rivest Cipher 4 (RC4) is a symmetric stream cipher used to encrypt and decrypt data. RC4 uses symmetric keys up to 128 bits in length for encryption. It is named for its creator, Ron Rivest.

TKIP   Temporal Key Integrity Protocol (TKIP) is a protocol specified in IEEE 802.11i that enhances the WEP/RC4 encryption in wireless networks. It was created in 2002. TKIP takes a PSK called the secret root key and combines it with a unique random or pseudorandom value called an initialization vector. TKIP also tracks the order of pieces of encrypted data using a sequence counter. This helps protect against an attack where the previous ciphertext is provided to a system to perform a transaction twice in what is known as a replay attack. Lastly, TKIP uses an integrity checking function called the message integrity code (MIC) to verify ciphertext in the communication stream.

RSA   Rivest, Shamir, Adleman (RSA) is an asymmetric stream cipher used to encrypt and decrypt data. It is named after its three creators, Ron Rivest, Adi Shamir, and Leonard Adleman, and was created in 1977. RSA uses asymmetric key pairs up to 4096 bits in length for encryption.

 EXAM TIP   Stream ciphers are faster than block ciphers.

Storage Security

Storage security is concerned with the security of data at rest or when it is stored on a cloud system. There are a large number of cloud services specifically dedicated to the storage of data, such as Dropbox, Google Drive, Amazon Drive, Microsoft OneDrive, and SpiderOak. For these services, storage is the business. For other cloud services, storage is one of the core building blocks on which the cloud service is architected, and it is important to implement effective security at this level.

From the cloud consumer perspective, storage security is built into the product offering, so cloud consumers do not need to implement these controls. It is, however, still important to understand cloud security controls to ensure that the cloud service meets organizational security and technology stipulations, contractual agreements, and regulatory requirements. Storage security is vital when setting up a private cloud or when providing cloud services to others, since storage is the underlying component behind cloud systems.

Granular Storage Resource Controls

Based on the storage technology utilized in the cloud system, security mechanisms can be put in place to limit access to resources over the network. This is important when setting up a private cloud or working for a cloud provider, since storage is the underlying component behind cloud systems. When using a storage area network (SAN), two techniques for limiting resource access are LUN masking and zoning. See Chapter 3 if you need a review on SANs and LUNs.

- **LUN masking** LUN masking allows access to resources, namely storage logical unit numbers (LUNs), to be limited by the utilization of a LUN mask either at the host bus adapter or the switch level.
- **Zoning** SANs can also utilize zoning, which is a practice of limiting access to LUNs that are attached to the storage controller.

LUN masking and zoning can be used in combination. Storage security is best implemented in layers, with data having to pass multiple checks before arriving at its intended target. All the possible security mechanisms, from software to operating system to storage system, should be implemented and configured to architect the most secure storage solution possible.

Securing Storage Resources

Data is the most valuable component of any cloud system. It is the reason that companies invest in these large, expensive infrastructures or services: to make certain that their users have access to the data they need to drive their business.

Storage is such a critical resource to the users of cloud models that special care must be taken with its security to make sure resources are available and accurate and accessible for users who have been authorized for access.

Digital and Information Rights Management

Digital rights management (DRM) is a set of technologies that enforces specific usage limitations on data, such as preventing a document from being printed or e-mailed or photos from being downloaded from a phone app. DRM is typically associated with consumer applications.

Similarly, information rights management (IRM) is a set of technologies that enforces specific usage limitations on data throughout enterprise systems, including cloud and distributed systems.

Protected Backups

Backups are copies of live data that are maintained in case something happens that makes the live data set inaccessible. Because it is a copy of valuable data, it needs to have the same protections afforded to it that the live data employs. It should be encrypted, password-protected, and kept physically locked away from unauthorized access. See Chapter 13 for more information on backups and backup strategies.

Network Security

Network security is the practice of protecting the usability, reliability, integrity, and safety of a network infrastructure and also the data traveling along it. As it does in many other areas, security in cloud computing has similarities to traditional computing models. If deployed without evaluating security, cloud systems may deliver against their functional requirements. Still, they will likely have many gaps that could lead to a compromised system.

Security systems are designed to protect the network against certain types of threats. One solution alone will not fully protect the company because attackers have multiple avenues for exploitation. Security systems should be used in conjunction with one another to protect against these avenues and to provide layers of security. If an attacker passes by one layer, he will not be able to exploit the network without bypassing another layer and so forth. Security systems will only overlap in some places, so having 20 security systems does not mean that the organization has 20 layers.

The security systems mentioned here, and many others, can exist either as networking/security hardware that is installed in a data center or as virtual appliances that are placed in hypervisors in much the same way as servers. Cloud environments can deploy virtual appliances to their networks easily with this method. Virtual appliances were covered in the "Component Updates" section of Chapter 10. The following sections cover the following important network security controls:

- Segmentation
- Firewalls
- Distributed denial of service (DDoS) protection
- Packet capture
- Intrusion prevention systems (IPSs)/intrusion detection systems (IDSs)
- Packet broker
- Network access control (NAC)
- APIs

Segmentation

Remember the phrase "don't put all of your eggs in one basket"? If you drop the basket, all the eggs are broken. Some networks today are like that basket. We call these flat networks. As you can see in Figure 11-3, they have all their computers, servers, and devices on one network, so when one device is compromised, all are placed at risk.

Segmentation can also have a performance impact. Have you ever tried to have a conversation in a full open room? It is very noisy and hard to talk. However, if you divide that room into many smaller spaces, talking becomes much easier. Similarly, if you divide the network into smaller sections, each one receives less communication. Thus each machine will be less burdened processing traffic that is not intended for it.

To segment a network, you will need to define a distinct subnet for the network and place a device capable of routing between the networks. Such devices include most commonly routers, firewalls, and layer 3 switches. You will then need to define the network segments using a protocol such as VLAN, VXLAN, NVGRE, STT, and GENEVE.

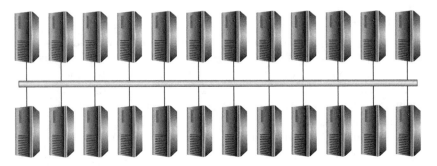

Figure 11-3   Flat network

These protocols were discussed in detail in Chapter 4. Figure 11-4 shows a network that is segmented into different networks for various purposes. This improves security because analytics data is not directly accessible to web servers, and development data cannot affect virtual desktops. Each segment is kept separate from the others, using a firewall to govern acceptable traffic flows between the segments.

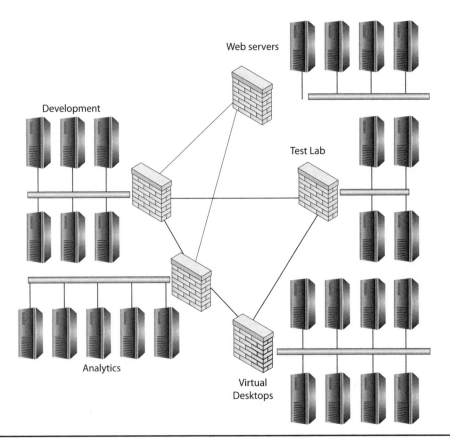

Figure 11-4   Segmented network

NOTE A layer 3 device is one that is capable of routing packets. Layer 3 comes from the OSI network model.

Firewall

A firewall is used to control traffic. Firewalls operate at OSI layer 3 or above, meaning that, at a minimum, they can analyze packets and implement filtering on packets based on the information contained in the packet header, such as source and destination IP addresses, lengths, and sizes. However, most firewalls operate at a much higher level.

Firewalls in a cloud environment are typically virtual appliances or software services offered to cloud consumers. Common public cloud providers offer layer 4 firewalls such as the Azure Network Security Group (NSG) and AWS EC2 Security Group. These are implemented simply by configuring them on an administrative dashboard.

Some firewall capabilities include the following:

- **NAT/PAT** Network address translation (NAT) consolidates the addresses needed for each internal device to a single valid public IP address, allowing all of the organization's employees to access the Internet using a single public IP address.

  Firewalls can be configured with multiple IP addresses, and NAT can be used to translate external IP addresses to internal IP addresses so that the host's actual IP address is hidden from the outside world.

  Port address translation (PAT) allows for the mapping of private IP addresses to public IP addresses, as well as for mapping multiple devices on a network to a single public IP address. PAT enables the sharing of a single public IP address between multiple clients trying to access the Internet. Each external-facing service has a port associated with it, and the PAT service knows which ones map to which internal servers. It repackages the data received on the outside network to the inside network, addressing it to the destination server. PAT makes this determination based on the port the data was sent to.

- **Port/service** The firewall can be configured to filter out traffic that is not addressed to an open port. For example, the firewall may be configured to allow traffic to HTTPS, port 443, and SMTP, port 25. If it receives data for HTTP on port 80, it will drop the packet.

- **DMZ** A demilitarized zone (DMZ) is a network segment that allows some level of access to its resources from the public Internet. DMZs are configured with ACLs that enforce specific security rules to allow only the traffic required for those DMZ systems. Externally facing web servers, remote access servers, or Internet file sharing systems are often housed in a DMZ.

- **Screened subnet** A screened subnet is a network segmentation technique that uses multiple networks to segment Internet-facing systems from internal systems. It is accomplished with multiple routers or firewalls or by using a triple-homed firewall (one with three interfaces). A typical scenario is to place public-facing web servers in a DMZ. ACLs are then defined to allow web traffic to the web servers but not anywhere else. The web servers may need to connect back to a database server on an internal cloud segment, so ACLs allow the web servers in the DMZ to talk to the database server in the internal cloud segment, but connections from the outside would not be able to talk to the database server directly. Similarly, other internal machines on the internal segment could not be contacted directly from outside resources.

- **Stateful packet inspection**   Stateful packet inspection evaluates whether a session has been created for a packet before it will accept it. This is similar to how an accounts receivable department looks to see if they issued a purchase order before paying an invoice. If there is no purchase order, no check is sent. If the firewall sees that an inside computer has established a connection with a handshake (SYN packet, then SYN + ACK, then ACK packet) with the target system, it allows the traffic to flow back to the inside machine that initiated the connection. Otherwise, the packets are dropped. Unfortunately, stateful firewalls can be subjected to SYN-based DDoS attacks, so DDoS mitigation controls are advised when using stateful packet inspection.

- **Stateless**   The cheaper alternative to a stateful firewall is the stateless firewall. This type of firewall does not analyze packets with as much rigor as the stateful firewall. Stateless firewalls do less processing of the traffic flowing through them, so they can achieve better performance.

- **IP spoofing detection**   Spoofing is the modification of the sending IP address in a packet to obscure the data transmission origin. Attackers will sometimes try to send data to a device to make it seem like the data came from another device on the local network. They spoof the sending IP address and give it some local address. Spoofing is the modification of the source IP address to obfuscate the original source. However, the firewall knows which addresses it has internally because they are contained in its routing table. If it sees data with a sender address from outside the network, it knows that data is spoofed.

  Spoofing is not limited to local addresses. Spoofing is often used in e-mail phishing to make e-mails appear as if they originated from a company's servers when they actually came from an attacker. Spoofing is also used in man-in-the-middle attacks so that data is routed through a middleman.

WAF

One specialized type of firewall is called a web application firewall (WAF). A WAF is a device that screens traffic intended for web applications. WAFs understand common web application attacks such as cross-site scripting (XSS) and SQL injection and can inspect traffic at the OSI model's application layer.

Cloud Access Security Broker

Organizations may choose to have a third-party screen traffic for cloud or on-premises systems. A cloud access security broker (CASB) is an on-premises or cloud service that operates as the gateway between users and cloud systems.

CASBs are configured with policies to determine what type of access is allowed to cloud services. The CASB screens incoming traffic for malicious content and anomalous behavior and prevents that traffic from being delivered to the cloud systems it services. A CASB can also be used as an on-premises proxy so that local user access is limited to specific cloud apps only.

Ingress and Egress Traffic Filtering

Firewalls filter traffic. This filtering is performed on both ingress and egress traffic. Ingress traffic flows from the outside to the inside, while egress traffic flows from the inside out. Some filtering methods include access control lists (ACLs), whitelisting, and blacklisting.

Cloud firewalls perform filtering with ACLs to a large extent. ACLs are made up of a series of access control entries (ACEs). Each ACE specifies the access rights of an individual principal or entity. An ACL comprises one or more ACEs.

The firewall processes the ACL in order from the first ACE to the last ACE. For example, the first ACE would say "allow traffic over HTTP to the web server." The second ACE would say "allow SMTP traffic to the e-mail server," and the third ACE would say "deny all traffic." If the firewall receives DNS traffic, it will go through the rules in order. ACE 1 is not matched because this is not HTTP traffic. ACE 2 is not matched because this is not SMTP traffic. ACE 3 is matched because it is anything else, so the firewall drops the packet. In the real world, ACLs are much more complex.

Another method of ingress and egress filtering is whitelisting and blacklisting. Whitelisting, also known as an allow list, denies all traffic unless it is on the whitelist. A company might have a system set up for remote access by employees from their homes. They could require users to provide them with their home IP address and then whitelist that address so the users can connect. If a connection request is received by an IP address that is not on the whitelist, it will be rejected.

The opposite approach is to blacklist, also known as a deny list. You could pull down a list of known bad sites or IP addresses from a public blacklist and instruct the firewall to drop any packets from these systems.

 EXAM TIP When a technology has multiple terms, be sure to memorize both so that you will be ready no matter which one is used on the test.

DDoS Protection

DDoS is an attack that targets a single system simultaneously from multiple compromised systems to make that system unavailable. The attack is distributed because it uses thousands or millions of machines that could be spread worldwide. The attack denies services or disrupts availability by overwhelming the system so that it cannot respond to legitimate connection requests.

Cloud firewalls or CASBs can often prevent DDoS traffic from reaching organizational cloud servers because the cloud vendor or CASB has the necessary bandwidth to withstand a DDoS attack. However, some DDoS attacks have been performed using the Mirai botnet that overwhelmed several of the world's largest networks.

Packet Capture

Packet capture devices collect the traffic traveling over a link, such as a firewall, to be analyzed later. Packet capture can be used to replay the traffic at a point in time for troubleshooting or investigation of a threat. Some monitoring systems automatically gather packet captures when certain events are triggered.

Network Flow

Network flow tools provide visibility into network traffic, where it is going, and how much traffic flows to the various network nodes. It is a useful tool for discovering congestion on the network or troubleshooting excessive network errors or dropped packets. You can also use network flows to identify abnormal traffic patterns that may be indicative of an attack.

IDS/IPS

An intrusion detection system (IDS) or an intrusion prevention system (IPS) looks at traffic to identify malicious traffic. IDSs and IPSs do this through two methods: signatures and heuristics. IDSs or IPSs in a cloud environment are typically virtual appliances or software services offered to cloud consumers. Azure and AWS have built-in IDS/IPS solutions in their environments that can be licensed and enabled as software configurations. They can also utilize third-party cloud solutions that are supported by the cloud provider. For example, in the AWS or Azure marketplace, you can deploy IDS/IPS solutions from companies like Alert Logic, Trend Micro, or McAfee.

Signatures are descriptions of what malicious data looks like. IDSs and IPSs review the data that passes through them and take action if the system finds data that matches a signature. The second screening method used is heuristics, which looks for patterns that appear malicious, such as many failed authentication attempts. Heuristics operates off an understanding of what constitutes normal on the network. A baseline is configured and periodically updated so the IDS or IPS understands what to expect from the network traffic. Anything else is an anomaly, and the device will take action.

So far, we have only said that these devices take action. IDSs and IPSs differ in how they react to the things they find. An IDS sends alerts and logs suspicious traffic but does not block the traffic. An IPS can send alerts and record log entries on activities observed. IPS can also block, queue, or quarantine the traffic. An IPS can be generically referred to as intrusion detection and prevention (IDP). This term is used in the same way that IPS is used.

In the cloud, firewalls and IDS/IPS functionality can be achieved with cloud-specific configuration settings or by deploying a virtual appliance from the cloud provider marketplace. IDSs and IPSs need to be in a position to collect network data. There are three types: network-based, host-based, and hybrid configurations.

Network-Based

A network-based IDS (NIDS) or IPS (NIPS) is placed next to a firewall or built into a perimeter firewall. A firewall is an ideal place because it processes all traffic going between the inside network and the outside. If the NIPS is a separate device, it will need to have the traffic forwarded to it and then relay back instructions, or it will need to be the first device to screen the information.

Host-Based

The second type of IDS or IPS is the host-based IDS (HIDS) or IPS (HIPS). These devices reside on endpoints such as cloud servers or a cloud virtual desktop infrastructure (VDI). A NIDS or NIPS can collect a lot of data, but it does not see everything because not all data passes through the perimeter. Consider malware that has infected a machine. It may reach out to other computers on the network without touching the perimeter device. A HIDS or HIPS would be able to identify this traffic when a NIDS or NIPS would not.

Hybrid

You can choose to implement both a host-based and network-based IDS or IPS. They will still operate independently but also send data to a collection point so that the data between the devices can be correlated to produce better intelligence on what is expected and abnormal. This is known as a hybrid IDS or IPS configuration.

Packet Broker

As you can imagine, all these tools, monitoring systems, packet capture devices, network flow, and IDSs/IPSs are receiving traffic from network devices. Some of this traffic is redundant and sent to multiple devices, while other traffic is unique to the system. It can be challenging for administrators to manage all these services that need to collect data as the network changes or when new systems are provisioned.

The packet broker is positioned between the network and the tools collecting data to manage and optimize the flow of data to those devices. Packet brokers combine traffic coming from multiple sources to more efficiently transmit the data to recipients. They can also filter network traffic using specific criteria for each recipient service so that services do not receive data that they will not ultimately use. This improves network performance overall and eases the management complexity of the systems.

APIs

Application programming interfaces (APIs) are used to expose functions of an application or cloud service to other programs and services. APIs allow for expansion of the original application's scope. They are used to integrate multiple applications together as part of an organization's cloud or security operations.

A vendor will create an API for its application and then release documentation so that developers and integrators know how to utilize that API. For example, Office 365, a cloud-based productivity suite that includes an e-mail application, has an API for importing and exporting contacts. Salesforce, a cloud-based customer relationship management (CRM) application, could integrate with Office 365 through that API so that contacts could be updated based on interactions in the CRM tool.

Effects of Cloud Service Models on Security Implementation

Cloud technologies have streamlined many aspects of security, but they have added their own complexities as well. Many security functions that were once performed in-house have now been delegated to the CSP, but this results in reduced visibility and control for the organization. They have to place a level of trust in the CSP.

In the cloud, companies may not need to provision their own security technologies. Rather, they use a self-service portal where they can simply select the systems they want deployed, and the CSP automates the process on their behalf. Similarly, consumers can browse through solutions in cloud marketplaces and begin using those systems almost immediately. These systems still need to be configured, but there is still far less work to go through than required in a traditional data center model.

Endpoint Protection

Vendors have created a vast number of applications to solve many endpoint security challenges, and many security applications are available as cloud services on your endpoints. IT administrators and security teams have many tools at their disposal. There are systems they can deploy to implement security or vendor applications. Each of these systems must be compatible with existing systems and services.

The following sections cover important endpoint security controls:

- Host-based firewall
- Antivirus/antimalware
- Endpoint detection and response
- Data loss prevention
- Hardening
- Application whitelisting

We will wrap this section up with a discussion on the impact security tools have on systems and services.

Host-Based Firewall

Firewalls often exist on the perimeter of the network, where they can screen the data that is going to and coming from the Internet. There is also a type of firewall called the host-based firewall that resides on an endpoint to screen the data that is received by the endpoint. If a device is not running as a web server, there is no reason for it to process web traffic. Web traffic sent to it is either malicious or sent by mistake, so it is either a waste of time to look at it or, more likely, a threat. The host-based firewall drops this traffic before it can do harm to the device.

Host-based firewalls can be configured based on policy so that many machines can use the same configuration. Chapter 10 covered how to automate configuring firewalls with scripting. You can also use Windows group policies to configure the Windows Defender firewall that comes with Windows.

Many antivirus vendors bundle a host-based firewall with their products, and these can be managed with a central management application or cloud portal if the licensing for that application or portal has been purchased.

Antivirus/Antimalware

Antivirus or antimalware looks at actions on a system to identify malicious activity. Antivirus or antimalware does this through the same two methods used by an IDS/IPS: signatures and heuristics. The terms antivirus and antimalware are used interchangeably. Both antivirus and antimalware software detect viruses, trojans, bots, worms, and malicious cookies. Some antivirus or antimalware software also identifies adware, spyware, and potentially unwanted applications.

Signatures are descriptions of what malicious actions look like. Antivirus and antimalware review the data in memory and scan data on the disk or disks plugged into them and take action if they find data that matches a signature.

The second screening method used is heuristics, which looks for patterns that appear malicious, such as a user-mode process trying to access kernel-mode memory addresses. Just as with the IDS and IPS, antivirus or antimalware heuristics operate off an understanding of what constitutes normal on the device. A baseline is configured and periodically updated so the antivirus or antimalware understands what to expect from the network traffic. Anything else is an anomaly, and the device will take action.

Many antivirus and antimalware vendors have a central management application or cloud portal option that can be purchased. These tools or portals are very valuable for ease of administration. Each antivirus or antimalware client reports into the portal, and administrators can view all machines in a set of dashboards. Dashboards, like the one shown in Figure 11-5, display things like machines with outdated signatures, number of viruses detected, virus detection rates, virus types, items in quarantine, number of files scanned, and much more.

These administration tools usually allow administrators to deploy antivirus or antimalware software to endpoints without walking to each machine.

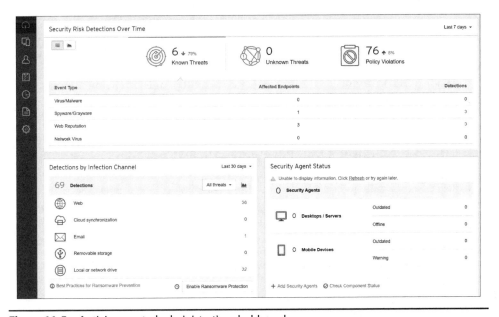

Figure 11-5 Antivirus central administration dashboard

Some antivirus and antimalware tools come with other services bundled in. These include host-based firewalls, data loss prevention, password vaults, e-mail scanners, web scanners, and other features.

Endpoint Detection and Response

Endpoint detection and response (EDR) is a system that resides on endpoints to continually collect data from them for real-time analysis. EDR automates elements of the incident response analysis by applying policy rules and workflow to events that are triggered along the way. This helps guard against more advanced threats that would typically evade the perimeter defenses and standard antivirus scans. Some primary functions of an EDR include:

- Collecting endpoint data based on established policy rules
- Identifying threat patterns in the collected data
- Performing workflow when events occur
- Collecting and preserving evidence of threats for forensic analysis and investigation

Data Loss Prevention

Data loss prevention (DLP) systems enforce policies for data flow and on managed devices. Data may be identified through tags that are embedded into documents or from searches performed on the data. Searches commonly use regular expressions to identify information of specific types, such as Social Security numbers, credit card numbers, or health records.

DLP policies define how the data can and cannot be used, and they can be used to enforce protections, such as encryption, on the data. For example, you could configure DLP to allow personally identifiable information (PII) to be e-mailed to others within the organization, but not to outside domain names. Department of Defense (DoD) contractors will often use DLP to ensure that data tagged as Controlled Unclassified Information (CUI) cannot be transferred to a computer unless it is on the whitelist. Cloud DLP solutions can enforce policies throughout their ecosystem. For example, Microsoft's DLP for Office 365 extends to e-mail, SharePoint, Teams, and OneDrive.

Exercise 11-1: Creating a DLP Policy for Office 365

In this exercise, we will create a DLP policy for Office 365 for U.S. Social Security numbers, taxpayer ID numbers, and passport numbers. This DLP policy will prevent the data from being shared with anyone outside the organization. Furthermore, it will send a notification to the user and data owners that this activity is prohibited.

1. Log into your Office 365 portal.

2. Select Admin at the bottom of the apps list on the left:

3. Expand the Data Loss Prevention section and select Policy. The Policy screen will now show the policies you have defined.

4. Select the Create A Policy button to start the DLP policy wizard.

5. We will first choose the information that the policy will be focused on. In this case, we want to protect U.S. PII, including Social Security numbers, taxpayer ID numbers, and passport numbers. Select Privacy and then scroll down and select U.S. Personally Identifiable Information (PII) Data, as shown here:

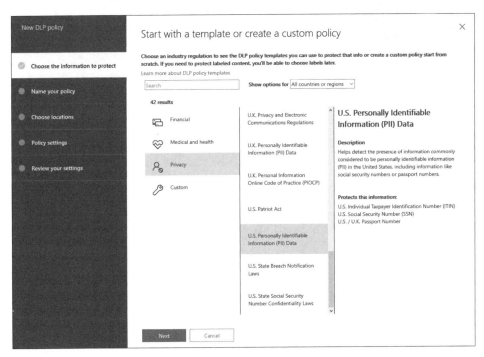

6. Click Next.

7. Enter a name and a description of the policy. In this example, we called the policy "PII Protection Policy" and gave it a short description, as shown in the following illustration. Click Next when finished.

8. You can now select the scope of the policy. Microsoft lets you enforce the policy throughout the Office 365 ecosystem, including e-mail, Teams, OneDrive, and SharePoint, or you can select only some of those locations. By default, all locations are enabled, as shown next. In this example, we will enforce protection on all locations, so you just need to click Next.

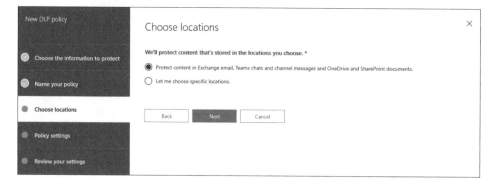

9. Select Use Advanced Settings and then click Next.

10. The advanced settings give you options for what to do when someone tries to share a small number of files and a large number of files, as shown next.

In this case, we will only apply one policy for whenever someone tries to share a document containing PII, so select Delete Rule under Low Volume Of Content Detected U.S. PII.

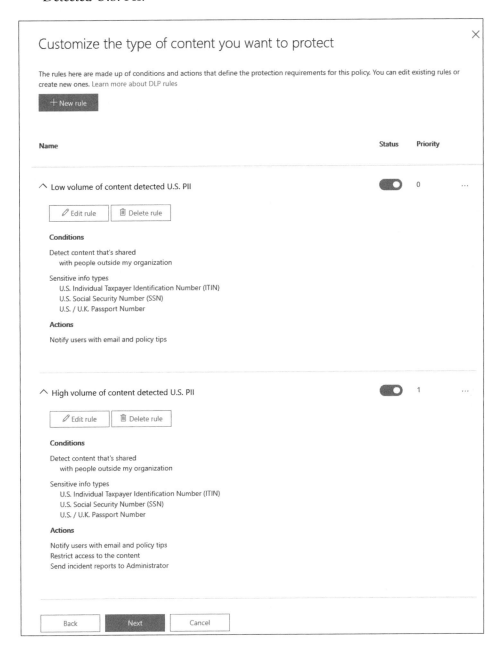

11. Select Yes in the dialog box that confirms whether you want to delete the object.

12. Click Edit Rule under High Volume Of Content Detected U.S. PII.

13. Change the name from "High volume of content detected U.S. PII" to "Content detected: U.S. PII."

14. Under Content Contains, change the instance count min from 10 to 1 for each of the information types by clicking on the 10 and changing it to a 1. When you are done, the section should look like this:

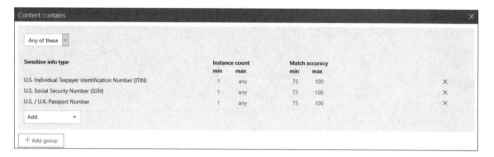

15. The Content Is Shared section is set to With People Outside My Organization by default. Leave this setting as is because we are looking for when users try to send such information outside the organization.

16. Under Actions, leave the default settings, as shown next. These include blocking people from sharing the content and enabling restrictions only for those outside the organization.

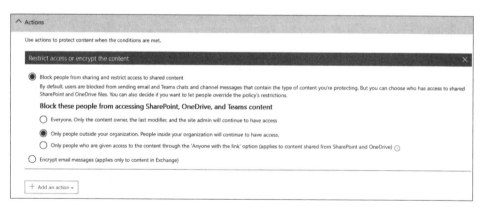

17. Scroll down to the User Notifications section and review the options. We will leave them at their default, but this is where you can change it to send notifications of the event to a custom list of people, such as a compliance person, internal audit, or the SOC team.

18. Under User Overrides, toggle the switch to Off so that users who see the tip cannot override the policy. The settings for steps 17 and 18 are shown here:

∧ User notifications

Use Notifications to inform your users and help educate them on the proper use of sensitive info.
Please note: Notifications for teams will be displayed in the chat client itself.

⬤◯ On

Email notifications

◯ Notify the user who sent, shared, or last modified the content.

◉ Notify these people:
  ☑ The person who sent, shared, or modified the content
  ☑ Owner of the SharePoint site or OneDrive account
  ☑ Owner of the SharePoint or OneDrive content

  Send the email to these additional people:

  Add or remove people

☐ Customize the email text

Policy tips
☐ Customize the policy tip text

∧ User overrides

Let people who see the tip override the policy and share the content.

◉◯ Off

19. At the bottom, click Save. This will bring you back to the policy settings step in the wizard.

20. Click Next.

21. On the last page, you are given a choice to test the policy out first, turn it on right away, or leave it off and turn it on later. DLP can have a significant impact on operations, so it is best to test the policy first before deploying it. You might choose to leave it off and turn it on later if you plan to enable it in downtime but want to get it configured ahead of time. For this example, select I'd Like To Test It Out First, as shown next, and then click Next.

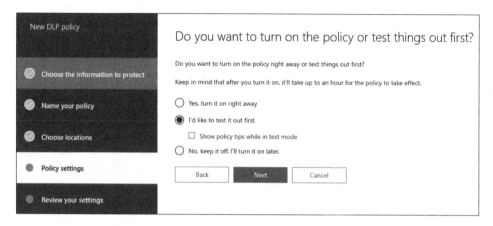

22. Click Create to create your policy in test mode. The policy will now show up on the policy screen.

NAC

NAC manages access to network resources based on policies. NAC can block computers from a network or connect them to networks based on their settings. It can screen computers before allowing their connection to the network. Computers are denied access unless they meet all the security requirements. Security requirements can include some of the following:

- Patch level
- Operating system type
- Antivirus signature version
- IDS/IPS signature version
- Host-based firewall status
- Geolocation

In some cases, the NAC system will provide limited access to systems that do not meet compliance with the policy to update their virus signatures or apply patches. Once they remediate the issues, they are allowed regular access.

The other use of NAC is to connect systems to resources based on their settings and organizational policy. NAC can automatically place Linux machines on a dedicated Linux network and Macs on another network. A popular use of NAC is to automatically place mobile phones on their own network so that their traffic is isolated from other computing devices. It can also be used to segment BYOD or IoT from other networks.

Hardening

The hardening of computer systems and networks, whether they are on-premises or in the cloud, involves ensuring that the host and guest computers are configured in such a way that it reduces the risk of attack from either internal or external sources. While the specific configuration steps for hardening vary from one system to another, the basic concepts involved are largely similar, regardless of the technologies that are being hardened. Some of these central hardening concepts are as follows:

- **Remove all software and services that are not needed on the system**   Most operating systems and all preloaded systems run applications and services that are not required by all configurations as part of their default. Systems deployed from standard cloud templates may contain services that are not required for your specific use case. These additional services and applications add to the attack surface of any given system and thus should be removed.

- **Maintain firmware and patch levels**   Security holes are continually discovered in both software and firmware, and vendors release patches as quickly as they can to respond to those discoveries. Enterprises, as well as cloud providers, need to apply these patches to be protected from the patched vulnerabilities.

- **Control account access**   Unused accounts should be either disabled or removed entirely from systems. The remaining accounts should be audited to make sure they are necessary and that they only have access to the resources they require. Default accounts should be disabled or renamed. If hackers are looking to gain unauthorized access to a system and guess the username, they already have half of the necessary information to log into that system.

  For the same reason, all default passwords associated with any system or cloud service should be changed. In addition to security threats from malicious users who are attempting to access unauthorized systems or data, security administrators must beware of the danger from a well-meaning employee who unknowingly accesses resources that shouldn't be made available to them or, worse yet, deletes data that he or she did not intend to remove.

- **Implement the principle of least privilege (POLP)**   POLP dictates that users are given only the amount of access they need to carry out their duties and no additional privileges above that for anything else. Protecting against potential insider threats and protecting cloud consumers in a multitenant environment require that privileged user management be implemented and that security policies follow the POLP.

- **Disable unnecessary network ports** As with software and service hardening, only the required network ports should be enabled to and from servers and cloud services to reduce the attack surface.

- **Deploy antivirus or antimalware software** Antivirus or antimalware software should be deployed to all systems that support it. The most secure approach to virus defense is one in which any malicious traffic must pass through multiple layers of detection before reaching its potential targets, such as filtering at the perimeter, through e-mail gateways, and then on endpoints such as cloud servers or end-user machines.

- **Configure logging** Logging should be enabled on all systems so that if an intrusion is attempted, it can be identified and mitigated or, at the very least, investigated. Cloud logging options can be leveraged to archive logs automatically, conserving space on servers and ensuring that data is available if needed. See Chapter 10 for more information on log automation.

- **Limit physical access** If a malicious user has physical access to a network resource, they may have more options for gaining access to that resource. Because of this, limitations that can be applied to physical access should be utilized. Some examples of physical access deterrents are locks on server room doors, network cabinets, and the network devices themselves. Additionally, servers need to be secured at the BIOS level with a password so that malicious users cannot boot to secondary drives and bypass operating system security.

- **Scan for vulnerabilities** Once the security configuration steps have been defined and implemented for a system, a vulnerability assessment should be performed using a third-party tool or service provider to make certain no security gaps were missed. Penetration testing can validate whether vulnerabilities are exploitable and whether other security controls are mitigating the vulnerability. Vulnerability scanning and penetration testing are discussed later in this chapter.

- **Deploy a host-based firewall** Software firewalls should be deployed to the hosts and guests that will support them. These software firewalls can be configured with ACLs and protection tools in the same fashion as hardware firewalls.

- **Deactivate default accounts** Many systems come provisioned with accounts that are used to initially set up the software or device. The usernames and passwords of such accounts are well known to attackers, so it is best to deactivate these default accounts. Deactivation is better than just changing the password because attackers still know the default username, which gives them one piece of the puzzle even if the password is changed.

- **Disable weak protocols and ciphers** Weak protocols and ciphers are those that can be broken or compromised. As computers get more powerful and as vulnerabilities are discovered in existing protocols, those are flagged as weak, and companies should stop using them. Computer systems may support several ciphers or encryption protocols. They will use the highest one that both sender and receiver support, so any enabled protocol can potentially be used.

- **Single function**   Systems should perform a single function so that it will be easier to limit the services, open ports, and software that must be updated.

- **Hardened baselines**   Ensure that the baselined systems and templates used to create new machines are hardened so that security vulnerabilities are not introduced into the environment when new devices are provisioned.

Application Whitelisting

Application whitelisting allows a company to restrict the applications that can be installed on a machine to only those that have been approved for use. Many applications are available to users, but a myriad of deployed applications can make it difficult for administrators to keep those applications up to date and ensure that they are sufficiently tested when changes are made.

For this reason, companies typically restrict applications to the ones that they have approved and placed on a whitelist. These applications are tested when new changes are rolled out, and administrators stay informed when new versions are released or when vulnerabilities are identified for those applications.

Impact of Security Tools to Systems and Services

Security tools can affect the systems they are installed on. Antivirus software could flag some legitimate applications as malicious or require additional steps to log on to tools. Security tools can take up a large amount of CPU or memory resources. Logging tools utilize a large amount of storage. Since cloud resource utilization often determines how much the cloud consumer is charged, resource utilization directly affects the bottom line.

Some security tools do not play well together. For example, it is never a good idea to install multiple antivirus tools on the same machine. Each tool will interpret the other tool as malicious because they each are scanning large numbers of files and trying to read memory. Some security tools may accidentally flag other security tools as malicious and cause problems running those tools. If this happens, whitelist the application in the security tool that blocks it. Some security tools can cause issues with backup jobs because the tools create locks when scanning files and folders that the backup job must wait for or try to snapshot.

Access Control

Access control is the process of determining who or what should be able to view, modify, or delete information. Controlling access to network resources such as files, folders, databases, and web applications relies upon effective access control techniques. Access control is accomplished by authenticating and authorizing both users and hosts.

Authentication means that an entity can prove that it is who or what it claims to be. Authorization means that an entity has access to all of the resources it is supposed to have access to and no access to the resources it is not supposed to have access to.

Authorization is the set of processes that determine who a claimant is and what they are allowed to do. These processes also log activity for later auditing. They are sometimes referred to as AAA, which stands for authentication, authorization, and accounting.

This section includes coverage of the following access control concepts:

- Identification
- Authentication
- Authorization
- Access control methodologies
- Multifactor authentication
- Single sign-on (SSO)
- Federation

Identification

Identification is the process of claiming an identity. In the medieval days, a guard would ask, "Who goes there?" if a stranger approached the gate, in response to which the stranger would reply, "Eric Vanderburg." Of course, the guard would not just take the stranger's word for it, and neither should a computer when a user or service tries to connect to it or log on. The next step is authentication.

Authentication

Authentication is the process of determining who or what is requesting access to a resource. When you log on to a computer, you present credentials that validate your identity to the computer, much like a driver's license or passport identifies your identity to a police officer or customs officer. And just as the police officer or customs officer compares the photo on the ID to your face, the computer will compare the credentials you offer with the information on hand to determine if you are who you claim to be. However, the computer may trust that you are who you say you are, but that doesn't necessarily mean that you are allowed to be there. The next step is to determine if the user identity is allowed access to the resource.

Authorization

Authorization determines if the authenticated individual should have the requested access to the resource. For example, after this book is published, if I go to a club to celebrate, bypass the line, and present my credentials to the bouncer, he or she will compare my name to a list of authorized individuals. If the club owner is a huge fan of this book, she might have put my name on the list, in which case, I will be granted access to the club. If not, the bouncer will tell me to get lost. Computer systems compare the identity to the resource ACL to determine if the user can access the resource.

ACLs define the level of access, such as read-only (RO), modify (M), or full control (FC). Read-only access allows a user to view the data but not make changes to it. Modify allows the user to read the data and change it. Full control allows the user to read data, change it, delete it, or change the permissions on it.

Organizations should implement approval procedures and access policies along with authorization techniques. Approval and access policy are discussed next.

 EXAM TIP Devices may exchange authorization data using the Security Assertion Markup Language (SAML).

Approval

Approval is an audit of the authorization function. In the bouncer example, imagine that the bouncer is a fan of this book, not the owner. A supervisor who is watching over a group of club staff members, including the bouncer, sees the bouncer letting us into the club and decides to check the list to verify that Eric Vanderburg is on it. If the supervisor finds that I am not on the list or sees my name written in with the bouncer's handwriting, sanctions are soon to follow, and I might not be welcome there anymore.

When implemented in the computer setting, approval would see a connection from a new user who is on the ACL. Since the user has not logged in before, a second authentication would occur, such as sending a text to the user's phone or an e-mail to their inbox. The user would enter the code from the text or e-mail to prove that they know the password from the first authentication and have access to the phone or e-mail. In future attempts, the approval step would not be needed since the user has logged in before. The concept of approval operates on a level of trust, which can be changed depending on organizational preferences. One company could decide that approval will take place not just for new connections but the lesser of every fifth time someone logs in or every two weeks. Implementations are quite flexible.

Access Policy

Access policy is the governing activities that establish authorization levels. Access policy determines who should have access to what. Access policy requires at least three roles. The first is the authorizer. This is the person or group that can define who has access. The second is the implementer. This is the person or group that assigns access based on an authorization. The third role is the auditor. This person or group reviews existing access to verify that each access granted is authorized.

Here is how an access policy plays out on the job: The organization typically defines access based on a job role. In this example, human resources (HR) is the authorizer, IT is the implementer, and audit is the auditor. When a new person is hired for a job in marketing, HR will notify IT of the new hire, their name, start date, and that they are in marketing. IT would then grant them access to the systems that others in marketing have access to. This is typically accomplished by creating the user account and then adding that account to an appropriate group.

Auditors will routinely review group memberships to determine if they match what has been defined by HR. Any inconsistencies would be brought to the attention of management. Access policies have a lifetime. Access is not provided forever, and at some point, access rights are revoked. In this example, HR would notify IT to revoke access, and IT would disable or remove the account when employees are terminated. On the next audit cycle, the auditor would verify that the account had been disabled.

Single Sign-On

As individuals, we have all had to remember multiple usernames and passwords for various software at work or even at home for multiple websites. Wouldn't it be great if we logged in only once and had access to everything without being prompted to log in again? This is what SSO is all about!

SSO can take the operating system, VPN, or web browser authentication credentials and present them to the relying party transparently, so the user does not even know it is happening. Modern Windows operating systems use the credential locker as a password vault to store varying types of credentials to facilitate SSO. Enterprise SSO solutions such as the open-source Shibboleth tool or Microsoft Active Directory Federation Services (ADFS) let cloud personnel implement SSO on a large scale. Cloud providers normally offer identity federation services to cloud customers.

The problem with SSO is that different software and websites may use other authentication mechanisms. This makes implementing SSO in a large environment difficult.

Federation

Federation uses SSO to authorize access for users or devices to potentially many very different protected network resources, such as file servers, websites, and database applications. The protected resources could exist within a single organization or between multiple organizations.

For business-to-business (B2B) relationships, such as between a cloud customer and a cloud provider, a federation allows the cloud customer to retain their own on-premises user accounts and passwords that can be used to access cloud services from the provider. This way, the user does not have to remember a username and password for the cloud services as well as for the local network. Federation also allows cloud providers to rent on-demand computing resources from other cloud providers to service their clients' needs.

Here is a typical B2B federation scenario (see Figure 11-6):

1. User Bob in company A attempts to access an application on the web application server 1 in company B.

2. If Bob is not already authenticated, the web application server in company B redirects Bob to the federation server in company B for authentication.

3. Since Bob's user account does not exist in company B, the federation server in company B sends an authentication redirect to Bob.

4. Bob is redirected to the company A federation server and gets authenticated since this is where his user account exists.

Figure 11-6
An example of
a B2B federation
at work

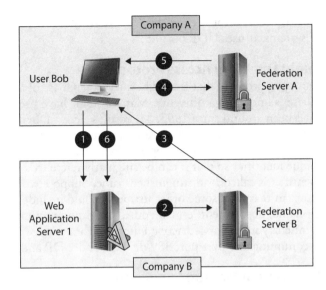

5. The company A federation server returns a digitally signed authentication token to Bob.

6. Bob presents the authentication token to the application on the web application server 1 and is authorized to use the application.

Access Control Protocols

Access control protocols are used to send authentication challenges and responses to and from resources and authenticators. Some common access control protocols include Kerberos, LDAP, and SAML.

Kerberos

Kerberos is an authentication protocol that uses tickets to validate whether an entity can access a resource. A Kerberos system consists of the following elements:

- **Authentication Server (AS)**   Clients send their credentials to the AS to verify them and then forward user information to the KDC.

- **Key Distribution Center (KDC)**   The KDC issues a TGT (discussed next) to clients after receiving identifying information from an AS for a client. These TGTs expire after a period of time and must be renewed.

- **Ticket Granting Ticket (TGT)**   The TGT is provided by the KDC. It can be used to get a session key from a TGS.

- **Ticket Granting Service (TGS)**   This service is associated with a resource. Clients request access to the resource by sending their TGT to the resource TGS's Service Principal Name (SPN).

Kerberos has been implemented by Microsoft Windows, macOS, FreeBSD, Linux, and other systems. It uses UDP port 88.

Lightweight Directory Access Protocol

LDAP is an open protocol that is used to query a database of authentication credentials. This database is known as a directory. Many systems have been based on LDAP, as this protocol has been around since 1993. Microsoft's Active Directory is based on LDAP.

An LDAP directory consists of entries that each has attributes. The directory schema defines which attributes will be associated with each type of entry. Each entry must have a unique identifier so that it can be singularly referenced within the directory. This unique identifier is called its distinguished name. Suppose we had an entry for a user in the directory. In that case, some of its attributes could include username, password, first name, last name, department, e-mail address, and phone number. Figure 11-7 shows a user account entry in Microsoft Active Directory for a service account.

LDAP communicates over port 389 on TCP and UDP and port 636 over SSL/TLS.

Security Assertion Markup Language

SAML is an authentication protocol that is used primarily for federated access and SSO. SAML allows identity providers, such as Azure Active Directory or Identity Access Management (IAM) solutions, to send a SAML assertion to service providers.

Figure 11-7
User account in
Microsoft Active
Directory

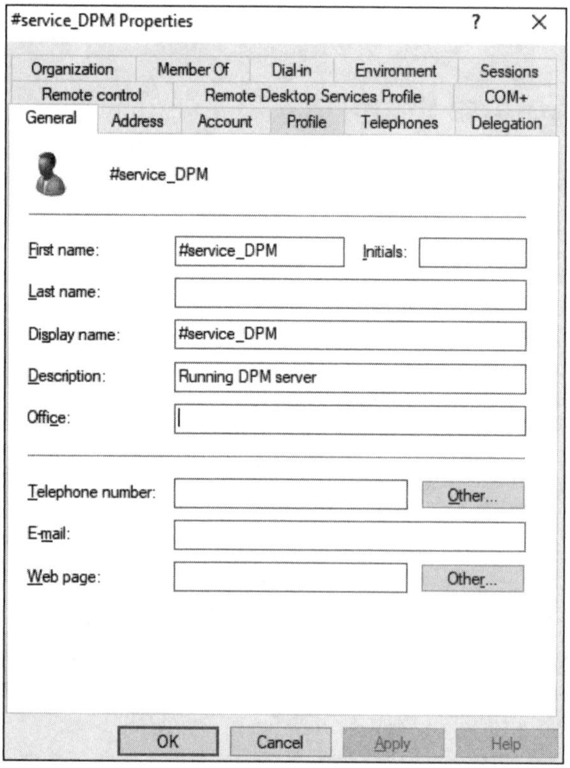

SAML assertions inform the provider that the user is who they say they are and that they have access to the selected resource. SAML assertions are formatted in Extensible Markup Language (XML), hence the ML part of the SAML acronym.

Access Control Methodologies

Several methodologies can be used to assign permissions to users so that they can use network resources. These methods include mandatory access control (MAC), discretionary access control (DAC), and nondiscretionary access control (NDAC). NDAC consists of role-based access control (RBAC) and task-based access control (TBAC). RBAC, MAC, and DAC are compared in Table 11-3.

As systems become more complex and distributed, the policies, procedures, and technologies required to control access privileges, roles, and rights of users across a heterogeneous enterprise can be centralized in an identity and access management (IAM) system.

	Mandatory Access Control (MAC)	Discretionary Access Control (DAC)	Nondiscretionary Access Control (NDAC)	
			Role-Based Access Control (RBAC)	Task-Based Access Control (TBAC)
Permissions	System or application determines who has access	Permissions are granted to users	Permissions are granted to groups or roles	Permissions are granted based on a task
Additional Requirements	Resources must be labeled for granular control	None	None	Discrete tasks must be identified along with required access
Scope	Suited for larger organizations	Suited for smaller organizations	Suited for larger organizations	Suited for smaller organizations
Resource Access	User attributes can determine resource access	Uses the identity of a subject to determine resource access	Users are added to groups or roles to gain access to resources	Permissions are granted to tasks
Advantages	Requires the need to know in addition to clearance	Easy to implement	Flexible and scales well	Useful when the person needing access changes frequently but the task remains the same
Disadvantages	Complicated to implement and manage	Considered less secure than MAC and RBAC	May not fit the unique access needs of an individual	Access to tasks may require a separate authentication

Table 11-3   Comparison of Access Control Methods

Mandatory Access Control

The word *mandatory* is used to describe this access control model because permissions to resources are controlled or mandated by the operating system (OS) or application, which looks at the requesting party and their attributes to determine whether access should be granted. These decisions are based on configured policies that are enforced by the OS or application.

With mandatory access control (MAC), data is labeled or classified, so only those parties with specific attributes can access it. For example, perhaps only full-time employees can access a particular portion of an intranet web portal. Alternatively, perhaps only human resources employees can access files classified as confidential.

Discretionary Access Control

With the DAC methodology, the power to grant or deny user permissions to resources lies not with the OS or an application, but rather with the data owner. Protected resources might be files on a file server or items in a specific web application.

 TIP Most network environments use both DAC and RBAC; the data custodian can give permissions to the resource by adding a group to the ACL.

There are no security labels or classifications with DAC; instead, each protected resource has an ACL that determines access. For example, we might add user RayLee with read and write permissions to the ACL of a specific folder on a file server so that she can access that data.

Nondiscretionary Access Control

With the NDAC methodology, access control decisions are based on organizational rules and cannot be modified by (at the discretion of) nonprivileged users. NDAC scales well because access control rules are not resource-specific and can be applied across the board to new resources such as servers, computers, cloud services, and storage as those systems are provisioned.

NDAC has been implemented in the RBAC and TBAC methodologies. RBAC is by far the most popular, but both are discussed in this section. RBAC relies on group or role memberships to determine access, while TBAC relies on the task that is being performed to make access decisions.

Role-Based Access Control For many years, IT administrators, and now cloud administrators, have found it easier to manage permissions to resources by using groups or roles. This is the premise of RBAC. A group or role has one or more members and that group or role is assigned permissions to a resource.

Permissions are granted either implicitly or explicitly. Any user placed into that group or role inherits its permissions; this is known as implicit inheritance. Giving permissions to individual users is considered an explicit permission assignment. Explicit permission assignment does not scale as well in larger organizations as RBAC does. RBAC is implemented in different ways depending on where it is being performed. Solutions such as IAM can manage identity across an enterprise, including on-premises and cloud systems. However, these systems tie into locally defined groups to assign generalized IAM groups to the local groups. IAM can significantly improve the time it takes to provision or remove users or change their roles across an enterprise.

Sometimes, cloud vendors define the groups or roles in RBAC through an IAM solution such as AWS IAM. RBAC can also be applied at the operating system level, as in a Microsoft Windows Active Directory group. RBAC can be used at the application level, as in the case of Microsoft SharePoint Server roles. In the cloud, roles may be defined by the cloud provider if cloud consumers are not using provider IAM solutions.

To illustrate how cloud-based RBAC would be implemented using an IAM solution, consider the following commands. AWS IAM can be managed through the web GUI or via the CLI. These commands can be used in the AWS IAM CLI. This first command creates a group called managers:

```
aws iam create-group --group-name Managers
```

The following command assigns the administrator policy to the managers group. AWS IAM has policies that package together a set of permissions to perform tasks. The administrator policy provides full access to AWS.

```
aws iam attach-group-policy --group-name Managers --policy-arn
arn:aws:iam::aws:policy/AdministratorAccess
```

We can then create a user named EricVanderburg with the following command:

```
aws iam create-user --user-name EricVanderburg
```

Last, we add the user EricVanderburg to the managers group with this command:

```
aws iam add-user-to-group --username EricVanderburg --group-name Managers
```

Task-Based Access Control The TBAC methodology is a dynamic method of providing access to resources. It differs significantly from the other NDAC methodology, RBAC, in that it is not based on subjects and objects (users and resources).

TBAC was created around the concept of least privilege. In other models, a user might have the ability to access a reporting system, but they use that system only once a month. For the majority of each month, the user has more access than they require. In TBAC, users have no access to resources by default and are only provided access when they perform a task requiring it, and access is not retained after the task is complete.

TBAC systems provide access just as it is needed, and it is usually associated with workflows or transactions. TBAC can also be efficient because tasks and their required access can be defined when new processes are defined, and they are independent of who performs them or how many times they are performed.

Multifactor Authentication

Authentication means proving who (or what) you are. Authentication can be done with the standard username and password combination or with a variety of other methods.

Some environments use a combination of the five authentication mechanisms (listed next), known as multifactor authentication (MFA). Possessing a debit card, along with knowledge of the PIN, comprises multifactor authentication. Combining these authentication methods is considered much more secure than single-factor authentication.

These are the five categories of authentication that can be combined in multifactor authentication scenarios:

- **Something you know**   Knowing your username and password is by far the most common. Knowing your first pet's name or the PIN for your credit card or your mother's maiden name all fall into this category.

- **Something you have**   Most of us have used a debit or credit card to make a purchase. We must physically have the card in our possession. For VPN authentication, a user would be given a hardware token with a changing numeric code synced with the VPN server. For cloud authentication, users could employ a mobile device authenticator app with a changing numeric code in addition to their username and password.

- **Something you do**   This measures how an individual performs a routine task to validate their identity. Handwriting analysis can determine if the user writes their name the same way, or the user could be asked to count to 10, and the computer would determine if this is the way they normally count to 10 with the appropriate pauses and inflection points.

- **Someplace you are**   Geolocation is often used as an authentication method along with other methods. The organization may allow employees to access certain systems when they are in the workplace or facility but not from home. Traveling employees might be able to access some resources in the country but not when traveling internationally.

- **Something you are**   This is where biometric authentication kicks in. Your fingerprints, your voice, your facial structure, the capillary pattern in your retinas—these are unique to you. Of course, voice impersonators could reproduce your voice, so some methods are more secure than others.

 EXAM TIP   Knowing both a username and password is not considered multifactor authentication because they are both "something you know."

Chapter Review

This chapter focused on data security, network security, and access control, all of which are of interest to cloud personnel. Assessing the network is only effective when comparing your results with an established baseline of typical configuration and activity. Auditing a network is best done by a third party, and you may be required to use only accredited auditors that conform to industry standards such as NIST or ISO 27000 and compliance requirements like HIPAA, GDPR, or PCI. All computing equipment must be patched and hardened to minimize the potential for compromise.

An understanding of data security measures and access control methods is also important for the exam. Data security must be in place both for data as it traverses a network and for stored data. Encrypting data prevents unauthorized access to the data, while digital signatures verify the authenticity of the data. Various encryption protocols are used to accomplish these objectives. The various access control models discussed in this chapter include role-based access control, mandatory access control, and discretionary access control.

Questions

The following questions will help you gauge your understanding of the material in this chapter. Read all the answers carefully because there might be more than one correct answer. Choose the best response(s) for each question.

1. You are invited to join an IT meeting where the merits and pitfalls of cloud computing are being debated. Your manager conveys her concerns about data confidentiality for cloud storage. What can be done to secure data stored in the cloud?

   A. Encrypt the data.

   B. Digitally sign the data.

   C. Use a stream cipher.

   D. Change default passwords.

2. Which of the following works best to encrypt variable-length data?

   A. Block cipher

   B. Symmetric cipher

   C. Asymmetric cipher

   D. Stream cipher

3. With PKI, which key is used to validate a digital signature?

   A. Private key

   B. Public key

   C. Secret key

   D. Signing key

4. Which of the following is related to nonrepudiation?

   A. Block cipher

   B. PKI

   C. Symmetric encryption

   D. Stream cipher

5. Which service does a firewall use to segment traffic into different zones?

   A. DMZ

   B. ACL

   C. Port/service

   D. NAT/PAT

6. Which device would be used in front of a cloud application to prevent web application attacks such as cross-site scripting (XSS) and SQL injection?

   A. IAM

   B. DLP

   C. WAF

   D. IDS/IPS

7. Which best practice configures host computers so that they are not vulnerable to attack?

   A. Vulnerability assessment

   B. Penetration test

   C. Hardening

   D. PKI

8. Which device would be used to identify potentially malicious activity on a network?

   A. IAM

   B. DLP

   C. WAF

   D. IDS/IPS

9. Sean configures a web application to allow content managers to upload files to the website. What type of access control model is Sean using?

   A. DAC

   B. MAC

   C. RBAC

   D. GBAC

10. You are the administrator of a Windows network. When creating a new user account, you specify a security clearance level of top secret so that the user can access classified files. What type of access control method is being used?

    A. DAC

    B. MAC

    C. RBAC

    D. GBAC

11. John is architecting access control for a custom application. He would like to implement a nondiscretionary access control method that does not rely upon roles. Which method would meet John's criteria?

    A. RBAC

    B. MAC

    C. TBAC

    D. DAC

Answers

1. A. Encrypting data at rest protects the data from those not in possession of a decryption key.

2. D. Stream ciphers encrypt data, usually a bit at a time, so this works well for data that is not a fixed length.

3. B. The public key of the signer is used to validate a digital signature.

4. B. PKI is related to nonrepudiation, which means that a verified digital signature proves the message came from the listed party. This is true because only the private key of the signing party could have created the validated signature.

5. A. A demilitarized zone (DMZ) is a segment that has specific security rules on it. DMZs are created to segment traffic.

6. C. A web application firewall (WAF) is a specialized type of firewall that screens traffic intended for web applications. WAFs understand common web application attacks such as XSS and SQL injection and can inspect traffic at the application layer of the OSI model.

7. C. Hardening configures systems such that they are protected from compromise.

8. D. IDS/IPS technologies look at traffic to identify malicious traffic.

9. C. Sean is using a role (content managers) to control who can upload files to the website. This is role-based access control (RBAC).

10. B. Mandatory access control (MAC) uses attributes or labels (such as "top secret") that enable computer systems to determine who should have access to what.

11. C. Task-based access control uses tasks instead of roles to determine the level and extent of access.

CHAPTER 12

Security Best Practices

In this chapter, you will learn about
- Cloud security engineering
- Security governance and strategy
- Vulnerability management
- Incident response

Cloud services make it easier for companies to adopt software, systems, and services. However, it can be easy to implement a cloud system that functions well but secures very little. Some practical steps can be taken to better secure systems and data in the cloud.

Cloud security engineering includes important information on how to protect cloud systems. Cloud security engineering involves host and guest computer hardening and layering security to provide multiple overlapping controls that an attacker would need to break through to get to systems and data. Additionally, systems should be designed so that users and services have only the privileges they need to function, in what is known as least privilege. Cloud security engineers must also divide elements of tasks among multiple people to minimize the risk of corruption. Lastly, cloud security engineering seeks to automate security tasks.

Security governance is the set of activities and guidelines an organization uses to manage technologies, assets, and employees. Security governance ensures that the right activities are performed and that those activities accomplish the security goals of the organization. This is performed through security policies that set organizational expectations and procedures that define how tasks will be performed. Established industry standards and regulations can be used to craft the right mix of technologies and policies to meet regulatory requirements or established best practices.

Organizations also need to perform vulnerability scanning and penetration testing. These functions together form the basis for vulnerability management. Vulnerability management is the process of identifying possible vulnerabilities and enacting controls to mitigate those threats that are probable.

Cloud Security Engineering

Cloud security engineering is the practice of protecting the usability, reliability, integrity, and safety of cloud data and infrastructure and the users utilizing cloud systems. As it does in many other areas, security in cloud computing has similarities to traditional computing models. If deployed without evaluating security, cloud systems may deliver against their functional requirements, but they will likely have many gaps that could lead to a compromised system.

As part of any cloud deployment, attention needs to be paid to specific security requirements so that the resources that are supposed to have access to data and software in the cloud system are the only resources that can read, write, or change it. This section provides coverage of the following practices and principles employed in cloud security engineering:

- Implementing layered security
- Protecting against availability attacks
- Least privilege
- Separation of duties
- Security automation

Implementing Layered Security

To protect network resources from threats, secure network design employs multiple overlapping controls to prevent unwanted access to protected cloud resources. Some layered security components include demilitarized zones, ACLs, and intrusion detection and prevention systems.

A demilitarized zone (DMZ) is a separate network that is layered in between an internal network and an external network to house resources that need to be accessed by both while preventing direct access from the outside network to the inside network. ACLs define the traffic that is allowed to traverse a network segment. Lastly, intrusion detection systems can detect anomalous network behavior and send alerts to system administrators to take action, while intrusion prevention systems can detect anomalies and take specific actions to remediate threats.

The real strength of demilitarized zones, ACLs, and intrusion detection and prevention systems (covered in Chapter 11) is that they can all be used together, creating a layered security system for the greatest possible security.

Consider an attacker trying to get to a cloud database. The attacker would need to first get through the firewall. A DMZ, along with appropriately configured ACLs, between networks would require the attacker to compromise a machine in the DMZ and then pivot from that machine to another machine in the internal network. However, networks with an IDS/IPS might detect this activity, notify administrators, and block the attacker from making the connection. In this way, these technologies work together to provide a layered solution to protect the cloud database.

Protecting Against Availability Attacks

Attacks on availability are those designed to take a system down so that users, such as customers or employees, cannot use it. Some availability attacks are used to cause a system to restart so that weaknesses in the system's startup routines can be exploited to inject code, start in a maintenance mode and reset passwords, or take other malicious actions.

Distributed Denial of Service

A distributed denial of service (DDoS) attack targets a single system simultaneously from multiple compromised systems. DDoS was introduced in Chapter 11 under the discussion on firewalls and cloud access security brokers (CASBs), but there are other protections against DDoS.

DDoS attacks are distributed because they use thousands or millions of machines that could be spread worldwide. Such an attack denies services or disrupts availability by overwhelming the system so that it cannot respond to legitimate connection requests. The distributed nature of these attacks makes it difficult for administrators to block malicious traffic based on its origination point and to distinguish approved traffic from attacking traffic. DDoS can quickly overwhelm network resources. However, large cloud systems can offer protection to cloud consumers.

Cloud DDoS protection solutions, such as those from Amazon, Microsoft, Verisign, or Cloudflare, not only protect cloud consumers from attack and loss of availability of resources but also protect against excessive usage charges, since many cloud providers charge for how much data is sent and received. Cloud providers offering services such as CASB, also introduced in Chapter 11, can screen out some traffic. They also have the bandwidth to soak up most DDoS traffic without becoming overwhelmed. There have been some high-profile DDoS attacks that caused a disruption, such as those committed with the Internet of Things (IoT) devices that took down large clouds. However, most DDoS attacks cannot commit resources at that scale.

Ping of Death

Ping of death (PoD) attacks send malformed ICMP packets with the intent of crashing systems that cannot process them and consequently shut down. Most modern cloud firewall packages, such as AWS Shield, DigitalOcean, and Zscaler, can actively detect these packets and discard them before they cause damage.

Ping Flood Attacks

Ping flood attacks are similar to DDoS attacks in that they attempt to overwhelm a system with more traffic than it can handle. In this variety, the attack is usually attempted by a single system, making the attack easier to identify and block. Defense strategies for ping floods are the same as those for DDoS, including cloud DDoS protection.

Least Privilege

Another essential security concept is the principle of least privilege. Employees should be granted only the minimum permissions necessary to do their job. No more, no less. Incorporating the principle of least privilege limits the potential misuse and risk of accidental mishandling or viewing of sensitive information by unauthorized people.

Separation of Duties

Separation of duties, also known as segregation of duties, divides the responsibilities required to perform a sensitive task among two or more people so that one person, acting alone, cannot compromise the system. The separation of duties needs to be carefully planned and implemented. If implemented correctly, it can act as an internal control to help reduce potential damage caused by the actions of a single administrator.

By limiting permissions and influence over key parts of the cloud environment, no one individual can knowingly or unknowingly exercise complete power over the system. For example, in an e-commerce organization with multiple layers of security comprised in a series of cloud solutions, separation of duties would ensure that a single person would not be responsible for every layer of that security, such as provisioning accounts, implementing ACLs, and configuring logging and alerting for the various cloud services and their integrations. Therefore, if that person were to become disgruntled, they would not have the ability to compromise the entire system or the data it contains; they would only have the ability to access their layer of the security model.

 EXAM TIP Separation of duties is the process of segregating tasks among two or more people. It prevents fraud because one person cannot compromise a system without colluding with others. Separation of duties is also called segregation of duties.

Security Automation

The last part of cloud security engineering is to automate security tasks. Security tasks must be performed at regular intervals, and they must be performed correctly each time. Additionally, it can be quite a job to secure many systems, and organizational security departments are supporting more systems and cloud services than ever before.

Security automation helps in both these areas. Automation ensures that tasks are performed the same way every time and performed precisely on schedule. Furthermore, automation frees up valuable security resources so that they can focus on other tasks. Automation uses scripting, scheduled tasks, and automation tools to perform routine tasks so that IT staff can spend more time solving real problems and proactively looking for ways to make things better and even more efficient.

This section discusses different security activities that can be automated to save time and standardize. They include the following:

- Disabling inactive accounts
- Eliminating outdated firewall rules
- Cleaning up outdated security settings
- Maintaining ACLs for target objects

Disabling Inactive Accounts

You can automate the disabling of inactive accounts. Use this quite sparingly because disabling an account will mean that the user cannot log in anymore. Choose to disable rather than remove an account because once you remove an account, creating it again is somewhat tricky. If you create another account with the same name, it will still have a different security identifier and will not really be the same account. That is why it is best to disable accounts first, and then at some later point, you can remove the account. Disabling it is also important if you need to take action on that account in the future, such as decrypting EFS encrypted files, viewing profile settings, or logging onto that person's e-mail. These are things that might need to be done for a terminated employee if that employee is under investigation; if the account were deleted, they would still be possible, but a bit more complicated.

The following PowerShell command disables all accounts that have not been logged into for over 30 days. Of course, if you were in Europe, some people take a holiday for longer than 30 days, but you can always enable the account when they return.

```
Search-ADAccount -AccountInactive -TimeSpan ([timespan]30d) -UsersOnly | Set-
ADUser -Enabled $false
```

Eliminating Outdated Firewall Rules

It is possible through the course of adding and removing programs or changing server roles that the Windows Firewall rules for a VM could become out of date. It can be challenging to automate the analysis of the rules and remove outdated rules, so the best course of action is to remove all rules and reassign rules based on the current roles.

As mentioned many times in this book, it is imperative to document. Document the firewall rules that you put in place for VMs and organize the rules by role. For example, you would have one set of standard rules for database servers, web servers, file servers, domain controllers, certificate servers, VPN servers, FTP servers, DHCP servers, and a separate role for each type of application server.

Each of the firewall rules for a defined role can be scripted. Here is an example configuration for a VM with the database role running Microsoft SQL Server 2016 with Analysis Services. This script allows remote management and communication over SQL Server ports. The last commands turn the firewall on, just in case it is not already on.

```
New-NetFirewallRule -DisplayName "SQL Database Management" -Direction Inbound -
Protocol UDP -LocalPort 1434 -Action allow
New-NetFirewallRule -DisplayName "SQL Server" -Direction Inbound -Protocol TCP -
LocalPort 1433 -Action allow
New-NetFirewallRule -DisplayName "SQL Service Broker" -Direction Inbound -Protocol
TCP -LocalPort 4022 -Action allow
New-NetFirewallRule -DisplayName "SQL Debugger/RPC" -Direction Inbound -Protocol
TCP -LocalPort 135 -Action allow
New-NetFirewallRule -DisplayName "SQL Analysis Services" -Direction Inbound -
Protocol TCP -LocalPort 2383 -Action allow
New-NetFirewallRule -DisplayName "SQL Browser" -Direction Inbound -Protocol TCP -
LocalPort 2382 -Action allow
New-NetFirewallRule -DisplayName "SQL Admin Connection" -Direction Inbound -
Protocol TCP -LocalPort 1434 -Action allow
New-NetFirewallRule -DisplayName "SQL Server Browse Button Service" -Direction
Inbound -Protocol UDP -LocalPort 1433 -Action allow
Set-NetFirewallProfile -DefaultInboundAction Block -DefaultOutboundAction Allow
-NotifyOnListen True -AllowUnicastResponseToMulticast True
```

Now, with the role descriptions and the scripts in hand, you can clear the configurations from a set of servers whose rules you believe are outdated, and then you can reapply the company standard firewall rules for that role. Here is the command to clear the rules from the server. Essentially, this command resets the Windows Firewall to its default out-of-the-box settings.

```
netsh advfirewall reset
```

Please note that the firewall configuration formerly used just the `netsh` command, but this command was deprecated. The new command is `netsh advfirewall`.

Firewalls are covered in more detail in the "Network Security" section of Chapter 11.

Cleaning Up Outdated Security Settings

VMware vSphere can be made much more secure by turning off some features for VMs. The first feature to disable is host guest file system (HGFS) file transfers. HGFS transfers files into the operating system of the VM directly from the host, and a hacker or malware could potentially misuse this feature to download malware onto a guest or to exfiltrate data from the guest. Script these commands for each VM:

```
keyword = isolation.tools.hgfsServerSet.disable
keyval = TRUE
```

The next feature to disable is the ability to copy and paste data between the remote console and the VM. This is disabled by default, but if someone turned it on, you could disable it again. Enabling copy and paste can allow for sensitive content to accidentally be placed on another machine. Script these commands for each VM:

```
keyword = isolation.tools.copy.disable
keyval = TRUE
keyword = isolation.tools.paste.disable
keyval = TRUE
keyword = isolation.tools.setGUIOptions.enable
keyval = FALSE
Limiting Exposure of Sensitive Data Copied to the Clipboard
keyword = isolation.tool.copy.disable
keyval = TRUE
keyword = isolation.tool.paste.disable
keyval = TRUE
```

The third item to disable is the ability for a user to disconnect VMware devices from the VM. When this is turned on, administrative users on the VM can run commands to disconnect devices such as network adapters, hard disk drives, and optical drives. Script these commands for each VM:

```
keyword = isolation.device.connectable.disable
keyval = TRUE
keyword = isolation.device.edit.disable
keyval = TRUE
```

The fourth item to disable is the ability of processes running in the VM to send configuration messages to the hypervisor. Processes on the VM that modify configuration settings can potentially damage the VM or cause it to be unstable. Script these commands for each VM:

```
keyword = isolation.tools.setinfo.disable
keyval = TRUE
```

Maintaining ACLs for Target Objects

You can script setting access control lists for objects by using the `cacls` command. ACL scripting can be useful if you want to change permissions for many files and folders. Here is the command to give a group called DevOps full control to the D:\ drive and all subfolders:

```
CACLS D:\ /E /T /C /G "DevOps":F
```

Security Governance and Strategy

Attackers keep coming up with innovative attacks, so the line for security best practices continues to move. A variety of government agencies and standards bodies publish security best practices and standards, such as the ISO/IEC 27001 or NIST SP 800-53. These can give an organization some guidance on security governance practices and valuable security strategies. Still, each organization needs to determine for itself what is appropriate for its security based on its specific operations.

Implementing a practice just because it is listed in a standard might improve security, but it might not improve it as much as something else. Budgets are tight, so it is crucial to choose the security controls that will give your organization the best protection for your budget. This section covers best practices for governance and strategy. This text has organized these best practices into the following sections:

- Developing company security policies
- Account management policies
- Documenting security procedures
- Assessment and auditing
- Leveraging established industry standards and regulations
- Applying platform-specific security standards
- Data classification
- Keeping employees and tools up to date
- Roles and responsibilities

Developing Company Security Policies

Security policies set the organizational expectations for certain functional security areas. Policies should be defined based on what the organization is committed to doing, not on what it might do. Once a policy is put in place, others will expect the company to adhere to it. Policies usually come with sanctions for those who do not follow the policy, such as oral or written warnings, coaching, suspensions from work, or termination.

Security policies often use the terms personally identifiable information (PII) and protected health information (PHI). PII is information that represents the identity of a person, such as name, phone number, address, e-mail address, Social Security number, and date of birth. PHI is similar to PII in the context of patient identity but is used in HIPAA compliance and other similar areas. The term PII is common in security policies of many types of organizations, whereas PHI is common in the security policies of healthcare organizations. Both terms are used in security policies to designate information that must not be disclosed to anyone who is not authorized to access it.

Some common security policies include the following:

- **Acceptable use policy**   States how organizational assets are to be used. This policy covers the use of corporate equipment such as computers, laptops, phones, and office equipment. More importantly, it covers which cloud and other Internet services employees can use, acceptable norms for e-mail, and use of social networking.

- **Audit policy**   Specifies how often audits occur, the differences between internal and external audits, who should handle audits, how they are reported on, and the level of access granted to auditors. Both internal and external audits would cover internal systems and cloud systems used by the company. The audit policy also covers how audit findings and exceptions are to be handled.

- **Backup policy**   Covers how the organization will back up the data that it has. This includes both data on-premise and in the cloud. The backup policy usually includes who is responsible for backing up data, how often backups will take place, the data types that will be backed up, and the recovery time objective (RTO) and recovery point objective (RPO) for each data type.

- **BYOD policy**   Specifies how employee-owned devices are to be used within the company and how they can be used if they access company cloud services and data.

- **Cloud services policy**   Defines which cloud services are acceptable for organizational use, how cloud services are evaluated, who is authorized to purchase cloud services, and how employees suggest or recommend cloud services to the review committee.

- **Data destruction policy**   Outlines how the organization will handle the disposal of equipment that houses data, such as computers, servers, and hard drives. It should specify how that data will be wiped or destroyed, what evidence will be retained on the disposal or destruction, and who is authorized to dispose of assets. This includes not only digital data but physical documents as well, so these documents must be shredded when the policy requires it.

- **Data retention policy**   Specifies how long data of various types will be kept on organizational systems or cloud systems the organization utilizes. For example, the data retention policy may specify that e-mail on Office 365 will be retained for two years, financial documents on SAP S/4HANA will be kept for seven years, and other data will be retained for one year.

- **Encryption policy**   Specifies what should be encrypted in the organization and in cloud systems used by the organization, how encryption systems are evaluated, which cryptographic algorithms are acceptable, how cryptographic keys are managed, and how keys are disposed of.

- **Mobile device policy**   Specifies which types of mobile devices can be used for organizational purposes, which person or role authorizes mobile devices, how those devices are to be protected, where they can be used, which cloud services can be accessed by mobile devices, how they are encrypted, and how organizational data will be removed from mobile devices when they are retired or when employees leave.

- **Privacy policy**   Includes what information the organization considers private; how the organization will handle that information; the purposes and uses of that information; and how that information will be collected, destroyed, or returned.

- **Remote access policy**   Specifies which types of remote access are acceptable, how remote access will take place, how employees are authorized for remote access, auditing of remote access, and how remote access is revoked.

There are hundreds of other policies that can be defined for more granular things. However, the best practice is to keep the number of policies to the minimum necessary so that employees can easily find the organization's expectations regarding a particular subject.

Some organizations choose to bundle policies together into a handbook or a comprehensive security policy. Compliance requirements may specify which policies an organization needs to have and the minimum standards for those policies. Be aware of which compliance requirements your organization falls under so that you can make sure your policies are in accordance with those requirements.

Account Management Policies

Account management policies establish expectations on how accounts and their associated credentials will be managed. Some simpler policies will be called a password policy. These policies deal only with the password elements of the account management policy and are often used when granularity on password requirements is needed.

 EXAM TIP   Account management policies and password policies should apply to organizational systems and cloud systems that house organizational data.

Account management policies stipulate how long passwords need to be and how often they should be changed. They also specify who should be issued an account and how accounts are issued to users. This includes which approvals are necessary for provisioning an account. There may be rare cases where a password can be shared, and account management policies will specify these circumstances, if any. These policies also establish requirements for how and when temporary passwords are issued and the process for how and when passwords can be reset.

Two other sections in the account management policy require a bit more attention. They include the lockout policy and password complexity rules. These are covered next in their own sections.

Lockout Policy

A lockout is the automatic disabling of an account due to some potentially malicious action. The most common reason for a lockout is too many incorrect password attempts. Lockout policy can be specified on a per-resource basis or a per-domain basis. When single sign-on (SSO) is used, a single lockout policy also applies.

When a user's password is entered incorrectly too often, either by the user or by an unauthorized person, the system will disable the user's account for a predefined period. In some cases, the account is disabled until an administrator unlocks it. Another system can be configured to lock out the account for a set amount of time that increases each time the account is subsequently locked out until a point when an administrator is required to unlock the account again.

You may wish to notify on account lockouts. For example, suppose you have a cloud-based application. In that case, you may want to send users an e-mail when they enter their password incorrectly too many times. This way, if someone else tries to log on as the user, the authorized user will become aware of the attempt and report that it was not authorized. Systems can be configured to automatically notify users when their account is locked out. Otherwise, users will find out their account is locked out when they are unable to log in.

Password Complexity Rules

Stealing or cracking passwords is one of the most common ways that attackers infiltrate a network and break into systems. People generally choose weak passwords because passwords are hard to remember. Most people try to create a password using information that is easy for them to remember, and the easiest thing to remember is something you already know, such as your address, phone number, children's names, or workplace. But this is also information that can be learned about you easily, so it is a poor choice for a password.

Password complexity has to do with how hard a password would be to break with brute force techniques, where the attacker tries all possible combinations of a password until they get the right one. If you look at just numbers, there are four combinations in a two-character password, while there are eight combinations in a three-character password.

Numbers alone are the easiest to break because there are only ten combinations for each digit (0–9). When you add letters into the mix, this creates more possibilities for the brute force attack to factor in. Special characters such as @#$%^&*&() expand that scope even further. The best passwords are ones that you can remember. However, they should be unrelated to anything someone would be able to figure out about you and to any security questions you may have answered. Passwords should contain a mix of numbers, uppercase and lowercase letters, and special characters.

For those with multiple-language keyboards and application support, a password that combines multiple character systems such as Chinese or Russian can make it even harder to crack.

Security practitioners have for decades tried to find a balance between password complexity and usability. On the one hand, stronger passwords are harder to guess and more difficult to brute force crack. However, these more complex passwords are harder to remember. This can lead users to circumvent best practices by writing passwords down.

Similarly, frequent change intervals can cause users to construct passwords that follow specific patterns such as Fire$ale4Dec in December, Fire$ale4Jan in January, and so forth. Since users have so many passwords to remember, some use the same password in many places and change them all at the same time. However, when a data breach occurs in one location, the usernames and passwords are often put in a database that attackers use to determine other likely passwords. In this example, the attacker might breach the database at the end of December, but then the user changes their passwords. An attacker reviewing the database in April would likely try Fire$ale4Apr and gain access to the system if the user continued with their pattern.

NIST has recognized these weaknesses in their special publication 800-63B. Here are some of the new guidelines. First, increase the maximum password length to at least 64 characters. Along with this, NIST recommends that password fields allow spaces and other printable characters in passwords. These two changes allow users to create longer but more natural passwords.

NIST has also relaxed some of the complexity rules and recommends that companies require just one uppercase, number, or symbol—not all three—and that passwords be kept longer with less frequent change intervals.

NIST also adds some requirements. They recommend that two-factor authentication be used, and they exclude SMS as a valid two-factor authentication method because of the ability for others to potentially obtain the unencrypted SMS authentication data. They also require that passwords be measured for how common and easy to guess they are. Authentication systems should restrict users from creating passwords that contain simple dictionary words, common phrases, or easily guessed information.

Documenting Security Procedures

Security policies specify the company's expectations and provide general guidelines for what to do, but they do not get into the specifics. This is where security procedures step in. Security procedures outline the individual steps required to complete a task. Furthermore, security procedures ensure that those who follow the procedures will do the following:

- Perform the task consistently.
- Take a predictable amount of time to perform the task.
- Require the same resources each time the task is performed.

Assessment and Auditing

A network assessment is an objective review of an organization's network infrastructure regarding current functionality and security capabilities. The environment is evaluated holistically against industry best practices and its ability to meet the organization's requirements. Once all the assessment information has been documented, it is stored as a baseline for future audits to be performed against.

Complete audits must be scheduled regularly to make certain that the configurations of all network resources are not changed to increase the risk to the environment or the organization.

Internal Audits

Internal audit teams validate that security controls are implemented correctly and that security systems are functioning as expected. Companies operate today in an environment of rapid change, and this increased frequency of change can result in an increase in mistakes leading to security issues. Internal audits can help catch these issues before they are exploited.

For example, the technologies enable administrators to move VMs between hosts with no downtime and minimal administrative effort. Because of this, some cloud environments have become extremely volatile. A side effect of that volatility is that the security posture of a guest on one cloud may not be retained when it has been migrated to a different yet compatible cloud. The audit team would have a specification of what the security posture should look like, and they would use that to determine if the machine met the requirements after being moved to the new cloud.

A change management system can help identify changes in an environment, but initial baseline assessments and subsequent periodic audits are still necessary. Such evaluations make it possible for administrators to correlate performance logs on affected systems with change logs, so they can identify configuration errors that may be causing problems. Change management will be covered in more detail in Chapter 14.

Utilizing Third-Party Audits

When assessing or auditing a network, it is best practice to use a third-party product or service provider. Using external resources is preferable to using internal resources. The latter often have both preconceived biases and preexisting knowledge about the network and security configuration.

Familiarity with the environment can produce unsuccessful audits because the internal resources already have an assumption about the systems they are evaluating. Those assumptions result in either incomplete or incorrect information. A set of eyes from an outside source not only eliminates the familiar as a potential hurdle but also allows for a different (and in many cases, broader or more experienced) set of skills to be utilized in the evaluation.

The results of an unbiased third-party audit are more likely to hold up under scrutiny. Many regulations and standards stipulate third-party audits.

Risk Register

A risk register is a document that tracks the risks that have been identified along with their likelihood. Some companies use risk management tools to maintain the risk register, but you can track risks in a spreadsheet too. A risk register contains the list of risks, a description of the risk, the impact the risk would have on the business if actualized, and the likelihood of the risk. The risk register might also prioritize the risks and assign a risk owner.

Figure 12-1
Computing
the risk value

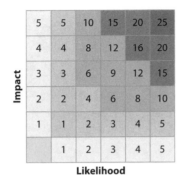

Risks are given a risk value. This value is a combination of the likelihood and impact, where risk = likelihood * impact. To make things simple, risk managers assign a number value to each and then multiply them together to get the risk value. These values can then be assigned a priority of low, medium, high, or critical.

Figure 12-1 shows a risk heat map. A risk heat map is a visualization of a risk's impact and likelihood values. The colors indicate which risks would be low, medium, high, or critical, based on the multiplication of the two rankings. In the diagram, green is low, yellow is medium, orange is high, and red is critical.

As risks are analyzed by business owners, they will make a determination on how to handle the risk. Some risks are too unlikely or have very little impact and the company may choose to accept them. Others might require action to remediate the risk. Still other risks can be transferred by purchasing insurance or utilizing a cloud service to perform the function that pertains to the risk. The last option is to avoid the risk by ceasing the function that produces the risk.

Risk registers may document mitigating controls that reduce the risk. If mitigating controls are mentioned, the register will then show what the residual risk is after the mitigating control is factored in. A sample risk register is shown in Tables 12-1 and 12-2.

Leveraging Established Industry Standards and Regulations

As cloud computing has become ubiquitous, various standards for best practice deployments of cloud computing infrastructures have been developed. Standards have been established to improve the quality of IT organizations. Some examples of standards include the Information Technology Infrastructure Library (ITIL) and the Microsoft Operations Framework (MOF).

Regulations specify security requirements for business systems and clouds. Noncompliance with regulations can lead to fines or the inability to do business in that industry or in the current capacity. Some regulations include the Payment Card Industry Data Security Standard (PCI DSS), the Sarbanes-Oxley Act (SOX), and the Health Insurance Portability and Accountability Act (HIPAA). Regulatory compliance is more expensive for IT organizations than adhering to a set of standards or best practices. Regulatory compliance requires not only for the organization to build solutions according to the regulatory requirements but also to demonstrate compliance to auditors. The tools and labor required to generate the necessary proof can be costly.

ID	Risk	Category	Mitigating Controls	Risk Owner
IR-01	Security incident occurs, and the security incident response plan is inadequate.	Incident Response	The company conducts analysis of incident-response processes to ensure adequate response and support-recovery activities.	Bob Jones
DR-01	Business continuity failure	Disaster Recovery	The company manages and tests its information security plans including incident response, business continuity, and disaster recovery.	Tina Smith
GV-03	The data classification policy is violated.	Governance	The company trains on its data classification policy and enforces policy sanctions.	George Larose
GV-05	Client data exposed if left on employee desks, printers, copiers, etc.	Governance	The company has a Clean Desk Policy requiring employees to secure client and firm data.	George Larose
GV-07	Inadequate cybersecurity insurance that does not cover a loss.	Governance	The company maintains a cybersecurity insurance policy that is regularly reviewed to maintain adequacy.	George Larose
VM-01	Vulnerabilities exploited by bad actors to gain access to its network.	Vulnerability Management	The company conducts quarterly vulnerability scans and annual penetration testing.	Craig Barton
BK-01	Data loss (back up data)	Backup	A robust backup schedule is in place for all resources. This is tested quarterly and upon changes to backup operations.	Tina Smith
TC-01	Malware/Virus	Technical Controls	Anti-virus software is installed on all company owned computers.	Henry Mills
PD-02	Unauthorized corporate wireless access	Perimeter Defense	Access to the Corporate wireless network is approved by the IT Committee, and only on an as-needed basis for a limited number of employees.	Bob Jones

Table 12-1   Risk Register Risk Documentation

ID	Risk	Residual Risk	Likelihood	Impact	Risk Value	Risk Rating	Management Decision
IR-01	Security incident occurs, and the security incident response plan is inadequate.	Incident response plan does not adequately address how to respond to an incident.	4	3	12	Medium	Mitigate
DR-01	Business continuity failure	The Company has not fully identified all possible disaster scenarios, and is unprepared to handle it appropriately.	4	4	16	High	Mitigate
GV-03	The data classification policy is violated.	Data classified incorrectly by an employee and thus is not handled or secured appropriately.	2	5	10	Medium	Mitigate
GV-05	Client data exposed if left on employee desks, printers, copiers, etc.	Employees do not secure sensitive and confidential documents.	3	4	12	Medium	Mitigate
GV-07	Inadequate cybersecurity insurance that does not cover a loss.	Insurance coverage is inadequate for a given security incident.	4	4	16	High	Insurance
VM-01	Vulnerabilities exploited by bad actors to gain access to its network.	Vulnerabilities exploited between patch cycles and scans.	4	4	16	High	Mitigate
BK-01	Data loss (back-up data)	Bad data is introduced into backups and persists throughout the entire rotation.	5	4	20	High	Mitigate
TC-01	Malware/Virus	Virus software has not been updated, so new viruses are not detected and removed.	3	5	15	High	Mitigate
PD-02	Unauthorized corporate wireless access	Little to none	2	2	4	Low	Accept

Table 12-2   Risk Register Showing Risk Ratings and Management Decisions

In addition to adopting published best practices, organizations can implement one of the many tools available to raise alerts when a deviation from these compliance frameworks is identified.

Applying Platform-Specific Security Standards

Many vendors have released their own security standards or device configuration guides. It is a good idea to follow the recommendations from these vendors. After all, Cisco created Cisco switches, so who better to recommend how to configure them? Seek out the configuration guides for the equipment you have and audit your device against those security guidelines.

Some vendors release multiple guidelines that are customized for different needs. For example, you may want to harden web application servers, so you look to your web hosting provider for guidance. However, they might offer different guidelines on configuring the server for HIPAA, PCI DSS, NIST, or their general security best practice or hardening guide. Which one you choose depends on which compliance areas you need to adhere to.

Data Classification

Data classification is the practice of sorting data into discrete categories that help define the access levels and type of protection required for that data set. These categories are then used to determine the disaster recovery mechanisms, cloud technologies needed to store the data, and the placement of that data onto physically or logically separated storage resources.

Data classification can be divided into four steps that can be performed by teams within an organization. The first step is to identify the present data within the organization. Next, the data should be grouped into areas with similar sensitivity and availability needs. The third step is to define classifications for each unique sensitivity and availability requirement. The last step is to determine how the data will be handled in each category.

Here are some of the different types of data that an organization would classify into categories such as public, trade secret, work product, financial data, customer data, strategic information, and employee data:

- Account ledgers
- Application development code
- Bank statements
- Change control documentation
- Client or customer deliverables
- Company brochures
- Contracts and SLAs
- Customer data
- HR records

- Network schematics
- Payroll
- Press releases
- Process documentation
- Project plans
- Templates
- Website content

Tagging

Tagging is a process of adding relevant metadata to files so that they can be tracked for compliance. Documents are often tagged so that policies can be applied to the data. For example, under the CMMC and NIST SP800-171, controlled unclassified information (CUI) must be tagged so that systems know it is CUI and can apply appropriate protections.

Of course, when creating policies for tagged data, the first step would be to establish a policy that prevents tags from being removed from the data. Otherwise, users can simply get around the policy by removing a tag and then doing whatever they want.

Legal Holds

Legal holds, also known as litigation holds, are orders to preserve electronically stored information (ESI) from deletion or change when the company has a reasonable expectation that those documents may be relevant to litigation. The company legal team will typically notify IT with the particulars on which documents, e-mails, or other information should be held.

It is important that the team quickly place the legal hold on the information. The company could be guilty of spoliation if the information is not preserved and the court determines that data relevant to the litigation was deleted or modified.

Tools are available from cloud providers that will preserve the data at the point when the legal hold is created on the ESI. Employees can continue working with the data as they usually would, changing or deleting files, but the system will still preserve the original data behind the scenes. Let's take a look at the process for creating a legal hold in Office 365.

Exercise 12-1: Creating a Legal Hold for a Mailbox in Office 365

In this exercise, we will create a legal hold for a mailbox in Office 365.

1. Log into your Office 365 portal.
2. Select admin at the bottom of the apps list on the left.
3. Expand the eDiscovery section and select eDiscovery. The screen will now show the cases you have defined.

4. Select the Create A Case button to start the eDiscovery wizard.

5. The first step is to give the case a name. For this example, we are calling the case CloudTest. The description is optional, so we are leaving it blank here.

6. Click Save to continue, and the new case will appear in the eDiscovery screen.

7. Click Open next to the CloudTest case.

8. Click the Holds tab.

9. On the Holds page, click the Create button.

10. Give the hold a name. In this example, we call it CloudTest Hold.

11. Click the Next button to move to the next step in the wizard. This next screen allows you to select the ESI that will be part of the legal hold.

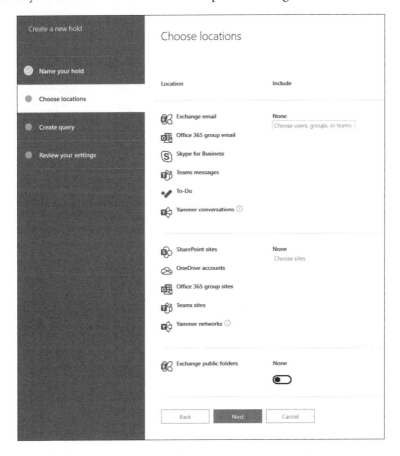

In this example, we are going to choose a user account. Your environment will be different from this example because you will not have the same user accounts. I will choose the Eric Vanderburg account for this example.

12. Click Choose Users, Groups, Or Teams, and a new window will appear.

13. Click Choose Users, Groups, Or Teams under Exchange e-mail in the new window.

14. Type the first few letters of the username until you see the account appear in the lower half of the screen where it says "users, groups, or teams."

15. Select the user account by checking the box next to it, and then click the Choose button at the bottom.

16. This takes you back to the previous screen, but now you should see the e-mail account you selected in step 15. Click the Done button.

17. You will now see the wizard's Choose Locations page, but it will show one user selected. Click the Next button to proceed to the Query page of the wizard.

18. On this page, you can establish keywords. Each e-mail that contains those keywords will be preserved as part of the legal hold. Enter these three keywords (note that each word is separated by a comma): **Cloud,server,infrastructure**

19. Click Next. This screen shows the options we selected. Click Create This Hold.

20. The legal hold will now appear in the Holds tab.

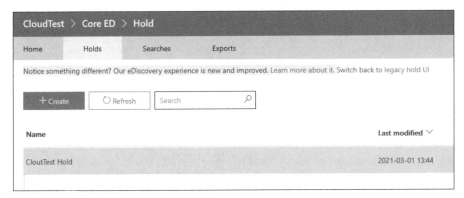

21. Wait a minute for statistics to be gathered and then click the hold to display its statistics in a window that will open on the right. In this example, we see the mailbox we enabled the hold on has 2,003 items. If you do not see the statistics, click the update statistics button.

Keeping Employees and Tools Up to Date

The rapidly evolving landscape of cloud technologies and virtualization presents dangers for cloud security departments that do not stay abreast of changes to both their toolsets and their training. Companies can use new virtualization technologies and tools to more rapidly deploy new software, leading to an acceleration of software development activities in fast-forward-type deployments, known as rapid deployment. See Chapter 9 for more details.

One hazard of rapid deployment is the propensity to either ignore security or proceed with the idea that the organization will enable the system's functionality immediately, then circle back and improve the security once it is in place. Typically, however, new functionality requests continue to take precedence, and security is rarely or inadequately revisited.

Many networks were initially designed to utilize traditional network security devices that monitor traffic and devices on a physical network. Suppose the intra–virtual machine traffic that those tools are watching for never routes through a physical network. In that case, it cannot be monitored by that traditional toolset. The problem with limiting network traffic to guests within the host is that if the tools are not virtualization or cloud-aware, they will not provide the proper information to make a diagnosis or suggest changes to the infrastructure. Therefore, monitoring and management toolsets (including cloud-based CLIs) must be updated as frequently as the technology that they are designed to control.

Roles and Responsibilities

Security is a complex discipline and involves securing a variety of components, including applications, storage, network connectivity, and server configuration. There are many various security functions, security controls, and security technologies, so it is unlikely that a single person will able to handle all of the company's security needs. It is also important to evaluate methods for implementing separation of duties, introduced earlier in this chapter, by splitting the responsibilities of those managing security procedures among various people.

There are some benefits to having a different person in charge of each facet of the cloud security environment. Having other people running additional configuration tests creates a system of checks and balances since not just one person has ultimate control. For example, a programmer would be responsible for verifying all of the code within their application and for making sure there are no security risks in the code itself, but the programmer would not be responsible for the web server or database server that is hosting or supporting the application. The person testing code security should be different from the person who wrote the code. Likewise, the person testing cloud service integration security should not be the person who configured it.

Vulnerability Management

In addition to comprehensive testing of all areas affecting service and performance, it is incumbent on an organization to test for vulnerabilities as well. Security testing in the cloud is a critical part of having an optimal cloud environment. It is similar to security testing in a traditional environment in that testing involves components like login security and the security layer in general.

Before doing any security tests, testers should always clearly define the scope, present it to the system owner, and get written permission to proceed. The contract in place with the cloud provider should then be reviewed to determine testing notification requirements. Inform the cloud provider of any planned security penetration testing before actually performing it unless the contract specifies otherwise.

Another thing for an organization to consider is that with a public cloud model, the organization does not own the infrastructure; therefore, the environment the resources are hosted in may not be very familiar. For example, if you have an application hosted in a public cloud environment, that application might make some application programming interface (API) calls back into your data center via a firewall, or the application might be entirely hosted outside of your firewall.

A primary security concern when using a cloud model is who has access to the organization's data in the cloud and what are the concerns and consequences if that data is lost or stolen. Being able to monitor and test access to that data is a primary responsibility of the cloud administrator and should be taken seriously, as a hosted account may not have all the proper security implemented. For example, a hosted resource might be running an older version of system software with known security issues, so keeping up with the security for the hosted resource and the products running on those resources is vital.

Security testing should be performed regularly to ensure consistent and timely cloud and network vulnerability management. Periodic security testing will reveal newly discovered vulnerabilities and recent configuration issues, enabling administrators to remediate them before (hopefully) attackers have an opportunity to exploit them.

Common testing scenarios include quarterly penetration testing with monthly vulnerability scanning or annual penetration testing with quarterly or monthly vulnerability scanning. It is absolutely necessary to run tests at intervals specified by compliance requirements. Testing should also be conducted whenever the organization undergoes significant changes.

Cloud vendors typically require notification before penetration testing is conducted on their networks. Microsoft Azure recently announced that it no longer needs such notification. Check with your cloud vendor before conducting vulnerability scanning or penetration testing to be sure you have permission.

In this section, you will learn about the following vulnerability management concepts:

- Black-box, gray-box, and white-box testing
- Vulnerability scanning
- Penetration testing
- Vulnerability management roles and responsibilities

Testing Methods

The three basic security testing types in a cloud environment are black-box, gray-box, and white-box testing. They differ based on the amount of information the tester has about the targets before starting the test and how much they cost. Since testing is typically done at regular intervals, companies often perform black-box testing the first time

	Black Box	Gray Box	White Box
Information provided to testers	Low	Medium	High
Relative cost/time and effort	High	Medium	Low

Table 12-3 Testing Methods

and then perform gray- or white-box testing after that, assuming the testing team already knows the information gained from the first black-box test.

Table 12-3 shows each of the testing methods and their level of information and cost/effort.

Black-Box Test

When performing a black-box test, the tester knows as little as possible about the system, similar to a real-world hacker. This typically includes only a company name or domain name. The testers then need to discover the devices to test and determine a priority.

Black-box testing is a good method when the goal is to simulate a real-world attack and uncovers vulnerabilities that are discoverable even by someone who has no prior knowledge of the environment. However, it may not be right for all scenarios because of the additional expense required for research and reconnaissance.

Gray-Box Test

In gray-box testing, the test team begins with some information on the targets, usually what attackers would reasonably be assumed to find out through research, such as the list of target IP addresses, public DNS records, and public-facing URLs. Roles and configurations are not provided to the testing team in a gray-box test.

Gray-box testing can be a cost-effective solution if one can reasonably assume that information such as the list of target IP addresses, public DNS records, and public-facing URLs would be obtained by an attacker. Gray-box testing is faster and cheaper than black-box testing because some research and reconnaissance work is reduced, but it is somewhat more expensive than white-box testing.

White-Box Test

White-box testing is done with an insider's view and can be much faster than black-box or gray-box testing. White-box testing makes it possible to focus on specific security concerns the organization may have because the tester spends less time figuring out which systems are accessible, their configurations, and other parameters.

Vulnerability Scanning

Vulnerability scanning is the process of discovering flaws or weaknesses in systems and applications. These weaknesses can range anywhere from host and service misconfiguration to insecure application design. Vulnerability scanning can be performed manually, but it is common to use a vulnerability scanning application to perform automated testing.

Automated vulnerability scanning utilizes software to probe a target system. The vulnerability scanning software will send connection requests to a computer and then monitor the responses it receives. It may insert different data types into web forms and analyze the results. This allows the software to identify potential weaknesses in the system.

Vulnerability scanning includes basic reconnaissance tools such as port scanning, a process that queries each TCP/UDP port on a system to see if it is capable of receiving data; footprinting, the process of enumerating the computers or network devices on a target network; and fingerprinting, a process that determines the operating system and software running on a device.

Management may review the vulnerabilities and determine which ones they want to remediate and who will be responsible for remediation. The vulnerability remediation request (VRR) is a formal request to change an application or system to remediate a known vulnerability.

Vulnerabilities are ranked with industry standards, such as the Common Vulnerability Scoring System (CVSS) numbers for vulnerability scoring. These rankings have a risk score associated with them. The CVSS numbers can be used to find additional threat and remediation information on the vulnerability in the National Vulnerability Database (NVD).

This remainder of this section discusses the phases, tools, and scope options for vulnerability scanning.

Phases

The vulnerability scanning process is organized into three phases: intelligence gathering, vulnerability assessment, and vulnerability validation. The phases are shown in Figure 12-2.

Intelligence Gathering   A vulnerability scanning project begins by gathering information about the targets. Intelligence gathering is a phase of information gathering that consists of passive and active reconnaissance. Depending on your level of knowledge of the targets and the type of test (black box, gray box, or white box), this step may not be necessary.

Vulnerability Assessment   The second phase is vulnerability assessment. Vulnerability scanning tools are used at this stage to scan targets for common weaknesses such as outdated or unpatched software, published vulnerabilities, and weak configurations. The vulnerability assessment then measures the potential impact of discovered vulnerabilities. Identified vulnerabilities are classified according to CVSS numbers for vulnerability scoring.

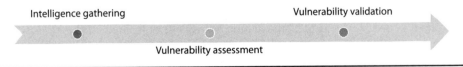

Figure 12-2   Vulnerability scanning phases

Vulnerability Validation   Automated scans alone do not represent a complete picture of the vulnerabilities present on the target machines. Automated scans are designed to be nondisruptive, so they tend to err on the side of caution when identifying the presence of security weaknesses. As a result, conditions that outwardly appear to be security flaws— but which in fact are not exploitable—are sometimes identified as being vulnerabilities. It takes experience in interpreting a tool's reports, as well as knowledge of the system, to identify vulnerabilities that are likely exploitable.

Some vulnerability validation can be performed with automated tools. Such automation reduces the manual testing burden, but there will still be cases where manual validation is required to ensure a quality deliverable. Tools are discussed in the next section.

Tools

Vulnerability scanning teams rely extensively on tools to perform tasks for them. The intelligence gathering and vulnerability scanning tasks are highly suited to automation through tools because they perform a consistent set of tasks against all targets and then output their results. A wide variety of tools can be used to perform these functions. This section discusses intelligence gathering tools first and then vulnerability assessment tools.

Intelligence Gathering   Intelligence gathering tools are used to obtain basic information on targets before other tasks are performed. Two main functions of intelligence gathering include port scanning and detecting service availability. Port scanning reveals the open ports on a machine. Port scans are typically executed against a large number of devices. Tools that detect service availability identify the services that are running behind ports and whether they will respond to commands or queries.

Testers will likely use most of the intelligence gathering tools to gather information about their targets. Snmpwalk uses SNMP messages to obtain information on targets through their MIB data. See Chapter 7 for more information on SNMP. Fierce is used to find internal and external IP addresses for a target DNS name.

Sam Spade is a tool that combines several command-line functions together. These functions include Whois, a command that identifies the owner of a domain name; ping, a tool that tests to determine if a host is responding to ICMP packets; IPBlock, a tool that performs whois operations on a block of IP addresses; dig, a command that obtains resource records for a domain (see Chapter 14); traceroute, a command that identifies each hop from source to destination (see Chapter 14); and finger, a tool that obtains information on the user logged into a target machine. Please note that finger has been disabled on most machines for years now, so this tool is unlikely to work on targets today, but it remains in the Sam Spade suite of tools.

Nmap, Zenmap, and Unicornscan are each used to map a network by identifying the hosts that are online, the operating system they are running, installed applications, and security configuration such as host-based firewalls.

Table 12-4 lists some of the information gathering tools along with their uses and whether they are free or paid.

Vulnerability Assessment Tools   Some of the vulnerability assessment tools are specific to certain cloud applications. For example, the Amazon Inspector would be used for AWS servers, while the Microsoft Azure Security Center would be used for servers in

Tool	Purpose	Cost
TCP Port Scanner	Port scanning	Free
PortQryUI	Port scanning	Free
NetScanTools	Network mapping, port scanning, service enumeration	Free
snmpwalk	SNMP enumeration	Free
Fierce	DNS discovery	Free
Sam Spade	Network reconnaissance	Free
Nmap	Network mapping, port scanning, service enumeration	Free
Zenmap	Network mapping	Free
Unicornscan	Network mapping	Free

Table 12-4   Information Gathering Tools

an Azure environment. Nessus, Nexpose, OpenVAS, and Security Center can scan cloud systems or on-premise systems. Of the four, OpenVAS is open source and available for free. OpenVAS is an excellent tool to use to get familiar with the process.

There are two methods of performing scanning that tools may employ. These are as follows:

- **Network-based scanning**   This form of scanning uses a centralized device that scans all machines that it can reach over the network. Network scans are fast and require no configuration on scan targets. Network scans can target most devices without the need for a compatibility check. However, network scans can be limited in what information they can obtain from devices.

- **Agent-based scanning**   These scans rely upon software that runs locally on each target to report back information on the system, its software, and configuration. Agent-based scanning can usually provide more details than network-based scans, but it requires more effort to deploy the agents to each machine and keep them updated. It is also limited because some systems may not support agents, such as IoT devices. Still others, such as personal laptops or phones, may not be managed by the organization, so agents would not be installed on them.

Table 12-5 lists some of the vulnerability scanning tools along with their uses and whether they are free or paid. A wide variety of the tools listed are open source. Some Linux distributions come with a large number of security tools preinstalled. The most popular security distribution is Kali, but others, such as DEFT, Caine, Pentoo, and the Samurai Web Testing Framework, offer similarly valuable toolsets, albeit with a somewhat different interface. These Linux security distributions can be used as a bootable DVD or can be installed on a system for permanent use. Linux security distributions contain hundreds of security tools, including many for penetration testing, vulnerability scanning, network analysis, and computer forensics.

Default and Common Credential Scanning   Default or commonly used credentials are a significant vulnerability if they are present on the network. It is common for

Tool	Purpose	Cost
Kali	A suite of scanning, forensic, and analysis tools	Free
Caine	A suite of scanning, forensic, and analysis tools	Free
Pentoo	A suite of scanning, forensic, and analysis tools	Free
Samurai Web Testing Framework	A suite of scanning, forensic, and analysis tools	Free
Microsoft Azure Security Center	Vulnerability scanning	Paid
OpenVAS	Vulnerability scanning	Free
Nikto	Application vulnerability scanning	Free
Amazon Inspector	Vulnerability scanning	Paid
WPScan	WordPress vulnerability scanning	Paid
Nessus	Vulnerability scanning	Paid
Nexpose	Vulnerability scanning	Paid
Google Cloud Security Scanner	Vulnerability scanning	Paid
Tenable SecurityCenter	Vulnerability scanning	Paid

Table 12-5 Vulnerability Scanning Tools

attackers to attempt password guessing on devices. Attackers try to get into systems by trying passwords in this order:

1. Try default credentials
2. Try commonly used passwords
3. Brute force or dictionary attack to reveal weak passwords

Companies can protect themselves by scanning their own systems or those they have in the cloud for default, commonly used, or weak credentials. They do this by submitting authentication requests using databases of potential passwords. The easiest way to get in is if a device is still using the password supplied by the manufacturer. These are known as the default credentials, and these are public knowledge because they are contained in user manuals and other documentation.

If a system does not accept the default credentials, the testing team will next try to gain access to systems using databases of commonly used credentials. These databases are built by analyzing password dumps from large-scale attacks. For example, the CyberNews investigation team analyzed some of these password dumps. It published the top ten most common passwords as of February 2021. These included the following:

1. 123456
2. 123456789
3. qwerty

4. password

5. 12345

6. qwerty123

7. 1q2w3e

8. 12345678

9. 111111

10. 1234567890

If neither of these methods works, the testing team may attempt to obtain access by performing brute force password cracking, where all possible combinations of passwords are tried, or a dictionary password cracking attack, where a list of passwords obtained from common dictionary words and permutations of those words with common dates, places, and other information is tried against the systems. Suppose users have set a weak password, such as one that is very short or not very complex. In that case, these cracking attempts will identify that password quickly.

Once the scans are complete, the team will provide the company with a list of identified credentials so that those credentials can be changed and users or administrators trained on better password practices.

Scope

A vulnerability scan can cover different scopes such as external scanning, internal scanning, web application scanning, or a combination.

- **External vulnerability scan**   An external scan is conducted from outside the company's internal network, on Internet-facing nodes such as web servers, e-mail servers, FTP servers, and VPN servers.

- **Internal vulnerability scan**   An internal vulnerability scan is conducted from within the company cloud, targeting servers, workstations, and other devices on the corporate cloud.

- **Web application vulnerability scan**   Web applications are often big targets because they are built to continually interface with the outside world. They often contain valuable information. Web application scans use a different set of tools geared toward assessing the web platforms and the types of applications and frameworks that run on them. Web applications require close attention by the testing team, as there can be significant variations in how each application works depending on its purpose and role. For example, an enterprise resource planning (ERP) system functions much differently than an asset tracking system. The ERP system has many more interconnections and is functionally more complex than the asset tracking system, just to name some of the differences.

Scans can be performed through the cloud provider's services such as Microsoft Azure Security Center, Google Cloud Security Scanner, or Amazon Inspector. Some of these tools are built to scan the types of systems that reside on the cloud vendor's network, while others are more flexible. For example, Google Cloud Security Scanner scans Google App Engine apps for vulnerabilities, while Amazon Inspector can analyze any applications running within Amazon Web Services (AWS).

Credentialed and Noncredentialed Scanning   Vulnerability scans can be performed with or without valid credentials to the resources. A scan without credentials is called a noncredentialed scan. This simulates what an attacker would see if they did not have access to a valid user session. Credentialed scanning uses one or more valid credentials to determine what vulnerabilities can be identified under that user context. Some scans will include multiple types of credentials, such as a standard user account, an administrative account, and a service account.

Credentialed scanning generally provides more information than a noncredentialed scan, and it can help to eliminate some false positives as well. It is common for noncredentialed scans to identify multiple possible operating systems for a target device or see surface-level vulnerabilities. In contrast, a credentialed scan can more accurately identify version information and configuration settings.

Penetration Testing

Penetration testing evaluates system security at a point in time by attacking target systems as an outside attacker would and then documenting which attacks were successful, how the systems were exploited, and which vulnerabilities were utilized. Penetration testing provides realistic, accurate, and precise data on system security.

A penetration test is a proactive and approved plan to measure the protection of a cloud infrastructure by using system vulnerabilities, together with operating system or software application bugs, insecure settings, and potentially dangerous or naïve end-user behavior to obtain access to systems. Such assessments also help confirm defensive mechanisms' effectiveness and assess end users' adherence to security policies.

Tests are usually performed using manual or automated technologies to compromise servers, endpoints, applications, wireless networks, network devices, mobile devices, and alternative potential exposure points. Once vulnerabilities are exploited on a particular system, pen testers might commit to using the compromised system to launch later exploits at other internal resources, in a technique known as pivoting. Pivoting is performed to incrementally reach higher security clearance levels and deeper access to electronic assets and data via privilege increase.

This section's remainder discusses the phases, tools, scope options, and testing limitations for penetration testing. The section concludes with a discussion on roles and responsibilities. Security testing requires specialized skill sets and should be performed by a team that is independent of DevOps.

Phases

The penetration testing process is organized into seven phases: intelligence gathering, vulnerability assessment, vulnerability validation, attack planning and simulation, exploitation, postexploitation, and reporting. The phases are shown in Figure 12-3.

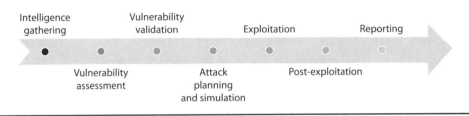

Figure 12-3   Penetration testing phases

As you can see, penetration testing begins with the three phases of vulnerability scanning, covered in the previous section, so they will not be covered again. We will start with phase 4: attack planning and simulation.

Attack Planning and Simulation   Once the vulnerabilities have been enumerated and validated, the next step is to determine how the vulnerabilities can best be used together to exploit systems. Some of this comes with experience as penetration testers learn to see the subtle relationships between hosts that automated tools and complex scripts cannot detect. An initial plan of attack is built from this data.

This phase also involves attack plan simulations. Simulations of the exploits outlined in the attack plan are performed in a test environment or automatically in penetration testing tools to eliminate lingering false-positive results and refine the attack plan through the simulations. A full attack strategy can then be put together to be employed in the exploitation phase.

Exploitation   In the exploitation phase, penetration testers establish access to a system or resource by employing exploit packages that take advantage of discovered vulnerabilities. Penetration testing activities are performed for the approved scope following the attack strategy.

Postexploitation   In this stage, evidence of exploitation of the vulnerabilities is collected and remnants from the exploits are removed. As part of this, penetration testers clean up accounts and resident files that were put in place to perform the exploits.

Reporting   The last phase of penetration testing is to put all the details of the tests, including what worked and what didn't, into the report. Information on the security vulnerabilities that were successfully exploited through penetration testing is collected and documented in the report. The report is provided to a risk manager or someone in charge of security in the organization. This person will then coordinate with other teams to remediate the vulnerabilities, track remediation, and possibly schedule validation tests to ensure that the vulnerabilities identified have been successfully remediated.

Reports rank findings by risk rating and provide recommendations on how to remediate the items.

Tools

A wide variety of tools can be used to perform penetration testing. Table 12-6 lists several popular penetration testing tools. Some tools are large suites with various components,

Tool	Purpose	Phase
Core Impact	Penetration testing suite	Exploitation
Metasploit Pro	OS- and application-level vulnerability exploitation	Exploitation
Kali	Collection of tools on a single bootable disk; can also be installed as an operating system	Exploitation
Social-Engineer Toolkit (SET)	Toolkit for performing social engineering	Exploitation

Table 12-6 Penetration Testing Tools

while others perform a particular task. Many tools are command-line driven, requiring familiarity with the command structure and usage.

Penetration testers may try to crack passwords in order to test the strength of passwords users have created. Brute force attempts are usually made on a password database that has been downloaded from a system. Testers first obtain access to the password database and download it. However, most password databases cannot be read because the passwords in them are hashed. Penetration testers use a computer with a powerful CPU or GPU or a network of distributed systems to try all possible combinations until they get in. The number of possible combinations increases exponentially as the number of characters in the password increases.

Scope

A penetration test can cover any of the following different scopes or a combination of them:

- **External penetration testing**   External penetration testing is conducted from the Web, from outside the company's internal network, with the targets being the company's web-facing hosts. This may sometimes include web servers, e-mail servers, FTP servers, and VPN servers.

- **Internal penetration testing**   Internal penetration testing is conducted from within the company network. Targets may include servers; workstations; network devices such as firewalls or routers; and IoT devices such as webcams, IP lighting, or smart TVs.

- **Web application penetration testing**   Web application penetration testing is concerned with evaluating web-based applications' security by issuing attacks against the site and supporting infrastructures, such as database servers, file servers, or authentication devices.

- **Wireless penetration testing**   Wireless penetration testing evaluates wireless access points and common weaknesses in a company's wireless network. This includes attempting to crack wireless passwords, capture traffic on the wireless network, capture authentication information, and obtain unauthorized access to the network through a wireless connection. Wireless penetration testing also scans for rogue access points and peer-to-peer wireless connections.

- **Physical penetration testing**   Physical penetration testing evaluates an outsider's ability to obtain direct access to company facilities and areas containing sensitive data.

- **Social engineering penetration testing**   Social engineering penetration testing can involve a person directly interacting with individuals, but it is more common to use remote social engineering tactics, since these are most often employed by attackers.

  Remote social engineering evaluates employee response to targeted phishing attacks. The penetration tester requests a listing of e-mail addresses to be tested. A custom phishing e-mail is crafted and sent employing a spoofed source e-mail address or an external one that appears legitimate to every employee. The e-mail message will encourage the user to perform a range of nonsecure activities like clicking a link, visiting an unauthorized website, downloading a file, or revealing their username and password.

Testing Limitations

Testing limitations affect the scope of penetration testing by defining types of testing that are not allowed. Typical testing restrictions exclude from the scope memory corruption tests and similar tests that are likely to cause instability. Such testing is an assumed limitation when testing production environments. Denial of service attacks are also often excluded from the scope of testing.

 EXAM TIP   The difference between a penetration test and a vulnerability assessment is that a penetration test simulates an attack on the environment.

Roles and Responsibilities

Security testing can be a complicated procedure and involves testing various components, including applications, storage, network connectivity, and server configuration. Security testing requires specialized skill sets and should be performed by a team that is independent of DevOps.

Vulnerability scanning is an easier task to perform than penetration testing, and penetration testing requires vulnerability scanning, so this is an obvious place to define roles. Vulnerability analysts detect and validate vulnerabilities and then pass that information to penetration testers who might be more familiar with specific areas such as operating systems, storage, software development, web services, communications protocols, and so forth. These penetration testers are also familiar with how such services can be exploited, and they stay up to date on new vulnerabilities, exploits, and tools.

The social engineering penetration tester may also be a different role, since this requires a knowledge of human behavior and what will most effectively entice victims to read phishing e-mails and follow the instructions given.

The most crucial detail is that the security testing team should be distinct and independent from the DevOps team. Such a separation of duties ensures that the test accurately represents what an attacker could do. Furthermore, it provides a level of objectivity. It reduces the likelihood of bias from internal knowledge or a conflict of interest that could arise if security testing team members have a personal stake, for example, in an application being launched on time.

Considerations Before You Scan or Test

Penetration tests and vulnerability scans should be designed to have minimal or no impact on the production environment. The following are some of the methods testers use to protect availability and data integrity:

- Confirming in-scope machines, testing times, and duration before testing to ensure that the correct devices are tested.

- Providing operations teams with the IP addresses testers use to conduct penetration tests. This allows the ops team to quickly determine if actions they observe result from penetration testing or an active attack from some other actor. This step will not be performed if the test is designed to test the operations team's responsiveness.

- Executing scans and other automated tasks slowly to not consume excessive network capacity or other computing resources.

- Subjecting vulnerability exploits to rigorous testing to eliminate methods that might cause harm to customer systems.

- Collecting the minimum evidence necessary to demonstrate the exploitability of a vulnerability.

- Documenting steps performed and actions taken.

Still, no process is perfect, and there is always the potential that something could happen in the test that would affect the availability or data integrity of the systems under test. The goal of a pen test is to identify and determine the exploitability of vulnerabilities in target systems. As such, there is a possibility that such exploits could make changes to customer systems. The following measures can help protect against unforeseeable outcomes in your pen test or vulnerability scan:

- If possible, perform testing on a nonproduction environment, such as a testing system or QA system. This environment should be an exact or very near duplicate of the production environment so that the risks identified in it can be extrapolated to the production environment. However, the environment should be separate so as to not cause interference with production data.

- Test the application for common malicious input before testing. Many unforeseeable issues are caused by a lack of input validation. This includes public-facing web forms that send e-mails or populate data in a database. If proper input validation is not performed on these, automated tests for injection vulnerabilities could result in excessive e-mails or junk data in a database.

- Keep in mind that account permissions will give the tester and any automated tool the ability to perform the same functions of that account. If you are aware of functions that may lead to lack of availability, provide the testing team with a listing of the function and the directory under which it is performed so they may take special care to avoid troublesome input concerning these functions. This may include testing this function individually or manually where necessary.

- Create a backup of this environment prior to testing. This includes, at a minimum, a snapshot of systems, as well as a database backup.

Incident Response

At some point, your company is going to have to deal with a cybersecurity incident. An incident is an event that is deemed to have caused harm to the company or harm to its customers, partners, or stakeholders via company systems or employees. This definition used the term harm a few times. I define harm as the diminished organizational effectiveness, value, or reputation or monetary, physical, reputational, or other tangible loss for employees, members, stakeholders, or partners. It is important to contrast an incident with an event. An event is an observed occurrence that is potentially suspicious. Security Operations Center (SOC) teams may investigate many events without any of them being an incident.

Incident response (IR) consists of the actions taken to handle an incident. This begins before an incident occurs by preparing for an incident. Following the discovery of an event classified as an incident, IR teams will go through a series of steps to resolve the incident. This section covers the preparation steps, followed by a description of different types of incidents. The section concludes by providing you with details on each major step in the incident response procedure. For more information, the National Institute of Standards and Technology (NIST) has produced special publication 800-61 titled "Computer Security Incident Handling Guide."

Preparation

It is best to prepare for an incident before one occurs. One of the most critical facets of incident handling is preparedness. Preparation allows for an organized and clear response to incidents. It also limits the potential for damage by ensuring that response plans are familiar to all employees.

Companies that prepare for an incident end up resolving incidents faster with fewer mistakes. This results in less impact to operations and their brand image and costs them less money.

Preparation begins with documenting an incident response plan and then training employees and contractors on the roles they will play. Lastly, tabletop exercises help familiarize staff with the plan and identify deficiencies before a real incident occurs.

Documentation

Incident documentation helps guide decision-making during an incident and record the actions taken to investigate and resolve the incident so that the company can provide evidence of their due diligence, properly notify affected individuals or companies, and continuously improve.

Essential incident documentation includes

- Incident response policy
- Incident response plan (IRP)
- Incident reporting form
- Chain of custody

Incident Response Policy   The incident response policy outlines the overall company approach to incident response. However, it does not get into how an incident will be handled or specific incident response steps. Those are addressed in the incident response plan. Critical elements of an incident response policy include

- **Definitions**   This includes definitions of what constitutes an event, incident, and a data breach.
- **Purpose**   This section describes why incident response is important and what the organization hopes to achieve with its incident response activities.
- **Incident reporting expectations**   This section outlines when reporting should be performed and who should be notified.
- **Roles and responsibilities**   This section outlines which team members will be involved in incident response and what their jobs will be. This may list people by name, but it is more common to put in their titles, such as CSO, director of information technology, or senior network engineer. Table 12-7 shows some roles and responsibilities that might be included in a policy. It is also essential to establish several incident response contacts who will review incident report forms and potentially contact others to initiate the IR.

Incident Response Plan   The IRP specifies the steps that will be performed to identify, investigate, and resolve information security incidents. This includes how long it will take to respond to an incident, recovery times, investigation times, the members of the incident response team, how employees are to notify the group of incident indicators, the indicators of an incident, and how the team will vet incidents. The IRP will go through each of the incident response procedures discussed later in this chapter and explain the steps that will be performed.

Data may need to be retrieved from multiple cloud vendors, so the incident response policy will specify how that will take place. This includes how data will be packaged from the cloud provider and how long it will take for it to be delivered to the cloud consumer.

Role	Responsibility
Incident Response Lead Primary Contact	Incident response lead/primary contact.
Senior Management	Executive officer/risk owner.
Information Technology	Contains malware, restores systems, reviews event information, and triages systems.
Forensics	Preserves evidence and chain of custody. Performs forensic analysis on systems.
Cybersecurity	Investigates incidents to identify the root cause. Advises on mitigation and remediation measures.
Public Relations / Spokesperson	Handles any external communications in relation to an incident. All external communications must be cleared by the CEO before distribution. Legal must work with marketing and communications on external communications.
Human Resources	Handles any personnel and disciplinary issues relating to security incidents.
Corporate Counsel	Handles any legal questions/issues relating to security incidents.
Facilities/Physical Security	Locks down areas, secures physical assets, and protects against related physical threats.
Insurance	Determines if a claim is warranted and provides services outlined in the insurance plan. This could include such services as ransomware negotiation or investigative assistance.

Table 12-7   IR Roles and Responsibilities

Toward the beginning of an IRP will be a contact list of each person who is a member of the IR team, their role, and contact information. Alternates will be listed for each person so that another person can be contacted if the primary is unavailable. You do not want to be in a situation where one role is not represented.

The IRP will next outline a call tree. This is a diagram showing how each person will be contacted. It does not make sense for one person to call everyone, because that would take too much time. Instead, one person might call two others, who will reach more people so that the message is quickly relayed to the entire team. Figure 12-4 shows a sample call tree. Each person is indicated by their role.

 EXAM TIP   The incident response plan must factor in the communication and coordination activities with each cloud provider. This can add significant time to an incident response timeline.

Incident Reporting Form   The incident reporting form documents who reported the incident, the date of the incident, and any pertinent facts identified when the incident was reported. The incident report is the document that is provided to the incident

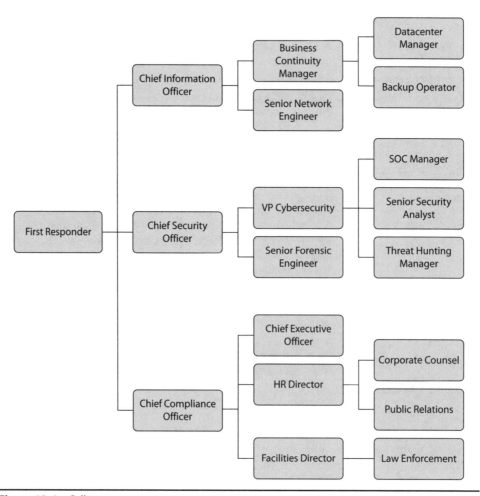

Figure 12-4 Call tree

response team when it is called together, so it will not contain all the details discovered in the course of the IR, but it will contain those details that were initially discovered. A sample reporting form is provided here.

1. Contact Information	
Name:	
Title:	
Location:	
Work Phone/Extension:	
Mobile Phone:	
E-mail address:	

2. Incident Description

3. Impact
☐ Destruction/Compromise of Data ☐ Damage to Systems ☐ System Downtime ☐ Financial Loss ☐ Third-Party Systems Affected ☐ Compliance Violation ☐ Unknown

4. Data Classification	
☐ Public ☐ Financial ☐ Business/Strategic	☐ Personal data (PII/PHI) ☐ Other

5. Who Else Has Been Notified?

6. Initial Steps Taken	
☐ None ☐ Disconnected system ☐ Scanned for malware ☐ Created ticket	☐ Restored backup ☐ Analyzed logs ☐ Other

Details:

7. Incident Details	
Specific location of the incident	
Number of sites affected:	
Number of computers affected:	
Number of users affected:	
Did this affect third-party systems, such as business partners, supply chain members, or customers?	

Chain of Custody Chain of custody documentation tracks when the evidence is acquired, who released the evidence to the forensic person, where the evidence is stored, and each time the evidence is accessed. A sample chain of custody form is shown in Figure 12-5.

Training

Appropriate training should be provided to technical operations personnel and other relevant staff regularly. Training helps update knowledge and skills in handling security incidents. Each time the incident response plan is updated, training should be performed to cover the changes that were made.

Examiner

Name	
Title	

Evidence Information

Computer/Device Name	Address
User Name	
Phone Number	**Email**
Password	

☐ Desktop ☐ Laptop ☐ Server ☐ Media (DVD/Flash) ☐ Hard Drive ☐ Other: ____________

Manufacturer:	
Model:	
Serial Number:	
Monitor:	**Keyboard:**
Mouse:	**Other:**
Other:	**Other:**

Media Information

Manufacturer	**Type**
Model Number	**Size**
Serial Number	

Chain of Custody

Date:	Time:	Released By:	Received By:	Electronically Logged
				☐
				☐
				☐
				☐
				☐
				☐

Figure 12-5 Chain of custody form

Tabletop Exercises

Tabletop exercises are a great way to test out an IRP and familiarize staff with the process they will need to follow when an actual incident occurs. A tabletop exercise is facilitated by someone who has prepared a scenario that the IR team then works through. For example, the IR team may explore all the steps they would follow in a ransomware incident. They work their way through the IRP and document any steps that are missing details, corrections, and improvements to the plan. The plan is then updated to include these elements.

Incident Types

A security incident involves events that occur either by accident or deliberately that affect systems negatively. An incident may be any event or set of circumstances that threaten the confidentiality, integrity, or availability of information, data, or services. For example, incidents could include unauthorized access to, use, disclosure, modification, or destruction of data or services used or provided by the company.

Additionally, incidents can be classified by the type of threat. These include internal and external threats.

- **Internal threat** An internal threat is one that occurs from a trusted employee or contractor. Examples of internal threats include users misusing resources, execution of malicious code, or attempts at unauthorized access by organizational accounts. The most severe internal threats involve highly privileged users, known as administrators, misusing their privileges or hiding unauthorized activities.

- **External threat** An external threat is one that occurs by an actor that is not associated with the organization. Examples of external threats include an unauthorized person attempting to gain access to systems, attacks on availability such as denial of service, phishing, and malware.

Incidents can be further classified into types based on the type of event or service that is targeted. Some of these are provided here as examples:

- **Data breach** A data breach is an incident involving the disclosure of sensitive information to an unauthorized party. Breaches require notification of affected individuals within a defined period following discovery and typically involve the expertise of an attorney to interpret the regulatory and contractual obligations.

- **Criminal activity** This could include the presence of illegal material on systems, such as child pornography or illegal software.

- **Denial of service** Attacks on the availability of systems or other resources.

- **Malware** Code that is designed to harm organizational systems. Malware includes viruses, Trojans, worms, bots, keyloggers, rootkits, or ransomware.

- **Policy violation**   Organizational policies specify how employees, contractors and others will work with information. Some policies can be enforced through technical controls, but others must be adhered to. When someone does not follow the policy, such as failing to verify ID before providing sensitive information, not encrypting data as required by policy, or failing to report indicators of an incident, the company and its customers can suffer harm.
- **Compliance violation**   This typically involves a privacy concern, such as not following HIPAA procedures or accidental disclosure of personal data to an unauthorized person.
- **Rogue services**   Unknown services, software, or systems identified could have been placed there by a malicious entity.
- **Phishing interaction**   A user that responds to a phishing message or opens attachments in a phishing message.
- **Unauthorized access**   Any access to files or systems from an unauthorized device or user account.
- **Vandalism**   Defacement of a website or destruction of property.

Incident Response Procedures

This section outlines the steps the IR team will go through when handling an incident. Each of these should be outlined in the IRP discussed earlier. These steps include

- Identification
- Preservation
- Investigation
- Containment
- Eradication
- Recovery
- Reflection

Identification

A security incident may not be recognized straightaway; however, there may be security breach indicators, system compromise, unauthorized activity, or signs of misuse within the environment, including cloud resources. Some indicators include

- Excessive or anomalous login activity
- Activity by accounts that have been disabled

- Significantly increased remote access activity
- Computers that are contacting a large number of other network systems
- Excessive file access or modification
- Identification of malware
- Tampering with security systems or other sensitive equipment, such as point of sale (POS) systems
- Lost or stolen devices
- Corrupt backups
- Lost or stolen backups

If a person suspects an incident, they should report the incident to their designated incident response contacts and complete the incident reporting form.

Preservation

The preservation phase is concerned with preserving evidence for the investigation so that important information is not lost. IT professionals are sometimes so concerned with getting things back up and running that they restore systems, eliminating valuable evidence that could help determine the root cause.

Evidence Acquisition　In the preservation phase, forensic teams will take forensic images of equipment or virtual machines. This could also include snapshots or forensic copies of log files, packet captures, memory captures, or e-mail exports.

Each piece of evidence that is collected must be tracked for the chain of custody. This ensures that evidence is not modified or handled by unauthorized individuals. Without the chain of custody, the integrity of the evidence cannot be assured. Chain of custody forms track when the evidence is acquired, who released the evidence to the forensic person, where the evidence is stored, and each time the evidence is accessed.

Investigation

The investigation phase is concerned with determining the root cause and the scope. Root cause analysis (RCA) is a process where information is gathered during the containment phase and additional information collected is analyzed. The team determines the factor or factors that led to the incident occurring, such as a vulnerable system, a user clicking on a phishing message, drive-by malware, or someone not following standard operating procedures. If a root cause cannot be determined, multiple potential reasons will be listed and ranked by likelihood.

Scope　Scope analysis is concerned with identifying affected individuals, such as the number of persons whose personal information was disclosed or how many credit card numbers were stolen. This information is then provided to legal counsel so that they can determine the company's notification requirements under the law.

Containment

The containment stage's primary objective is to limit the scope and magnitude of an incident as quickly as possible. The first step is to determine whether to isolate affected machines and the method for doing so. There are usually three considerations here:

1. Shut down the system.

2. Disconnect the system from the network or disable its network port. In the case of a large number of systems, the switch or switches they are connected to can be turned off.

3. Allow the device to continue to run. This option is only selected when you wish to monitor the system to potentially track attackers or malicious insiders so that they can be prosecuted. The decision of whether to allow this depends on the risk continued operation of the system presents to the company.

One common incident is malware. In such cases, companies will typically move quickly to eradicate malicious code, such as viruses, bots, Trojans, or worms.

Eradication

The next priority, after containing the damage from a security incident, is to remove the cause of the incident. In the case of a virus incident, the company will remove the virus from all systems and media by using one or more proven commercial virus eradication applications or OS reinstallation, as needed. Some of these steps include

- **Improve defenses** In this step, the IR team implements appropriate protection techniques such as firewall and router access control lists. It will continue monitoring the intrusion detection system.

- **Run vulnerability scans** The IR team will scan the system for vulnerabilities to shore up defenses and potentially identify an avenue that could've been used in the attack.

Recovery

In the recovery phase, the company brings systems back to normal functional states. The recovery steps depend on the nature of the incident, but some include removing malicious code, restoring systems, blocking IP addresses or regions, failing over to secondary equipment or sites, or deploying new systems.

Once systems have been recovered, the next step is to verify that the operation was successful and that the system is back to its normal operating condition. This involves testing the systems and monitoring them for anomalous activity or other indicators of compromise that may have escaped detection. This level of monitoring should be greater than standard monitoring for organizational systems.

Reflection

The last step is to follow up on an incident after recovery to improve incident response procedures. This involves documenting how well the team responded to the incident, as well as the costs associated with the incident. Understanding the costs will help in determining whether it makes sense to invest additional money or other resources into prevention technologies, procedures, or training.

Debrief   Following the incident, it is best to sit down with the IR team to review the incident and identify lessons learned throughout the process. This aids in improving future incident response and refining the IRP. The debrief pays particular attention to questions like these:

- Were we sufficiently prepared for the incident?
- Did we meet our time objectives for discovering the incident, resolving the incident, restoration of systems, etc.?
- Would other tools have helped us resolve the incident more quickly?
- Was the incident effectively contained?
- How could we have better communicated during the incident?

Document Costs   Following the debrief, the company will review the staff time required to address incidents, losses due to lost productivity, lost customers, regulatory fines, legal work, increased insurance premiums, ransom payments, and other costs associated with the incident. The goal here is to determine whether additional funds should be budgeted for security efforts.

Chapter Review

This chapter covered the concepts of cloud security engineering, security governance and strategy, and vulnerability management. Cloud security engineering is the practice of protecting the usability, reliability, integrity, and safety of information systems, including network and cloud infrastructures and the data traversing and stored on such systems.

One method of engineering secure cloud systems is to harden them. Hardening involves ensuring that the host or guest is configured to reduce the risk of attack from either internal or external sources. Another method is to layer security technologies on top of one another so that systems are protected even if one security system fails because others guard against intrusion. Next, incorporate the principle of least privilege by granting employees only the minimum permissions necessary to do their job. Along with least privilege is a concept called separation of duties, a process that divides the responsibilities required to perform a sensitive task among two or more people so that one person, acting alone, cannot compromise the system.

Security governance and strategy begin with the creation of company security policies. Security policies set the organizational expectations for certain functional security areas.

Data classification can help companies apply the correct protection mechanisms to the data they house and maintain. Data classification is the practice of sorting data into discrete categories that help define the access levels and type of protection required for that data set. An organization establishes security policies to set its expectations for certain functional security areas. Some of these expectations may come out of standards, best practices, or compliance requirements.

Companies perform assessments and audits to identify areas where they are not meeting organizational expectations, contractual agreements, best practices, or regulatory requirements. Regulations such as HIPAA, SOX, and PCI DSS specify requirements for security controls, procedures, and policies that some organizations must comply with.

Cloud security professionals have limited time and much to do. Consider how existing security management processes can be automated. Some examples include removing inactive accounts, eliminating outdated firewall rules, cleaning up obsolete security settings, and maintaining ACLs for target objects.

It is essential to test systems for vulnerabilities and to remediate those vulnerabilities so that systems will be protected against attacks targeting those vulnerabilities. Vulnerability management consists of vulnerability scanning and penetration testing to identify weaknesses in organizational systems and the corresponding methods and techniques to remediate those weaknesses. Vulnerability scanning consists of intelligence gathering, vulnerability assessment, and vulnerability validation. Penetration testing includes the steps in vulnerability scanning, as well as attack planning and simulation, exploitation, postexploitation, and reporting.

Lastly, companies need to prepare for an incident by developing plans, training on those plans, and then executing incident response procedures. These procedures include identification, preservation, investigation, containment, eradication, recovery, and reflection.

Questions

The following questions will help you gauge your understanding of the material in this chapter. Read all the answers carefully because there might be more than one correct answer. Choose the best response(s) for each question.

1. You have been asked to harden a crucial network router. What should you do? (Choose two.)

   A. Disable the routing of IPv6 packets.

   B. Change the default administrative password.

   C. Apply firmware patches.

   D. Configure the router for SSO.

2. You are responsible for cloud security at your organization. The chief compliance officer has mandated that the organization utilize layered security for all cloud systems. Which of the following would satisfy the requirement?

 A. Implementing ACLs and packet filtering on firewalls

 B. Configuring a DMZ with unique ACLs between networks and an IDS/IPS

 C. Specifying separation of duties for cloud administration and training additional personnel on security processes

 D. Defining a privacy policy, placing the privacy policy on the website, and e-mailing the policy to all current clients

3. Which policy would be used to specify how all employee-owned devices may be used to access organizational resources?

 A. Privacy policy

 B. Mobile device policy

 C. Remote access policy

 D. BYOD policy

4. Which policy or set of rules temporarily disables an account when a threshold of incorrect passwords is attempted?

 A. Account lockout policy

 B. Threshold policy

 C. Disabling policy

 D. Password complexity enforcement rules

5. Which type of test simulates a network attack?

 A. Vulnerability assessment

 B. Establishing an attack baseline

 C. Hardening

 D. Penetration test

6. Which of the following phases are unique to penetration testing? (Choose all that apply.)

 A. Intelligence gathering

 B. Vulnerability validation

 C. Attack planning and simulation

 D. Exploitation

7. Which of the following describes a brute force attack?

 A. Attacking a site with exploit code until the password database is cracked

 B. Trying all possible password combinations until the correct one is found

 C. Performing a denial of service (DoS) attack on the server authenticator

 D. Using rainbow tables and password hashes to crack the password

Answers

1. **B, C.** Changing the default passwords and applying patches are important steps in hardening a device.

2. **B.** Layered security requires multiple overlapping controls that are used together to protect systems. Configuring a DMZ with ACLs along with an IDS/IPS provides multiple layers because an attacker would have to compromise a machine in the DMZ and then pivot from that machine to another machine in the internal network. However, IDS/IPS systems might detect this activity, notify administrators, and block the attacker from making the connection.

3. **D.** The BYOD policy is the correct answer here. Bring your own device (BYOD) is a device that is employee owned, not owned by the company; this policy governs how those devices may be used to access organizational resources.

4. **A.** An account lockout policy temporarily disables an account after a certain number of failed logons. For example, if the policy were set to 3, then a user's account would be temporarily disabled (locked out) after three failed tries until an administrator unlocks it.

5. **D.** Penetration tests simulate a network attack.

6. **C, D.** Penetration testing includes all the steps from vulnerability scanning. The two steps that are unique to penetration testing here are attack planning and simulation and exploitation.

7. **B.** A brute force attack tries all possible combinations of a password. A brute force attack relies on the ability to try thousands or millions of passwords per second. For example, at the time of this writing, the password cracking system that is used at TCDI for penetration testing can try 17 million passwords per minute in a brute force attack.

CHAPTER 13

Business Continuity and Disaster Recovery

In this chapter, you will learn about
- Business continuity methods
- Disaster recovery methods
- Backup and recovery

An organization's data must be backed up, and key processes like payroll and billing need to be continually available even if the organization's data center is lost due to a disaster. Choosing a disaster recovery method is an important step in a reliable cloud implementation. A cloud computing model can be seen as an alternative to traditional disaster recovery. Cloud computing offers a more rapid recovery time and helps to reduce the costs of a disaster recovery model.

Protecting organizational data requires different methods depending on the situation. Business continuity (BC) is the set of plans, procedures, and technologies necessary to ensure continued business operations or minimal disruption when incidents, technology failures, or mistakes happen.

BC is different from disaster recovery (DR) in that BC is a holistic way of keeping things running, while DR addresses major events that can take down a company if the right controls are not in place. Organizations typically have a disaster recovery plan (DRP) that can be followed for specific major events.

Backup and recovery are integral to both BC and DR. These functions are also useful for events that do not strain the business, such as when a user accidentally overwrites a non-urgent file and needs it recovered. Backup and recovery are used for significant and major events, as well as those not affecting business continuity and disaster recovery scenarios.

Business Continuity Methods

BC encompasses the activities that enable an organization to continue functioning, including offering services, delivering products, and conducting other activities deemed integral to running the business during and following a disruptive incident such as data corruption, employee mistakes, a malware breach, a malicious insider attack, a system hack, or a major component failure.

Business continuity is also concerned with recovering data or systems if and when they are harmed.

Business Continuity Plan

An organization makes its guidelines known through a business continuity plan (BCP), and it enacts its guidelines through business continuity management (BCM). BCM is the process the organization goes through to create procedures to deal with threats to data integrity, data exfiltration, data confidentiality, data availability, employee safety, asset integrity, brand image, and customer relationships. The process defines the threats to those organizational resources and outlines the safeguards and practices designed to protect them from harm.

BCM is concerned with protecting organizational resources from harm and relies on contingency and resiliency.

Contingency

A major portion of the BCP is concerned with contingency. Contingency planning involves establishing alternative practices, sites, and resources that can be used in an emergency or to establish high availability (discussed later in this section).

In the contingency component of the BCP, the organization establishes a generalized capability and readiness to cope effectively with whatever events compromise business operations. The BCP plans for, documents, and maps out steps to be taken if and when contingency events should occur.

Alternatives

Alternative preparations are the organization's response if resilience and recovery arrangements prove inadequate to address the contingency event. Still, if a BCP is to be complete, it must have documented, planned for, and mapped out how it will handle alternatives when primary resources are unavailable. There are many factors to consider in a business continuity event, and some of those factors may affect whether certain parts of the plan will function as expected. When this happens, alternatives will be implemented.

Alternative Sites

Alternative sites are an essential part of business continuity. For example, hot and warm sites require replication to keep data consistent. Hot sites require continuous replication, while a warm site requires scheduled replication at certain points throughout the day, week, or month.

Using a remote site helps provide a more advanced business continuity solution, since the entire site is protected in case of a disaster. Multisite configurations rely on a backup site where a company can quickly relocate its computer equipment if a disaster occurs at its primary location and data center. The backup site needs to be either another location that the company owns and has available to implement additional equipment or a space that it rents from another provider for an annual or monthly fee.

There are three types of backup sites an organization can use: a cold site, a hot site, and a warm site. The difference between each site is determined by the administrative effort to implement and maintain them and the costs involved with each type.

Cold Site   Of the three backup site options, the least expensive is the cold site. A cold site does not include any backup copies of data from the organization's original data center. When an organization implements a cold site, it does not have readily available hardware at the site; it has only the physical space and network connectivity for recovery operations and is responsible for providing the hardware. Because there is no hardware at the backup site, the cost for a cold site is lower; however, not having readily available hardware at the cold site is also one of its downfalls. Since there is no hardware set up and ready to use at the backup site, it takes the organization longer to get up and operating after a disaster, which could end up costing it more than the extra expense of a warm or hot site, depending on the type of organization.

Hot Site   A hot site, on the other hand, is a duplicate of the original site of the organization and has readily available hardware and a near-complete backup of the organization's data. A hot site can have real-time synchronization between the original site and the backup site and can be used to mirror the original data center completely.

If the original site is affected by a disaster, the hot site is available for the organization to quickly relocate to, with minimal impact on the normal operations of the organization. A hot site is the most expensive type of alternative site to maintain. However, it is popular with organizations that need the highest level of disaster recovery, such as financial institutions and e-commerce providers.

EXAM TIP   A hot site is the most expensive multisite configuration but provides the quickest recovery time in the event of a disaster.

Warm Site   A warm site is somewhere on the continuum between a cold site and a hot site. It has readily available hardware but on a much smaller scale than the original site or a hot site. Warm sites will also have backups at the location, but they may not be complete backups, or they might be a few days old.

Determining an acceptable recovery time objective (RTO) for an organization helps a cloud administrator choose between the three types of backup sites. A hot site might have an RTO of a few hours, whereas a cold site might have an RTO of a day or more. It is important that the organization and the cloud administrator completely understand the RTO of an application or service and the cost required to operate at that RTO.

A hot site provides faster recovery time but also has a much higher cost than a warm site. A cold site costs the least to set up, but it takes the longest to implement in the event of a disaster. Understanding the benefits and costs of each of the three types of backup sites will help an organization determine which backup type best fits its needs and which backup strategy it should implement.

Site Mirroring

A mirror site is either a hosted website or set of files that is an exact copy of the original site and resides on one or more separate computers from the original. This mirror copy ensures that the website or files are accessible from multiple locations to increase availability and reduce network traffic on the original site. It is updated regularly to reflect changes in content from the original site.

A set of distributed mirrored servers can be set up to reflect geographic discrepancies, making it faster to download from various places throughout the world in what is known as a content delivery network (CDN). For example, a site that is heavily used in the United States might have multiple mirror sites throughout the country, or even a mirror site in Germany, so that end users who are trying to download the files can access a site that is in closer proximity to their location.

Sites that offer a large array of software downloads and have a large amount of network traffic can use mirror sites to meet the demand for the downloads and improve response time for the end user. For example, Microsoft often has multiple mirror sites available for users to download its software, and Download.com (http://download.cnet.com) often has mirror sites so that end users can retrieve files from a location that is closer to them.

Resiliency

The BCP should define how the organization will implement resiliency. Resiliency requires designing systems that can still service the company when problems arise. It accomplishes this primarily through redundancy. Cloud service providers achieve resiliency by architecting cloud and information systems that can withstand assault or faults. Security controls protect against assault (see Chapter 11), and redundancy protects against component failure or failure of integrated or dependent third-party systems such as the power grid, hosting provider, or key toolset.

Redundant components protect the system from a failure and can include power supplies, switches, network interface cards, and hard disks. An example of a redundant system is RAID, which employs methods to guard against single or multiple drive failure, depending on the RAID level. Review Chapter 2 if this seems unfamiliar.

Another example is NIC teaming, where two or more NICs are combined into one logical NIC. If the cable, NIC, or switch link for one fails, the others will still remain to service the server.

A redundant component means you have more of that component than you need. For example, a virtualization host computer might have two power supplies to make it redundant, but it can function with a single power supply. A data center may have four connections to four different ISPs, but it can function with any one of them, except that it would incur bursting charges for additional bandwidth used.

Redundant does not mean that there is not an impact to performance or a cost if a component fails; it means that service can be restored to working condition (although the condition may be in a degraded state) without the need for external components. Redundancy differs from fault tolerance (FT) in that FT allows the system to tolerate a fault and continue running in spite of it. Fault tolerance is discussed in more detail later in the chapter.

Once an organization has established the BCP and created redundant systems, it can implement high availability.

High Availability

High availability (HA) is a method of designing systems to ensure that they are continuously available for a predefined length of time. Organizations need to have their applications and services available to end users at all times. If end users cannot access a service or application, it is considered to be unavailable, and the period during which it is unavailable is commonly referred to as downtime.

Downtime comes in two different forms: scheduled downtime and unscheduled downtime. Scheduled downtime is downtime that has been predefined in a service contract that allows an administrator to perform routine maintenance on a system, like installing critical updates, firmware, or service packs.

Unscheduled downtime usually involves an interruption to a service or application due to a physical event, such as a power outage, hardware failure, or security breach. Most organizations exclude scheduled downtime from their availability calculation for an application or service as long as the scheduled maintenance does not affect the end users.

Having an infrastructure that is redundant and highly available helps an organization provide a consistent environment and a more productive workforce. Determining which systems require the investment to be highly available is up to each organization. There will be some systems or applications that do not need to be highly available and do not warrant the cost involved to make them so.

One of the benefits of a public cloud model is that the cost of making the systems highly available falls on the cloud provider and allows the cloud consumer to take advantage of that highly available system.

If a system is not highly available, it means that the system will fail if a single component fails. For example, suppose a system that is not highly available has a single power supply and that power supply fails. In that case, the entire system will be unavailable until the power supply can be replaced.

Determining which systems and which applications require redundancy can help reduce costs and administrative overhead. A policy should be created to determine the expected availability for each application. This will govern whether HA features are required on the systems housing the application.

An organization might use a scale of zero to four to rate the availability requirements of an application. In that scenario, an application that has a rating of zero would need to be available 99.99 percent, whereas an application with a rating of four might only have to be available 98 percent. Creating a scale allows an organization to prioritize its applications and appropriately distribute costs so that it can maximize its compute resources.

Fault Tolerance

FT allows a computer system to function as normal in the event of a failure in one or more of the system's components. Fault-tolerant systems are designed for HA and reliability by installing redundant hardware components. For example, a virtualization host computer would have multiple CPUs, power supplies, and hard disks in the same physical computer. If a component fails, the spare component would take over without bringing the system down. However, having a system that is truly fault-tolerant does result in greater expense because the system requires additional components to achieve fault-tolerant status.

 EXAM TIP   Fault tolerance allows the system to tolerate a fault and to continue to run in spite of it.

Clustering   Connecting multiple computers to provide parallel processing and redundancy is known as clustering. Clustering allows for two or more computers to be connected to act as a single computer. The computers are connected over a fast local area network (LAN), and each node (i.e., each computer used as a server) constituting the cluster runs its own operating system. Clusters can thereby improve performance and availability as compared to using a single computer, and clusters are often used in the cloud for Big Data analysis.

Geo-clustering   Geo-clustering allows for the clustering of multiple redundant computers while those computers are located in different geographical locations. The cluster performs as one node to the outside world, but internally, it is distributed across multiple sites. Geo-clustering allows an organization to support enterprise-level continuity by providing a system that is location-independent. Geo-clustered sites could be contained within a single cloud but distributed across multiple regions, a multicloud solution, or a hybrid cloud solution. Some organizations that have existing regional data centers may opt for a hybrid cloud approach that also involves clustering of systems in their own regionally distributed data centers.

Geo-clustering requires that the devices in the cluster have a persistent connection to one another. In the case of multiple data centers, a wide area network (WAN) would be established between them. In a multicloud setup, a VPN might be used, whereas geographically distributed resources in the same cloud could use a VPC to connect them. In each of these cases, the nodes still appear as a single highly available system.

Failover   Failover uses a constant communication mechanism between two systems called a heartbeat. As long as this heartbeat continues uninterrupted, failover to the redundant system will not initiate. If the heartbeat between the systems fails, the redundant system will take over processing for the primary system.

Failback   When primary systems become operational again, the organization can initiate a failback. Failback is the process of restoring the processing back to the original node. If this were a failure situation, failback would revert processing to the node that had failed once it has been fixed.

Multipathing

Having a fault-tolerant system is a great start to achieving HA, but it is not the only requirement. When planning for HA, all aspects of the network must be considered.

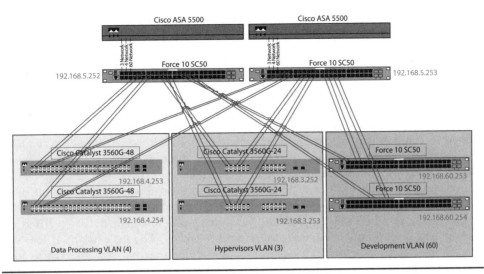

Figure 13-1 Redundant network connections

If the connection between the fault-tolerant systems is a single point of failure, then it is limiting the high availability of the system. Implementing multipathing allows for the configuration of multiple paths for connectivity to a device, providing redundancy for the system to connect to the others.

Figure 13-1 shows a sample network where each distribution switch is redundantly cabled to the core switches, which also are redundantly connected to two clustered firewalls. The servers and other endpoints would be connected to both switches for their subnet. This protects against a single NIC, cable, switch, or firewall failure.

Load Balancing

Another component of HA is load balancing. Load balancing allows you to distribute a workload across multiple computers, networks, and disk drives. Load balancing helps to optimize workloads and resources, allowing for maximum throughput, and helps minimize response times for the end user. Load balancing can also help to create reliability with the use of multiple computers instead of a single computer and is delivered either with dedicated software or hardware.

Load balancing uses the resources of multiple systems to provide a single, specific Internet service. It can be used with any type of internal or public-facing TCP or UPD service to distribute the load of web or file requests between two or more servers. Load balancing can distribute incoming HTTP requests across multiple web servers in a server farm, which can help distribute the load across multiple servers to prevent overloading any single server. Suppose one of the servers in the server farm starts to become overwhelmed. In that case, load balancing begins to distribute HTTP requests to another node in the server farm so that no one node becomes overloaded.

Load balancers are supplied with an IP address and fully qualified domain name (FQDN) that is typically mapped through NAT and a firewall to an external DNS name for cloud resources. This IP address and FQDN represent the load balancer, but client connections are handled by one of the members of the load-balanced system. Internally the load balancer tracks the individual IP addresses of its members.

Load balancing can be performed on software that runs on each device or performed on a dedicated device.

Load Balancers   Load balancers are devices that perform load balancing. Load balancers may be physical hardware, but more often, they are virtual appliances or services offered by cloud providers that can be easily added on to other services in your cloud.

Load balancers can be used to direct traffic to a group of systems to spread the traffic evenly across them. They operate at the OSI transport layer (layer 4). The advantage of cloud load balancers over software load balancing is that load balancers reduce the overhead of having software on each machine to manage the load balancing.

Load balancers make their decisions on which node to direct traffic to based on rulesets and node status obtained through health probes. The load balancer does not modify the URL. It just passes it on to the internal resource that best matches its load balancing rule.

Azure Load Balancer can be used to distribute the load across machines hosted in Microsoft Azure. In AWS, use Elastic Load Balancing.

Application Delivery Controller

Application delivery controllers (ADCs) have more functionality than a load balancer. ADC operates at the OSI application layer (layer 7) and can make delivery decisions based on the URL. Examples of ADC include the Azure Application Gateway (AGW), the AWS Application Load Balancer, and Citrix ADC. Some functions of an ADC include

- URL translation
- Content-based routing
- Hybrid cloud support

URL Translation   ADCs allow companies to deploy a web application that runs on dedicated VMs for each client but maintain a single URL for the clients to access their instances. Each client would access the site from https://mainappurl.com/clientname/, and the ADC would interpret the client name in the URL and know which servers on the back end to direct the traffic to. In such cases, the ADC will rewrite the URL, translating https://mainappurl.com/clientname/ to the internal URL. This may seem simplistic, but as clients use the system, the URL string will be much longer, so the ADC needs to pick out that part of it and rewrite only a portion of the string.

For example, if a client Bob's Hats connects to https://inventorycontrol.com/bobshats/, this might be internally translated to https://BHWeb01.clientsites.local. Later, a request for a resource in the session may look like this: https://inventorycontrol.com/bobshats/hatsearch/query.aspx?gender=mens&type=fedora. This would be translated to https://BHWeb01.clientsites.local/hatsearch/query.aspx?gender=mens&type=fedora.

Content-Based Routing   In another example, you may have different types of data hosted on dedicated resources to better handle storage. If a request comes in for standard HTML content, the ADC can send them to one set of servers, whereas if a request comes in for video, the ADC will direct that traffic to a different set of servers. Each time it directs the traffic, it could still load-balance across the pool of video servers or web servers, but it makes that initial determination by looking at the application layer request to understand the content that is requested.

Another use of ADC is to terminate SSL/TLS sessions at the ADC so that back-end traffic is sent unencrypted. This method is used when trying to cut down on the SSL/TLS processing load on back-end web servers.

CAUTION   Terminating SSL/TLS sessions at the ADC may seem like a good idea, but unencrypted sessions, even on the back end, do present a vulnerability that can be exploited if malicious code or unauthorized access is obtained to internal systems. This can result in a data breach or man in the middle attack.

Hybrid and Multicloud Support   Hybrid and multiclouds are another area where ADCs are used. The ADC can distribute traffic between a combination of different cloud providers or local data centers based on traffic load or other factors. The ADC may require agent software to reside on resources so that it will have visibility into the health and other status of resources. You will also need to configure firewall rules to allow the ADC traffic, such as DNS lookups, health queries, and HTTP/HTTPS requests.

High Availability Network Functions

Without network connectivity, the cloud becomes useless to consumers. That is why it is so important to have reliable network resources. A primary method of establishing this reliability is through HA network functions.

HA in networking equipment involves improving resiliency at the device level and adding redundant units. HA networking equipment will often have FT components. These components are redundant or modular to increase resiliency if a component fails. Some FT components include

- Power supplies
- Control modules
- Interface cards
- Fan trays

A device configured for FT will have two or more of each of these components. Modular devices often allow for hot-swapping of components. This means that a hot-swap interface card or power supply can be removed and replaced while the device is running, with no interruption in service.

Another method of achieving HA is the use of link aggregation. Link aggregation combines two or more network interfaces into one logical unit. This allows the connection to achieve greater throughput because data can be transferred over all of the link aggregated ports at once. This throughput is equal to the total capacity of all the links aggregated. More importantly, link aggregation increases resiliency because the link will still operate, although at a slower speed, as long as one port in the link aggregation is operational.

Some networking equipment that is commonly configured for HA includes switches, routers, and firewalls.

Switches Switches connect servers and other resources to the network. As such, a switch failure would interrupt service to all the devices connected to it if redundant devices were not available. Switch resiliency can be achieved through FT, as described in the preceding section. This involves selecting devices with modular, hot-swappable, redundant components. Figure 13-2 shows the front of a modular switch. The interface cards have latches on the sides so that they can be released from the unit and swapped out. In the picture, the lower interface card has been pulled out so you can see how it slides into the unit. The power supplies at the top of the unit can be pulled and hot-swapped as well.

Figure 13-2   Modular switch front

Multiple switches can be cabled to each device, and then these switches are connected together. This is known as path resiliency. Switches must use protocols to allow for them to dynamically enable or disable links so that broadcast messages are not endlessly repeated over redundant pathways. Such protocols include Rapid Spanning Tree Protocol (RSTP) and Open Shortest Path First (OSPF).

Some switches are stackable. This does not mean that they can sit on top of one another. Stacking is a networking term where multiple devices are connected together at the backplane so that they operate as a single device. Stacking also offers higher throughput between the switches than could be achieved by cabling them together using some of the available switch ports.

Routers   If you recall from Chapter 4, a router is used to connect multiple networks together and allows a network to communicate with the outside world. Without redundancy, a router failure would disrupt connectivity to an entire network. Router resiliency can be achieved as described in the preceding section, with modular, hot-swappable, redundant components.

You can also configure redundant devices to protect against device failure. There are three protocols that allow for multiple routers to operate as one default gateway. These protocols are known as First Hop Redundancy Protocols (FHRPs). These protocols are limited to a single subnet, so they do not modify the routing table or advertise networks other than the one used for the gateway.

The first of these is the Virtual Router Redundancy Protocol (VRRP). With VRRP, multiple routers share the same virtual IP address. These routers collectively are known as a virtual router. The devices that make up the virtual router are known as a VRRP group. One router in the group is the master, and the other routers are backups to that router. Each router is given a priority between 1 and 254, so that if the master fails, the one with the highest priority takes over as the master. The routers communicate with each other and determine their state (operational or not) over the multicast IP 224.0.0.18. These multicast packets will have 112 in the protocol field of the IPv4 header. VRRP is an open standard, so any router vendor can choose to support it. Some mainstream routers that support it include those from Juniper and Brocade.

Hot Standby Router Protocol (HSRP) is another protocol that operates much like VRRP. HSRP, however, is a Cisco proprietary protocol, so it is implemented when you are working with Cisco routers. However, due to the widespread use of Cisco routers, HSRP is a very well-known protocol. Some of the terminology is different, but the process is much the same as VRRP. Instead of a master device, the one that services requests is known as the active device. A standby device will take over if the master fails. Any other routers in the group are known as listening routers.

The third protocol is Gateway Load Balancing Protocol (GLBP). GLBP is another Cisco proprietary protocol. The advantage of GLBP over VRRP and HSRP is that, rather than having an active/standby model where only one router is doing the work and the others are just waiting, each of the routers in the GLBP group can route packets, so the load is shared among them. Figure 13-3 depicts how these three protocols operate.

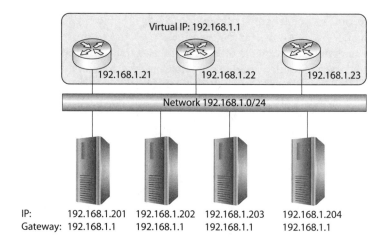

Figure 13-3
First Hop
Redundancy
Protocols

The status of each router is not shown in the diagram because that is how they differ. If it were a GLBP setup, each of the routers would be servicing traffic. If VRRP or HSRP were being used, one would service the traffic and the others would wait until it failed.

Firewalls Firewalls route traffic and enforce security rules governing the traffic flow. Similar to a router, without HA, a firewall failure would disrupt connectivity to an entire network. Routers can be configured for FT with modular, hot-swappable, redundant components to provide device resiliency. They can also be clustered together to protect against single device failure. Some clusters allow for both devices to service traffic together (active/active), whereas others operate with one servicing traffic while the other waits to take control if a failure occurs (active/passive).

Service-Level Agreements for BCP and HA

A service-level agreement (SLA) is a contract that specifies the level of uptime that will be supported by the service provider. SLAs are used with Internet service providers, cloud solutions, and a variety of other technology solutions.

Review the SLA damage clauses when purchasing a complete HA solution. SLAs include provisions for how the service provider will compensate customers if SLAs are not met. At a minimum, these include some monetary compensation for the time the system was down that may be credited toward future invoices. Sometimes the provider must pay fines or damages for lost revenue or lost customer satisfaction. Ensure that the SLA specifies the expected amount of uptime and that damages for SLA violations are sufficient to cover losses due to unexpected downtime.

Similarly, when providing a solution to customers, ensure that you construct SLAs that are consistent with the HA capabilities of your systems. For example, you would not want to create an SLA that states five 9s of availability if the underlying systems can only provide four 9s.

Disaster Recovery Methods

When an organization is choosing a disaster recovery method, it has to measure the level of service required. This means understanding how critical the application or server is and then determining the proper disaster recovery method. When implementing disaster recovery, it is important to form DRPs that will describe how the organization is going to deal with potential disasters such as fires, floods, earthquakes, complete site failure, or blackouts.

It is first necessary to focus on those applications or servers that are mission critical in the DRP. A mission-critical system is any system whose failure would result in the failure of business operations. These systems need to be identified and prioritized in the DRP so that recovery methods are documented commensurate with their criticality level so that losses are minimized.

Location is also important. The company will need to determine where to place the disaster recovery center. Geographic diversity should be taken into account when planning for a disaster that may affect a particular geographic region. Disasters come in many forms, including natural disasters, so placing the disaster recovery center in a location that is 1000 miles away might prevent the same natural disaster from destroying both the primary data center and the disaster recovery data center.

Corporate Guidelines/Documentation

Corporate guidelines should be established so that employees understand the company's expectations for how a disaster will be handled and their own responsibilities if a disaster were to occur. Corporate guidelines are expressed through a set of plans and policies that have been approved by company leadership such as a CEO, CSO, CIO, or an executive group such as an information security steering committee.

The first of these documents is the DRP. An organization makes its DR guidelines known through the DRP, and it is likely the most comprehensive DR document. Other documents are usually created by departments in support of DR initiatives, such as employee rosters, emergency checklists, emergency contact numbers, system documentation, system dependency sheets, triage lists, and so forth. This section will focus mainly on the DRP, but it is good to be aware of some of the documents just mentioned.

After a discussion on the DRP, this section introduces metrics that the organization can use to determine when components might fail or cause problems. These metrics are good to know because they will likely appear in some of the documents mentioned previously. Lastly, DR defines parameters for what losses are acceptable during recovery in terms of how much data can be lost and how much time can be spent recovering. These are defined as the recovery time objective (RTO) and the recovery point objective (RPO). Both concepts are explained in their own subsection at the end of this section.

Disaster Recovery Plan

An organization makes its guidelines for how a disaster will be handled in a DRP. The DRP outlines the procedures to deal with large-scale threats to data, systems, and employees. The DRP defines the threats to those organizational resources and outlines the safeguards and practices designed to allow the company to operate in a different location, using different resources, while primary resources are being restored.

The DRP establishes a generalized capability and readiness to cope effectively with potential disasters. Disaster preparations constitute a last-resort response if resilience and recovery (elements of the BCP) should prove inadequate in practice. Still, if the DRP is to be complete, it must have documented, planned for, and mapped out contingencies.

A DRP typically contains the following sections:

- Business risk evaluation
- Impact analysis
- Roles and responsibilities
- Damage assessment process
- Disaster declaration process
- RTO and RPO (covered later in this section)
- Call trees
- Communication protocols
- Prearranged communication templates
- Testing methods
- Training methods
- Impact and likelihood of each identified disaster scenario
- Recovery steps for each identified disaster scenario

Disaster Recovery Metrics

Another factor to consider when planning for DR is hardware health metrics. Some important hardware health metrics include

- Mean time between failures (MTBF)
- Mean time to repair (MTTR)
- Self-monitoring, analysis, and reporting technology (SMART)

MTBF is the average length of time a device will function before it fails. MTBF can be used to determine approximately how long a hard drive will last in a server. It can also be used to project how long it might take for a particular hardware component to fail and thereby help with the creation of a DRP.

MTTR, on the other hand, is the average length of time that it takes to repair a failed hardware component. MTTR needs to be a factor in the DRP, as it is often part of the maintenance contract for the virtualization host computers. An MTTR of 24 hours or less would be appropriate for a higher-priority server, whereas a lower-priority server might have an MTTR of seven days.

Lastly, SMART is a set of hard disk metrics used to predict failures by monitoring over 100 metrics such as read error rate, spin-up time, start and stop count, reallocated sectors count, and seek error rate. SMART has predefined thresholds for each metric, and those thresholds are used to determine if a drive is in an OK, warning, or error status. All of these factors need to be considered in the DRP for the organization to have a successful disaster recovery environment.

RTO

The RTO is the maximum tolerable amount of time between an outage and the restoration of the service before an organization suffers unacceptable losses. RTO will involve many tasks. The following is the general sequence of tasks that must be performed:

1. Notify IT or cloud backup operations of the need for a restore.

2. Locate restoration archive or media that contains the required data, such as cloud storage, local storage, a remote data center, or tape. If tape, identify if the tape is on-site or off-site. If the tape is off-site, pick it up and bring it to the location where the restoration will take place.

3. Conduct the restore.

4. Validate the restore to confirm that the data is accessible, free from error, and ready for use. If errors are encountered, try restoring again. If errors continue, attempt the restore from another backup.

Figure 13-4 shows a flowchart of all the activities that could be required depending on where the data is located and how the activities contribute to RTO.

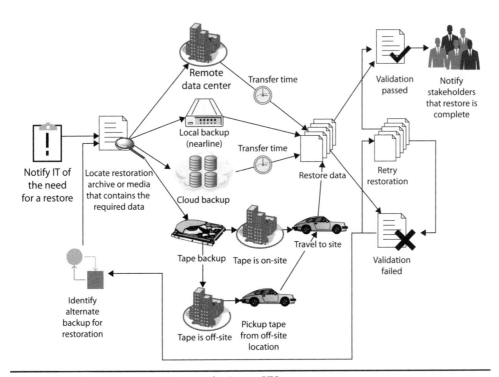

Figure 13-4   Restoration activities contributing to RTO

RPO

The RPO is the maximum amount of time in which data can be lost for a service due to a major incident. The RPO determines how often backups should take place. For example, if the RPO is 24 hours, then backups would occur daily.

The organization should not treat all data the same. Some data might need to have a different RPO because it has different availability needs. For example, a database of customer orders might have an RPO of one minute, whereas the RPO for web files might be 24 hours because updates are made no more than once per day and web files are also located in web developer repositories.

One of the things that should be considered and that can help meet expected RTO and RPO is redundancy. A redundant system can be used to provide a backup to a primary system in the case of failure.

Disaster Recovery Kit

A DR kit is a container packed with the essential items you will need in a disaster. One item should be the disaster recovery plan. Some other items to include are

- Water
- Dry food (nuts, protein bars, etc.)
- Flashlight
- First aid kit
- Batteries
- Whistle
- Cellular hotspot
- Charging brick
- Tool kit

Playbook

A DR playbook is a document that outlines the steps necessary for resolving a particular situation. This may sound like the DRP, but a playbook differs from a DRP in that a playbook only lists the steps required for one situation. For example, a DRP would list steps required in general for a disaster along with particulars for certain things, but it can be hard to find the information you need when a document gets so large. Playbooks, on the other hand, are shorter, situation-specific references that show employees what they need without all the extra details that do not pertain to the situation at hand. A company would develop playbooks for events like fires, floods, hurricanes, tornados, critical infrastructure failure, pandemics, or active shooter situations.

Network Diagram

A network diagram is a picture that explains how the network is laid out, how systems, such as firewalls, routers, switches, IoT, servers, and other computers, are interconnected. Each device is labeled with its name and possibly an IP address or other information on the system, such as the operating system, role, services, open ports, or subnet. There are two types of network diagrams: logical and physical.

Logical Network Diagram   The logical network diagram is concerned with information flow and how systems communicate. Figure 13-5 shows a logical network diagram. It shows several networks that are each connected together. The resources on each server are defined, but the physical connections are not shown.

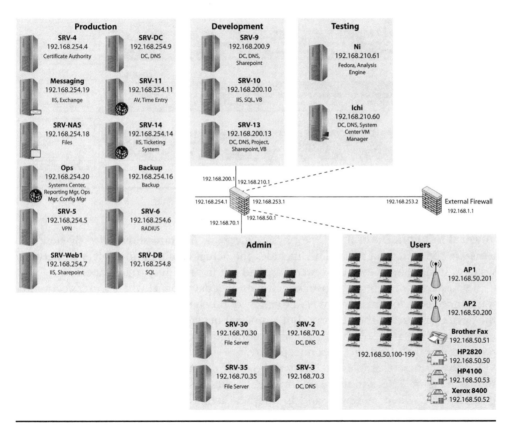

Figure 13-5   Logical network diagram

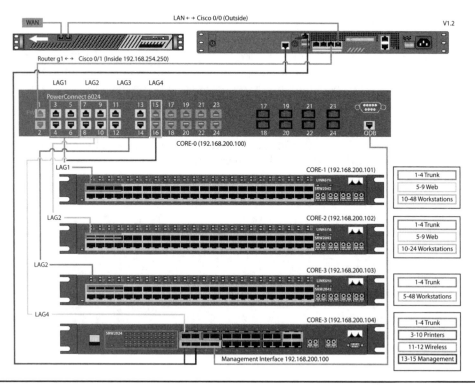

Figure 13-6 Switch port diagram

Physical Network Diagram The physical network diagram shows directly how systems are connected together. This includes the actual cabling and devices in between systems. It may also show how systems are laid out in proximity to one another.

If you were trying to track down which port on a patch panel where a user's computer was connected, a logical diagram would not be of much use. It would only show you that the device was part of the network, but a physical network diagram could show the jack number of the wall port, the patch panel termination point, and the switch name and port number that the device is connected to.

Consider these examples of physical network diagrams. A switch port diagram is shown in Figure 13-6. This diagram includes labeling for LAG groups that are connected back to a core switch, a firewall, and an Internet filter. This diagram would help network engineers understand how the switch backbone is laid out and where to look if they were encountering issues with the switch fabric.

Figure 13-7 depicts a rack diagram of three racks in a data center. Each item is labeled with its model number. Most of the equipment is facing the front of the racks, but a few pieces are mounted facing the back side, and those are noted. This diagram would

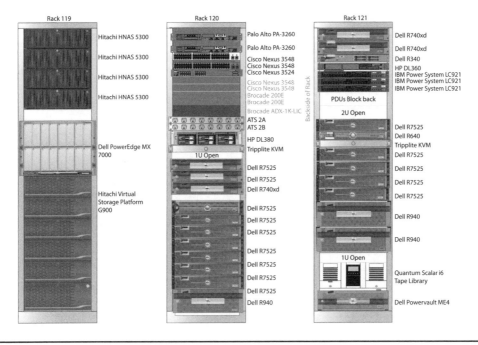

Figure 13-7 Rack diagram

be helpful when planning for new equipment in the racks or when determining optimal data center cable runs. It would also help if you were to give instructions to a technician on where to find a server that has a spared drive or requires some other maintenance.

Figure 13-8 shows a patch panel diagram. Each wall port is described with its purpose, color, and where it is patched in the wiring closet. If a port stopped working, technicians could use the diagram to determine where the port terminates in the wiring closet and then could troubleshoot the port, cable, or switch it is connected to.

Replication

Replication transfers data between two or more systems so that any changes to the data are made on each node in the replica set. A replica set consists of the systems that will all retain the same data. Replication can occur between systems at the same site, termed intrasite replication, or between systems at different sites, termed intersite replication. Multiple sites are used to protect data when a single site is unavailable and to ensure low-latency availability by serving data from sources that are close to the end user or application.

Outlet:	Patch Panel	Patch Plug	Purpose:	Wall Port Label:	Type:	Cable/Jack Color:	Wall Port Name:
1	A	1	Data A	A1-A	Workstation	Blue	A1 - Chris
2	A	2	VOIP	A1-B	VOIP	Brown	A1 - Chris
3	A	3	Data A	A2-A	Workstation	Blue	A2 - Tom
4	A	4	VOIP	A2-B	VOIP	Brown	A2 - Tom
5	A	5	Data C	A3-A	Protected	Yellow	A3 - Paula
6	A	6	VOIP	A3-B	VOIP	Brown	A3 - Paula
7	A	7	Data A	A4-A	Workstation	Blue	A4 - Hans
8	A	8	VOIP	A4-B	VOIP	Brown	A4 - Hans
9	A	9	Data A	A5-A	Workstation	Blue	A5 - Conference East
10	A	10	VOIP	A5-B	VOIP	Brown	A5 - Conference East
11	A	11	Data A	A6-A	Workstation	Blue	A6 - Conference South
12	A	12	VOIP	A6-B	VOIP	Brown	A6 - Conference South
13	A	13	Data A	A7-A	Workstation	Blue	A7 - Joe
14	A	14	VOIP	A7-B	VOIP	Brown	A7 - Joe
15	A	15	Data A	A8-A	Workstation	Blue	A8 - Bill
16	A	16	VOIP	A8-B	VOIP	Brown	A8 - Bill
17	A	17	Data A	A9-A	Workstation	Blue	A9 - Lynda
18	A	18	VOIP	A9-B	VOIP	Brown	A9 - Lynda
19	A	19	IoT A	A10-A	Camera	Orange	A10 - NW Ceiling 01
20	A	20	IoT B	A10-B	Camera	Orange	A10 - NW Ceiling 02
21	A	21	Data C	A11-A	Public	Red	A11 - Reception
22	A	22	VOIP	A11-B	VOIP	Brown	A11 - Reception
23	A	23	Data A	A12-A	Workstation	Blue	A12 - Workroom West
24	A	24	VOIP	A12-B	VOIP	Brown	A12 - Workroom West
25	B	1	Data A	B1-A	Workstation	Blue	B1 - Workroom East
26	B	2	VOIP	B1-B	VOIP	Brown	B1 - Workroom East
27	B	3	Data A	B2-A	Camera	Orange	B2 - NE Ceiling 01
28	B	4	VOIP	B2-B	Camera	Orange	B2 - NE Ceiling 02
29 Through 40	B B B						
41	C	13	Inet	Internet - A	Internet	White	
42	C	14	Inet	Internet - B	Internet	White	
43	C	15	Inet	Internet - C	Internet	White	
44	C	16	Inet	Internet - D	Internet	White	

Figure 13-8 Patch panel diagram

As discussed in Chapter 3, two forms of replication can be used to keep replica sets consistent. Synchronous replication writes data to the local store and then immediately replicates it to the replica set or sets. The application is not informed that the data has been written until all replica sets have acknowledged receipt and storage of the data. Asynchronous replication stores the data locally and then reports back to the application that the data has been stored. It then sends the data to replication partners at its next opportunity.

File Transfer

In lieu of some backups, an organization may choose to perform a file transfer or a scheduled synchronization of files instead. This is quite common in replication scenarios. It is important when synchronizing files for the intent of archiving that you configure them to not synchronize deletes. Additionally, changes on one side are going to be reflected on the other side, so synchronizations are not useful in preserving those changes.

A one-time file transfer is a great way to get a point-in-time copy for data that does not change so that you do not need to keep backing it up with every full backup that occurs. A one-time backup can be performed and then stored away for whenever it is needed. If data has remained unchanged since the one-time backup, the backup will still be consistent even though it has not been updated.

One-time backups can reduce space on backup drives and reduce the length of time required to perform backups. Ensure that if you do a one-time file transfer that you lock the files so that they cannot be changed in production. Otherwise, you might find at some later date that people have been changing the files but there is no active backup for the data.

Network Configurations

Network devices can take a long time to configure properly, but a saved configuration can be applied to a device in minutes. Save device configurations to a central location that is backed up regularly so that you will be able to retrieve device configurations and reapply them if necessary.

If you have a failed device but a spare is available, it can be placed into service, cabled up just like the failed unit, and then the configuration can be applied to it to make it functional.

 CAUTION Ensure that you apply firmware updates to bring a device to the same firmware level before applying a configuration. Configuration files may not work correctly if the firmware versions differ between the one whose configuration was exported and the one you are importing it to.

Service-Level Agreements for DR

As mentioned earlier in this chapter, an SLA is a contract that specifies the level of uptime that will be supported by the service provider. SLAs should be obtained for each of the systems that will be relied upon for the DR solution. It would be a shame to fail over to a DR site only to find that the site did not meet availability expectations. Customers who have recently suffered a downtime do not want to experience other downtimes shortly thereafter, so you want to ensure that your DR site will provide the required service level.

Backup and Recovery

A backup set is a secondary copy of the organization's data and is used to replace the original data in the event of a loss. The backup process needs to be monitored just like any other process that is running in the environment. Proper monitoring of the backup system helps to ensure that the data is available if there is a disaster.

Backups are only as good as their accompanying restore strategies. Testing the restoration process of all the backups in an organization should be done on a scheduled and routine basis. Backups can be fully automated with schedules, so that they can run without interaction from an administrator.

Proper DRP and data retention plans should be established to ensure that data loss is consistent with the RPO if a disaster occurs. The backup plan should include how the data is to be stored and if the data is going to be stored off-site, how long it is kept off-site and how many copies are kept at the off-site facility. The backup plan should also specify how the data will be recovered.

Selecting the appropriate backup solution is a critical piece of a properly configured disaster recovery implementation. Creating a backup is simply the process of copying and archiving data so that the data is available to be restored to either the original location or an alternative location should the original data be lost, modified, or corrupted.

Creating backups of data serves two primary purposes. The first purpose of a backup is to restore data that is lost because either it was deleted or it became corrupt. The second purpose of a backup is to enable the recovery of data from an earlier time frame.

An organization should have a data retention policy that specifies how long data needs to be kept. For example, if an organization has a data retention policy that specifies all data must be kept for two weeks, an end user who needs to have a document restored from ten days ago could do so.

When selecting a backup policy, several things need to be taken into consideration. First, the organization must determine how the backups will be stored, whether on tape, optical media, NAS, external disk, or a cloud-based storage system. Cloud storage can emulate a virtual tape library (VTL) so that existing on-premises backup solutions can see it.

If data is stored on removable media such as tapes, optical media, or external disks, first determine if the backups should be stored at an offsite location. Storing backups at an offsite location allows for recovery of the data in the event of a site disaster. After choosing a media type, the next step is to choose the style of backup.

Cloud backups exist in the cloud provider's data center, so they are already outside of the organization and thus "off-site." Cloud backups are an effective way to perform off-site backups without an extensive infrastructure. Files from cloud backups are easier to manage and often faster to retrieve than off-site tapes or removable media.

The available backup types are discussed next. Each backup type has its own set of advantages and disadvantages.

Backup Types

An organization can structure backups in multiple ways to strike a balance between the length of time it takes to conduct a backup and the length of time it takes to perform a restore operation. Backup types also offer different levels of recoverability, with some requiring the presence of another backup to be functional. The available backup types include the following:

- Full backup
- Differential backup

- Incremental backup
- Snapshot
- Bit-for-bit backup
- Imaging

Backups utilize features such as change or delta tracking and can be stored online or offline. We will discuss those topics before covering the various backup types.

Change/Delta Tracking

Some backup types archive information depending on whether it has been backed up recently or if it has changed since the last backup. File change status is tracked using a flag on files called the archive bit. When a full backup is performed, the archive bit is set to 0. If that file changes, the archive bit is set to 1.

Online and Offline Backups

Online backups are those that are available to restore immediately, while offline backups must be brought online before they are available to restore. Some offline backups include tape backups and removable hard drives. A backup tape is offline because it must be retrieved and inserted into a tape drive before it is available to restore. Similarly, a backup hard drive stored in a safe deposit box is offline.

Online backups include nearline and cloud backups. Nearline backups are written to media on the network, such as a NAS, a local backup server, or shared storage on a server. In the cloud, nearline storage is rated at a lower availability. (Google lists their nearline at 99.95 percent, whereas standard storage is 99.99 percent available.) These backups are online because they can be retrieved without having to insert media. Cloud backups are also online backups because they are always available. Both of these online options can be restored at any time.

Full Backup

A full system backup backs up the entire system, including everything on the hard drive. It makes a copy of all the data and files on the drive in a single process. A full backup takes up the most space on storage media because it does a full drive copy every time the backup is executed. Performing a full backup every day requires the same amount of space on the backup media as the drive being backed up without backup compression or deduplication. Multiple backup iterations usually have many duplicates and so deduplication ratios can be 100:1 or higher. A 100:1 reduction ratio reduces the space required for further backups by 99 percent. If a full backup takes 300GB, the next full backup would take 3GB with the 100:1 reduction ratio.

The benefit to a full backup is that an organization can take any of the backups from any day they were executed and restore data from a single backup media. The full backup resets the archive bit on all files on the computer to zero. Figure 13-9 shows an example of how a full system backup would look after four backups.

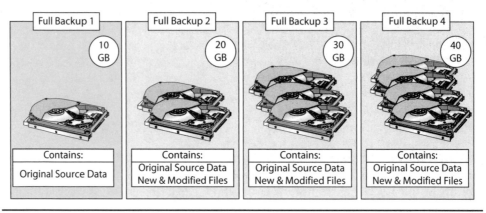

Figure 13-9   Illustration of a full system backup

Differential Backup

The differential backup backs up only those changes that were made since the last full backup was executed. To perform a differential backup, a full backup must have been performed on the data set previously.

After the full backup is executed, every differential backup executed thereafter will contain only the changes made since the last full backup. The differential backup knows which data has been changed because of the archive bit. Each changed file results in a file with an archive bit set to 1. The differential backup does not change the archive bit when it backs up the files, so each successive differential backup includes the files that changed since the last full backup because full backups do reset the archive bit.

One of the disadvantages to differential backups is that the time it takes to complete the backup will increase as files change between the last full backup. Another disadvantage is that if the organization wants to restore an entire system to a particular point in time, it must first locate the last full backup taken prior to the point of failure and the last differential backup since the last full backup.

For example, if full backups are taken every Friday night and differentials are taken each night in between, restoring a system on Wednesday to the Tuesday backup would require the full backup and the Tuesday differential. Figure 13-10 shows an example of how a differential backup looks after three days.

 EXAM TIP   Differential backups require more space to store the backup and take more time to complete than an incremental backup. They are still faster to perform than a full backup. Differential backups require less time to perform a restoration than does an incremental backup.

Incremental Backup

An incremental backup also backs up only those files that have changed since the last backup was executed, but the last backup can be either a full backup or an incremental backup. Incremental backups do reset the archive bit to 0 when they back up files, so the

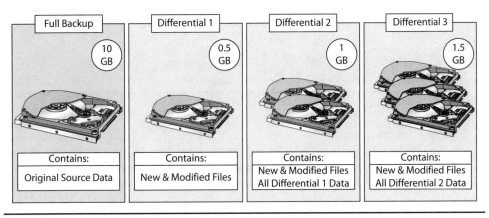

Figure 13-10   Illustration of a differential backup

next incremental backup does not back up that file again unless it has changed again. To perform an incremental backup, a full backup must have been carried out on the data set previously.

Backing up only files that have changed since the last backup makes incremental backups faster and requires less space than a full or differential backup. However, the time it takes to perform a restoration is longer because many backup files could need to be processed. Restores require the last full backup and all the incremental backups since the last full backup.

For example, if full backups are taken every Friday night, and incremental backups are taken each night in between, to restore a system on Wednesday to the Tuesday backup would require the full backup, Saturday incremental, Sunday incremental, Monday incremental, and Tuesday incremental. Figure 13-11 shows an example of how an incremental backup would look after three backups.

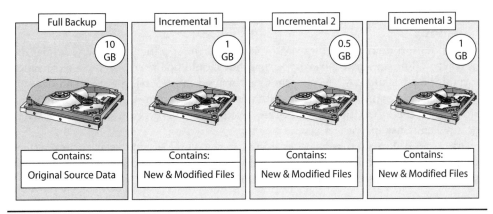

Figure 13-11   Illustration of an incremental backup

	Full	Differential	Incremental
Size	High	Medium to Low	Low
Backup Duration	Long	Moderately Short	Short
Restore Duration	Short	Moderately Short	Longest

Table 13-1   Comparison of Full, Differential, and Incremental Backups

 EXAM TIP   Incremental backups require less space to store the backup than differential or full backups. Incremental backups also complete much more quickly but require more time to perform a restoration.

Table 13-1 shows the full, differential, and incremental backup types and their size, backup duration, and restore duration.

3-2-1 Rule

The 3-2-1 rule is a general principle to follow when designing backups. It requires that you keep at least three copies of your data, that two of the backups reside on different types of storage, and that at least one copy is stored off-site.

For example, you might have your production data hosted in the cloud and configure backups with a third-party cloud provider. You also have a backup job that makes a weekly copy of the backup to store on a removable hard drive rotation.

The 3-2-1 rule is easy to remember and very practical. If your data is lost or corrupted and you have to go to backup, you want to have some assurance that you will have another option if your backup fails. The second copy is that assurance. Furthermore, it is stored off-site because that helps to separate it from the same risks that the first backup copy faces. For example, if the cloud provider goes bankrupt, it wouldn't help if you had multiple backup copies stored with them because they all would be inaccessible. Similarly, if all your backups are stored in a vault at the office and the building burns down, you want to have another copy at a different location to restore from.

Snapshot

A snapshot captures the state of a VM or volume at the specific time when the snapshot was taken. While similar to a backup, a snapshot should not be considered a replacement for traditional backups. A VM snapshot can be used to preserve the state and data of a VM at a specific point in time. A snapshot can be taken before a major software installation, and if the installation fails or causes issues, the VM can be restored to the state it was in when the snapshot was taken.

Other cloud data such as websites hosted in the cloud or cloud data stores perform storage snapshots that operate similarly to a VM snapshot except that they are only concerned with the data stored in the snapped location.

Multiple snapshots can be taken. A series of snapshots are organized into a snapshot chain. A snapshot keeps a delta file of all the changes after the snapshot was taken. The delta file records the differences between the current state of the disk and the state the disk was in when the snapshot was taken. A marker in the chain allows the cloud provider to know which points represent snapshots.

Snapshots and snapshot chains can be created and managed in a variety of different ways. It is possible to create snapshots, revert to any snapshot in the chain, mount snapshots as data stores to view individual files, or even delete snapshots.

Since snapshots are not a replacement for regular backups, they should only be kept for a short period, preferably a few days. A snapshot continues to record from its point of origin, so if the snapshot is kept for long periods, the file will continue to grow larger and might eventually become too large to remove or cause disk storage constraints. This can cause performance issues for the cloud resource. If there is a need to keep a snapshot longer than a few days, it is recommended to create a full system backup.

Bit-for-Bit Backups
Another type of backup is the bit-for-bit backup, which captures the entire hard drive bit by bit. Because the whole hard drive was captured, the image can be used to restore an entire server in the event of a disaster, allowing the image to be restored on new hardware.

Creating a bit-for-bit backup of a server differs from the file-based backups discussed earlier in that the file-based backups only allow you to restore what was configured to be backed up, whereas a bit-for-bit backup allows for the entire restoration of the server, including files, folders, and operating system. Even if a file backup contains all the data on a drive, it cannot restore partition tables and data to the exact places and states they were in when the backup was taken, and this can cause problems if you try to do a file-level restore on a server's operating system drive or on transactional data such as e-mail mailboxes or databases.

Bit-for-bit backups can be scheduled much like other backup jobs and can be an excellent method for returning a system to a previous state. Bit-for-bit backups are typically used for physical machines in much the same way as a snapshot is used for VMs.

Imaging
Images are like bit-for-bit backups in that they are a bit-for-bit copy of the hard drive. However, images are usually taken as a one-time operation rather than a normal scheduled task. Images are taken of machines prior to deploying them to end users. Administrators may restore from the image if the user has issues with the machine at a later date. Some administrators may choose to restore rather than troubleshoot an issue if the issue appears complex. Applying an image can quickly and easily bring a system back to the organizationally approved operating system build and software set. Images can also be used to bring systems back to a standard approved state.

Images can be taken of machines that are prepped for deployments. Suppose the IT department receives 900 workstations with the same hardware configuration. They would configure the first one with all the software, configure it for use, update the system with the latest patches, and then harden the system. They would then image the system and deploy the image to the other 899 machines.

Images can be used for remote deployments as well. Similar to the situation just described, the IT department would configure the first machine with the software, configuration, and updates and then create an image. That image would be deployed to the network, and computers could PXE boot to the image repository, and the image would be deployed to them.

Clone

A clone is similar to an image, but it is often made as part of an ongoing process. A clone is a copy of the data on a logical or physical drive. Clones can be created through storage management software or via software tools. Figure 13-12 shows an example of a clone used

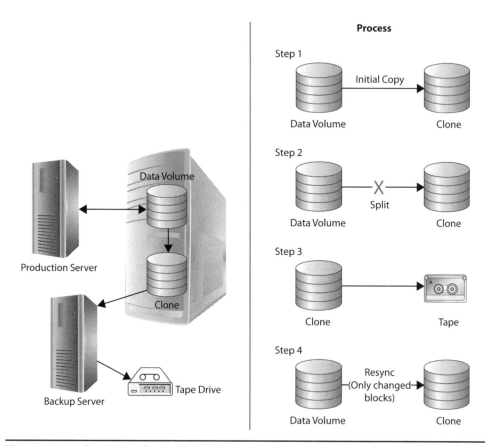

Figure 13-12   Illustration of a clone used in backup operations

as part of an ongoing backup operation. A clone is made of the production server data and kept synchronized using the storage software. When the backup server needs to write the data to tape, rather than copy the data over the network, the clone is split from the production volume so that new changes are not recorded to it and then mounted to the backup server. The backup server writes the data to tape and then takes the volume offline so that it can be resynced with the data volume.

Backup Target

A backup target is a destination for a backup job. A backup target could be a local folder on another drive, a folder on the network, a cloud drive, a remote site, or a tape, for example. Choose a target that will offer low enough latency to complete backup jobs in the required amount of time and that is fast enough to meet the RTO.

Backup targets are sometimes confused with replicas. The two differ in that backup targets are the destination for a backup, whereas replicas are used to create a mirrored copy of the data between the initial target and a replica target.

Local

Local targets are those that are on the same network as the source data. These are also called nearline backups. Local targets include backups to another drive on the same machine, backups to a NAS on the local network, or backups to a file server on the local network. This could also include a local cloud appliance with local storage, which is then replicated to the cloud.

Remote

To help reduce downtime in case of a disaster, an organization can set up and configure backups or replication to another site or a cloud service that is off-premises. It is less likely that an event affecting the source data will also affect a remote target. For example, a forklift that knocks over a server rack in the data center would not affect the cloud backup. Remote targets include cloud backups, remote data centers, and tapes that are taken off-site.

Exercise 13-1: Cross-Region Replication

In this exercise, we will establish cross-region replication between two AWS S3 buckets.

1. Log in to your AWS account. You will be presented with the management console, which will show the available services you can choose from.

2. Go to the storage section and select S3.

3. You will be presented with a screen showing your existing buckets:

Enable replication for the source bucket

4. Select the cloud-example bucket we created in Exercise 3-1 by clicking on the blue hyperlinked name. If you do not have that bucket, please go back to Exercise 3-1 in Chapter 3 to create it.

5. The details of the cloud-example bucket will be displayed. Select the Properties tab, as shown here:

6. You can see that bucket versioning is disabled. We will enable it. Click the Edit button under Bucket Versioning.

7. When the Edit Bucket Versioning screen loads, select Enable, as shown next, and then click Save Changes.

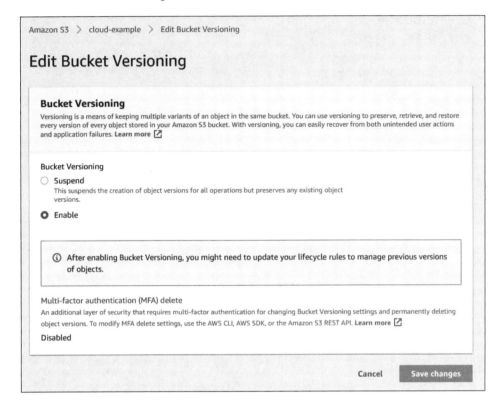

Create a destination bucket and enable versioning

8. We will now create a destination bucket for the replication. Click the Buckets link on the left side of the screen. It is directly underneath the Amazon S3 label.

9. Choose Create Bucket.

10. Give the bucket a name. In this example, we call the bucket **cloud-test-destination**.

11. Select a different AWS region from the first bucket. In this example, the cloud-test bucket resides in the US East (Ohio) us-east-2 region. The replication bucket will reside in the US West (N. California) us-west-1 region.

12. Under bucket versioning, select the Enable radio button. Your selections should look like this:

Amazon S3 > Create bucket

Create bucket

Buckets are containers for data stored in S3. Learn more ↗

General configuration

Bucket name

cloud-test-destination

Bucket name must be unique and must not contain spaces or uppercase letters. **See rules for bucket naming** ↗

AWS Region

US West (N. California) us-west-1   ▼

Copy settings from existing bucket - *optional*
Only the bucket settings in the following configuration are copied.

Choose bucket

Block Public Access settings for this bucket

Public access is granted to buckets and objects through access control lists (ACLs), bucket policies, access point policies, or all. In order to ensure that public access to this bucket and its objects is blocked, turn on Block all public access. These settings apply only to this bucket and its access points. AWS recommends that you turn on Block all public access, but before applying any of these settings, ensure that your applications will work correctly without public access. If you require some level of public access to this bucket or objects within, you can customize the individual settings below to suit your specific storage use cases. **Learn more** ↗

☑ **Block *all* public access**
     Turning this setting on is the same as turning on all four settings below. Each of the following settings are independent of one another.

☑ Block public access to buckets and objects granted through *new* access control lists (ACLs)
     S3 will block public access permissions applied to newly added buckets or objects, and prevent the creation of new public access
     ACLs for existing buckets and objects. This setting doesn't change any existing permissions that allow public access to S3 resources
     using ACLs.

☑ Block public access to buckets and objects granted through *any* access control lists (ACLs)
     S3 will ignore all ACLs that grant public access to buckets and objects.

☑ Block public access to buckets and objects granted through *new* public bucket or access point policies
     S3 will block new bucket and access point policies that grant public access to buckets and objects. This setting doesn't change any
     existing policies that allow public access to S3 resources.

☑ Block public and cross-account access to buckets and objects through *any* public bucket or access point
     policies
     S3 will ignore public and cross-account access for buckets or access points with policies that grant public access to buckets and
     objects.

Bucket Versioning

Versioning is a means of keeping multiple variants of an object in the same bucket. You can use versioning to preserve, retrieve, and restore every version of every object stored in your Amazon S3 bucket. With versioning, you can easily recover from both unintended user actions and application failures. **Learn more** ↗

Bucket Versioning

◉ Disable

◯ Enable

13. Scroll to the bottom of the page and select Create Bucket.

14. Select the Management tab.

15. Under Replication Rules, select Create Replication Rule.

16. Give it a name. For this exercise, we will call it **cloud-test-bucket-replication**.

17. Under Source Bucket, choose This Rule Applies To All Objects In The Bucket.

18. Under Destination, click the Browse S3 button to select the destination bucket we created in steps 8 to 13.

19. Choose the cloud-test-destination bucket by clicking the radio button next to it and click Choose Path.

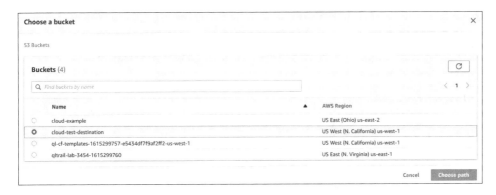

20. Scroll to the bottom of the screen and click Save. The replication rule will be displayed.

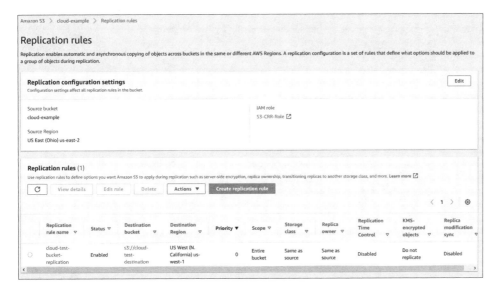

Upload files

21. You will be presented with the Buckets screen again. Open the cloud-example bucket.

22. Create three text files on your desktop called **test1**, **test2**, and **test3**. Select those files and upload them to the bucket by clicking the Upload button, which will open the Upload screen, and then click Add Files, as shown here.

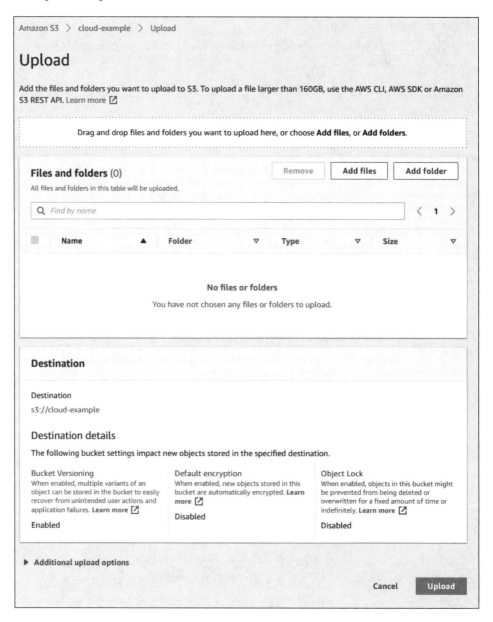

23. Click the Amazon S3 link in the upper left to return to the list of buckets.

24. Select the three text files and choose the Open button. The files will populate in the Upload screen.

25. Click Upload and the files will be placed into the bucket. The Upload Status screen will be displayed and you should see a status of Succeeded next to each of the files, as shown next.

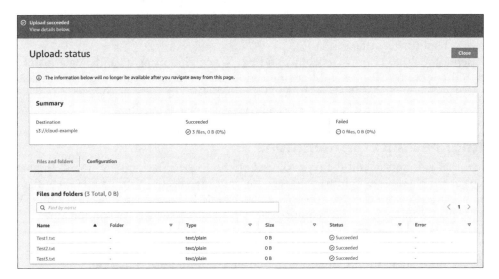

26. Click the Close button, and the cloud-example bucket details will be displayed.

27. Click the Amazon S3 link in the upper left to return to the list of buckets.

28. Open the cloud-test-destination bucket, and you will see that the three test files we uploaded are now in the destination bucket too.

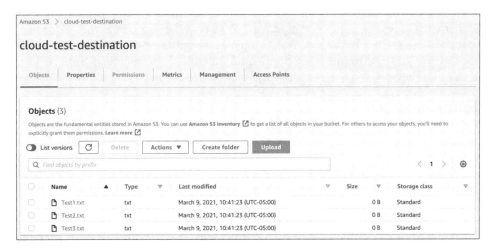

Replicas

The closer the target is to the source, the faster the backup will run. It will also be faster to restore the data when the target is closer to the source. However, closer targets are riskier because an event that could disrupt services or corrupt the source data might also do the same to the local backup. You do not want to be in a situation where both production systems and backups are unavailable.

Typically, companies will perform a backup to a local data store in the same data center so that the backup job completes quickly and so the data is available close to the source if necessary. However, this data will then be replicated to a replica such as a cloud service, remote site, or tape.

Replicas help to improve reliability and FT. When replicating data, the data is stored on multiple storage devices at different locations so that if one location suffers a disaster, the other location is available with the exact same data. Remote sites are costly to own and operate, so cloud backups have become very popular as a replica.

Other Backup Considerations

Now that you understand the types of backups and where backups are stored, the next steps are to choose the right backup type for your organization and its RTO, configure the backups to store the right objects, and schedule backups to run at ideal times. Be aware that restoring data may require some dependencies such as backup software, catalogs, decryption keys, and licensing.

It is also important to ensure that connectivity from source to target is sufficient to back up the data in the required time frame and with minimal impact on other services that may be operating concurrently. Some companies may find that latency is preventing them from meeting backup windows, in which case they can employ edge sites to reduce the latency.

Next, procure the necessary equipment to conduct backups and restores. If you find that the cost of the equipment is prohibitive for your organization, look to contract with a third party or cloud provider to conduct backups. You will also want to be aware of the availability cost of performing backups or restores and make others aware of activities that could cause performance degradation. The availability cost is the performance impact incurred when backup or restore operations produce contention for available resources. Backup and restore operations could potentially prevent users from performing tasks, or they could make systems less desirable to use.

Backup Schedules

Backup jobs must run on a schedule to be effective. A one-time backup can be useful, but it does little to protect company information that changes rapidly. Scheduled jobs allow for backups to operate at regular intervals to back up the files that have changed since the last backup or to back up all files. The determination as to what is backed up in the job is based on the backup type discussed earlier, such as a full backup, incremental backup, differential backup, snapshot, or bit-for-bit backup.

Backup schedules should be structured such that they do not affect production activities. Backups can consume a lot of disk and network I/O. Compressed and encrypted backups consume CPU as well. Compression and decompression can place a heavy burden on the server and cause disruptions or poor performance for users if backups run during peak times.

Most backups will not require downtime, but they could still affect the performance of the VM and the applications that run on top of it. For this reason, it is best to plan backups for times when the load on the system is minimal.

For example, it would be a bad idea to back up a domain controller at the beginning of the day when users are logging into systems because that is when the domain controller must authenticate each request. Users would likely see service interruptions if a backup were to take place during such a peak time.

Virtualized and cloud systems may have users spread across the globe. Additionally, it may be necessary to coordinate resources with cloud vendors or with support personnel in different global regions. In such cases, time zones can be a large constraint for performing backups. It can be challenging to coordinate a time that works for distributed user bases and maintenance teams. In those cases, you might need to provision enough resources on machines so that backups can run concurrently with a full traffic load.

Configurations

As you choose a schedule for the backup jobs, you will also need to configure the appropriate backup type to minimize the impact on production systems and applications, yet meet backup frequency requirements, RTO, and RPO.

Some common scenarios include performing a full backup weekly and incrementals or differentials daily. Others might choose to do a full backup nightly with hourly incrementals or differentials. Bandwidth and system resources may determine which options are available to you. Of course, if company policy specifies a specific configuration, you may need to upgrade equipment to meet the requirements.

Objects

One of the most important decisions when designing backups is determining what to back up. Each item selected for backup is an object. Should you back up the company intranet? What about local machines if the policy states that data should only be stored on the network? The selection of backup objects is one that should be approved by data and application owners. Ensure that senior management sees the list and ensures that all data and application owners are represented. You may receive sign-off from the intranet application owner and the end-user support manager to back up local machines and the intranet, but if you forgot to include the e-mail application owner, you might be in trouble when the e-mail server goes down. We cannot stress how important it is to choose the right backup objects.

Dependencies

Just having a backup is not always enough. You also need to have the dependencies necessary to restore that backup in an emergency. Dependencies include backup software, catalogs, decryption keys, and licensing.

Backup software is the first dependency. Each vendor stores its backup data in a different format. Usually, one vendor's backup software cannot read the backup software of another vendor, so you will need to have the backup software that initially created the backup or a newer version of the software to perform the restore.

Catalogs are also necessary. Catalogs are indexes of the data on backup media or backup files. When you want to restore data, you may not know which file contains the data you are looking for, so you query the backup system, and it uses a catalog to find the file or media, and then you can load that media or select that file to do the restore. The good news is that you can catalog media or files if the catalog does not exist. However, if you have 1000 backup files pulled from an old backup drive, the backup software will need to catalog all of them for you to know what is on each one.

Encryption is an important factor when storing backups. Many controls may be in place to protect data on production systems, but if backups are not encrypted, that data could be lost simply by exploiting the backup connection, backup media, or backup systems. For this reason, many companies encrypt their backups. To do the restore, you will need to provide the decryption keys, so keep these safe.

Licensing is also necessary for backup and restore operations. If you back up to a cloud service and then let the contract lapse, you will not be able to do a restore until you renew that license. Also, there is no guarantee that your backups will still be available if you let the contract lapse.

Connectivity

Backups, especially full ones, can take a lot of bandwidth depending on the size and type of the backup object. When migrating over a 1 Gbps or 10 Gbps Ethernet network, this is not as much of a concern, but bandwidth can be a huge constraint when performing backups over a low-speed WAN link such as a 5 Mbps Multiprotocol Label Switching (MPLS) connection.

Evaluate backup objects and their data sizes and then estimate how much time it will take to back them up over the bandwidth available. Be sure to factor in other traffic as well. You do not want the backup to affect normal business operations in the process.

Edge Sites

As information systems become more critical, companies are backing them up more often, even continuously. Latency can be an issue in ensuring timely backup completion when backing up to the cloud. The solution to latency with cloud backups is to select a vendor with edge sites close in proximity to the data that is being backed up. Edge sites are data centers closer to the customer.

Edge sites sometimes service requests and then synchronize back to the primary data center at a later time. Edge sites can also keep data close to the customer in their country of operation to meet data sovereignty requirements.

Equipment

You will need appropriate hardware to do the restoration. If the data is on tape media, you will need a compatible tape device to perform the restore. LTO drives can typically read two versions behind their stated version, and they can write to the stated version and one level down so that an LTO 7 drive can read LTO 5, 6, and 7, and it can write to LTO 6 and 7.

You will also need enough storage space to do a restore. If you archived data to free up space but then later need it, you might need to purchase and install more storage first. You will also need enough bandwidth to copy down data from cloud backups.

Availability

It is imperative to understand if the chosen backup requires downtime. Images of machines can sometimes fail when they are in use, so some image jobs are performed from boot disks when a server is offline.

Backups that require the system to be unavailable must be performed during a downtime. Downtime needs to be scheduled with stakeholders, such as end users and customers, and the stakeholders need to understand how long the downtime is expected to take.

If you anticipate performance degradation due to backups or restores, let stakeholders know. Some can adapt if they are aware of the issues, while some cannot, but they will at least know what is going on. A restore will likely be a higher priority than normal operations, but the helpdesk and other operations teams will need to be aware of the cause of the performance degradation.

Partners or Third Parties

You may use a third party or partner to perform backup services. The most common scenario is to use a cloud provider as the third-party backup service. It is important to understand your contract with the cloud vendor or other third party. Understand what their responsibilities are to you in the case of an emergency and how quickly data can be transferred from their site to yours.

If contracted, an IT service provider or CSP performs backups for you. You will need to determine whether they will be available overnight or on weekends to perform emergency work if necessary. You don't want to be in a situation where you hire a firm to manage your backups, but then find that no one is available to do a restore when you need it.

Block-Level Backups and Transfers

Block-level backups reduce the time it takes to transfer data to the cloud. They are especially useful when dealing with large files. A block-level backup understands each of the individual blocks that make up the files in a backup set. When a file changes, the only data that is replicated to the cloud includes the individual blocks that changed, rather than the entire file. A large 60GB file might be divided into many small 512KB blocks. A small change to the file would result in some of those blocks changing, and those alone would be replicated to the cloud.

Restoration Methods

The whole point of having a backup is so that you can restore if necessary. While we all hope that day is far away, it helps to be prepared for how to handle it efficiently and effectively. There are a few methods you can use to restore data. They include

- **Restoring in place**   An in-place restore will restore data to its original location on primary storage. The restore operation will overwrite the currently existing data with the data on the backup medium. Choose this option if the data you are overwriting no longer has value. For example, you may restore a database in place if the current database is corrupt and cannot be fixed. In-place restores are also used when granular selection is used, such as in the case of restoring only a few files.

- **Restoring to an alternative location**   This restore places the data in a different location so that the currently existing data remains untouched. This is useful when you want to compare the restored data to the current data to merge it or overwrite selectively following the restore. For example, you might restore files from a backup to an alternative location and then allow users to pull data from the restored folder if they need it.

- **Restoring files**   Restore operations do not have to restore all files that were backed up in the backup operation. File restores selectively choose one or more files from within a backup set to restore.

- **Restoring snapshots**   Restoring snapshots rejects or undoes the changes made since the snapshot was taken. This is most often performed for virtual machines. You could take a snapshot before performing maintenance and then restore the snapshot if errors are encountered following the maintenance.

Archiving

Archiving is another important function to reduce the costs of storage and backup operations. Organizations keep a lot of data, and some data is kept on the off chance that it is ever needed. This data does not need to reside on primary storage and can be moved to the cloud or to archival media instead, such as a hard drive, tape, optical media, or a flash drive. Cloud archiving options offer inexpensive ways to archive data to a data store that is available whenever users have an Internet connection. Cloud archiving options are best for portable machines such as laptops or mobile devices because they do not need to be connected to the corporate network to be archived. This preserves valuable organizational data for users on the go.

Local storage administrators should ensure that the media chosen is adequately protected against harm and that it is logged and cataloged so that it can be found if and when needed. Cloud backups should be verified periodically to ensure that data can be effectively retrieved in an acceptable amount of time.

Chapter Review

This chapter covered methods for protecting data and systems against issues that may come up such as mistakes, component failures, malicious activity, and disasters. Business continuity (BC) encompasses the activities that enable an organization to continue functioning, including offering services, delivering products, and conducting other activities deemed integral to running the business, during and following a disruptive incident.

Achieving a highly available computing environment is something that takes careful planning and consideration. Multiple devices need to be considered and multiple components in each device need to be redundant and fault tolerant to achieve a highly available environment. High availability helps to prevent unplanned downtime and maintain service-level agreements. An organization can set up a multisite configuration to have a hot site, warm site, or cold site so that in the event something happens to the primary data center, the organization can migrate to a secondary data center and continue to operate.

Disaster recovery (DR) is the activities that are performed when a highly disruptive event occurs, such as an outage for a complete site, fires, floods, or hurricanes. These events cause damage to information resources, facilities, and possibly personnel. A proper disaster recovery plan (DRP) can help an organization plan for and respond to a disaster through replication and restoration at alternative sites. Metrics such as the recovery time objective (RTO) and the recovery point objective (RPO) help organizations specify how much data can be lost and how long it should take to restore data and bring systems back to a functioning state. These decisions should be made based on the potential impact on the business so that impact is limited to acceptable levels.

This chapter wrapped up by discussing backup and recovery. A backup set is a secondary copy of the organization's data and is used to replace the original data in the event of a loss in a process known as restoration.

Questions

The following questions will help you gauge your understanding of the material in this chapter. Read all the answers carefully because there might be more than one correct answer. Choose the best response(s) for each question.

1. Which of the following would be considered a cold site?

   A. A site with no heating system

   B. A site that has a replication enabled

   C. A site that is fully functional and staffed

   D. A site that provides only network connectivity and a physical location

2. You are designing a disaster recovery plan that includes a multisite configuration. The backup site must include all necessary hardware and current backups of the original site. Which type of site do you need to design?

   A. Cold site

   B. Warm site

   C. Hot site

   D. Virtual site

3. Which of the following is a documented set of procedures that defines how an organization recovers and protects its IT infrastructure in the event of a disaster?

   A. MTBF

   B. MTTR

   C. RPO

   D. DRP

4. An organization recently had a disaster, and the data center failed over to the backup site. The original data center has been restored, and the administrator needs to migrate the organization back to the primary data center. What process is the administrator performing?

   A. Failover

   B. Failback

   C. DRP

   D. RTO

5. You have been tasked with distributing incoming HTTP requests to multiple servers in a server farm. Which of the following is the easiest way to achieve that goal?

   A. Mirror site

   B. Fault tolerance

   C. Redundancy

   D. Load balancing

6. When replicating data in a multisite configuration from the primary site to a backup site, which form of synchronization requires the system to wait before proceeding with the next data write?

   A. Asynchronous replication

   B. Synchronous replication

   C. Failover

   D. Mirror site

7. Which of the following terms can be used to describe a system that is location independent and provides failover?

   A. Clustering

   B. Load balancing

   C. Geo-clustering

   D. Failover

8. Which term is used to describe the target amount of time that a system can be down after a failure or a disaster occurs?

   A. RPO

   B. RTO

   C. BCP

   D. MTBF

9. Which of the following processes allows a system to automatically switch to a redundant system in the event of a disaster at the primary site?

   A. Failback

   B. DRP

   C. Failover

   D. Redundancy

10. Which of the following backup processes needs the last backup and all additional backups since that backup to perform a restore?

    A. Incremental

    B. Differential

    C. Full

    D. Image

11. Which of the following backups could be restored without any additional backups?

    A. Incremental

    B. Differential

    C. Full

    D. Image

12. What is the easiest method for an administrator to capture the state of a VM at a specific point in time?

    A. Backup

    B. Snapshot

    C. Image

    D. Clone

Answers

1. **D.** A cold site does not include any backup copies of data from the organization's original data center. When an organization implements a cold site, it does not have readily available hardware at the site; the site only includes the physical space and network connectivity for recovery operations, and it is the organization's responsibility to provide the hardware.

2. **C.** A hot site is a duplicate of the original site of the organization and has readily available hardware and a near-complete backup of the organization's data. A hot site can contain a real-time synchronization between the original site and the backup site and can be used to completely mirror the organization's original data center.

3. **D.** A DRP (disaster recovery plan) describes how an organization is going to deal with recovery in the event of a disaster.

4. **B.** Failback is the process of switching back to the primary site after the environment has been shifted to the backup site.

5. **D.** Load balancing distributes workloads across multiple computers to optimize resources and throughput and to prevent a single device from being overwhelmed.

6. **B.** Synchronous replication writes data to the local store and then immediately replicates it to the replica set or sets. The application is not informed that the data has been written until all replica sets have acknowledged receipt and storage of the data.

7. **C.** Geo-clustering uses multiple redundant systems that are located in different geographical locations to provide failover and yet appear as a single highly available system.

8. **B.** RTO (recovery time objective) is the target amount of time a system can be down after a failure or disaster.

9. **C.** Failover is the process of switching to a redundant system upon failure of the primary system.

10. **A.** An incremental backup backs up the files that have changed since the last full or incremental backup and requires all incremental backups to perform a restore.

11. **C.** A full backup backs up the entire system, including everything on the hard drive. It does not require any additional backups to perform a restore.

12. **B.** Snapshots can be used to capture the state of a VM at a specific point in time. They can contain a copy of the current disk state as well as memory state.

CHAPTER 14

Testing, Automation, and Changes

In this chapter, you will learn about
- Testing techniques
- Automation and orchestration
- Change and configuration management

One of the challenges of a cloud environment is service and maintenance availability. When organizations adopt a cloud model instead of hosting their own infrastructure, it is important for them to know that the services and data they need to access are available whenever and wherever they need them, without experiencing undue delays. Therefore, organizations need procedures for testing the cloud environment. Testing is a proactive measure to ensure consistent performance and operations of information systems.

Because maintenance tasks associated with on-premises technology are assumed by the cloud provider, operational and specific business rules need to be employed to best leverage the cloud technology to solve business problems. Standard maintenance tasks can take a significant amount of time, time that many companies just do not have. IT resources are typically stretched thin. This is where automation and orchestration step in. Automation and orchestration are two ways to reduce time spent on tasks, increase the speed of technological development, and improve efficiencies. Automation uses scripting, scheduled tasks, and automation tools to programmatically execute workflows that were formerly performed manually. Orchestration manages automation workflows to optimize efficiencies and ensure effective execution.

Improper documentation can make troubleshooting and auditing extremely difficult. Additionally, cloud systems can become extremely complex as they integrate with more systems, so a change in one place can affect systems across the enterprise if not managed correctly. Change and configuration management address these issues by tracking change requests, establishing a process for approval that considers the risks and impacts, and tracking the changes that are actually made.

Testing Techniques

Availability does not just mean whether services are up or down. Rather, availability is also concerned with whether services are operating at expected performance levels. Cloud consumers have many options, and it is relatively easy for them to switch to another model, so it is important for cloud providers to consistently provide the level of service users expect.

Ensuring consistent performance and operation requires vigilant testing of services such as cloud systems or servers, virtual appliances, virtual networking, bandwidth, and a host of more granular metrics. Together, this data can paint a picture of where constraints may lie and how performance changes when conditions change. In this section, you will learn about the following testing techniques:

- Baseline comparisons
- Performance testing
- Configuration testing
- Testing in the cloud landscape
- Validating proper functionality
- SLA comparisons
- Testing sizing changes
- Testing high availability
- Testing connectivity
- Verifying data integrity
- Evaluating replication
- Testing load balancing

Baseline Comparisons

A baseline can be compared with actual performance metrics at any point following the collection of the baseline to determine if activity represents the norm. The purpose of establishing a baseline is to create a sample of resources that are being consumed by the cloud services, servers, or VMs over a set period and to provide the organization with a point-in-time performance chart of its environment.

Establish a baseline by selecting a sampling interval and the objects to monitor and then collecting performance data during that interval. Continue to collect metrics at regular intervals to get a chart of how systems are consuming resources.

Cloud providers offer the ability for each cloud VM to send performance metrics to a central monitoring location in the cloud, such as with AWS CloudWatch. This also provides aggregated metrics for apps that consist of multiple VMs.

Procedures to Confirm Results

It is important to establish procedures to evaluate performance metrics in a baseline both in testing and production to confirm the accuracy of testing baselines. Load testing, stress testing, and simulated user behavior utilize workload patterns that are automated and standard, but these workloads may not be the same as actual user activity. Therefore, baseline comparisons from load testing, stress testing, or simulations could differ significantly from production baselines. Understand how baselines were obtained so that you do not use these baselines in the wrong context.

Decision-makers use baselines to determine initial and max resource allocations, gauge scalability, and establish an application or service cost basis, so baseline numbers need to be accurate. Evaluate metrics for critical resources, including CPU, memory, storage, and network utilization.

CPU Utilization   CPU utilization may change as systems are moved from test to production and over time as overall utilization changes. Collect CPU metrics once systems have been moved to production and track the metrics according to system load so that numbers can be compared to testing baselines. The following list includes some of the metrics to monitor:

- **CPU time**   Shows the amount of time a process or thread spends executing on a processor core. For multiple threads, the CPU time of the threads is additive. The application CPU time is the sum of the CPU time of all the threads that run the application. If an application runs multiple processes, a CPU time will be associated with each process, and these will need to be added together to get the full value.

- **Wait time**   Shows the amount of time that a given thread waits to be processed.

Memory Utilization   Memory utilization is also subject to changes in test versus production environments. Collect memory metrics once systems have been moved to production and track the metrics according to system load so that numbers can be compared to testing baselines. Some metrics to monitor include

- **Paged pool**   Shows the amount of data that has been paged to disk. Paging from disk is performed when there is insufficient memory available, and it results in lower performance for each page fault.

- **Page faults**   Shows the total number of times data was fetched from disk rather than memory since process launch. A high number of page faults could indicate that memory needs to be increased.

- **Peak memory usage**   Shows the memory used by a process since it was launched.

Storage Utilization   After evaluating CPU and memory performance compared to proposed resources, an organization must also test the performance of the storage system. Identifying how well the storage system is performing is critical in planning for growth and proper storage management. Collect storage utilization data in production.

The performance metrics can be compared to baselines if load values can be associated with each metric for common comparison. Some metrics to monitor include

- **Application read IOPS**   Shows how much storage read I/O was performed by the application process per second. Storage read I/O is when data is pulled from the disk for the application. If an application runs multiple processes, a read IOPS value will be associated with each process, and these values will need to be added together to get the full value.

- **Application write IOPS**   Shows how much storage write I/O was performed by the application process per second. Storage write I/O is when the application saves data to disk. Similar to read IOPS, if an application runs multiple processes, a write IOPS value will be associated with each process.

- **Read IOPS**   Shows how much storage read I/O was performed by the system per second.

- **Write IOPS**   Shows how much storage write I/O was performed by the system per second.

Network Utilization   The fourth item to consider is network utilization. This also can change from test to production and as systems mature. Collect network metrics once systems have been moved to production. You can use network collection tools or collect statistics from network devices or the VMs themselves. Sometimes it is useful to collect network metrics at different points and then compare the results according to system load so that numbers can be compared to testing baselines. Some metrics to monitor include

- **Physical NIC average bytes sent/received**   Tracks the average amount of data in bytes that was sent and received over the physical network adapter per second.

- **Physical NIC peak bytes sent/received**   Tracks the largest values for the average amount of data in bytes that were sent and received over the physical network adapter. Peak values can show whether the adapter is getting saturated.

- **Virtual switch average bytes sent/received**   Tracks the average amount of data in bytes that were sent and received over the virtual switch per second. Track this for each virtual switch you want to monitor.

- **Virtual switch peak bytes sent/received**   Tracks the largest values for the average amount of data in bytes that were sent and received by the virtual switch. Track this for each virtual switch you want to monitor. Peak values can show whether the virtual switch is getting saturated.

- **Virtual NIC average bytes sent/received**   Tracks the average amount of data in bytes that were sent and received over the virtual NIC per second. Track this for each virtual NIC in the VMs you want to monitor.

Exercise 14-1: Collecting Windows Metrics with Performance Monitor

In this exercise, we will create counters to collect performance metrics on a Windows machine using the Performance Monitor tool.

1. Log in to a Windows computer or VM.

2. Start the Performance Monitor application. From Windows 10, click the search button or bar in the lower left and then type **performance monitor**. Select the Performance Monitor application.

3. The Performance Monitor application will load, as shown here.

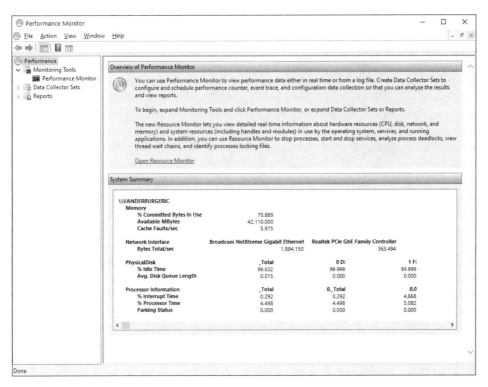

4. Select Performance Monitor on the left side of the application. This will display the chart with the current counters. It may have some counters already defined, or it could be blank. In this example, a single processor time counter has been set so you can see the chart of its activity.

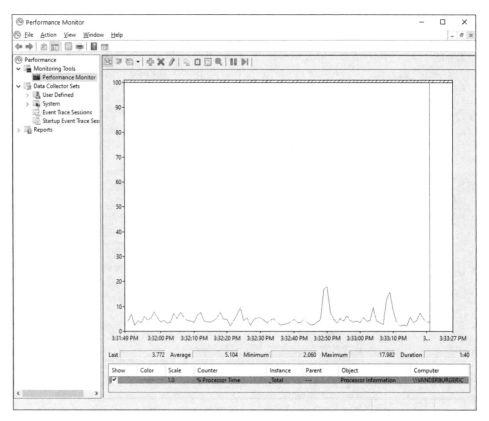

5. Click the plus sign icon to add more counters. Scroll through the list to see the available counters. Depending on the role the computer fills, you might have some additional counters. For example, the computer used for this example has Hyper-V on it, so a range of counters can be set for it, as shown here.

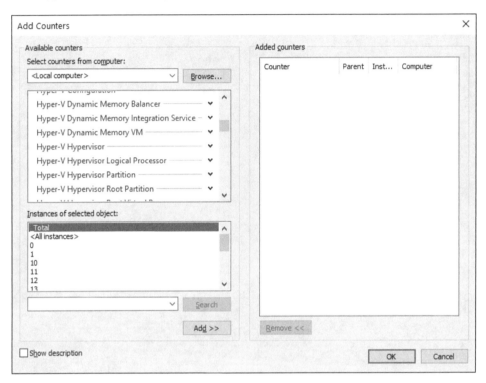

6. Expand Memory and then select Pages/Sec, then click the Add button.

7. Expand Physical Disk and then select Avg. Disk Sec/Read, then click the Add button.

8. Repeat this process for Avg. Disk Sec/Write. Your screen should now look like this:

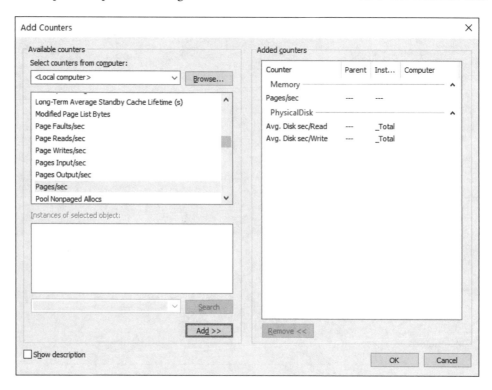

9. Click OK and those counters will now be displayed in the Performance Monitor:

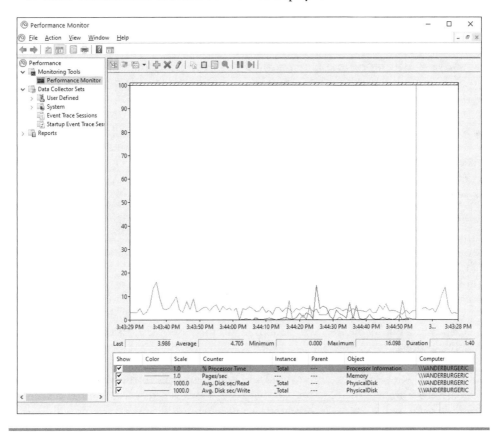

Patch Version   Performance baselines can change following patch deployment. Patches can change the way the system processes data or the dependencies involved in operations. Security patches, in particular, can add overhead to common system activities, necessitating an update of the baseline on the machine.

Application Version   Performance baselines can change following application updates. Application vendors introduce new versions and patches when they want to address vulnerabilities, fix bugs, or add features. Each of these could result in performance changes to the application as the code changes. Applications may process data in a different way or require more processing to implement more secure encryption algorithms, more storage to track additional metadata, or more memory to load additional functions or feature elements into RAM.

Auditing Enabled   Enabling auditing functions can significantly affect performance baselines. Auditing logs record events when certain actions are taken, such as failed logins, privilege use, error debug data, and other information useful for evaluating security or operational issues. However, tracking and storing this data increases the overhead of running processes and applications on the server and can have a big impact on the baseline.

If auditing is temporary, schedule auditing and baselining activities to occur on different dates if possible. If not, make operations aware that baseline values will be affected due to auditing.

Management Tool Compliance   Management tools improve the process of collecting and analyzing data on performance metrics from testing, production, and other metrics and baselines collected as time progresses by putting all the data in one place where it can be easily queried, analyzed, and reported on.

Management tools can provide a dashboard of metrics that can be tweaked for operations teams to see changes, trends, and potential resource problems easily. Management tools may need to interface with cloud APIs or have an agent running on hypervisors to collect the data.

Performance Testing

A common item that is tested is how well the program or system performs. Cloud adoption is a combination of new systems and migrations of existing physical or virtual systems into the cloud. New systems will need to have new benchmarks defined for adequate performance. However, you can start with some generic role-based performance benchmarks until the applications have been tested under full load and actual performance data has been captured.

Existing systems should have performance metrics associated with ideal operational speed already, so implementers will be looking to meet or exceed those metrics in cloud implementations.

Performance metrics on systems without a load can show what the minimum resource requirements will be for the application, since the resources in use without activity on the machine represent the bare operational state. However, to get a realistic picture of how the system will perform in production and when under stress, systems will need to go through load testing and stress testing.

Load Testing

Load testing evaluates a system when the system is artificially forced to execute operations consistent with user activities at different utilization levels. Load testing emulates expected system use and can be performed manually or automatically. Manual load testing consists of individuals logging into the system and performing normal user tasks on the test system. In contrast, automated testing uses workflow automation and runtimes to execute normal user functions on the system.

Stress Testing

Stress testing is a form of load testing that evaluates a system under peak loads to determine its max data or user handling capabilities. Stress testing is used to determine how the application will scale. Stress testing can also be used to determine how many standard VM configurations of different types can exist on a single hypervisor. This can help in planning for ideal resource allocation and host load balancing.

Systems can be tested as a whole, or they can be tested in isolation. For example, testing of the web server in a test system may have allowed testers to identify the max load the web server can handle. However, in production, the operations team will deploy web servers in a load-balanced cluster. The data so far tells how many servers would be needed in the cluster for the expected workload, but the testing team needs to determine how many database servers would be required for the workload as well. Rather than spin up more web servers, the team can run a trace that captures all queries issued to the database server in the web server testing. They can then automate issuing those same queries multiple times over to see how many database servers would be required for the number of web servers.

Continuing the example, let's assume that testing revealed that the web server could host up to 150 connections concurrently. The traffic from those 150 connections was captured and then replayed to the database server in multiples until the database server reached max load. The testing team might try doubling the traffic, then tripling it, and so forth until they reach the max load the database server can handle; for this example, we will say that it is five times the load, or the load of 750 end-user connections. The testing team would typically build in a buffer, since it is not good to run systems at 100 percent capacity, and then they would document system scalability requirements. In this example, assuming the ideal load is 80 percent or 120 connections instead of 150, the team would document that one web server should be allocated for each 120 concurrent user connections and that one database server should be allocated for every 600 concurrent user connections.

Taking this just a little bit further, the organization could configure rules to spin up a new VM from a template based on concurrent connections so that the system as a whole auto-scales.

Remote Transactional Monitoring

After systems are deployed, operations teams will want to know how different functions within the application are performing. End users do not typically provide the best information on what is actually causing a performance problem, but remote transactional monitoring can simulate user activity and identify how long it takes to perform each task. Cloud-based options can be deployed at different locations around the world to simulate the user experience in that region.

Remote transactional monitoring, deployed in this fashion, can be used by operations teams to isolate tasks that exceed established thresholds and determine whether thresholds differ around the globe. They can then isolate the individual system processes that are contributing to the performance issue and determine whether the performance issue is localized to the edge.

Available vs. Proposed Resources

The elasticity associated with virtualization and cloud computing can result in different resources being available to a VM than were proposed in requirements. Elastic computing allows computing resources to vary dynamically to meet a variable workload. (See Chapter 6 for more details.) Operations teams typically deploy machines with fewer resources than were proposed, but with a ceiling for growth.

Compute   It is best to allocate one vCPU to a VM and then monitor performance, adding more vCPUs as needed. When a VM attempts to use a vCPU, the hypervisor must wait for the physical CPU associated with that vCPU to become available. The VM believes that vCPU to be idle and will attempt to spread the load around if the application is configured for multiprocessing, but this can have an adverse impact on VM performance if the physical CPU has a large number of processes in the queue. Furthermore, even idle processors place some load on the hypervisor from host management processes, so it is best not to provision more than will be necessary.

Where possible, monitor hypervisor metrics to determine if overcommitment bottlenecks are occurring. The most important metric to watch is the CPU ready metric. CPU ready measures the amount of time a VM has to wait for a physical CPU to become available. It is also important to monitor CPU utilization within each VM and on the host. High CPU utilization might indicate the need for additional vCPUs to spread the load, while high host CPU utilization could indicate whether VMs are properly balanced across hosts. If one host has high CPU utilization and others have available resources, it may be best to migrate some of the VMs to another host to relieve the burden on the overtaxed host.

Memory   When configuring dynamic memory on VMs, ensure that you set both a minimum and a maximum. Default configurations typically allow a VM to grow to the maximum amount of memory in the host unless a maximum is set. There are hypervisor costs to memory allocation that you should be aware of. Based on the memory assigned, hypervisors will reserve some amount of overhead for the VM kernel and the VM. VMware has documented overhead for VMs in its "VM Right-Sizing Best Practice Guide." According to VMware's guide, one vCPU and 1GB of memory allocated to a VM produce 25.90MB of overhead for the host.

There is also the burden of maintaining overly large shadow page tables. Shadow page tables are how hypervisors map host memory to VMs and how the VM perceives the state of memory pages. This is necessary to prevent VMs from accessing host memory directly. If VMs could access the host memory directly, they could potentially access the memory of other VMs. These constraints can put unnecessary strain on a hypervisor if resources are overallocated. For this reason, keep resources to a minimum until they are actually required.

Configuration Testing

Configuration testing allows an administrator to test and verify that the cloud environment runs at optimal performance levels. Configuration testing needs to be done regularly and should be part of a weekly or monthly routine. When testing a cloud environment, a variety of aspects need to be verified.

Data Access Testing

The ability to access data stored in the cloud and hosted with a cloud provider is an essential function of a cloud environment. Accessing that data needs to be tested for efficiency and compliance so that an organization has confidence in the cloud computing model.

Network Testing

Testing network latency measures the amount of time between a networked device's request for data and the network's response from the requester. This helps an administrator determine when a network is not performing at an optimal level.

In addition to testing network latency, it is essential to test the network's bandwidth or speed. The standard practice for measuring bandwidth is to transfer a large file from one system to another and measure the amount of time it takes to complete the transfer or to copy the file. The throughput, or the average rate of a successful message delivery over the network, is then determined by dividing the file size by the time it takes to transfer the file and is measured in megabits or kilobits per second. However, this test does not provide a maximum throughput and can be misleading because of overhead factors.

When determining bandwidth and throughput, it is important to understand that overhead needs to be accounted for, like network latency and system limitations. Dedicated software can be used to measure the throughput (e.g., NetCPS and iPerf) to get a more accurate measure of maximum bandwidth. Testing the bandwidth and latency of a network that is supporting a cloud environment is important since the applications and data that are stored in the cloud would not be accessible without the proper network configurations.

Application Testing

After moving an application to the cloud or virtualizing an application server in the cloud, testing that application or server will need to be performed regularly to ensure consistent operation and performance. There are various ways to test an application: some can be done manually, and some are automated.

Containerization is exceptionally effective at this point. Application containers are portable runtime environments containing an application and dependencies such as frameworks, libraries, configuration files, and binaries. These are all bundled into the container, which can run on any system with compatible container software. This allows application testing teams to deploy multiple isolated containers to the cloud for simultaneous testing.

Performance counters are used to establish an application baseline and verify that the application and the application server are performing at expected levels. Monitor performance metrics and set alerting thresholds to know when applications are nearing limits. Baselines and thresholds are discussed in more detail in the "Monitoring Techniques" section of Chapter 10. Batch files or scripts can easily automate checking the availability of an application or server or collecting performance metrics.

Applications need to be delivered seamlessly so that the end user is unaware the application is being hosted in a cloud environment. Tracking this information can help determine just how seamless that delivery process is.

A variety of diagnostic tools can be used to collect information about how an application is performing. To test application performance, an organization needs to collect information about the application, including requests and the number of connections. The organization also needs to track how often the application is being utilized, as well as overall resource utilization (memory and CPU).

Performance monitoring tools are valuable in evaluating application performance. Such tools can create reports on how quickly an application loads or spins up and analyze performance data on each aspect of the application as it is being delivered to the end user.

Follow this simple process in assessing application performance:

- Evaluate which piece of an application or service is taking the most time to process.
- Measure how long it takes each part of the program to execute and how the program is allocating its memory.
- Test the underlying network performance, storage performance, or performance of cloud virtual infrastructure components if using IaaS or PaaS.

In addition to testing the I/O performance of its storage system, a company can use a variety of tools for conducting a load test to simulate what happens to the storage system as the load is increased. Testing the storage system allows the organization to be more proactive than reactive with its storage and helps it plan for when additional storage might be required.

Testing in the Cloud Landscape

Cloud resources can be used as a "sandbox" of sorts to test new applications or new versions of applications without affecting the performance or even the security of the production landscape. Extensive application and application server testing can be performed on applications migrated to the cloud landscape before making cloud-based applications available to the organization's users. Testing application and application server performance in the cloud is a critical step to ensuring a successful user experience. Performance issues can be identified before they are rolled out. This helps avoid user complaints and bad publicity.

Cloud landscape testing should include testing the application from the server hosting the application and its connection to the end user's device. These testing procedures should use the application, and everything in between is critical success factors in testing the cloud environment.

Functional Testing

Systems are created to solve some business problem or to enhance an essential business process. It is important, therefore, to test the execution of those activities to ensure that they function as expected. Functional testing is used to verify that an application meets the requirements set forth when the application was authorized. Functional testers will establish what output would be expected given a specific input and then verify that the program exhibits this behavior.

Functionality can be tested with the steps shown in Figure 14-1. These steps include identifying actions the program should perform, defining test input, defining expected output, running through each test case, and comparing the actual output against the expected output.

Quality assurance (QA) teams create a list of test cases, each with an established input that should produce a specific output. For example, if we create a user, a report of all users should display the user. If we instruct the application to display the top ten customer

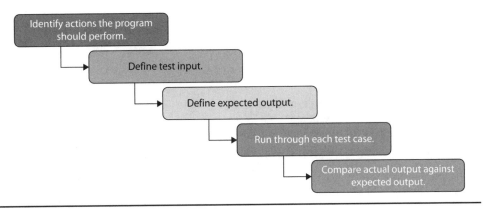

Figure 14-1 Functional testing steps

accounts with the largest outstanding balances, we should be able to verify that the ones displayed actually have the highest balances.

Regression Testing

Regression testing is used to determine whether code modifications break application features or functionality. With CI/CD, updates are produced rapidly and regularly so regression testing needs to be a part of the process. Cloud tools are available to automate portions of regression testing. Automation schedules are sometimes configured on a set schedule or based on triggers, such as when new code is placed in the repository.

Automated regression testing tools can compare the UI of the new build with the baseline build to identify changes. With record-playback features, an application can monitor the actions you take within the system and then perform those same steps during the test. Not only will it alert on failures, but it can also record response time metrics for each step to identify performance issues.

Regression tools can also automatically capture screenshots or video of failed or successful actions for documentation. This can aid developers in fixing issues. Some cloud regression testing tools include Selenium, Appium, Sikuli, JMeter, and ZapTest.

Regression testing differs from functional testing in that functional testing is performed on a new application, whereas regression testing is performed for application changes.

Usability Testing

Usability testing is geared toward determining if the application is easy for users to work with. Usability testing concentrates a lot on the user interface and can be broken down into four tests. Each one starts with a P so that they are easier to remember.

- **Productivity**   Testing the effectiveness of the system.
- **Performance**   Testing application efficiency. If an application is too slow to use, it will not be usable, so usability testing will determine if the application performs well enough for users to accept it.

- **Precision**   Testing system accuracy
- **Pleasantness**   Testing user-friendliness

SLA Comparisons

A service level agreement (SLA) is a contract that specifies the level of uptime that will be supported by the service provider, as well as expected performance metrics. SLAs include provisions for how the service provider will compensate cloud consumers if SLAs are not met. At a minimum, these include some monetary compensation for the time the system was down that may be credited toward future invoices. Sometimes the provider must pay fines or damages for lost revenue or lost customer satisfaction.

SLAs are specific to a cloud service, meaning that the SLA for cloud storage might differ from the SLA for cloud databases, cloud VMs, and so on.

A multilevel SLA is used when different types of cloud consumers use the same services. These are a bit more complicated to read, and cloud consumers must understand which type they are to understand their expectations for availability. Multilevel SLAs are useful for cloud providers that provide a similar solution to different customer types because the same SLA can be delivered to each customer. For example, a web hosting company may have different levels of service that are specified based on the customer type.

A service-based SLA describes a single service that is provided for all customers. There is no differentiation between customer expectations in a service-based SLA, unlike a multilevel SLA. For example, an Internet service provider (ISP) has specified the same SLA terms for each nonbusiness customer.

In comparison, a customer-based SLA is an agreement that is unique between the customer and service provider. Since business terms can vary greatly, the ISP in this example may use customer-based SLAs for business customers and the service-based SLA for home users.

It is crucial to understand which SLAs are in place. As a customer, you should be aware of what your availability expectations are so that you can work around downtime. As a provider, you need to understand your responsibility for ensuring a set level of availability and the consequences of not living up to that agreement. The establishment of SLAs is an important part of ensuring adequate availability of key resources so that the company can continue doing business and not suffer excessive losses.

Testing Sizing Changes

Sizing is performed for hosts and their guests. First, the host must be provisioned with sufficient resources to operate the planned VMs with a comfortable buffer for growth. This step is not necessary if you are purchasing individual machines from a cloud vendor because it is the cloud vendor's responsibility to size the hosts that run the machines it provides to you. However, this is an important step if you rent the hypervisor itself (this is called "dedicated hosting") in the cloud, as many companies do, in order to give them flexibility and control in provisioning.

One of the many benefits of virtualization is the ability to provision VMs on the fly as the organization's demands grow, making the purchase of additional hardware unnecessary. If the host computer is not sized correctly, however, it is not possible to add VMs without adding compute resources to the host computer or purchasing additional resources from the cloud vendor.

It is a best practice to allocate fewer resources to VMs and then analyze performance to scale as necessary. It would seem that overallocating resources would not be a problem if the resources are available, and many administrators have fallen for this misconception. Overallocating resources results in additional overhead to the hypervisor and sometimes an inefficient use of resources.

For example, overallocating vCPUs to a VM could result in the VM dividing work among multiple vCPUs only to have the hypervisor queue them up because not enough physical cores are available. Similarly, overallocating memory can result in excessive page files consuming space on storage and hypervisor memory overhead associated with memory page tracking.

Test each resource independently so that you can trace the performance impact or improvement to the resource change. For example, make a change to the vCPU and then test before changing memory.

Testing High Availability

High availability (HA) was introduced in Chapter 13. As HA systems are deployed, they should also be tested to ensure that they meet availability and reliability expectations. Test the failure of redundant components such as CPU, power supplies, Ethernet connections, server nodes, and storage connections.

The HA system should continue to function when you simulate the failure of a redundant component. It is also important to measure the performance of a system when components fail. When a drive fails in parity-based RAID (RAID 5, RAID 6, RAID 50), the RAID set must rebuild. This can have a significant performance impact on the system as a whole. Similarly, when one node in an active/active cluster fails, all applications will run on the remaining node or nodes. This can also affect performance. Ensure that scenarios such as these are tested to confirm that performance is still acceptable under the expected load when components fail.

You can test the drive rebuild for a RAID set by removing one drive from the set and then adding another drive. Ensure that the disk you add is the same as the one removed. You can simulate the failure of one node in a cluster by powering that node down or by pausing it in the cluster.

Testing Load Balancing

When hosting an application in the cloud, there may be times where an organization uses the cloud as a load balancer. As discussed in previous chapters, load balancing with dedicated software or hardware allows for the distribution of workloads across multiple computers. Using multiple components can help improve reliability through redundancy, with multiple devices servicing the workload.

If a company uses load balancing to improve the availability or responsiveness of cloud-based applications, it needs to test the effectiveness of a variety of characteristics, including TCP connections per second, HTTP/HTTPS connections per second, and traffic loads simulated to validate performance under high-traffic scenarios. Testing all aspects of load balancing helps ensure that the computers can handle the workload and that they can respond in the event of a single server outage.

Testing Connectivity

In addition to this end-to-end testing, an organization needs to be able to test the connectivity to the cloud service. Without connectivity to the cloud that services the organization, the organization could experience downtime and costly interruptions to its data. It is the cloud administrator's job to test the network for things such as network latency and replication and to make sure that an application hosted in the cloud can be delivered to the users inside the organization.

Verifying Data Integrity

Data integrity is the assurance that data is accurate and that the same information that is stored in the cloud is the data that is later retrieved. The data remains unchanged by unauthorized processes. Application data is valuable and must be protected against corruption or incorrect alteration that could damage its integrity. Data integrity testing can be combined with other testing elements to ensure that data does not change unless specified. For example, functional testing reviews each test case along with the specified input and output. Data integrity testing would detect data integrity issues with the direct test case, but automated integrity checks could also be built in to verify that all other data has not changed in the process.

Similarly, when performing load testing, ensure that data does not change as the system reaches its max capacity. Performance constraints can sometimes result in a cascade failure, and you want to ensure that data is adequately protected in such a case.

Evaluating Replication

Some situations require an organization to replicate or sync data between its internal data center and a cloud provider. Replication is typically performed for fault tolerance or load-balancing reasons. After testing network latency and bandwidth, it is important to check and verify that the data is replicating correctly between the internal data center and the cloud provider or between multiple cloud services.

Test by making a change on one replication partner and then confirm that the change has taken place on the other replication partners. Measure how long it takes to complete replication by creating replication metrics. Combine replication testing with load testing to ensure that replication can stay consistent even under heavy loads and to determine at what point replication performance decreases.

Automation and Orchestration

Organizations are adopting numerous cloud technologies that offer a myriad of services to them and often involve exchanging data through them. While the cloud provider is responsible for standard maintenance tasks associated with its on-premises technology, each organization is responsible for managing the cloud services it consumes, including implementing operational rules and specific business rules to best leverage the cloud technology to fulfill its operational needs. Automation and orchestration are two ways for an organization's IT staff to reduce the time spent on tasks, increase the speed of technological development, and improve efficiencies. The two concepts of automation and orchestration work well together, but they are not the same thing.

Automation uses scripting, scheduled tasks, and automation tools to programmatically execute workflows that were formerly performed manually. Orchestration manages automation workflows to optimize efficiencies and ensure effective execution.

Orchestration integrates organizational systems to provide more value to the organization. In orchestration, workflow automations are called runbooks, and each discrete step in a runbook is called an activity.

As an example of orchestration integration, an IT person working on a customer trouble ticket could generate change requests from within the ticketing system by selecting the type of change and providing relevant details. This would prompt a set of activities to get the change approved. Once approved, the runbook could be automatically executed if one exists for the task, with the input provided by the IT person in the ticket. The output from the runbook could then be placed into the change management system and documented on employee timesheets while metrics are gathered for departmental meetings. This is the power of orchestration!

Orchestration requires integration with a variety of toolsets and a catalog of sufficiently developed runbooks to complete tasks. Orchestration often involves a cloud portal or other administrative center to provide access to the catalog of workflows along with data and metrics on workflow processes, status, errors, and operational efficiency. The orchestration portal displays useful dashboards and information for decision-making and ease of administration.

In this scenario, orchestration ensures that tickets are handled promptly, tasks are performed according to SOPs, associated tasks such as seeking change approval and entering time are not forgotten, and the necessary metrics for analytics and reporting are collected and made available to managers.

Interrelationships are mapped between systems and runbooks, along with requirements, variables, and dependencies for linked workflows. This facilitates the management of cloud tools and integration of tools and processes with a variety of legacy tools. Management options are improved with each new workflow that automates management that once would have required logging into many different web GUIs, workstations, servers, or traditional applications or sending SSH commands to a CLI to accomplish.

This section is organized into the following subsections:

- Event orchestration
- Scripting

- Custom programming
- Runbook management for single nodes
- Orchestration for multiple nodes and runbooks
- Automation activities

Event Orchestration

Event logs used to be reviewed by IT analysts who understood the servers and applications in their organization and had experience solving a variety of problems. These individuals commonly used knowledge bases of their own making or those created by communities to identify whether an event required action to be taken and what the best action was for the particular event.

The rapid expansion of the cloud and IT environments, as well as the increasing complexity of technology and integrations, has made manual event log analysis a thing of the past. However, the function of event log analysis and the corresponding response to actionable events is still something companies need to perform. They accomplish this through event orchestration.

Event orchestration collects events from servers and devices such as firewalls and virtual appliances in real time. It then parses events, synchronizes time, and executes correlation rules to identify commonalities and events that, together, could form a risk. It ranks risk items, and if they exceed specific thresholds, it creates alerts on the events to notify administrators. Some events may result in runbook execution. For example, excessive login attempts from an IP address to an FTPS server could result in runbook execution to add the offending IP address to IP blocklists. Similarly, malware indicators could quarantine the machine by initiating one runbook to disable the switch port connected to the offending machine and another runbook to alert local incident response team members of the device and the need for an investigation.

Scripting

Scripting languages offer a simple way to accomplish tasks without developing an entire program. Scripts can be used to perform something as simple as a single task, such as displaying a message, to complex operations, like deploying services. This makes them quite flexible and easy to apply to a diverse set of solutions.

There are a wide variety of scripting languages, and some may be more applicable to certain uses. Most orchestration tools support a large number of scripting languages, so feel free to use the tools that are most effective for the task or those that you are most familiar with. The advantage of scripting languages is that they are relatively simple to learn, they can run with a small footprint, they are easy to update, and they are widely supported. Some popular scripting languages include

- CoffeeScript
- ECMAScript

- Go
- JavaScript
- Perl
- PHP
- Python
- Ruby
- SQL
- VBScript and VBA

OS and Application-Specific Scripting Languages

A host of languages are specific to certain applications, operating systems, or functions. For example, Google Apps Script can be used in the Google Workspace (formerly G Suite) to automate functions, PL/SQL with Oracle databases, Advanced Business Application Programming (ABAP) for SAP reporting, forms, and data manipulation or LotusScript for Lotus software applications.

Job Control Languages and Shells

Another type of scripting language is known as job control languages or shells. These languages are interpreted by an application running on the platform. Table 14-1 shows some of the common job control languages and the platform they work on.

Custom Programming

Full-fledged programming languages can be used to create runbooks as well as hook into cloud-based APIs. Programming languages offer more capabilities than scripting languages, and there are powerful development environments that can allow for more extensive testing. Programming languages are also good to use when runbook programs

Job Control Language/Shell	Platform
PowerShell	Microsoft Windows, Linux, macOS
Bash	Unix and Linux
Bourne Shell	Unix and Linux
C shell (CSH)	Unix and Linux
KornShell (KSH)	Unix and Linux
AppleScript	Apple OS X and macOS
F-Script	macOS
HAScript	IBM mainframe systems

Table 14-1 Job Control Languages and Shells

are increasingly complex because programs can be organized into flexible modules. Some popular languages include

- Basic
- C, C++, and C#
- ColdFusion
- Java
- Lisp
- Python
- Scala
- PHP

Runbook Management for Single Nodes

As previously stated, runbooks are workflows organized into a series of tasks called activities. Runbooks begin with an initiation activity and end with some activity to disconnect and clean up. In-between activities may include processing data, analyzing data, debugging systems, exchanging data, monitoring processes, collecting metrics, and applying configurations. Runbook tools such as Microsoft System Center Orchestrator include plug-in integration packs for Azure and AWS cloud management.

Single-node runbooks are those that perform all activities on a single server or device. For example, this runbook would perform a series of maintenance activities on a database server:

1. Connect to the default database instance on the server.
2. Enumerate all user databases.
3. Analyze indexes for fragmentation and page count.
4. Identify indexes to optimize.
5. Rebuild indexes.
6. Reorganize indexes.
7. Update index statistics.
8. Perform database integrity checks.
9. Archive and remove output logs older than 30 days.
10. Remove rows from the commandlog table older than 30 days.
11. Disconnect from the default database instance on the server.

Orchestration for Multiple Nodes and Runbooks

Multiple-node runbooks are those that interface with multiple devices or servers. For example, this runbook would patch all VMs on all hosts in the customer cloud:

1. Enumerate VMs on each host.
2. Create a snapshot of VMs.
3. Add VMs to the update collection.
4. Scan for updates.
5. Apply updates to each machine, restarting load-balanced servers and domain controllers one at a time.
6. Validate service states.
7. Validate URLs.
8. Remove snapshot after 24 hours of successful runtime.

Automation Activities

A wonderful thing about runbooks is that there is a great deal of community support for them. You can create your own runbooks—and you definitely will have to do that—but you also can take advantage of the many runbooks that others have created and made available in runbook communities. Some of these can be used as templates for new runbooks to save valuable development time. Consider contributing your own runbooks to the community to help others out as well. Microsoft maintains a gallery of runbooks that can be downloaded for implementation on the Microsoft Azure cloud computing platform. Other vendors have set up community runbook repositories as well.

Routine Operations

Here are some runbook activities that are used for routine operations.

- **Snapshots**   Activities can be created to take snapshots of VMs or remove existing snapshots or snapshot chains from VMs. Runbooks might use this activity when making changes to a VM. The snapshot could be taken first, and then the maintenance would be performed. If things ran smoothly, the snapshot could be removed. Otherwise, the runbook could execute the activity to apply the snapshot taken at the beginning of the runbook.

- **Cloning**   Activities can be created to make a clone of a VM. A runbook using this activity might combine it with an activity to create a template from the clone, or an activity to archive the clone to secondary storage, or an activity to send the clone to a remote replication site and create a VM from it.

- **User account creation**   Activities can be created to create a user account based on form input. For example, the activity could create the account in Windows Active Directory and on several cloud services and then add the user account to groups based on the role provided on the form input.

- **Permission setting**   Activities can be created to apply permissions to a group of files, folders, and subfolders.

- **Resource access**   Activities can be created to assign resources to a device such as storage LUNs, virtual NICs, or other resources. This can be useful for runbooks that provision VMs or provision storage.

- **User account management**   Activities can be created to reset user account passwords, disable accounts, unlock accounts, or activate accounts.

- **Shutdowns**   You may want to shut down a large number of systems to perform maintenance on them. This could also be performed as a containment action in the case of an intrusion or malware. If there is a power outage, battery systems may be configured to automatically shut down systems that are attached to them once battery levels reach a low threshold so that systems are shut down in a controlled manner instead of simply losing power.

- **Restarts**   Restarting systems may be required for changes to take effect or as part of patch deployment. Still other systems may need a periodic restart just to ensure that they operate at a consistent level. These are easy tasks to automate.

- **Create internal APIs**   Internal APIs can be created based on workflow or self-service operations.

- **Scaling**   When performance metrics hit thresholds, systems can be configured to receive additional resources, such as RAM or CPU, to ensure that performance does not degrade.

Change and Configuration Management

The process of making changes to the cloud environment from its design phase to its operations phase in the least impactful way possible is known as change management. Configuration management ensures that the assets required to deliver services are adequately controlled and that accurate and reliable information about those assets is available when and where it is needed.

Change management and configuration management support overall technology governance processes to ensure that cloud systems are managed appropriately. All change requests and configuration items need to be documented to make certain that the requirements documented as part of the strategy phase are fulfilled by its corresponding design phase.

Change Management

Change management is a collection of policies and procedures that are designed to mitigate risk by evaluating change, ensuring thorough testing, providing proper communication, and training both administrators and end users.

A change is defined as the addition, modification, or removal of anything that could affect cloud services. This includes modifying system configurations, adding or removing users, resetting accounts, changing permissions, and a host of other activities that are part of the ordinary course of cloud operations, and also includes conducting project tasks associated with upgrades and new initiatives. It is important to note that this definition is not restricted to cloud components; it should also be applied to documentation, people, procedures, and other nontechnical items that are critical to a well-run cloud environment. The definition is also important because it debunks the notion that only "big" changes should follow a change management process. However, it is often the little things that cause significant problems, and thus change management needs to be applied equally to both big and small changes.

Change management maximizes business value through modification of the cloud environment while reducing disruption to the business and unnecessary cloud expense due to rework. Change management helps ensure that all proposed changes are both evaluated before their implementation and recorded for posterity. Change management allows companies to prioritize, plan, test, implement, document, and review all changes in a controlled fashion according to defined policies and procedures.

Change management optimizes overall business risk. It does this by building a process of evaluating both the risks and the benefits of a proposed change in the change procedure and organizational culture. Identified risks contribute to the decision to either approve or reject the change.

Lastly, change management acts as a control mechanism for the configuration management process by ensuring that all changes to configuration item baselines in the cloud environment are updated in the configuration management system (CMS).

A change management process can be broken down into several constituent concepts that work together to meet these objectives. These concepts are as follows:

- Change requests
- Change proposals
- Change approval or rejection
- Change scheduling
- Change documentation
- Change management integration

Change Requests

A request for change (RFC) is a formal request to make a modification that can be submitted by anyone who is involved with or has a stake in that particular item or service. IT leadership may submit changes focused on increasing the profitability of a cloud service; a systems administrator may file a change to improve system stability, and an end user may submit a change that requests additional functionality for their job role. All are valid requests for change.

Change Request Types   Change request types are used to categorize both the amount of risk and the amount of urgency each request carries. There are three types of changes: normal changes, standard changes, and emergency changes.

Normal changes are changes that are evaluated by the defined change management process to understand the benefits and risks of any given request. Standard changes request a type of change that has been evaluated previously and now poses little risk to the health of the cloud services. Because it is well understood, poses a low risk, and the organization does not stand to benefit from another review, a standard change is preauthorized. For example, resetting a user's password is a standard task. It still requires approval to ensure it is tracked and not abused, but it does not require the deliberation other changes might.

Emergency changes, as the name suggests, are used in case of an emergency and designate a higher level of urgency to move into operation. Even if the change is urgent, all steps of the process for implementing the change must be followed. However, the process can be streamlined. The review and approval of emergency changes, however, is usually executed by a smaller group of people than is used for a normal change to facilitate moving the requested change into operation.

Change Proposals

Change proposals are similar to RFCs but are reserved for changes that have the potential for major organizational impact or severe financial implications. The reason for a separate designation for RFCs and change proposals is to make sure that the decision-making for highly strategic changes is handled by the right level of leadership within the organization.

Change proposals are managed by the CIO or higher position in an organization. They are a high-level description of the change requiring the approval of those responsible for the strategic direction associated with the change. Change proposals help IT organizations stay efficient by not wasting resources on the intensive process required by an RFC to analyze and plan the proposed change if it is not in the strategic best interest of the organization to begin with.

Change Approval or Rejection

The change manager is the individual who is directly responsible for all the activities within the change management process. The change manager is ultimately responsible for the approval or rejection of each RFC and for making sure that all RFCs follow the defined policies and procedures as a part of their submission. The change manager will evaluate the change and decide to approve the change or reject it.

Change managers cannot be expected to know everything, nor to have full knowledge of the scope and impact of the change, despite the documentation provided in the change request because systems are highly integrated and complex. One small change to one system could have a big impact on another system. For this reason, the change manager assembles the right collection of stakeholders to help advise on the risks and benefits of a given change and to provide the input that will allow the change manager to make the right decision when he or she is unable to decide autonomously.

Change Advisory Board   The body of stakeholders that provides input to the change manager about RFCs is known as the change advisory board (CAB). This group of stakeholders should be composed of members from all representative areas of the business, as well as customers who might be affected by the change (see Figure 14-2). As part of their evaluation process for each request, the board needs to consider the following:

- The reason for the change
- The benefit of implementing the change
- The risks associated with implementing the change
- The risks associated with not implementing the change
- The resources required to implement the change
- The scheduling of the implementation
- The impact of the projected service outage concerning established SLAs
- The planned backout strategy in case of a failed change

Figure 14-2
The entities represented by a change advisory board (CAB)

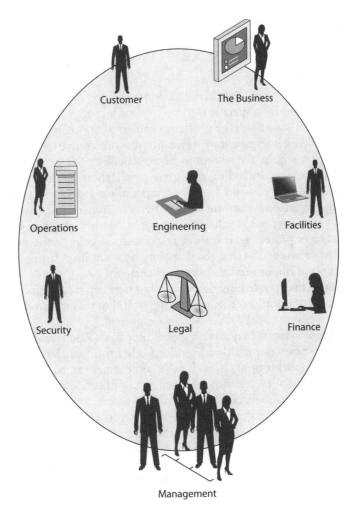

While this may seem like it involves a lot of people and time to consider each change to the environment, these policies and procedures pay off in the long run. They do so by limiting the impact of unknown or unstable configurations going into a production environment.

Emergency Change Advisory Board   A CAB takes a good deal of planning to get all the stakeholders together. In the case of an emergency change, there may not be time to assemble the full CAB. For such situations, an emergency change advisory board (ECAB) should be formed. This emergency CAB should follow the same procedures as the standard CAB; it is just a subset of the stakeholders who would usually convene for the review. Often the ECAB is defined as a certain percentage of a standard CAB that would be required by the change manager to make sure they have all the input necessary to make an informed decision about the request.

EXAM TIP   When implementing a change that requires expedited implementation approval, an emergency change advisory board should be convened.

Change Scheduling

Approved changes must be scheduled. Some changes can take place right away, but many must be planned for a specific time and date when appropriate team members are available and when stakeholders have been notified of the change.

Not all changes require downtime, but it is imperative to understand which ones do. Changes that require the system to be unavailable need to be performed during downtime. Stakeholders, including end users, application owners, and other administrative teams, need to be consulted prior to scheduling a downtime so that business operations are not adversely affected. They need to understand how long the downtime is anticipated to take, what value the change brings to them, and the precautions that are being taken to protect against risks. For customer-facing systems, downtimes need to be scheduled or avoided so that the company does not lose customer confidence by taking a site, application, or service down unexpectedly.

Upgrades may not require downtime, but they could still affect the performance of the VM and the applications that run on top of it. For this reason, it is best to plan changes for times when the load on the system is minimal.

Enterprise systems may have a global user base. Additionally, it may be necessary to coordinate resources with cloud vendors, other third parties, or with support personnel in different global regions. In such cases, time zones can be a considerable constraint for performing upgrades. It can be difficult to coordinate a time that works for distributed user bases and maintenance teams. For this reason, consider specifying in vendor contracts and SLAs an upgrade schedule so that you are not gridlocked by too many time zone constraints and are unable to perform an upgrade.

Working hours should also be factored in when scheduling change implementation. For example, if a change is to take three hours of one person's time, then it must be scheduled at least three hours prior to the end of that person's shift, or the task will need to be transitioned to another team member while still incomplete. It generally takes more time to transition a task from one team member to another, so it is best to try to keep this to a minimum.

It is also important to factor in some buffer time for issues that could crop up. In this example, if the change is expected to take three hours and you schedule it exactly three hours before the employee's shift ends, that provides no time for troubleshooting or error. If problems do arise, the task would be transitioned to another team member, who would need to do the troubleshooting that might require input from the first team member to avoid rework, since the second employee may not know everything that was done in the first place.

If those implementing the change run into difficulties, they should document which troubleshooting steps they performed as well. This is especially important if others will be assisting the individual in troubleshooting the issue. This can also be helpful when working with technical support. This leads us to the next step in the change management process: documentation.

Change Documentation

It is important to keep a detailed log of what changes were made. Sometimes the impact of a change is not seen right away. Issues could crop up sometime down the road, and it helps to be able to query a system or database to view all the changes related to current issues.

After every change has been completed, it must go through a defined procedure for both change review and closure. This review process is intended to evaluate whether the objectives of the change were accomplished, whether the users and customers were satisfied, and whether any new side effects were produced. The review and closure process is also intended to evaluate the resources expended in the implementation of the change, the time it took to implement, and the overall cost so that the organization can continue to improve the efficiency and effectiveness of the cloud IT service management processes.

Change documentation could be as simple as logging the data in a spreadsheet, but spreadsheets offer limited investigative and analytical options. It is best to invest in a configuration management database (CMDB) to retain documentation on requests, approvals or denials, and change implementation. The CMDB is discussed in the upcoming "Configuration Management" section.

Change Management Integration

The change process may sound bureaucratic and cumbersome, but it does not have to be. Integrate change management into your organization in a way that fits with your organizational culture. Here are some ideas.

Users could submit change requests through a web-based portal, which would send an e-mail to the change approvers. Change approvers could post requests to the change approval board on Slack or some other medium to solicit feedback and then use that feedback to approve or reject the change in the system. Communication on the issue could include a hashtag (a feature of Slack) with the change ID so that it could be easily tracked. Another channel could be used to communicate with stakeholders to schedule the time and resources for the change.

Some workflow can be built into the system to help automate scheduling. You can also use tools to help capture details of changes, such as scripts that dump firewall configurations to the configuration management database when they are made and archival tools to export the CAB discussions to the database. When changes are complete, they can be updated in the same system so that everything is tracked.

Essentially, the entire process can be streamlined and still offer robust checks and balances. Don't be afraid of change management. Look for ways to integrate it into your company.

Configuration Management

Change management offers value to both information technology organizations and their customers. One problem when implementing change management, however, lies in how the objects that are being modified are classified and controlled. To this end, we introduce configuration management, which deals with cloud assets and their relationships to one another.

The purpose of the configuration management process is to ensure that the assets and configuration items (CIs) required to deliver services are adequately controlled and that accurate and reliable information about those assets and CIs is available when and where it is needed. CIs are defined as any asset or document that falls within the scope of the configuration management system. Configuration management information includes details of how the assets have been configured and the relationships between assets.

The objectives of configuration management are as follows:

- Identifying CIs
- Controlling CIs
- Protecting the integrity of CIs
- Maintaining an accurate and complete CMS
- Maintaining information about the state of all CIs
- Providing accurate configuration information

The implementation of a configuration management process results in improved overall service performance. It is also important for optimization of both the costs and risks that can be caused by poorly managed assets, such as extended service outages, fines, incorrect license fees, and failed compliance audits. Some of the specific benefits to be achieved through its implementation are the following:

- A better understanding on the part of cloud professionals of the configurations of the resources they support and the relationships they have with other resources, resulting in the ability to pinpoint issues and resolve incidents and problems much faster
- A much richer set of detailed information for change management from which to make decisions about the implementation of planned changes

- Greater success in the planning and delivery of scheduled releases
- Improved compliance with legal, financial, and regulatory obligations with less administration required to report on those obligations
- Better visibility to the true, fully loaded cost of delivering a specific service
- Ability to track both baselined configuration deviation and deviation from requirements
- Reduced cost and time to discover configuration information when required

Although configuration management may appear to be a straightforward process of just tracking assets and defining the relationships among them, you will find that it has the potential to become very tricky as we explore each of the activities associated with it.

At the very start of the process implementation, configuration management is responsible for defining and documenting which assets of the organization's cloud environments should be managed as configuration items. This is a highly important decision, and careful selection at this stage of the implementation is a critical factor in its success or failure. Once the items that will be tracked as CIs have been defined, the configuration management process has many CI-associated activities that must be executed. For each CI, it must be possible to do the following:

- Identify the instance of that CI in the environment. A CI should have a consistent naming convention and a unique identifier associated with it to distinguish it from other CIs.
- Control changes to that CI through the use of a change management process.
- Report on, periodically audit, and verify the attributes, statuses, and relationships of any and all CIs at any requested time.

If even one of these activities is not achievable, the entire process fails for all CIs. Much of the value derived from configuration management comes from a trust that the configuration information presented by the CMS is accurate and does not need to be investigated. Any activity that undermines that trust and requires a stakeholder to investigate CI attributes, statuses, or relationships eliminates the value the service is intended to provide.

Configuration Management Database

A CMDB is a database used to store configuration records throughout their life cycle. The configuration management system maintains one or more CMDBs, and each database stores attributes of CIs and relationships with other configuration items.

Record all the attributes of the CI in a CMDB. A CMDB is an authority for tracking all attributes of a CI. An environment may have multiple CMDBs that are maintained under disparate authorities, and all CMDBs should be tied together as part of a larger CMS. One of the key attributes that all CIs must contain is ownership. By defining an owner for each CI, organizations can achieve asset accountability. This accountability imposes responsibility for keeping all attributes current, inventorying, financial reporting, safeguarding, and other controls necessary for optimal maintenance, use, and disposal of the CI. The defined owner for each asset should be a key stakeholder in any CAB that deals with a change that affects the configuration of that CI, thus providing the owner with configuration control.

Playbook

A configuration management playbook is a method for automating configuration management procedures. It is similar to a runbook but applied to configuration management activities, such as deploying new systems, software, or code.

Configuration management tools maintain an inventory of systems and the software versions running on them. Deploying new software to a group is then as simple as defining the software version to deploy and the set of machines from the inventory. The configuration management tool will then determine if the software needs to be deployed to those systems (they might already be running the defined version) and which upgrade package to deploy to bring them to the desired level. Figure 14-3 shows configuration management software managing computers, containers, databases, mobile devices, servers, and cloud services.

One popular platform for configuration management is Ansible. Ansible playbooks are YAML statements that define the automation procedures. YAML is a recursive acronym that stands for YAML Ain't Markup Language.

 NOTE Some configuration management tools use different terminology. For example, Chef calls its automation function a cookbook.

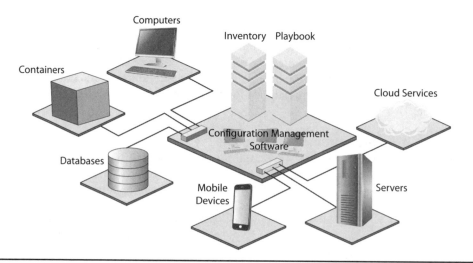

Figure 14-3 Configuration management software

Chapter Review

The first part of this chapter covered testing techniques. The ability to test the availability of a cloud deployment model allows an organization to be proactive with the services and data that it stores in the cloud.

Automation and orchestration are two ways to reduce time spent on tasks, increase the speed of technological development, and improve efficiencies. Automation uses scripting, scheduled tasks, and automation tools to programmatically execute workflows that were formerly performed manually. Orchestration manages automation workflows to optimize efficiencies and ensure effective execution. Orchestration integrates organizational systems to provide more value to the organization. In orchestration, workflow automations are called runbooks, and each discrete step in a runbook is called an activity.

The chapter ended with a discussion on change and configuration management. A change is defined as the addition, modification, or removal of anything that could affect cloud services. Configuration management, on the other hand, is concerned with controlling cloud assets and their relationships to one another through CIs.

Questions

The following questions will help you gauge your understanding of the material in this chapter. Read all the answers carefully because there might be more than one correct answer. Choose the best response(s) for each question.

1. Which configuration test measures the amount of time between a networked device's request for data and the network's response?

    A. Network bandwidth

    B. Network latency

    C. Application availability

    D. Load balancing

2. Which of the following items is not included in a baseline?

    A. Performance

    B. Vulnerabilities

    C. Availability

    D. Capacity

3. Which of the following would be used in orchestration to execute actions to automatically perform a workflow?

    A. Simulator

    B. Workplan

    C. Runbook

    D. Scheduled task

4. Which of the following is a scripting language?

   A. Cobol

   B. C++

   C. Java

   D. PowerShell

5. Which of the following are objectives of change management?
   (Choose all that apply.)

   A. Maximize business value.

   B. Ensure that all proposed changes are both evaluated and recorded.

   C. Identify configuration items (CIs).

   D. Optimize overall business risk.

6. Which of the following are objectives of configuration management?
   (Choose all that apply.)

   A. Protect the integrity of CIs.

   B. Evaluate performance of all CIs.

   C. Maintain information about the state of all CIs.

   D. Maintain an accurate and complete CMS.

7. Dieter is a systems administrator in an enterprise IT organization. The servers
   he is responsible for have recently been the target of a malicious exploit, and the
   vendor has released a patch to protect against this threat. If Dieter would like to
   deploy this patch to his servers right away without waiting for the weekly change
   approval board meeting, what should he request to be convened?

   A. ECAB

   B. Maintenance window

   C. Service improvement opportunity

   D. CAB

Answers

1. **B.** Testing network latency measures the amount of time between a networked
   device's request for data and the network's response. Testing network latency helps
   an administrator determine when a network is not performing at an optimal level.

2. **B.** Vulnerabilities are discovered in vulnerability management, which is not a
   function of baselining. Organizations may track the number of vulnerabilities
   and remediation of those vulnerabilities, but as a business metric, not a baseline.
   A baseline is used to better understand normal performance so that anomalies can
   be identified.

3. C. A runbook is a workflow automation that can be used in orchestration tools.

4. D. PowerShell is a scripting language for Windows, Linux, and macOS.

5. A, B, D. Maximizing business value, ensuring that all changes are evaluated and recorded, and optimizing business risk are all objectives of change management.

6. A, C, D. The objectives of configuration management are identifying CIs, controlling CIs, protecting the integrity of CIs, maintaining an accurate and complete CMS, and providing accurate configuration information when needed.

7. A. Dieter would want to convene an emergency change advisory board (ECAB). The ECAB follows the same procedures that a CAB follows in the evaluation of a change; it is just a subset of the stakeholders that would usually convene for the review. Because of the urgency for implementation, convening a smaller group assists in expediting the process.

CHAPTER 15

Troubleshooting

In this chapter, you will learn about
- Troubleshooting methodology
- Troubleshooting steps
- Documentation and analysis
- Troubleshooting tools

Service and maintenance availability must be a priority when choosing a cloud provider. Having the ability to test and troubleshoot the cloud environment is a critical step in providing the service availability an organization requires. This chapter introduces you to troubleshooting tools, discusses documentation and its importance to company and cloud operations, and presents a troubleshooting methodology with various sample scenarios and issues that you might face in your career and on the CompTIA Cloud+ exam.

Troubleshooting Methodology

CompTIA has established a troubleshooting methodology consisting of six steps, as shown in Figure 15-1. They are as follows: First, identify the problem. This is followed by establishing a theory of probable causes. Next, you test the theory to determine the cause. Fourth, establish a plan of action to resolve the problem and implement the solution. Fifth, verify full system functionality and, if applicable, implement preventative measures. Last, document your findings, actions, and outcomes.

Step 1: Identify the problem.   The first step in the CompTIA troubleshooting methodology is to identify the problem. There are four parts to this, as follows:

1. Interview the user
2. Reproduce the issue
3. Preserve the state
4. Identify changes precipitating the issue

Interview the User   Talk with the user experiencing the issue to understand it. Identify the problem's scope, including which machines and network devices, subnets, sites, or domains are affected. Identifying the scope may involve interviewing others in the

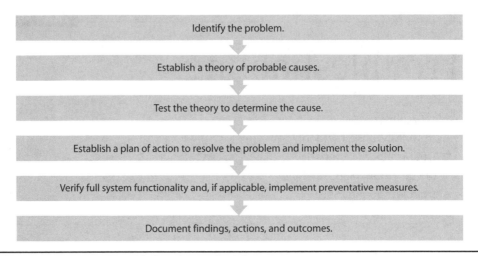

Figure 15-1 CompTIA troubleshooting methodology

department or company. You will also need to find out when the issue first began. Did this occur last week, earlier in the day, or is this a chronic issue that they are finally reporting? Try to get as precise a time as possible because this will make it easier to isolate changes and conditions that occurred surrounding that time.

Since both of these steps require asking the user or others questions, it is important to be courteous and respectful. Show the user that you are concerned about the problem by actively listening to what they have to say. All too often, IT professionals want to run off as soon as a problem is mentioned so that they can begin fixing it. However, in a rush to fix the problem, they may not truly understand the problem and give the user the impression that their situation is not important.

Reproduce the Issue   A critical step in identifying the problem is to ask the user to demonstrate what is not working for them. If they say the Internet is not working on their cloud virtual desktop, ask them to demonstrate. In this way, both you and the user can better understand the scope of the problem, and the user might be able to do more while you troubleshoot.

Sometimes a user will describe a scenario that you cannot reproduce. For example, they may have trouble visiting a site, and you can get there fine until they show you and you see they are using a different, out-of-date browser. Similarly, they may show you that a particular site does not come up, but when you ask them to go to another site, it loads correctly.

It can be frustrating if you cannot reproduce the error with the user. If this happens, be patient and try several more times. If you still cannot reproduce it, ask them to notify you when it happens again and to note other things that happen around that time. It could be that the issue only occurs when certain conditions are met, such as a high load on the network, a specific time of day, or when other applications are open.

Preserve the State   Before moving to further steps, ensure that a backup is taken of the system. You want to preserve the state the machine is in so that you can get back to this state later, if necessary. This allows you to revert back if changes make the problem worse as you are troubleshooting.

Identify Changes Precipitating the Issue   Lastly, determine what has changed recently. Evaluate whether those changes could have contributed to the issue. Some things to consider include

- New software installations.
- Applying patches or updates.
- New users logging on.
- The machine was moved to a new location.
- Connections to new Wi-Fi networks.
- Operating system changes were made.
- New hardware was added, or hardware was removed. This could include something as simple as plugging in a portable hard drive or flash drive or removing a webcam.
- Connections to new network resources, such as network shares or printers.
- The system was damaged in some way, or the user noticed signs of damage.
- The user noticed signs of tampering or tampering alarms were triggered.

Step 2: Establish a theory of probable causes.   The second step in the CompTIA troubleshooting methodology is to establish a theory of probable causes. There are three parts to this, as follows:

1. List and prioritize possible causes
2. Question the obvious
3. Conduct research based on symptoms

List and Prioritize Possible Causes   The information gathered in step 1 should help in generating possible causes. Ask yourself what is common between devices that are experiencing the issue. Do they share a common connection or resource?

Question the Obvious   Be sure to question the obvious (the simple things). Sometimes, problems can be solved by something relatively simple such as plugging in an Ethernet cable, verifying that users are typing a URL or UNC correctly, or verifying that target systems are turned on. Don't spend your time working out potential complex solutions until you have eliminated the simple solutions.

Conduct Research Based on Symptoms   Next, research the symptoms the user is experiencing. Documentation comes in very handy when performing this research. Be sure to review records on how systems should be configured and compare these with the actual configuration.

Depending on the issue, you may need to review vendor manuals as well. For example, if this is an issue with a software application, check the vendor manual for that application. It is essential to know where to find this information. For this reason, keep manuals and other documentation in a central location, typically on a network share or a shared cloud folder that can be easily updated and accessed.

 NOTE Make sure you identify the product version number that the user is running so that you can refer to the correct vendor document.

Step 3: Test the theory to determine the cause. At this point, you will likely have multiple theories on what might be the problem. Only one of those theories will be correct, so you will need to test the theories to identify which one it is. Systematically go through the theories, testing them to either confirm or reject them. Figure 15-2 shows the process.

Start by testing the simplest theories before thinking through the complex ones. As mentioned in the previous step, most issues are caused by simple things, and simple things are easier to test. Ensure that the system you use for testing is similar enough to the one experiencing issues, and ensure that you can replicate the issue on the test system before attempting a fix. Some IT professionals have worked hard to deploy a solution to a system that was not experiencing the problem. They then falsely believe they fixed the issue when they later test. For each theory, determine if you can confirm or reject it. If you reject the theory, move on to the next one. If you confirm it, move on to step 4.

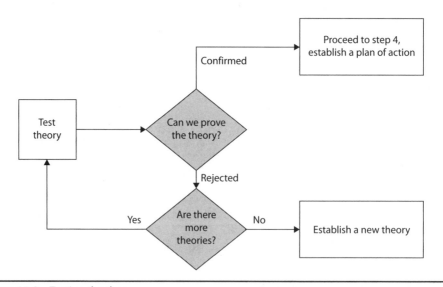

Figure 15-2 Testing the theory

If you need to have the user test some things, be sure to ask politely. Phrase your request so as not to cause the user to think that you are blaming them for the problem, even if you believe it is a user error. If you are incorrect and it is not a user error, you will look foolish, and the user might be offended.

If you end up rejecting all the theories, you will need to establish a new theory. Go back to step 2 and consider the situation from angles that you did not consider before. If you are unable to think of new theories, solicit help from others.

Step 4: Establish a plan of action to resolve the problem and implement the solution. Document the steps that you want to take to resolve the problem. Ensure that you can demonstrate that your tests confirmed a nonworking condition and then a working condition following the proposed actions' implementation. Review the plan with others and ensure that change controls are followed. The change management process was discussed in Chapter 14. Lastly, after approval has been given to implement the change, perform the outlined steps to fix the problem.

Step 5: Verify full system functionality and, if applicable, implement preventative measures. Check with all users who were experiencing the issue to ensure that they are no longer experiencing the problem. Also, check with others around them to ensure that you have not created other issues by implementing the fix. Lastly, implement restrictions or additional controls to prevent the problem from occurring in the future. This could involve retraining the user or placing technical controls on the system to prevent such actions from happening again. In some cases, permissions may need to be changed or system configurations updated. System changes should follow the same change control process as the troubleshooting change did.

Step 6: Document findings, actions, and outcomes. This last step is critical to ensure that you or others at your company do not continue to solve the same problems from scratch over and over. If you are anything like us, you will need to write down what you did so that you can remember it again later. IT professionals lead busy lives, and there never seems to be time to document. However, if you do not document, you will find that you spend time performing the same research when you could have simply consulted your documentation.

The CompTIA troubleshooting steps provided here will be demonstrated in the scenarios that follow to help you understand better how the troubleshooting methodology is applied to real-world problems.

In the course of your career, you will run into a wide variety of issues that you will need to troubleshoot. No book could be comprehensive enough to cover all of them, so I have selected a few problems that you are likely to see. The issues are also ones that you are likely to see on the CompTIA Cloud+ exam.

Troubleshooting Steps

Troubleshooting is a broad subject because there are so many things that can go wrong. This is complicated with the many complex systems in use today. No matter the issue, remember to try to break the problem down to the smallest parts so that you can work on just those. This is why it is crucial to identify the issue as precisely as possible.

This section discusses some of the potential issues you might face in the following main areas:

- Security
- Deployment
- Connectivity
- Performance
- Capacity
- Automation and orchestration

Security Issues

Security issues can cause significant problems for system availability and data confidentiality or integrity. Some security issues you should be aware of are as follows:

- **Federations, domain trusts, and single sign-on**   Federations, domain trusts, and single sign-on (SSO) are each technologies that extend authentication and authorization functions across multiple interdependent systems.

- **External attacks**   External attacks can be minimized using firewalls, intrusion detection systems, hardening, and other concepts discussed in Chapter 11.

- **Internal attacks**   Separation of duties and least privilege can help reduce the likelihood of internal attacks.

- **Privilege escalation**   System vulnerabilities, incorrectly configured roles, or software bugs can result in situations where malicious code or an attacker can escalate their privileges to gain access to resources that they are unauthorized to access.

- **External role change**   Role change policies should extend out to procedures and practices employed to change authorizations for users to match changes in job roles for employees.

- **Incorrect hardening settings**   Hardening, discussed in Chapter 11, reduces the risk to devices.

- **Weak or obsolete security technologies**   Security technologies age quickly. Those technologies that are out of support may not receive vendor patches and will be unsafe to use in the protection of corporate assets.

This section explores three common security topics in more detail, along with scenarios that utilize CompTIA's troubleshooting methodology to help you become familiar with the process in practice. These topics include authorization and authentication issues, malware, and certificate issues. Lastly, certificates are used to secure communication between devices and verify the identity of communication partners. When certificates or the systems around them fail, communication failures are sure to follow, significantly affecting business operations.

Insufficient Security Controls and Processes

Security controls are technologies, procedures, or services that reduce security risk. As you can imagine, there are a wide variety of security controls. They are generally divided into three types as follows:

- Preventative controls
- Detective controls
- Corrective controls

Preventative Controls   Preventative controls are designed to stop harmful activity from occurring. Some examples include firewalls that block malicious traffic from entering the network, encryption that prevents other parties from viewing data or a communication stream, hardening that closes unused ports and disables unused services, or patch management that keeps systems up-to-date with fixes for discovered vulnerabilities in software.

Insufficient preventative controls increase the likelihood that an attacker will exploit the area the control is designed to protect against. Table 15-1 shows the example preventative controls, action they perform, and potential results of insufficient controls. Some controls perform actions that fit into multiple categories, such as antimalware software that both detects and corrects malware by identifying it and then removing it.

Control	Action Performed	Potential Harm If Insufficient
Firewall	Block malicious traffic	Malicious traffic is allowed onto the network, potentially compromising machines, denying access to services, or stealing data.
Encryption	Prevents other parties from viewing data or a communication stream	Unauthorized parties are able to view sensitive data.
Hardening	Closes unused ports and disables unused services	Unused ports or services are utilized to compromise the machine.
Patch management	Keeps systems up-to-date with fixes for discovered vulnerabilities in software	Vulnerabilities are exploited to compromise the machine, install malware, mine bitcoin, or perform some other malicious task.
Input validation	Restricts the input that can be entered into web forms.	Web forms are manipulated to modify data on the database or send data that the user should not be able to view. Garbage data is inserted into the database. Thousands of e-mails are sent in response to automated web form entries, clogging user mailboxes and making it hard for those employees to respond to legitimate messages.

Table 15-1   Preventative Controls and the Harm They Prevent

Control	Action Performed	Potential Harm If Insufficient
DLP	Alerts on data handling that violates acceptable handling policies.	Privacy breach, such as a nurse viewing data on a patient not under his or her care. Data loss through improper communication of sensitive or protected data. Theft of information by an insider.
Internet filtering	Detects attempts to access restricted Internet content.	The company is unaware of malicious code that is executed in a browser. The company and employee are unaware that an employee has entered sensitive or personal information into a form on a fake website.
IDS	Identifies malicious network activity and alerts on it.	Malicious network traffic goes undetected, potentially leading to a compromised system, malware, or data breach.
SIEM	Analyzed log data and other information collected from systems to identify and alert on attacks. Allows security operations teams to investigate potential security events.	Security incidents last much longer without being detected, resulting in much greater harm to the company, its customers, and its stakeholders.

Table 15-2   Detective Controls and the Harm They Prevent

Detective Controls   Detective controls are designed to identify and alert on harmful activity. For example, DLP would alert on activity that violates policies. It could also be configured to block such activity, so it would fall into a preventative control as well. Similarly, Internet filtering can detect attempts to access restricted Internet content that could contain harmful material, but it can also be configured to block that access. The mode that each of these runs in can be audit only or audit and protect.

Insufficient preventative controls result in the company being unaware of ongoing attacks or misuse of company resources. Table 15-2 shows the example preventative controls, the action they perform, and the potential results of insufficient controls.

Corrective Controls   Corrective controls are designed to bring systems or data back to a normal operating state following a security event. Some corrective controls include antivirus software that removes malware for which it has a signature, backup software that restores data or systems, and patch management that applies fixes for known vulnerabilities.

Insufficient corrective controls increase the harm of a security event, including loss of data, extended system outages, or more expensive recovery. Table 15-3 shows the example corrective controls, the action they perform, and the potential results of insufficient controls.

Control	Action Performed	Potential Harm If Insufficient
Antivirus software	Removes malware for which it has a signature or a heuristic match.	Malware infects one or more machines.
Backup software	Creates copies of data and systems that can be restored if necessary.	Data loss. Systems need to be restored manually, resulting in a much longer period of system unavailability.
Patch management	Applied vendor released fixes for known vulnerabilities.	Known vulnerabilities could be exploited on systems.
Account lockout	Locks out accounts when certain conditions are met, such as a threshold of incorrect password attempts.	Brute force password cracking is allowed to continue, and user or service credentials are obtained by an attacker.
Failover site	Operate services on alternative hardware.	Users are unable to access systems when the primary systems are unavailable.

Table 15-3   Corrective Controls and the Harm They Prevent

Privilege Issues

Privileges are the rights to perform actions on an information system. Privileges can be assigned to users or other entities, such as service accounts. These privileges may allow users to access files, run programs, or use services.

Privilege issues can sometimes arise when employees change positions and their privileges are not correctly updated. It could also happen when files are restored and older permissions are restored with them, or permissions are not carried along with the restored files. Whatever the cause, permission issues result in a lack of access to resources that affect authorized user or system activities.

Privilege issues may reveal themselves when a user or service attempts to perform an action that they are authorized to perform, but they cannot do so. For example, a user may try to access a share that they are supposed to be able to access, but they are given an access denied error. Service accounts can also cause issues. Service accounts are created for very specific uses, and their permissions are usually granularly defined. However, as needs change, so must the permissions. These privileges would need to be updated to grant the permissions to resources a service account can access and what the service can do with that resource.

Let's demonstrate the CompTIA troubleshooting methodology with a scenario: A service account is used to log into a database server. It issues queries to three databases. The service can add data to the tables of one database but cannot modify the table structure. This account works fine for operating the application, but upgrading the application results in an error stating that tables could not be updated.

Step 1: Identify the problem.   The application upgrade fails when updating tables.

Step 2: Establish a theory of probable causes.   You theorize that this could be due to a permissions issue with the person running the upgrade or with the service account.

You run a trace on the database as the application is upgraded. You identify the account used to perform the upgrade and the queries that fail. The queries are related to adding new fields.

Step 3: Test the theory to determine the cause.   You review the permissions for the account and find that it does not have permission to modify the table structure, and adding new fields is a change to the structure.

Step 4: Establish a plan of action to resolve the problem and implement the solution.   You recommend that an account with permission to modify the table structure should be used to install the application. Management agrees, and you put in a service ticket to have an account created with the appropriate permissions and roles. Once the account is created, you provide the credentials to the application team.

Step 5: Verify full system functionality and, if applicable, implement preventative measures.   The application team reports that the application installs correctly with the new credentials. You confirm that the application upgrade is complete and then submit a ticket to have the account disabled until the application team needs it again.

Step 6: Document findings, actions, and outcomes.   You document the account that needs to be used for application updates and the process that must be followed to enable the account.

 EXAM TIP   In this example, you could add the permissions to the account that runs the application, but this would not be the best approach. The application does not need that permission regularly, and something that exploited the application or service could use that to modify the table structure and do more harm to the application. It is best to exercise the principle of least privilege in both user and service accounts.

Security Groups   Permissions are typically assigned to a group associated with a role rather than giving permissions directly to a user account. This makes it easier to add others to a role because they can just be added to the group, rather than copying all the permissions assigned to another user. Similarly, making changes to the permissions can be done in one place, rather than for each user that has access. However, security groups can become complex to troubleshoot when users are members of many groups and those groups have overlapping permissions.

In most systems, permissions are cumulative unless a deny permission is applied. Let's look at an example. You will likely find that as systems grow over time, some convoluted data organization methods can evolve that result in some cumbersome privileges. Consider a situation where Todd is unable to access the R&D share. Todd is a member of the employees and management groups. Figure 15-3 shows the folder structure for the company data.

Figure 15-3
Shared folder
structure

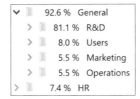

This data is stored within OneDrive, and permissions to the folders are assigned to groups. The folder permissions for each group are shown in Figure 15-4.

For this scenario, consider the troubleshooting methodology and walk through it on your own. Think through each step. You may need to make some assumptions as you move through the process since this is a sample scenario.

Step 1. Identify the problem.

Step 2. Establish a theory of probable causes.

Step 3. Test the theory to determine the cause.

Step 4. Establish a plan of action to resolve the problem and implement the solution.

Step 5. Verify full system functionality and, if applicable, implement preventative measures.

Step 6. Document findings, actions, and outcomes.

Todd is a member of the employees and management groups, but he would not be able to access the R&D share because the deny read and write permission from his membership in the employees group would override his read permission as a member of the management group. You could resolve this by removing Todd from the employees group, but this could cause issues with other resources he needs to access. The best thing to do would be to move the R&D folder out from under the general share. The employees group could then be removed from the permissions on the R&D folder so that a deny permission would not be required there.

General share	
Group	Permission
Employees	Full control
Research	Full control

HR share	
Group	Permission
HR share	Full control

R&D share	
Group	Permission
Research	Full control
Employees	Deny read, Deny write
Management	Read

Figure 15-4 Folder permissions

Authorization and Authentication Issues

Authentication is the process of validating an identity, and authorization validates that the identity has the required privileges to perform the requested action. Authorization and authentication issues include scenarios such as systems that are deployed without proper service accounts or account lockouts.

Authentication issues can be as simple as users locking their accounts by entering their credentials incorrectly several times consecutively. The user's account will need to be unlocked before they can access network resources. If many users report permission problems, check services like DNS and Active Directory, or LDAP on Linux servers, to verify that they are functioning. Problems with these services can prevent users from authenticating to domain services.

Consider a scenario where a user reports that they are unable to log into their Office 365 mailbox and their OneDrive but they can access other resources.

For this scenario, consider the troubleshooting methodology and walk through it on your own. Think through each step. You may need to make some assumptions as you move through the process since this is a sample scenario.

Step 1. Identify the problem.

Step 2. Establish a theory of probable causes.

Step 3. Test the theory to determine the cause.

Step 4. Establish a plan of action to resolve the problem and implement the solution.

Step 5. Verify full system functionality and, if applicable, implement preventative measures.

Step 6. Document findings, actions, and outcomes.

Malware

Another security issue you might face is the presence of malware. Malware impact can range from low, such as malware that slows a machine, to high-risk malware that results in a data breach. Malware infects machines through infected media that is plugged into a computer or other device, through website downloads or drive-by malware that executes from infected websites, or malicious ads known as malvertizing. Malware is also distributed through a variety of methods, as shown in Figure 15-5.

Computers infected with malware might run slowly or encounter regular problems. Ransomware, a particularly troublesome form of malware, encrypts data on the user's machine and on network drives the machine has write access to.

Let's demonstrate the CompTIA troubleshooting methodology with a scenario: Aimee, a cloud security engineer, receives reports that user files are being encrypted on the network.

Step 1: Identify the problem.　　Files are being encrypted on the company NAS. Access logs from the NAS around the time of the encryption show connections from a computer called LAB1014. LAB1014 has many encrypted files on its local drive. No other

Figure 15-5 Malware distribution methods

users report encrypted files on their machines, and a spot check by another administrator confirms no encrypted files on a sample of other devices.

Step 2: Establish a theory of probable causes. This could be due to a rogue script or ransomware running on LAB1014.

Step 3: Test the theory to determine the cause. Both theories have the same response. LAB1014 needs to be quarantined immediately so that the problem does not spread and continue. If it is the cause of a rogue script, the activity will cease after LAB1014 is quarantined. If it is the result of ransomware, the LAB1014 will continue encrypting files on its local drive, but uninfected machines on the network and the NAS will continue operating normally.

Step 4: Establish a plan of action to resolve the problem and implement the solution. The first step is to isolate LAB1014 from the network so that it cannot infect any other machines. Next, check other computers, starting with devices that were connected to the infected machine, such as file servers or departmental servers and surrounding workstations. Isolate all machines that have malware on them.

Next, make a forensic copy of LAB1014 in case an investigation is required. Once the forensic image is verified, you can begin identifying the malware through virus scanning and removing the malware using virus scanning tools or specific malware removal tools. It is best to scan the LAB1014 computer with installed antivirus tools and with bootable media that can scan the machine from outside the context of the installed operating system. Sometimes malware tricks the operating system into thinking parts of its code are legitimate. It might even tell the operating system that its files do not exist. Virus scanning tools installed on the operating system rely on the operating system to provide them with accurate information, but this is not always the case. Bootable antivirus tools work independently from the operating system, so they do not suffer from these potential limitations.

Step 5: Verify full system functionality and, if applicable, implement preventative measures. Verify that the ransomware has been removed from LAB1014 and any other machines that may have been identified as containing ransomware in the course of troubleshooting and that new devices are not being infected. Next, restore data to the machines where data was encrypted.

Step 6: Document findings, actions, and outcomes. Create a report of the impact and actions taken.

Key and Certificate Issues

Certificates are used to encrypt and decrypt data, as well as to digitally sign and verify the integrity of data. Each certificate contains a unique, mathematically related public and private key pair. During the standard authentication process to a website, a client is presented with a certificate from a website. It then verifies that the certificate is in its trusted root store, thus trusting the certificate was signed by a trusted certificate authority. Afterward, the client confirms that the certificate is coming from the correct web server.

When the certificate is issued, it has an expiration date; certificates must be renewed before the expiration date. Otherwise, they are not usable. Expired certificates or certificates that are misconfigured can make sites unavailable or available with errors for end users.

Misconfigured certificates include sites that have a different name from their certificate, such as a site with the URL www.example.com configured with a certificate, for example.com. The missing "www" in the certificate name would result in certificate errors for site visitors.

Consider a scenario with a certificate issue and how the CompTIA troubleshooting methodology could be applied to resolve the issue: Users report that the company website shows security errors and customers are afraid to go to the website. Some customers on Twitter are saying that the company site has been hacked.

Step 1: Identify the problem. You open the site and see that the site is displaying a certificate error.

Step 2: Establish a theory of probable causes. The certificate either is expired or has been revoked.

Step 3: Test the theory to determine the cause. View the certificate on the web server to see if it is expired. If it is not expired, check the certificate revocation list (CRL) to see if it has been revoked. In this case, the certificate expired.

Step 4: Establish a plan of action to resolve the problem and implement the solution. Discuss renewal of the certificate and receive approval to perform the renewal and a purchase order to purchase the certificate renewal. Complete the renewal of the server certificate.

Step 5: Verify full system functionality and, if applicable, implement preventative measures. Log onto the site to confirm that certificate errors are no longer displayed.

Step 6: Document findings, actions, and outcomes. Identify all certificates in use at the company and when they expire. Discuss which ones are still required and establish a process to review certificates needed at least annually. Next, create a schedule with alerts so that certificates are renewed before they expire. Share the schedule with management so that they can budget for the certificate renewal cost.

Misconfigured or Misapplied Policies

In this context, policies do not refer to documents, but to rules given to security systems. Some of these include

- **DLP** Data loss prevention (DLP) uses policies to define acceptable and unacceptable ways of working with data.

- **IAM** Identity access management (IAM) systems have policies that define how resources can be accessed.

- **IDS/IPS** IDS/IPS systems have policies that define the actions taken when traffic matches a signature.

- **Remote access** VPN and other remote access technologies, such as Microsoft's Remote Desktop Gateway, have policies that define conditions that allow access, such as group membership, location, or time.

Table 15-4 shows each of these systems and some of the issues that could arise with misconfiguration or misapplication of policies.

	DLP	IAM	IDS/IPS	Remote Access
Misconfigured Policy	• Incorrect data handling • Employees are not able to work with data to do their jobs	• Users lack access to needed resources • Users have access to restricted resources	• Legitimate traffic is blocked • Malicious traffic is allowed	• Users are denied remote access • Unauthorized users are allowed to connect
Misapplied Policy	• Policy not enforced • Policy not enforced on all required data types • Policy not enforced for all required users	• Applications, systems, or sites no longer authenticate users	• Traffic is not screened • Alerts are not sent	• No users can connect remotely

Table 15-4 Misconfigured or Misapplied Policies

Exercise 15-1: Using the Google Cloud Policy Troubleshooter

In this exercise, we will create the Google Cloud Policy Troubleshooter to determine if an account has the required permissions for a resource under the current IAM policies. The tool will show whether the user can perform the selected action and which policies give them that right. If they do not have permission, it will state that access is denied and then specify the required role the user would need to be able to perform the action.

1. Log in to your Google Cloud Platform and then click the menu button in the upper left. Select IAM & Admin and then Policy Troubleshooter.

2. The Policy Troubleshooter screen will load. Type in a user account to test and then select the resource and the desired permission. This will test to see if the user account entered can perform that action on the resource. For this example, I have selected a sample account cloudtest@vanderburg.com. We will see if the account has the ability to approve requests through the cloud resource manager API. To do this, we entered the e-mail shown and then selected the cloud resource manager API and the accessapproval.requests.approve permission.

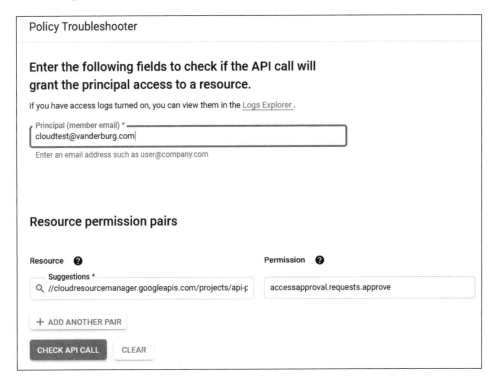

3. Click Check API Call. The troubleshooter will then assess whether that account has the selected access. In this example, the account does not have access. It shows that the role required for that permission is the owner role and that there is currently only one member of that role. The member has been blurred to protect privacy, but it is the value following "user:," shown here.

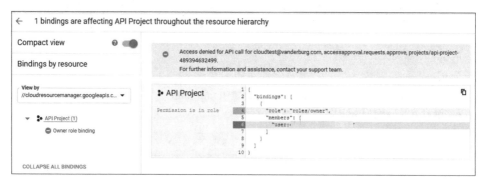

If we were having difficulty with this account performing approvals using the API, one solution would be to add them to the owner's role. However, this role likely contains permissions that the user does not need, so the best solution would be to create a new role and then assign the permissions to that role and grant the user that role.

Data Security Issues

A major component of security is protecting the data on systems from compromise, including unauthorized access, deletion, or corruption. Data security issues are those that result in some compromise of the data. Some data security issues you should be aware of are as follows:

- **Unencrypted data** Sensitive data transmitted or stored in an unencrypted format could potentially be exposed to unauthorized parties. For example, a backup tape containing sensitive information is lost, and the tape is not encrypted.

- **Data breach** When data is stolen from a company, it is known as a data breach. Data breaches require an investigation to determine the scope and impact of the breach and root causes so that those can be remediated. For example, a customer service rep opens a phishing e-mail containing a malicious attachment that provides access to an attacker. The attacker then uses the customer service rep's credentials to retrieve the personal information on customers from the company database.

- **Misclassification** Data classifications are used to properly handle data. However, if the data is misclassified, incorrect handling rules and procedures will be applied to it. For example, controlled unclassified information (CUI) is received and misclassified as normal data. DLP policies based on the data classification tags are then not applied to it.

- **Unencrypted protocols**   We have covered a wide variety of protocols used for communication over the Internet, on a local network, over VPNs, and back-end storage networks. Some of these protocols used encryption to protect the data in transit, while others were unencrypted. A data security issue could arise when an unencrypted protocol is used to send sensitive data over a public Internet link or a shared medium.

- **Insecure ciphers**   A cipher is a mathematical formula used to convert plaintext (unencrypted) data into ciphertext (encrypted data). As ciphers age, weaknesses in their implementation are sometimes discovered that render them unsafe to use. In other cases, the power of computing renders them obsolete because faster computers may break the encryption using brute force methods.

Exposed Endpoints

Endpoints can be exposed to security threats if they are misconfigured, lack security updates, or lack essential security software such as host-based firewalls and antivirus protection. An exposed endpoint can lead to the compromise of the credentials of users on the machine or data that resides on the endpoint.

Misconfigured or Failed Security Appliances

Security appliances are hardware or virtual appliances that are used to secure the network infrastructure and systems. Misconfigured devices may not provide the level of security needed, or they could prevent legitimate services from operating correctly. This section discusses issues that could be seen with IDS/IPS, NAC, and WAF.

- **IDS/IPS**   A misconfigured intrusion prevention system (IPS) or intrusion detection system (IDS) could result in blocked traffic or false alarms on traffic.

- **NAC**   Misconfigured network access control (NAC) could result in machines that do not meet the NAC policy to connect, or it may block legitimate connections that do meet the NAC policy.

- **WAF**   Web application firewalls (WAFs) screen traffic destined for web applications. A misconfigured WAF could block legitimate traffic or allow unauthorized traffic to the site. For example, suppose an administrator wants to remove encrypted HTTP access for a website used to accept customer orders. They log into the firewall and remove the access control list (ACL) that allows HTTPS traffic rather than the one for HTTP.

Deployment Issues

Application deployment issues are relatively commonplace. Most applications will be deployed without issue, but you will deploy so many apps that deployment issues will be something that you see quite often.

Missing or Incorrect Tags

Tags can be used to represent resources in the cloud. Policy rules can be defined on the tags to more efficiently manage the resources. For example, you could tag each IP that represents a web server. Then, you could deploy a new version of Apache to each system with the web server tag. However, you can run into a real mess if tags are missing or if the wrong devices are tagged.

Imagine deploying the wrong software or code to machines. You could have servers with completely different roles running software that serves no purpose. This creates an attack surface on those machines that would likely not be protected by appropriate controls. The machines that really do need the software would not have it, resulting in services that would not work properly.

Troubleshooting this would require verifying tags against system documentation to ensure that the correct machines are tagged. You would also want to check the change management system to see which changes were made recently to the tags and cross-reference this with the logs. The system might show that 192.168.1.60 was added to the web servers, but the logs show that 192.168.1.50 was added. You could then remove 50 and add 60 to correct the problem.

Application Container Issues

When deploying containers, there are a wide range of issues you might encounter. One issue you might face is incompatible host and container images. The base image version of a container must match the OS of the system you are deploying it to. If the versions do not match, the deployment will fail or will not operate correctly. Failed deployments will have the following error code: 0xc0370101.

Host and container image versions must match because the host and the container share a single kernel. On Windows, the versions must match at the build level. You can check the version of the container and the host to compare. You can query the version of a system with the ver command at the command prompt, as shown in Figure 15-6.

Windows build numbers are divided into four sections, as shown in Figure 15-7. The first three sections must match. These are the major, minor, and build numbers. The revision numbers can differ.

Another issue you might see is attempting to deploy a container from a missing or mistyped image. If you encounter this, verify that the specified image exists at the location specified and that you typed the name correctly.

Figure 15-6
Querying the
Windows version

```
Microsoft Windows [Version 10.0.19042.867]
(c) 2020 Microsoft Corporation. All rights reserved.

C:\Users\Eric>ver

Microsoft Windows [Version 10.0.19042.867]
```

Figure 15-7
Windows version
breakdown

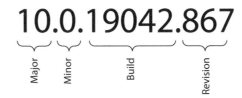

10.0.19042.867

Major Minor Build Revision

You will need to have enough resources available to deploy the image. If you lack suffi-cient CPU or memory, the container deployment will fail. If you encounter errors related to resource availability, try one of the following:

- Deploy the container to a different host
- Reduce the CPU or memory specified for the container
- Reduce the CPU or memory of other containers on the host
- Migrate other containers to a different host

Incompatible or Missing Dependencies

Missing or incompatible dependencies can make an application fail to install or not work correctly. They can also cause software upgrades to fail. For example, you may want to upgrade the version of WordPress running on your hosted site, but the upgrade fails because it requires an upgrade to PHP and MySQL first.

When deploying a web application, ensure that programming libraries are installed first. Windows applications written in a .NET programming language such as C# will require a particular version of .NET on the machine. Other applications may require PHP or Java to be installed. Read through deployment documentation carefully to ensure that you meet all the requirements. Of course, you will also need Internet Information Services (IIS) and any other operating system roles and features. Ensure that all this is in place before application installation.

The Java Runtime Environment (JRE) can be particularly troublesome when running multiple Java-based applications on the same machine because they might not all sup-port the same version. For example, three applications are installed on the server, and you upgrade the first one. You read through the documentation before upgrading and find that you need to update the Java version first. The Java upgrade completes successfully, and then you deploy the new version of the application. Testing confirms that the new app works fine, but a short time later, users report that the other two applications are no longer working. Upon troubleshooting, you find that they do not support the new version of Java that was deployed.

The most straightforward fix to this issue is to deploy dedicated VMs for each applica-tion. You can also use application containers to host each application so that dependen-cies can be handled individually for each container. Containers are more lightweight, quicker to deploy (less disk space, since OS is generally not in the container), and start up much more quickly than VMs.

Now that you understand the potential problem, let's try a scenario: You have been asked to set up a new website for your company. You purchase a hosted cloud solution and create a host record in your company's hosted DNS server to point to the hosted cloud server's IP address. You test the URL and see the default setup page. You then use the cloud marketplace to install some website applications and themes. However, when you navigate to your website, you now receive the following error message:

```
Warning: Creating default object from empty value in customizer.php
```

Step 1: Identify the problem.   New applications and themes were installed since the site last came up correctly, so the error is most likely related to the latest software and themes.

Step 2: Establish a theory of probable causes.   You research the error online and see issues relating to missing PHP files. You theorize that PHP is installed incorrectly or that the PHP dependency is missing.

Step 3: Test the theory to determine the cause.   To test these theories, you can reinstall PHP on the server or install it if it is missing. You first identify the required level of PHP from the software that you installed earlier. Then you log onto the cloud server and check the PHP version. You find that PHP is not installed, so it seems like installing the required PHP version will solve the problem.

Step 4: Establish a plan of action to resolve the problem and implement the solution.   You log into the cloud management portal and go to the marketplace. After locating the PHP version required by the software, you review the release notes to determine if it is compatible with your other software and system. You find that your cloud vendor maintains a database of compatible applications and software, and it has already queried your systems and noted that this version of PHP is compatible with your cloud installation.

You place a change request to install PHP and include relevant documentation on why the software is needed. Once the change request is approved, you proceed to install the software from the marketplace and then verify that the software installs correctly.

Note that because this is a new installation, no users are accessing the site. If this were a production site, installing a significant dependency like PHP would take the site down, so you would need to perform the install in a downtime.

Step 5: Verify full system functionality and, if applicable, implement preventative measures.   You open a web browser, navigate to the company website URL, and verify that you can access the site. The installation of the PHP dependency solved the problem. Additionally, you find that you can enable the system to automatically install dependencies in the future so that you can avoid such a situation. You create another change request to enable this feature and wait for the approval. Once approval is provided, you enable the feature.

Step 6: Document findings, actions, and outcomes.   You update both change request tickets to indicate that the work was completed successfully and that no other changes were required. Additionally, you send a memo to the other team members noting the issue and what was done to resolve it and that dependencies will be installed automatically moving forward.

Integration Issues with Different Cloud Platforms

Cloud applications typically do not reside on their own. They are often integrated with other cloud systems with APIs. A vendor will create an API for its application and then release documentation so that developers and integrators know how to utilize that API. For example, Office 365, a cloud-based productivity suite that includes an e-mail application, has an API for importing and exporting contacts. Salesforce, a cloud-based customer relationship management (CRM) application, could integrate with Office 365 through that API so that contacts could be updated based on interactions in the CRM tool. However, APIs must be implemented correctly, or the integration will not work.

Let's try the CompTIA troubleshooting methodology with a scenario: You receive an e-mail from Microsoft informing you of a new API that works with Salesforce. You log into Salesforce and configure Salesforce to talk to Office 365. You educate users on the new integration and that contacts created in Salesforce will be added to Office 365 and that tasks in Salesforce will be synchronized with Office 365 tasks. However, a user reports that their contacts are not being updated and that tasks are not being created. You also find when opening your tasks that there are hundreds of new tasks that should belong to other users.

For this scenario, consider the troubleshooting methodology and walk through it on your own. Think through each step. You may need to make some assumptions as you move through the process since this is a sample scenario.

Step 1. Identify the problem.

Step 2. Establish a theory of probable causes.

Step 3. Test the theory to determine the cause.

Step 4. Establish a plan of action to resolve the problem and implement the solution.

Step 5. Verify full system functionality and, if applicable, implement preventative measures.

Step 6. Document findings, actions, and outcomes.

Script Misconfiguration

Deployment scripts need to be absolutely correct, or they will deploy the wrong thing or fail altogether. Scripts can be developed for a wide variety of applications, but it is a best practice to build in checks so that changes can be validated as the script executes. If a step in the process fails, the script should be able to roll back the changes and send notifications to appropriate personnel to investigate. Developing scripts like this takes much more time, but it can help avoid many headaches in the future and provide additional details when troubleshooting. Ensure the following to help avoid or prevent script misconfiguration issues:

- **Referencing the right objects**   Ensure that object names are correctly spelled and that they exist.

- **Using accounts with the necessary privileges**   The script will need to use accounts that have sufficient privileges to perform the operation.

- **Referencing the right resources**   Ensure that the resource names are correctly spelled, that they exist, and that there are sufficient resources for the operation. Some resources include storage locations, network security groups, or virtual networks.

- **Correct networking**   Ensure that the script configures the correct networking settings for the desired deployment location. This is easier if you are using DHCP, but in many cases, servers will not use DHCP so you will need to ensure the IP address, subnet mask, and default gateway work on the deployment network.

- **Deploying resources in the correct order**   Ensure that you create each resource so that dependencies are met.

If your script fails, check your logs to see which step in the process failed. For example, you may find that a step for creating the database fails, so you would then check the logs on the database. If those logs show that the database drive is full, you could correct that issue and then try the script again.

CAUTION   Be sure to clean up or roll back changes your script may have made if it fails before fully completing. These changes, if not rolled back, could prevent the script from running in the future.

Consider a scenario where you attempt to run a deployment script but encounter an AuthorizationFailed error. For this scenario, use the troubleshooting methodology and walk through it on your own. Think through each step. You may need to make some assumptions as you move through the process since this is a sample scenario.

Step 1. Identify the problem.

Step 2. Establish a theory of probable causes.

Step 3. Test the theory to determine the cause.

Step 4. Establish a plan of action to resolve the problem and implement the solution.

Step 5. Verify full system functionality and, if applicable, implement preventative measures.

Step 6. Document findings, actions, and outcomes.

Incorrect Configuration

Computer programs need to be configured perfectly for them to run. There is really no margin for error. An extra character in a UNC path or a mistyped password is all that is required for the program to crash and burn. It is important to double-check all configuration values to ensure that they are correct. If you run into issues, go back to the configuration and recheck it, maybe with another person who can offer some objectivity. Compare configuration values to software documentation and ensure that the required services on each server supporting the system are running.

Let's look at this in a scenario and consider how the CompTIA troubleshooting methodology would help in solving a configuration issue: Your company is consolidating servers from two cloud environments into one for easier manageability. The transition team is responsible for moving the servers and the shares. The transition team successfully moves the servers to the new location and consolidates the shares onto a single server. A web application retrieves files from one of the shares, but users of the site report that they can no longer access files within the system. You are part of the troubleshooting team, and you are assigned the trouble ticket.

Step 1: Identify the problem.   The problem is that users cannot access files in the application. You send a message to the user base informing them of the problem and that you are actively working to resolve it.

Step 2: Establish a theory of probable causes.   Several changes were made when the servers were moved over from one cloud to another. The servers were exported into files and then imported into the new system. Each server was tested, and they worked following the migration. You check the testing notes and verify that the website was working correctly following the migration. The shares were consolidated after that. However, you do not see testing validation following the share consolidation. It is possible that the application is pointing to a share that no longer exists.

Step 3: Test the theory to determine the cause.   You log into the server hosting the application and review the configuration. The configuration for the files points to a UNC path. You attempt to contact the UNC path but receive an error. You then message the transition team, asking them if the UNC referenced in the application still exists or if it changed. They send you a message stating that the UNC path has changed, and they provide you with the new path.

Step 4: Establish a plan of action to resolve the problem and implement the solution.   You plan to change the application configuration to point to the new path. You put in a change request to modify the application configuration, and the change request is approved. You then adjust the application settings, replacing the old UNC path with the new one.

Step 5: Verify full system functionality and, if applicable, implement preventative measures.   You log into the site and verify that files are accessible through the application. You then reach out to several users and request they test as well. Each user reports that they can access the files successfully. Finally, you message the users and let them know that the issue has been resolved.

Step 6: Document findings, actions, and outcomes.   You update the change request ticket to indicate that the work was completed successfully and that no other changes were required. Additionally, you send a memo to the transition team members noting the issue and what was done to resolve it. Management then creates a checklist for application transitions that includes a line item for updating the UNC path in the application if the back-end share path changes.

Template Misconfiguration

When an organization is migrating its environment to the cloud, it requires a standardized installation policy or profile for its virtual servers. The VMs need to have a similar base installation of the operating system, so all the devices have the same security patches, service packs, and base applications installed.

VM templates provide a streamlined approach to deploying a fully configured base server image or even an entirely configured application server. VM templates help decrease the installation and configuration costs when deploying VMs and lower ongoing maintenance costs, allowing for faster deploy times and lower operational costs. However, incorrectly configuring templates can result in a large number of computers that all have the same flaw.

Now that you understand the potential problems, let's try a scenario: Karen is creating VM templates for common server roles, including a web server with network load balancing (NLB), a database server, an application server, and a terminal server. Each server will be running Windows Server 2016 Standard. She installs the operating system on a VM, assigns the machine a license key, and then installs updates to the device in offline mode.

Karen applies the standard security configuration to the machine, including locking down the local administrator account, adding local certificates to the trusted store, and configuring default firewall rules for remote administration. She then shuts down the VM and makes three copies of it using built-in tools in her cloud portal. She renames the machines and starts each up.

She then installs the server roles for web services and NLB on the web server, SQL Server 2016 on the database server along with Microsoft Message Queuing (MSMQ), SharePoint on the application server, and Remote Desktop Session Host services on the terminal server. She applies application updates to each machine and then saves the virtual hard disks to be used as a template.

A month later, Karen is asked to set up an environment consisting of a database server and a web server. She uses the built-in tools in her cloud portal to make copies of her database and web server templates. She gives the new machines new names and starts them up. She then assigns IP addresses to them. Both are joined to the company domain under their assigned names. However, server administrators report that the servers are receiving a large number of authentication errors.

Step 1: Identify the problem.   The servers are receiving a large number of authentication errors.

Step 2: Establish a theory of probable causes.   Karen theorizes that the authentication errors could be caused by incorrect licensing on the machines or by duplicate security identifiers.

Step 3: Test the theory to determine the cause. Karen issues unique license keys to both machines and activates them. However, the authentication errors still continue. She then clones another web server and runs Sysprep on it. She adds it to the domain and observes its behavior. The new machine does not exhibit the authentication errors.

Step 4: Establish a plan of action to resolve the problem and implement the solution. Karen proposes to remove faulty machines from the domain, run Sysprep on the defective machines to regenerate their security identifiers, and then add them back in. She puts change requests in for each activity and waits for approval. Upon receiving authorization, Karen implements the proposed changes.

Step 5: Verify full system functionality and, if applicable, implement preventative measures. Server administrators confirm that the authentication errors have ceased after the changes were made.

Step 6: Document findings, actions, and outcomes. Karen updates the change management requests and creates a process document outlining how to create templates with the Sysprep step included.

CSP/ISP Outage

An outage with a cloud service provider (CSP) or an Internet service provider (ISP) may result in some of your systems being unavailable to users. Check the website of the CSP or ISP to see if they are experiencing an outage. Sometimes downed limbs in bad weather or construction mistakes can break buried or hanging network cabling. Similarly, power outages at your ISP could prevent them from operating. If you do not see a notice, create a trouble ticket with them, describing the outage and any other details you have, such as subscriber ID or site ID.

If you have a business continuity plan, this is the time to enact it. You may need to fail resources over to a different region or availability zone. If you have redundant services running on multiple clouds, switch to an alternative cloud to continue service. Internal users may need to use another method for accessing the Internet, such as hotspots. Enact these measures while staying in contact with the CSP or ISP so that you can switch back to normal operations once service has been restored.

Vendor Issues

You could have issues that arise from vendor-supported systems. Not all issues are under your control. The issues could be related to a configuration you have applied, or they could be the result of some issue on the provider's systems. If so, you will need to be able to accurately describe the issues to the vendor so that they can fix them. It is also helpful to have documentation on what responses your application expects from standard input. Companies will routinely provide testing teams with sheets that show what results should be expected from test searches or transactions involving specific items or users. You may have automated this testing process. If so, check your workflow to identify which parts are failing to provide this information to the vendor.

Some vendor issues you might experience include vendor or platform misconfiguration, integration issues, API request limits, or cost or billing issues.

Vendor or Platform Misconfiguration   Vendor or platform misconfigurations can be a big headache for teams deploying new systems or software. If you experience this, start by analyzing log files and monitoring systems to determine where the problem lies. If you suspect that the configuration may be at fault, go back to vendor documentation to verify that you have the system configured properly. Vendors often supply best practice guides for different implementation types, so consider these when deploying and troubleshooting systems. If you do not find your solution on the documentation, consider the following additional resources:

- Reviewing the vendor's FAQ.
- Checking forums on the vendor or platform. Vendors sometimes have their own official forums, or you can seek out forums where other professionals discuss their systems, problems, and resolutions.
- Create a trouble ticket.

Vendor or Platform Integration Issues   Cloud services increasingly are part of a much larger enterprise ecosystem, consisting of multiple clouds and on-premise equipment. This requires a high degree of interoperability between the systems. An upgrade of one cloud or component can sometimes break the integration between these systems.

Stay on top of release notes and updates from vendors on the changes they are making and those they plan to make so that you can ensure that updates are made to other systems that integrate with them. It is also a good idea to try to stick to vendor best practices when configuring the integration. If the vendor has gone through the process of developing a best practice document for the solution, they are invested enough to keep you informed on how those best practices change with updates and additions to their service offering. It can also be much easier to troubleshoot down the road.

Ensure that you are using the same standard on both ends of a connection between clouds. CSPs often support many protocols for communication, but you will need to choose the same one on both ends. Also, make sure that you keep keys and secrets up to date. Expired keys or secrets will not work for encrypting the communication between systems, so those communication sessions will fail. Effective secret management can help keep these up to date with no or minimal effort on your part.

API Request Limits   Your cloud provider may set limits on the number of application programming interface (API) requests that will be serviced over time, such as 100 per second or 10 million per month. Requests that exceed these limits will not be processed.

If you are experiencing an API issue, a reasonable place to look is at the request capacity to see if you have hit the limit. You should increase the limit if this is something that you expect to happen again. Alternatively, you could balance requests across multiple APIs. It is a good practice to monitor API usage and capacity to avoid these issues before they happen.

Cost or Billing Issues   It is an unfortunate fact that you can have a fine-running solution come to a crashing halt with something as simple as an expired credit card. Make sure you keep billing information up to date in cloud systems so that you can avoid such issues.

CSPs often process payments shortly before the renewal date and will notify you of issues or retry payment methods. However, if you do not address the issue before the renewal period, these services may become unavailable.

System Clock Differences

Networked computer systems rely on time synchronization to communicate. When computers have different times, some may not be able to authenticate to network resources, they may not trust one another, or they may reject data sent to them.

Using the CompTIA troubleshooting methodology, let's consider a scenario: Eddie is a cloud administrator managing over 40 servers in a hosted cloud. His monitoring system frequently sends out alerts that servers are unavailable. He restarts the machines, and the problem goes away, but the problem comes back a few days later. He scripts restarts for each of the servers but realizes that this is a short-term fix at best.

Step 1: Identify the problem.   Servers lose connectivity periodically.

Step 2: Establish a theory of probable causes.   Eddie theorizes that there could be connectivity issues on the cloud backend. There also could be an issue with the template that each of the machines was produced from. Lastly, the machines could be losing time synchronization.

Step 3: Test the theory to determine the cause.   Eddie creates a support ticket with the cloud provider and provides the necessary details. The cloud provider runs several tests and reports no issues. Eddie creates another machine from the template and finds that it also exhibits the same problems. However, he is not sure where the problem might lie in the template. Lastly, he configures a scheduled job to run three times a day that sends him the system time for each of the servers.

As he reviews the output from the scheduled job, it becomes clear that the domain controller is getting out of sync with most of the network every few hours. Upon analyzing the configuration of the servers that go out of sync and the others, he finds that some are configured to obtain their time from the cloud provider NTP server, while others are set to obtain their time from a different server.

Step 4: Establish a plan of action to resolve the problem and implement the solution.   Eddie proposes to set all servers to the same time server. He creates a change request documenting the proposed change and receives approval to move forward with the change during a scheduled downtime. He makes the change.

Step 5: Verify full system functionality and, if applicable, implement preventative measures.   Eddie monitors the output from the scheduled task and confirms that each server remains in sync.

Step 6: Document findings, actions, and outcomes.   Eddie documents the NTP server settings on a standard setup configuration document. He mentions the issue in a standup IT meeting the following Friday, and the document is circulated around and placed on the company intranet for reference.

Connectivity Issues

Connectivity issues can create a broad range of problems, since most systems do not operate in isolation. There is a myriad of interdependencies on the modern issues of networking, and connectivity can be a digital monkey wrench that breaks a plethora of systems.

The first indicator that there is a connectivity problem will be the scope of the issue. Because everything is connected, connectivity issues usually affect a large number of devices. Ensure that affected devices have an IP address using the ipconfig (Windows) or ifconfig (Linux) command described later in this chapter. Suppose they do not have an IP address. In that case, it could be a problem with DHCP or with DHCP forwarders or cloud-based virtual network IP address ranges, firewall ACLs, and routing tables.

For example, the DHCP scope could be full, so the administrator might need to expand the scope or reduce the lease interval so that computers do not keep their addresses for as much time. A user may reside in a different subnet from the DHCP server, and no forwarder exists on the subnet to direct DHCP requests to the DHCP server. The connection may be on a different cloud-based virtual network IP address range from the servers it wishes to contact, and there are no rules defined to allow traffic between these ranges. There could be firewall ACLs that need to be defined to allow traffic between two nodes that are not communicating. Lastly, the default gateway or VPN concentrator, if the issue is with a VPN connection, may not have the correct information on the destination network in its routing table.

When identifying the problem, determine the scope by using the ping command described earlier in this chapter. Ping devices on the network starting with your default gateway. If the default gateway pings, try another hop closer to the Internet or to where others are experiencing issues. Try to connect to other devices that report problems as well. If the default gateway will not ping, attempt to ping something else on the same network. If neither will ping, it is likely an issue with the switch that connects both devices. If you can ping the other machine but not the gateway, it might be a problem with the gateway.

Connectivity issues could be part of the CSP's responsibility, but determining whether it is the CSP's responsibility or yours requires that you accurately determine the source of the connectivity issue.

Network Security Group Misconfiguration

Users may not be able to connect to resources if they lack the required membership in security groups. For example, suppose users cannot connect to the Azure VPN. You could check the groups the user belongs to and then check the settings in Azure to see if those groups are allowed access. Figure 15-8 shows the Azure VPN compliance policy.

ACL   Firewalls screen traffic using ACLs. A misconfigured ACL could create a connectivity issue by blocking legitimate traffic. For example, suppose an administrator sees a large number of new connections coming from an IP address, so they block that address. Later, in an IT staff meeting, they find that the DevOps team deployed a new application that started working and then failed for some reason. Upon investigation, the administrator realizes that the IP they blocked was the new application.

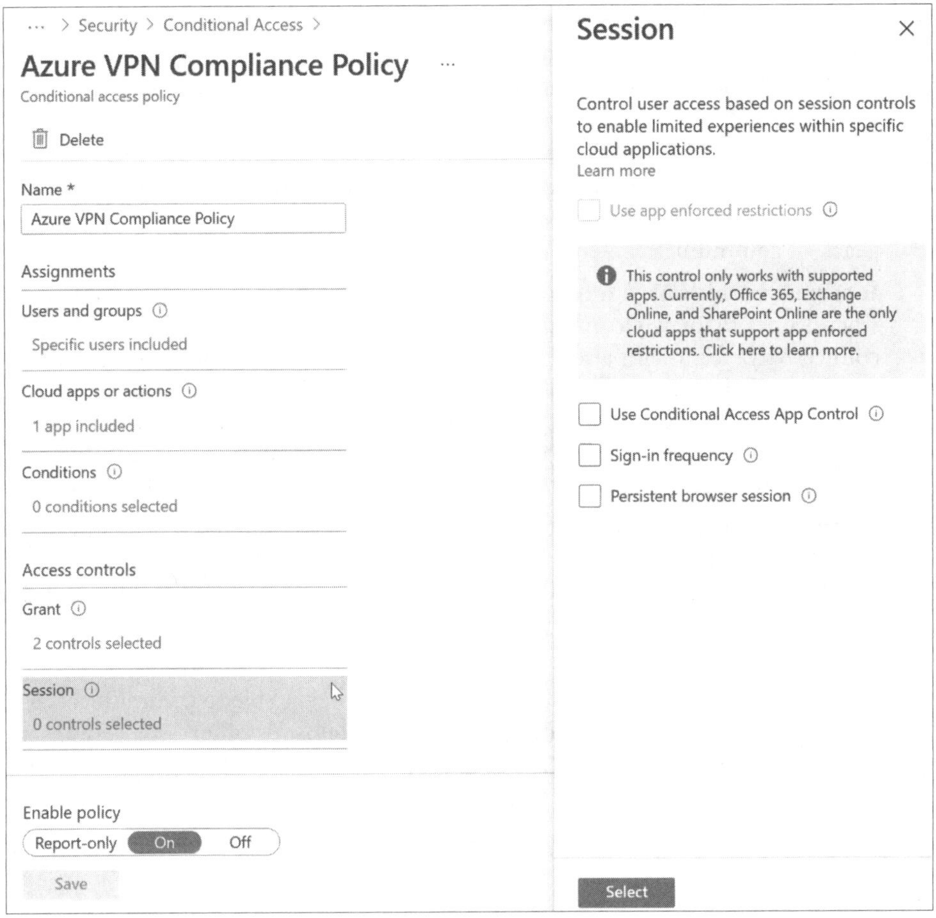

Figure 15-8 Azure VPN compliance policy

Inheritance Inheritance issues can prevent connectivity to files and folders. Inheritance is when the permissions of a higher-level folder are applied to subfolders or files. Permissions on subfolders are inherited by default until different permissions are assigned to those subfolders. However, the subfolders can be changed to inherit permissions again of higher-level folders and overwrite permissions of subfolders.

Sometimes changes to higher-level folders on a file system will be propagated down to subfolders, overwriting more granular permissions. For example, you might have a marketing folder that is only available to the marketing team under a general shared folder. If someone changes the permissions on the general shared folder and forces those permissions to be applied to all subfolders and files, the custom permissions for the marketing folder would be lost.

Network Configuration Issues

Network configuration issues may cause connectivity loss, slowness, or excessive latency in applications. Some network configuration issues to be aware of include

- **Peering**   Incorrect peering will result in a loss of communication between VPCs.

- **Incorrect subnet**   An incorrect subnet will either result in communication over the wrong network if the nearest routing device has connectivity to that subnet or a lack of communication entirely if there is no connectivity to that subnet.

- **Incorrect IP address**   You may accidentally assign a duplicate IP address where either the newly configured machine or an existing machine will lose connectivity. You might also assign an IP address that does not have the correct mappings. For example, firewall rules or other ACLs may be defined for a specific IP address or IP address range. If you assign a different one, these rules will not be triggered for traffic going to and from that system. The same case would occur if tagging has been applied for one IP address, but you assigned a different one.

- **Incorrect IP space**   You may be managing multiple IP address spaces for different sites and subnets. Some administrators use systems like IP Address Management (IPAM) to help manage these IP address spaces. If you assign an IP address for the wrong IP address space, it will not communicate with its network peers.

- **Incorrect routing**   The most common routing mistake is to assign the wrong default gateway. This will result in the computer being able to communicate with its local peers, but not with any external systems. Another issue is the misconfiguration of routing information on routers or firewalls. This will result in packets not being delivered to certain networks.

Firewall Issues

Some firewall issues to be aware of include

- **Incorrectly administered micro-segmentation**   Micro-segmentation isolates application communication by implementing specific rules governing application traffic. Incorrect micro-segmentation configurations can result in a loss of connectivity to the application or to portions of the application. Review the Syslog for blocked connections, or review the application log on the application server for failed connections to troubleshoot or identify such issues.

- **NAT issues**   Network address translation (NAT) allows one or more public IP addresses to be used to service internal addresses. NAT issues could prevent connectivity between internal systems and the Internet. Test NAT for the internal IP address scope and test for source or destination connectivity issues by verifying communication from the outside in and from the inside out. The firewall should show a hit on the NAT rule when connecting. You may need to enable enhanced logging on the NAT rule in testing to ensure that you get this information.

- **VPN**   Issues with a virtual private network (VPN) can result in a loss of connectivity between cloud sites or between users and a cloud. Review the VPN log or console to identify VPN issues. Verify that users or sites have the correct VPN configuration. Ensure also that secrets or keys are updated on both ends.

Load Balancer Issues

Load balancer issues could be the result of misconfiguration of one of the following components:

- **Methods**   Load balancers use a variety of methods to perform their balancing. Some methods differ based on the way they distribute traffic, and others differ based on the services they can offer. Some methods include DNS, database, round robin, SIP, and link load balancing. You will want to pair the method you use with the resources you are load balancing. For example, round robin is often used for load balancing connections between web servers. SIP load balancing would most likely be used for messaging services, and link load balancing would be used for optimizing traffic between multiple ISP links. Database load balancing would be used for distributing traffic across nodes in a database cluster.

- **Headers**   The IP address headers are changed when packets are processed by the load balancers and then sent on to their destination system. Load balancing modifies the X-Forwarded-For, X-Forwarded-Proto, and X-Forwarded-Port portion of the header. Ensure that your end systems are configured to work with this data.

- **Protocols**   There is a wide range of load balancing protocols. Some protocols include Direct Routing (DR), NAT-based, layer 4 tunneling, Source Network Address Translation (SNAT), or HAProxy. You may experience issues with an application if the wrong load balancing protocol is used. For example, simple DR load balancing would not allow for cookie persistence over HTTPS, so an application relying on cookies would not function properly.

- **Encryption**   If you are using encryption, such as SSL/TLS, ensure that load balancers will be able to process this traffic. Load balancing will fail if the load balancers are not configured to handle the decryption of such traffic. Load balancers will need to be able to decrypt the data to properly direct it. They can then be configured to re-encrypt the data on its way to the destination or send data to the back-end systems unencrypted.

- **Backends**   The load balancers need to be configured to send traffic to a set of systems that will receive and process the information. If this is not configured, the load balancer will not be able to properly direct traffic.

- **Frontends**   Firewalls or WAFs will need to be configured to send traffic to the load balancers, not the end machines. If this is not configured, traffic will not be delivered to the load balancers. Similarly, the load balancers will need to be configured to accept the desired traffic. Otherwise, they will reject the traffic.

DNS Record Issues

Domain Name System (DNS) is used to translate the name of a system to its IP address so that devices can communicate with one another. As IP addresses change, DNS will need to be updated to reflect that. Some systems are configured to automatically update DNS entries when DHCP leases change. Others require manual updates. Also, you may advertise some services through DNS, and these will need to be kept up to date if you make changes to the IP addresses of those services.

Another issue you could face is the resolution of stale entries. Stale entries are records for systems that no longer exist. Automated processes can be enabled to remove stale entries from DNS to avoid this issue.

VLAN or VXLAN Misconfiguration

VLANs and VXLANs were discussed back in Chapter 4. Both the VLAN and VXLAN partition a network to create logical separation between subnetworks. Connectivity problems can appear when VLANs or VXLANs are misconfigured. For example, machines must be on the same VLAN or have inter-VLAN routing configured for the two machines to communicate. It is common to configure virtual networks with specific VLANs or to add VLAN tagging to virtual networks. Incorrectly setting these values could allow devices to talk to machines they are not supposed to talk to, and they would be unable to communicate with others. Subnets are usually assigned per VLAN, so if the IP address is configured manually for one subnet on the machine and it is placed on the wrong VLAN, it will not be able to communicate with any of its neighbors.

Let's demonstrate the CompTIA troubleshooting methodology with a scenario: Geoff configures three VLANs named VLAN1, VLAN2, and VLAN3. He has four servers that are running on a virtual network, and he plans on cloning those servers several times and then assigning the servers to each of the VLANs for use. He performs the clones and then assigns the machines to the appropriate VLANs but finds that they are unable to communicate with one another.

Step 1: Identify the problem.   The cloned servers cannot communicate with each other.

Step 2: Establish a theory of probable causes.   Geoff determines that the VLANs could be misconfigured, the tagging could be incorrectly set, the virtual switches could be misconfigured, or the IP addresses could be incorrectly assigned.

Step 3: Test the theory to determine the cause.   Geoff tries to ping a single server called VM-DC1 from each of the other machines. None of the computers can communicate with the server. Geoff then creates a testing strategy where he will rotate VLANs and test. He explains the strategy to his manager and receives approval to proceed. Geoff then rotates the VLAN that is assigned to VM_DC1 and tries the tests again. He is unable to connect to the machine on any of the three VLANs. Geoff then removes VLAN tagging from the virtual switch configuration on VM_DC1 and receives an IP address conflict on the main VM_DC1 computer. Geoff suddenly realizes that the

IP addresses are hard-coded into each of the machines and that they do not correspond to their assigned VLAN.

Step 4: Establish a plan of action to resolve the problem and implement the solution. Geoff documents IP addresses to assign to each of the machines in each VLAN. He then creates a change request to modify the IP addresses for each of the computers and explains why the change needs to be made. Once approval is given, Geoff modifies the IP addresses on each machine as planned.

Step 5: Verify full system functionality and, if applicable, implement preventative measures. Geoff verifies that each machine can talk to other devices on the same VLAN and that computers cannot talk to those on other VLANs.

Step 6: Document findings, actions, and outcomes. Geoff notifies his manager that the machines are now functioning. He also updates the change control ticket to note that the change corrected the issue.

Incorrect Routing and Misconfigured Proxies

Internetwork traffic, traffic that moves from one network to another, requires routers to direct the traffic to the next leg of its journey toward its destination. Routers do this because they have an understanding of where different networks reside and the possible paths to reach those networks. Incorrect routing can result in a loss of connectivity between one or more devices. In some cases, a proxy will be used to manage communications between nodes on behalf of one or more members.

Let's now consider a routing/proxy issue and how it can be resolved using the CompTIA troubleshooting methodology: Pam is responsible for the network infrastructure, but her company recently moved many of the company servers to Amazon Web Services (AWS). A consultant configured VLANs and routing, but cloud administrators report that machines cannot communicate with devices on the Internet. Pam is asked to troubleshoot AWS routing for the VLANs. Pam confirms that devices can communicate with other devices on the same VLAN and that computers cannot communicate with the Internet.

Step 1: Identify the problem. Traffic from VLANs is not being routed externally to the Internet.

Step 2: Establish a theory of probable causes. Pam considers the possible causes and comes up with several theories. The problem could be that routing is not configured for the VLANs. It might also be possible that the default route was removed. Pam also theorizes that access lists could be preventing inside traffic from exiting the network.

Step 3: Test the theory to determine the cause. Pam uses the traceroute command from one of the machines exhibiting the problem to test the path from that machine to google.com, as shown in this example:

```
C:\Users\Pam>tracert google.com
Unable to resolve target system name google.com.
```

Pam issues the nslookup command on google.com to see if she can resolve the name to an IP address. She receives a nonauthoritative answer with an IP address, shown here:

```
C:\Users\Pam>nslookup google.com
Server:  box.local
Address:  192.168.1.21
Non-authoritative answer:
Name:    google.com
Addresses:  2607:f8b0:4009:812::200e
            172.217.6.110
```

She then issues the traceroute command again with the IP address instead of the name. The traceroute command shows a hop to the local proxy called box.local and then a connection to the default gateway 192.168.1.1, but the connection times out:

```
C:\Users\Pam>tracert 172.217.6.110
Tracing route to ord37s03-in-f110.1e100.net [172.217.6.110]
over a maximum of 30 hops:
  1     3 ms     3 ms     3 ms  box.local [192.168.1.21]
  2     3 ms     4 ms     3 ms  192.168.1.1
  3      *        *        *     Request timed out.
```

Pam disables the proxy to test whether that is the issue and runs tracert again, but the request times out immediately after hitting the default gateway. Pam then logs into the AWS Virtual Private Cloud (VPC) console and observes the Route Tables page. She finds that the main route table was modified to include routes between the subnets, but the route to the virtual private gateway was replaced when these changes were made.

Step 4: Establish a plan of action to resolve the problem and implement the solution. Pam believes the problem lies with the missing route to the virtual private gateway, so she submits a change request to add this route.

Step 5: Verify full system functionality and, if applicable, implement preventative measures. Pam's change request is approved, so she makes the change and then issues a traceroute along with the –d switch to skip resolving host names so that the trace will run faster. She issues the command from the same machine she was using to test and receives this output:

```
C:\Users\Pam>tracert -d 172.217.6.110
Tracing route to 172.217.6.110 over a maximum of 30 hops
  1    11 ms     7 ms    11 ms  192.168.1.21
  2     4 ms     3 ms     3 ms  192.168.1.1
  3    12 ms    12 ms    15 ms  142.254.157.249
  4    85 ms    45 ms    21 ms  24.164.114.225
  5    16 ms    11 ms    18 ms  24.33.103.92
  6    21 ms    22 ms    20 ms  65.29.1.97
  7    20 ms    14 ms    15 ms  65.29.1.32
  8    48 ms    42 ms    44 ms  66.109.6.70
  9    42 ms    47 ms    47 ms  66.109.6.30
 10    42 ms    42 ms    45 ms  107.14.17.202
 11    45 ms    40 ms    39 ms  216.6.87.149
 12    42 ms    47 ms    43 ms  72.14.198.28
 13    43 ms    43 ms    43 ms  108.170.246.81
 14    45 ms    47 ms    47 ms  216.239.50.93
```

```
15    36 ms    42 ms    34 ms    209.85.253.248
16    36 ms    47 ms    38 ms    209.85.241.122
17    35 ms    40 ms    40 ms    108.170.238.91
18    34 ms    34 ms    35 ms    172.217.6.110
Trace complete.
```

Step 6: Document findings, actions, and outcomes.   Pam notifies her manager that the machines are now functional. She then updates the change control ticket to note that the change corrected the issue. See Chapter 4 for more information on routing.

QoS Issues

Quality of service (QoS) is a set of technologies that can identify the type of data in data packets and divide those packets into specific traffic classes that can be prioritized according to defined service levels. QoS was introduced back in Chapter 9. QoS technologies enable administrators to meet their service requirements for a workload or an application by measuring network bandwidth, detecting changing network conditions, and prioritizing the network traffic accordingly. QoS can be targeted at a network interface, toward a given server's or router's performance, or regarding specific applications. Incorrectly configured QoS can result in performance degradation for specific services and, consequently, irate users.

Let's demonstrate how the CompTIA troubleshooting methodology can help resolve QoS issues: Marco is a cloud administrator for Big Top Training, a company that produces fireworks safety videos that are streamed by subscribers from the company's cloud. Marco has been reading about QoS, and he thinks it can significantly improve the cloud network's performance. He discusses it with his boss and receives approval to test QoS settings in a lab environment set up on another cloud segment. Marco configures QoS priorities and tests several types of content, including streaming video, data transfers, active directory replication, and DNS resolution. He shows the results of his tests to Dominick, his manager, and they agree to roll the changes out to the rest of the network. A couple of weeks later, the backup administrator, Teresa, mentions that some backup jobs have been failing because they cannot complete in their scheduled time window and are terminated. She suggests that QoS might be the problem because the timeouts started happening the day after the QoS changes were put in place. Dominick tells Marco to look into the problem.

Step 1: Identify the problem.   Marco identifies the problem as backups are unable to complete in scheduled time windows.

Step 2: Establish a theory of probable causes.   Marco theorizes that the backup issues could be caused by a lack of a backup profile since the lab environment he worked in did not have any backups scheduled for it.

Step 3: Test the theory to determine the cause.   Marco walks Dominick through his theory. Dominick suggests that he collect baseline data on traffic from the production network and then use that to build additional QoS rules. Marco collects the data for the baseline and then reviews the data with Teresa and Dominick.

Step 4: Establish a plan of action to resolve the problem and implement the solution. Marco, Teresa, and Dominick find that backup traffic communicates over a port that does not have a QoS rule, as Marco theorized. They also identify five other services that have no QoS rules defined. Hence, they map out priorities for those items as well. The planned changes are put into the change management system, and Dominick schedules a downtime in the evening for the changes to be made. Dominick informs stakeholders of the downtime, and Marco implements the new QoS rules during the planned downtime.

Step 5: Verify full system functionality and, if applicable, implement preventative measures. Marco notifies Teresa when the work has been completed, and Teresa manually executes the failing backup jobs to confirm that they do run within the normal time allotted. Marco and Teresa inform Dominick that the jobs now work, and the downtime is concluded.

Step 6: Document findings, actions, and outcomes. Marco creates a QoS document outlining each of the priorities and the traffic that fits into each priority. He also schedules a time to collect a more intensive baseline to confirm that all critical services have been accounted for.

For more information on baselines, see Chapter 10, and for more information on QoS, see Chapter 9.

Time Synchronization Issues

Many network protocols rely on timestamps in order to communicate. They use timestamps to ensure the orderly delivery of packets and to prevent replay attacks. For this reason, computers need to have consistent time so that packets are not rejected.

Computers get their time from the system clock. Administrators can ensure that system clocks are kept in sync on VMs by installing hypervisor guest tools and then enabling time synchronization between host and guest. Virtual, physical, and cloud servers can synchronize time by configuring them to point to an external Network Time Protocol (NTP) server. Each computer will set its time to the time specified by the NTP server. The servers will poll the NTP server periodically to verify that their clocks are still in sync and avoid time synchronization issues.

Proxy Issues

Proxies make connections to resources on behalf of other machines to obscure the source of the connection. Proxied communication may fail if the destination system has blacklisted proxy addresses or proxy communication.

Latency

Latency is the time delay encountered while data is being sent from one point to another. It takes time for the physical impulses that comprise communication over a medium, such as copper or fiber cabling, to travel down the line—latency increases in accordance with the distance between source and destination.

Figure 15-9
Measuring
latency with the
ping command

```
C:\Users\Eric>ping google.com

Pinging google.com [172.217.4.110] with 32 bytes of data:
Reply from 172.217.4.110: bytes=32 time=42ms TTL=114
Reply from 172.217.4.110: bytes=32 time=42ms TTL=114
Reply from 172.217.4.110: bytes=32 time=44ms TTL=114
Reply from 172.217.4.110: bytes=32 time=45ms TTL=114

Ping statistics for 172.217.4.110:
    Packets: Sent = 4, Received = 4, Lost = 0 (0% loss),
Approximate round trip times in milli-seconds:
    Minimum = 42ms, Maximum = 45ms, Average = 43ms
```

Latency is generally associated with performance, but it can cause connectivity issues if the latency is so high that it exceeds thresholds on either end of the communication. In this case, the communication sessions will time out, and the connection will not be established.

Latency metrics are essential for ensuring responsive services and applications and avoiding performance or availability problems. One way to see the latency between your device and another is to use the ping command, discussed later in this chapter. As you can see in Figure 15-9, each of the pings shows a time in milliseconds (ms). This time is the latency, or how long it took for the ping. There is a summary following all of the pings that shows the minimum, maximum, and average latency for each of the pings.

Misconfigured MTU/MSS

The maximum transmission unit (MTU) is the largest packet or frame that can be sent over the network. Frames operate at the data link layer, while packets operate at the network layer. Segments also have a maximum size. Segments operate at the transport layer, and their maximum size is specified as the maximum segment size (MSS). MTU and MSS are typically measured in bytes.

Higher-level protocols may create packets larger than a particular link supports, so the TCP divides the packets into several pieces in a process known as fragmentation. Each fragment is given an ID so that the fragments can be pieced back together in the correct order. However, not all applications support fragmentation. When this routinely happens, the solution is to adjust the MSS so that packets are not fragmented. MSS is adjusted because it operates at a higher layer than the frames and packets. Hence, the data provided to the lower-level protocols ends up an appropriate size and does not need to be fragmented.

Let's look at this in a scenario and use the CompTIA troubleshooting methodology to resolve the situation: You configure a new VPN for your company using L2TP over IPSec. However, performance over the VPN is much slower than expected. You run a packet capture on the data over the network link using the tcpdump tool. You capture packets less than 64 bytes with the following command:

```
tcpdump < 64
```

You then you capture packets greater than 60,000 bytes (the max packet size is 65,535 bytes) with this command:

```
tcpdump > 60000
```

For this scenario, consider the troubleshooting methodology and walk through it on your own. Think through each step. You may need to make some assumptions as you move through the process since this is a sample scenario.

Step 1. Identify the problem.

Step 2. Establish a theory of probable causes.

Step 3. Test the theory to determine the cause.

Step 4. Establish a plan of action to resolve the problem and implement the solution.

Step 5. Verify full system functionality and, if applicable, implement preventative measures.

Step 6. Document findings, actions, and outcomes.

Performance Issues

Performance issues can be a nightmare for users and administrators alike. No administrator appreciates receiving tickets for slow systems because it can be challenging to identify which components are contributing to the slowness and what the user means by slow, as some users report slowness when application performance is within normal tolerances. When troubleshooting issues, attention needs to be paid to replication, scaling, applications, and latency.

Replication

Slow replication can cause systems to process requests inconsistently. For example, Active Directory uses replication to keep user, service, and computer account information synchronized between domain controllers. When replication is slow, users who change their password will not be able to log in with their new credentials on all systems until the new credentials have been replicated to all sites.

In transactional systems, such as banking, replication needs to occur before a transaction can be marked complete. Slow replication can result in slow application performance for users. To troubleshoot replication, look at replication logs and test connectivity between replication partners.

Scaling

Applications and systems should scale appropriately with demand. However, suppose an application does not scale or does not scale in a timely manner. In that case, the application will underperform, resulting in a poor experience for users.

Application Issues

Application issues can also result in poor performance. Some application issues include memory management and service overload.

Memory Management   Memory management is concerned with providing the required memory to applications and reclaiming memory when the application no longer needs it. Poorly written applications may suffer from one of these issues:

- **Memory leaks**   Memory leaks occur when a program allocates memory for tasks and never releases that memory. This slowly consumes more and more memory as the application runs, and the system will eventually run out of memory. This can cause the application and potentially other applications to crash.

- **Memory fragmentation**   Ideally, a program will release memory before memory allocation processes so that new memory needs can be allocated from the same memory address space. Memory fragmentation occurs when memory is not released quickly enough, so new memory is allocated from a different memory address space. This is less efficient for the application and results in slower application performance.

- **Memory corruption**   Memory corruption occurs when reference variables are not reset. This leaves dangling memory pointers to memory locations that have already been freed.

Depending on the programming language, software developers may be able to use resource management mechanisms so that they do not need to code specific memory allocation and release processes. Monitor memory usage for applications to detect such behavior.

Service Overload   Services can become overloaded when they receive more requests than they are equipped to handle. This results in the slow processing of new requests or dropping new requests entirely. Service overload can be prevented by properly sizing resources and properly scaling systems.

You may also experience service overload in a distributed denial of service (DDoS) attack. These can be prevented with DDoS mitigation services. Such services absorb junk traffic and send legitimate traffic on to the application servers.

Latency

As mentioned earlier, latency is the time delay encountered while data is being sent from one point to another. When it is excessive, network latency can create bottlenecks that prevent data from using the maximum capacity of the network bandwidth, resulting in slower cloud application performance.

EXAM TIP   Pay close attention to latency metrics to identify latency issues. Many tools will provide latency values, but you can also use the ping command to determine latency between two systems.

Let's consider a scenario: You recently configured synchronous replication of a key ERP database to another site 2000 miles away. However, the ERP system is now running extremely slowly. Performance metrics on the servers that make up the ERP system show plenty of capacity and very low utilization of system resources. Management is upset and demands a resolution ASAP.

For this scenario, consider the troubleshooting methodology and walk through it on your own. Think through each step. You may need to make some assumptions as you move through the process since this is a sample scenario.

Step 1. Identify the problem.

Step 2. Establish a theory of probable causes.

Step 3. Test the theory to determine the cause.

Step 4. Establish a plan of action to resolve the problem and implement the solution.

Step 5. Verify full system functionality and, if applicable, implement preventative measures.

Step 6. Document findings, actions, and outcomes.

See Chapter 4 for more information on latency.

Capacity Issues

Capacity issues can be found with compute, storage, networking, and licensing. Considerable attention needs to be paid to the design of compute, storage, and networking systems. The design phase must ensure that all service levels are understood and that the capacity to fulfill them is incorporated into its configurations. Once those configurations have been adequately designed and documented, operations can establish a baseline. This baseline is a measuring stick against which capacity can be monitored to understand both the current demand and trend for future needs.

Capacity issues can result in system or application slowdowns or complete unavailability of systems. Alerts should be configured on devices to inform cloud administrators when capacity reaches thresholds (often 80 percent or so). Define thresholds low enough that you will be able to correct the capacity issue before the available capacity is fully consumed.

Compute

Appropriately distributing compute resources is an integral part of managing a cloud environment. Planning for future growth and the ability to adjust compute resources on demand is key to avoiding compute capacity issues. One potential capacity issue is overconsumption by customers. Because compute resources are limited, cloud providers must protect them and make sure that their customers only have access to the amount that they are contracted to provide. Two methods used to deliver no more than the contracted amount of resources are quotas and limits.

Now that you understand the potential problem, try a scenario: Tim manages the cloud infrastructure for hundreds of cloud consumers. He notices that some of the consumers are utilizing far more resources than they should be allocated.

For this scenario, consider the troubleshooting methodology and walk through it on your own. Think through each step. You may need to make some assumptions as you move through the process since this is a sample scenario.

Step 1. Identify the problem.

Step 2. Establish a theory of probable causes.

Step 3. Test the theory to determine the cause.

Step 4. Establish a plan of action to resolve the problem and implement the solution.

Step 5. Verify full system functionality and, if applicable, implement preventative measures.

Step 6. Document findings, actions, and outcomes.

Storage

Companies are producing data at a rate never seen before. Keeping up with data growth can be quite a challenge. It is best to set thresholds and alerts on storage volumes so that you can proactively expand the storage when they reach a threshold (often 80 percent or so). Set more aggressive thresholds and alerts on physical storage because physical storage cannot be extended as easily on the fly. Physical storage expansion requires the purchase of additional hardware, approval, and other red tape associated with the purchase, shipping time, and installation. You want to make sure that you have enough of a buffer so that you do not run out of space while additional storage is on order.

Let's demonstrate the CompTIA troubleshooting methodology with a scenario: Sharon, a cloud administrator, receives reports that users are experiencing sluggish performance and slow response times when accessing the company ERP systems that reside in their hybrid cloud.

Step 1: Identify the problem.   Sharon identifies the problem as unacceptable application performance.

Step 2: Establish a theory of probable causes.   Sharon collects metrics while users experience the issues. She then compares the metrics to the baseline to see if performance is within normal tolerances. The anomalies not only confirm that there is a problem but they tell where the problem might lie. The baseline comparison indicates that disk input/output operations per second (IOPS) are well below the baseline for several LUNs.

Step 3: Test the theory to determine the cause.   Sharon isolates the LUNs that are outside of their normal IOPS range. Each of the LUNs was created from the same RAID group, and an analysis of the disk IOPS shows that a RAID group is rebuilding, causing the performance issues.

Step 4: Establish a plan of action to resolve the problem and implement the solution. Sharon discusses the risks and performance hit the rebuild is causing, and her manager agrees that the rebuild can be paused for the two hours that remain in the workday and that they should resume at 5:00 P.M. Sharon pauses the rebuild.

Step 5: Verify full system functionality and, if applicable, implement preventative measures. Sharon confirms that application performance has returned to normal. At 5:00 P.M., she resumes the rebuild, and performance drops for the next few hours until the rebuild completes.

Step 6: Document findings, actions, and outcomes. Sharon documents the experience in the company's knowledge management system.

Networking

Each device that is attached to the network is capable of generating traffic. A single user used to have only one or two devices attached to the network, but now, many users have a desktop, laptop, multiple tablets, phones, and other devices that may connect through wired or wireless connections. Many of these devices connect to cloud services and request data from them. Some cloud services may be used to keep such systems in sync. The rapid growth of devices and increasing use of cloud services can result in contention for valuable network resources.

Now that you understand some potential network contention problems, let's try a scenario: You work in the company's operations center. Metrics show that nodes on a particular network segment are consuming a high amount of network bandwidth. You also receive alerts for many network collisions on the segment, and the network switch for the segment shows spanning tree errors.

For this scenario, consider the troubleshooting methodology and walk through it on your own. Think through each step. You may need to make some assumptions as you move through the process since this is a sample scenario.

Step 1. Identify the problem.

Step 2. Establish a theory of probable causes.

Step 3. Test the theory to determine the cause.

Step 4. Establish a plan of action to resolve the problem and implement the solution.

Step 5. Verify full system functionality and, if applicable, implement preventative measures.

Step 6. Document findings, actions, and outcomes.

Bandwidth

Bandwidth is the network's speed, measured as how much data can be sent or received over a period of time, such as megabits per second (Mbps). Ensure that your bandwidth is sufficient for the number of concurrent connections you expect to your application and the amount of data that will be sent, on average, to and from these connections.

Oversubscription

If you recall from Chapter 5, oversubscription is where you assign more resources to VMs than are physically available to the system. Oversubscription is possible because not all VMs will require full utilization of these resources simultaneously, so you can make better use of resources through oversubscription.

However, oversubscription can result in contention for CPU resources when multiple machines attempt to utilize all their vCPUs at the same time. This results in reduced performance for the virtual machines and the applications that run on them. For this reason, it is essential to understand what a reasonable oversubscription ratio is. Some of the resources you can oversubscribe include the CPU, GPU, memory, and NIC.

- **CPU**   It is generally safe to maintain an oversubscription ratio of 5:1, with three vCPUs for each physical CPU, so a server with four physical CPU cores could assign up to 20 vCPUs.

- **GPU**   There is no standard oversubscription ratio for GPU. The ratio depends on the GPU model, so you will need to determine the maximum vGPUs supported for the GPUs you are considering.

- **Memory**   It is generally safe to maintain an oversubscription ratio of 1.25:1, with 125 percent of physical memory allocated to virtual machines. Thus, a server with 256GB of memory could assign up to 320GB of memory to virtual machines.

- **NIC**   It is generally safe to maintain an oversubscription ratio of 10:1, but as with other resources, pay attention to network utilization metrics and tweak this if utilization stays consistently high so that you can avoid contention.

Licensing

Purchased software and cloud services operate based on a license. The license grants specific uses of the software for a period. Software typically checks for compliance with licensing and may revoke access to service when the software vendor or cloud provider deems that compliance has not been met. Additionally, groups such as BSA | The Software Alliance (www.bsa.org) can perform license investigations and assess fines for companies that are not in compliance. Hence, companies need to ensure that they are adhering to license requirements.

Software licenses may be per user of the software, or they could be based on the physical or virtual resources that are allocated to the software. For example, some products are licensed based on the number of CPU cores or vCPUs. It is important to know how many CPU cores you are licensed for when assigning resources so that you do not violate your license or cause a program to fail activation checks.

Let's demonstrate the CompTIA troubleshooting methodology with a scenario: Your organization has a self-service portal where administrators can create new VMs based on VM templates. The portal has been very popular, but now over 500 VMs have been deployed to the environment, and the machines deployed over the last 30 days are unable to activate Windows.

For this scenario, consider the troubleshooting methodology and walk through it on your own. Think through each step. You may need to make some assumptions as you move through the process since this is a sample scenario. We have provided step 1 for you.

Step 1. Identify the problem.

Systems are unable to activate, and the organization may have exceeded available licenses. The company has ten hypervisors in a cluster and 10 Server 2016 data center edition licenses, as well as 100 Server 2016 standard edition licenses. An assessment of the VMs shows that there are 200 CentOS Linux servers and 312 Server 2016 Standard edition servers.

Step 2. Establish a theory of probable causes.

Step 3. Test the theory to determine the cause.

Step 4. Establish a plan of action to resolve the problem and implement the solution.

Step 5. Verify full system functionality and, if applicable, implement preventative measures.

Step 6. Document findings, actions, and outcomes.

API Request Limits

In order to guard against abuse or malicious use of APIs, companies set request limits, usually per IP address or subnet. This limits the ability of a single client to utilize too much of the service. Some misuse of API calls might be an attempt to scrape resources, input malformed content to trigger buffer overflows, or disrupt API availability.

Let's look at this in a scenario and consider how the CompTIA troubleshooting methodology would help in solving a configuration issue: You work for a consulting company as a developer on the DevOps team. Senior leadership has expressed concerns that some consultants may not be billing out all their time. They assume that this is just due to forgetfulness, since many do not enter their time each day, but wait until the weekend to enter most of it. You have developed an application that tracks e-mail usage against calendar entries and time entries to confirm that employees do not forget to put in billable time. The application ties into several APIs designed by the e-mail and time entry software companies. Your application works fine in testing. However, when you deploy it to production, the application works for about 30 minutes and then it ceases functioning. You need to figure out why the application ceases functioning and correct it.

For this scenario, consider the troubleshooting methodology and walk through it on your own. Think through each step. You may need to make some assumptions as you move through the process since this is a sample scenario.

Step 1. Identify the problem.

Step 2. Establish a theory of probable causes.

Step 3. Test the theory to determine the cause.

Step 4. Establish a plan of action to resolve the problem and implement the solution.

Step 5. Verify full system functionality and, if applicable, implement preventative measures.

Step 6. Document findings, actions, and outcomes.

Automation and Orchestration Issues

Automation and orchestration can be incredibly complex. The advantage of automation and orchestration over manual processes is that automation performs the task the exact same way every time. Unfortunately, things do not stay the same, and processes will need to be updated from time to time.

When automation or orchestration changes, evaluate the process and run a change management report to identify all changes made recently to the resources the automation depends on. Usually, something has changed in the environment that is not reflected in the automation workflow. Some issues that can arise in automation and orchestration include

- Account mismatches
- Change management failures
- Server name changes
- IP address changes
- Location changes
- Version or feature mismatch or deprecation
- Automation tool incompatibility
- API version incompatibility
- Job validation issues
- Patching failure
- Batch job scheduling issues

Account Mismatches

The actions taken in automation and orchestration will require credentials to be performed. Account mismatches happen when the specified service account in the automation or orchestration does not exist or does not have the appropriate privileges to perform the action.

If you receive an account mismatch error, verify all credentials used in the automation to first ensure that they are named correctly; second, ensure that they have the correct permissions; third, check that you have specified the correct password; and fourth, verify that they are not locked out.

Change Management Failures

Change management failures occur when unauthorized changes are made to systems or when authorized changes are not performed. There can be legitimate reasons for why some authorized changes are not made. Several changes could be authorized to be performed in a downtime, but one change may make it impossible for the other change to be made concurrently. For example, assume that a SQL Server version upgrade and a storage LUN expansion on the database server were scheduled for the same downtime. Once the storage team takes the LUN offline for expansion, the database team cannot perform the upgrade because they have no access to the disks.

Unauthorized changes should be avoided if at all possible. The most common occurrence of unauthorized changes occurs when there is an urgent issue that the team is trying to fix. For example, consider a situation where users cannot access the file shares because the DFS root is unavailable. A systems engineer restarts the DFS server and then updates the DFS server's DNS record to correct the issue. However, neither of these changes were submitted into the change management system, nor were they approved before they were performed. In this situation, the emergency change advisory board should have been called to approve the changes once they were put into the system. In this way, the changes could still be made relatively quickly, but the change management process would still be followed. This helps avoid issues where an urgent issue causes an even greater problem when mistakes are made in the heat of the moment. The change advisory team is better equipped to offer more objective, tactical, and objective feedback.

Server Name Changes

Server name changes can cause problems with automation and orchestration if the related automation and orchestration steps are not also updated. These steps will fail if the named server is not available, or they could perform the steps on the wrong server if another server has been created with the same name as the previous server that was set up for automation.

Be sure to document places where the server name exists so that you can properly update such workflow.

IP Address Changes

IP address changes sometimes happen when the IP addressing scheme changes or when you expand subnets or add more subnets. It is important to update DNS following these changes so that automation and orchestration retrieve the latest IP address for the system. If DNS is not updated following these changes, the automation steps will likely fail.

Location Changes

Changing the location of resources can affect automation and orchestration because the pointers to the resource will no longer be valid. Ensure that you also update the automation steps to point to the correct resource or to point to a new resource in the same region or zone if resources have been moved elsewhere.

You can also run into issues if you move an automation to a new location. The resources and systems there may differ, and the orchestration or automation will likely need to be modified for it to work properly there. It helps to have environments that were configured using Infrastructure as Code (IaC) so that you have greater assurance of the configuration parameters and naming conventions of a site.

Version or Feature Mismatch or Deprecation

Some automation and orchestration steps are dependent upon a specific software version. They may use functionality that is in place in one version but deprecated in a newer version. If that software is upgraded to the point where the functionality is deprecated, the orchestration or automation will fail. You will then need to update the orchestration to use a newer supported function.

It is important to document the automation and orchestration used and to review release notes for new software versions before deploying them to ensure that you update such steps. The change advisory board should help identify items like this before they are approved and implemented.

Automation Tool Incompatibility

Sometimes updates and patches will break automation or orchestration. When this happens, the first place you should look is at the change management system to find out what was changed. If patches were applied, review the release notes for those patches to see if changes were made to functions utilized by automation or orchestration.

API Version Incompatibility

API version incompatibilities result when the CSP or API provider updates their API, but you have not yet updated the automation or orchestration interfacing with that API. If you find that an API suddenly is not working, check the vendor or CSP's API notes to see if they made changes to it. They should have documentation on what changes are necessary to update your automation or orchestration to continue using it. If you cannot find information on how to update your system, consider contacting the vendor or opening a ticket with them to get more information.

Job Validation Issue

Job validation is the last step in an automation or orchestration. The validation step runs checks on the system to ensure that it is operating as expected. If you are deploying updated software, verify that the current version matches that of the deployed software. If you are updating records, take the number of additional records added and the previous value and compare it to the current number of records to ensure that all were added. If you are manipulating data, check the values to ensure that they are correct.

It is a best practice to build in functions to roll back the changes and send notifications to appropriate personnel to investigate if a step in the validation process fails. Developing automation and orchestration like this will help you avoid many headaches in the future and provide additional details when troubleshooting.

Patching Failure

The application of patches is a commonly automated activity. However, sometimes patch deployments will fail. Since patches often address vulnerabilities, it is important to check to make sure that patches were applied correctly and to all machines that were scheduled for patching.

If a patch fails, try to run the patch again. You may need to roll back other patches or revert to a snapshot before trying the patch again. If it still fails, check the log to see where it is erroring out. A third-party dependency could be causing the issue, or it could be related to resource constraints or contention with running processes. If so, you can update the third-party software, add more resources, or stop contenting processes before performing the upgrade again.

Batch Job Scheduling Issues

Batch jobs can sometimes encounter scheduling issues as data volumes grow, utilization increases, or new jobs are added. These issues can be avoided through proper capacity planning and forecasting.

Now that you understand the potential problems let us try a scenario to see how the CompTIA troubleshooting methodology can help: John is working for a small company that heavily uses cloud services. He has been working for the company for about a month after the previous IT administrator left. The previous administrator automated a number of tasks. John has been receiving an e-mail each morning stating that space has been added to several VMs based on their usage. However, this morning, he received a message that stated the job has failed. When he checked the orchestration, no error trapping was present.

For this scenario, consider the troubleshooting methodology and walk through it on your own. Think through each step. You may need to make some assumptions as you move through the process since this is a sample scenario. We have provided step 1 for you.

Step 1. Identify the problem.

John investigates the hypervisor cluster that the VMs reside on and finds that the virtual disks have been expanded using a large pool on a shared storage device. The logs on the device show expansions corresponding to the e-mails he has been receiving. He also finds alerts in the logs showing that the storage pool is full. John sees that the machines that were expanded each have 25 percent free space. He also finds that there is an additional 2.3TB available on the SAN that hosts the shared storage.

Step 2. Establish a theory of probable causes.

Step 3. Test the theory to determine the cause.

Step 4. Establish a plan of action to resolve the problem and implement the solution.

Step 5. Verify full system functionality and, if applicable, implement preventative measures.

Step 6. Document findings, actions, and outcomes.

Documentation and Analysis

Being able to use the proper tools is a good start when troubleshooting cloud computing issues. Correctly creating and maintaining the correct documentation makes the troubleshooting process quicker and easier. It is important for the cloud administrator to document every aspect of the cloud environment, including its setup and configuration and which applications are running on which host computer or VM. Also, the cloud administrator should assign responsibility for each application and its server platform to a specific support person, who can respond quickly if an issue should arise that affects the application.

When issues come up, cloud professionals need to know where to look to find the data they need to solve the problem. The primary place they look is in log files. Operating systems, services, and applications create log files that track certain events as they occur on the computer. Log files can store a variety of information, including device changes, device driver loading and unloading, system changes, events, and much more.

Documentation

Documentation needs to be clear and easy to understand for anyone who may need to use it and should be regularly reviewed to ensure that it is up to date and accurate. I was once asked to create documentation for an application that was going to be monitored in a distributed application diagram within Microsoft SharePoint. To have a satisfactory diagram to display inside Microsoft SharePoint for the entire organization to view, I needed to collect as much information as possible. The company wanted to monitor the application from end to end, so I needed to know which server the application used for the web server, which server it used for the database server, which network devices and switches the servers connected to, the location of the end users who used the application, and so on.

The information-gathering process took me from the developer who created the application to the database administrator who could explain the back-end infrastructure to the server administrator and then the network administrator and so on. As you can see, to truly document and monitor an application, you need to talk to everyone who is involved in keeping that application operational.

From the documentation, the organization was given a clear picture of precisely what systems were involved with keeping that application operational and functioning at peak performance. It made it easier to troubleshoot and monitor the application and set performance metrics. It also allowed for an accurate diagram of the application with true alerting and reporting of any disruptions. As new administrators joined the organization, they could use the documentation to understand better how the application and the environment work together and which systems support each other.

Documentation should include the application owner, application locations, and device configurations.

Application Owner

Documenting the person responsible for creating and maintaining the application, otherwise known as the application owner, is the first step. This person should be able to tell you the details of the application, such as where it is hosted. The application owner may also be the person who provisions accounts for new users. These are all things that should be included in the documentation. Documenting these items is a good process that saves valuable time when troubleshooting any potential issues with the cloud environment.

Device Configurations

In addition to documenting the person responsible for the application and hosting the computer, an organization needs to record device configurations. This provides a quick and easy way to recover a device in case of failure. By utilizing a document to swap a faulty device and mimic its configuration quickly, the company can immediately replace the failed device.

When documenting device configuration, it is imperative that the document is updated every time a significant change is made to that device. Otherwise, coworkers, auditors, or other employees might operate off out-of-date information. For example, let's say you are working on a firewall that has been in place and running for the last three years. After making the required changes, you then update or re-create the documentation so that there is a current document listing all the device settings and configurations for that firewall. This makes it easier to manage the device if there are problems later on, and it gives you a hard copy of the settings that can be stored and used for future changes.

Also, the firewall administrator would likely rely on your documented configuration to design new configuration changes. If you failed to update the documentation after making a change, the firewall administrator would be operating off old information and wouldn't factor in the changes that you made to the configuration.

Configuration management tools are available that can automatically log changes to rule sets. These, along with orchestration tools and runbooks, can be used to update documentation programmatically following an approved change.

Log Files

Logs files are extremely important in troubleshooting problems. Operating systems, services, and applications create log files that track certain events as they occur on the computer. Log files can store a variety of information, including device changes, device drivers, system changes, events, and much more.

Log files allow for closer examination of events that have occurred on the system over a more extended period. Some logs keep information for months at a time, allowing a cloud administrator to go back and see when an issue started and if any issues seem to coincide with a software installation or a hardware configuration change.

Figure 15-10 shows the Event Viewer application for a Microsoft Windows system. The Event Viewer application in this screenshot is displaying the application log, and an error is highlighted for the Microsoft Photos application that failed due to a problem with a .NET module.

A variety of software applications can be used to gather the system logs from a group of machines and send those records to a central administration console, making it possible for the administrator to view the logs of multiple servers from a single console.

Logs can take up much space on servers, but you will want to keep logs around for a long time in case they are needed to investigate a problem or a security issue. Logs are set by default to grow to a specific size and then roll over. Rolling over overwrites the oldest log entries with new ones. This can cause considerable problems when you need to research what has been happening to a server because rollover can cause valuable log data to be overwritten.

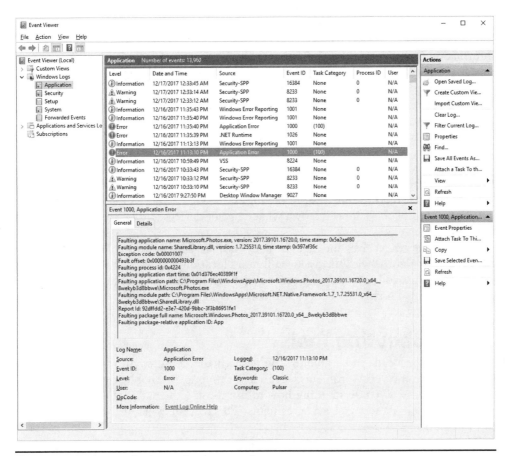

Figure 15-10   An error in the application event log

For this reason, you might want to archive logs to a cloud logging and archiving service such as Logentries, OpenStack, Sumo Logic, Syslog-ng, Amazon S3, Amazon CloudWatch, or Papertrail. These services will allow you to free up space on your cloud servers while still retaining access to the log files when needed. Some of these services also allow for event correlation, or they can tie into event correlation services.

Event correlation can combine authentication requests from domain controllers, incoming packets from perimeter devices, and data requests from application servers to gain a more complete picture of what is going on. Software exists to automate much of the process. Such software, called security information and event management (SIEM), archives logs and reviews them in real time against correlation rules to identify possible threats or problems.

Network Device and IoT Logs

Log files are not restricted to servers. Network devices, even IoT devices, have log files that can contain helpful information in troubleshooting issues. These devices usually have a smaller set of logs. These logs may have settings for how much data is logged.

If the standard log settings do not seem to provide enough information when trouble-shooting an issue, you can enable verbose logging. Verbose logging records more detailed information than standard logging but is recommended only for troubleshooting a particular problem, since it tends to fill up the limited space on network and IoT devices. To conserve space and prevent essential events from being overwritten, verbose logging should be disabled after the issue is resolved so that it does not affect the performance of the application or the computer.

Syslog

Network devices can generate events in different formats, and they often have very little space to store logs. Most devices only have room for system and configuration data. This means that if you want to store the logs somewhere, you will need to use Syslog. The Syslog protocol is supported by a wide range of devices and can log different types of events.

A Syslog server receives messages sent by various devices and collects those. Each machine is configured with the Syslog collector's location, and each sends his or her logs to that server for collection. Syslog can be analyzed in place, or it can be archived to a cloud logging and archiving service, just like other logs.

Troubleshooting Tools

An organization needs to be able to troubleshoot the cloud environment when there are issues or connectivity problems. A variety of tools are available to troubleshoot the cloud environment. Understanding how to use those tools makes it easier for a company to maintain its service level agreements. This section explains the common usage of those tools.

There are many tools to choose from when troubleshooting a cloud environment. Sometimes a single tool is all that is required to troubleshoot the issue; other times, a combination of tools might be needed. Knowing when to use a particular tool makes the troubleshooting process easier and faster. As with anything, the more you use a particular troubleshooting tool, the more familiar you become with the tool and its capabilities and limitations.

Connectivity Tools

Connectivity tools are used to verify if devices can talk to one another on a network. These include ping, traceroute, and nslookup. Ping verifies that a node is talking on the network, traceroute displays the connections between source and destination, and nslookup performs DNS queries to resolve names to IP addresses.

Ping

One of the most common and previously most utilized troubleshooting tools is the ping utility. Ping is used to troubleshoot the lack of reachability of a host on an IP network. Ping sends an Internet Control Message Protocol (ICMP) echo request packet to a specified IP address or host and waits for an ICMP reply.

Figure 15-11
Ping command
output

```
Microsoft Windows [Version 10.0.15063]
(c) 2017 Microsoft Corporation. All rights reserved.

C:\Users\Vanderburg>ping comptia.org

Pinging comptia.org [198.134.5.6] with 32 bytes of data:
Reply from 198.134.5.6: bytes=32 time=35ms TTL=49
Reply from 198.134.5.6: bytes=32 time=35ms TTL=49
Reply from 198.134.5.6: bytes=32 time=34ms TTL=49
Reply from 198.134.5.6: bytes=32 time=40ms TTL=49

Ping statistics for 198.134.5.6:
    Packets: Sent = 4, Received = 4, Lost = 0 (0% loss),
Approximate round trip times in milli-seconds:
    Minimum = 34ms, Maximum = 40ms, Average = 36ms
```

Ping can also be used to measure the round-trip time for messages sent from the originating workstation to the destination and to record packet loss. Ping generates a summary of the information it has gathered, including packets sent, packets received and lost, and the amount of time taken to receive the responses. Starting with Microsoft Windows XP Service Pack 2, Windows Firewall was enabled by default and blocks ICMP traffic and ping requests. Figure 15-11 shows an example of the output received when you use the ping utility to ping comptia.org.

EXAM TIP   Ping allows an administrator to test the availability of a single host.

Traceroute

Traceroute is a troubleshooting tool that is used to determine the path that an IP packet has to take to reach a destination. Unlike the ping utility, traceroute displays the path and measures the transit delays of packets across the network to reach a target host.

The command in Microsoft Windows is written as tracert. Issuing the traceroute command followed by an FQDN or IP address will print the list of hops from source to destination. Some switches that can be used with traceroute include the following:

- **–d**   Disables host name resolution
- **–h**   Specifies the maximum number of hops to trace
- **–j**   Specifies an alternative source address, so traceroute executes from that node instead of the one from which you are issuing commands
- **–w**   Specifies the timeout to use for each reply

Traceroute sends packets with gradually increasing time-to-live (TTL) values, starting with a TTL value of 1. The first router receives the packet, decreases the TTL value, and drops the packet because it now has a value of zero. The router then sends an ICMP "time exceeded" message back to the source, and the next set of packets is given a TTL value of 2, which means the first router forwards the packets and the second router drops them and replies with its own ICMP "time exceeded" message. Traceroute then uses

```
C:\Users\Vanderburg>tracert comptia.org

Tracing route to comptia.org [198.134.5.6]
over a maximum of 30 hops:

  1    10 ms    13 ms     6 ms  box.local [192.168.1.21]
  2    18 ms    17 ms    63 ms  192.168.1.1
  3    35 ms    19 ms    24 ms  142.254.157.249
  4    22 ms    37 ms    31 ms  24.164.114.229
  5    16 ms    16 ms    16 ms  be23.bathoh0601r.midwest.rr.com [24.33.103.94]
  6    19 ms    23 ms    30 ms  be12.pltsohae01r.midwest.rr.com [65.29.1.89]
  7    34 ms    28 ms    43 ms  be25.clmkohpe01r.midwest.rr.com [65.29.1.28]
  8    48 ms    46 ms    42 ms  107.14.17.252
  9    43 ms    41 ms    49 ms  bu-ether11.chcgildt87w-bcr00.tbone.rr.com [66.109.6.20]
 10    73 ms    35 ms    82 ms  0.ae1.pr1.chi10.tbone.rr.com [107.14.17.194]
 11    44 ms    52 ms    49 ms  ix-ae-27-0.tcore2.CT8-Chicago.as6453.net [64.86.79.97]
 12    36 ms    36 ms    36 ms  if-ae-22-2.tcore1.CT8-Chicago.as6453.net [64.86.79.2]
 13    46 ms    75 ms    36 ms  p5-1.ir1.chicago2-il.us.xo.net [206.111.2.33]
 14    34 ms    37 ms    35 ms  vb2001.rar3.chicago-il.us.xo.net [207.88.13.130]
 15    41 ms    33 ms    39 ms  216.156.16.199.ptr.us.xo.net [216.156.16.199]
 16    53 ms    43 ms    80 ms  216.55.11.62
 17    47 ms    48 ms    42 ms  198.134.5.6

Trace complete.
```

Figure 15-12   Tracert command output

the returned ICMP "time exceeded" messages with the source IP address of the expired intermediate device to create a list of routers until the destination device is reached and returns an ICMP echo reply.

Most modern operating systems support some form of the traceroute tool: as mentioned, on a Microsoft Windows operating system, it is named tracert; Linux has a version named trace; on Internet protocol version 6 (IPv6), the tool is called traceroute6. Figure 15-12 displays an example of the tracert command being used to trace the path to comptia.org.

Nslookup and Dig

Another tool that can be used to troubleshoot network connection issues is the nslookup command. With nslookup, it is possible to obtain domain name or IP address mappings for a specified DNS record. Nslookup uses the computer's local DNS server to perform the queries. Using the nslookup command requires at least one valid DNS server, which can be verified by using the ipconfig /all command.

The domain information groper (dig) command can also be used to query DNS name servers and can operate in interactive command-line mode or be used in batch query mode on Linux-based systems. The host utility can also be used to perform DNS lookups. Figure 15-13 shows an example of the output using nslookup to query comptia.org.

Figure 15-13
Nslookup query

```
C:\Users\Vanderburg>nslookup comptia.org
Server:  box.local
Address:  192.168.1.21

Non-authoritative answer:
Name:    comptia.org
Address:  198.134.5.6
```

Configuration Tools

Configuration tools are used to modify the configuration of network settings such as the IP address, DHCP, DNS, gateway, or routing settings. Three important configuration tools you should know are ifconfig, ipconfig, and route.

ifconfig

ifconfig is a Linux command used to configure the TCP/IP network interface from the command line, which allows for setting the interface's IP address and netmask or even disabling the interface. ifconfig displays the current TCP/IP network configuration settings for a network interface.

Figure 15-14 shows the ifconfig command standard output, which contains information on the system's network interfaces. The system this command was executed on has an Ethernet adapter called enp2s0 and a wireless adapter called wlp3s0. The item labeled "lo" is the loopback address. The loopback address is used to test networking functions and does not rely on physical hardware.

EXAM TIP   ifconfig lacks some command-line switches that ipconfig has that allow you to perform more advanced tasks, like clearing the DNS cache and obtaining a new IP address from DHCP, rather than just displaying TCP/IP configuration information.

```
eric@Neptune:~$ ifconfig
enp2s0: flags=4099<UP,BROADCAST,MULTICAST>  mtu 1500
        ether 10:c3:7b:1a:c5:2f  txqueuelen 1000  (Ethernet)
        RX packets 0  bytes 0 (0.0 B)
        RX errors 0  dropped 0  overruns 0  frame 0
        TX packets 0  bytes 0 (0.0 B)
        TX errors 0  dropped 0 overruns 0  carrier 0  collisions 0

lo: flags=73<UP,LOOPBACK,RUNNING>  mtu 65536
        inet 127.0.0.1  netmask 255.0.0.0
        inet6 ::1  prefixlen 128  scopeid 0x10<host>
        loop  txqueuelen 1000  (Local Loopback)
        RX packets 210  bytes 15568 (15.5 KB)
        RX errors 0  dropped 0  overruns 0  frame 0
        TX packets 210  bytes 15568 (15.5 KB)
        TX errors 0  dropped 0 overruns 0  carrier 0  collisions 0

wlp3s0: flags=4163<UP,BROADCAST,RUNNING,MULTICAST>  mtu 1500
        inet 192.168.1.199  netmask 255.255.255.0  broadcast 192.168.1.255
        inet6 fe80::adf1:d21b:7b0f:c02f  prefixlen 64  scopeid 0x20<link>
        ether 80:86:f2:90:32:bf  txqueuelen 1000  (Ethernet)
        RX packets 145168  bytes 215239452 (215.2 MB)
        RX errors 0  dropped 0  overruns 0  frame 0
        TX packets 24143  bytes 2361712 (2.3 MB)
        TX errors 0  dropped 0 overruns 0  carrier 0  collisions 0
```

Figure 15-14   Viewing interfaces using ipconfig

Ipconfig

Ipconfig is a Microsoft Windows command used to configure a network interface from the command line. Ipconfig can display the network interface configuration, release or renew IP version 4 and 6 addresses from DHCP, flush the cache of DNS queries, display DNS queries, register a DHCP address in DNS, and display class IDs for IP versions 4 and 6. Figure 15-15 shows the command-line switch options available with the ipconfig command.

```
C:\Users\Vanderburg>ipconfig /?

USAGE:
    ipconfig [/allcompartments] [/? | /all |
                                 /renew [adapter] | /release [adapter] |
                                 /renew6 [adapter] | /release6 [adapter] |
                                 /flushdns | /displaydns | /registerdns |
                                 /showclassid adapter |
                                 /setclassid adapter [classid] |
                                 /showclassid6 adapter |
                                 /setclassid6 adapter [classid] ]

where
    adapter             Connection name
                        (wildcard characters * and ? allowed, see examples)

    Options:
       /?               Display this help message
       /all             Display full configuration information.
       /release         Release the IPv4 address for the specified adapter.
       /release6        Release the IPv6 address for the specified adapter.
       /renew           Renew the IPv4 address for the specified adapter.
       /renew6          Renew the IPv6 address for the specified adapter.
       /flushdns        Purges the DNS Resolver cache.
       /registerdns     Refreshes all DHCP leases and re-registers DNS names
       /displaydns      Display the contents of the DNS Resolver Cache.
       /showclassid     Displays all the dhcp class IDs allowed for adapter.
       /setclassid      Modifies the dhcp class id.
       /showclassid6    Displays all the IPv6 DHCP class IDs allowed for adapter.
       /setclassid6     Modifies the IPv6 DHCP class id.

The default is to display only the IP address, subnet mask and
default gateway for each adapter bound to TCP/IP.

For Release and Renew, if no adapter name is specified, then the IP address
leases for all adapters bound to TCP/IP will be released or renewed.

For Setclassid and Setclassid6, if no ClassId is specified, then the ClassId is removed.

Examples:
    > ipconfig                       ... Show information
    > ipconfig /all                  ... Show detailed information
    > ipconfig /renew                ... renew all adapters
    > ipconfig /renew EL*            ... renew any connection that has its
                                         name starting with EL
    > ipconfig /release *Con*        ... release all matching connections,
                                         eg. "Wired Ethernet Connection 1" or
                                             "Wired Ethernet Connection 2"
    > ipconfig /allcompartments      ... Show information about all
                                         compartments
    > ipconfig /allcompartments /all ... Show detailed information about all
                                         compartments
```

Figure 15-15   Ipconfig options

Route

The route command can be used to view and manipulate the TCP/IP routing tables of Windows operating systems. The routes displayed show how to get from one network to another. A computer connects to another over a series of devices, and each step from source to destination is called a hop. The route command can display the routing tables so that you can troubleshoot connectivity issues between devices or configure routing on a device that is serving that function.

Modification of a route requires modifying a routing table. A routing table is a data table stored on a system that connects two networks together. It is used to determine the destination of network packets it is responsible for routing. A routing table is a database that is stored in memory. It contains information about the network topology that is located adjacent to the router hosting the routing table.

When using earlier versions of Linux, the route command and the ifconfig command can be used together to connect a computer to a network and define the routes between the networks; later versions of Linux have replaced the ifconfig and route commands with the iproute2 command, which adds functionality such as traffic shaping. Figure 15-16 shows the route command using the print switch to display the current IP versions 4 and 6 routing tables.

```
C:\Users\Vanderburg>route print
===========================================================================
Interface List
 10...50 e5 49 c5 cd 4e ......Realtek PCIe GBE Family Controller
  1...........................Software Loopback Interface 1
===========================================================================

IPv4 Route Table
===========================================================================
Active Routes:
Network Destination        Netmask          Gateway       Interface  Metric
          0.0.0.0          0.0.0.0      192.168.1.21    192.168.1.162     25
        127.0.0.0        255.0.0.0         On-link         127.0.0.1    331
        127.0.0.1  255.255.255.255         On-link         127.0.0.1    331
  127.255.255.255  255.255.255.255         On-link         127.0.0.1    331
      192.168.1.0    255.255.255.0         On-link     192.168.1.162    281
    192.168.1.162  255.255.255.255         On-link     192.168.1.162    281
    192.168.1.255  255.255.255.255         On-link     192.168.1.162    281
        224.0.0.0        240.0.0.0         On-link         127.0.0.1    331
        224.0.0.0        240.0.0.0         On-link     192.168.1.162    281
  255.255.255.255  255.255.255.255         On-link         127.0.0.1    331
  255.255.255.255  255.255.255.255         On-link     192.168.1.162    281
===========================================================================
Persistent Routes:
  Network Address          Netmask  Gateway Address  Metric
          0.0.0.0          0.0.0.0      192.168.1.1  Default
===========================================================================

IPv6 Route Table
===========================================================================
Active Routes:
 If Metric Network Destination        Gateway
  1    331 ::1/128                  On-link
 10    281 fe80::/64                On-link
 10    281 fe80::44e2:6bf1:10bb:f30d/128
                                    On-link
  1    331 ff00::/8                 On-link
 10    281 ff00::/8                 On-link
===========================================================================
Persistent Routes:
  None
```

Figure 15-16   The route command displaying current routing tables

Query Tools

Query tools are used to view the status of network services. The two commands you should be familiar with are netstat and arp. Netstat displays network connections, routing tables, and network protocol statistics. Arp displays the MAC addresses that a computer or network devices know about.

Netstat

If you want to display all active network connections, routing tables, and network protocol statistics, you can use the netstat command. Available in most operating systems, the netstat command can be used to detect problems with the network and determine how much network traffic there is. It can also display protocol and Ethernet statistics and all the currently active TCP/IP network connections. Figure 15-17 shows the options available with the netstat command.

```
C:\Users\Vanderburg>netstat /?

Displays protocol statistics and current TCP/IP network connections.

NETSTAT [-a] [-b] [-e] [-f] [-n] [-o] [-p proto] [-r] [-s] [-x] [-t] [interval]

  -a            Displays all connections and listening ports.
  -b            Displays the executable involved in creating each connection or
                listening port. In some cases well-known executables host
                multiple independent components, and in these cases the
                sequence of components involved in creating the connection
                or listening port is displayed. In this case the executable
                name is in [] at the bottom, on top is the component it called,
                and so forth until TCP/IP was reached. Note that this option
                can be time-consuming and will fail unless you have sufficient
                permissions.
  -e            Displays Ethernet statistics. This may be combined with the -s
                option.
  -f            Displays Fully Qualified Domain Names (FQDN) for foreign
                addresses.
  -n            Displays addresses and port numbers in numerical form.
  -o            Displays the owning process ID associated with each connection.
  -p proto      Shows connections for the protocol specified by proto; proto
                may be any of: TCP, UDP, TCPv6, or UDPv6.  If used with the -s
                option to display per-protocol statistics, proto may be any of:
                IP, IPv6, ICMP, ICMPv6, TCP, TCPv6, UDP, or UDPv6.
  -q            Displays all connections, listening ports, and bound
                nonlistening TCP ports. Bound nonlistening ports may or may not
                be associated with an active connection.
  -r            Displays the routing table.
  -s            Displays per-protocol statistics.  By default, statistics are
                shown for IP, IPv6, ICMP, ICMPv6, TCP, TCPv6, UDP, and UDPv6;
                the -p option may be used to specify a subset of the default.
  -t            Displays the current connection offload state.
  -x            Displays NetworkDirect connections, listeners, and shared
                endpoints.
  -y            Displays the TCP connection template for all connections.
                Cannot be combined with the other options.
  interval      Redisplays selected statistics, pausing interval seconds
                between each display.  Press CTRL+C to stop redisplaying
                statistics.  If omitted, netstat will print the current
                configuration information once.
```

Figure 15-17   The netstat command displaying the active connections

Figure 15-18
The ARP cache
with the Internet
and the physical
addresses
displayed

```
C:\Users\Vanderburg>arp -a

Interface: 192.168.1.162 --- 0xa
  Internet Address      Physical Address      Type
  192.168.1.1           14-cc-20-ec-2d-8e     dynamic
  192.168.1.9           00-08-9b-cf-d0-3e     dynamic
  192.168.1.10          00-08-9b-c7-64-03     dynamic
  192.168.1.11          00-08-9b-d2-56-b6     dynamic
  192.168.1.21          e8-44-7e-00-74-f4     dynamic
  192.168.1.100         b8-e9-37-af-e1-dc     dynamic
  192.168.1.104         b8-3e-59-48-39-6d     dynamic
  192.168.1.113         00-0e-58-11-c0-ca     dynamic
  192.168.1.117         d8-d4-3c-f9-56-76     dynamic
  192.168.1.168         00-6b-9e-4f-0c-77     dynamic
  192.168.1.172         a4-77-33-f5-5d-56     dynamic
  192.168.1.185         f0-79-59-2b-b1-8d     dynamic
  192.168.1.199         80-86-f2-90-32-bf     dynamic
  192.168.1.209         d0-bf-9c-b4-10-8d     dynamic
  192.168.1.233         6c-3b-e5-01-51-41     dynamic
  192.168.1.234         f0-1d-bc-3d-7f-80     dynamic
  192.168.1.255         ff-ff-ff-ff-ff-ff     static
  224.0.0.2             01-00-5e-00-00-02     static
  224.0.0.22            01-00-5e-00-00-16     static
  224.0.0.251           01-00-5e-00-00-fb     static
  224.0.0.252           01-00-5e-00-00-fc     static
  224.0.1.60            01-00-5e-00-01-3c     static
  239.255.188.44        01-00-5e-7f-bc-2c     static
  239.255.255.250       01-00-5e-7f-ff-fa     static
  255.255.255.255       ff-ff-ff-ff-ff-ff     static
```

Arp Command

Another helpful troubleshooting tool is the arp command. The arp command uses the Address Resolution Protocol (ARP) to resolve an IP address to either a physical address or a media access control (MAC) address. The arp command makes it possible to display the current ARP entries or the ARP table and to add a static entry. Figure 15-18 uses the arp –a command to view the ARP cache of a computer.

Remote Administration Tools

Remote administration tools allow connectivity to systems or network devices. The two tools you should know about for troubleshooting are used to connect to network devices such as switches and routers. They include Telnet and Secure Shell (SSH).

Telnet

If a user wants to connect their computer to another computer or server running the Telnet service over the network, they can enter commands via the Telnet program, and the commands are executed as if they were being entered directly on the server console. Telnet enables the user to control a server and communicate with other servers over the network.

Figure 15-19 A telnet session

A valid username and password are required to activate a Telnet session; nonetheless, Telnet has security risks when it is used over any network because credentials and data are exchanged in plaintext. Figure 15-19 shows an example of a Telnet session established with a remote server.

 EXAM TIP Telnet and SSH both allow an administrator to connect to a server remotely, the primary difference being that SSH offers security mechanisms to protect against malicious intent.

SSH

SSH is another protocol that enables the user to securely control a server and communicate with other servers over the network. Secure Shell and its most recent version, Secure Shell version 2 (SSHv2), have become a more popular option for providing a secure remote command-line interface than Telnet because they encrypt credentials and data.

Figure 15-20 shows an example of an SSH session established with a remote server 192.168.254.254. In this screenshot, a connection has been established, and the remote server is asking for a username to log in. After a username is provided, the system will ask for a password.

Figure 15-20 SSH session

Chapter Review

This chapter introduced you to troubleshooting tools, described documentation and its importance to company and cloud operations, and explained CompTIA's troubleshooting methodology. Troubleshooting tools can be used to help identify issues, validate troubleshooting theories, and refine theories. Some tools include ping, traceroute, nslookup, ifconfig, ipconfig, route, netstat, arp, Telnet, and SSH. Understanding which tools are best suited to troubleshoot different issues as they arise with a cloud deployment model saves an administrator time and helps maintain service level agreements set forth by the organization.

Documentation is another important concept for cloud and systems administrators. Documentation needs to be clear and easy to understand for anyone who may need to use it and should be regularly reviewed to ensure that it is up to date and accurate. Documenting the person responsible for creating and maintaining the application and where it is hosted is a good process that saves valuable time when troubleshooting any potential issues with the cloud environment.

Lastly, the CompTIA troubleshooting methodology provides an effective means for evaluating problems, identifying potential solutions, testing those solutions, and putting them into practice. The methodology is broken down into six steps as follows: Step 1: Identify the problem. Step 2: Establish a theory of probable causes. Step 3: Test the theory to determine the cause. Step 4: Establish a plan of action to resolve the problem and implement the solution. Step 5: Verify full system functionality and, if applicable, implement preventative measures. Step 6: Document findings, actions, and outcomes.

Questions

The following questions will help you gauge your understanding of the material in this chapter. Read all the answers carefully because there might be more than one correct answer. Choose the best response(s) for each question.

1. Which of the following command-line tools allows for the display of all active network connections and network protocol statistics?

   A. Netstat

   B. Ping

   C. Traceroute

   D. Ipconfig and ifconfig

2. You need to verify the TCP/IP configuration settings of a network adapter on a VM running Microsoft Windows. Which of the following tools should you use?

   A. Ping

   B. ARP

   C. Tracert

   D. Ipconfig

3. Which of the following tools can be used to verify if a host is available on the network?

   A. Ping

   B. ARP

   C. Ipconfig

   D. Ipconfig and ifconfig

4. Which tool allows you to query DNS to obtain domain name or IP address mappings for a specified DNS record?

   A. Ping

   B. Ipconfig

   C. Nslookup

   D. Route

5. You need a way to remotely execute commands against a server that is located on the internal network. Which tool can be used to accomplish this objective?

   A. Ping

   B. Dig

   C. Traceroute

   D. Telnet

6. You need to modify a routing table and create a static route. Which command-line tool can you use to accomplish this task?

   A. Ping

   B. Traceroute

   C. Route

   D. Host

7. Users are complaining that an application is taking longer than normal to load. You need to troubleshoot why the application is experiencing startup issues. You want to gather detailed information while the application is loading. What should you enable?

   A. System logs

   B. Verbose logging

   C. Telnet

   D. ARP

8. How often should documentation be updated?

   A. Annually

   B. Quarterly

   C. It depends on how many people are working on the project

   D. Whenever significant changes are made

9. Fred manages 50 cloud servers in Amazon Web Services. Each cloud server is thin provisioned, and Fred pays for the amount of space his servers consume. He finds that the logs on the servers are rolling over and that each server has only about six days of logs. He would like to retain 18 months of logs. What should Fred do to retain the logs while conserving space on local hard disks?

   A. Compress the log files

   B. Request that the cloud provider deduplicate his cloud data

   C. Purchase and configure a cloud log archiving service

   D. Log in to the server every five days and copy the log files to his desktop

10. Which is not the name of a step in the CompTIA troubleshooting methodology?

    A. Seek approval for the requested change

    B. Identify the problem

    C. Document findings, actions, and outcomes

    D. Seek approval for change requests

11. Which step in the CompTIA troubleshooting methodology implements the solution?

    A. Step 1

    B. Step 2

    C. Step 3

    D. Step 4

    E. Step 5

    F. Step 6

Answers

   1. A. The netstat command can be used to display protocol statistics and all of the currently active TCP/IP network connections, along with Ethernet statistics.

   2. D. Ipconfig is a Microsoft Windows command that displays the current TCP/IP network configuration settings for a network interface.

   3. A. The ping utility is used to troubleshoot the reachability of a host on an IP network. Ping sends an ICMP echo request packet to a specified IP address or host and waits for an ICMP reply.

   4. C. Using the nslookup command, it is possible to query the Domain Name System to obtain domain name or IP address mappings for a specified DNS record.

   5. D. Telnet allows you to connect to another computer and enter commands via the Telnet program. The commands will be executed as if you were entering them directly on the server console.

   6. C. You can use the route command to view and manipulate the TCP/IP routing tables and create static routes.

7. **B.** Verbose logging records more detailed information than standard logging and is recommended to troubleshoot a specific problem.

8. **D.** Each time a significant change is made, the documentation should be updated to reflect the change. Otherwise, coworkers, auditors, or other employees might operate off out-of-date information.

9. **C.** A cloud log archiving service would allow Fred to retain the logs on the archiving service while freeing up space on the local disks. The log archival space would likely be cheaper than the production space, and log archiving services offer additional analytical and searching tools to make reviewing the logs easier.

10. **D.** Change requests were discussed in the previous chapter, and it is important to seek approval for changes before making them. However, this is not the name of a step in the CompTIA troubleshooting methodology.

11. **D.** Step 4 implements the solution. The steps in the CompTIA troubleshooting methodology are as follows: Step 1: Identify the problem. Step 2: Establish a theory of probable causes. Step 3: Test the theory to determine the cause. Step 4: Establish a plan of action to resolve the problem and implement the solution. Step 5: Verify full system functionality and, if applicable, implement preventative measures. Step 6: Document findings, actions, and outcomes.

Objective Map

Exam CV0-003

Official Exam Objective	Chapter No.	All-in-One Coverage
1.0 Cloud Architecture and Design		
1.1 Compare and contrast the different types of cloud models.	1	Cloud service models
Deployment models	1	Cloud deployment models and services
Service models	1	Cloud service models
Advanced cloud services	1	Advanced cloud services
Shared responsibility model	1	Accountability and the shared responsibility model
1.2 Explain the factors that contribute to capacity planning.	10	Capacity management
Requirements	10	Capacity management
Standard templates	10	Capacity management
Licensing	10	Standardization
User density	10	Capacity management
System load	10	Thresholds
Trend analysis	10	Trending
Performance capacity planning	10	Capacity management
1.3 Explain the importance of high availability and scaling in cloud environments.	13	High availability
Hypervisors	9	Processor CPU affinity CPU anti-affinity
Oversubscription	5	CPU oversubscription ratio GPU oversubscription ratio Memory oversubscription ratio NIC oversubscription ratio

Official Exam Objective	Chapter No.	All-in-One Coverage
Regions and zones	3	Failover zones Regional replication Multiregional replication
Applications	13	High availability
Containers	13	High availability
Clusters	13	Clustering Geo-clustering
High availability of network functions	13	High-availability network functions
Avoid single points of failure	13	Multipathing
Scalability	9	Scalability
1.4 Given a scenario, analyze the solution design in support of the business requirements.	7	Requirement analysis
Requirement analysis	6 7	Requirements gathering Requirement analysis
Environments	10 10	Deployment landscapes Deployment methodologies
Testing techniques	8	Phase 3: testing
2.0 Security		
2.1 Given a scenario, configure identity and access management.	11	Data security
Identification and authorization	11 11	Identification Authorization
Directory services	7	Directory services
Federation	11	Federation
Certificate management	11	Certificate management
Multifactor authentication (MFA)	11	Multifactor authentication
Single sign-on (SSO)	11	Single sign-on (SSO)
Public key infrastructure (PKI)	11	Public key infrastructure (PKI)
Secret management	11	Secret management
Key management	11	Key management
2.2 Given a scenario, secure a network in a cloud environment.		
Network segmentation	11	Segmentation
Protocols	11 4 11 11	Access control protocols Network ports and protocols Tunneling protocols Encryption protocols
Network services	4	Network ports and protocols

Official Exam Objective	Chapter No.	All-in-One Coverage
Log and event monitoring	10	Logging
Network flows	11	Network flow
Hardening and configuration changes	11 14	Hardening Configuration management
2.3 Given a scenario, apply the appropriate OS and application security controls.		
Policies	12	Account management policies
User permissions	11	Access control
Antivirus/antimalware/endpoint detection and response (EDR)	11 11	Antivirus/antimalware Endpoint detection and response (EDR)
Host-based IDS (HIDS)/host-based IPS (HIPS)	11	IDS/IPS
Hardened baselines	10	Baselines
File integrity	2 14	Resilient file system Verifying data integrity
Log and event monitoring	10	Logging
Configuration management	14	Configuration management
Builds	8	Builds
Operating system (OS) upgrades	10	Operating system (OS) upgrades
Encryption	11	Encryption
Mandatory access control	11	Mandatory access control
Software firewall	11	Firewall
2.4 Given a scenario, apply data security and compliance controls in cloud environments.		
Encryption	11	Encryption
Integrity	2 11 14	Resilient file system Digital signatures Verifying data integrity
Classification	12	Data classification
Segmentation	4	Network segmentation and micro-segmentation
Access control	11	Access control
Impact of laws and regulations	8	Impact of regulation and legal changes
Records management	10	Records management
Data loss prevention (DLP)	11	Data loss prevention (DLP)
Cloud access security broker (CASB)	11	Cloud access security broker (CASB)

Official Exam Objective	Chapter No.	All-in-One Coverage
2.5 Given a scenario, implement measures to meet security requirements.		
Tools	12	Tools
Vulnerability assessment	12	Vulnerability assessment
Security patches	10	Patch management
Risk register	12	Risk register
Prioritization of patch application	10	Prioritization of patch application
Deactivate default accounts	11	Hardening
Impacts of security tools on systems and services	11	Impacts of security tools on systems and services
Effects of cloud service models on security implementation	11	Effects of cloud service models on security implementation
2.6 Explain the importance of incident response procedures.	12	Incident response
Preparation	12	Preparation
Incident response procedures	12	Incident response procedures
3.0 Deployment		
3.1 Given a scenario, integrate components into a cloud solution.		
Subscription services	7 7	Service model solutions Solutions
Provisioning resources	3	Storage provisioning
Application	1	Serverless
Deploying virtual machines (VMs) and custom images	7	Deploying virtual machines
Templates	7	Templates
Identity management	7	Identity management
Containers	7	Containers
Auto-scaling	1	Auto-scaling
Post-deployment validation	7	Post-deployment validation
3.2 Given a scenario, provision storage in cloud environments.		
Types	3	Storage types and technologies
Tiers	3	Storage tiers
Input/output operations per second (IOPS) and read/write	3 9	IOPS IOPS
Protocols	3	Storage access protocols

Official Exam Objective	Chapter No.	All-in-One Coverage
Redundant array of inexpensive disks (RAID)	2	Redundant array of inexpensive disks (RAID)
Storage system features	4 4 4	Compression Deduplication Replication
User quotas	9	Quotas and limits
Hyperconverged	5	Hyperconverged systems and infrastructure
Software-defined storage (SDS)	6	Software-defined storage (SDS)
3.3 Given a scenario, deploy cloud networking solutions.		
Services	4 4 4 4 4	DHCP NTP DNS CDN IPAM
Virtual private networks (VPNs)	7	Virtual private networks (VPNs)
Virtual routing	7	Virtual routing
Network appliances	7	Appliances
Virtual private cloud (VPC)	7	Virtual private cloud (VPC)
VLAN/VXLAN/GENEVE	4	Network segmentation and micro-segmentation
3.4 Given a scenario, configure the appropriate compute sizing for a deployment.		
Virtualization	5	Hypervisor
Central processing unit (CPU)/virtual CPU (vCPU)	5	CPU
Graphics processing unit (GPU)	5	GPU
Clock speed/instructions per cycle (IPC)	5	CPU
Hyperconverged	5	Hyperconverged systems and infrastructure
Memory	5	Memory
3.5 Given a scenario, perform cloud migrations.		
Physical to virtual (P2V)	6	Physical to virtual (P2V)
Virtual to virtual (V2V)	6	Virtual to virtual (V2V)
Cloud-to-cloud migrations	6	Cloud provider migrations
Storage migrations	6	Storage migrations
Database migrations	6	Database migrations

Official Exam Objective	Chapter No.	All-in-One Coverage
4.0 Operations and Support		
4.1 Given a scenario, configure logging, monitoring, and alerting to maintain operational status.		
Logging	10	Logging
Monitoring	10	Monitoring techniques
Alerting	10	Common alert methods/messaging
	10	Alerting based on deviation from baseline
	10	Policies to communicate alerts properly
4.2 Given a scenario, maintain efficient operation of a cloud environment.		
Confirm completion of backups	13	Backup and recovery
Life cycle management	8	Life cycle management
Change management	14	Change management
Asset management	14	Change and configuration management
	14	Configuration management database (CMDB)
Patching	10	Patch management
Impacts of process improvements on systems	8	Life cycle management
Upgrade methods	10	Deployment methodologies
Dashboard and reporting	10	Dashboards
4.3 Given a scenario, optimize cloud environments.		
Right-sizing	1	Auto-scaling technology
	9	Scalability
Compute	5	VM sizing considerations
Storage	5	VM sizing considerations
Network	5	VM sizing considerations
Placement	5	VM sizing considerations
Device drivers and firmware	5	Virtualization host
4.4 Given a scenario, apply proper automation and orchestration techniques.	14	Automation and orchestration
Infrastructure as Code	8	Infrastructure as Code
	14	Automation and orchestration
Continuous integration/continuous deployment (CI/CD)	8	Continuous integration/continuous deployment (CI/CD)
	14	Automation and orchestration

Official Exam Objective	Chapter No.	All-in-One Coverage
Version control	8	Code updates
	14	Automation and orchestration
Configuration management	14	Automation and orchestration
Containers	14	Automation and orchestration
Automation activities	14	Automation and orchestration
Secure scripting	14	Automation and orchestration
Orchestration sequencing	14	Automation and orchestration
4.5 Given a scenario, perform appropriate backup and restore operations.	13	Backup and recovery
Backup types	13	Backup types
Backup objects	13	Backup and recovery
Backup targets	13	Backup targets
Backup and restore policies	13	Corporate guidelines/documentation
Restoration methods	13	Restoration methods
4.6 Given a scenario, perform disaster recovery tasks.	13	Disaster recovery methods
Failovers	13	Failover
Failback	13	Failback
Restore backups	13	Restoration methods
Replication	13	Replication
Network configuration	13	Network configuration
On-premises and cloud sites	13	Alternate sites
	13	Site mirroring
Requirements	13	RPO
	13	RTO
	13	Service level agreements for DR
Documentation	13	Corporate guidelines/documentation
Geographical data center requirements	13	Disaster recovery methods
5.0 Troubleshooting		
5.1 Given a scenario, use the troubleshooting methodology to resolve cloud-related issues.	15	Troubleshooting methodology
Always consider corporate policies, procedures, and impacts before implementing changes.	14	Change management
1. Identify the problem	15	Identify the problem
2. Establish a theory of probable cause (question the obvious)	15	Theorize probable cause

Official Exam Objective	**Chapter No.**	**All-in-One Coverage**
5.4 Given a scenario, troubleshoot connectivity issues.	15	Connectivity issues
Network security group misconfigurations	15	Network security group misconfigurations
Common networking configuration issues	15	Networking configuration issues
Network troubleshooting tools	15	Troubleshooting tools
5.5 Given a scenario, troubleshoot common performance issues.	15	Performance issues
Resource utilization	15 15	Capacity issues Scaling
Application	15	Application issues
Incorrectly configured or failed load balancing	15	Load balancer issues
5.6 Given a scenario, troubleshoot automation or orchestration issues.	15	Automation and orchestration issues
Account mismatches	15	Account mismatches
Change management failures	15	Change management failures
Server name changes	15	Server name changes
IP address changes	15	IP address changes
Location changes	15	Location changes
Version/feature mismatch	15	Version or feature mismatch or deprecation
Automation tool incompatibility	15	Automation tool incompatibility
Job validation issue	15	Job validation issue
Patching failure	15	Patching failure

About the Online Content

This book comes complete with TotalTester Online customizable practice exam software with more than 200 practice exam questions including 10 simulated performance-based questions and a bonus glossary.

System Requirements

The current and previous major versions of the following desktop browsers are recommended and supported: Chrome, Microsoft Edge, Firefox, and Safari. These browsers update frequently, and sometimes an update may cause compatibility issues with the TotalTester Online or other content hosted on the Training Hub. If you run into a problem using one of these browsers, please try using another until the problem is resolved.

Your Total Seminars Training Hub Account

To get access to the online content, you will need to create an account on the Total Seminars Training Hub. Registration is free, and you will be able to track all your online content using your account. You may also opt in if you wish to receive marketing information from McGraw Hill or Total Seminars, but this is not required for you to gain access to the online content.

Privacy Notice

McGraw Hill values your privacy. Please be sure to read the Privacy Notice available during registration to see how the information you have provided will be used. You may view our Corporate Customer Privacy Policy by visiting the McGraw Hill Privacy Center. Visit the **mheducation.com** site and click **Privacy** at the bottom of the page.

Single User License Terms and Conditions

Online access to the digital content included with this book is governed by the McGraw Hill License Agreement outlined next. By using this digital content you agree to the terms of that license.

Access   To register and activate your Total Seminars Training Hub account, simply follow these easy steps.

1. Go to this URL: **hub.totalsem.com/mheclaim**

2. To register and create a new Training Hub account, enter your e-mail address, name, and password on the **Register** tab. No further personal information (such as credit card number) is required to create an account.

   If you already have a Total Seminars Training Hub account, enter your e-mail address and password on the **Log in** tab.

3. Enter your Product Key: **f3pt-qnpv-hzbp**

4. Click to accept the user license terms.

5. For new users, click the **Register and Claim** button to create your account. For existing users, click the **Log in and Claim** button.

   You will be taken to the Training Hub and have access to the content for this book.

Duration of License   Access to your online content through the Total Seminars Training Hub will expire one year from the date the publisher declares the book out of print.

Your purchase of this McGraw Hill product, including its access code, through a retail store is subject to the refund policy of that store.

The Content is a copyrighted work of McGraw Hill, and McGraw Hill reserves all rights in and to the Content. The Work is © 2021 by McGraw Hill.

Restrictions on Transfer   The user is receiving only a limited right to use the Content for the user's own internal and personal use, dependent on purchase and continued ownership of this book. The user may not reproduce, forward, modify, create derivative works based upon, transmit, distribute, disseminate, sell, publish, or sublicense the Content or in any way commingle the Content with other third-party content without McGraw Hill's consent.

Limited Warranty   The McGraw Hill Content is provided on an "as is" basis. Neither McGraw Hill nor its licensors make any guarantees or warranties of any kind, either express or implied, including, but not limited to, implied warranties of merchantability or fitness for a particular purpose or use as to any McGraw Hill Content or the information therein or any warranties as to the accuracy, completeness, correctness, or results to be obtained from, accessing or using the McGraw Hill Content, or any material referenced in such Content or any information entered into licensee's product by users or other persons and/or any material available on or that can be accessed through the licensee's product (including via any hyperlink or otherwise) or as to non-infringement of third-party rights. Any warranties of any kind, whether express or implied, are disclaimed. Any material or data obtained through use of the McGraw Hill Content is at your own discretion and risk and user understands that it will be solely responsible for any resulting damage to its computer system or loss of data.

Neither McGraw Hill nor its licensors shall be liable to any subscriber or to any user or anyone else for any inaccuracy, delay, interruption in service, error or omission, regardless of cause, or for any damage resulting therefrom.

In no event will McGraw Hill or its licensors be liable for any indirect, special or consequential damages, including but not limited to, lost time, lost money, lost profits or good will, whether in contract, tort, strict liability or otherwise, and whether or not such damages are foreseen or unforeseen with respect to any use of the McGraw Hill Content.

TotalTester Online

TotalTester Online provides you with a simulation of the CompTIA Cloud+ CV0-003 exam. Exams can be taken in Practice Mode or Exam Mode. Practice Mode provides an assistance window with hints, references to the book, explanations of the correct and incorrect answers, and the option to check your answer as you take the test. Exam Mode provides a simulation of the actual exam. The number of questions, the types of questions, and the time allowed are intended to be an accurate representation of the exam environment. The option to customize your quiz allows you to create custom exams from selected domains or chapters, and you can further customize the number of questions and time allowed.

To take a test, follow the instructions provided in the previous section to register and activate your Total Seminars Training Hub account. When you register, you will be taken to the Total Seminars Training Hub. From the Training Hub Home page, select your certification from the Study drop-down menu at the top of the page, or from the list of Your Topics on the Home page, and then click on the Total Tester link to launch the Total Tester. You can then select the option to customize your quiz and begin testing yourself in Practice Mode or Exam Mode. All exams provide an overall grade and a grade broken down by domain.

Performance-Based Questions and Other Resources

In addition to multiple-choice questions, the CompTIA Cloud+ (CV0-003) exam includes performance-based questions (PBQs), which, according to CompTIA, are designed to test your ability to solve problems in a simulated environment. More information about PBQs is provided on CompTIA's website. You can access the PBQs included with this book by navigating to the **Resources** tab and selecting the quiz icon. You can also access them by navigating to and selecting **CompTIA Cloud+ All-in-One (CV0-003) Resources** from the Study drop-down menu at the top of the page or from the list of Your Topics on the Home page. After you have selected the PBQs, an interactive quiz will launch in your browser.

A bonus glossary is also provided. Click the **Glossary PDF** link on the **Book Resources** tab. For your convenience, you may view it online or download a PDF.

Technical Support

For questions regarding the TotalTester or operation of the Training Hub, visit **www.totalsem.com** or e-mail **support@totalsem.com**.

For questions regarding book content, visit **www.mheducation.com/customerservice**.

INDEX

P